X.media.publishing

T0155820

For further volumes:
www.springer.com/series/5175

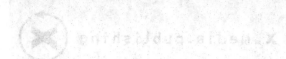

Christian Wöhler

3D Computer Vision

Efficient Methods and Applications

Second Edition

Christian Wöhler
Department of Electrical Engineering and IT
Technical University of Dortmund
Dortmund
Germany

ISSN 1612-1449   X.media.publishing
ISBN 978-1-4471-5944-5   ISBN 978-1-4471-4150-1 (eBook)
DOI 10.1007/978-1-4471-4150-1
Springer London Heidelberg New York Dordrecht

Printed on acid-free paper

Springer is part of Springer Science+Business Media (www.springer.com)

To Katja, Alexander, and Sebastian

Preface

This work provides an introduction to the foundations of three-dimensional computer vision and describes recent contributions to the field, which are methodical and application-specific in nature. Each chapter of this work provides an extensive overview of the corresponding state of the art, into which a detailed description of new methods or evaluation results in application-specific systems is embedded.

Triangulation-based approaches to three-dimensional scene reconstruction (cf. Chap. 1) are primarily based on the concept of bundle adjustment, which has been developed in the domain of photogrammetry. The three-dimensional scene structure and the intrinsic and extrinsic camera parameters are determined such that the Euclidean backprojection error in the image plane is minimised, usually relying on a nonlinear optimisation procedure. In the field of computer vision, an alternative framework based on projective geometry has emerged during the last two decades, which allows one to use linear algebra techniques for three-dimensional scene reconstruction and camera calibration purposes. With special emphasis on the problems of stereo image analysis and camera calibration, these fairly different approaches are related to each other in the presented work, and their advantages and drawbacks are stated. In this context, various state-of-the-art camera calibration and self-calibration methods as well as recent contributions towards automated camera calibration systems are described. An overview of classical and new feature-based, correlation-based, dense, and spatio-temporal methods for establishing point correspondences between pairs of stereo images is given. Furthermore, an analysis of traditional and newly introduced methods for the segmentation of point clouds and for the three-dimensional detection and pose estimation of rigid, articulated, and flexible objects in the scene is provided (cf. Chap. 2).

A different class of three-dimensional scene reconstruction methods consists of intensity-based approaches (cf. Chap. 3), which evaluate the pixel grey values in the image to infer the three-dimensional scene structure. Basically, these methods can be divided into shape from shadow, photoclinometry and shape from shading, photometric stereo, and shape from polarisation. As long as sufficient information about the illumination conditions and the surface reflectance properties is available, these methods may provide dense depth maps of object surfaces.

In a third, fundamentally different class of approaches the behaviour of the point spread function of the optical system used for image acquisition is exploited in order to derive depth information about the scene (cf. Chap. 4). Depth from defocus methods determine the position-dependent point spread function, which in turn yields absolute depth values for the scene points. A semi-empirical framework for establishing a relation between the depth of a scene point and the observed width of the point spread function is introduced. Depth from focus methods use as a reference the distance between the camera and the scene at which a minimum width of the point spread function is observed, relying on an appropriate calibration procedure.

These three classes of approaches to three-dimensional scene reconstruction are characterised by complementary properties; thus it is favourable to integrate them into unified frameworks that yield more accurate and robust results than each of the approaches alone (cf. Chap. 5). Bundle adjustment and depth from defocus are combined to determine the absolute scale factor of the scene reconstruction result, which cannot be obtained by bundle adjustment alone if no a priori information is available. Shading and shadow features are integrated into a self-consistent framework to reduce the inherent ambiguity and large-scale inaccuracy of the shape from shading technique by introducing regularisation terms that rely on depth differences inferred from shadow analysis. Another integrated approach combines photometric, polarimetric, and sparse depth information, yielding a three-dimensional reconstruction result which is equally accurate on both large and small scales. An extension of this method provides a framework for stereo image analysis of non-Lambertian surfaces, where traditional stereo methods tend to fail. Furthermore, a method is proposed to integrate photometric information and absolute depth data acquired using an active range scanning device. In the context of monocular three-dimensional pose estimation, the integration of triangulation, photopolarimetric, and defocus cues is demonstrated to behave more robustly and to provide significantly more accurate results than techniques exclusively relying on triangulation-based information.

The developed three-dimensional scene reconstruction methods are examined in different application scenarios. A comparison to state-of-the-art systems is provided where possible. In the context of industrial quality inspection (cf. Chap. 6), the performance of pose estimation is evaluated for rigid objects (e.g. plastic caps and electric plugs) as well as flexible objects (e.g. tubes and cables). The integrated surface reconstruction methods are applied to the inspection of different kinds of metallic surfaces.

The developed techniques for object detection and tracking in three-dimensional point clouds and for pose estimation of articulated objects are evaluated in the context of partially automated industrial production scenarios requiring a safe interaction between humans and industrial robots (cf. Chap. 7). Furthermore, we determine how the developed three-dimensional detection and pose estimation techniques are related to state-of-the-art gesture recognition methods in human–robot interaction scenarios, and typical action recognition results are presented in a realistic industrial scenario.

The third addressed application scenario is completely different and regards remote sensing of the lunar surface by preparing elevation maps (cf. Chap. 8).

While the spatial scales involved differ by many orders of magnitude from those encountered in the industrial quality inspection domain, the underlying physical processes are fairly similar. An introductory outline of state-of-the-art approaches to topographic mapping of solar system bodies is given. The estimation of impact crater depths and shapes is an issue of especially high geological relevance. It is demonstrated for lunar craters that three-dimensional surface reconstruction based on integrated methods yields topographic maps of high resolution, where at several places a comparison with recent topographic data (orbital laser altimetry and stereophotogrammetry) is performed. Another geologically relevant field is the three-dimensional reconstruction of lunar volcanic edifices, especially lunar domes.

Finally (cf. Chap. 9), the main results of the presented work and the most important conclusions are summarised, and possible directions of future research are outlined.

Dortmund, Germany   Christian Wöhler

Acknowledgements

First of all, I wish to express my gratitude to my wife, Khadija Katja, and my sons, Adnan Alexander Émile and Sebastian Marc Amin, for their patience and continuous encouragement.

I am grateful to Prof. Dr. Gerhard Sagerer (Technical Faculty, Bielefeld University), Prof. Dr. Reinhard Klette (Computer Science Department, University of Auckland), and Prof. Dr. Rainer Ott (Faculty of Computer Science, Electrical Engineering, and Information Technology, Stuttgart University) for providing their reviews for the first edition.

Moreover, I wish to thank Prof. Dr. Gerhard Sagerer, Prof. Dr. Franz Kummert, Dr. Joachim Schmidt, and Dr. Niklas Beuter from Bielefeld University for a fruitful collaboration. I gratefully acknowledge the opportunity to be a visiting lecturer at the Technical Faculty of Bielefeld University from 2005–2010. I also wish to thank Prof. Dr. Horst-Michael Groß from the Technical University of Ilmenau for his long-lasting cooperation.

I would like to thank my former colleagues in the Environment Perception department at Daimler Group Research and Advanced Engineering in Ulm for providing a lively and inspiring scientific environment, especially to Dr. Lars Krüger (to whom I am extraordinarily indebted for his critical reading of the manuscript of the first edition), Prof. Dr. Rainer Ott, Dr. Ulrich Kreßel, Dr. Frank Lindner, and Kia Hafezi, to our (former and current) Ph.D. students, Dr. Pablo d'Angelo, Dr. Marc Ellenrieder, Dr. Björn Barrois, Dr. Markus Hahn, Christoph Hermes, Eugen Käfer, and Matthias Hillebrand, and to our former Diplom students, Clemens von Bank, Dr. Annika Kuhl, Tobias Gövert, and Melanie Krauß. I am also indebted to Claus Lörcher and his team colleagues, Werner Progscha, Dr. Rolf Finkele, and Mike Böpple, for their continuous support.

I also wish to thank my current Ph.D. students of the Image Analysis Group at TU Dortmund, Steffen Herbort, Arne Grumpe, and Armin Staudenmaier, for their help and cooperation.

Furthermore, I am grateful to the members of the Geologic Lunar Research Group, especially Dr. Raffaello Lena, Dr. Charles A. Wood, Paolo Lazzarotti, Dr. Jim Phillips, Michael Wirths, K. C. Pau, Maria Teresa Bregante, and Richard

Evans, for sharing their experience in many projects concerning lunar observation and geology.

My thanks are extended to the Springer editorial staff, especially Hermann Engesser, Ralf Gerstner, Dorothea Glaunsinger, Gabi Fischer, Viktoria Meyer, and Donatas Akmanavičius, for their advice and cooperation.

Contents

Part I
Methods of 3D Computer Vision

Chapter 1
Triangulation-Based Approaches to Three-Dimensional Scene Reconstruction

Triangulation-based approaches to three-dimensional scene reconstruction are primarily based on the concept of bundle adjustment, which allows the determination of the three-dimensional point coordinates in the world and the camera parameters based on the minimisation of the reprojection error in the image plane. A framework based on projective geometry has been developed in the field of computer vision, where the nonlinear optimisation problem of bundle adjustment can to some extent be replaced by linear algebra techniques. Both approaches are related to each other in this chapter. Furthermore, an introduction to the field of camera calibration is given, and an overview of the variety of existing methods for establishing point correspondences is provided, including classical and also new feature-based, correlation-based, dense, and spatio-temporal approaches.

1.1 The Pinhole Model

The reconstruction of the three-dimensional structure of a scene from several images relies on the laws of geometric optics. In this context, optical lens systems are most commonly described by the pinhole model. Different models exist, describing optical devices such as fisheye lenses or omnidirectional lenses. This work, however, is restricted to the pinhole model, since it represents the most common image acquisition devices. In the pinhole model, the camera lens is represented by its optical centre, corresponding to a point situated between the three-dimensional scene and the two-dimensional image plane, and the optical axis, which is perpendicular to the plane defined by the lens and passes through the optical centre (cf. Fig. 1.1). The intersection point between the image plane and the optical axis is called the 'principal point' in the computer vision literature (Hartley and Zisserman, 2003). The distance between the optical centre and the principal point is called the 'principal distance' and is denoted by b. For real lenses, the principal distance b is always larger than the focal length f of the lens, and the value of b approaches f if the object distance Z is much larger than b. This issue will be further examined in Chap. 4.

In this work we will utilise a notation similar to the one by Craig (1989) for points, coordinate systems, and transformation matrices. Accordingly, a point $\mathbf{x}$ in

C. Wöhler, *3D Computer Vision*, X.media.publishing,
DOI 10.1007/978-1-4471-4150-1_1, © Springer-Verlag London 2013

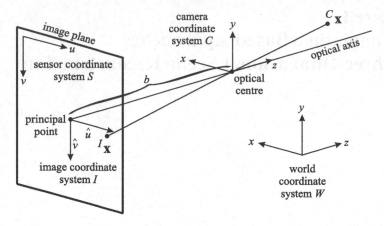

Fig. 1.1 The pinhole model. A scene point $^C\mathbf{x}$ defined in the camera coordinate system is projected into the image point $^I\mathbf{x}$ located in the image plane

the camera coordinate system C is denoted by $^C\mathbf{x}$, where the origin of C corresponds to the principal point. Similarly, a transformation of a point in the world coordinate system W into the camera coordinate system C is denoted by a transformation $^C_W T$, where the lower index defines the original coordinate system and the upper index the coordinate system into which the point is transformed. The transformation $^C_W T$ corresponds to an arbitrary rotation and translation. In this notation, the transformation is given by $^C\mathbf{x} = ^C_W T\, ^W\mathbf{x}$. A scene point $^C\mathbf{x} = (x, y, z)^T$ defined in the camera coordinate system C is projected on the image plane into the point $^I\mathbf{x}$, defined in the image coordinate system I, such that the scene point $^C\mathbf{x}$, the optical centre, and the image point $^I\mathbf{x}$ are connected by a straight line in three-dimensional space (Fig. 1.1). Obviously, all scene points situated on this straight line are projected into the same point in the image plane, such that the original depth information z is lost. Elementary geometrical considerations yield for the point $^I\mathbf{x} = (\hat{u}, \hat{v})$ in the image coordinate system the relations

$$\frac{\hat{u}}{b} = \frac{x}{z}$$
$$\frac{\hat{v}}{b} = \frac{y}{z}$$

(1.1)

(Horn, 1986). The coordinates $\hat{u}$ and $\hat{v}$ in the image plane are measured in the same metric units as x, y, z, and b. The principal point is given in the image plane by $\hat{u} = \hat{v} = 0$. In contrast, pixel coordinates in the coordinate system of the camera sensor are denoted by u and v.

While it may be useful to regard the camera coordinate system C as identical to the world coordinate system W for a single camera, it is favourable to explicitly define a world coordinate system as soon as multiple cameras are involved. The orientation and translation of each camera i with respect to this world coordinate system is then expressed by $^{C_i}_W T$, transforming a point $^W\mathbf{x}$ from the world coordinate system W into the camera coordinate system C_i. The transformation $_W^{C_i}T$ is composed of a rotational part R_i, corresponding to an orthonormal matrix of size 3×3 determined by three independent parameters, e.g. the Euler rotation angles (Craig, 1989), and a translation vector $\mathbf{t}_i$ denoting the offset between the coordinate systems. This decomposition yields

$$^{C_i}\mathbf{x} = {_W^{C_i}T}(^W\mathbf{x}) = R_i{^W\mathbf{x}} + \mathbf{t}_i. \tag{1.2}$$

Furthermore, the image formation process is determined by the intrinsic parameters $\{c_j\}_i$ of each camera i, some of which are lens-specific while others are sensor-specific. For a camera described by the pinhole model and equipped with a digital sensor, these parameters comprise the principal distance b, the effective number of pixels per unit length k_u and k_v along the horizontal and the vertical image axes, respectively, the pixel skew angle θ, and the coordinates u_0 and v_0 of the principal point in the image plane (Birchfield, 1998). For most modern camera sensors, the skew angle amounts to $\theta = 90°$ and the pixels are of quadratic shape with $k_u = k_v$.

For a real lens system, however, the observed image coordinates of scene points may deviate from those given by (1.1) due to the effect of lens distortion. In this work we employ the lens distortion model by Brown (1966, 1971) which has been extended by Heikkilä and Silvén (1997) and by Bouguet (1999). According to Heikkilä and Silvén (1997), the distorted coordinates $^I\mathbf{x}_d$ of a point in the image plane are obtained from the undistorted coordinates $^I\mathbf{x}$ by

$$^I\mathbf{x}_d = \left(1 + k_1 r^2 + k_3 r^4 + k_5 r^6\right){^I\mathbf{x}} + \mathbf{d}_t, \tag{1.3}$$

where $^I\mathbf{x} = (\hat{u}, \hat{v})^T$ and $r^2 = \hat{u}^2 + \hat{v}^2$. If radial distortion is present, straight lines in the object space crossing the optical axis still appear straight in the image, but the observed distance of a point in the image from the principal point deviates from the distance expected according to (1.1). The vector

$$\mathbf{d}_t = \begin{pmatrix} 2k_2\hat{u}\hat{v} + k_4(r^2 + 2\hat{u}^2) \\ k_2(r^2 + 2\hat{v}^2) + 2k_4\hat{u}\hat{v} \end{pmatrix} \tag{1.4}$$

is termed tangential distortion. The occurrence of tangential distortion implies that straight lines in the object space crossing the optical axis appear bent in some directions in the image.

When a film is used as an imaging sensor, $\hat{u}$ and $\hat{v}$ directly denote metric distances on the film with respect to the principal point, which has to be determined by an appropriate calibration procedure (cf. Sect. 1.4). When a digital camera sensor is used, the transformation

$$^S\mathbf{x} = {_I^S T}(^I\mathbf{x}) \tag{1.5}$$

from the image coordinate system into the sensor coordinate system is defined in the general case by an affine transformation $_I^S T$ (as long as the sensor has no 'exotic' architecture such as a hexagonal pixel raster, where the transformation would be still more complex). The corresponding coordinates $^S\mathbf{x} = (u, v)^T$ are measured in pixels.

1.2 Geometric Aspects of Stereo Image Analysis

The reconstruction of three-dimensional scene structure based on two images acquired from different positions and viewing directions is termed stereo image analysis. This section describes the 'classical' Euclidean approach to this important field of image-based three-dimensional scene reconstruction (cf. Sect. 1.2.1) as well as its formulation in terms of projective geometry (cf. Sect. 1.2.2).

1.2.1 Euclidean Formulation of Stereo Image Analysis

In this section, we begin with an introduction in terms of Euclidean geometry, following the derivation described by Horn (1986). It is assumed that the world coordinate system is identical with the coordinate system of camera 1; i.e. the transformation matrix $_W^{C_1}T$ corresponds to unity while the relative orientation of camera 2 with respect to camera 1 is given by $_W^{C_2}T$ and is assumed to be known (in Sect. 1.4 we will regard the problem of camera calibration, i.e. the determination of the extrinsic and intrinsic camera parameters). The three-dimensional straight line (ray) passing through the optical centre of camera 1, which is given by the equation

$$^{C_1}\mathbf{x} = \begin{pmatrix} x_1 \\ y_1 \\ z_1 \end{pmatrix} = \begin{pmatrix} \hat{u}_1 s \\ \hat{v}_1 s \\ bs \end{pmatrix}, \tag{1.6}$$

with s as a positive real number, is projected into the point $^{I_1}\mathbf{x} = (\hat{u}_1, \hat{v}_1)^T$ in image 1 for all possible values of s. In the coordinate system of camera 2, according to (1.2) the points on the same ray are given by

$$^{C_2}\mathbf{x} = \begin{pmatrix} x_2 \\ y_2 \\ z_2 \end{pmatrix} = R^{C_1}\mathbf{x} + \mathbf{t} = \begin{pmatrix} (r_{11}\hat{u}_1 + r_{12}\hat{v}_1 + r_{13}b)s + t_1 \\ (r_{21}\hat{u}_1 + r_{22}\hat{v}_1 + r_{23}b)s + t_2 \\ (r_{31}\hat{u}_1 + r_{32}\hat{v}_1 + r_{33}b)s + t_3 \end{pmatrix} \tag{1.7}$$

with r_{ij} as the elements of the orthonormal rotation matrix R and t_i as the elements of the translation vector $\mathbf{t}$ (cf. (1.2)). In the image coordinate system of camera 2, the coordinates of the point $^{I_2}\mathbf{x} = (\hat{u}_2, \hat{v}_2)^T$ are given by

$$\frac{\hat{u}_2}{b} = \frac{x_2}{z_2} \quad \text{and} \quad \frac{\hat{v}_2}{b} = \frac{y_2}{z_2}, \tag{1.8}$$

assuming an identical principal distance b for both cameras.

For the point $^{I_1}\mathbf{x}$ in image 1, the corresponding scene point $^W\mathbf{x} = {}^{C_1}\mathbf{x}$ is located on the ray defined by (1.6), but its associated value of s is unknown. The point $^{I_2}\mathbf{x}$ in image 2 which corresponds to the same scene point must be located on a line which is obtained by projecting the points on the ray into image 2 for all values of $0 \le s < \infty$. The point on the ray with $s = 0$ corresponds to the optical centre $^{C_1}\mathbf{c}_1$ of camera 1. It projects into the point $^{I_2}\mathbf{c}_1$ in image 2 and the

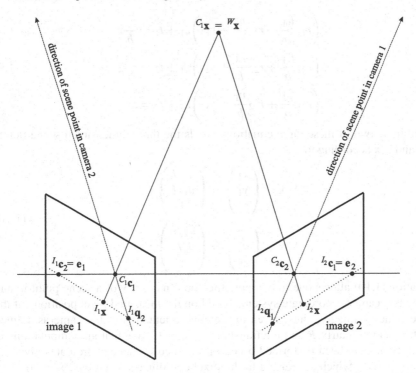

Fig. 1.2 Definition of epipolar geometry according to Horn (1986). The *epipolar lines* of the image points $^{I_1}\mathbf{x}$ and $^{I_2}\mathbf{x}$ are drawn as *dotted lines*

point on the ray at infinity ($s \to \infty$) into $^{I_2}\mathbf{q}_1$ (cf. Fig. 1.2). The point $^{I_2}\mathbf{x}$ in image 2 is located on the line connecting $^{I_2}\mathbf{c}_1$ and $^{I_2}\mathbf{q}_1$ (drawn as a dotted line in Fig. 1.2), which is the 'epipolar line' corresponding to the point $^{I_1}\mathbf{x}$ in image 1. For image 1, an analogous geometrical construction yields the line connecting the points $^{I_1}\mathbf{c}_2$ and $^{I_1}\mathbf{q}_2$ (where $^{I_1}\mathbf{c}_2$ is the optical centre of camera 2 projected into image 1) as the epipolar line corresponding to the point $^{I_2}\mathbf{x}$ in image 2. Alternatively, the epipolar lines can be obtained by determining the intersection lines between the image planes and the 'epipolar plane' defined by the scene point $^{C_1}\mathbf{x}$ and the optical centres $^{C_1}\mathbf{c}_1$ and $^{C_2}\mathbf{c}_2$ (cf. Fig. 1.2). From the fact that each epipolar line in image 1 contains the image $^{I_1}\mathbf{c}_2$ of the optical centre of camera 2 it follows that all epipolar lines intersect in the point $^{I_1}\mathbf{c}_2$, and analogously for image 2. Hence, the points $^{I_1}\mathbf{c}_2 = \mathbf{e}_1$ and $^{I_2}\mathbf{c}_1 = \mathbf{e}_2$ are termed epipoles, and the restriction on the image positions of corresponding image points is termed the epipolar constraint.

Horn (1986) shows that as long as the extrinsic relative camera orientation given by the rotation matrix R and the translation vector $\mathbf{t}$ are known, it is straightforward to compute the three-dimensional position of a scene point $^{W}\mathbf{x}$ with image coordinates $^{I_1}\mathbf{x} = (\hat{u}_1, \hat{v}_1)^T$ and $^{I_2}\mathbf{x} = (\hat{u}_2, \hat{v}_2)^T$, expressed as $^{C_1}\mathbf{x}$ and $^{C_2}\mathbf{x}$ in the two camera coordinate systems. Inserting (1.8) into (1.7) yields

$$\left(r_{11}\frac{\hat{u}_1}{b} + r_{12}\frac{\hat{v}_1}{b} + r_{13} \right) z_1 + t_1 = \frac{\hat{u}_2}{b} z_2$$

$$\left(r_{21}\frac{\hat{u}_1}{b} + r_{22}\frac{\hat{v}_1}{b} + r_{23} \right) z_1 + t_2 = \frac{\hat{v}_2}{b} z_2 \qquad (1.9)$$

$$\left(r_{31}\frac{\hat{u}_1}{b} + r_{32}\frac{\hat{v}_1}{b} + r_{33} \right) z_1 + t_3 = z_2.$$

Combining two of these three equations yields the three-dimensional scene points $^{C_1}\mathbf{x}$ and $^{C_2}\mathbf{x}$ according to

$$^{C_1}\mathbf{x} = \begin{pmatrix} x_1 \\ y_1 \\ z_1 \end{pmatrix} = \begin{pmatrix} \hat{u}_1/b \\ \hat{v}_1/b \\ 1 \end{pmatrix} z_1$$

$$^{C_2}\mathbf{x} = \begin{pmatrix} x_2 \\ y_2 \\ z_2 \end{pmatrix} = \begin{pmatrix} \hat{u}_2/b \\ \hat{v}_2/b \\ 1 \end{pmatrix} z_2. \qquad (1.10)$$

Equation (1.10) allows one to compute the coordinates $^{C_i}\mathbf{x}$ of a scene point in any of the two camera coordinate systems based on the measured pixel positions of the corresponding image points, given the relative orientation of the cameras defined by the rotation matrix R and the translation vector $\mathbf{t}$. Note that all computations in this section have been performed based on the metric image coordinates given by $^{I_i}\mathbf{x} = (\hat{u}_i, \hat{v}_i)^T$, which are related to the pixel coordinates given by $^{S_i}\mathbf{x} = (u_i, v_i)^T$ in the sensor coordinate system by (1.5).

1.2.2 Stereo Image Analysis in Terms of Projective Geometry

To circumvent the nonlinear formulation of the pinhole model in Euclidean geometry, it is advantageous to express the image formation process in the more general mathematical framework of projective geometry.

1.2.2.1 Definition of Coordinates and Camera Properties

This section follows the description in the overview by Birchfield (1998) [detailed treatments are given e.g. in the books by Hartley and Zisserman (2003) and Schreer (2005), and other introductions are provided by Davis (2001) and Lu et al. (2004)]. Accordingly, a point $\mathbf{x} = (x, y)^T$ in two-dimensional Euclidean space corresponds to a point $\tilde{\mathbf{x}} = (X, Y, W)^T$ defined by a vector with three coordinates in the two-dimensional projective space $\mathcal{P}^2$. The norm of $\tilde{\mathbf{x}}$ is irrelevant, such that $(X, Y, W)^T$ is equivalent to $(\beta X, \beta Y, \beta W)^T$ for an arbitrary value of $\beta \neq 0$. The Euclidean vector $\mathbf{x}$ corresponding to the projective vector $\tilde{\mathbf{x}}$ is then given by $\mathbf{x} = (X/W, Y/W)^T$. The transformation is analogous for projective vectors in the three-dimensional space $\mathcal{P}^3$ with four coordinates.

According to the definition by Birchfield (1998), the transformation from the coordinate system I_i of camera i into the sensor coordinate system S_i is given by the matrix

$$A_i = \begin{bmatrix} \alpha_u & \alpha_u \cot\theta & u_0 \\ 0 & \alpha_v/\sin\theta & v_0 \\ 0 & 0 & 1 \end{bmatrix}, \tag{1.11}$$

with α_u, α_v, θ, u_0, and v_0 as the intrinsic parameters of camera i. In (1.11), the scale parameters α_u and α_v are defined according to $\alpha_u = -bk_u$ and $\alpha_v = -bk_v$.

The coordinates of an image point in the image coordinate system I_i corresponding to a scene point $^{C_i}\tilde{\mathbf{x}}$ defined in a world coordinate system W corresponding to the coordinate system C_i of camera i are obtained by

$$^{I_i}\tilde{\mathbf{x}} = \begin{bmatrix} -b & 0 & 0 & 0 \\ 0 & -b & 0 & 0 \\ 0 & 0 & 1 & 0 \end{bmatrix} {}^{C_i}\tilde{\mathbf{x}}, \tag{1.12}$$

which may be regarded as the projective variant of (1.1).

The complete image formation process can be described in terms of the projective 3×4 matrix P_i which is composed of the intrinsic and extrinsic camera parameters according to

$$^{S_i}\tilde{\mathbf{x}} = P_i {}^{W}\tilde{\mathbf{x}} = A_i [R_i \mid \mathbf{t}_i] {}^{W}\tilde{\mathbf{x}}, \tag{1.13}$$

such that $P_i = A_i [R_i \mid \mathbf{t}_i]$. For each camera i, the linear projective transformation P_i describes the image formation process in projective space.

1.2.2.2 The Essential Matrix

At this point it is illustrative to regard the derivation of the epipolar constraint in the framework of projective geometry. Birchfield (1998) describes two cameras regarding a scene point $^{W}\tilde{\mathbf{x}}$ which is projected into the vectors $^{I_1}\tilde{\mathbf{x}}'$ and $^{I_2}\tilde{\mathbf{x}}'$ defined in the two image coordinate systems. Since these vectors are projective vectors, $^{W}\tilde{\mathbf{x}}$ is of size 4×1 while $^{I_1}\tilde{\mathbf{x}}'$ and $^{I_2}\tilde{\mathbf{x}}'$ are of size 3×1. The cameras are assumed to be pinhole cameras with the same principal distance b, and $^{I_1}\tilde{\mathbf{x}}'$ and $^{I_2}\tilde{\mathbf{x}}'$ are given in normalised coordinates; i.e. the vectors are scaled such that their last (third) coordinates are 1. Hence, their first two coordinates represent the position of the projected scene point in the image with respect to the principal point, measured in units of the principal distance b, respectively. As a result, the three-dimensional vectors $^{I_1}\tilde{\mathbf{x}}'$ and $^{I_2}\tilde{\mathbf{x}}'$ correspond to the Euclidean vectors from the optical centres to the projected points in the image planes.

Following the derivation by Birchfield (1998), the normalised projective vector $^{I_1}\tilde{\mathbf{x}}'$ from the optical centre of camera 1 to the image point of $^{W}\tilde{\mathbf{x}}$ in image 1, the normalised projective vector $^{I_2}\tilde{\mathbf{x}}'$ from the optical centre of camera 2 to the image point of $^{W}\tilde{\mathbf{x}}$ in image 2, and the vector $\mathbf{t}$ connecting the two optical centres are coplanar. This condition can be written as

$$^{I_1}\tilde{\mathbf{x}}'^{T} \left(\mathbf{t} \times R \, {}^{I_2}\tilde{\mathbf{x}}' \right) = 0 \tag{1.14}$$

with R and $\mathbf{t}$ as the rotational and translational parts of the coordinate transformation from the first into the second camera coordinate system. Now $[\mathbf{t}]_\times$ is defined as the 3×3 matrix for which it is $[\mathbf{t}]_\times \mathbf{y} = \mathbf{t} \times \mathbf{y}$ for an arbitrary 3×1 vector $\mathbf{y}$. The matrix $[\mathbf{t}]_\times$ is called the 'cross product matrix' of the vector $\mathbf{t}$. For $\mathbf{t} = (d, e, f)^T$, it is

$$[\mathbf{t}]_\times = \begin{bmatrix} 0 & -f & e \\ f & 0 & -d \\ -e & d & 0 \end{bmatrix}. \tag{1.15}$$

Equation (1.14) then becomes

$$^{I_1}\tilde{\mathbf{x}}'^{T} \left([\mathbf{t}]_\times R\,^{I_2}\tilde{\mathbf{x}}'\right) = \,^{I_1}\tilde{\mathbf{x}}'^{T} \, E\,^{I_2}\tilde{\mathbf{x}}' = 0, \tag{1.16}$$

with

$$E = [\mathbf{t}]_\times R \tag{1.17}$$

as the 'essential matrix' describing the transformation from the coordinate system of one camera into the coordinate system of the other camera. Equation (1.16) shows that the epipolar constraint can be written as a linear equation in homogeneous co-ordinates. Birchfield (1998) states that E provides a complete description of how corresponding points are geometrically related in a pair of stereo images. Five parameters need to be known to compute the essential matrix; three correspond to the rotation angles describing the relative rotation between the cameras, while the other two denote the direction of translation. It is not possible to recover the absolute magnitude of translation, as increasing the distance between the cameras can be compensated by increasing the depth of the scene point by the same amount, thus leaving the coordinates of the image points unchanged. The essential matrix E is of size 3×3 but has rank 2, such that one of its eigenvalues (and therefore also its determinant) is zero. The other two eigenvalues of E are equal (Birchfield, 1998).

1.2.2.3 The Fundamental Matrix

It is now assumed that the image points are not given in normalised coordinates but in sensor pixel coordinates by the projective 3×1 vectors $^{S_1}\tilde{\mathbf{x}}$ and $^{S_2}\tilde{\mathbf{x}}$. According to Birchfield (1998), distortion-free lenses yield a transformation from the normalised camera coordinate system into the sensor coordinate system as given by (1.11), leading to the linear relations

$$\begin{aligned} ^{S_1}\tilde{\mathbf{x}} &= A_1\,^{I_1}\tilde{\mathbf{x}}' \\ ^{S_2}\tilde{\mathbf{x}} &= A_2\,^{I_2}\tilde{\mathbf{x}}'. \end{aligned} \tag{1.18}$$

The matrices A_1 and A_2 contain the pixel size, pixel skew, and pixel coordinates of the principal point of the cameras, respectively. If lens distortion has to be taken into account, e.g. according to (1.3) and (1.4), the corresponding transformations may become nonlinear. Birchfield (1998) shows that (1.16) and (1.18) yield the expressions

$$\left(A_2^{-1\,S_2}\tilde{\mathbf{x}}\right)^T \left(\mathbf{t} \times RA_1^{-1\,S_1}\tilde{\mathbf{x}}\right) = 0$$

$$^{S_2}\tilde{\mathbf{x}}^T A_2^{-T} \left(\mathbf{t} \times RA_1^{-1\,S_1}\tilde{\mathbf{x}}\right) = 0 \qquad (1.19)$$

$$^{S_2}\tilde{\mathbf{x}}^T F^{\,S_1}\tilde{\mathbf{x}} = 0,$$

where

$$F = A_2^{-T} E A_1^{-1} \qquad (1.20)$$

is termed the 'fundamental matrix' and provides a representation of both the intrinsic and the extrinsic parameters of the two cameras. The 3×3 matrix F is always of rank 2 (Hartley and Zisserman, 2003); i.e. one of its eigenvalues is always zero. Equation (1.19) is valid for all corresponding image points $^{S_1}\tilde{\mathbf{x}}$ and $^{S_2}\tilde{\mathbf{x}}$ in the images.

According to Hartley and Zisserman (2003), the fundamental matrix F relates a point in one stereo image to the line of all points in the other stereo image that may correspond to that point according to the epipolar constraint. In a projective plane, a line $\tilde{\mathbf{l}}$ is defined such that for all points $\tilde{\mathbf{x}}$ on the line the relation $\tilde{\mathbf{x}}^T\tilde{\mathbf{l}} = 0$ is fulfilled. At the same time, this relation indicates that in a projective plane, points and lines have the same representation and are thus dual with respect to each other. Specifically, the epipolar line $^{S_2}\tilde{\mathbf{l}}$ in image 2 which corresponds to a point $^{S_1}\tilde{\mathbf{x}}$ in image 1 is given by $^{S_2}\tilde{\mathbf{l}} = F^{\,S_1}\tilde{\mathbf{x}}$. Equation (1.19) immediately shows that this relation must be fulfilled since all points $^{S_2}\tilde{\mathbf{x}}$ in image 2 which may correspond to the point $^{S_1}\tilde{\mathbf{x}}$ in image 1 are located on the line $^{S_2}\tilde{\mathbf{l}}$. Accordingly, the line $^{S_1}\tilde{\mathbf{l}} = F^T {}^{S_2}\tilde{\mathbf{x}}$ in image 1 is the epipolar line corresponding to the point $^{S_1}\tilde{\mathbf{x}}$ in image 2 (Birchfield, 1998; Hartley and Zisserman, 2003).

Hartley and Zisserman (2003) point out that for an arbitrary point $^{S_1}\tilde{\mathbf{x}}$ in image 1 except the epipole $\tilde{\mathbf{e}}_1$, the epipole $\tilde{\mathbf{e}}_2$ in image 2 is a point on the epipolar line $^{S_2}\tilde{\mathbf{l}} = F^{\,S_1}\tilde{\mathbf{x}}$. The epipoles $\tilde{\mathbf{e}}_1$ and $\tilde{\mathbf{e}}_2$ are defined in the sensor coordinate system of camera 1 and camera 2, respectively, such that $\tilde{\mathbf{e}}_2^T (F^{\,S_1}\tilde{\mathbf{x}}) = (\tilde{\mathbf{e}}_2^T F)^{\,S_1}\tilde{\mathbf{x}} = 0$ for all points $^{S_1}\tilde{\mathbf{x}}$ on the epipolar line, which implies $\tilde{\mathbf{e}}_2^T F = 0$. Accordingly, $\tilde{\mathbf{e}}_2$ is the eigenvector belonging to the zero eigenvalue of F^T (i.e. its 'left null-vector'). The epipole $\tilde{\mathbf{e}}_1$ in image 1 is given by the eigenvector belonging to the zero eigenvalue of F according to $F\tilde{\mathbf{e}}_1 = 0$ (i.e. the 'right null-vector' of F).

1.2.2.4 Projective Reconstruction of the Scene

This section follows the presentation by Hartley and Zisserman (2003). In the framework of projective geometry, image formation by the pinhole model is defined by the projection matrix P of size 3×4 as defined in (1.13). A projective scene reconstruction by two cameras is defined by $(P_1, P_2, \{^W\tilde{\mathbf{x}}_i\})$, where P_1 and P_2 denote the projection matrix of camera 1 and 2, respectively, and $\{^W\tilde{\mathbf{x}}_i\}$ are the scene points reconstructed from a set of point correspondences. Hartley and Zisserman (2003) show that a projective scene reconstruction is always ambiguous up to a projective transformation H, where H is an arbitrary 4×4 matrix. Hence, the projective reconstruction given by $(P_1, P_2, \{^W\tilde{\mathbf{x}}_i\})$ is equivalent to the one defined by $(P_1 H, P_2 H, \{H^{-1}{}^W\tilde{\mathbf{x}}_i\})$.

It is possible to obtain the camera projection matrices P_1 and P_2 from the fundamental matrix F in a rather straightforward manner. Without loss of generality, the projection matrix P_1 may be chosen such that $P_1 = [I \mid \mathbf{0}]$, i.e. the rotation matrix R is the identity matrix and the translation vector $\mathbf{t}$ is zero, such that the world coordinate system W corresponds to the coordinate system C_1 of camera 1. The projection matrix of the second camera then corresponds to

$$P_2 = \left[[\tilde{\mathbf{e}}_2]_\times F \mid \tilde{\mathbf{e}}_2 \right]. \tag{1.21}$$

A more general form of P_2 is

$$P_2 = \left[[\tilde{\mathbf{e}}_2]_\times F + \tilde{\mathbf{e}}_2 \mathbf{v}^T \mid \lambda \tilde{\mathbf{e}}_2 \right], \tag{1.22}$$

where $\mathbf{v}$ is an arbitrary 3×1 vector and $\lambda \neq 0$. Equations (1.21) and (1.22) show that the fundamental matrix F and the epipole $\tilde{\mathbf{e}}_2$, which is uniquely determined by F since it corresponds to the eigenvector belonging to the zero eigenvalue of F^T, determine a projective reconstruction of the scene (Hartley and Zisserman, 2003).

If two corresponding image points are situated exactly on their respective epipolar lines, (1.19) is exactly fulfilled, such that the rays described by the image points $^{S_1}\tilde{\mathbf{x}}$ and $^{S_2}\tilde{\mathbf{x}}$ intersect in the point $^W\tilde{\mathbf{x}}$ which can be determined by triangulation in a straightforward manner. We will return to this scenario in Sect. 1.5 in the context of stereo image analysis in standard geometry, where the fundamental matrix F is assumed to be known. The search for point correspondences only takes place along corresponding epipolar lines, such that the world coordinates of the resulting scene points are obtained by direct triangulation. If, however, an unrestricted search for correspondences is performed, (1.19) is generally not exactly fulfilled due to noise in the measured coordinates of the corresponding points, and the rays defined by them do not intersect. Hartley and Zisserman (2003) point out that the projective scene point $^W\tilde{\mathbf{x}}$ in the world coordinate system is obtained from $^{S_1}\tilde{\mathbf{x}}$ and $^{S_2}\tilde{\mathbf{x}}$ based on the relations $^{S_1}\tilde{\mathbf{x}} = P_1{}^W\tilde{\mathbf{x}}$ and $^{S_2}\tilde{\mathbf{x}} = P_2{}^W\tilde{\mathbf{x}}$. These expressions yield the relation

$$G^W\tilde{\mathbf{x}} = 0. \tag{1.23}$$

The cross product $^{S_1}\tilde{\mathbf{x}} \times (P_1{}^W\tilde{\mathbf{x}}) = \mathbf{0}$ determines the homogeneous scale factor and allows us to express the matrix G as

$$G = \begin{bmatrix} u_1 \tilde{\mathbf{p}}_1^{(3)T} - \tilde{\mathbf{p}}_1^{(1)T} \\ v_1 \tilde{\mathbf{p}}_1^{(3)T} - \tilde{\mathbf{p}}_1^{(2)T} \\ u_2 \tilde{\mathbf{p}}_2^{(3)T} - \tilde{\mathbf{p}}_2^{(1)T} \\ v_2 \tilde{\mathbf{p}}_2^{(3)T} - \tilde{\mathbf{p}}_2^{(2)T} \end{bmatrix}, \tag{1.24}$$

where $^{S_1}\tilde{\mathbf{x}} = (u_1, v_1, 1)^T$, $^{S_2}\tilde{\mathbf{x}} = (u_2, v_2, 1)^T$, and $\tilde{\mathbf{p}}_i^{(j)T}$ corresponds to the jth row of the camera projection matrix P_i. Equation (1.23) is overdetermined since $^W\tilde{\mathbf{x}}$ only has three independent components due to its arbitrary projective scale, and generally

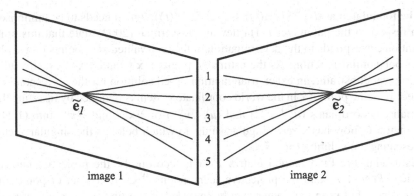

Fig. 1.3 In each of the two images, the epipolar lines form a pencil of lines. The *intersection points* correspond to the epipoles $\tilde{e}_1$ and $\tilde{e}_2$. Corresponding pairs of epipolar lines are numbered consecutively

only a least-squares solution exists due to noise in the measurements of $^{S_1}\tilde{x}$ and $^{S_2}\tilde{x}$. The solution for $^{W}\tilde{x}$ corresponds to the singular vector of the matrix G normalised to unit length which belongs to the smallest singular value (Hartley and Zisserman, 2003).

However, as merely an algebraic error rather than a physically motivated geometric error is minimised by this linear approach to determine $^{W}\tilde{x}$, Hartley and Zisserman (2003) suggest a projective reconstruction of the scene points by minimisation of the reprojection error in the sensor coordinate system. While $^{S_1}\tilde{x}$ and $^{S_2}\tilde{x}$ correspond to the measured image coordinates of a pair of corresponding points, the estimated point correspondences which exactly fulfil the epipolar constraint (1.19) are denoted by $^{S_1}\tilde{x}^{(e)}$ and $^{S_2}\tilde{x}^{(e)}$. We thus have $^{S_2}\tilde{x}^{(e)T} F \,^{S_1}\tilde{x}^{(e)} = 0$. The point $^{S_1}\tilde{x}^{(e)}$ lies on an epipolar line $^{S_1}\tilde{l}$ and $^{S_2}\tilde{x}^{(e)}$ lies on the corresponding epipolar line $^{S_2}\tilde{l}$. However, for any other pair of points lying on the lines $^{S_1}\tilde{l}$ and $^{S_2}\tilde{l}$, the epipolar constraint $^{S_2}\tilde{l}^T F \,^{S_1}\tilde{l} = 0$ is also fulfilled. Hence, the points $^{S_1}\tilde{x}^{(e)}$ and $^{S_2}\tilde{x}^{(e)}$ have to be determined such that the sum of the squared Euclidean distances $d^2(^{S_1}\tilde{x}, {}^{S_1}\tilde{l})$ and $d^2(^{S_2}\tilde{x}, {}^{S_2}\tilde{l})$ in the sensor coordinate system between $^{S_1}\tilde{x}$ and $^{S_1}\tilde{l}$ and between $^{S_2}\tilde{x}$ and $^{S_2}\tilde{l}$, respectively, i.e. the reprojection error, is minimised. Here, $d(^{S}\tilde{x}, {}^{S}\tilde{l})$ denotes the distance from the point $^{S}\tilde{x}$ to the line $^{S}\tilde{l}$ orthogonal to $^{S}\tilde{l}$. This minimisation approach is equivalent to bundle adjustment (cf. Sect. 1.3) as long as the distance $d(^{S}\tilde{x}, {}^{S}\tilde{l})$ is a Euclidean distance in the image plane rather than merely in the sensor coordinate system, which is the case for image sensors with zero skew and square pixels.

According to Hartley and Zisserman (2003), in each of the two images the epipolar lines in the two images form a 'pencil of lines', which is an infinite number of lines which all intersect in the same point (cf. Fig. 1.3). For the pencils of epipolar lines in images 1 and 2, the intersection points correspond to the epipoles $\tilde{e}_1$ and $\tilde{e}_2$. Hence, the pencil of epipolar lines can be parameterised by a single parameter t according to $^{S_1}\tilde{l}(t)$. The corresponding epipolar line $^{S_2}\tilde{l}(t)$ in image 2 then follows directly from the fundamental matrix F. Now the reprojection error term can be formulated as $d^2({}^{S_1}\tilde{\mathbf{x}}, {}^{S_1}\tilde{\mathbf{l}}(t)) + d^2({}^{S_2}\tilde{\mathbf{x}}, {}^{S_2}\tilde{\mathbf{l}}(t))$, which needs to be minimised with respect to the parameter t. Hartley and Zisserman (2003) state that this minimisation corresponds to the determination of the real-valued zero points of a sixth-order polynomial function. As the estimated points ${}^{S_1}\tilde{\mathbf{x}}^{(e)}$ and ${}^{S_2}\tilde{\mathbf{x}}^{(e)}$ exactly fulfil the epipolar constraint, an exact, triangulation-based solution for the corresponding projective scene point ${}^{W}\tilde{\mathbf{x}}$ in the world coordinate system is obtained by inserting the normalised coordinates $(u_1^{(e)}, v_1^{(e)})$ and $(u_2^{(e)}, v_2^{(e)})$ of ${}^{S_1}\mathbf{x}^{(e)}$ and ${}^{S_2}\mathbf{x}^{(e)}$ into (1.24). The matrix G now has a zero singular value, to which belongs the singular vector representing the solution for ${}^{W}\tilde{\mathbf{x}}$.

Estimating the fundamental matrix F and, accordingly, the projective camera matrices P_1 and P_2 and the projective scene points ${}^{W}\tilde{\mathbf{x}}_i$ from a set of point correspondences between the images can be regarded as the first (projective) stage of camera calibration. Subsequent calibration stages consist of determining a metric (Euclidean) scene reconstruction and camera calibration. These issues will be regarded further in Sect. 1.4.6 in the context of self-calibration of camera systems.

1.3　The Bundle Adjustment Approach

In the following, the general configuration is assumed: K three-dimensional points ${}^{W}\mathbf{x}_k$ in the world appear in L images acquired from different viewpoints, and the corresponding measured image points are denoted by their sensor coordinates ${}^{S_i}\mathbf{x}_k$, where $i = 1, \ldots, L$ and $k = 1, \ldots, K$ (Triggs et al., 2000; Hartley and Zisserman, 2003; Lourakis and Argyros, 2004).

A nonlinear function $\mathcal{Q}({}^{C_i}_W T, \{c_j\}_i, {}^{W}\mathbf{x})$ is defined such that it yields the modelled image coordinates by transforming the point ${}^{W}\mathbf{x}$ in world coordinates into the sensor coordinate system of camera i using (1.1)–(1.5) based on the camera parameters denoted by ${}^{C_i}_W T$ and $\{c_j\}_i$ and the coordinates of the K three-dimensional points ${}^{W}\mathbf{x}_k$ (Lourakis and Argyros, 2004; Kuhl et al., 2006) (cf. also Sect. 5.1). For estimating all or some of these parameters, a framework termed 'bundle adjustment' has been introduced, corresponding to a minimisation of the reprojection error

$$E_{\text{BA}} = \sum_{i=1}^{L} \sum_{k=1}^{K} \left\| {}^{S_i}_{I_i} T^{-1}\left(\mathcal{Q}({}^{C_i}_W T, \{c_j\}_i, {}^{W}\mathbf{x}_k)\right) - {}^{S_i}_{I_i} T^{-1}\left({}^{S_i}\mathbf{x}_k\right) \right\|^2, \quad (1.25)$$

which denotes the sum of squared Euclidean distances between the modelled and the measured image point coordinates (Lourakis and Argyros, 2004, cf. also Triggs et al., 2000). The transformation by ${}^{S_i}_{I_i} T^{-1}$ in (1.25) ensures that the reprojection error is measured in Cartesian image coordinates. It can be omitted if a film is used for image acquisition, on which Euclidean distances are measured in a Cartesian coordinate system, or as long as the pixel raster of the digital camera sensor is orthogonal ($\theta = 90°$) and the pixels are quadratic ($\alpha_u = \alpha_v$). This special case corresponds to ${}^{S_i}_{I_i} T$ in (1.5) describing a similarity transform.

1.4 Geometric Calibration of Single and Multiple Cameras

Camera calibration aims for a determination of the transformation parameters between the camera lens and the image plane as well as between the camera and the scene based on the acquisition of images of a calibration rig with a known spatial structure. This section first outlines early camera calibration approaches as described by Clarke and Fryer (1998) (cf. Sect. 1.4.1). It then describes the direct linear transform (DLT) approach (cf. Sect. 1.4.2) and the methods by Tsai (1987) (cf. Sect. 1.4.3) and Zhang (1999a) (cf. Sect. 1.4.4), which are classical techniques for simultaneous intrinsic and extrinsic camera calibration especially suited for fast and reliable calibration of standard video cameras and lenses commonly used in computer vision applications, and the camera calibration toolbox by Bouguet (2007) (cf. Sect. 1.4.5). Furthermore, an overview of self-calibration techniques is given (cf. Sect. 1.4.6), and the semi-automatic calibration procedure for multi-camera systems introduced by Krüger et al. (2004) (cf. Sect. 1.4.7), which is based on a fully automatic extraction of control points from the calibration images, and the corner localisation approach by Krüger and Wöhler (2011) (cf. Sect. 1.4.8) are described.

1.4.1 Methods for Intrinsic Camera Calibration

According to the detailed survey by Clarke and Fryer (1998), early approaches to camera calibration in the field of aerial photography in the first half of the twentieth century mainly dealt with the determination of the intrinsic camera parameters, which was carried out in a laboratory. This was feasible in practise due to the fact that aerial (metric) camera lenses are focused to infinity in a fixed manner and do not contain iris elements. The principal distance, in this case being equal to the focal length, was computed by determining the angular projection properties of the lens, taking a plate with markers as a reference. An average 'calibrated' value of the principal distance was selected based on measurements along several radial lines in the image plane, best compensating the effects of radial distortion, which was thus only taken into account in an implicit manner. The position of the principal point was determined based on an autocollimation method. In stereoplotting devices, radial distortion was compensated by optical correction elements. Due to the low resolution of the film used for image acquisition, there was no need to take into account tangential distortion.

Clarke and Fryer (1998) continue with the description of an analytic model of lens distortion based on a power series expansion which has been introduced by Brown (1966), and which is still utilised in modern calibration approaches (cf. also (1.3) and (1.4)). These approaches involve the simultaneous determination of lens parameters, extrinsic camera orientation, and coordinates of control points in the scene in the camera coordinate system, based on the bundle adjustment method. A different method for the determination of radial and tangential distortion parameters outlined by Clarke and Fryer (1998) is plumb line calibration (Brown, 1971), exploiting the fact that straight lines in the real world remain straight in the image. Radial and tangential distortions can be directly inferred from deviations from straightness in the image. These first calibration methods based on bundle adjustment, which may additionally determine deviations of the photographic plate from flatness or distortions caused by expansion or shrinkage of the film material, are usually termed 'on-the-job calibration' (Clarke and Fryer, 1998).

1.4.2 The Direct Linear Transform (DLT) Method

In its simplest form, the direct linear transform (DLT) calibration method introduced by Abdel-Aziz and Karara (1971) aims for a determination of the intrinsic and extrinsic camera parameters according to (1.1). This goal is achieved by establishing an appropriate transformation which translates the world coordinates of known control points in the scene into image coordinates. This section follows the illustrative presentation of the DLT method by Kwon (1998). Accordingly, the DLT method assumes a camera described by the pinhole model, for which, as outlined in the introduction given in Sect. 1.1, it is straightforward to derive the relation

$$
\begin{pmatrix} \hat{u} \\ \hat{v} \\ -b \end{pmatrix} = cR \begin{pmatrix} x - x_0 \\ y - y_0 \\ z - z_0 \end{pmatrix}. \tag{1.26}
$$

In (1.26), R denotes the rotation matrix as described in Sect. 1.1, $\hat{u}$ and $\hat{v}$ the metric pixel coordinates in the image plane relative to the principal point, and x, y, z are the components of a scene point ${}^W\mathbf{x}$ in the world coordinate system. The values x_0, y_0, and z_0 can be inferred from the translation vector $\mathbf{t}$ introduced in Sect. 1.1, while c is a scalar scale factor. This scale factor amounts to

$$
c = -\frac{b}{r_{31}(x - x_0) + r_{32}(y - y_0) + r_{33}(z - z_0)}, \tag{1.27}
$$

where the coefficients r_{ij} denote the elements of the rotation matrix R. Assuming rectangular sensor pixels without skew, the coordinates of the image point in the sensor coordinate system, i.e. the pixel coordinates, are given by $u - u_0 = k_u \hat{u}$ and $v - v_0 = k_v \hat{v}$, where u_0 and v_0 denote the position of the principal point in the sensor coordinate system. Inserting (1.27) into (1.26) then yields the relations

$$
\begin{aligned}
u - u_0 &= -\frac{b}{k_u} \frac{r_{11}(x - x_0) + r_{12}(y - y_0) + r_{13}(z - z_0)}{r_{31}(x - x_0) + r_{32}(y - y_0) + r_{33}(z - z_0)} \\
v - v_0 &= -\frac{b}{k_v} \frac{r_{21}(x - x_0) + r_{22}(y - y_0) + r_{23}(z - z_0)}{r_{31}(x - x_0) + r_{32}(y - y_0) + r_{33}(z - z_0)}
\end{aligned} \tag{1.28}
$$

Rearranging (1.28) results in expressions for the pixel coordinates u and v which only depend on the coordinates x, y, and z of the scene point and 11 constant parameters that comprise intrinsic and extrinsic camera parameters:

$$u = \frac{L_1 x + L_2 y + L_3 z + L_4}{L_9 x + L_{10} y + L_{11} z + 1}$$
$$v = \frac{L_5 x + L_6 y + L_7 z + L_8}{L_9 x + L_{10} y + L_{11} z + 1}. \tag{1.29}$$

If we use the abbreviations $b_u = b/k_u$, $b_v = b/k_v$, and $D = -(x_0 r_{31} + y_0 r_{32} + z_0 r_{33})$, the parameters $L_1 \ldots L_{11}$ can be expressed as

$$L_1 = \frac{u_0 r_{31} - b_u r_{11}}{D}$$

$$L_2 = \frac{u_0 r_{32} - b_u r_{12}}{D}$$

$$L_3 = \frac{u_0 r_{33} - b_u r_{13}}{D}$$

$$L_4 = \frac{(b_u r_{11} - u_0 r_{31}) x_0 + (b_u r_{12} - u_0 r_{32}) y_0 + (b_u r_{13} - u_0 r_{33}) z_0}{D}$$

$$L_5 = \frac{v_0 r_{31} - b_v r_{21}}{D}$$

$$L_6 = \frac{v_0 r_{32} - b_v r_{22}}{D} \tag{1.30}$$

$$L_7 = \frac{v_0 r_{33} - b_v r_{23}}{D}$$

$$L_8 = \frac{(b_v r_{21} - v_0 r_{31}) x_0 + (b_v r_{22} - v_0 r_{32}) y_0 + (b_v r_{23} - v_0 r_{33}) z_0}{D}$$

$$L_9 = \frac{r_{31}}{D}$$

$$L_{10} = \frac{r_{32}}{D}$$

$$L_{11} = \frac{r_{33}}{D}.$$

It is straightforward but somewhat tedious to compute the intrinsic and extrinsic camera parameters from these expressions for $L_1 \ldots L_{11}$.

Radial and tangential distortions introduce offsets Δu and Δv with respect to the position of the image point expected according to the pinhole model. Using the polynomial laws defined in (1.3) and (1.4) and setting $\xi = u - u_0$ and $\eta = v - v_0$, these offsets can be formulated as

$$\Delta u = \xi \left(L_{12} r^2 + L_{13} r^4 + L_{14} r^6 \right) + L_{15} (r^2 + 2\xi^2) + L_{16} \eta \xi$$
$$\Delta v = \eta \left(L_{12} r^2 + L_{13} r^4 + L_{14} r^6 \right) + L_{15} \eta \xi + L_{16} (r^2 + 2\eta^2). \tag{1.31}$$

The additional parameters $L_{12} \ldots L_{14}$ describe the radial and L_{15} and L_{16} the tangential lens distortion, respectively.

Kwon (1998) points out that by replacing in (1.29) the values of u by $u + \Delta u$ and v by $v + \Delta v$ and defining the abbreviation $Q_i = L_9 x_i + L_{10} y_i + L_{11} z_i + 1$, where x_i, y_i and z_i denote the world coordinates of scene point i ($i = 1, \ldots, N$), an equation for determining the parameters $L_1 \ldots L_{16}$ is obtained according to

$$\left[\begin{array}{ccccccccccc} \frac{x_1}{Q_1} & \frac{y_1}{Q_1} & \frac{z_1}{Q_1} & \frac{1}{Q_1} & 0 & 0 & 0 & 0 & \frac{-u_1x_1}{Q_1} & \frac{-u_1y_1}{Q_1} & \frac{-u_1z_1}{Q_1} \\[2mm] 0 & 0 & 0 & 0 & \frac{x_1}{Q_1} & \frac{y_1}{Q_1} & \frac{z_1}{Q_1} & \frac{1}{Q_1} & \frac{-v_1x_1}{Q_1} & \frac{-v_1y_1}{Q_1} & \frac{-v_1z_1}{Q_1} \\[1mm] \vdots & \vdots & \vdots & \vdots & \vdots & \vdots & \vdots & \vdots & \vdots & \vdots & \vdots \\[1mm] \frac{x_N}{Q_N} & \frac{y_N}{Q_N} & \frac{z_N}{Q_N} & \frac{1}{Q_N} & 0 & 0 & 0 & 0 & \frac{-u_Nx_N}{Q_N} & \frac{-u_Ny_N}{Q_N} & \frac{-u_Nz_N}{Q_N} \\[2mm] 0 & 0 & 0 & 0 & \frac{x_N}{Q_N} & \frac{y_N}{Q_N} & \frac{z_N}{Q_N} & \frac{1}{Q_N} & \frac{-v_Nx_N}{Q_N} & \frac{-v_Ny_N}{Q_N} & \frac{-v_Nz_N}{Q_N} \end{array}\right.$$

$$\left.\begin{array}{ccccc} \xi_1 r_1^2 & \xi_1 r_1^4 & \xi_1 r_1^6 & r_1^2+2\xi_1^2 & \eta_1\xi_1 \\[1mm] \eta_1 r_1^2 & \eta_1 r_1^4 & \eta_1 r_1^6 & \eta_1\xi_1 & r_1^2+2\eta_1^2 \\[1mm] \vdots & \vdots & \vdots & \vdots & \vdots \\[1mm] \xi_N r_N^2 & \xi_N r_N^4 & \xi_N r_N^6 & r_N^2+2\xi_N^2 & \eta_N\xi_N \\[1mm] \eta_N r_N^2 & \eta_N r_N^4 & \eta_N r_N^6 & \eta_N\xi_N & r_N^2+2\eta_N^2 \end{array}\right] \left(\begin{array}{c} L_1 \\ \vdots \\ L_{16} \end{array}\right) = \left(\begin{array}{c} \frac{u_1}{Q_1} \\[1mm] \frac{v_1}{Q_1} \\[1mm] \vdots \\[1mm] \frac{u_N}{Q_N} \\[1mm] \frac{v_N}{Q_N} \end{array}\right).$$

$$\tag{1.32}$$

Equation (1.32) is of the form

$$\mathbf{ML} = \mathbf{B}, \tag{1.33}$$

where M is a rectangular matrix of size $2N \times 16$, $\mathbf{B}$ a column vector of length $2N$, and $\mathbf{L}$ a column vector of length 16 containing the parameters $L_1 \ldots L_{16}$. The number of control points in the scene required to solve (1.33) amounts to eight if all 16 parameters are desired to be recovered. In the absence of lens distortions, only 11 parameters need to be recovered based on at least six control points. It is of course favourable to utilise more than the minimum necessary number of control points since the measured pixel coordinates u_i and v_i are not error-free. In this case, equation (1.33) is overdetermined, and the vector $\mathbf{L}$ is obtained according to

$$\mathbf{L} = \left(M^T M\right)^{-1} M^T \mathbf{B}, \tag{1.34}$$

where the matrix $(M^T M)^{-1} M^T$ is the pseudoinverse of M. Equation (1.34) yields a least-squares solution for the parameter vector $\mathbf{L}$. It is important to note that the coefficient matrix A in (1.33) contains the values Q_i, which in turn depend on the parameters L_9, L_{10}, and L_{11}. Initial values for these parameters have to be chosen, and the solution (1.34) has to be computed iteratively.

It is worth noting that the control points must not be coplanar but have to obtain a volume in three-dimensional space if the projection of arbitrary scene points onto the image plane is required. Otherwise, the pseudoinverse of M does not exist. A reduced, two-dimensional DLT can be formulated by setting $z = 0$ in (1.29) for scene points situated on a plane in three-dimensional space. In this special case it is always possible to choose the world coordinate system such that $z = 0$ for all regarded scene points (Kwon, 1998).

The DLT method is a simple and easy-to-use camera calibration method, but it has two essential drawbacks. The first one is that the computed elements of the matrix R do not form an orthonormal matrix, as would be expected for a rotation matrix. Incorporating orthonormality constraints into the DLT scheme would require nonlinear optimisation methods instead of the simple iterative linear solution scheme defined by (1.34). Another drawback is the fact that the optimisation scheme is not equivalent to bundle adjustment. While bundle adjustment minimises the reprojection error in the image plane, (1.32) illustrates that the DLT method minimises the error of the backprojected scaled pixel coordinates $(u_i/Q_i, v_i/Q_i)$. It is not guaranteed that this somewhat arbitrary error measure is always a reasonable choice.

1.4.3 The Camera Calibration Method by Tsai (1987)

Another important camera calibration method is introduced by Tsai (1987), which estimates the camera parameters based on a set of control points in the scene (here denoted by $^W\mathbf{x} = (x, y, z)^T$) and their corresponding image points (here denoted by $^I\mathbf{x} = (\hat{u}, \hat{v})$). According to the illustrative presentation by Horn (2000) of that approach, in the first stage of the algorithm by Tsai (1987) estimates of several extrinsic camera parameters (the elements of the rotation matrix R and two components of the translation vector $\mathbf{t}$) are obtained based on the equations

$$\frac{\hat{u}}{b} = s \frac{r_{11}x + r_{12}y + r_{13}z + t_x}{r_{31}x + r_{32}y + r_{33}z + t_z} \tag{1.35}$$

$$\frac{\hat{v}}{b} = \frac{r_{21}x + r_{22}y + r_{23}z + t_y}{r_{31}x + r_{32}y + r_{33}z + t_z} \tag{1.36}$$

following from the pinhole model (cf. Sect. 1.1), where s is the aspect ratio for rectangular pixels, the coefficients r_{ij} are the elements of the rotation matrix R, and $\mathbf{t} = (t_x, t_y, t_z)^T$. Following the derivation by Horn (2000), dividing (1.35) by (1.36) leads to the expression

$$\frac{\hat{u}}{\hat{v}} = s \frac{r_{11}x + r_{12}y + r_{13}z + t_x}{r_{21}x + r_{22}y + r_{23}z + t_y} \tag{1.37}$$

which is independent of the principal distance b and the radial lens distortion, since it only depends on the direction from the principal point to the image point. Equation (1.37) is then transformed into a linear equation in the camera parameters. This equation is solved with respect to the elements of R and the translation components t_x and t_y in the least-squares sense based on the known coordinates of the control points and their observed corresponding image points, where one of the translation components has to be normalised to 1 due to the homogeneity of the resulting equation.

Horn (2000) points out that the camera parameters have been estimated independently, i.e. the estimated rotation matrix is generally not orthonormal, and describes a method which yields the most similar orthonormal rotation matrix. The orthonormality conditions allow the determination of s and the overall scale factor of the solution. The principal distance b and the translation component t_z are then obtained based on (1.35) and (1.36). For the special case of a planar calibration rig, the world coordinate system can always be chosen such that $z = 0$ for all control points, and (1.35)–(1.37) are applied accordingly. This special case only yields a submatrix of size 2×2 of the rotation matrix, which nevertheless allows us to estimate the full orthonormal rotation matrix.

The second calibration stage of the method by Tsai (1987) is described by Horn (2000) as a minimisation of the reprojection error in the image plane (cf. Sect. 1.3), during which the already estimated parameters are refined and the principal point (u_0, v_0) and the radial and tangential distortion coefficients (cf. Sect. 1.1) are determined based on nonlinear optimisation techniques.

1.4.4 The Camera Calibration Method by Zhang (1999a)

The camera calibration method by Zhang (1999a) is specially designed for utilising a planar calibration rig which is viewed by the camera at different viewing angles and distances. This calibration approach is derived in terms of the projective geometry framework.

For a planar calibration rig, the world coordinate system can always be chosen such that we have $Z = 0$ for all points on it. The image formation is then described by Zhang (1999a) in homogeneous normalised coordinates by

$$\begin{pmatrix} u \\ v \\ 1 \end{pmatrix} = A[R \mid \mathbf{t}] \begin{pmatrix} X \\ Y \\ 0 \\ 1 \end{pmatrix} = A[\mathbf{r}_1 \mid \mathbf{r}_2 \mid \mathbf{t}] \begin{pmatrix} X \\ Y \\ 1 \end{pmatrix}, \tag{1.38}$$

where the vectors $\mathbf{r}_i$ denote the column vectors of the rotation matrix R. A point on the calibration rig with $Z = 0$ is denoted by $\mathbf{M} = (X, Y)^T$. The corresponding vector in normalised homogeneous coordinates is given by $\tilde{\mathbf{M}} = (X, Y, 1)^T$. According to (1.38), in the absence of lens distortion the image point $\tilde{\mathbf{m}}$ can be obtained from its corresponding scene point $\tilde{\mathbf{M}}$ by applying a homography H. A homography denotes a linear transform of a vector (of length 3) in the projective plane. It is given by a 3×3 matrix and has eight degrees of freedom, as a projective transform is unique only up to a scale factor (cf. Sect. 1.1). This leads to

$$\tilde{\mathbf{m}} = H\tilde{\mathbf{M}} \quad \text{with } H = A[\mathbf{r}_1 \quad \mathbf{r}_2 \quad \mathbf{t}]. \tag{1.39}$$

To compute the homography H, Zhang (1999a) proposes a nonlinear optimisation procedure which minimises the Euclidean reprojection error of the scene points projected into the image plane. The column vectors of H are denoted by $\mathbf{h}_1$, $\mathbf{h}_2$, and $\mathbf{h}_3$. We obtain

$$[\mathbf{h}_1 \quad \mathbf{h}_2 \quad \mathbf{h}_3] = \lambda A[\mathbf{r}_r \quad \mathbf{r}_2 \quad \mathbf{t}], \tag{1.40}$$

with λ as a scale factor. It follows from (1.40) that $\mathbf{r}_1 = (1/\lambda)A^{-1}\mathbf{h}_1$ and $\mathbf{r}_2 = (1/\lambda)A^{-1}\mathbf{h}_2$ with $\lambda = 1/\|A^{-1}\mathbf{h}_1\| = 1/\|A^{-1}\mathbf{h}_2\|$. The orthonormality of $\mathbf{r}_1$ and $\mathbf{r}_2$ yields $\mathbf{r}_1^T \cdot \mathbf{r}_2 = 0$ and $\mathbf{r}_1^T \cdot \mathbf{r}_1 = \mathbf{r}_2^T \cdot \mathbf{r}_2$, implying

$$\begin{aligned} \mathbf{h}_1^T A^{-T} A^{-1} \mathbf{h}_2 &= 0 \\ \mathbf{h}_1^T A^{-T} A^{-1} \mathbf{h}_1 &= \mathbf{h}_2^T A^{-T} A^{-1} \mathbf{h}_2 \end{aligned} \tag{1.41}$$

as constraints on the intrinsic camera parameters. In (1.41), the expression A^{-T} is an abbreviation for $(A^T)^{-1}$.

Zhang (1999a) derives a closed-form solution for the extrinsic and intrinsic camera parameters by defining the symmetric matrix

$$B = A^{-T} A^{-1}, \tag{1.42}$$

which can alternatively be defined by a six-dimensional vector $\mathbf{b} = (B_{11}, B_{12}, B_{22}, B_{13}, B_{23}, B_{33})$. With the notation $\mathbf{h}_i = (h_{i1}, h_{i2}, h_{i3})^T$ for the column vectors $\mathbf{h}_i$ of the homography H, we obtain

$$\mathbf{h}_i^T B \mathbf{h}_j = \mathbf{v}_{ij} \mathbf{b}, \tag{1.43}$$

where the six-dimensional vector $\mathbf{v}_{ij}$ corresponds to

$$\mathbf{v}_{ij} = (h_{i1}h_{j1}, h_{i1}h_{i2} + h_{j1}, h_{i2}h_{j2}, h_{i3}h_{j1} + h_{i1}h_{j3}, h_{i3}h_{j2} + h_{i2}h_{j3}, h_{i3}h_{j3})^T. \tag{1.44}$$

Equation (1.41) is now rewritten in the following form:

$$\begin{pmatrix} \mathbf{v}_{12}^T \\ (\mathbf{v}_{11} - \mathbf{v}_{22})^T \end{pmatrix} \mathbf{b} = 0. \tag{1.45}$$

Acquiring n images of the planar calibration rig yields n equations of the form (1.45), leading to the homogeneous linear equation

$$V\mathbf{b} = 0 \tag{1.46}$$

for $\mathbf{b}$, where V is a matrix of size $2n \times 6$. As long as $n \leq 3$, (1.46) yields a solution for $\mathbf{b}$ which is unique up to a scale factor. Zhang (1999a) shows that for $n = 2$ images and an image sensor without skew, corresponding to the matrix element A_{12} being zero, adding the appropriate constraint $(0, 1, 0, 0, 0, 0)\mathbf{b} = 0$ also yields a solution for $\mathbf{b}$ in this special case. If only a single calibration image is available, Zhang (1999a) proposes to assume a pixel sensor without skew ($A_{12} = 0$), set the principal point given by u_0 and v_0 equal to the image centre, and estimate only the two matrix elements A_{11} and A_{22} from the calibration image. It is well known from linear algebra that the solution to a homogeneous linear equation of the form (1.46) corresponds to the eigenvector of the 6×6 matrix $V^T V$ which belongs to the smallest eigenvalue.

Using the obtained value of $\mathbf{b}$, Zhang (1999a) determines the intrinsic camera parameters based on the relation $B = v A^{-T} A$, where v is a scale factor, as follows:

$$\begin{aligned}
v_0 &= A_{23} = (B_{12}B_{13} - B_{11}B_{23})/(B_{11}B_{22} - B_{12}^2) \\
v &= B_{33} - [B_{13}^2 + v_0(B_{12}B_{13} - B_{11}B_{23})]/B_{11} \\
\alpha_u &= A_{11} = \sqrt{v/B_{11}} \\
\alpha_v &= A_{22} = \sqrt{v B_{11}/(B_{11}B_{22} - B_{12}^2)} \\
\alpha_u \cot\theta &= A_{12} = -B_{12}\alpha_u^2 \alpha_v/v \\
u_0 &= A_{13} = A_{12}v_0/\alpha_v - B_{13}\alpha_u^2/v
\end{aligned} \tag{1.47}$$

(note that in (1.47) the matrix elements according to (1.11) are used). The extrinsic parameters for each image are then obtained according to

$$
\begin{aligned}
\mathbf{r}_1 &= \lambda A^{-1}\mathbf{h}_1 \\
\mathbf{r}_2 &= \lambda A^{-1}\mathbf{h}_2 \\
\mathbf{r}_3 &= \mathbf{r}_1 \times \mathbf{r}_2 \\
\mathbf{t} &= \lambda A^{-1}\mathbf{h}_3.
\end{aligned}
\tag{1.48}
$$

The matrix R computed according to (1.48), however, does not necessarily fulfill the orthonormality constraints imposed on a rotation matrix. For initialisation of the subsequent nonlinear bundle adjustment procedure, a technique is suggested by Zhang (1998) to determine the orthonormal rotation matrix which is closest to a given 3×3 matrix in terms of the Frobenius norm.

Similar to the DLT method, the intrinsic and extrinsic camera parameters computed so far have been obtained by minimisation of an algebraic error measure which is not physically meaningful. Zhang (1999a) uses these parameters as initial values for a bundle adjustment step which is based on the minimisation of the error term

$$
\sum_{i=1}^{n}\sum_{j=1}^{m}\left\|\mathbf{m}_{ij} - A(R_i\mathbf{M}_j + \mathbf{t})\right\|^2.
\tag{1.49}
$$

In the optimisation, a rotation R is described by the Rodrigues vector $\mathbf{r}$. The direction of this vector indicates the direction of the rotation axis, and its norm denotes the rotation angle in radians. Zhang (1999a) utilises the Levenberg-Marquardt algorithm (Press et al., 2007) to minimise the bundle adjustment error term (1.49).

To take into account radial lens distortion, Zhang (1999a) utilises the model defined by (1.3). Tangential lens distortion is neglected. Assuming small radial distortions, such that only the coefficients k_1 and k_3 in (1.3) are significantly different from zero, the following procedure is suggested for estimating k_1 and k_3: An initial solution for the camera parameters is obtained by setting $k_1 = k_3 = 0$, which yields projected control points according to the pinhole model. The parameters k_1 and k_3 are computed in a second step by minimising the average Euclidean distance in the image plane between the projected and the observed image points, based on an overdetermined system of linear equations. The final values for k_1 and k_3 are obtained by iteratively applying this procedure.

Due to the observed slow convergence of the iterative technique, Zhang (1999a) proposes an alternative approach to determine lens distortion by incorporating the distortion parameters appropriately into the error term (1.49) and estimating them simultaneously with the other camera parameters.

1.4.5 The Camera Calibration Toolbox by Bouguet (2007)

Bouguet (2007) provides a toolbox for the calibration of multiple cameras implemented in Matlab. The calibration images should display a chequerboard pattern, where the reference points have to be selected manually. The toolbox then determines the intrinsic and extrinsic parameters of all cameras. It is also possible to rectify pairs of stereo images into standard geometry. The toolbox employs the camera model by Heikkilä and Silvén (1997), where the utilised intrinsic and extrinsic parameters are similar to those described in Sect. 1.1.

1.4.6 Self-calibration of Camera Systems from Multiple Views of a Static Scene

The camera calibration approaches regarded so far (cf. Sects. 1.4.2–1.4.5) all rely on a set of images of a calibration rig of known geometry with well-defined control points that can be extracted at high accuracy from the calibration images. Camera calibration without a dedicated calibration rig, thus exclusively relying on feature points extracted from a set of images of a scene of unknown geometry and the established correspondences between them, is termed 'self-calibration'.

1.4.6.1 Projective Reconstruction: Determination of the Fundamental Matrix

This section follows the presentation by Hartley and Zisserman (2003). The first step of self-calibration from multiple views of an unknown static scene is the determination of the fundamental matrix F between image pairs as defined in Sect. 1.2.2. This procedure immediately allows us to compute a projective reconstruction of the scene based on the camera projection matrices P_1 and P_2 which can be computed with (1.21) and (1.22). As soon as seven or more point correspondences $(^{S_1}\tilde{x}, {}^{S_2}\tilde{x})$ are available, the fundamental matrix F can be computed based on (1.19). We express the image points $^{S_1}\tilde{x}$ and $^{S_2}\tilde{x}$ in normalised coordinates by the vectors $(u_1, v_1, 1)^T$ and $(u_2, v_2, 1)^T$. Each point correspondence provides an equation for the matrix elements of F according to

$$u_1 u_2 F_{11} + u_2 v_1 F_{12} + u_2 F_{13} + u_1 v_2 F_{21} + v_1 v_2 F_{22} + v_2 F_{23} + u_1 F_{31} + v_1 F_{32}$$
$$+ F_{33} = 0. \tag{1.50}$$

In (1.50), the coefficients of the matrix elements of F only depend on the measured coordinates of $^{S_1}\tilde{x}'$ and $^{S_2}\tilde{x}'$. Hartley and Zisserman (2003) define the vector $\mathbf{f}$ of length 9 as being composed of the matrix elements taken row-wise from F. Equation (1.50) then becomes

$$(u_1 u_2, u_2 v_1, u_2, u_1 v_2, v_1 v_2, v_2, u_1, v_1, 1)\mathbf{f} = 0. \tag{1.51}$$

A set of n point correspondences then yields a system of equations for the matrix elements of F according to

$$
Gf = \begin{bmatrix} u_1^{(1)}u_2^{(1)} & u_2^{(1)}v_1^{(1)} & u_2^{(1)} & u_1^{(1)}v_2^{(1)} & v_1^{(1)}v_2^{(1)} & v_2^{(1)} & u_1^{(1)} & v_1^{(1)} & 1 \\ \vdots & \vdots & \vdots & \vdots & \vdots & \vdots & \vdots & \vdots & \vdots \\ u_1^{(n)}u_2^{(n)} & u_2^{(n)}v_1^{(n)} & u_2^{(n)} & u_1^{(n)}v_2^{(n)} & v_1^{(n)}v_2^{(n)} & v_2^{(n)} & u_1^{(n)} & v_1^{(n)} & 1 \end{bmatrix} f
$$
$$
= 0. \tag{1.52}
$$

The scale factor of the matrix F remains undetermined by (1.52). A unique solution (of unknown scale) is directly obtained if the coefficient matrix G is of rank 8. However, if is it assumed that the established point correspondences are not exact due to measurement noise, the rank of the coefficient matrix G is 9 even if only eight point correspondences are taken into account, and the accuracy of the solution for F generally increases if still more point correspondences are regarded. In this case, the least-squares solution for $\mathbf{f}$ is given by the singular vector of G which corresponds to its smallest singular value, for which $\|Gf\|$ becomes minimal with $\|\mathbf{f}\| = 1$.

Hartley and Zisserman (2003) point out that a problem with this approach is the fact that the fundamental matrix obtained from (1.52) is generally not of rank 2 due to measurement noise, while the epipoles of the image pair are given by the left and right null-vectors of F, i.e. the eigenvectors belonging to the zero eigenvalues of F^T and F, respectively. These do not exist if the rank of F is higher than 2. The constraint that F is of rank 2 can be taken into account by replacing the solution obtained based on the singular value decomposition (SVD) of the coefficient matrix G as defined in (1.52) by the matrix $\bar{F}$ which minimises $\|F - \bar{F}\|_F$ with $\det \bar{F} = 0$. The term $\|A\|_F$ is the Frobenius norm of a matrix A with elements a_{ij} given by

$$
\|A\|_F^2 = \sum_{i=1}^{m}\sum_{j=1}^{n}|a_{ij}|^2 = \text{trace}(A^*A) = \sum_{i=1}^{\min(m,n)} \sigma_i^2 \tag{1.53}
$$

with A^* as the conjugate transpose of A and σ_i as its singular values. If it is assumed that $F = UDV^T$ is the SVD of F with D as a diagonal matrix $D = \text{diag}(r, s, t)$, where $r \geq s \geq t$, the matrix $\bar{F}$ which minimises the Frobenius norm $\|F - \bar{F}\|_F$ is given by $\bar{F} = U\text{diag}(r, s, 0)V^T$.

At this point, Hartley and Zisserman (2003) propose an extension of this "eight-point algorithm" to determine the fundamental matrix F. Since the elements of the fundamental matrix may be of strongly different orders of magnitude, it is favourable to normalise by a translation and scaling transformation in each image the sensor (pixel) coordinates of the image points, given by $(u_i^{(j)}, v_i^{(j)}, 1)^T$ with $i \in \{1, 2\}$ indicating the image index and j denoting the index of the pair of corresponding points. Hence, the average of the image points, which are given in normalised homogeneous coordinates, is shifted to the origin of the sensor coordinate system, and their root-mean-square distance to the origin obtains the value $\sqrt{2}$. This transformation is performed according to

$$\begin{pmatrix} \breve{u}_i^{(j)} \\ \breve{v}_i^{(j)} \\ 1 \end{pmatrix} = T_i \begin{pmatrix} u_i^{(j)} \\ v_i^{(j)} \\ 1 \end{pmatrix}, \tag{1.54}$$

where the transformation matrices T_i are given by

$$T_i = \begin{bmatrix} s_i & 0 & -s_i \langle u_i^{(j)} \rangle_j \\ 0 & s_i & -s_i \langle v_i^{(j)} \rangle_j \\ 0 & 0 & 1 \end{bmatrix}$$

$$\text{with } s_i = \frac{\sqrt{2}}{\sqrt{\langle (u_i^{(j)} - \langle u_i^{(j)} \rangle_j)^2 + (v_i^{(j)} - \langle v_i^{(j)} \rangle_j)^2 \rangle_j}}. \tag{1.55}$$

A normalised fundamental matrix $\check{F}$ is then obtained based on (1.52), where the image points $(u_i^{(j)}, v_i^{(j)}, 1)^T$ are replaced by the normalised image points $(\breve{u}_i^{(j)}, \breve{v}_i^{(j)}, 1)^T$, followed by enforcing the singularity constraint on $\check{F}$ using the SVD-based procedure described above. Denormalisation of $\check{F}$ according to $F = T_2^T \check{F} T_1$ then yields the fundamental matrix F for the original image points.

The linear methods to determine the fundamental matrix F all rely on error measures which are purely algebraic rather than physically motivated. In contrast, the 'gold standard method' described by Hartley and Zisserman (2003) yields a fundamental matrix which is optimal in terms of the Euclidean distance in the image plane between the measured point correspondences $^{S_1}\tilde{\mathbf{x}}_i$ and $^{S_2}\tilde{\mathbf{x}}_i$ and the estimated point correspondences $^{S_1}\tilde{\mathbf{x}}_i^{(e)}$ and $^{S_2}\tilde{\mathbf{x}}_i^{(e)}$, which exactly satisfy the relation $^{S_2}\tilde{\mathbf{x}}_i^{(e)T} F^{S_1}\tilde{\mathbf{x}}_i^{(e)} = 0$. It is necessary to minimise the error term

$$E_G = \sum_i [d^2(^{S_1}\tilde{\mathbf{x}}_i, {}^{S_1}\tilde{\mathbf{x}}_i^{(e)}) + d^2(^{S_2}\tilde{\mathbf{x}}_i, {}^{S_2}\tilde{\mathbf{x}}_i^{(e)})]. \tag{1.56}$$

In (1.56), the distance measure $d(^S\tilde{\mathbf{x}}, {}^S\tilde{\mathbf{x}}^{(e)})$ describes the Euclidean distance in the image plane between the image points $^S\tilde{\mathbf{x}}$ and $^S\tilde{\mathbf{x}}^{(e)}$, i.e. the reprojection error. To minimise the error term (1.56), Hartley and Zisserman (2003) suggest defining the camera projection matrices as $P_1 = [I \mid \mathbf{0}]$ (called the canonical form) and $P_2 = [M \mid \mathbf{t}]$ and the set of three-dimensional scene points that belong to the measured point correspondences $^{S_1}\tilde{\mathbf{x}}_i$ and $^{S_2}\tilde{\mathbf{x}}_i$ as $^W\mathbf{x}_i$. It then follows that $^{S_1}\tilde{\mathbf{x}}_i^{(e)} = P_1{}^W\tilde{\mathbf{x}}_i$ and $^{S_2}\tilde{\mathbf{x}}_i^{(e)} = P_2{}^W\tilde{\mathbf{x}}_i$. The Euclidean error term E_G according to (1.56) is minimised with respect to the projection matrix P_2, defined by the matrix M and the vector $\mathbf{t}$, and the scene points $^W\tilde{\mathbf{x}}_i$. Due to the special form of camera matrix P_1, the matrix F follows as $F = [\mathbf{t}]_\times M$. The correspondingly estimated image points $^{S_1}\tilde{\mathbf{x}}_i^{(e)}$ and $^{S_2}\tilde{\mathbf{x}}_i^{(e)}$ exactly satisfy the relation $^{S_1}\tilde{\mathbf{x}}_i^{(e)T} F^{S_2}\tilde{\mathbf{x}}_i^{(e)} = 0$. The Euclidean error term (1.56) is minimised with a nonlinear optimisation algorithm such as the Levenberg–Marquardt method (Press et al., 2007).

1.4.6.2 Metric Self-calibration

This section describes how a metric self-calibration can be obtained based on the projective reconstruction of the scene, following the presentation by Hartley and Zisserman (2003). In a metric coordinate system, the cameras are calibrated and the scene structure is represented in a Euclidean world coordinate system. Each of the m cameras is defined by its projection matrix $P_i^{(M)}$, for which a scene point $^W\tilde{\mathbf{x}}_i^{(M)}$ yields the image point $^{S_i}\tilde{\mathbf{x}}_i^{(M)} = P_i^{(M)}\, ^W\tilde{\mathbf{x}}_i^{(M)}$. The index M denotes that the projection matrices as well as the scene and image points, although given in homogeneous coordinates, are represented in Euclidean coordinate systems. The projection matrices can be written as $P_i^{(M)} = A_i[R_i \mid \mathbf{t}_i]$ for $i = 1, \ldots, m$. The projective reconstruction according to Sect. 1.2.2 yields projection matrices P_i from which the corresponding Euclidean matrices $P_i^{(M)}$ are obtained by

$$P_i^{(M)} = P_i H \tag{1.57}$$

for $i = 1, \ldots, m$, with H as a 4×4 projective transformation. According to Hartley and Zisserman (2003), the aim of metric self-calibration is the determination of H in (1.57).

Hartley and Zisserman (2003) assume that the world coordinate system is identical to the coordinate system of camera 1, i.e. $R_1 = I$ and $\mathbf{t}_1 = \mathbf{0}$. The matrices R_i and the translation vectors $\mathbf{t}_i$ denote the rotation and translation of camera i with respect to camera 1. Furthermore, we have $P_1^{(M)} = A_1[I \mid \mathbf{0}]$. The projection matrix P_1 is set to its canonical form $P_1 = [I \mid \mathbf{0}]$. If H is written as

$$H = \begin{bmatrix} B & \mathbf{t} \\ \mathbf{v}^T & k \end{bmatrix}. \tag{1.58}$$

Equation (1.57) reduces to the simplified form $[A_1 \mid \mathbf{0}] = [I \mid \mathbf{0}]H$, from which it can be readily inferred that $B = A_1$ and $\mathbf{t} = \mathbf{0}$. To prevent the matrix H from becoming singular, it is required that its element $H_{44} = k \neq 0$. A favourable choice is to set $H_{44} = k = 1$, which yields

$$H = \begin{bmatrix} A_1 & \mathbf{0} \\ \mathbf{v}^T & 1 \end{bmatrix}. \tag{1.59}$$

Under these conditions, the plane at infinity corresponds to

$$\tilde{\pi}_\infty = H^{-T} \begin{pmatrix} 0 \\ 0 \\ 0 \\ 1 \end{pmatrix} = \begin{bmatrix} A_1^{-T} & -A_1^{-T}\mathbf{v} \\ \mathbf{0}^T & 1 \end{bmatrix} \begin{pmatrix} 0 \\ 0 \\ 0 \\ 1 \end{pmatrix} = \begin{pmatrix} -A_1^{-T}\mathbf{v} \\ 1 \end{pmatrix} \tag{1.60}$$

and hence $\mathbf{v}^T = -\mathbf{p}^T A$ with the upper triangular matrix $A \equiv A_1$ denoting the intrinsic calibration of the first camera (Hartley and Zisserman, 2003). Equation (1.59) then becomes

$$H = \begin{bmatrix} A & \mathbf{0} \\ -\mathbf{p}^T A & 1 \end{bmatrix}. \tag{1.61}$$

The metric reconstruction then consists of a determination of the three components of $\mathbf{p}$ and the five independent matrix elements of A (Hartley and Zisserman, 2003).

The Basic Equations for Self-calibration and Methods for Their Solution To determine the basic equations for self-calibration, Hartley and Zisserman (2003) suggest to denote the camera projection matrices of the projective reconstruction as $P_i = [B_i \mid \mathbf{b}_i]$. Combining (1.57) and (1.58) then yields

$$A_i R_i = \left(B_i - \mathbf{b}_i \mathbf{p}^T\right) A_1 \qquad (1.62)$$

for $i = 2, \ldots, m$, which corresponds to $R_i = A_i^{-1}(B_i - \mathbf{b}_i \mathbf{p}^T) A_1$. It follows from the orthonormality of the rotation matrices that $R R^T = I$ and thus

$$A_i A_i^T = \left(B_i - \mathbf{b}_i \mathbf{p}^T\right) A_1 A_1^T \left(B_i - \mathbf{b}_i \mathbf{p}^T\right)^T. \qquad (1.63)$$

This important expression yields the basic equations of self-calibration. Knowledge about the elements of the camera matrices A_i, e.g. the position of the principal point (u_0, v_0) or the skew angle θ, yields equations for the eight unknown parameters of $\mathbf{p}$ and A_1 based on (1.63).

A special case of high practical relevance is the situation where all cameras have the same intrinsic parameters. Equation (1.63) then becomes

$$AA^T = \left(B_i - \mathbf{b}\mathbf{p}^T\right) AA^T \left(B_i - \mathbf{b}\mathbf{p}^T\right)^T. \qquad (1.64)$$

Since each side of (1.64) is a symmetric 3×3 matrix and the equation is homogeneous, each view apart from the first provides five additional constraints, such that a solution for the eight unknown parameters and thus for A can be obtained for $m \geq 3$ images (Hartley and Zisserman, 2003).

In the context of the basic equations of self-calibration, several geometric entities are introduced by Hartley and Zisserman (2003). In projective geometry, the general representation of curves resulting from the intersection between a plane and a cone, i.e. circles, ellipses, parabolas, and hyperbolas, is given by a conic. The projective representation of a conic is a matrix C with $\tilde{\mathbf{x}}^T C \tilde{\mathbf{x}}$ for all points $\tilde{\mathbf{x}}$ on the conic C. The dual of a conic is also a conic, because a conic can either be defined by the points belonging to it, or by the lines (in $\mathcal{P}^2$) or planes (in $\mathcal{P}^3$) which are dual to these points and thus form the 'envelope' of the conic (Hartley and Zisserman, 2003).

The absolute conic Ω_∞ is situated on the plane at infinity $\tilde{\pi}_\infty$. An important entity is the dual of the absolute conic Ω_∞, which is termed absolute dual quadric and is denoted by Q_∞^*. In a Euclidean coordinate system, Q_∞^* obtains its canonical form $Q_\infty^* = \tilde{I} = \operatorname{diag}(1, 1, 1, 0)$, while its general form corresponds to $Q_\infty^* = H \tilde{I} H^T$ (Hartley and Zisserman, 2003).

Two entities which are relevant in the context of metric self-calibration are the 'image of the absolute conic' (IAC) and the 'dual image of the absolute conic' (DIAC), which are denoted by ω and ω^*, respectively. Hartley and Zisserman (2003) show that they are given in terms of the matrix A comprising the intrinsic camera parameters (cf. (1.11)) according to

$$\omega = \left(AA^T\right)^{-1} = A^{-T} A^{-1} \quad \text{and} \quad \omega^* = \omega^{-1} = AA^T. \qquad (1.65)$$

Once the matrix ω^* is known, the matrix A is readily obtained based on Cholesky factorisation (Press et al., 2007). In terms of the intrinsic camera parameters themselves, the DIAC $\omega^* = AA^T$ can be expressed as

$$\omega^* = \begin{bmatrix} \alpha_u^2 + \alpha_u^2 \cot^2\theta + u_0^2 & \alpha_u\alpha_v \cos\theta/\sin^2\theta + u_0v_0 & u_0 \\ \alpha_u\alpha_v \cos\theta/\sin^2\theta + u_0v_0 & \alpha_v^2/\sin^2\theta + v_0^2 & v_0 \\ u_0 & v_0 & 1 \end{bmatrix} \quad (1.66)$$

when A is defined according to Birchfield (1998) (cf. (1.11)). Written in terms of the IACs ω_i and the DIACs ω_i^*, the basic equations of self-calibration (1.63) become

$$\omega_i^* = \left(B_i - \mathbf{b}_i\mathbf{p}^T\right)\omega_1^*\left(B_i - \mathbf{b}_i\mathbf{p}^T\right)^T$$
$$\omega_i = \left(B_i - \mathbf{b}_i\mathbf{p}^T\right)^{-T}\omega_1\left(B_i - \mathbf{b}_i\mathbf{p}^T\right)^{-1}. \quad (1.67)$$

Hartley and Zisserman (2003) show that the image of the absolute dual quadric Q_∞^* is identical to the DIAC and can be expressed as

$$\omega^* = PQ_\infty^* P^T \quad (1.68)$$

with P as the projection matrix of the camera, where (1.68) is shown to be equivalent to the basic equations of self-calibration (1.67). At this point, metric self-calibration based on the absolute dual quadric according to Hartley and Zisserman (2003) proceeds as follows:

1. Determine Q_∞^* based on known elements, especially zero-valued elements, of ω^* and the known projection matrix P using (1.68). As an example, for a known principal point (u_0, v_0) the sensor coordinate system can be translated such that $u_0 = v_0 = 0$, leading to $\omega_{13}^* = \omega_{23}^* = \omega_{31}^* = \omega_{32}^* = 0$. In addition, a zero skew angle, i.e. $\theta = 90°$, yields $\omega_{12}^* = \omega_{21}^* = 0$.
2. Determine the transformation H based on an eigenvalue decomposition of the absolute dual quadric Q_∞^* according to $Q_\infty^* = H\tilde{I}H^T$ with $\tilde{I} = \mathrm{diag}(1, 1, 1, 0)$.
3. Determine the metric camera projection matrix $P^{(M)} = PH$ and the metric scene point coordinates ${}^W\tilde{\mathbf{x}}_i^{(M)} = H^{-1}\,{}^W\tilde{\mathbf{x}}_i$.

Since the solution for $P^{(M)}$ and ${}^W\tilde{\mathbf{x}}_i^{(M)}$ is obtained based on a merely algebraic rather than a physically meaningful error term, it is advantageous to perform a refinement by a full bundle adjustment step. A summary of the scene reconstruction and self-calibration methods based on projective geometry described so far in this section is given in Fig. 1.4.

An alternative approach to self-calibration is based on the Kruppa equations. According to Hartley and Zisserman (2003), they were originally introduced by Kruppa (1913) and modified by Hartley (1997) to establish a relation based on an SVD of the fundamental matrix F which yields quadratic equations in the parameters of the DIACs. The main advantage of this technique is that it does not require a projective reconstruction. Another approach, termed 'stratified self-calibration' by Hartley and Zisserman (2003), is to proceed stepwise from projective to affine and finally to metric reconstruction. A detailed description of these methods is beyond the scope of this section.

Essential matrix: Fundamental matrix:

$$^{I_1}\tilde{\mathbf{x}}'^T\, E\, {}^{I_2}\tilde{\mathbf{x}}' = 0 \qquad {}^{S_2}\tilde{\mathbf{x}}^T\, F\, {}^{S_1}\tilde{\mathbf{x}} = 0 \qquad F = A_2^{-T} E A_1^{-1}$$

Epipoles: Projective reconstruction (linear method):

$$\tilde{\mathbf{e}}_2^T F = 0 \qquad F \tilde{\mathbf{e}}_1 = 0 \qquad P_1 = \begin{bmatrix} I \mid \vec{0} \end{bmatrix} \qquad P_2 = \begin{bmatrix} [\tilde{\mathbf{e}}_2]_\times F \mid \tilde{\mathbf{e}}_2 \end{bmatrix}$$

Projection matrices in Euclidean coordinate system:

$$P_i^{(M)} = P_i H \qquad\qquad G\,{}^W\tilde{\mathbf{x}} = 0 \qquad G = \begin{bmatrix} u_1 \tilde{\mathbf{p}}_1^{(3)T} - \tilde{\mathbf{p}}_1^{(1)T} \\ v_1 \tilde{\mathbf{p}}_1^{(3)T} - \tilde{\mathbf{p}}_1^{(2)T} \\ u_2 \tilde{\mathbf{p}}_2^{(3)T} - \tilde{\mathbf{p}}_2^{(1)T} \\ v_2 \tilde{\mathbf{p}}_2^{(3)T} - \tilde{\mathbf{p}}_2^{(2)T} \end{bmatrix}$$

$$H = \begin{bmatrix} A_1 & \mathbf{0} \\ \mathbf{v}^T & 1 \end{bmatrix}$$

Nonlinear projective reconstruction is based on minimising Euclidean distances in the image plane.

Image of the absolute conic (IAC):   Dual image of the absolute conic (DIAC):

$$\omega = (AA^T)^{-1} = A^{-T}A^{-1} \qquad\qquad \omega^* = \omega^{-1} = AA^T$$

Basic equations of self-calibration:

$$\omega_i^* = \left(B_i - \mathbf{b}_i\, \mathbf{p}^T\right) \omega_1^* \left(B_i - \mathbf{b}_i\, \mathbf{p}^T\right)^T$$

$$\omega_i = \left(B_i - \mathbf{b}_i\, \mathbf{p}^T\right)^{-T} \omega_1 \left(B_i - \mathbf{b}_i\, \mathbf{p}^T\right)^{-1} \qquad \text{where} \quad P_i = \begin{bmatrix} B_i \mid \mathbf{b}_i \end{bmatrix}$$

Self-calibration based on the absolute dual quadric:

$$\omega^* = P Q_\infty^* P^T \qquad\qquad Q_\infty^* = H \tilde{I} H^T \qquad$$ determination of H based on eigenvalue decomposition of the absolute dual quadric

$$P^{(M)} = P H \qquad\qquad {}^W\tilde{\mathbf{x}}_i^{(M)} = H^{-1}\, {}^W\tilde{\mathbf{x}}_i \qquad$$ transformation into Euclidean coordinates

---

Fig. 1.4 Summary of projective techniques for scene reconstruction and self-calibration

Notably, all metric self-calibration methods yield the three-dimensional scene structure only in arbitrary units. Consequently, the absolute scale of the reconstruction remains unknown as long as the camera positions are unknown or unless scene knowledge is available (Wöhler et al., 2009), since an increase of the mutual distances between the scene points by a constant factor can be compensated by increasing the mutual distances between the cameras and their distances to the scene accordingly (cf. Wöhler et al., 2009 and Sect. 5.1, where the issue of scene reconstruction at absolute scale is examined further).

1.4.6.3 Self-calibration Based on Vanishing Points

The self-calibration methods described so far require a large number of point correspondences between the acquired images. In certain scenes, especially those containing human-made objects such as buildings, it may be more convenient to extract lines instead of well-defined points from the acquired images.

Two parallel lines in the scene intersect at infinity. The projected images of the lines are generally not parallel and intersect at an image point $^S\tilde{\mathbf{v}}$ with well-defined image coordinates, called the 'vanishing point'. Cipolla et al. (1999) present a framework to directly estimate the intrinsic camera parameters based on three vanishing points, the associated directions of which are orthogonal with respect to each other. They suggest that parallel lines are extracted manually from the image.

According to Hartley and Zisserman (2003), vanishing points denoting orthogonal directions allow a determination of the IAC ω, and for two such vanishing points with the sensor coordinates $^S\tilde{\mathbf{v}}_1$ and $^S\tilde{\mathbf{v}}_2$ the relation $^S\tilde{\mathbf{v}}_1^T \omega\, ^S\tilde{\mathbf{v}}_2 = 0$ is valid. Three vanishing points denoting orthogonal directions allow one to estimate the parameters of ω for quadratic pixels.

As it is fairly unlikely that three mutually orthogonal vanishing points can be reliably detected in a single image, Grammatikopoulos et al. (2004) extend the approach based on vanishing points towards a framework involving several images acquired independently with the same camera (thus not necessarily all showing the same object), each displaying two orthogonal vanishing points. The lines extracted from the images to determine the vanishing points are also used to infer the lens distortion coefficients. An automated version of this technique is described by Grammatikopoulos et al. (2006). Lines are extracted and vanishing points are determined automatically. Multiple images acquired independently with the same camera, each displaying either two or three mutually orthogonal vanishing points, are utilised for this method.

1.4.7 Semi-automatic Calibration of Multiocular Camera Systems

In principle, all intrinsic and extrinsic camera parameters can be determined by self-calibration as a 'by-product' of the three-dimensional reconstruction of the scene based on a large number of point correspondences between the images. However, not every distribution of scene points is equally well suited for an accurate determination of camera parameters based on self-calibration—as an example, many linear methods fail if the scene points do not occupy a volume in space. As a consequence, during the camera calibration phase a 'cooperative' scene from which scene points and their mutual correspondences can be extracted at high accuracy and reliability is desirable.

Especially in self-calibration scenarios, false correspondences are a serious problem. When they remain undetected, the final reconstruction result may display gross errors. Outlier rejection methods such as RANSAC (Fischler and Bolles, 1981) or robust optimisation techniques like M-estimators (Rey, 1983) are often unable to fully solve this problem. In some cases, the scene may even contain no well-defined point features at all, e.g. if it is desired to reconstruct a weakly textured or textureless surface. Furthermore, the majority of automatic methods for establishing point correspondences assume that the surfaces of the objects in the scene are Lambertian, while most realistic surface materials also have a specular component. This specular component may lead to inaccurate image point measurements—if e.g. a specular

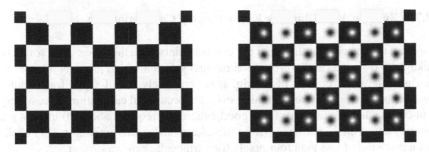

Fig. 1.5 *Left*: The calibration rig proposed by Bouguet (2007). *Right*: The non-ambiguous calibration rig proposed by Krüger et al. (2004)

reflection is detected as a point feature in one image, it will be associated with a different physical surface point in an image acquired from another viewpoint, leading to inaccuracies or even gross errors in the measured image coordinates of the corresponding points. Under unfavourable circumstances, the determination of point correspondences may become impossible, since the specular object surface may look completely different from different viewpoints (the problem of stereo image analysis in the presence of specularly reflecting surfaces and the physically correct determination of point correspondences is regarded in detail in Sect. 5.4).

This section therefore describes the semi-automatic camera calibration approach by Krüger et al. (2004) which is employed in the application scenarios described in Chaps. 6 and 7. The presentation is adopted from Krüger et al. (2004). In contrast to self-calibration techniques relying on point features extracted from a scene of unknown geometry, this method requires a calibration rig with accurately known control points, but no user interaction is necessary since the control points are automatically extracted from the calibration images. A camera calibration is then performed which is similar to the methods of Heikkilä and Silvén (1997) and Zhang (1999a) for determination of the intrinsic and extrinsic camera parameters.

1.4.7.1 The Calibration Rig

The calibration rig as proposed by Bouguet (2007) consists of a planar chequerboard pattern, e.g. as generated by a laser printer. The parts of this rig will be named as follows: The term 'square' denotes the black or white fields of the rig, which do not need to be square but may be rectangular. A 'corner' is a point where four squares touch, while a 'rig corner' denotes the outermost four corners where one large and three small squares touch. This calibration rig is very simple to generate but does not provide an orientation, which is required for camera systems where the cameras are not arranged in standard geometry. With a slight modification consisting of acentrical marks without sharp edges, an orientation can be obtained even if only a part of the rig is visible. Figure 1.5 illustrates the original calibration rig by Bouguet (2007) and the calibration rig proposed by Krüger et al. (2004).

1.4.7.2 Existing Algorithms for Extracting the Calibration Rig

To extract the image coordinates of the control points from the images, the software package by Bouguet (2007) provides a manual solution which prompts the user to click near the outer corners of the rig. It is completely out of scope for an automatic calibration process, and it makes even the occasional calibration process very cumbersome and prone to errors. A good calibration requires about 20 images per camera. At four clicks per image (if no mistake is made), this amounts to 240 clicks with a precision of less than four pixels for a trinocular camera system.

The OpenCV library[1] provides a corner detection algorithm as well. It is based on an initial scanning process with a subsequent subpixel accurate search of the corners. The initial scanning process operates on binary images, extracts the potential corner candidates, and tries to sort them with a polygonal approximation in a loop. If all expected corners are determined, the result is assigned to the subpixel accurate location. It is a gradient minimum search with a relocation of a neighbourhood window until the centre stays within a given threshold. In practise, this contour analysis turns out to be rather instable. The OpenCV algorithm is not able to properly detect and sort the corners under outdoor lighting conditions or under those in an industrial production environment. In order to avoid singularities due to parallel image and calibration rig planes, the calibration rig must be imaged at a certain obliquity. The corner analysis of the OpenCV implementation often fails if the angle or the camera-to-rig distance is too large, mainly due to an imprecise polygon approximation.

Two proprietary implementations based on cross-correlation template matching, line fitting, and subsequent precise position estimation at subpixel accuracy have been conceived as the predecessors of the algorithm described in Sect. 1.4.7.3. The first one operates on the assumption of a fully visible calibration rig. Hence, it extracts a number of most prominent features, equal to the number of corners in the calibration rig, by means of cross-correlation matching (Aschwanden, 1993). Subsequently, an outlier detection is performed based on a Hough transform (Jähne, 2005) and geometric constraint evaluation. Upon this, the lines are approximated by least-squares methods. Independent of the previously detected features, the line intersections are used as coarse corner guesses, and a maximum search followed by fitting a paraboloid to the correlation coefficients is performed. The second method discards the assumption of a fully visible calibration rig. Instead of extracting a fixed number, it selects features according to their reliability. The coarse feature sorting and outlier detection is performed as described above; then, for each potential rig corner, it is determined if a rig-corner template is displayed. The final sorting before the determination of feature position at subpixel accuracy is performed by accumulating features along line segments into approximated lines.

These two state-of-the-art algorithms are very robust with respect to occlusion, illumination, and noise. Due to the efficient implementation of the correlation process

---

[1]The OpenCV library is accessible at http://opencv.willowgarage.com.

they are fast enough for real-time processing. The limit of usability is the assumption that the straight lines through the corners appear approximately straight in the image. Once the lens distortion effects are comparable to the corner spacing in the image, this assumption is not valid, since it is only true for lenses with weak distortion. If it is required to cope with wide angle lenses, lens distortion increases. In the image, lens distortion makes straight lines appear bent. This effect directly leads to blurring in the Hough accumulator of the first sorting stage when compared to a lens with weak distortion. In the blurred Hough accumulator, maxima cannot be detected precisely, such that false positive lines appear or existing lines remain undetected. Obviously, this behaviour is directly related to the fact that the Hough transform is a global algorithm. One way to cope with the distortion is to change from a global approach to a local approach.

1.4.7.3 A Graph-Based Rig Extraction Algorithm

Outline of the Rig Finding Algorithm   The proposed algorithm is based on the previously mentioned features, i.e. the cross-correlation coefficient between the image and a corner mask. The local extrema are identified, and their position is determined at subpixel accuracy by means of weighted mean or bivariate quadratic interpolation.

The major difference from the existing approaches is the integration of these local extrema to a complete rig. Both the Hough transform and the proposed algorithm are bottom-up algorithms: Starting with atomic features, more complex entities are constructed, cumulating in the complete rig. The integration in this algorithm is done using topological methods. This approach is guided by a general principle: It is preferable to discard the whole image rather than accept a false positive identification of the corners. This strategy results from the fact that images are easy to acquire, while errors are hard to cope with during subsequent processing stages.

One observes that positive and negative correlation coefficient peaks interchange. Each positive peak has four negative neighbours directly connected along the black/white edges of the squares and vice versa. This effect is shown in Fig. 1.6. The first step is to identify this neighbourhood relation, which is illustrated in Fig. 1.7a showing a close-up of the image in Fig. 1.6.

The next steps verify the resulting directed graph according to a few simple rules that eliminate the edges to false positive corners and cut the graph such that the rig becomes a single graph component, where each corner candidate contains the edges to the four neighbours, labelled with the respective directions (left, right, up, down).

The first filter is used to eliminate non-bidirectional graph edges. Figures 1.7a and b illustrate a situation where a false positive is eliminated this way.

The second filter checks for circles of length 4. These circles in the graph map directly to the edges of the squares. Figure 1.7 illustrates incomplete circles (e.g. Fig. 1.7b, top row, leftmost corner) and complete circles only (cf. Fig. 1.7c).

The third filter eliminates graph edges that have an exceptional difference in length. The lengths are compared along one axis only, i.e. left/right and up/down.

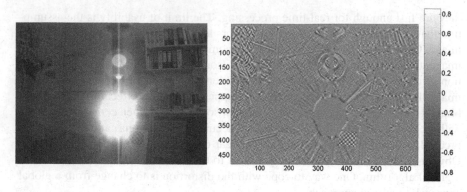

Fig. 1.6 *Left*: Image of the calibration rig under unfavourable illumination conditions which may, however, occur in real-world environments such as industrial production facilities. *Right*: Resulting cross-correlation coefficient

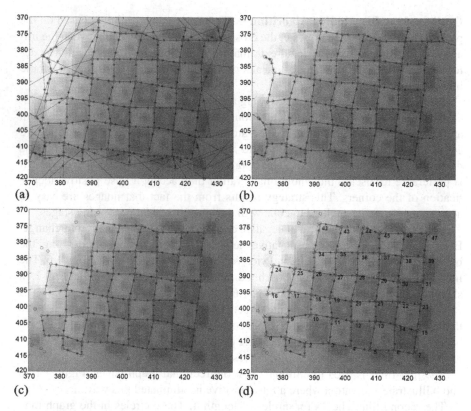

Fig. 1.7 Results of the first two topological filters and the corner enumeration. The images display an enlargement of the relevant part of Fig. 1.6, demonstrating the performance of the processing steps under difficult conditions. The *asterisks* denote the direction of the edges. (**a**) Initial graph. (**b**) Graph without non-bidirectional edges. (**c**) Graph containing *circles* only. (**d**) Final corner enumeration

This avoids problems with extremely tilted rigs and false positives next to the rig (not shown here). Another run of the circle filter is performed to eliminate corners which have become unconnected due to differences in length.

At this point the rig is assumed to be one component of the graph. The next step is to identify the component which describes the rig. This is done by traversing the graph component starting from all rig corner candidates. During the traversal each square corner is assigned its presumed number (cf. Fig. 1.7d). A single inconsistency in this enumeration starting from different rig corners discards the complete image. During the traversal the number of vertices per component is counted. The largest component is assumed to be the rig. If the number of corners is not the expected one, the complete image is discarded. If the rig is rectangular, the algorithm checks for the correct size in both axes; i.e. a rig turned by 90° is discarded.

The last step is to detect the direction marks on the rig and change the corner enumeration accordingly. If marks are expected and cannot be found, the complete image is discarded.

Definition of the Graph   The individual processing steps operate on a directed graph G defined as

$$G = \{V, E\} \tag{1.69}$$

$$V = \left\{ {}^S\mathbf{x}_i = \begin{pmatrix} u_i \\ v_i \end{pmatrix} \middle| i = 1, \ldots, N_v \right\} \tag{1.70}$$

$$E = \big\{ \mathbf{e}_i = (s_i, t_i, d_i) \mid i = 1, \ldots, N_e;$$

$$s_i, t_i \in 1, \ldots, N_v;$$

$$d_i \in D = \{\text{left,right,up,down}\} \big\}. \tag{1.71}$$

The vertices ${}^S\mathbf{x}_i$ are estimated at subpixel accuracy as described in the following section. The graph edges $\mathbf{e}_i$ contain the numerical identifiers of the source vertex s_i and target vertex t_i along with the symbolic direction d_i of the point from source to target.

Extraction of Corner Candidates   Generating corner candidates from the image is the most time-consuming processing step due to the iconic nature of the algorithm. A fast implementation is crucial to the real-time application of the algorithm. It is desired to find the corners by computing the correlation coefficient between the image and the corner template. Since the correlation coefficient is a normalised value, in terms of both brightness and contrast, the actual grey values of the templates are not important; they are chosen to be -1 for the black parts and $+1$ for the white parts. The empirical normalised cross-correlation coefficient is defined as

$$c = \frac{\sum_{i=1}^n x_i y_i - \frac{1}{n}(\sum_{i=1}^n x_i)(\sum_{i=1}^n y_i)}{\sqrt{[\sum_{i=1}^n x_i^2 - \frac{1}{n}(\sum_{i=1}^n x_i)^2][\sum_{i=1}^n y_i^2 - \frac{1}{n}(\sum_{i=1}^n y_i)^2]}}, \tag{1.72}$$

where x_i is a grey value of the input image and $y_i \in \{-1, +1\}$ is a pixel of the template. It is assumed that the black and white areas in the template have an equal number of pixels, i.e. $\sum_{i=1}^{n} y_i = 0$. With a total area of n pixels, this simplifies (1.72) to

$$c = \frac{\sum_{i=1}^{n} x_i y_i}{\sqrt{[\sum_{i=1}^{n} x_i^2 - \frac{1}{n}(\sum_{i=1}^{n} x_i)^2]n}}. \qquad (1.73)$$

This leads to the following optimisation: The pixel sums $\sum_{i=1}^{n} x_i y_i$, $\sum_{i=1}^{n} x_i^2$, and $\sum_{i=1}^{n} x_i$ are computed using integral images. In an integral image each pixel contains the grey value sum of the top left subimage including the pixel itself. The respective sum is computed by reading the value of four corner pixels of the area, which results in a computationally efficient implementation in terms of memory accesses per pixel. The runtime of this algorithm is independent of the size of the corner template. This allows for improvements in terms of detection robustness and subpixel accuracy. As soon as the integral images are computed, the recomputation of the correlation coefficient takes very little time. One could try different mask sizes and select one or integrate the results of all of them.

Candidate Filter and Graph Construction   The corner candidates in the correlation coefficient image are obtained by a straightforward non-maximum suppression followed by false-positive removal. The non-maximum suppression is performed by counting the number of pixels with a lower absolute value than the centre pixel in the eight-neighbourhood. If the count exceeds a threshold (default: 6) and the centre value exceeds another threshold (default: 0.75), the pixel is assumed to be a corner candidate. This simple non-maximum suppression provides a robust detection with a reasonable amount of false positives. The false positives are the neighbouring pixels of the true positive. Deciding which of the pixels is the true positive is done during the position estimation at subpixel accuracy. As soon as this position is available, the same data are used to determine the interpolated cross-correlation value. The candidate with the larger cross-correlation value is assumed to be the true positive.

Two algorithms for computing the subpixel position are investigated: Weighted mean (WM) and bivariate quadratic interpolation (BVI). The subpixel position of WM is the average of the eight-neighbourhood positions weighted by the corresponding correlation coefficients. The interpolated value is the mean of the correlation coefficients involved. The subpixel position of BVI is the location of the extremum of the bivariate quadratic function, assuming it is appropriately shaped and does not form a saddle point. The interpolated cross-correlation value is the function value at the extremum. This procedure yields the set V in (1.69). The corresponding set E is constructed by finding the nearest neighbour t of each vertex s in the respective direction d. The correlation coefficients of v_s and v_t must be of opposite sign.

Non-bidirectional Edge Elimination   This procedure consists of deleting all graph edges $e = (s, t, d)$ subject to $(t, s, \text{opposite}(d)) \notin E$ (cf. Fig. 1.7b). The func-

Table 1.1 Definitions of the graph functions used by the edge circle filter

d	$\text{cw}(d)$	$\text{ccw}(d)$	Opposite(d)
Left	Up	Down	Right
Up	Right	Left	Down
Right	Down	Up	Left
Down	Left	Right	Up

tions $\text{cw}(d)$ (clockwise), $\text{ccw}(d)$ (counter-clockwise), and opposite(d) are defined according to Table 1.1.

Edge Circle Filter The filter is implemented as a mark-and-sweep algorithm. In the first run, all corner candidates are marked which are part of at least one circle of length 4. The second run eliminates all candidates that are not marked. The circle check is performed as follows: A vertex $^S\mathbf{x}$ which either fulfils the conditions in (1.74)–(1.78)

$$e_1 = \left(^S\mathbf{x}, {}^S\mathbf{x}_1, d\right) \in E \quad \text{for all } d \in D \tag{1.74}$$

$$e_2 = \left(^S\mathbf{x}_1, {}^S\mathbf{x}_2, d_1 = \text{cw}(d)\right) \in E \tag{1.75}$$

$$e_3 = \left(^S\mathbf{x}_2, {}^S\mathbf{x}_3, d_2 = \text{cw}(d_1)\right) \in E \tag{1.76}$$

$$e_4 = \left(^S\mathbf{x}_3, {}^S\mathbf{x}_4, d_3 = \text{cw}(d_2)\right) \in E \tag{1.77}$$

$$^S\mathbf{x} = {}^S\mathbf{x}_4 \tag{1.78}$$

or (1.79)–(1.83)

$$e_1 = \left(^S\mathbf{x}, {}^S\mathbf{x}_1, d\right) \in E \quad \text{for all } d \in D \tag{1.79}$$

$$e_2 = \left(^S\mathbf{x}_1, {}^S\mathbf{x}_2, d_1 = \text{ccw}(d)\right) \in E \tag{1.80}$$

$$e_3 = \left(^S\mathbf{x}_2, {}^S\mathbf{x}_3, d_2 = \text{ccw}(d_1)\right) \in E \tag{1.81}$$

$$e_4 = \left(^S\mathbf{x}_3, {}^S\mathbf{x}_4, d_3 = \text{ccw}(d_2)\right) \in E \tag{1.82}$$

$$^S\mathbf{x} = {}^S\mathbf{x}_4 \tag{1.83}$$

is marked.

Edge Length Filter For each vertex with edges oriented in opposite directions, i.e. $(s, t_1, d) \in E$ and $(s, t_2, \text{opposite}(d)) \in E$, the lengths $l_1 = \|{}^S\mathbf{x}_s - {}^S\mathbf{x}_{t_1}\|$ and $l_2 = \|{}^S\mathbf{x}_s - {}^S\mathbf{x}_{t_2}\|$ are determined. If the condition of (1.84) is not fulfilled, the lengths of the edges are assumed to be so strongly different that this difference cannot be explained as a result of lens distortion or a slanted calibration rig. The threshold δ (default value: 0.6) depends on the expected lens distortion. The larger the distortion, the smaller should be the threshold value:

$$\frac{\min(l_1, l_2)}{\max(l_1, l_2)} > \delta. \tag{1.84}$$

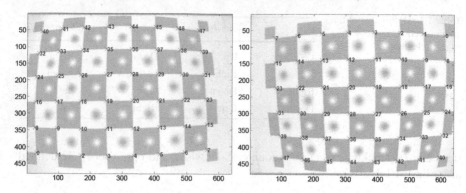

Fig. 1.8 Typical rig extraction results for images acquired with the Point Grey Digiclops wide-angle camera system. Strong lens distortion effects are apparent

Corner Enumeration   The corner enumeration algorithm assigns a number to each corner candidate that can be used to assign rig coordinates to a corner candidate. It performs multiple runs starting at different assumed rig corners and neglects the image if the enumerations are not identical.

Notch Direction Detector   The direction marks resolve the 180° ambiguity of the rig orientation. In order to detect the direction of each notch, the grey values along two lines are extracted. These lines start in the middle of one square border and end in the middle of the opposite square border. The grey levels on the horizontal line lead to a higher standard deviation than those on the vertical line if the rig is horizontal, as shown in Fig. 1.6. Additionally, the weighted mean of these grey values yields a position that clearly detects them to be off-centre. It is possible to threshold the standard deviation to detect missing notch marks if the processing options require them. In this case the image is discarded because expected notch marks cannot be found.

Rig Direction   The direction of the rig is determined by computing the mean direction vector from the intersection points of the two lines to the centre of gravity. The direction of the mean vector is quantised into four directions (left, right, up, down), and the corner identifiers obtained in the previous step are adjusted accordingly based on the square counts.

A typical rig extraction result is shown in Fig. 1.8 for the trinocular Point Grey Digiclops wide-angle camera system with a field of view of 70°. The size of each square amounts to 30×30 mm^2. The rig was printed out at 600 dpi and attached to a wooden board.

1.4.7.4 Discussion

The proposed method for calibration rig extraction successfully performs the difficult task of automatically assigning the control points on the rig to their counterparts in the acquired calibration images. It has been used for the convergent stereo camera setup employed in some of the three-dimensional surface inspection scenarios described in Chap. 6, which consists of two Baumer CCD cameras of 1032×776 pixel image size equipped with Cosmicar video lenses of $f = 25$ mm, for the trinocular Point Grey Digiclops system used for the three-dimensional reconstruction of flexible objects in Chap. 6, and for the trinocular camera system used in the application scenario of human–robot interaction described in Chap. 7. In the first scenario, the distance to the scene amounts to about 0.5 m, in the second scenario to approximately 1 m, and in the third to 2–7 m. The uncertainty of the measured image coordinates of the control points due to pixel noise is examined in Sect. 1.4.8.

The quality of camera calibration strongly depends on the number of images available for calibration and on the positions in space where the calibration rig is located during image acquisition. In this context, Krüger (2007) states the following four 'rules of thumb' to yield a suitable set of calibration images.

1. In order to be able to determine the lens distortion coefficients, images in which the calibration rig completely fills the image must be acquired for each camera.
2. Images of the rig should be acquired when the rig is positioned at the near side, in the middle, and at the far side of the space in which three-dimensional scene reconstruction is performed.
3. For all three distances, the calibration rig should also be placed such that it appears close to the corners of the images, respectively.
4. At each selected position, the orientation of the calibration rig should be perpendicular to the optical axis as well as rotated by an angle of about $\pm 30°$ around the horizontal and the vertical axis.

As additional examples, Fig. 1.9 shows the result of automatic calibration rig extraction from images acquired with somewhat 'exotic' lenses, an omnidirectional catadioptric lens and a fisheye lens. The proposed graph-based rig extraction algorithm performs well despite the strongly distorted shape of the calibration rig in the images. Even when not all control points are found (cf. Fig. 1.9a), the assignment of the extracted control points is nevertheless correct. Hence, the proposed method can be used for automatic calibration rig extraction for a variety of lens architectures.

1.4.8 Accurate Localisation of Chequerboard Corners

This section provides a comparison between different calibration pattern types and describes a model-based method for estimating the image position of chequerboard patterns which provides highly accurate results even in the presence of strong distortions. The section is adopted from Krüger and Wöhler (2011).

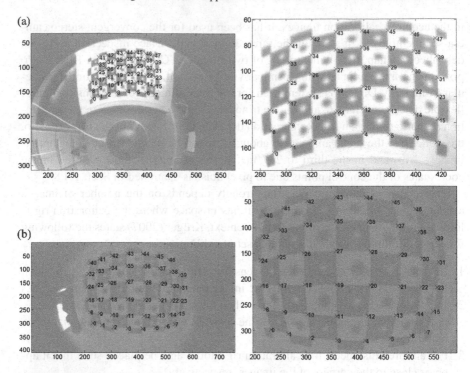

Fig. 1.9 (a) Extraction of the calibration rig in an image acquired with a catadioptric omnidirectional camera. (b) Extraction of the calibration rig in an image acquired with a fisheye lens. For both examples, the full image and an enlarged section are shown. The contrast has been reduced for visualisation

1.4.8.1 Different Types of Calibration Targets and Their Localisation in Images

Throughout this section it is assumed that the positions of targets are already known up to a few pixels. This can be achieved by various detectors (Jähne, 2005; Krüger et al., 2004). Given the positions of the targets in a set of images and their known world coordinates, a least-mean-squared error between the projected scene points and the measured image points is minimised. This requires suitable initial parameters such as the per-image transformation or the parameters of the camera model for each camera to be calibrated. For planar calibration rigs and pinhole cameras these parameters can be estimated using homographies (Heikkilä and Silvén, 1997). Salvi et al. (2002) provide a systematic comparison of the accuracies of several camera calibration techniques relying on nonlinear, linear, and two-step optimisation approaches for the determination of the intrinsic and extrinsic camera parameters. As a measure for the quality of calibration they use the average reprojection error in the image plane and the three-dimensional reconstruction error of selected points in the scene. For their comparative analysis, a unique set of points extracted from the images is used for all regarded calibration methods, and no comparison between

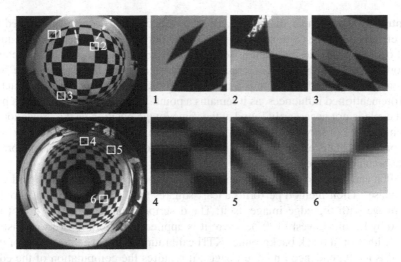

Fig. 1.10 *Top*: Image of a chequerboard pattern acquired with a camera of 1.9 megapixel image size, equipped with a fisheye lens of 185° field of view. *Bottom*: Image taken with a catadioptric omnidirectional camera of 640 × 480 pixel resolution. Enlarged example corners are shown *on the right*, respectively

several target localisation approaches is performed. Similar techniques can be used to reconstruct the spatial positions of the targets along with the camera parameters.

Four aspects of this process influence the accuracy of the ensuing calibration: the suitability of the camera model for the given cameras and lenses, the accuracy of the calibration rig, the accuracy of the target localisation algorithm, and the placement of the rig with respect to the camera. The accuracy of the calibration rig is a procurement or manufacturing problem and will not be discussed here. Different camera models have been regarded before, e.g. by Brown (1966). The placement strategy of the calibration rig is partially covered by Mason (1994) and Krüger (2007). This study therefore examines the localisation accuracy in image space of the novel technique and three reference approaches.

Photogrammetric applications usually deal with nearly ideal pinhole cameras. This results in higher hardware costs but better image quality. Computer vision applications are often concerned with optics that display stronger distortion effects. In particular, mobile robotic systems often employ non-pinhole optical systems such as fisheye lenses or catadioptric optics.

Usually, one of the following three target types is used: corners, chequerboard corners, or circular dots. Examples of images displaying a chequerboard pattern, acquired with non-pinhole optical systems, are shown in Fig. 1.10 along with typical chequerboard corners extracted from these images.

Corners are commonly used in the domain of computer vision, whereas the use of circular targets for camera calibration, often consisting of retro-reflecting material, is the standard approach in photogrammetry (Luhmann, 2006). A comparison between corner targets and circular targets is provided by Mallon and Whelan (2006). The chequerboard corners are found to be bias-free with respect to projective transformations and nonlinear distortions. By contrast, circular dots are influenced by these effects. A simple explanation for this behaviour relies on the fact that chequerboard corners are scale invariant as long as the localisation window only contains the corner. The coordinate of interest is the intersection of the edges of the four adjacent chequerboard fields, thus a point. The projection of a point is invariant to the aforementioned influences, as it remains a point. In contrast, the centre of a projected circle is not necessarily found at the same image position as the projection of the centre of the observed circle; thus circular targets suffer from a bias in their centre coordinates. This effect becomes increasingly pronounced when lens distortion effects become stronger.

Mallon and Whelan (2006) present an edge-based nonlinear chequerboard corner localiser. Their method performs a least-squares fit of a parametric model of the edge image with the edge image itself. The described approach makes use of the method by Li and Lavest (1995), where it is applied to calibration rigs consisting of white lines on a black background (KTH calibration cube). The drawback of this method is its dependence on edge images; it requires the computation of the edge image of the input image, which is an additional (but small) computational burden. Furthermore, the original method by Li and Lavest (1995) uses a rather ad hoc approach to the modelling of the corner image, as it relies on 11 parameters compared to our 7 parameters. The 4 additional parameters account for an illumination gradient, different reflectivities of the white lines, and different line widths. These additional parameters put an unnecessary computational burden on the optimiser. In general more model parameters increase the probability of getting stuck in local minima.

One of the popular algorithms for finding the centre of a circular white target is the computation of the centre of gravity of a window around the detected position (Luhmann, 2006). Here, the square of the grey value serves as the weight of a pixel. The ensuing algorithm is simple and fast. It is, however, sensitive to inhomogeneous grey values caused e.g. by defects of the target or non-uniform incident light. We will use this method as a reference in this study.

Locating a chequerboard corner can be achieved by various methods. Chen and Zhang (2005) use the intermediate values computed in the corner detection phase to obtain the second-order Taylor expansion of the image and find its saddle point. The underlying corner model is restricted to orthogonal corners. The result is invariant to rotation, translation, contrast, and brightness, but not to projective transformations or nonlinear distortions.

The method by Lucchese and Mitra (2002) performs a least-squares fit of a second-order polynomial to a low-pass version of the input image. The position of the saddle point is obtained from the polynomial coefficients. The underlying model is invariant to affine transformations, contrast, and brightness. If the neighbourhood of the corner is chosen small enough, the affine invariance yields a suitable approximation in the presence of projective transformations and nonlinear distortions. We will use this method as a reference in this paper. The method is able to cope with the distortions introduced by fisheye lenses, but requires a careful tuning of the size of the low-pass filter and at the same time the window size for fitting. The low-pass parameters depend mostly on the width of the point spread function (PSF) of the lens.

Krüger et al. (2004) utilise intermediate information of the corner detector. A correlation coefficient between the image and a corner template is computed for each pixel. Peaks in this correlation coefficient image indicate the presence of chequerboard corners. The subpixel accurate position is obtained by computing the position of the local extremum by fitting a second-order polynomial. Incidentally, this operation is identical to the method by Lucchese and Mitra (2002), but it operates on different input data. For this reason we include the method by Krüger et al. (2004) as another reference approach.

In the following section we derive a chequerboard corner model and fitting procedure that copes with strong distortions and different PSF widths while providing a high accuracy. As a by-product we obtain the radius of the PSF along with the target position.

Olague and Hernández (2005) present a technique that can be seen as a precursor to the method proposed in this study. They model an L-corner by two overlapping smoothed step functions. They use a Gaussian kernel as the smoothing operator and therefore model their step function by the Gaussian error function. We are using a similar step function model in our approach, but provide an additional approximation. Since the Gaussian error function is provided by most numerical libraries as a piecewise polynomial approximation, it is quite slow to compute. We propose using the sigmoid function, which is based on a single exponential that exists as a floating-point operation in many processor architectures and is therefore fast to compute. Furthermore, we use chequerboard corners instead of L-corners and assume a circular PSF, thus reducing the number of parameters to 7, compared to 12 by Olague and Hernández (2005).

We will compare our approach to the methods by Lucchese and Mitra (2002), Krüger et al. (2004), and the centre of gravity method according to Luhmann (2006) for circular targets. The comparison between accuracies achieved with the same camera system under identical illumination conditions for corner targets and circular targets is of high interest due to the fact that circular targets are commonly used for camera calibration in photogrammetry. In the literature, such comparisons are generally performed using synthetically generated images (Luhmann, 2006). Instead, we rely on a set of real images labelled with the displacement in metric units, where the independently determined pixel scale is used to compute the displacement in pixels as a ground truth. Our direct comparative method differs from previous indirect evaluation approaches that compare the reprojection error of a subsequent bundle adjustment stage (Triggs et al., 2000; Salvi et al., 2002; Luhmann, 2006), the three-dimensional reconstruction error of selected points in the scene (Salvi et al., 2002), or the variances of camera parameters obtained by a subsequent extrinsic calibration stage (Olague and Hernández, 2005).

1.4.8.2 A Model-Based Method for Chequerboard Corner Localisation

We regard a square image window I^* with a width and height of $(2r + 1)$ pixels. The central pixel is assumed to have the coordinates $(0, 0)$ and to be the location of the most likely position of the corner as computed by the corner detector. An ideally sharp image $\hat{I}$ of a corner with a brightness of -1 in the dark and $+1$ in the bright areas can be modelled by the product of two oriented step functions according to

$$\hat{I}(x, y) = \delta(x \cos\alpha_1 + y \sin\alpha_1)\delta(x \cos\alpha_2 + y \sin\alpha_2)$$

$$\text{with } x, y \in \mathbb{R} \quad \text{and} \quad \delta(t) = \begin{cases} -1 & \text{if } t < 0 \\ +1 & \text{otherwise.} \end{cases} \quad (1.85)$$

The angles α_1 and α_2 denote the directions of the normals to the black-white edges. This notation is identical to the affine transformation of an orthogonal, infinitely large corner. Since it is assumed that r is sufficiently small (e.g. $r = 9$ pixels), the affine transformation is a suitable approximation of the projective transform and the lens distortions. Otherwise, the straight line edges may be replaced by a different model such as cubic curves.

The ideal image $\hat{I}$ is subject to blurring by the lens. An exact description of the PSF due to diffraction of monochromatic light at a circular aperture is given by the radially symmetric Airy pattern $A(r) \propto [J_1(r)/r]^2$, where $J_1(r)$ is a Bessel function of the first kind of first order (Pedrotti, 1993). Consequently, the image of a point light source is radially symmetric and displays an intensity maximum at its centre and concentric rings surrounding the maximum with brightnesses which decrease with increasing ring radius. It is explained in more detail in Chap. 4 that for practical purposes a radially symmetric Gaussian function is a reasonable approximation to the PSF. It is thus assumed that the PSF is an ideal circular Gaussian filter G of radius σ. Hence, the continuous image $\tilde{I}(x, y)$ of the ideal chequerboard corner $\hat{I}(x, y)$ corresponds to

$$\tilde{I}(x, y) = G\left(\sqrt{x^2 + y^2}, \sigma\right) * \hat{I}(x, y) \quad \text{with } G(t, \sigma) = \frac{1}{\sqrt{2\pi}\sigma} e^{-\frac{t^2}{2\sigma^2}}. \quad (1.86)$$

It is formed by convolving the step image with the circular Gaussian filter. Since the Gaussian filter is separable, we may exchange the step function $\delta(t)$ in $\hat{I}(x, y)$ by the step response of the Gaussian filter in $\tilde{I}(x, y)$. Hence, the observed intensity pattern corresponds to the step response $H(t, \sigma)$ of the PSF $G(t, \sigma)$ with

$$H(t, \sigma) = \text{erf}\left(\frac{t}{\sqrt{2}\sigma}\right). \quad (1.87)$$

The error function $\text{erf}(t)$ is twice the integral of the Gaussian distribution with zero mean and variance $1/2$, i.e. $\text{erf}(t) = \frac{2}{\sqrt{\pi}} \int_0^t e^{-s^2} ds$. It is scaled such that its infimum and supremum are $+1$ and -1, respectively. A model of the observed chequerboard corner is then given by

$$\tilde{I}(x, y) = H(x \cos\alpha_1 + y \sin\alpha_1, \sigma)H(x \cos\alpha_2 + y \sin\alpha_2, \sigma). \quad (1.88)$$

The error function $\text{erf}(t)$ is of sigmoidal shape but cannot be expressed in closed form. In practise it is approximated numerically and quite expensive to compute.

Fig. 1.11 True step response
$H(t, \sigma)$ with $\sigma = 1$ (*solid
curve*) and approximation by
the function $S(t, \tilde\sigma)$ with
$\tilde\sigma = \sigma\sqrt{\pi/8}$ (*dashed curve*)

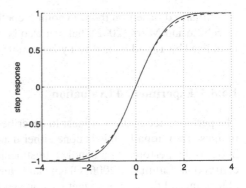

In order to achieve an acceptable computational performance of the implementation we approximate the Gaussian error integral by the function $S(t, \tilde\sigma)$ according to

$$\tilde I(x, y) \approx S(x\cos\alpha_1 + y\sin\alpha_1, \tilde\sigma)\, S(x\cos\alpha_2 + y\sin\alpha_2, \tilde\sigma)$$

$$\text{with } S(t, \tilde\sigma) = \frac{2}{1 + e^{-t/\tilde\sigma}} - 1. \tag{1.89}$$

The function $S(t, \tilde\sigma)$ is also of sigmoidal shape and similar to the logistic function $L(t) = 1/(1 + e^{-t})$. In (1.89), $\tilde\sigma$ is a scaling factor which is proportional to the width parameter σ of the Gaussian PSF $G(t, \sigma)$. Setting $\tilde\sigma = \sigma\sqrt{\pi/8}$ yields an identical slope of $H(t, \sigma)$ and $S(t, \tilde\sigma)$ at $t = 0$ (Fig. 1.11). Note that the function $S(t, \tilde\sigma)$ defined in (1.89) can also be expressed as

$$S(t, \tilde\sigma) = \tanh\left(\frac{t}{2\tilde\sigma}\right). \tag{1.90}$$

To determine the discrete model I_{uv} of the image, assume a linear camera response is assumed, described by the gain β and offset γ and the sample $\tilde I(x, y)$ at the integer-valued pixel positions (u, v) according to

$$I_{uv} = \beta \tilde I(u + u_0, v + v_0) + \gamma \quad \text{with } u, v \in \mathbb{N} \text{ and } u_0, v_0 \in \mathbb{R}. \tag{1.91}$$

Again this is an approximation, as each pixel of the sensor actually performs an integral over the area that it covers. Since the corner model has been fixed to the previously detected corner point, we have to move the corner with respect to the centre pixel of I_{uv}. In order to obtain the subpixel accurate corner position (u_0, v_0) of the corner in the input image I_{uv}^* we find the simulated corner image I_{uv} that is the best approximation of I_{uv}^* in the least-mean-squares sense by determining

$$\arg\min_{u_0, v_0, \beta, \gamma, \tilde\sigma, \alpha_1, \alpha_2} \left(\sum_{u, v}[I_{uv} - I_{uv}^*]^2\right) \tag{1.92}$$

using the Levenberg–Marquardt algorithm. For clarity, the dependence of I_{uv} on u_0, v_0, β, γ, $\tilde\sigma$, α_1, and α_2 has been omitted in (1.92). The gain and offset are initialised from the minimum and maximum grey values in I_{uv}^*. The angles α_1 and α_2

are initialised based on the polynomial coefficients obtained with the approach by Lucchese and Mitra (2002), but can also be set to fixed values. The parameter $\tilde{\sigma}$ is initialised by 1, and u_0 and v_0 by zero values.

1.4.8.3 Experimental Evaluation

The performance of the nonlinear fit described in Sect. 1.4.8.2 is evaluated using real images. Traditionally, this is done either using synthetic data (Lucchese and Mitra, 2002) or by performing a bundle adjustment-based scene reconstruction or camera calibration (Luhmann, 2006; Olague and Hernández, 2005). We do not compare our algorithm and the reference methods on synthetic data for two major reasons.

1. Synthetic data only show how well the synthesis and the analysis algorithms match and may—to a limited extent—provide quantitative information about the noise sensitivity.
2. The number of influencing parameters that have to be modelled is quite large. Apart from general and statistical influences (e.g. brightness, contrast, digitalisation noise) there are a lot of local influences with even more parameters (e.g. brightness gradient, inhomogeneity of illumination and pattern). Modelling all these influences realistically in a way that does not accidentally favour one method over another is difficult, if not unfeasible.

In a bundle adjustment-based calibration (Olague and Hernández, 2005), the various sources of error (e.g. camera model, calibration rig error) are mixed; thus clear distinctions between them are hard or even impossible to obtain when it is desired to determine the accuracy of the employed technique for chequerboard corner localisation.

For these reasons images of real planar patterns were recorded. The patterns were photoset on non-glossy paper from 8-bit greyscale images. The prints were attached to the planar surface of a high-precision xy-table. The xy-table allows a motion in either direction with a gauge stepping of 10 μm. In order to obtain accurate displacements we only used full 10 μm steps in the x (horizontal) direction.

A batch of 100 images was recorded depicting the pattern (cf. Fig. 1.12 for some examples), then we moved the pattern in front of the camera with the high-precision xy-table, and recorded the next set of images. In order to attribute the images with the relative motion in pixels we obtained the overall scaling factor by measuring the subpixel accurate width of the box of size 64×48 mm^2 around the targets. The grey levels of the box borders along a row were each approximated by a parabola, and the positions of the local extrema were used to compute the width d_p of the box in pixels at an accuracy of about 0.2 pixel. The resulting horizontal pixel scale amounts to $s_x = 8.910 \pm 0.003$ pixels/mm on the surface of the xy-table, implying a maximum systematic error of the chequerboard corner displacements due to inaccurate knowledge of the pixel scale s_x of about 0.03 %.

The images were acquired with a Sony DFW-V500 VGA 8-bit grey level camera using a 12.5 mm lens, giving a horizontal field of view of 21.7°. The camera was mounted at a distance of 190 mm from the xy-table with the optical axis

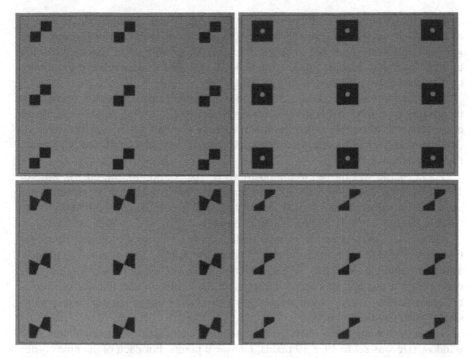

Fig. 1.12 Example input images for the evaluation of the examined chequerboard corner localisation methods. The x axis is in the horizontal and the y axis in the vertical image direction

parallel to the normal of its surface. Specifically, our mechanical setup ensures that the deviations β_x and β_y from orthogonality of the optical axis with respect to the x and y axes of the xy-table are smaller than $0.5°$. If it is assumed that the optical axis of the camera is inclined horizontally by the angle β_x, perspective foreshortening of the surface of the xy-table implies an unforeshortened horizontal pixel scale $s_x^{(0)} = s_x / \cos \beta_x$ as long as β_x is smaller than a few degrees (for larger angles the finite distance of the camera from the xy-table would become relevant). At the same time, a horizontal displacement Δx in millimetres on the xy-table translates into a horizontal displacement Δu in pixel coordinates of $\Delta u = \Delta x s_x^{(0)} \cos \beta_x = \Delta x s_x$. Hence, systematic errors of the pixel scale s_x and the horizontal displacement Δu in pixel coordinates due to a small nonzero horizontal deviation β_x from orthogonality compensate each other, and no systematic errors are introduced.

A nonzero deviation β_y of the optical axis from orthogonality in the y direction has the effect that the upper and lower rows of targets (cf. Fig. 1.12) have effective horizontal pixel scales which are different from the value s_x determined for the middle row. For $\beta_y = 0.5°$, the relative differences amount to 0.1 % in our setup but compensate each other on the average—when the pixel scale is higher for the top row it is lower by the same relative amount for the bottom row, and vice versa.

Based on a standard calibration of the intrinsic camera parameters (Krüger et al., 2004), it was found that the lens displays only insignificant distortions. The lens distortion was measured to be less than 0.2 pixel between the distorted and the undistorted image near the image corners, leading to a maximum relative shortening of displacements in the image corners of 0.1 %.

As the random scatter (standard deviation) of all chequerboard corner localisation techniques examined in this study is always higher than 1 % of the displacement and corresponds to about 10 % for the most accurate method when averaged over all displacements, it can be safely assumed that the ground truth is sufficiently accurate for our evaluation.

The xy-table was moved to the positions 0, 10, 20, 30, 40, 50, 60, 70, 80, 90, 100, 150, 200, 250, 300, and 400 μm along the horizontal axis, translating into horizontal displacements of 0.00, 0.09, 0.18, 0.27, 0.36, 0.45, 0.53, 0.62, 0.71, 0.80, 0.89, 1.34, 1.78, 2.23, 2.67, and 3.56 pixels.

The camera was operated in automatic exposure mode. Controlled illumination was provided by ceiling-mounted fluorescent lamps. This resulted in a fairly uniform illumination of the targets, but on some targets local intensity gradients occurred. We did not attempt to compensate these effects and did not use retro-reflective targets in order to illustrate the robustness of our method with respect to slightly uneven illumination.

The images were processed beginning with manually entered starting points. The window size was set to 19×19 pixels, i.e. $r = 9$ pixels. For each of the nine corner targets in each image we computed the location using the methods of Lucchese and Mitra (2002), Krüger et al. (2004), and Sect. 1.4.8.2. For the circular targets, the position was computed using the weighted mean method with the square of the grey levels as weights.

As we have no absolute positions in the ground truth—but accurate displacements—the ground truth displacements were compared with the displacements estimated by the various operators. This was accomplished by selecting two random images of the same target and computing the pixel distance between the estimated absolute corner positions. Identical image pairs were selected for different operators.

The stability of the three methods with respect to the starting position was also evaluated. The subpixel accurate corner position was computed starting from the eight pixels around the manually selected starting position and the starting position itself along with the resulting error due to offset from the manually selected starting position. The Tukey box plots in Figs. 1.13, 1.14, 1.15 display the median, the 25 % and 75 % quantiles, and the minimum and maximum values of the error between ground truth and estimated displacement for all four methods. Each error bar was computed based on 10^6 image pairs. The error depending on the target position in the image (centre, edge, corner), on the target rotation, and on the target shear is also displayed. All targets were acquired with two different contrasts (white on black and light grey on dark grey). Another set shows the targets with a different PSF, which was obtained by acquiring slightly defocused images.

Table 1.2 relates the methods to the plot labels. An intuitive measure of the localisation error is the difference between the 75 % and the 25 % quantiles, depicted in

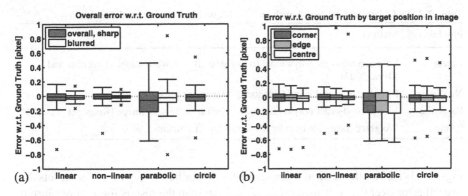

Fig. 1.13 Tukey box plots of the deviations between the measured and the true target displacement for the different methods, regarding (**a**) image blur and (**b**) target position in the image

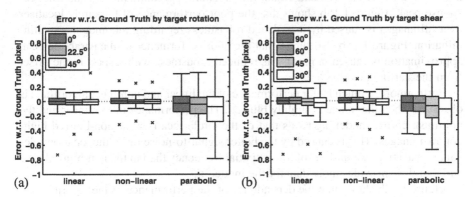

Fig. 1.14 Tukey box plots of the deviations between the measured and the true target displacement for the different methods, regarding (**a**) target rotation and (**b**) target shear

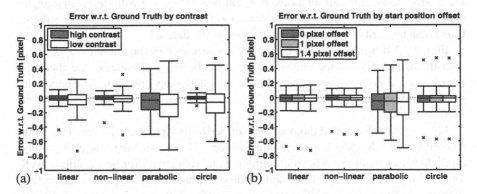

Fig. 1.15 Tukey box plots of the deviations between the measured and the true target displacement for the different methods, regarding (**a**) target contrast and (**b**) the offset of the initial corner detector

Table 1.2 Plot labels and examined methods for chequerboard corner localisation

Plot label	Method
Linear	Fit a second-order polynomial to low-pass filtered input image (Lucchese and Mitra, 2002)
Nonlinear	Fit a corner model using Levenberg–Marquardt (this section)
Parabolic	Fit a second-order polynomial to correlation coefficient image (Krüger et al., 2004)
Circle	Weighted mean (for circular markers only) (Luhmann, 2006)

Figs. 1.13–1.15 by the vertical extensions of the error boxes. Figure 1.13a depicts the overall error over the well-focused images along with the results for a set of blurred images. The proposed nonlinear fitting algorithm is about two times more accurate than both the linear algorithm and the centre of gravity-based circle localiser. It is about three times more accurate than the parabolic approximation of the filter response peak. Figure 1.15b shows that the poor performance of the circle localiser over all images is caused by its reduced robustness regarding inhomogeneous illumination. Figure 1.15b also shows that the poor performance of the parabolic peak approximation is caused in part by its reduced robustness with respect to the offset from the starting position.

Furthermore, a much better performance of the linear and nonlinear algorithms is observed when the image is slightly blurred. The performance of the linear and the nonlinear corner modelling rivals that of the circle localiser for non-blurred high-contrast images. This is caused by the better signal-to-noise ratio; the location relevant signal (step response) is of lower spatial frequency than in the non-blurred case and therefore provides more data for the model fit.

Figure 1.13b shows that the dependence of the performance of the algorithms is virtually independent of the target position in the image. The slight differences can be attributed to random variations. Figure 1.14a shows that the linear and nonlinear chequerboard corner localisers are basically rotation invariant, as the error values are nearly identical for all rotations. A slight bias increasing with decreasing angle can be observed. This trend is of minor importance compared to the error values; thus it can be attributed to random variations in the data set.

Figure 1.14b again depicts the superior performance of the nonlinear algorithm over the linear fit. Even for an angle of only 30° between the sides of the chequerboard corner it performs better than the linear fit under any condition. The parabolic peak approximation again has an error value about three times larger than the other methods.

Figure 1.15a shows that the nonlinear fit performs significantly better than both reference methods under low-contrast conditions. The fact that the centre-of-gravity circle localiser requires uniform illumination and reflectivity for best results is well known from the literature (Luhmann, 2006). In practise this requires constructive measures such as retro-reflective targets and confocal illumination. Our experiment did not provide these in order to investigate the influences of a realistic imaging situation typically encountered in computer vision scenarios. Although the nonlinear fit results in a higher error value and a slight bias due to the inhomogeneous illumination, the performance drop is not as pronounced as for the reference methods. The nearly quadrupled error of the circle localiser along with a bias larger than the error of the corresponding high-contrast result illustrate the superior robustness of the nonlinear fit, which shows only an insignificant bias.

The peak approximation is not significantly influenced by the contrast, as the correlation coefficient is brightness and contrast invariant. Even in the low-contrast setting the peak approximation is outperformed by both the linear and the nonlinear corner models.

Figure 1.15b shows that three of the examined algorithms are robust to variations of the initial position in a 3×3 neighbourhood. The peak approximation shows a clear trend regarding its error and the accuracy of the initial corner detector. If the corner detector is off by only 1 pixel diagonally, the error increases by about one third.

At this point, note that all stated accuracies refer to displacements, and thus the differences of target positions. According to the law of error propagation (Bronstein and Semendjajew, 1989) and assuming identical error distributions for the position measurements used to determine a set of differences, the actual errors of the corner positions are smaller by a factor of $1/\sqrt{2}$ than the displacement errors stated above.

1.4.8.4 Discussion

The nonlinear chequerboard corner localisation algorithm proposed by Krüger and Wöhler (2011) attains an overall error value (half the difference between the 75 % and 25 % quantiles) of 0.032 pixel averaged over image contrast, target rotation, shear, and position in the image. The error values are 0.024 and 0.043 pixel for high- and low-contrast images, respectively, and becomes as low as 0.016 pixel for slightly blurred images. For comparison, the classical photogrammetric method based on circular targets achieves 0.045 pixel in the average case, and 0.017 pixel for high and 0.132 pixel for low image contrast. All these error values refer to differences between pairs of corner positions. No evidence was found for systematic errors for any of the examined chequerboard corner localisation methods.

The proposed algorithm is also suitable to evaluate the focusing of lenses and would allow the calibration of the Depth-Defocus-Function (Kuhl et al., 2006) for the computation of depth from defocus based on the estimation of the parameter $\tilde{\sigma}$ in (1.89).

The evaluation based on real test images has shown that the proposed nonlinear algorithm is more robust with respect to unfavourable imaging conditions (e.g. low image contrast) than the linear algorithm by Lucchese and Mitra (2002) and the centre-of-gravity-based localiser for circular targets according to Luhmann (2006). Furthermore, it can be applied earlier in the image processing chain than a model-fitting circle localiser, e.g. as proposed by Heikkilä and Silvén (1997), as it is independent of the camera model. A further advantage over the linear algorithm is that the input images do not need to be low-pass filtered. The main advantage stated by

Krüger et al. (2004) for the parabolic peak approximation, its invariance to contrast and brightness, becomes irrelevant, as both the linear and nonlinear corner models are about three times more accurate, even for low-contrast images.

Hence, the proposed algorithm allows camera calibration under more complex conditions and with a larger variety of optical systems than the centre-of-gravity circular target localisation algorithm or the classical methods for chequerboard corner localisation.

1.5 Stereo Image Analysis in Standard Geometry

When the intrinsic and extrinsic camera parameters are known or can be inferred from a reference set of point correspondences, it is advantageous to rectify the stereo image pair to standard geometry, corresponding to parallel optical axes, identical principal distances, collinear horizontal image axes, and image planes which are orthogonal to the optical axes and parallel to the stereo baseline. Accordingly, pairs of corresponding epipolar lines become parallel to each other and to the horizontal image axes. The important advantage of performing stereo analysis in image pairs rectified to standard geometry is the fact that the search for point correspondences needs to be performed only along corresponding pixel rows of the rectified images.

1.5.1 Image Rectification According to Standard Geometry

In a first step, the original images are warped such that the radial and tangential lens distortions described by (1.3) and (1.4) are compensated. Image rectification then essentially corresponds to determining a projective transformation for each image such that the conditions stated above are fulfilled. To obtain parallel epipolar lines, Hartley and Zisserman (2003) propose a method to project both epipoles to points at infinity and determine a corresponding projective transformation for each image based on a set of point correspondences. Their approach does not require the extrinsic camera parameters to be known. A more compact algorithm for the rectification of stereo image pairs, requiring calibrated cameras, i.e. knowledge about their intrinsic parameters A_i and their extrinsic parameters R_i and $\mathbf{t}_i$, is introduced by Fusiello et al. (2000). Basically, geometric camera calibration is achieved by applying the principle of bundle adjustment to a reference object of known size and shape. An overview of geometric camera calibration methods is given in Sect. 1.4. In the algorithm by Fusiello et al. (2000), the image formation process of camera i is defined by the corresponding projective transformation

$$P_i = A_i[R_i \mid \mathbf{t}_i] = [B_i \mid \mathbf{b}_i] \quad \text{with } B_i = A_i R_i \text{ and } \mathbf{b}_i = A_i \mathbf{t}_i \qquad (1.93)$$

which is shown to yield the relation

$$\mathbf{b}_i = -B_i{}^W \mathbf{c}_i \qquad (1.94)$$

for the optical centre $^W\mathbf{c}_i$ of camera i in the world coordinate system. The image point $^{S_i}\tilde{\mathbf{x}}$, defined in pixel coordinates in image i, is obtained from the corresponding scene point $^W\tilde{\mathbf{x}}$ by $^{S_i}\tilde{\mathbf{x}} = P_i\,^W\tilde{\mathbf{x}}$. The three-dimensional straight line ("ray") running through the optical centre $^W\mathbf{c}_i$ and the three-dimensional scene point $^W\tilde{\mathbf{x}}$ is then given by

$$\mathbf{s} = {^W}\mathbf{c}_i + \lambda B_i^{-1}\,{^{S_i}}\tilde{\mathbf{x}} \tag{1.95}$$

with λ as a real number.

It is assumed by Fusiello et al. (2000) that the projective transformations P_1 and P_2 of the two cameras are given. They introduce a pair of projective transformations $P_1^{(s)}$ and $P_2^{(s)}$ which describe a rotation of the original cameras such that both image planes and also the baseline lie in the same plane. This operation also leads to parallel epipolar lines, while the optical centres remain unchanged. Furthermore, it is required that the epipolar lines run horizontally in both images and a pair of corresponding epipolar lines is associated with identical vertical image coordinates. This configuration is obtained by requiring identical intrinsic parameters for both new cameras, i.e. $A_1 = A_2 \equiv A$. The new projective transformations $P_i^{(s)}$ are then given by

$$P_i^{(s)} = A[R \mid -R\,{^W}\mathbf{c}_i]. \tag{1.96}$$

The optical centres $^W\mathbf{c}_i$ are obtained by $^W\mathbf{c}_i = -B_i^{-1}\mathbf{b}_i$ according to (1.94). The fact that the optical axes are parallel implies an identical rotation matrix R, which is defined by Fusiello et al. (2000) in terms of its row vectors according to

$$R = \begin{bmatrix} \mathbf{r}_1^T \\ \mathbf{r}_2^T \\ \mathbf{r}_3^T \end{bmatrix}. \tag{1.97}$$

The vectors $\mathbf{r}_1$, $\mathbf{r}_2$, and $\mathbf{r}_3$, which are mutually orthogonal and of unit norm due to the orthonormality of the rotation matrix R, denote the x, y, and z axes, respectively, of the camera coordinate system in the world coordinate system. At this point, the vector $\mathbf{r}_1$ (which defines the new x axis) has the same direction as the baseline and is thus set to $\mathbf{r}_1 = ({^W}\mathbf{c}_1 - {^W}\mathbf{c}_2)/\|{^W}\mathbf{c}_1 - {^W}\mathbf{c}_2\|$. Fusiello et al. (2000) then define a unit vector $\mathbf{k}$ which points into the direction of the z axis of the original coordinate system of camera 1. Accordingly, $\mathbf{r}_2 = \mathbf{k} \times \mathbf{r}_1$ corresponds to the y axis and $\mathbf{r}_3 = \mathbf{r}_1 \times \mathbf{r}_2$ to the z axis of the new coordinate system. Notably, this algorithm only yields a solution as long as the optical axes are not pointing in the same direction as the baseline.

For a rectification of image i, the transformation between the original image plane defined by $P_i = [B_i \mid \mathbf{b}_i]$ to the new image plane defined by $P_i^{(s)} = [B_i^{(s)} \mid \mathbf{b}_i^{(s)}]$ is required. For an arbitrary scene point $^W\mathbf{x}$ the expressions $^{S_i}\tilde{\mathbf{x}} = P_i\,^W\tilde{\mathbf{x}}$ and $^{S_i^{(s)}}\tilde{\mathbf{x}} = P_i^{(s)}\,^W\tilde{\mathbf{x}}$ are valid. The scene point $^W\mathbf{x}$ is located on both three-dimensional lines corresponding to the two image points $^{S_i}\tilde{\mathbf{x}}$ and $^{S_i^{(s)}}\tilde{\mathbf{x}}$, corresponding to

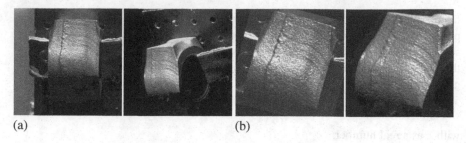

(a)   (b)

Fig. 1.16 (a) Pair of stereo images, acquired by two cameras with non-parallel optical axes. (b) Image pair rectified to standard geometry

$$
\begin{aligned}
{}^{W}\mathbf{x} &= {}^{W}\mathbf{c}_i + \lambda B_i^{-1} S_i \tilde{\mathbf{x}} \quad \text{and} \\
{}^{W}\mathbf{x} &= {}^{W}\mathbf{c}_i + \lambda^{(s)} \left(B_i^{(s)} \right)^{-1} S_i^{(s)} \tilde{\mathbf{x}},
\end{aligned}
\tag{1.98}
$$

which directly implies the rectification equation

$$
S_i^{(s)} \tilde{\mathbf{x}} = \frac{\lambda}{\lambda^{(s)}} B_i^{(s)} B_i^{-1} S_i \tilde{\mathbf{x}}
\tag{1.99}
$$

(Fusiello et al., 2000).

At this point it is necessary to compute a grey value for each pixel of the rectified image, where the pixel coordinates are integer-valued. The pixel coordinates in the original image obtained according to (1.99), however, are real-valued. Accordingly, an interpolation technique such as bilinear interpolation has to be applied (Fusiello et al., 2000). An example of a stereo image pair originally acquired with a convergent camera setup and rectified to standard geometry is shown in Fig. 1.16.

The first two coordinates of the projective vector $S_i^{(s)} \tilde{\mathbf{x}}$ correspond to the rectified pixel values $u_i^{(s)}$ and $v_i^{(s)}$. The row $v_1^{(s)}$ of image 1 and the row $v_2^{(s)} = v_1^{(s)}$ of image 2 now form a corresponding pair of epipolar lines. As a consequence, the problem of stereo image analysis becomes a problem of establishing corresponding points along image rows. We will now regard the computation of three-dimensional scene structure from the coordinates of image points measured in stereo image pairs rectified to standard geometry. Without loss of generality, at this point the coordinate system of camera 1 is used as the world coordinate system, such that the corresponding rotation matrix R_1 corresponds to the identity matrix and the translation vector $\mathbf{t}_1$ is zero, and we define $\mathbf{t} \equiv \mathbf{t}_2$. The distance $\|\mathbf{t}\|$ between the optical centres of the two cameras corresponds to the baseline distance of the stereo camera system. As the images are rectified to standard geometry, both optical axes are orthogonal to the baseline (Horn, 1986). Due to the rectification to standard geometry, both cameras have the same effective principal distance b_0.

The image coordinates in standard geometry are denoted by $u_1^{(s)}$ and $v_1^{(s)}$ in image 1 and by $u_2^{(s)}$ and $v_2^{(s)}$ in image 2, respectively. As it is assumed that the world coordinate system corresponds to the coordinate system of camera 1, a scene point can be described by ${}^{W}\mathbf{x} = {}^{C_1}\mathbf{x} = (x, y, z)^T$. We furthermore assume square pixels with $k_u = k_v$, corresponding to a pixel edge length $d_p = 1/k_u$, and without skew. On the basis of Horn (1986), (1.1) then implies the equations

$$\frac{d_p u_1^{(s)}}{b_0} = \frac{x}{z}$$

$$\frac{d_p u_2^{(s)}}{b_0} = \frac{x - \|\mathbf{t}\|}{z} \tag{1.100}$$

$$\frac{d_p v_1^{(s)}}{b_0} = \frac{d_p v_2^{(s)}}{b_0} = \frac{y}{z}$$

which yield the expressions

$$x = \|\mathbf{t}\| \frac{u_1^{(s)}}{u_1^{(s)} - u_2^{(s)}}$$

$$y = \|\mathbf{t}\| \frac{v_1^{(s)}}{u_1^{(s)} - u_2^{(s)}} \tag{1.101}$$

$$z = \|\mathbf{t}\| \frac{b_0}{d_p} \frac{1}{u_1^{(s)} - u_2^{(s)}}$$

for the coordinates x, y, and z. The difference $d = u_1^{(s)} - u_2^{(s)}$ occurring in (1.101) is termed 'disparity'. Accordingly, the depth z is characterised by an inverse proportionality to the disparity.

1.5.2 The Determination of Corresponding Points

In this section it is assumed that the regarded pair of stereo images has been rectified to standard geometry. Hence, the problem of three-dimensional scene reconstruction basically becomes a problem of establishing point correspondences along epipolar lines, i.e. corresponding image rows. Under these preconditions, the problem of three-dimensional scene reconstruction is solved as soon as a disparity map has been generated, i.e. disparity values have been determined for all image pixels or a subset of them.

For selecting the correct correspondences from the multitude of possible correspondences, certain constraints are applied by most stereo vision systems. Marr and Poggio (1979) introduced the 'uniqueness constraint' and the 'continuity constraint'. According to the uniqueness constraint, a point in the first image can be brought into correspondence with either one single point in the second image or no point at all. The continuity constraint postulates that the disparity map should not display abrupt changes (except at the borders of objects). According to the so-called 'monotonicity of edge order' introduced by Baker and Binford (1981), also known as the 'ordering constraint', the relative positions of corresponding points along the epipolar lines are the same in both images, i.e. the lateral sequential arrangement of points in image 1 is the same as that of their corresponding points in image 2.

The following parts of this section describe a variety of classical as well as recently developed methods for generating disparity maps.

1.5.2.1 Correlation-Based Blockmatching Stereo Vision Algorithms

Correlation-based blockmatching stereo algorithms rely on a determination of the similarity S between image regions located on corresponding epipolar lines with

$$S(u_1, u_2) = C\big(I_1\big(V_s(u, v)\big), I_2\big(V_s\big(u - d(u, v), v\big), v\big)\big), \qquad (1.102)$$

where I_1 is the intensity image 1, I_2 is the intensity image 2, $d(u, v)$ is the disparity, and V_s is a vector of pixels in a spatial neighbourhood of the pixel situated at (u, v) in image 1 and of the pixel situated at $(u - d(u, v), v)$ in image 2. An early description of this basic principle is provided by Horn (1986). As examples of the function C, Vincent and Laganière (2001) describe the variance-normalised cross-correlation and the average squared difference correlation. Franke and Joos (2000) rely on the sum of squared differences and the sum of absolute differences to express the similarity, which allows for a computationally efficient similarity estimation.

A broad overview of correlation-based stereo methods is provided by Faugeras et al. (2012). Their presentation especially emphasises the aspect of real-time implementation of such algorithms using special hardware, allowing an integration into mobile robotic systems.

According to the algorithm suggested by Franke and Joos (2000), the image regions which display a sufficient amount of texture are extracted with an interest operator, e.g. a Sobel detector for vertical edges. In a second step, point correspondences are established at pixel accuracy along corresponding epipolar lines by determining the optimum of the similarity measure. A hierarchical correspondence analysis at different resolution levels may significantly decrease the processing time. In a third step, the inferred integer disparity values can be refined to subpixel accuracy based on an interpolation of the measured similarity values by fitting a parabola to the local neighbourhood of the optimum.

Blockmatching algorithms are computationally efficient and thus favourably used in real-time vision systems. However, it is pointed out by Horn (1986) that the depth maps generated by such methods tend to be inaccurate for surfaces not orthogonal to the optical axes, where pixels with different associated depths comprise a correlation window. Similarly, Hirschmüller et al. (2002) state that abrupt depth discontinuities at the borders of objects appear diffuse in the depth map. Hirschmüller (2001) and Hirschmüller et al. (2002) propose a method which aims at correcting or decreasing the effects of depth discontinuities due to object borders. A large correlation window is replaced by a configuration of smaller, possibly overlapping windows, where windows that generate inconsistent similarity values are neglected. The correlation windows are bisected, and the correlation values obtained from the resulting partial windows are analysed in order to obtain refined disparity values associated with object borders. Only correspondences which pass a left–right consistency check are retained. It is shown experimentally by Hirschmüller et al. (2002) that the proposed method yields a clearly improved depth map when compared to standard correlation-based stereo.

1.5.2.2 Feature-Based Stereo Vision Algorithms

General Overview   In the framework of feature-based stereo, correspondences between pairs of stereo images are established based on the similarity between features extracted for certain pixels of interest, such as conspicuous points or lines.

A comparative discussion of stereo algorithms based on corner feature points is provided by Vincent and Laganière (2001). They describe the Plessey operator introduced by Harris and Stephens (1988) as an important detector for corner points. Here, however, we follow the original presentation of that detector as given by Harris and Stephens (1988), who formulate the underlying structure tensor as

$$M = \begin{bmatrix} \left(\frac{\partial I}{\partial x}\right)^2 * w & \left(\frac{\partial I}{\partial x}\frac{\partial I}{\partial y}\right) * w \\ \left(\frac{\partial I}{\partial x}\frac{\partial I}{\partial y}\right) * w & \left(\frac{\partial I}{\partial y}\right)^2 * w \end{bmatrix} \qquad (1.103)$$

with I as the pixel grey value and '$\ldots * w$' as a convolution with an image window function w of predefined size, where a radially symmetric Gaussian shape of the function w is given as an example. The eigenvalues of M are denoted by λ_1 and λ_2. Harris and Stephens (1988) point out that edges are characterised by the occurrence of one large and one small eigenvalue, while large values of both eigenvalues indicate a corner. Furthermore, Harris and Stephens (1988) suggest to use the value $R = \det(M) - k \cdot [\text{trace}(M)]^2$ as a threshold value for corner extraction, where the parameter k governs the sensitivity of the corner detector, instead of determining and analysing the eigenvalues of M.

Vincent and Laganière (2001) point out that the eigenvalues λ_1 and λ_2 of M denote the curvatures of the intensity profile at an extracted corner point. In this context, they present the method by Kung and Lacroix (2001), who define the 'cornerness' as $c = |\lambda_1^2 + \lambda_2^2|$ and establish correspondences between pixels in the stereo images based on the smaller divided by the larger associated cornerness value. In a different approach, Vincent and Laganière (2001) note that the directions of the eigenvectors of the matrix M correspond to the directions of the edges which form the corner. The average vector of the two eigenvectors then defines the 'corner orientation', which can be used as a criterion for establishing a correspondence between two corner points.

As a further feature point detector, Vincent and Laganière (2001) mention the 'univalue segment assimilating nuclei' (USAN) approach introduced by Smith and Brady (1997). According to the presentation by Smith and Brady (1997), the USAN area is computed by regarding a circular mask around a central pixel, called the 'nucleus', and determining the number of pixels inside the mask which have a similar grey value. For uniform image areas, this value is similar to the area of the mask, while it decreases at edges and further decreases at corners. These considerations give rise to the concept of 'smallest univalue segment assimilating nuclei' (SUSAN), which allows one to identify minima of the USAN area with edges and corners in the image.

Zhang and Gimel'farb (1999) use the SUSAN-based corner detector according to Smith and Brady (1997) to determine feature points in uncalibrated stereo image

(a)   (b)   (c)

Fig. 1.17 (**a**) Pair of stereo images. (**b**) Classified image pixels. The pixel brightness encodes the class index. (**c**) Distance image. The pixel brightness is proportional to the distance. Images are from Franke et al. (1999)

pairs as potentially corresponding pixels. As an alternative, they propose a method which determines a measure of the uniqueness of the appearance of a small image region around a given pixel. Their measure is based on the maximum cross-correlation coefficient between the regarded image region and neighbouring image regions. If this value is low, the corresponding pixel is highly unique and is regarded as a feature point, where only regions with strong grey value gradients are taken into account. Zhang and Gimel'farb (1999) show experimentally that both approaches behave in a similar manner with respect to image rotation, scaling, shift, and contrast adaptations.

Medioni and Nevatia (1985) propose an edge-based framework for establishing correspondences between pairs of stereo images. Using the method of Nevatia and Babu (1980), they detect edge pixels using appropriate filters for different edge orientations; a non-maximum suppression of the detected edge pixels is performed, gaps are filled, and linear segments are adapted. Medioni and Nevatia (1985) establish correspondences between these segments based on the coordinates of the points at which they start and terminate, their direction in the image plane, and their contrast. At this point it may be necessary to violate the uniqueness constraint and allow correspondences between single edge segments in the first image and multiple edge segments in the second image, as some edge segments may become decomposed into several parts. Another edge-based approach, where correspondences are established between groups of connected edges, is proposed by Baker and Binford (1981).

An example of a real-time feature-based stereo algorithm applied in the context of a vision-based driver assistance system is outlined by Franke and Kutzbach (1996) and Franke et al. (1999). According to Franke et al. (1999), each pixel is assigned to a class based on the grey values of its four nearest neighbours. The class assignment depends on the information about the relative intensities of the regarded pixel and its neighbours, i.e. which neighbour is significantly brighter or darker or of similar intensity. Essentially, the pixel classes denote edges and corners of different orientations. Correspondences are established by identifying pixels that belong to the same class and are located on corresponding epipolar lines (cf. Fig. 1.17). In the case of several possible correspondences, the pair of corresponding points with the smallest disparity is selected in order to avoid the formation of spurious obstacles at small distances.

A similar assignment scheme is proposed by Stein (2004) in the context of real-time optical flow analysis. This method regards local neighbourhoods of arbitrary size. The relation between the intensities of the central pixel and the neighbouring pixels is encoded as a chain of digits, called the 'signature vector'. Each digit denotes if the corresponding pixel is significantly darker, of similar brightness, or significantly brighter than the central pixel. This scheme can be regarded as an extension of the census transform introduced by Zabih and Woodfill (1994). Correspondences are established by determining pixels in the two images with identical signature vectors, where regions with many highly ambiguous assignments, such as areas of uniform intensity, are excluded. Furthermore, point correspondences are preferentially established based on signature vectors that do not occur frequently in the images. Outliers are removed based on a temporal analysis of the resulting optical flow vectors. Stein (2004) points out that the proposed assignment scheme can also be used for establishing stereo correspondences.

A Contour-Based Stereo Vision Algorithm   A feature-based stereo vision approach relying on the analysis of object contour segments is introduced by Wöhler and Krüger (2003) in the context of surveillance of working areas in industrial production. The presentation in this section is adopted from that work. This contour-based stereo vision (CBS) algorithm is based on the comparison of the current image pair with a pair of reference images. To detect changes between the current image and the reference image, we compute the absolute difference image. There are much more complex methods of change detection; cf. e.g. Durucan (2001) for an overview. Generally, however, these cannot guarantee that a zero image resulting from change detection is equivalent to the fact that the current and the reference image are identical. A zero difference image guarantees that the current and the reference image are exactly identical, which is of significant importance for the application scenario, as a person in the surveillance area must not be missed under any circumstances.

The image pair is rectified to standard geometry. We transform the pair of difference images into binary images by thresholding with

$$\theta_0 = q\sigma_d \quad \text{with } \sigma_d = \sqrt{2}\sigma_p, \tag{1.104}$$

where the pixel noise σ_p is the standard deviation of a camera pixel signal over time, given a constant input intensity, and the noise $\sigma_d = \sqrt{2}\sigma_p$ is the resulting pixel noise of the difference image. In our experiments, we set $q = 3$ in order to detect only changes which are with 99 % certainty significant with respect to pixel noise.

The image regions with pixel grey values above θ_0 are segmented using the binary connected components (BCC) algorithm (Mandler and Oberländer, 1990) which yields, among others, the properties area, centre coordinates, and a contour description for each blob. This computation yields n_1 blobs on the right and n_2 blobs on the left image with centre coordinates $(U_1^{(i)}, V_1^{(i)})$, $i = 1, \ldots, n_1$ and

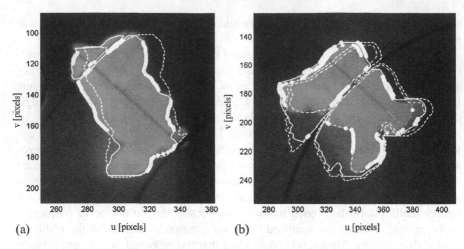

Fig. 1.18 (**a**) Contours extracted from absolute difference image with $\theta_0 = 100$. The *solid contours* have been extracted from the *right image* of the stereo pair, the *dashed contours* from the *left image*. Contour points on the *solid contour* for which a disparity value has been determined are marked by *solid dots*. Only the contours obtained with binary threshold θ_0 are shown. (**b**) Contours extracted from absolute difference image. The *solid* (binary threshold $\theta_0 = 50$) and the *dotted* (adaptive binary threshold derived from intensity histogram) *contours* have been extracted from the *right image* of the stereo pair, the *dashed and the dash-dotted contours* in a corresponding manner from the *left image*. The *solid and the dashed contours* are partially determined by shadow structures on the floor rather than by 'real' object contours. Contour points for which a disparity value has been determined are marked by *solid dots*

$(U_2^{(j)}, V_2^{(j)})$, $j = 1, \ldots, n_2$. The extracted contours are smoothed by B-spline interpolation. Subsequently, we calculate the u (column) coordinates at which the interpolated contour intersects the rows in the v range covered by the corresponding B-spline in order to obtain subpixel accuracy (cf. Fig. 1.18). Hence, the contours are represented as sets $\{\mathbf{c}_{2,a}^{(m)}\}$ and $\{\mathbf{c}_{1,b}^{(n)}\}$ of points for the left and the right image, respectively:

$$
\begin{aligned}
\mathbf{c}_{1,b}^{(n)} &= \left(\bar{u}_{1,b}^{(n)}, \bar{v}_{1,b}^{(n)}\right) \\
\mathbf{c}_{2,a}^{(m)} &= \left(\bar{u}_{1,a}^{(m)}, \bar{v}_{2,a}^{(m)}\right),
\end{aligned}
\tag{1.105}
$$

where $a = 1, \ldots, n_1$ and $b = 1, \ldots, n_2$ are the blob indices in the images and m and n the point indices in the respective contours. The values $\bar{u}_{1,b}^{(n)}$ and $\bar{u}_{2,a}^{(m)}$ are real numbers, while the values $\bar{v}_{1,b}^{(n)}$ and $\bar{v}_{2,a}^{(m)}$ denote image rows and thus are integer numbers.

In the following, a pair of blobs mutually assigned by the previously described procedure is regarded. For each epipolar line in the range covered by both blobs, the numbers of intersections between the contour and the epipolar line are calculated for both images. These intersection counts are denoted by $e_1(v)$ for the right and $e_2(v)$ for the left image of the stereo pair. Along with these values, the u coordinates of the epipolar intersections, $u_1^{(i)}(v)$, $i = 1, \ldots, e_1(v)$ for the right image and $u_2^{(j)}(v)$, $j = 1, \ldots, e_2(v)$ for the left image, are determined. They are known to subpixel accuracy due to the B-spline representation of the contours. The contour indices in the sets $\{\mathbf{c}_{1,b}^{(n)}\}$ and $\{\mathbf{c}_{2,a}^{(m)}\}$ corresponding to these epipolar intersections are denoted by $w_1^{(i)}$ and $w_2^{(j)}$, respectively. For each epipolar line v, the epipolar intersections are sorted in ascending order according to their respective $u_1^{(i)}$ and $u_2^{(j)}$ values. Assuming that the ordering constraint is valid, the following three cases must be distinguished.

1. The contours in both images have an identical number of epipolar intersections, i.e. $e_1(v) = e_2(v)$. Then epipolar intersection $\tilde{i}$ on the right image will be assigned to epipolar intersection $\tilde{j}$ on the left image with $\tilde{i} = \tilde{j}$, respectively.
2. The contours on both images do not have an identical number of epipolar intersections, i.e. $e_1(v) \neq e_2(v)$, and either $e_1(v)$ or $e_2(v)$ is odd. In this case, the epipolar line is a tangent to the respective B-spline contour and is thus discarded.
3. The contours on both images do not have an identical number of epipolar intersections, i.e. $e_1(v) \neq e_2(v)$, and both $e_1(v)$ and $e_2(v)$ are even. Without loss of generality it is assumed that $e_1 > e_2$. An even intersection index denotes an inward transition and an odd intersection index an outward transition. Hence, an intersection with even index j on the left image may only be assigned to an intersection with even index i on the right image, and analogously for odd indices, to account for the topology of the segmented blob features. According to the ordering constraint, we will always assign pairs of neighbouring intersections in the right image to pairs of neighbouring intersections in the left image, i.e. if intersection j is assigned to intersection i, intersection $j + 1$ will be assigned to intersection $i + 1$. According to these rules, $((e_1 - e_2)/2 + 1)$ assignments are allowed, for each of which we compute the sum of square differences:

$$S_j = \sum_{k=1}^{e_2} \left(u_1^{(k+2(j-1))} - u_2^{(k)} - d_{\min} \right)^2 \quad \text{for } j = 1, \dots, (e_1 - e_2)/2 + 1.$$

$$(1.106)$$

Epipolar intersection $\tilde{i}$ on the right image will consequently be assigned to intersection $\tilde{j} = \arg\min_j \{S_j\}$ on the left image. This heuristic rule helps to avoid spurious objects situated near to the camera; similar heuristics are used in state-of-the-art correlation-based blockmatching algorithms (Franke and Joos, 2000).

The mutual assignment of contour points on epipolar line v results in pairs of indices of the form $(\tilde{i}, \tilde{j})$. A disparity measure d_s that involves a single epipolar line v can be obtained in a straightforward manner by

$$d_s = u_2^{(\tilde{j})}(v) - u_1^{(\tilde{i})}(v).$$

$$(1.107)$$

This disparity measure, however, may significantly change from one epipolar line to the next, as the contours are often heavily influenced by pixel noise. Furthermore, d_s becomes inaccurate for nearly horizontal contour parts. An example of a disparity image obtained by using (1.107) is shown in Fig. 1.20.

To obtain a less noisy and more accurate disparity value, we define a contour segment-based disparity measure which relies on an evaluation of L_S neighbouring epipolar lines. The two contour segments of length L_S are denoted by the sets $\{\mathbf{s}_1^{(i)}\}_{i=1,\dots,L_S}$ and $\{\mathbf{s}_2^{(j)}\}_{j=1,\dots,L_S}$ with

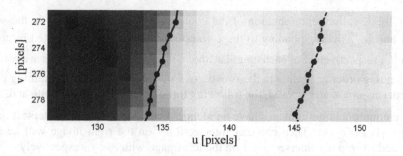

Fig. 1.19 Two contour segments of length $L_S = 8$ which are used to compute the disparity for the two contour points marked by *black circles* according to the contour segment-based scheme given by (1.110). The *solid contour* has been extracted from the *right image*, the *dashed contour* from the *left image* of the stereo pair

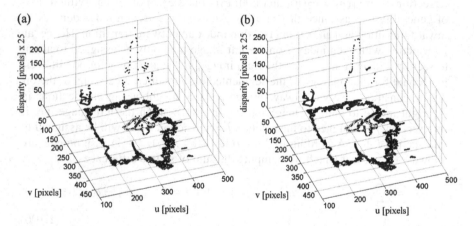

Fig. 1.20 (a) Disparity image obtained with binary threshold $\theta_0 = 7$ and $N_T = 3$ adaptive thresholds derived from the bounding box of each segmented blob, respectively. The contours are shown on the $d_s = 0$ plane of the three-dimensional plot. The disparities have been computed according to the contour point-based scheme given by (1.107). (b) Disparity image of the same scene, computed according to the contour segment-based scheme given by (1.110) with contour segment length $L_S = 8$, cross-correlation threshold $\theta_{\mathrm{corr}} = 0.7$, and absolute slope threshold $\theta_{\mathrm{slope}} = 0.5$. It is obvious that the contour segment-based method yields a significantly less noisy disparity image than the contour point-based method

$$s_1^{(i)} = c_1^{(w_1^{(\tilde{i})} - L_S/2 + i)} \quad \text{for } i = 1, \dots, L_S \tag{1.108}$$

$$s_2^{(j)} = c_2^{(w_2^{(\tilde{j})} - L_S/2 + j)} \quad \text{for } j = 1, \dots, L_S. \tag{1.109}$$

For an illustration of this contour segment extraction procedure, see Fig. 1.19. The contour segment-based disparity d_c is then defined by

$$d_c = \frac{1}{L_S} \sum_{i=1}^{L_S} \left(\bar{u}_2^{(w_2^{(\tilde{j})} - L_S/2 + i)} - \bar{u}_1^{(w_1^{(\tilde{i})} - L_S/2 + i)} \right). \tag{1.110}$$

To avoid false correspondences or inaccurate disparities, the value of d_c computed according to (1.110) is only accepted if the four following conditions are fulfilled.

1. The i-th point of both contour segments is on the same epipolar line, respectively, for all values of i:

$$\bar{v}_1^{(w_1^{(\tilde{i})}-L_S/2+i)} = \bar{v}_2^{(w_2^{(\tilde{j})}-L_S/2+i)} \quad \text{for } i = 1, \dots, L_S. \tag{1.111}$$

2. The average absolute slopes of both contour segments are above a threshold θ_{slope}:

$$\frac{1}{L_S} \sum_{i=2}^{L_S} \left| \frac{\bar{v}_1^{(w_1^{(\tilde{i})}-L_S/2+i)} - \bar{v}_1^{(w_1^{(\tilde{i})}-L_S/2+i-1)}}{\bar{u}_1^{(w_1^{(\tilde{i})}-L_S/2+i)} - \bar{u}_1^{(w_1^{(\tilde{i})}-L_S/2+i-1)}} \right| > \theta_{\text{slope}} \tag{1.112}$$

   and analogously for the left image.

3. The absolute cross-correlation coefficient of the contour segments (Heisele, 1998) exceeds a threshold θ_{corr}:

$$\left| \frac{1 - |\lambda_1 - \lambda_2|}{\lambda_1 + \lambda_2} \frac{\sum_{i=1}^{L_S} (s_1^{(i)} - \langle s_1 \rangle) \cdot (s_2^{(i)} - \langle s_2 \rangle)}{\sqrt{\sum_{i=1}^{L_S} |s_1^{(i)} - \langle s_1 \rangle|^2 \sum_{i=1}^{L_S} |s_2^{(i)} - \langle s_2 \rangle|^2}} \right| > \theta_{\text{corr}}, \tag{1.113}$$

   where $\lambda_1 = \sum_{i=2}^{L_S} |s_1^{(i)} - s_1^{(i-1)}|$ and $\lambda_2 = \sum_{i=2}^{L_S} |s_2^{(i)} - s_2^{(i-1)}|$ denote the length of the contour segments and $\langle s_1 \rangle^{(i)}$ and $\langle s_2 \rangle^{(i)}$ the corresponding contour segment averages. This condition ensures that only contour segments which run approximately parallel are matched.

4. The intensity gradient in the difference image exceeds a threshold θ_{grad}:

$$\nabla_g \left(\bar{u}_1^{(w_1^{(\tilde{i})})}, \bar{v}_1^{(w_1^{(\tilde{i})})} \right) > \theta_{\text{grad}}. \tag{1.114}$$

This condition ensures that only contour pixels are accepted whose position is characterised by intensity changes, i.e. transitions from the background to an object, rather than by pixel noise in nearly uniform areas of the difference image. It is assumed that the surfaces of the objects that may enter the scene, e.g. persons, are arced rather than flat, such that an intensity difference between object and background is still perceivable due to shading even if the corresponding reflectivities are identical. This shading contrast determines the value of θ_{grad}.

The segmentation obtained with binary threshold θ_0 often does not yield contours around the objects in the scene, but around secondary structures such as shadows indirectly caused by the objects (Fig. 1.18b). Hence, for the bounding box of each blob segmented with binary threshold θ_0, the described procedure is repeated with N_T different adaptive threshold values $\theta_a^{(q)}$, $q = 1, \dots, N_T$ which are derived from the intensity histogram of the corresponding bounding box. The values of the adaptive thresholds may be chosen to be equally spaced between θ_0 and the maximum possible grey value, or to lie within a suitable range around the minimum of the intensity histogram, which is in many cases a binary threshold value that can separate

(a)   (b)

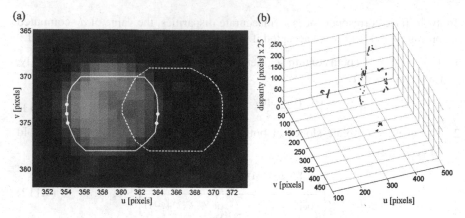

Fig. 1.21 (a) Contour segment-based stereo analysis of a ball of 10 cm diameter, painted in the same colour as the floor. The *solid contour* is valid for the *right image*, the *dashed contour* for the *left image* of the stereo pair. Image points for which disparity values have been computed are denoted by white *filled circles*. (b) Disparity map of the same scene as shown in Fig. 1.20, obtained with the correlation-based real-time stereo algorithm described in Franke and Joos (2000), which has been applied to the stereo pair of absolute difference images. Obviously, the disparity map is more noisy than the one obtained with the CBS algorithm (cf. Fig. 1.20b). This correlation-based stereo vision algorithm, however, does not necessarily depend on reference images of the scene

dark from bright image regions. Thus, disparity information is obtained from $N_T + 1$ isophotes in the pair of absolute difference images. These isophotes are determined by θ_0 and the chosen values of $\theta_a^{(q)}$.

Figure 1.18a displays contours extracted from the stereo image pair with a relatively high binary threshold value of $\theta_0 = 100$. In Fig. 1.18b the contours extracted from the stereo image pair with $\theta_0 = 50$ are partially determined by shadows cast by the object rather than by the object itself (solid and dashed contours, respectively). For these parts of the contours no disparity value is computed, as the gradient at the corresponding positions in the image is too small to exceed the threshold θ_{grad} that depends on the minimum shading contrast; in our experiments we set $\theta_{\mathrm{grad}} = 1$. Hence, the contour extraction procedure is repeated with an adaptive threshold derived from the intensity histogram of the bounding box of the solid contour, yielding the dotted and the dashed-dotted contours, which are now fully characterised by the object boundary. Figure 1.20 shows the resulting disparity map based on single contour points and based on contour segments with length $L_S = 8$. In the second example, we set the thresholds to the not very restrictive values $\theta_{\mathrm{corr}} = 0.7$ and $\theta_{\mathrm{slope}} = 0.5$, i.e. two corresponding contour segments may be oriented at an angle of up to 45°, provided that they are running at an angle of more than 30° with respect to the image rows. Note that changing these thresholds does not change the disparity value of a certain three-dimensional point but may only add it to or remove it from the disparity map. For this rather complex scene, the computation time of our C++ implementation of the CBS algorithm amounts to 80 ms on a 1.8 GHz Pentium IV processor. Figure 1.20 illustrates that the contour segment-based method yields a significantly less noisy disparity image than the contour point-based method. Compared to the correlation-based real-time stereo algorithm described by Franke and Joos (2000), which does not make use of a reference image, the disparity values are more accurate and less noisy (Fig. 1.21b). In Fig. 1.21a the CBS algorithm is applied to a scene displaying a ball of 10 cm diameter and painted in the same colour as the floor, therefore appearing as a small circle only eight pixels in diameter in the stereo images. This very difficult object is detected by means of its shading contrast only.

1.5.2.3 Dense Stereo Vision Algorithms

Correlation-based blockmatching and feature-based stereo vision algorithms usually generate sparse depth maps, i.e. depth information is only derived for parts of the scene in which a sufficient amount of texture is observed, such that enough information is available to achieve a meaningful comparison between image windows along corresponding epipolar lines. In contrast, stereo vision algorithms which generate a depth value for each image pixel are termed dense stereo vision algorithms. An early dense stereo vision approach by Horn (1986) relies on the direct comparison of pixel grey values along corresponding epipolar lines instead of a comparison between image windows or local features. Since the intensity-based criterion alone leads to a highly ambiguous solution, a smooth depth map is assumed, i.e. there are no large differences between the disparity values assigned to neighbouring pixels. This line of thought leads to the minimisation of the error term

$$e = \sum_{u,v} \left[\left(\nabla^2 d(u,v) \right)^2 + \lambda \left(I_1 \left(u + d(u,v)/2, v \right) - I_2 \left(u - d(u,v)/2, v \right) \right)^2 \right],$$

(1.115)

where λ is a weight parameter and $\nabla^2 d(u, v)$ denotes the Laplace operator applied to the disparity map—at this point, Horn (1986) states that using the first instead of the second derivative of the disparity in the first term of (1.115) would lead to a too smooth solution. Based on the Euler equation of (1.115), a differential equation for $d(u, v)$ of fourth order in u and v is derived and solved numerically.

Another stereo vision algorithm that constructs dense depth maps is based on dynamic programming (Cox et al., 1996). It makes use of the ordering constraint which requires that for opaque surfaces the order of neighbouring point correspondences on two corresponding epipolar lines is always preserved. Cox et al. (1996) assume that if two pixels correspond to the same scene point, the distribution of the intensity difference with respect to all mutually corresponding pixels is Gaussian. A maximum likelihood criterion then defines an overall cost function which is minimised by the dynamic programming algorithm. While in the approach suggested by Cox et al. (1996) each epipolar line is processed independently, the graph cut or maximum flow method optimises the solution globally (Roy and Cox, 1998). Instead of the ordering constraint, a more general constraint termed 'local coherence constraint' is introduced by Roy and Cox (1998), where it is assumed that the disparity values are always similar in the neighbourhood of a given point independent of the direction in the image. Correspondences are then established based on the maximisation of flow in a graph.

A survey about dense stereo methods and an evaluation framework essentially based on synthetic images to assess their performance is provided by Scharstein and Szeliski (2001). Van der Mark and Gavrila (2006) examine dense stereo algorithms with respect to their applicability in vehicle-based real-time vision systems. Based on synthetic image data that mimic the properties of real vehicle-based images and also on real-world images acquired during test drives in the urban traffic scenario, they show that algorithms which rely on global optimisation of the disparity map suffer more strongly from the variability of the encountered conditions under which the scene is imaged than approaches relying on simpler selection criteria to establish point correspondences. Furthermore, it is demonstrated by Van der Mark and Gavrila (2006) that the method proposed by Hirschmüller et al. (2002) in the context of correlation-based blockmatching stereo vision (cf. Sect. 1.5.2.1) shows the best performance of all examined algorithms when applied in a real-time setting for the analysis of traffic scenes.

A general drawback of dense stereo algorithms is the fact that the established depth values tend to be inaccurate for parts of the surface that do not show any surface texture at all, or for corresponding parts of the stereo image pair which do not display a similar structure. The latter behaviour may e.g. occur as a consequence of specular reflectance properties leading to a different appearance of the respective surface part in the stereo images. In such cases of missing or contradictory texture information, dense stereo algorithms usually interpolate the surface across the ambiguous image parts, leading to an inaccurate three-dimensional reconstruction result for the corresponding region. This problem is addressed explicitly by Hirschmüller (2006), who proposes the semi-global matching method which establishes correspondences based on similar pixel grey values to obtain plausible disparity values for surface parts free of small-scale structures. Furthermore, Hirschmüller (2006) suggests an interpolation approach which maintains sharp depth discontinuities rather than blurring them and which is able to fill regions in the disparity map where the disparity information is unavailable or incorrect. In the presence of systematic differences between the pixel grey values of corresponding points, Hirschmüller (2008) suggests the use of mutual information as a similarity measure for disparity estimation. An important advantage of the semi-global matching approach by Hirschmüller (2006, 2008) is that it has high computational efficiency, while also providing disparity estimates of high subpixel accuracy.

1.5.2.4 Model-Based Stereo Vision Algorithms

A higher level stereo method which is complementary to the previously described approaches is model-based stereo. The approach introduced by Tonko and Nagel (2000) relies on establishing correspondences between grey value gradients in the image ('edge elements') and edges of object models in the scene ('model segments'). The detected objects are tracked using an extended Kalman filter. In the context of three-dimensional reconstruction of the human hand, an articulated model derived from human anatomy is introduced by Lee and Kunii (1993), relying on planar kinematic chains consisting of rigid elements. The appearance of the hand in a pair of stereo images is modelled and compared with the appearance in the observed image. Heap and Hogg (1996) propose to represent the complete surface of the hand by a deformable model. In the application scenario of three-dimensional face reconstruction, a linear morphable model is adapted by Amberg et al. (2007) to the object appearance in a stereo image pair based on silhouettes, colour variations, and manually defined reference points.

1.5.2.5 Spacetime Stereo Vision and Scene Flow Algorithms

General Overview   An extension of the classical pairwise frame-by-frame approach to stereo vision towards a spatio-temporal analysis of a sequence of image pairs has been introduced quite recently as spacetime stereo by several researchers (Zhang et al., 2003; Davis et al., 2005). Both studies present a framework that aims for a unification of stereo vision with active depth from triangulation methods such as laser scanning and coded structured light by generalising a spatial similarity measure according to (1.102) to the spatio-temporal domain. Zhang et al. (2003) suggest to utilise pixel grey values changing over time to establish disparity maps of increased accuracy. They show that assuming a disparity value $d(u_c, v_c, t_c)$ which is constant throughout a spatio-temporal image window centred at (u_c, v_c, t_c) can only be assumed for a surface oriented parallel to the image plane. For surfaces of arbitrary orientation which do not move, a linear expansion for the disparity is introduced by Zhang et al. (2003), corresponding to

$$d(u, v, t) = d(u_c, v_c, t_c) + \frac{\partial d}{\partial u}(u - u_c) + \frac{\partial d}{\partial v}(v - v_c) + \cdots. \quad (1.116)$$

For moving scenes, this representation is extended according to

$$d(u, v, t) = d(u_c, v_c, t_c) + \frac{\partial d}{\partial u}(u - u_c) + \frac{\partial d}{\partial v}(v - v_c) + \frac{\partial d}{\partial t}(t - t_c) + \cdots \quad (1.117)$$

since the disparity may change over time as a result of a radial velocity of the object. These expressions for the disparity are inserted into a similarity measure defined by (1.102). Dynamic programming followed by Lucas-Kanade flow (Lucas and Kanade, 1981) is utilised to establish point correspondences and estimate the disparities as well as their spatial and temporal first derivatives $\partial d/\partial u$, $\partial d/\partial v$, and $\partial d/\partial t$. A significant improvement over classical stereo analysis is achieved by Zhang et al. (2003) when a static scene is illuminated by a temporally variable illumination pattern which is not necessarily strictly controlled. In these cases, their three-dimensional reconstruction method exhibits a similar amount of detail as three-dimensional data acquired by a laser scanner. For images displaying objects which are illuminated in a non-controlled manner, their spacetime stereo approach performs similarly to classical stereo vision approaches that do not go into the temporal domain, but it requires smaller matching windows.

The spacetime stereo framework described by Davis et al. (2005) is fairly similar to the one presented by Zhang et al. (2003). However, the spatial and temporal derivatives of the disparity are not estimated. Davis et al. (2005) concentrate on the determination of the optimal spatio-temporal size of the matching window for static scenes and scenes with moving objects. For static scenes illuminated with temporally variable but not strictly controlled structured light patterns, they conclude that after acquiring only a short sequence of about 25 images, it is no longer necessary to use spatially extended matching windows, since a purely temporal matching vector turns out to yield the highest reconstruction accuracy. Scenes with linearly moving and with rotating objects are illuminated with light patterns varying at high frequency, generated with an uncalibrated LCD projector. Davis et al. (2005) find that the optimum temporal window size is smaller and the optimum spatial window size is larger for a scene with a linearly moving object than for a scene displaying a rotating object. The optimum temporal extension decreases with increasing speed of the motion. For illumination with a temporally variable light pattern, Davis et al. (2005) conclude that for scenes with very fast motion, purely spatial stereo analysis is favourable, while static scenes should be analysed based on the purely temporal variations of the pixel grey values.

For obstacle avoidance in the context of driver assistance and mobile robotic systems, which require an extraction of depth information and the robust and fast detection of moving objects, Franke et al. (2005) introduce a framework termed 6D vision, addressing the integration of stereo and optical flow. For each individual extracted scene point, the three-dimensional world coordinates and the three-dimensional velocity vector are determined based on Kalman filters. Vedula et al. (2005) introduce the concept of scene flow, which contains the three-dimensional positions of the scene points along with their three-dimensional velocities. Hence, projecting the scene flow into the image plane yields the classical two-dimensional optical flow. Therefore, the 6D vision method by Franke et al. (2005) yields sparse scene flow information. Huguet and Devernay (2007) determine dense scene flow using an integrated simultaneous determination of the optical flow in both stereo images and a dense disparity map (cf. Fig. 1.22). A variational approach yields a system of partial differential equations that simultaneously determine the disparities and the optical flow field, which allows the method to cope with discontinuities of the disparities and the three-dimensional velocity field. Applying this method to multiple resolution levels eventually yields a numerical solution of the partial differential equations. While previous variational approaches, e.g. by Pons et al. (2005), estimate the three-dimensional scene point coordinates and the three-dimensional velocity field separately, they are computed simultaneously in a single adjustment stage by Huguet and Devernay (2007).

A computationally very efficient method for the computation of the scene flow is introduced by Wedel et al. (2008a, 2008b) and is refined and extended by Wedel et al. (2011). In contrast to Huguet and Devernay (2007), who determine the scene flow in an integrated manner by an optimisation of the disparity and the optical flow

Fig. 1.22 Determination of scene flow information (adapted from Huguet and Devernay, 2007)

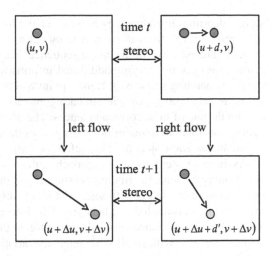

field over two stereo image pairs acquired at subsequent time steps, Wedel et al. (2008a) propose a separate determination of disparity and optical flow while keeping both estimates consistent with each other. At the same time, individual methods which are optimal e.g. with respect to accuracy or computational efficiency can be employed for each of these two parts of the scene flow estimation problem. The epipolar constraint is exploited for the computation of disparity and the vertical component of the optical flow. An energy functional consisting of the weighted sum of a first term describing the difference between the grey values in the left and the right image at the current and the subsequent time step, respectively ('data term'), and a second term favouring small absolute values of the gradients of the optical flow components and the disparity ('smoothness term') is minimised by a variational approach. An extensive experimental evaluation is performed by Wedel et al. (2008b), regarding image sequences synthetically generated with a ray tracing software, such that ground truth data are available, and real-world urban traffic scenes. Wedel et al. (2011) compare several disparity estimation approaches in the context of their scene flow computation framework, namely the sparse methods by Franke and Joos (2000) and by Stein (2004) as well as the semi-global matching approach based on mutual information by Hirschmüller (2008), where the best results are obtained using the method by Hirschmüller (2008). An experimental evaluation regarding synthetically generated image sequences and real-world traffic scenes, including long stereo image sequences, is presented by Wedel et al. (2011). The mean errors of the estimated optical flow components and the disparity values are typically well below 1 pixel, with standard deviations ranging from some tenths of a pixel to about 2 pixels. Furthermore, the scene flow field is used by Wedel et al. (2011) for extracting objects from the scene which move in a manner different from the background, relying on a graph cut-based segmentation approach.

Local Intensity Modelling   In contrast to the previously described spacetime stereo approaches, which exploit a pixel-based similarity measure, the spacetime stereo algorithm introduced by Schmidt et al. (2007), which is described in this section, relies on the fit of a parametric model to the spatio-temporal neighbourhood of each interest pixel in an image sequence. This method yields a cloud of three-dimensional points carrying additional information about the motion properties of the corresponding scene part. Hence, point correspondences may be resolved which would remain ambiguous without taking into account the temporal domain, thus reducing the rate of false correspondences. The additional motion cues may be used to support optional subsequent processing steps dealing with three-dimensional scene segmentation and object tracking (cf. Sect. 2.3).

As in most stereo vision approaches that establish correspondences between small image regions, the first processing step of our algorithm consists of determining interest pixels in order to select the image regions for which three-dimensional information is computed in a later step. The interest operator may e.g. consist of the local grey value variance or an edge detector. In this case, interest pixels correspond to image regions with small-scale intensity variations, implying the presence of image structures such as object boundaries upon which a correspondence analysis can be based. The presentation in this section is adopted from Schmidt et al. (2007).

The image sequence is defined in $(uvtg)$ space, where u and v denote the pixel coordinates, t the time coordinate, and g the pixel grey value. To the local spatio-temporal neighbourhood of each interest pixel a parameterised function $h(\mathbf{P}, u, v, t)$ is adapted, where the vector $\mathbf{P}$ denotes the parameters of the function. The interest operator preferentially extracts image regions along the boundaries of objects in the scene.

Ideally, an object boundary is described by an abrupt intensity change. In real images, however, one does not observe such discontinuities, since they are blurred by the point spread function of the optical system. Therefore, the intensity change at an object boundary is modelled by a 'soft' function of sigmoidal shape like the hyperbolic tangent (cf. Sect. 1.4.8.2). Without loss of generality it will be assumed here that the epipolar lines are parallel to the image rows. As the image regions inside and outside the object are usually not of uniform intensity, the pixel grey values around an interest pixel are modelled by a combined sigmoid–polynomial approach:

$$h(\mathbf{P}, u, v, t) = p_1(v, t)\tanh\big[p_2(v, t)u + p_3(v, t)\big] + p_4(v, t). \qquad (1.118)$$

The terms $p_1(v, t)$, $p_2(v, t)$, $p_3(v, t)$, and $p_4(v, t)$ denote polynomials in v and t. Here it is assumed that the stereo camera system is calibrated (Krüger et al., 2004) and the stereo image pairs are rectified to standard geometry (cf. Sect. 1.5).

The polynomial $p_1(v, t)$ describes the amplitude and $p_2(v, t)$ the steepness of the sigmoid function, which both depend on the image row v, while $p_3(v, t)$ accounts for the row-dependent position of the model boundary. The value of $p_2(v, t)$ is closely related to the sign of the intensity gradient and to how well it is focused, where large values describe sharp edges and small values blurred edges. The polynomial $p_4(v, t)$ is a spatially variable offset which models local intensity variations across the object and in the background, e.g. allowing the model to adapt to a cluttered background. All described properties are assumed to be time-dependent. An interest pixel is rejected if the residual of the fit exceeds a given threshold.

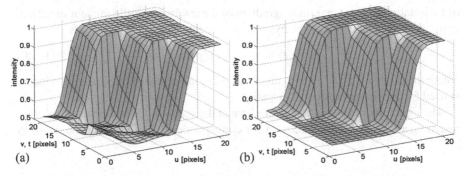

Fig. 1.23 (a) Spatio-temporal intensity profile of a moving object boundary, measured over a time interval of 3 time steps. The size of the spatio-temporal matching window is $21 \times 7 \times 3$ pixels. For visualisation, the (v, t) axis is divided such that each time step comprises an interval of 7 pixels. (b) Modelling result according to (1.119), with $p_2(v, t)$ of first order and $p_3(v, t)$ of second order in v and t

The parametric model according to (1.118) in its general form requires that a non-linear least-mean-squares optimisation procedure be applied to each interest pixel, which may lead to a prohibitively high computational cost of the method. It is possible, however, to transform the nonlinear optimisation problem into a linear problem by making the following simplifying assumptions:

1. The offset $p_4(v, t)$ is proportional to the average pixel grey value $\bar{I}$ of the spatio-temporal matching window, i.e. $p_4(v, t) = w\bar{I}$,
2. The amplitude $p_1(v, t)$ of the sigmoid is proportional to the standard deviation σ_I of the pixel grey values in the spatio-temporal matching window with $p_1(v, t) = k\sigma_I$.

These simplifications yield the model equation

$$p_2(v, t)u + p_3(v, t) = \operatorname{artanh}\left[\frac{I(u, v, t) - w\bar{I}}{k\sigma_I}\right] \equiv \tilde{I}(u, v, t), \quad (1.119)$$

where the model parameters, i.e. the coefficients of the polynomials $p_2(v, t)$ and $p_3(v, t)$, can be determined by a linear fit to the transformed image data $\tilde{I}(u, v, t)$. Real-time processing speed is achieved by implementing the artanh function as a look-up table.

Pixels with $|[I(u, v, t) - w\bar{I}]/[k\sigma_I]| > \theta$ are excluded from the fit, where θ is a user-defined threshold with $\theta < 1$, since arguments of the artanh function close to 1 would lead to a strong amplification of noise in the original pixel grey values. The factors k and w are further user-defined parameters of the algorithm. A typical spatio-temporally local modelling result for a moving object boundary is shown in Fig. 1.23.

Equation (1.118) allows for a direct computation of the location u_e of the epipolar intersection, i.e. the position of the intensity change at subpixel accuracy in the u direction. This value is essential for a precise determination of disparity. The value of u_e is defined by the maximum gradient of the intensity profile in the u direction, corresponding to the root of the hyperbolic tangent. This condition yields

$$u_e(v,t) = -p_3(v,t)/p_2(v,t), \tag{1.120}$$

where the value $u_e(v_c, t_c)$ with v_c and t_c denoting the centre of the matching window is used for the determination of disparity.

The direction δ of the intensity gradient at the location of the interest pixel, representing a feature that will be used for correspondence analysis later on, is given by

$$\delta = \left. \frac{\partial u_e}{\partial v} \right|_{v_c,t_c}. \tag{1.121}$$

The velocity μ of the intensity gradient along the epipolar line corresponds to the temporal derivative

$$\mu = \left. \frac{\partial u_e}{\partial t} \right|_{v_c,t_c} \tag{1.122}$$

of the location of the epipolar transection. Such explicit motion information is not revealed by the purely correlation-based spacetime approach described by Davis et al. (2005). The approach described by Franke et al. (2005) yields motion information for each three-dimensional point but requires a separate processing stage for individually tracking the corresponding positions and velocities.

For the purpose of correspondence analysis, a similarity measure between two interest pixels located on the same epipolar line v is determined based on the functions $h(\mathbf{P}_{\text{left}}, u, v, t)$ and $h(\mathbf{P}_{\text{right}}, u, v, t)$ fitted in the left and the right image to the spatio-temporal matching windows of the interest pixels, respectively, where the obtained function parameters are denoted by the vectors $\mathbf{P}_{\text{left}}$ and $\mathbf{P}_{\text{right}}$.

Similarity measures analogous to those well known from classical correlation-based stereo vision approaches (Franke and Joos, 2000), such as the sum of squared differences (SSD), the sum of absolute differences (SAD), or the cross-correlation coefficient, can be adapted to this spacetime stereo algorithm. This is achieved by comparing the fitted functions $h(\mathbf{P}_{\text{left}}, u, v, t)$ and $h(\mathbf{P}_{\text{right}}, u, v, t)$ rather than the pixel grey values themselves Davis et al. (2005). As an example, the SSD similarity measure then reads

$$S_{\text{SSD}} = \int \left[h\left(\mathbf{P}_l, u - u_e^{\text{left}}(v_c, t_c), v, t\right) - h\left(\mathbf{P}_r, u - u_e^{\text{right}}(v_c, t_c), v, t\right) \right]^2 du\, dv\, dt, \tag{1.123}$$

where u, v, and t traverse the spatio-temporal matching windows of the left and the right interest pixel, respectively. Analogous expressions are obtained for the SAD or cross-correlation similarity measure.

Once a correspondence between two interest pixels on the same epipolar line has been established by searching for the best similarity measure e.g. according to (1.123), the disparity d corresponds to the difference between the epipolar transections u_e^{left} and u_e^{right} computed according to (1.120) for the left and the right interest pixel, respectively:

$$d = u_e^{\text{left}}(v_c, t_c) - u_e^{\text{right}}(v_c, t_c). \tag{1.124}$$

To increase the accuracy of the determined disparity values, it is advantageous to establish the correspondences based on the spacetime approach by searching for the minimum value of the similarity measure along the epipolar line but to compute the corresponding disparities without utilising temporal information. This prevents the disparity value from becoming inaccurate when the true motion behaviour is not closely approximated by the model function.

Given the optical and geometrical parameters of the camera system, the velocity component $\bar{\mu}$ parallel to the epipolar lines (in pixels per time step) amounts to

$$\bar{\mu} = \frac{1}{2}\left(\mu^{\text{left}} + \mu^{\text{right}}\right). \tag{1.125}$$

In metric units, the epipolar velocity $U = \partial x/\partial t$ is given by

$$U = \frac{\partial x}{\partial t} = \|\mathbf{t}\| \frac{\bar{\mu}d - \frac{1}{2}(u_e^{\text{left}}(v_c, t_c) + u_e^{\text{right}}(v_c, t_c))\frac{\partial d}{\partial t}}{d^2}. \tag{1.126}$$

The vertical velocity component $V = \partial y/\partial t$ cannot be inferred pointwise from the spacetime stereo data due to the aperture problem. The velocity component $\partial z/\partial t$ along the depth axis depends on the first temporal derivative of the disparity, which is obtained according to

$$\frac{\partial d}{\partial t} = \mu^{\text{left}} - \mu^{\text{right}} \tag{1.127}$$

(cf. (1.122) and (1.124)). Inserting (1.127) into (1.101) yields for the velocity W along the z axis

$$W = \frac{\partial z}{\partial t} = -\frac{\|\mathbf{t}\| \, b_0(\mu^{\text{left}} - \mu^{\text{right}})}{d_p \, d^2}. \tag{1.128}$$

Note, however, that small relative errors of μ^{left} and μ^{right} may lead to large relative errors of $\partial d/\partial t$ and $\partial z/\partial t$. The relative difference between the temporal derivative $\partial d/\partial t$ of the disparity computed according to (1.127) and the manually measured average disparity variation per time step is of the order of 10 % or less (cf. Gövert, 2006 for further details).

Experimental results of the local spatio-temporal intensity modelling approach by Schmidt et al. (2007) outlined in this section are described in Chap. 7 in the context of three-dimensional scene segmentation and object tracking.

Like the approach described in this section, the spacetime stereo method by Zhang et al. (2003) estimates the temporal derivative $\partial d/\partial t$ of the disparity for each established point correspondence. However, no quantitative evaluation but merely a qualitative discussion is given in their study; thus a direct comparison is not possible. The spacetime stereo approach by Davis et al. (2005) does not take into account the temporal derivative of the disparity.

An important advantage of the spacetime stereo method described in this section is the fact that no explicit correspondences need to be established over time. Furthermore, the motion parameters are available nearly instantaneously (after acquisition of three images in the presented examples) since no tracking stage is involved—tracking systems usually require a certain settlement phase after initialisation before the estimated motion parameters become reliable. In Chap. 7 it is demonstrated that spacetime stereo is a useful technique in the context of three-dimensional scene segmentation and object tracking. Especially in the presence of several objects in the scene which all move in a different manner, it is often difficult to assign parts of the three-dimensional point cloud to specific objects when only spatial information is available. Adding motion cues to the point cloud introduces new information that may allow one to distinguish unambiguously between the objects in the scene even when they come close to each other or mutually overlap.

1.6 Resolving Stereo Matching Errors due to Repetitive Structures Using Model Information

It is a 'universal problem' of stereo vision that repetitive structures may lead to spurious objects in front of or behind the true scene (cf. Fig. 1.24), which may cause severe problems in scenarios involving mobile robot navigation or human–robot interaction. To alleviate this problem, a model-based method is proposed by Barrois et al. (2010) which is independent of the specific stereo algorithm used. The basic idea is the feedback of application-dependent model information into the correspondence analysis procedure without losing the ability to reconstruct scene parts not described by the model. The description in this section is adopted from Barrois et al. (2010).

Many stereo algorithms attempt to avoid false correspondences by using well-known techniques such as the ordering constraint, the smoothness constraint, the geometric similarity constraint, or a left–right consistency check (Fua, 1993). Regarding repetitive structures, Di Stefano et al. (2004) assess the quality of the minimum of the cost function and the related disparity value by introducing a distinctiveness and a sharpness test to resolve ambiguities. Some approaches handle erroneous stereo correspondences explicitly. Murray and Little (2004) use the RANSAC algorithm (Fischler and Bolles, 1981) to fit planes to the three-dimensional points in order to detect and eliminate gross errors. Sepehri et al. (2004) use a similar approach to fit a plane to the three-dimensional points of an object using an M-estimator technique (Rey, 1983).

Barrois et al. (2010) present a novel method to cope with repetitive structures in stereo analysis, which can be applied independent of the specific stereo algorithm used. In a first step, a three-dimensional reconstruction of the scene is determined by conventional correspondence analysis, leading to correct and incorrect three-dimensional points. An application-dependent scene model or object model is adapted to the initial three-dimensional points, which yields a model pose. The

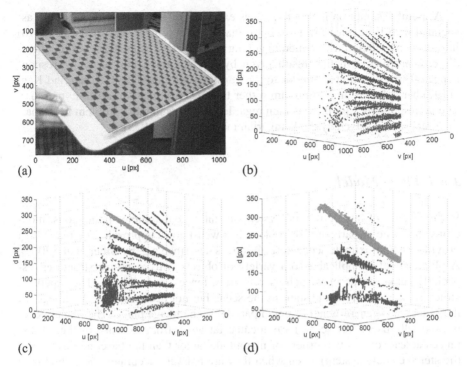

Fig. 1.24 Mismatches in the *marked area* produced by different stereo methods. *Light grey points*: correct disparities; *dark grey points*: incorrect disparities. The three-dimensional points are shown in disparity space, where u and v are the image coordinates of a pixel in the *right image* and d denotes the associated disparity value. (**a**) *Right image* of a stereo pair, area with repetitive structures marked in *light grey*. (**b**) Feature-based method (spacetime stereo algorithm; Schmidt et al., 2007). (**c**) Intensity-based method (blockmatching stereo algorithm; Horn, 1986). (**d**) Global method (semi-global matching algorithm; Hirschmüller, 2005)

model pose is used to perform a refined correspondence analysis. This analysis is governed by a cost function which takes into account the distances of the three-dimensional points from the model.

In this section, the stereo approach introduced by Schmidt et al. (2007) based on spatio-temporal local intensity modelling (cf. Sect. 1.5.2.5) is used, where different stereo constraints can be taken into account to find the correct matches. A comparison of the results of the well-known uniqueness (Marr and Poggio, 1979) and ordering constraints (Baker and Binford, 1981) (cf. Sect. 1.5.2) is performed. Furthermore, a model-based stereo method similar to the approach by Tonko and Nagel (2000) is regarded for comparison. It uses the model surface and the pose parameters to obtain the homographies that determine corresponding image points in both images. Image windows of predefined size around a given number of points in one stereo image are reprojected into the other image based on these homographies induced by the model surface. The similarities between corresponding image windows are maximised by variation of the pose parameters.

A useful assumption is that the edges extracted by the interest operator are associated with the same objects in both images. Accordingly, Barrois et al. (2010) introduce the minimum weighted matching constraint, which determines the three-dimensional reconstruction result given by the maximum number of correspondences. This constraint is similar to the constraint proposed by Fielding and Kam (1997) but is based on a minimum rather than a maximum overall SSD measure. The correspondence problem is then regarded as an assignment problem in a bipartite graph and is solved by the Hungarian method (Kuhn, 1955).

1.6.1 Plane Model

In the domain of mobile robotic systems or intelligent vehicle applications, modelling the scene or parts of it by a plane is a well-known approach. The plane then provides an approximate scene description, as described e.g. by Biber et al. (2004). A plane model is applicable to a variety of objects with repetitive structures, especially human-made ones such as wall tiles, fences, or buildings. The repetitive structures are usually equidistant in the scene but not necessarily in the image, as the objects are generally not oriented parallel to the image plane. The plane model is especially useful for scene parts located far away from the camera (i.e. at distances at least one to two orders of magnitude larger than the baseline distance of the stereo camera system), even when they are not very accurately described by a plane. In such a case, the repetitive structures are associated with the background of the scene, which is modelled by the plane at infinity. The deviations in disparity space from the configuration implied by a plane can then be assumed to be small due to the smallness of the disparity values themselves.

1.6.1.1 Detection and Characterisation of Repetitive Structures

Repetitive structures are characterised by a repeating grey value pattern which leads to a significant peak in the associated amplitude spectrum, which is favourably determined by a fast Fourier transform (FFT). Horizontal image lines of fixed length, e.g. 128 pixels, are extracted from each image row with an overlap of half the length of a line. In the amplitude spectrum, the maximum peak apart from the zero-frequency component is extracted if its significance exceeds a given threshold that depends on the mean and the standard deviation of the spectrum, and the corresponding wavelength is calculated. To obtain a continuous representation, a plane is adapted to the extracted wavelengths using an M-estimator technique. Outliers are eliminated, and image areas displaying repetitive structures are marked in the image based on the determined wavelengths. The same procedure is applied to vertical image lines extracted in an analogous manner. The results of these horizontal and vertical spectral analyses are image areas displaying repetitive structures and plane functions $\lambda_h(U, V)$ and $\lambda_v(U, V)$ providing a wavelength value for each marked image position with coordinates (U, V).

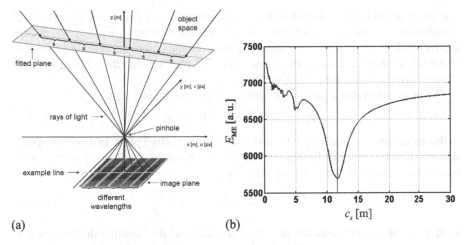

Fig. 1.25 Illustration of the model adaptation procedure for the plane model. (**a**) Plane fit based on repetitive structures. The 'wavelength' of the repetitive structures in scene space is denoted by s. (**b**) Dependence of the disparity error E_{ME} according to (1.135) on the offset parameter c_s for scene 1 (fence with person) regarded in Sect. 1.6.4

1.6.1.2 Determination of Model Parameters

In three-dimensional scene space spanned by the world coordinates x, y, and z, the plane with repetitive structures is determined based on modelling rays of light using the previously determined wavelength information. These rays describe the relation between the repetitive structures in the scene and their appearance in the image. The coordinates $U_{i,j}$ and $V_{i,j}$ of the intersections of the rays with the image plane are determined by

$$U_{i,j} = U_{i,j-1} + \lambda_h(U_{i,j-1}, V_{i,j-1}) \tag{1.129}$$

$$V_{i,j} = V_{i-1,j} + \lambda_v(U_{i-1,j}, V_{i-1,j}), \tag{1.130}$$

where i denotes the index of the ray in a column, j the index of the ray in a row, $U_{i,0} = 0$, and $V_{0,j} = 0$.

The connection between these intersection points and the optical centre leads to modelled rays which are characteristic for the repetitive structure. Assuming equidistant repetitive structures in the scene leads to the criterion that the mutual distances between the intersection points on the plane have to be equal. At this point we explicitly assume that these structures are repetitive in scene space and not just a reasonably regular high spatial frequency pattern in image space. The distance parameter is denoted by s in Fig. 1.25a. This condition yields the normal vector of the plane in three-dimensional space. However, the offset parameter of the plane cannot be determined based on the intersection point approach and has to be estimated based on the initial three-dimensional point cloud.

We found by inspection of the measurement uncertainties of the pixel coordinates of the three-dimensional points as well as their measured disparity values that they can be assumed to be distributed in a Gaussian manner. In contrast, the resulting coordinates x, y, and z in scene space show distributions which are not symmetrical. Correct and incorrect three-dimensional points are thus more favourably separated according to their disparity values, since the distance between the camera and the plane is inversely proportional to the disparity.

If it is assumed that a part of the scene can be modelled by a plane

$$\varepsilon_s : z(x, y) = a_s x + b_s y + c_s \tag{1.131}$$

in the scene space spanned by x, y, and z, the corresponding plane in disparity space spanned by the pixel coordinates u and v and the disparity d follows from the basic equations of the pinhole model according to

$$\frac{x}{z} = \frac{u}{f}, \qquad \frac{y}{z} = \frac{v}{f}, \qquad z = \frac{lf}{d} \tag{1.132}$$

with f as the camera constant in pixel units and l as the baseline distance of the stereo camera system in metric units. Inserting the expressions for x, y, and z derived from (1.132) into (1.131) yields a transformed plane in disparity space according to

$$\varepsilon_d : d(u, v) = a_d u + b_d v + c_d \tag{1.133}$$

with

$$a_d = -\frac{l}{c_s} a_s, \qquad b_d = -\frac{l}{c_s} b_s, \qquad c_d = \frac{lf}{c_s}. \tag{1.134}$$

The offset parameter c_s of the plane $z(x, y)$ in scene space, whose normal vector is given by the previously determined parameters a_s and b_s, is obtained by transforming it into disparity space according to (1.133) and (1.134) and then computing the mean distance between all three-dimensional points with coordinates (u, v) covered by the plane ε_d in disparity space and the disparities describing that plane (cf. (1.133)). The distances between the three-dimensional points and the plane are weighted according to the M-estimator method (Rey, 1983), resulting in the error function

$$E_{\mathrm{ME}}(c_s) = \left\langle \left\{ M \left(d_i - \left[-\frac{a_s l}{c_s} u_i - \frac{b_s l}{c_s} v_i + \frac{lf}{c_s} \right] \right) \right\}^2 \right\rangle_{(u_i, v_i) \in \varepsilon_d} \tag{1.135}$$

with $M(x) = 1 - (1 + |x/k_{\mathrm{ME}}|)^{-1}$. The brackets $\langle \dots \rangle$ denote the average. The function $E_{\mathrm{ME}}(c_s)$ is minimised with respect to the distance parameter c_s of the plane ε_s in scene space using the nested intervals method. The parameter k_{ME} is user defined. The behaviour of $E_{\mathrm{ME}}(c_s)$ is shown in Fig. 1.25b for scene 1 regarded in Sect. 1.6.4.

The plane model adaptation method described in this section does not require initial pose parameters. The image region characterised by repetitive structures and its metric extension in scene space are extracted without a priori knowledge about the scene. The normal vector of the plane is determined based on the assumption that the repetitive structures are characterised by a uniform distance parameter in scene space. Only the offset parameter of the model plane is estimated based on the three-dimensional point cloud generated by model-free stereo analysis; the experimental evaluation in Sect. 1.6.4 will show that a matching error rate of the stereo algorithm of 50–70 % still allows a good estimate.

1.6.2 Multiple-plane Hand–Arm Model

To show that the framework proposed in this study is also able to cope with complex objects that may have internal degrees of freedom, we also regard the problem of three-dimensional pose estimation of parts of the human body. This application is closely related to the scenario of safe human–robot interaction (Schmidt et al., 2007): In an industrial safety system, e.g. monitoring the collaboration between a human worker and an industrial robot, false correspondences due to repetitive structures are rather unfavourable as they cause spurious objects that may result in an emergency stop of the robot. As an example, we adapt the articulated three-dimensional model introduced by Hahn et al. (2007, 2010a), which consists of a kinematic chain of five truncated cones and one complete cone (cf. Sect. 2.2.3), to a motion-attributed three-dimensional point cloud according to the method by Barrois and Wöhler (2008) (cf. Sect. 2.3.3). Their three-dimensional pose estimation approach is inspired by the iterative closest point (ICP) algorithm introduced by Besl and McKay (1992).

It is assumed that the arm is moving in the scene. The spacetime stereo approach described by Schmidt et al. (2007) then yields a motion-attributed three-dimensional point cloud. This point cloud is clustered in the space spanned by the four coordinates x, y, z, and the epipolar velocity, and the hand–arm model is adapted to the largest moving cluster (here one might of course use more sophisticated cluster selection techniques). To reduce the complexity of our further analysis, the fairly complex hand–arm model is then approximated by three connected planes representing the fingers, the hand, and the arm, respectively. These three connected planes still provide a reasonable representation of the correct disparities in the image regions associated with the hand–arm limb. The approximation of the full model by a set of connected planes is acceptable, because the deviation between the simplified model and the true object in disparity space is negligible compared to the disparity errors occurring due to the repetitive structures (cf. Sect. 1.6.4). In the three-dimensional reconstruction context regarded in this study, models composed of several connected partial planes are a fairly general, approximative "tessellated" description of more complex objects.

1.6.3 Decision Feedback

The initial correspondence analysis is based on the matrix E_{SSD}. In the presence of repetitive structures the SSD values are small and quite similar for all possible correspondences, resulting in a large number of false correspondences. Based on the model, an additional disparity error is computed. If a point is situated in an image region with repetitive structures, the disparities of all possible correspondences are determined and compared to the model, which leads to the matrix E_d of disparity errors. These two matrices are merged into the total error matrix E_t according to

$$E_t = E_{SSD} + \lambda_e E_d, \tag{1.136}$$

involving the weight parameter λ_e. The refined correspondence analysis is performed based on the matrix E_t, using the same constraints (uniqueness, uniqueness and ordering, minimum weighted matching) as for the initial stereo analysis. The influence of the deviation between the three-dimensional points and the model on the resulting three-dimensional point cloud increases with the increasing value of λ_e. It is shown in Sect. 1.6.4, however, that the three-dimensional reconstruction result is not strongly sensitive with respect to the chosen value of λ_e and that a significant improvement of the initial stereo analysis is achieved for a variety of scenes using a unique value of λ_e.

Since correspondence analysis based on the matrix E_t involves the computation of disparity differences between three-dimensional points and the model, and since our experimental evaluation requires an assignment of three-dimensional points to the model or a foreground object based on a disparity difference threshold, it is necessary to examine to which extent inaccuracies of the estimated parameters a_s, b_s, and c_s of a model plane in scene space translate into inaccurate model disparities. For the errors Δa_d, Δb_d, and Δc_d of the model plane parameters in disparity space, the law of error propagation yields the following relations:

$$\Delta a_d = \left| \frac{\partial a_d}{\partial c_s} \right| \Delta c_s + \left| \frac{\partial a_d}{\partial a_s} \right| \Delta a_s = \frac{l a_s}{c_s^2} \Delta c_s + \frac{l}{c_s} \Delta a_s \tag{1.137}$$

$$\Delta b_d = \left| \frac{\partial b_d}{\partial c_s} \right| \Delta c_s + \left| \frac{\partial b_d}{\partial b_s} \right| \Delta b_s = \frac{l b_s}{c_s^2} \Delta c_s + \frac{l}{c_s} \Delta b_s \tag{1.138}$$

$$\Delta c_d = \left| \frac{\partial c_d}{\partial c_s} \right| \Delta c_s = \frac{l f}{c_s^2} \Delta c_s. \tag{1.139}$$

For an approximate quantitative error analysis a camera constant of $f = 1350$ pixels and a baseline of $l = 0.1$ m (cf. Sect. 1.6.4) are assumed. The average distance to the repetitive structures approximately corresponds to the value of c_s, which amounts to about 10 m for the outdoor scene and 1 m for the indoor scenes regarded in Sect. 1.6.4. Under the fairly pessimistic assumption that the value of c_s can be estimated at an accuracy of 5 %, the resulting error of c_d according to (1.139) amounts to 0.7 pixel for the outdoor scene and 6.8 pixels for the indoor scenes.

The extension of the object in the image is denoted by g and typically corresponds to 100–300 pixels, such that we may set $g = 200$ pixels. The maximum disparity error Δd_{max} due to an inaccuracy Δa_d of the model parameter a_d in disparity space then corresponds to $\Delta d_{max} = g \cdot \Delta a_d$. For simplicity, it is assumed that for the true model plane we have $a_s = b_s = 0$, i.e. the model plane is parallel to the image plane. If we (again pessimistically) assume that $\Delta a_s = 0.6$, corresponding to an angular error of more than 30° in the case of the frontoparallel plane, we obtain

$\Delta a_d = 0.006$ and $\Delta d_{max} = 1.2$ pixels for the outdoor scene and $\Delta a_d = 0.060$ and $\Delta d_{max} = 12$ pixels for the indoor scenes.

Based on this error analysis, in Sect. 1.6.4 the minimum wavelength of the repetitive structures allowed to apply the proposed method is estimated for the outdoor and the indoor scenario, respectively.

1.6.4 Experimental Evaluation

In this section we describe an experimental evaluation of the proposed method for resolving stereo matching errors. For image acquisition, we utilised a Point Grey Digiclops camera system with an image size of 1024×768 pixels, a camera constant of 6 mm (corresponding to $f = 1350$ pixels), and a baseline distance of $l = 100$ mm. The images were rectified to standard epipolar geometry based on the algorithm by Fusiello et al. (2000). We regard three different scenes, each showing a small object in front of a pronounced repetitive structure. The right image of each stereo pair is shown in Fig. 1.26a. Scene 1 displays a person standing in front of a large fence, scene 2 shows a keyboard with a hand in front of it, scene 3 displays an arm showing repetitive structures due to a pattern on the clothes with a bar in front of it, and scene 4 shows a typical urban environment with a person standing in front of a building. Scenes 1 and 4 are outdoor scenes while scenes 2 and 3 are indoor scenes. For scenes 1, 2, and 4 the plane model (cf. Sect. 1.6.1) is used; for scene 3 the articulated hand–arm model (cf. Sect. 1.6.2) is used.

For quantitative evaluation of the resulting three-dimensional point clouds, we have generated ground truth data by manual labelling (cf. Fig. 1.26). For each initial three-dimensional point cloud, the adaptation result of the plane model (scenes 1, 2, and 4) and the hand–arm model (scene 3) is shown in Fig. 1.27. In all four examples, the model adaptation is performed accurately, and the spurious objects arising due to the repetitive structures are clearly evident. The fact that the local stereo algorithm is not able to provide an appropriate three-dimensional reconstruction of the scene would lead to an unsatisfactory behaviour of subsequent processing stages such as scene segmentation and object detection, e.g. in a mobile robotic system, as the spurious objects would then result in spurious obstacles.

For comparison, the result of the model-based stereo approach is shown in Fig. 1.28 for scene 1. This technique yields a good three-dimensional reconstruction of the fence but of course fails to capture the person standing in front of it, as it is not part of the model. However, an initial pose which is already fairly close to the final result has to be known a priori, where the initial configuration shown in Fig. 1.28 already corresponds to the maximum offset for which the model-based stereo algorithm converges. In contrast, the plane model adaptation approach described in Sect. 1.6.1 does not require initial values for the pose parameters. Hence, both complementary standard approaches (local and model-based stereo) cannot provide a satisfactory simultaneous three-dimensional reconstruction of the scene part displaying repetitive structures and the object in front of it.

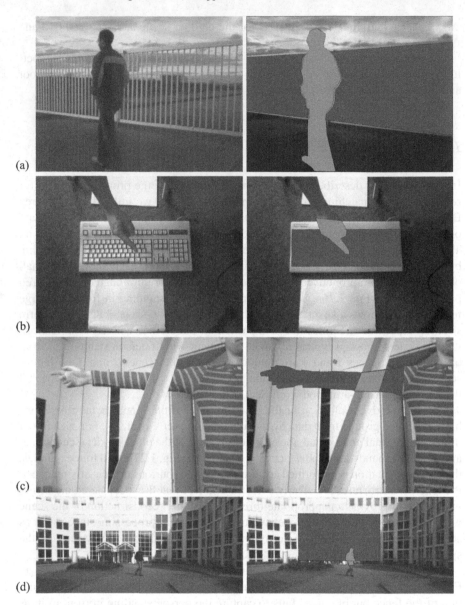

Fig. 1.26 Example scenes evaluated in Sect. 1.6.4. *Left column*: *Right image* of each stereo pair. *Right column*: Manually labelled scene parts. *Dark grey*: image area displaying repetitive structures. *Light grey*: object in front of the repetitive structures. (**a**) Scene 1 (fence with person). (**b**) Scene 2 (keyboard with hand). (**c**) Scene 3 (arm with bar). (**d**) Scene 4 (building with person)

The quality of the three-dimensional scene reconstruction result of the decision feedback approach described in Sect. 1.6.3 is depicted in a form similar to a receiver operating characteristics (ROC) curve representing the fraction F_{rep} of three-

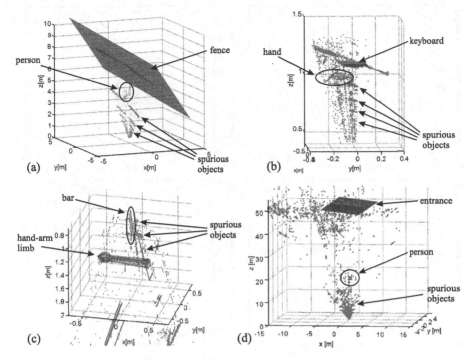

Fig. 1.27 Initial three-dimensional point clouds (corresponding to $\lambda_e = 0$) in scene space along with the adapted models, using the combined uniqueness and ordering constraint. (**a**) Scene 1 (fence with person). (**b**) Scene 2 (keyboard with hand). (**c**) Scene 3 (arm with bar). (**d**) Scene 4 (building with person)

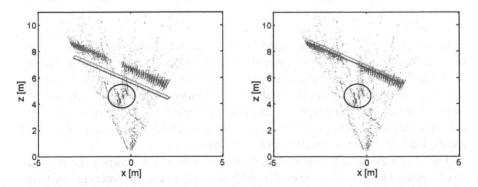

Fig. 1.28 Initialisation (*top*) and final result (*bottom*) for scene 1 of the model-based stereo method. For comparison, the three-dimensional point cloud illustrates the result of the feature-based spacetime stereo algorithm described in Sect. 1.5.2.5 with $\lambda_e = 0$, where the three-dimensional points belonging to the person are marked by a *circle*. The depicted initial configuration corresponds to the highest offset from the final solution for which convergence of the model-based stereo algorithm is achieved. This approach does not capture the object in front of the scene part displaying repetitive structures

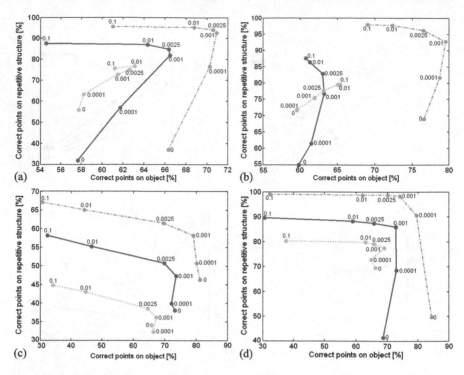

Fig. 1.29 Three-dimensional reconstruction results for the three examined scenes. The *solid curve* is obtained by evaluating the correspondence matrix E_t defined in (1.136) with the uniqueness constraint, the *dashed curve* by applying the combined uniqueness and ordering constraint, and the *dotted curve* by applying the minimum weighted matching constraint. The numbers on the curves denote the corresponding values of the weight parameter λ_e. (**a**) Scene 1 (fence with person). (**b**) Scene 2 (keyboard with hand). (**c**) Scene 3 (arm with bar). (**d**) Scene 4 (building with person)

dimensional points correctly assigned to the scene part displaying repetitive structures versus the fraction F_{obj} of three-dimensional points correctly assigned to the object in front of it, varying the value of the weight parameter λ_e defined in (1.136). See Fig. 1.29. Each three-dimensional point is evaluated with respect to its association with the area showing repetitive structures or the object in front of it, where the maximum allowed disparity deviation from the correct value amounts to ± 5 pixels for the outdoor scenes and ± 10 pixels for the indoor scenes.

For all four examined example scenes, the evaluation of the correspondence matrix E_t defined in (1.136) based on the combined uniqueness and ordering constraint always yields the highest fraction of correct points in the image area with repetitive structures and correct points on the object (cf. Table 1.3). Setting $\lambda_e = 0$ is equivalent to neglecting the model information. Increasing λ_e to a value of 0.001 strongly increases the value of F_{rep}, while the fraction F_{obj} remains largely constant. If λ_e is increased further, F_{rep} only slightly increases further while F_{obj} decreases strongly. As a consequence, the intuitively best result is obtained by setting λ_e to values

Table 1.3 Number of extracted 3D points for the regarded example scenes when neglecting model information ($\lambda_e = 0$) and taking it into account ($\lambda_e = 0.01$)

Scene	Constraint	$\lambda_e = 0$	$\lambda_e = 0.01$
Fence with person	Uniqueness	23317	24755
	Uniqueness + ordering	15509	22752
	Min. weighted matching	25354	25463
Keyboard with hand	Uniqueness	9392	9924
	Uniqueness + ordering	7613	9029
	Min. weighted matching	9980	10145
Arm with bar	Uniqueness	9164	9587
	Uniqueness + ordering	8329	8601
	Min. weighted matching	9604	10064
Building with person	Uniqueness	5023	5651
	Uniqueness + ordering	3270	5136
	Min. weighted matching	5648	5654

between 0.001 and 0.01 for all four example scenes. Hence, the choice of the parameter λ_e does not critically depend on the regarded scene.

In contrast to classical outlier rejection approaches, applying the proposed technique does not decrease the absolute number of three-dimensional points but actually increases it for all four regarded scenes. This increase is most significant when using the combined uniqueness and ordering constraint (cf. Table 1.3).

In Fig. 1.30, the resulting three-dimensional point clouds are shown in disparity space for the four example scenes, setting $\lambda_e = 0$ (i.e. model information is neglected) and $\lambda_e = 0.01$. In scene 1 (fence with person, cf. Fig. 1.30a), only a small number of 'spurious fence' points remain visible once we set $\lambda_e = 0.01$, while the object in front of the fence is extracted correctly. A similar behaviour occurs for scene 2 (keyboard with hand, cf. Fig. 1.30b), where an even smaller number of incorrectly assigned points on the repetitive structures remains for $\lambda_e = 0.01$, which do not form clusters but are more or less evenly distributed in disparity space. In scene 3 (arm and bar, cf. Fig. 1.30c), the effect of the proposed method is less pronounced than for scenes 1 and 2, but the density of the remaining incorrectly assigned points on the repetitive structure still decreases, and especially the clusters of three-dimensional points clearly apparent for $\lambda_e = 0$ at $u \approx 750$ pixels and disparities of 140 and 175 pixels, respectively, disappear or become less dense for $\lambda_e = 0.01$. The number of incorrectly assigned points on the object increases (these points are assigned a disparity that approximately corresponds to that of the arm), but the object between the camera and the arm remains represented by two dense clusters of three-dimensional points. For scene 4 (urban scene showing a person in front of a building, cf. Fig. 1.30d), increasing λ_e to values between 0.001 and 0.0025 strongly increases the fraction of correct points on the building, such that the spurious objects disappear, while the fraction of correct points on the person decreases only moderately.

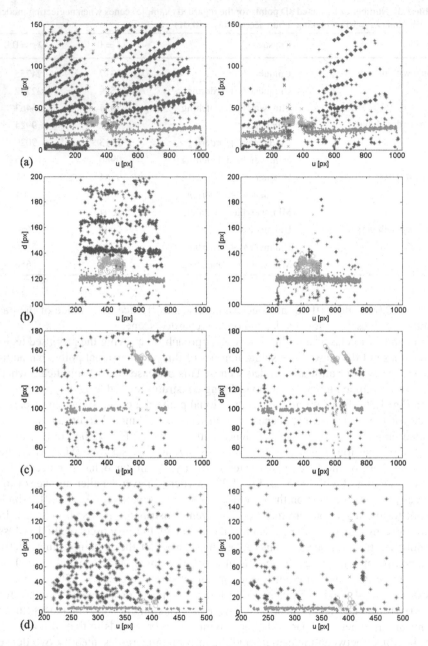

Fig. 1.30 Three-dimensional point clouds obtained with $\lambda_e = 0$ (*left column*), i.e. without using model information, and $\lambda_e = 0.01$ (*right column*). (**a**) Scene 1 (fence with person). (**b**) Scene 2 (keyboard with hand). (**c**) Scene 3 (arm with bar). (**d**) Scene 4 (building with person). *Dots* denote correct and *stars* incorrect points in the scene part displaying repetitive structures, while *circles* correspond to correct and *crosses* to incorrect points on the object

In all four example scenes, the number of three-dimensional points forming spurious objects is significantly reduced; in particular, clusters of incorrectly assigned points disappear. Accordingly, in mobile robot navigation or human–robot interaction scenarios the proposed method is useful for distinguishing between real objects between the camera and the repetitive structures and spurious objects, which would otherwise induce a halt of the robot motion in such systems.

The applicability of the proposed technique is limited by high spatial frequencies of the repetitive structures, corresponding to wavelengths (in pixels) comparable to or shorter than the typical disparity differences between the model plane and the corresponding three-dimensional points. The disparity difference between the spurious objects and the true object corresponds to the wavelength of the repetitive structures. Hence, given the typical inaccuracies of the model parameters derived in Sect. 1.6.3, the wavelength of the repetitive structures should be larger than about 2 pixels for the outdoor scenario and larger than about 20 pixels for the indoor scenario to ensure that the adapted model does not extend into the spurious objects. These minimum values decrease linearly with increasing accuracy of the estimated model parameters. They do not imply strong restrictions for the proposed method: In the indoor scenario, the minimum required wavelength of the repetitive structures is one order of magnitude larger than the resolution limit of the image, while in the outdoor scenario it approximately corresponds to the image resolution.

1.6.5 Discussion

The described model-based method by Barrois et al. (2010) for resolving stereo matching ambiguities is independent of the specific stereo algorithm used. Scene models have been applied which are represented by a single plane or several connected planes. In three example scenes with extended areas of very strongly pronounced repetitive structures, the proposed model-based refinement procedure decreases the fraction of false correspondences in the scene part displaying repetitive structures by factors of up to 30, while the fraction of three-dimensional points correctly assigned to the object decreases only moderately. In the example scene showing an object in front of an outstretched arm, the improvement is somewhat less pronounced but still significant. Furthermore, it has been shown that a state-of-the-art model-based stereo approach is also able to provide a three-dimensional reconstruction of scene parts displaying repetitive structures without generating spurious objects, at least as long as initial pose parameters and information about the metric extension of that scene part are provided. However, that method fails to capture scene parts or objects which are not part of the model. In contrast, the method described in this section has proven capable of suppressing spurious objects while at the same time achieving a correct three-dimensional reconstruction of objects in front of the scene part displaying repetitive structures.

Chapter 2
Three-Dimensional Pose Estimation and Segmentation Methods

In the previous chapter it has been described how a three-dimensional reconstruction of a scene can be obtained from point correspondences between images, and how this problem is related with the problem of determining the intrinsic and extrinsic camera parameters. In this context, the reconstruction result is always obtained as a cloud of three-dimensional points. This point cloud contains information about the presence of matter at a certain position in space. However, no information is available about the presence or even the position and orientation of objects in the scene.

Hence, this chapter provides an analysis of traditional and newly introduced methods for the segmentation of point clouds and for the three-dimensional detection and pose estimation of rigid, articulated, and flexible objects in a scene based on single or multiple calibrated images, where it is assumed that a (more or less detailed) model of the object is available.

For rigid objects, pose estimation refers to the estimation of the six degrees of freedom of the object, i.e. three rotation angles and three translation components (cf. Sect. 2.1). For objects with a limited number of internal degrees of freedom ('articulated objects') and objects with an infinite number of internal degrees of freedom ('non-rigid objects') pose estimation may correspond to a much higher dimensional optimisation problem (cf. Sect. 2.2.1.2). Here, the three-dimensional object detection is based directly on the acquired images of the scene or suitable features derived from them. A class of complementary approaches deals with the analysis of point clouds obtained e.g. by stereo image analysis with respect to their three-dimensional structure and motion behaviour, aiming for a segmentation into physically meaningful domains representing individual objects or object parts. Such methods are regarded in Sect. 2.3.

2.1 Pose Estimation of Rigid Objects

To estimate the pose of a rigid object, a set of three-dimensional scene points with coordinates given by a geometry model of the object is brought into corre-

C. Wöhler, *3D Computer Vision*, X.media.publishing,
DOI 10.1007/978-1-4471-4150-1_2, © Springer-Verlag London 2013

spondence with points in the image such that the rotation angles and the translation of the object with respect to the camera can be determined by minimising a suitable error measure, e.g. the reprojection error of the model points. Accordingly, pose estimation of rigid objects is equivalent to the problem of determining the extrinsic camera parameters (cf. Sect. 1.4). This is an important insight, since all approaches described in Sect. 1.4 in the context of camera calibration can in principle be applied to pose estimation as well. Hence, an important issue in the context of pose estimation is to establish reliable correspondences between model points and points in the image. This section provides an overview of pose estimation techniques for rigid objects based on point features but also on edges or lines, and then regards in more detail the edge-based hierarchical template matching approach to pose estimation introduced by von Bank et al. (2003).

2.1.1 General Overview

2.1.1.1 Pose Estimation Methods Based on Explicit Feature Matching

A seminal work in the domain of three-dimensional pose estimation is provided by Haralick et al. (1989). They introduce several classes of pose estimation problems: 2D–2D pose estimation determines the pose of a two-dimensional object from an image, while 3D–3D pose estimation deals with three-dimensional data points from which the pose of a three-dimensional object is inferred. The estimation of the six pose parameters from a single two-dimensional image of the object, given a geometry model, or an estimation of the relative camera orientation based on two or more images of the object without making use of a geometry model of the object, corresponds to 2D–3D pose estimation. The solutions proposed by Haralick et al. (1989) are based on point correspondences between the images and the object model. They rely on a minimisation of the distances in three-dimensional space between the model points and the observed rays to the corresponding scene points. A linear method based on singular value decomposition is proposed to determine the rotation angles, and it is demonstrated that using a robust M-estimator technique instead of least-mean-squares minimisation may increase the performance of the optimisation procedure, as a reasonable pose estimation result is still obtained when the rate of outliers is as high as 50 %.

Image features beyond points are examined in the classical work by Lowe (1987). Linear structures, whose appearance does not change significantly even with strongly varying camera viewpoints, are grouped according to geometric criteria such as their similarity in orientation or the distances between their end points, a process termed 'perceptual organisation' by Lowe (1987). The three-dimensional model is projected into the image plane. The complexity of the subsequent step, during which correspondences between the model and the extracted image features are established, is reduced by prioritising those correspondences which involve features that are known to have a high probability of occurrence.

A further important classical approach to 2D–3D pose estimation, introduced by Lamdan and Wolfson (1988), is geometric hashing. An object is represented in terms of its geometric features, where coordinate systems are constructed based on specific features, especially points. For example, for a set of points lying in a plane, an orthogonal coordinate system is given by any pair of points on the plane, and the other points can be expressed in that coordinate system. All point pair-specific sets of coordinates ('models') along with the points that define them ('basis pair') are stored in what is called the 'hash table'. Non-planar objects are assumed to be composed of planar parts by Lamdan and Wolfson (1988). The pose estimation process is then performed based on a random selection of pairs of observed scene points, where all other scene points are again expressed in the correspondingly defined coordinate system. Each selected pair of scene points increments a counter for one such model and basis pair stored in the hash table. All entries of the hash table for which the counter is larger than a previously defined minimum value are regarded as occurrences of the modelled object in the observed scene, where the parameters of the corresponding coordinate system denote the pose parameters, respectively.

An important edge-based approach to 2D–3D pose estimation is proposed by Lowe (1991). The object model is assumed to be composed of plane parts of polygonal shape as an approximation to the true surface shape. The contours of the object in the image are obtained by projecting the silhouette of the object into the image plane. Edge segments are extracted from the utilised greyscale image with the Canny edge detector (Canny, 1986). The error function is given by the sum of the perpendicular distances in the image plane between the extracted edge segments and the nearest projected object contour line. The pose parameters, including internal degrees of freedom of the object, are obtained by least-mean-squares minimisation of the error function with the Gauß–Newton method or alternatively with the Levenberg-Marquardt algorithm (Press et al., 2007), where the latter generally displays a more robust convergence behaviour.

A similar 2D–3D pose estimation approach based on point and line correspondences is described by Phong et al. (1996). They propose a quadratic error function by expressing the pose parameters in terms of a quaternion. Minimisation of the error function to determine the pose parameters is performed using a trust-region method, which yields a superior performance when compared with the Gauß–Newton method.

In the framework developed by Grebner (1994), 2D–3D pose estimation of industrial parts is performed based on edges and corner points, where the parameter search, corresponding to the minimisation of an appropriately chosen cost function, is performed using the A* algorithm (cf. e.g. Sagerer, 1985 for an overview).

2.1.1.2 Appearance-Based Pose Estimation Methods

A different class of methods consists of the appearance-based approaches, which directly compare the observed image with the appearance of the object at different poses without explicitly establishing correspondences between model features and parts of the image.

Methods Based on Monocular Image Data   A probabilistic approach to simultaneous pose estimation and object recognition is proposed by Niemann and Hornegger (2001). However, they only regard the problem of 2D–2D pose estimation. They follow a statistical approach to object recognition, while localisation is performed based on estimating the corresponding parameters. An object model is represented by the position-dependent and typically multimodal probability densities of the pixel grey values in an image that displays an object of a certain class. Relying on empirical data, the number of the components of these multimodal distributions is determined by vector quantisation, while the parameters of the distribution are obtained with the expectation–maximisation algorithm. Hence, pose estimation is performed based on a maximum likelihood estimate.

In the monocular system of Kölzow and Ellenrieder (2003), a unified statistical approach for the integration of several local features, such as edges or textures, is employed. The utilised object model consists of CAD data complemented by the local features, resulting in an 'operator model'. The six pose parameters of a rigid object are then obtained by adaptation of the visible model features to the image. The accuracy of the obtained pose estimation results is discussed in Sect. 6.1.

Other pose estimation algorithms rely on geometric (edges) and on intensity (surface radiance) information. In this context, Nayar and Bolle (1996) introduce an object representation based on reflectance ratios, which is used for object recognition using monocular greyscale images. Pose estimation is performed relying on the reflectance ratio representation and a three-dimensional object model, thus taking into account physical properties of the object surface in addition to purely geometric information.

Another technique which relies on the simultaneous extraction of edge and shading information for 2D–3D pose estimation is the appearance-based approach proposed by Nomura et al. (1996), who utilise synthetic edge and intensity images generated based on an object model. A nonlinear optimisation procedure based on a comparison between the observed and the synthetic images yields the pose parameters. The accuracy of the obtained pose estimation results is discussed in Sect. 6.1.

The approach by Ando et al. (2005) is based on a set of grey value images of an object with known associated three-dimensional poses. After reducing the dimension of the images by principal component analysis, the rotational pose parameters of the object are learned directly from the image data using support vector regression.

The integrated 2D–3D pose estimation approach by Barrois and Wöhler (2007), which in addition to edges and surface brightness also takes into account polarisation and defocus features, is discussed in Sects. 5.6 and 6.1.

The three-dimensional pose estimation method of Lagger et al. (2008) is based on an 'environment map', i.e. a direction-dependent map of the light intensity and colour incident on the object surface. An image sequence showing the object is acquired, where a three-dimensional model of the object is available. For each image, the diffuse reflection component is separated from the specular component, where the latter is then used to infer the corresponding environment map. The pose parameters are refined by minimising an error measure which consists of a weighted sum of the negative normalised cross-correlation coefficients between the pixel grey values of the first and the current image and the squared differences between the corresponding environment maps.

Chang et al. (2009) propose two appearance-based methods for estimating the three-dimensional pose of objects with specularly reflecting surfaces based on CAD data. A mirror-like reflectance behaviour of the object surface is assumed. The first approach is based on the determination of the position and appearance of specular reflections in the image by rendering and a subsequent comparison with the observed image. The second technique relies on the 'specular flow', i.e. the optical flow associated with specularly reflecting surface parts. The accuracy of the obtained three-dimensional pose estimation results is discussed in Sect. 6.1.

Methods Based on Multiocular Image Data   Classical monocular pose estimation approaches have in common that they are not able to estimate the distance to an object at high accuracy, since the only available depth information is the scale of a known object in the resulting image, and the appearance of the object in the image is not very sensitive to small depth variations. In comparison, for a convergent stereo setup with a baseline similar to the object distance, for geometrical reasons a depth accuracy of the same order as the lateral translational accuracy is obtainable. Accordingly, a variety of three-dimensional pose estimation methods relying on multiple images of the scene have been proposed.

The system of Bachler et al. (1999) performs a pose estimation of industrial parts based on a pair of stereo images in the context of taking the parts out of a bin with an industrial robot. In a first step, planes are detected in the scene relying on the projection of structured light. After isolating an object based on the plane detection result, the rotation angle around the optical axis is determined. Furthermore, the translational pose parameters parallel to the image plane are estimated using a CAD model, while the distance to the object is assumed to be known. The accuracy of the approach is discussed in Sect. 6.1.

A fast tracking algorithm for estimating the pose of an automotive part using a pair of stereo images is presented by Yoon et al. (2003). This method is regarded further in the application scenario of industrial quality inspection in Sect. 6.1.

Rosenhahn et al. (2003) introduce a method for appearance-based three-dimensional pose estimation from several images, regarding objects characterised by free-form surfaces modelled in terms of Fourier descriptors, thus providing a computationally favourable approximate representation on large spatial scales. The pose parameters are determined in the framework of conformal geometric algebra. The optimisation of the pose parameters is performed based on the appearance of the object contour projected into the image, applying the iterative closest point (ICP) algorithm by Zhang (1999b), which is especially designed for analysing free-form surfaces (cf. also Sect. 2.3).

Rosenhahn et al. (2006) compare the ICP algorithm for three-dimensional pose estimation in stereo image pairs with a level set approach formulated in terms of a computational technique from the field of optical flow analysis. The pose estimation is based on silhouettes. A quantitative evaluation of the two methods and their combination is performed. It demonstrates that the highest performance is achieved by a combination of both approaches, especially when regarding the convergence radius, i.e. the ability to converge towards the true pose from a considerably different initial pose.

The method of von Bank et al. (2003), which is described in detail in Sect. 2.1.2, is extended by Krüger (2007) to a multiocular setting characterised by three calibrated cameras. The accuracy of the three-dimensional pose estimation results obtained by Krüger (2007) is discussed in Sect. 6.1.

The object recognition and pose estimation system proposed by Collet et al. (2011) for the manipulation of objects by a robot relies on one or several calibrated images of the scene. Three-dimensional models of the objects are constructed using a structure from motion approach, where a model is associated with a set of features. The three-dimensional scene reconstruction and the estimation of the pose parameters are performed simultaneously based on the 'iterative clustering estimation' algorithm, where features detected in the images are clustered and associated with objects and their corresponding pose parameters in an iterative manner by employing robust optimisation methods. Collet et al. (2011) use the mean-shift algorithm as proposed by Cheng (1995) for clustering. The resulting object hypotheses are again clustered, using the 'projection clustering' approach, and a pose refinement is applied, which yields the objects in the scene with their associated pose parameters. An optimised hardware architecture using graphical processing units for the computationally complex parts of the algorithm, such as the feature detection step, results in cycle times of about two seconds for a real-world image sequence with 60 objects per image. The pose estimation accuracy of the system is discussed in Sect. 6.1.

2.1.2 Template-Based Pose Estimation

Many industrial applications of pose estimation methods for quality inspection purposes impose severe constraints on the hardware to be used with respect to robustness and easy maintenance. Hence, it is often not possible to utilise multiocular camera systems since they have to be recalibrated regularly, especially when the sensor unit is mounted on an industrial robot. As a consequence, employing a monocular camera system may be favourable from a practical point of view, while nevertheless a high pose estimation accuracy is required to detect subtle deviations between the true and the desired object pose.

The presentation in this section is adopted from von Bank et al. (2003). The appearance-based 2D–3D pose estimation method described in this section involves a viewer-centred representation of the image data. The views are generated automatically from a three-dimensional object model by rendering, and the pose parameters of each view are stored in a table. Edge templates are computed for each view. For the input image, the best-fitting template and thus the corresponding pose parameters are determined by a template matching procedure. The difficult trade-off between the tessellation constant, i.e. the difference between the pose parameters of neighbouring views, and the accuracy of pose estimation is alleviated by a technique for hierarchical template matching (Gavrila and Philomin, 1999).

The input image first undergoes an edge detection procedure. A distance transform (DT) then converts the segmented binary edge image into what is called a distance image. The distance image encodes the distance in the image plane of each image point to its nearest edge point. If we denote the set of all points in the image as $A = \{{}^S\mathbf{a}_1, \ldots, {}^S\mathbf{a}_N\}$ and the set of all edge points as $B = \{{}^S\mathbf{b}_1, \ldots, {}^S\mathbf{b}_M\}$ with $B \subseteq A$, then the distance $d({}^S\mathbf{a}_n, B)$ for point ${}^S\mathbf{a}_n$ is given by

$$d({}^S\mathbf{a}_n, B) = \min_m \left(\left\| {}^S\mathbf{a}_n - {}^S\mathbf{b}_m \right\| \right), \tag{2.1}$$

where $\| \ldots \|$ is a norm on the points of A and B (e.g. the Euclidean norm). For numerical simplicity we use the chamfer-2–3 metric (Barrow, 1977) to approximate the Euclidean metric.

The chamfer distance $D_C(T, B)$ between an edge template consisting of a set of edge points $T = \{{}^S\mathbf{t}_1, \ldots, {}^S\mathbf{t}_Q\}$ with $T \subseteq A$ and the input edge image is given by

$$D_C(T, B) = \frac{1}{Q} \sum_{n=1}^{Q} d({}^S\mathbf{t}_n, B). \tag{2.2}$$

A correspondence between a template and an image region is assumed to be present once the distance measure ('dissimilarity') $D(T, B)$ becomes smaller than a given threshold value θ. To reduce false detections, the distance measure was extended to include oriented edges (Gavrila and Philomin, 1999).

In order to recognise an object with unknown rotation and translation, a set of transformed templates must be correlated with the distance image. Each template is derived from a certain rotation of the three-dimensional object. In previous work, a uniform tessellation often involved a difficult choice for the value of the tessellation constant. If one chooses a relatively large value, the views that lie 'in between' grid points on the viewing sphere are not properly represented in the regions where the aspect graph is undergoing rapid changes. This decreases the accuracy of the measured pose angles. On the other hand, if one chooses a relatively small value for the tessellation constant, this results in a large number of templates to be matched online; matching all these templates sequentially is computationally intensive and prohibitive to any real-time performance. The difficult trade-off regarding tessellation constant is alleviated by a technique for hierarchical template matching, introduced by Gavrila and Philomin (1999). That technique, designed for distance transform-based matching, in an offline stage derives representation which takes into account the structure of the given distribution of templates, i.e. their mutual degrees of similarity. In the online stage, this approach allows an optimisation of the matching

Fig. 2.1 Sketch of the robot-based inspection system with a definition of the pose angles ε (roll), λ (pitch), and ρ (yaw) in the camera coordinate system

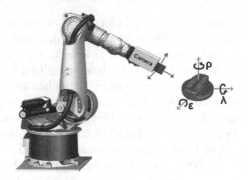

procedure by representing a group of similar templates by a single prototype template and a distance parameter. A recursive application of this grouping scheme eventually results in a hierarchy of templates, which is generated in a bottom-up manner using simulated annealing-based partitional clustering. Each node of the hierarchical tree of templates requires matching of a prototype template **p** with a part of the image. To avoid an exhaustive search, locations of interest for the nodes in the hierarchy one level below a certain prototype template ('children nodes') are determined by selecting the positions for which the distance measure between the respective prototype and the image falls below a predefined threshold θ_p. This procedure is repeated for the children nodes until the tree has been traversed. If, on the other hand, the distance measure exceeds θ_p, the search is not continued in the next level of the tree. The high computational efficiency of this method results from the fact that, according to the hierarchical approach, only a small fraction of the templates actually need to be matched with parts of the image.

In our system, we do not need to estimate scale—the distance to the object is assumed to be known at an accuracy of better than 3 % due to the fact that the system is designed for an industrial quality inspection scenario in which the approximate position of the parts is provided by CAD data. Template matching does not have to search all scales explicitly. Hence, the original pose estimation problem of determining six degrees of freedom can be reduced to a five-degree-of-freedom (three pose angles and two image position coordinates) problem.

For pose fine-tuning, the pose angles are interpolated between the n_b 'best' template matching solutions, with $n_b = 30$ in our system. This is justified, because in our pose estimation scenario the dissimilarity values of the 30 best solutions usually do not differ by more than about 20 %, and thus all these solutions contain a significant amount of information about the pose.

In many applications, templates are generated from real-world image data (Demant, 1999). For inspection tasks, however, one can assume that a CAD model of the object to be inspected is available. We therefore generate realistic two-dimensional templates from CAD data using the public domain software POVRAY, simulating the properties of the surface material and the illumination conditions by employing ray tracing techniques. The pose of the object is defined by the three angles ε (roll), λ (pitch), and ρ (yaw), as shown in Fig. 2.1. Typical matching results are shown

Fig. 2.2 Matching results
(best solution) for several
example poses

for an automotive part in Fig. 2.2. A quantitative evaluation of the described edge-based pose estimation technique is performed in the scenario of industrial quality inspection in Sect. 6.1.1.

To improve the robustness of monocular pose estimation in the presence of a cluttered background, the edge-based method is extended by Barrois and Wöhler (2007) to appearance-based monocular pose estimation based on geometric, photopolarimetric, and defocus cues (cf. Sect. 5.6).

2.2 Pose Estimation of Non-rigid and Articulated Objects

In contrast to rigid objects, articulated objects consist of several rigid subparts which are able to move with respect to each other. Methods that aim for a pose estimation of such objects need to determine these internal degrees of freedom in addition to the six rotational and translational degrees of freedom encountered for rigid objects. Non-rigid objects have no rigid subparts at all and therefore have an infinite number of internal degrees of freedom. In this section we first give an overview of pose estimation methods for articulated and non-rigid objects. Then we regard the contour-based algorithm of d'Angelo et al. (2004) for three-dimensional reconstruction of non-rigid objects such as tubes and cables, which may be regarded as a multiocular extension of the concept of active contours (Blake and Isard, 1998). Subsequently, the multiocular contracting curve density algorithm (Hahn et al., 2007, 2010a) is described, which allows a three-dimensional reconstruction of non-rigid objects and a pose estimation of articulated objects in the presence of a cluttered background.

2.2.1 General Overview

2.2.1.1 Non-rigid Objects

The extraction of two-dimensional object contours from images is an essential part of image segmentation. A classical approach to this problem is that of active contours or snakes. The original snake algorithm by Kass et al. (1988) determines a curve for which an optimisation is performed simultaneously in terms of its length or curvature and its correspondence with edges in the image. Many variations and improvements of the original snake algorithm have been proposed, such as 'balloon snakes' (Cohen, 1991), 'ziplock snakes' (Neuenschwander et al., 1997), 'gradient vector field snakes' (Xu and Prince, 1998), and implicit active contour models (Caselles et al., 1995, 1997; Sethian, 1999).

In the balloon snake approach of Cohen (1991), the adaptation of the curve to intensity gradients in the image is based on an 'inflation force', which increases the robustness of the contour adaptation in the presence of small edge segments which do not correspond to the true object border. The ziplock snake algorithm of Neuenschwander et al. (1997) is described in Sect. 2.2.2. Xu and Prince (1998) adapt a contour to the intensity gradients in the image based on a 'generalised gradient vector field'. In their approach, the process of the adaptation of the curve to the image is described by a set of partial differential equations modelling a force exerted on the contour, which decreases smoothly with increasing distance from an intensity gradient. In the approach by Caselles et al. (1997), the contour adaptation process is performed in a Riemannian space with a metric defined according to the image intensities. The contour adaptation thus corresponds to the minimisation of the length of a curve in that space, leading to a set of partial differential equations describing the adaptation of the curve to the image.

In many medical imaging applications, volumetric data need to be analysed, leading to the three-dimensional extension of the snake approach by Cohen and Cohen (1993). For pose estimation of non-rigid objects from multiple images, it is assumed by most approaches that the non-rigid object is adequately described by a one-dimensional curve in three-dimensional space. Such techniques are primarily useful for applications in medical imaging, e.g. for the extraction of blood vessels from a set of angiographies (Cañero et al., 2000) or for the inspection of bonding wires on microchips (Ye et al., 2001). A related method for extracting the three-dimensional pose of non-rigid objects such as tubes and cables from stereo image pairs of the scene based on three-dimensional ribbon snakes is described in detail later in this section.

For the segmentation of synthetic aperture radar images, which typically display strong noise, Gambini et al. (2004) adapt B-spline curves to the fractal dimension map extracted from the image, where gradients of the inferred fractal dimension are assumed to correspond to the borders of contiguous image regions.

Mongkolnam et al. (2006) perform a colour segmentation of the image in a first step and then adapt B-spline curves to the resulting image regions. The border points extracted by the colour segmentation step do not have to lie on the adapted curve, such that the approach yields smooth borders of the extracted regions.

Another approach to two-dimensional curve fitting is the contracting curve density (CCD) algorithm introduced by Hanek and Beetz (2004). The CCD algorithm employs a likelihood function as a quantitative measure of how well a curve is able to describe the boundary between different image regions, where the degree of similarity is described by the local probability distributions of the pixel grey values determined based on the local vicinity of the expected curve. The posterior probability density is iteratively maximised with respect to the parameters of the curve model, which are defined by a Gaussian distribution rather than a set of sharply defined quantities. Adapting this 'blurred curve model' (Hanek and Beetz, 2004) to the local statistical properties of the pixel grey values yields a large convergence radius and at the same time a high accuracy of the determined boundary. As a result, the CCD algorithm is capable of separating objects with ill-defined outlines from a cluttered background. Section 2.2.3 describes in detail a multiocular variant of the CCD algorithm developed by Hahn et al. (2007, 2010a).

Ellenrieder (2004) proposes a three-dimensional active contour method which incorporates a technique similar to the shape from texture approach (Jiang and Bunke, 1997) to estimate the normal of a surface displaying a pronounced texture (e.g. the surface of a tube laminated by textile material) based on spatial variations of the amplitude spectrum of the surface texture. In the context of industrial quality inspection of tubes and cables, Ellenrieder (2005) introduces a method for three-dimensional pose estimation of non-rigid objects which is based on the analysis of the contour of the shadow of the non-rigid object cast on a surface of known shape under known illumination conditions.

An approach to the computation of the derivatives of the bundle adjustment error function (1.25) for non-rigid objects is introduced by Krüger (2007), who adapts the model to the image based on a gradient descent scheme. The method relies on the sign of the gradient of the error function, and its determination reduces to one look-up per feature for which a correspondence with the image is established in a table that is computed offline. Once the space of pose parameters is divided into appropriate sections, it is sufficient to memorise one bit, denoting the sign of the gradient of the error function, for each pixel, each pose parameter of the regarded pose estimation problem, and each defined section in the pose parameter space. These bit matrices, which are termed 'gradient sign tables' by Krüger (2007), have the same size as the image. The computational complexity of this optimisation approach is quite low, while its memory demand may become fairly high.

2.2.1.2   Articulated Objects

Most pose estimation approaches regarding articulated objects address the scenario of human body pose estimation (cf. e.g. Moeslund et al. (2006) for an introduction to and overview of the large field of pose estimation and tracking of the human body).

Many approaches, especially those aiming for gesture recognition in the context of human–robot interaction, rely on monocular image sequences. A more detailed overview of such techniques is thus given in Sect. 7.1.2. As an example, Schmidt et al. (2006) adapt a three-dimensional articulated body model consisting of chains of cylinders to monocular colour images of the person, where the optimisation of the pose parameters basically relies on skin colour detection as well as on intensity, edges, and the spatially varying statistical distribution of colour cues. Sminchisescu (2008) provides a broad discussion of the advantages and limitations resulting from monocular body pose estimation. Specifically, the problem of ambiguities of the appearance of the object in the image as a result of the projection from the three-dimensional scene into the two-dimensional image plane is addressed, which may lead to reconstruction errors, especially when partial self-occlusions of the body occur. Body pose estimation methods are divided by Sminchisescu (2008) into generative algorithms, relying on a model of the observation likelihood which is supposed to obtain its maximum value once the pose parameters have been estimated correctly, and discriminative algorithms, which learn the probability distribution of the pose parameters from examples and predict them using Bayesian inference.

An early approach by Gavrila and Davis (1996) to full body pose estimation involves template matching in several distance-transformed images acquired from different viewpoints distributed around the person. Plänkers and Fua (2003) and Rosenhahn et al. (2005) apply multiple-view three-dimensional pose estimation algorithms which are based on silhouette information.

Plänkers and Fua (2003) make use of three-dimensional data generated by a stereo camera to obtain a pose estimation and tracking of the human upper body. The upper body is modelled with implicit surfaces, and silhouettes are used in addition to the depth data to fit the surfaces. Lange et al. (2004) propose a method for tracking the movements of a human body in a sequence of images acquired by at least two cameras based on the adaptation of a three-dimensional stick model with a stochastic optimisation algorithm. A comparison between the appearance of the stick model after projection into the image plane with the acquired images yields an appropriate error function. A refinement of the correspondingly estimated joint angles of the stick model is obtained based on several pairs of stereo images.

Rosenhahn et al. (2005) track the upper body of a person, which is represented by a three-dimensional model with 21 body pose parameters consisting of connected free-form surfaces. The pose estimation is based on silhouettes which are extracted using level set functions. Tracking is performed by using the pose in the last frame as the initial pose in the current frame. Using images acquired synchronously by four cameras distributed around the person, they achieve a high reconstruction accuracy of about 2° for the joint angles under laboratory conditions without a cluttered background. As a ground truth, the joint angles determined by a commercial marker-based tracking system with eight cameras are used. In an extension of this method by Brox et al. (2008), the silhouette of the person is inferred from a single image or several images acquired by cameras distributed around the person, and a three-dimensional model representing the body surface is adapted to the silhouettes. The procedures of pose estimation and silhouette extraction based on level sets are alternated in order to allow tracking in scenes with a non-uniform and non-static background. In this context, Bayesian inference involving the local probability density models of image regions with respect to different features such as grey value, RGB colour values, or texture is used for simultaneously extracting a contour and a set of pose parameters. For large pose differences between successive images, prediction of the pose is achieved based on the optical flow. Since the pose estimation yields correspondences between the two-dimensional silhouettes in the images and the three-dimensional body model, while the optical flow yields correspondences between two-dimensional image positions in the current and the subsequent time step, the three-dimensional pose of the body model which is consistent with the optical flow can be predicted for the subsequent time step. A priori knowledge about likely and unlikely configurations of joint angles is used to impose constraints on the pose by learning the probability distribution of the joint angles from examples and incorporating it as an a priori probability into the Bayesian inference scheme.

Rosenhahn et al. (2008a) propose a method for tracking the motion of dressed persons by integrating a kinematic simulation of clothes covering parts of the body into a silhouette-based system for body pose estimation. The body pose is determined by minimising an appropriately defined error function, where the correspondences between the observed and modelled silhouettes, the parameters of the kinematic chain defining the body model, the appearance of the clothes on the body, and the forces exerted on the clothes are taken into account. A fairly detailed modelling is performed, since parameters of the clothes of the person such as the length of a skirt are extracted during the optimisation process, and physical kinematic modelling of the motion of the clothes resulting e.g. from wind is performed. A quantitative evaluation demonstrates that despite the fact that parts of the tracked body are occluded by clothes, the error of the proposed method is less than one degree higher than typical inaccuracies of tracking systems relying on markers attached to the person.

Grest and Koch (2008) adapt a three-dimensional body model consisting of rigid fixed body parts to a three-dimensional point cloud extracted from a pair of stereo images with a dynamic programming-based dense stereo technique. A maximum number of 28 pose parameters is estimated for the human body model using a 3D–3D pose estimation technique based on the ICP algorithm. The Gauß–Newton, gradient descent, and stochastic meta-descent optimisation methods are compared with respect to their convergence behaviour, where the Gauß–Newton method is found to be the superior approach.

A markerless system for three-dimensional body pose estimation specifically designed for the distinction between normal and pathological motion behaviour of a person is described by Mündermann et al. (2008). It is based on an ICP technique involving an articulated surface model designed such that the exact positions at which the articulated motion is performed within the joints can be refined (within certain limits) during the model adaptation procedure, where multiple (between 4 and 64) images of the scene acquired from viewpoints distributed around the person are used. Segmentation of the person from the background is performed by applying an intensity and colour threshold to the background-subtracted images, which yields a three-dimensional visual hull of the person to which the articulated model is adapted. A direct comparison to a marker-based body pose estimation system yields accuracies of 10.6 ± 7.8 mm, 11.3 ± 6.3 mm, and 35.6 ± 67.0 mm for the full body and 8.7 ± 2.2 mm, 10.8 ± 3.4 mm, and 14.3 ± 7.6 mm for the lower limbs of the human body for 64, 8, and 4 cameras, respectively.

Gall et al. (2009) rely on silhouette and colour features and assume the existence of an accurate three-dimensional model of the analysed human body. They utilise a local optimisation technique for three-dimensional pose estimation which is similar to the approach introduced by Rosenhahn et al. (2005), combined with a global stochastic optimisation and filtering stage based on a technique named 'interacting simulated annealing'.

Hofmann and Gavrila (2009) suggest an extraction of three-dimensional human body pose parameters from single images based on a hierarchical matching scheme similar to the one described by Gavrila and Philomin (1999) and a simultaneous adaptation of the parameters of the human body model based on multiple image sequences acquired from different viewpoints distributed around the observed persons. The results are integrated over time relying on representative sequences of three-dimensional pose parameters extracted from the acquired image sequences, which are used to generate a model of the apparent surface texture of the person. Texture information is used in combination with contour information to arrive at a final estimate of the three-dimensional pose parameters.

Salzmann and Urtasun (2010) introduce a method which combines discriminative approaches (such as regression or classification techniques) estimating the three-dimensional pose of an articulated object and the three-dimensional shape of an arbitrary surface with the minimisation of a likelihood function depending on the image information (such as the reprojection error or the distances between edges generated by the three-dimensional model pose and those observed in the image). 'Distance preservation constraints' are introduced by Salzmann and Urtasun (2010) into the estimation of the three-dimensional pose parameters. These constraints impose constant distances between reference points, i.e. the joints in the case of an articulated human body model and the mesh points in the case of a surface model.

Approaches like those introduced by Plänkers and Fua (2003), Rosenhahn et al. (2005), and Brox et al. (2008) determine a single pose which is updated at every time step. A more refined tracking scheme is proposed by Ziegler et al. (2006), who employ an unscented Kalman filter for tracking the pose parameters of the body. An ICP-based approach to estimate the pose of the upper human body is used, relying on a comparison of a three-dimensional point cloud generated by the analysis of several pairs of stereo images with a synthetically rendered depth map, obtained with a polygonal model of the upper body using the z-buffer technique. The system of Ziegler et al. (2006) determines the position of the torso along with the joint angles of the upper arms at the shoulders and the joint angles characterising the postures of the forearms relative to the upper arms.

To increase the robustness of tracking, other approaches such as those proposed by Deutscher et al. (2001) and Schmidt et al. (2006) rely on the particle filter approach introduced by Isard and Blake (1998) in order to take into account multiple pose hypotheses simultaneously. In this probabilistic framework, the probability distribution of the parameters to be estimated is modelled by a (typically large) number of random samples ('particles'). For tracking the human body based on a small number of particles, Deutscher et al. (2001) introduce an approach inspired by the optimisation technique of simulated annealing, termed 'annealed particle filtering', which allows one to determine the absolute maximum of the (generally multimodal) probability distribution of the pose parameters by introducing several subsequent annealing stages. For weighting the particles, edge detection and background subtraction are used. A relatively small number of at least 100 and typically a few hundreds of particles are sufficient for tracking an articulated model of the human body with 29 pose parameters. For three-dimensional body tracking, Schmidt et al. (2006) employ the 'kernel particle filter', which approximates the probability density in state space by a superposition of Gaussian kernels. They use 150 particles to track a three-dimensional model of the upper human body defined by 14 pose parameters, relying on monocular colour images. The particles are weighted by the use of colour cues which are combined with ridge and edge cues. Due to the monocular approach, pose ambiguities may be encountered in this framework.

To alleviate the ambiguity of the three-dimensional pose estimation result of the human body, Pons-Moll et al. (2011) propose a method which combines image information with data acquired by inertial sensors attached to the body. The inertial sensors provide information about the orientation of the body parts to which they are attached, which are converted into three-dimensional poses based on an inverse kinematics approach. This technique allows one to reduce the number of pose parameters of the utilised human body model, corresponding to 31, to an effective number of 16 parameters when employing five inertial sensors. Three-dimensional pose hypotheses consistent with the inertial sensor data are compared by Pons-Moll et al. (2011) with the observed image features, especially silhouette information, using a particle filter framework, where the sensor noise is modelled by the von Mises–Fisher distribution. The experimental evaluation shows a high accuracy and robustness of the correspondingly obtained three-dimensional pose estimation results.

At this point it is illustrative to mention methods for three-dimensional pose estimation and tracking of the human hand, which also represents a complex articulated object with a large number of degrees of freedom. From the methodical point of view, methods for hand pose estimation tend to be fairly similar to many of the previously described full body pose estimation approaches. The extensive survey by Erol et al. (2007) provides an overview of hand pose estimation techniques. They divide methods for hand modelling into geometric techniques, usually involving a considerable number of pose parameters, and kinematic approaches that learn typical dynamical patterns of the hand motion, where they point out that in most systems a manual user-specific calibration of the kinematic hand model is required. Furthermore, they distinguish between two-dimensional and three-dimensional methods for hand pose estimation, where the three-dimensional techniques may rely on colour, edges, point correspondences, disparity information, or actively scanned range data. A further distinction is made by Erol et al. (2007) between tracking of single hypotheses, typically using a Kalman filter, and tracking of multiple hypotheses, e.g. involving an extended or unscented Kalman filter or a particle filter. For details refer to Erol et al. (2007) and references therein.

The work by Stößel (2007) is one of the few studies that examine the problem of three-dimensional pose estimation of articulated objects in the context of industrial quality inspection. The described system performs a three-dimensional pose estimation of objects which consist of several connected rigid parts, termed 'multi-part assemblies' by Stößel (2007), relying on a monocular image, where the corresponding articulated object models are characterised by up to 29 pose parameters. The method is based on the minimisation of the Hausdorff distance between edges observed in the image and those inferred from the model projected into the image, taking into account mutual occlusions of different parts of the articulated object. For minimisation of the error function, the 'extended kernel particle filter' approach is introduced by Stößel (2007) and employed as a stochastic optimisation technique.

2.2.2 Three-Dimensional Active Contours

This section is adopted from d'Angelo et al. (2004), who describe a parametric active contour framework for recovering the three-dimensional contours of rotationally symmetric objects such as tubes and cables. The proposed algorithm is a three-dimensional ziplock ribbon active contour algorithm based on multiple views.

2.2.2.1 Active Contours

In the snake approach by Kass et al. (1988), the basic snake is a parametric function $\mathbf{p}$ representing a contour curve or model:

$$\mathbf{p} = \mathbf{v}(s) \quad \text{for } s \in [0, l], \tag{2.3}$$

where $\mathbf{p}$ is a contour point for a certain value of the length parameter s. An energy function E_C is minimised over the contour $\mathbf{v}(s)$ according to

$$E_C = \int_0^l E_{\text{snake}}(\mathbf{v}(s)) \, ds. \tag{2.4}$$

The snake energy E_{snake} is separated into four terms:

$$E_{\text{snake}}(\mathbf{v}(s)) = \alpha E_{\text{cont}}(\mathbf{v}(s)) + \beta E_{\text{curv}}(\mathbf{v}(s)) + \gamma E_{\text{ext}}(\mathbf{v}(s)) + \delta E_{\text{con}}(\mathbf{v}(s)). \tag{2.5}$$

The 'internal energy' $E_{\text{int}} = \alpha E_{\text{cont}}(\mathbf{v}(s)) + \beta E_{\text{curv}}(\mathbf{v}(s))$ regularises the problem by favouring a continuous and smooth contour. The 'external energy' E_{ext} depends on the image at the curve point $\mathbf{v}(s)$ and thus links the contour with the image. Here we use the negative gradient magnitude of the image as the external energy, which then becomes $E_{\text{ext}} = -\|\nabla I(\mathbf{v}(s))\|$. E_{con} is used in the original snake approach by Kass et al. (1988) to introduce constraints, e.g. linking of points of the active contour to other contours or springs. Balloon snake techniques (Cohen, 1991) use E_{con} to 'inflate' the active contour in order to compensate for the shrinking induced by the internal energy E_{int}. The weight factors α, β, γ, and δ can be chosen according to the application.

The dependence of the snake model on its parameterisation may lead to numerical instabilities and self-intersection problems when it is applied to complex segmentation tasks. Such problems are avoided by implicit active contour models (Caselles et al., 1995, 1997). Furthermore, a contour is not necessarily a single curve, and modifications to extract ribbon structures consisting of parallel lines, like roads in aerial images (Fua and Leclerc, 1990) or blood vessels in angiographic images (Hinz et al., 2001), have been proposed in the literature. Snakes can also be used as a segmentation tool in an interactive manner, where a human operator provides a rough estimate of the initial contour and can move the snake such that local minima of the energy function are avoided (Kass et al., 1988).

For the method described in this section, the greedy active contours approach introduced by Williams and Shah (1992) is used as the basis for the three-dimensional snake framework. The contour is modelled by a polyline consisting of n points, and finite differences are used to approximate the energy terms E_{cont} and E_{curv} at each point $\mathbf{p}_s$, $s = 1, \ldots, n$ according to

$$E_{\text{cont}}\big(\mathbf{v}(s)\big) \approx \big|\, \|\mathbf{p}_s - \mathbf{p}_{s-1}\| - h \big|$$
$$E_{\text{curc}}\big(\mathbf{v}(s)\big) \approx \|\mathbf{p}_{s-1} - 2\mathbf{p}_s + \mathbf{p}_{s+1}\|, \tag{2.6}$$

where h is the mean distance between the polyline points. The greedy minimisation algorithm is an iterative algorithm which selects the point of minimal energy inside a local neighbourhood. The greedy optimisation is applied separately to each point, from the first point at $s = 0$ to the last point at $s = l$. The energy $E_C(\mathbf{v}(s))$ is calculated for each candidate point $\mathbf{p}$ in a neighbourhood grid $H \in \mathbb{R}^d$, where d is the dimensionality of the curve. The point $\mathbf{p}_{\text{min}}$ of minimum energy inside H is selected as the new curve point at $\mathbf{v}(s)$. This procedure is repeated until all points have reached a stable position or a maximum number of iterations has been reached.

Since the greedy optimisation algorithm does not necessarily find a global minimum, it needs a good initialisation to segment the correct contours. Especially in segmenting non-rigid objects, however, providing a suitable initialisation along the whole contour might not always be feasible. In such cases, the ziplock snake algorithm introduced by Neuenschwander et al. (1997) is used. Ziplock snakes are initialised by the end points of the contour segment to be extracted and the tangents of the curve at these points. The contour consists of active parts, which are subject to the full energy term E_{snake}, and inactive parts, which are influenced only by the internal energy E_{int}. The 'force boundaries' between the active and inactive parts of the snake start close to the end points of the contour segments and move towards each other in the course of the optimisation.

2.2.2.2   Three-Dimensional Multiple-View Active Contours

If volumetric images are available, the image energy E_{ext} of a three-dimensional contour can be calculated directly from the volumetric data. In industrial quality inspection applications, volumetric data are not available, but it is usually possible to obtain images acquired from multiple viewpoints. In that case E_{ext} can be calculated by projecting the contour into the image planes of the cameras (Fig. 2.3a). The camera system is calibrated with the method of Krüger et al. (2004) (cf. Sect. 1.4). An arbitrary number N of images ($i = 1, \ldots, N$) can be used for this projection. The intrinsic and extrinsic parameters of each camera are assumed to be known.

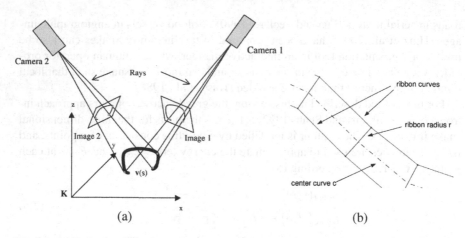

Fig. 2.3 (**a**) Projection of the three-dimensional curve model $\mathbf{v}(s)$ into multiple images. Two cameras are observing the scene. Calculation of the external energy requires the contour curves in the image planes of all cameras. (**b**) Sketch of a ribbon snake

Each scene point $^{W}\mathbf{p}$ is projected to the corresponding image point $^{S_i}\mathbf{p}$ defined in the sensor coordinate system. The energy term E_{ext} that connects the contour with the images is calculated based on the projection of the contour into each image plane according to $E_{\text{ext}}^* = \sum_{i=1}^{N} E_{\text{ext}}(^{S_i}\mathbf{p})$. Hence, generating different active contours separately for each image or a depth map determined e.g. by stereo image analysis is not necessary. All image and constraint information is used by the energy minimisation step in the model parameter space. In our examples, we use the image gradient as the external energy term, i.e. $E_{\text{ext}}(^{S_i}\mathbf{p}) = -\|\nabla I_i(^{S_i}\mathbf{p})\|$. Occlusions of the object are not considered during modelling, but the algorithm copes with partial occlusions and holes in the contour if they do not appear excessively. The energy terms E_{int} and E_{con} are independent of occlusions that may occur in some views.

The described approach requires that either the points of the extracted three-dimensional snake correspond to the same scene points, respectively, or that the object displays certain symmetries. In our scenario of inspection of tubes and cables, the objects to be segmented are rotationally symmetric with respect to a centreline, such that their silhouette is similar from multiple viewpoints and can be described by a centre curve $(x(s), y(s), z(s))^T$ and a radius $r(s)$, leading to $\mathbf{v}(s) = (x, y, z, r)^T$ (Fig. 2.3b). In this case, the contour model is not a simple curve and cannot be projected into the images as described above. Instead, the centreline $(x, y, z)^T$ is projected into the images while the corresponding ribbon curves are calculated by projecting the radius r into the image planes.

If prior knowledge about the contour is available, it can be integrated into the snake optimisation algorithm to improve its convergence. In an industrial production environment, CAD models of the parts that are subject to quality inspection are available and can be used to provide prior knowledge to the active contour segmentation. If the shape of objects should be recovered, only constraints that are invariant to the possible shapes of the object should be used. For quality inspection of tubes, this includes elasticity, length, radius, and sometimes the mounting position, depending on the application. The model information is introduced into the optimisation process in two ways. The first is by adding additional energy terms, the second by using a constrained optimisation algorithm. Additional model-based energy terms that favour a certain shape of the contour can be added to E_{con}. For example, the approximate radius of a cable is known, but it may vary at some places due to labels or constructive changes.

As a first approach, we utilise a three-dimensional ribbon snake to detect the cable shape and position. Hence, $E_{con} = E_{rib} = [r(s) - r_{model}(s)]^2$ can be used as a 'spring energy' to favour contours with a radius r close to a model radius given by the function $r_{model}(s)$. However, adding constraint terms to the objective function may result in an ill-posed problem with poor convergence properties and adds more weight factors that need to be tuned for a given scenario (Fua and Brechbühler, 1996). The second approach is to enforce model constraints through optimiser constraints. In the greedy algorithm this is achieved by intersecting the parameter search region H and the region C permitted by the constraints to obtain the allowed search region $H_c = H \cup C$. This ensures that these constraints cannot be violated (they are also called hard constraints).

For some applications like glue line detection, the surface in which the contour is located is known, for example from CAD data. In other cases, the bounding box of the object can be given. This knowledge can be exploited by a constraint that restricts the optimisation to the corresponding surface or volume. Model information can also be used to create suitable initial contours—for example, tubes are often fixed with brackets to other parts. The pose of these brackets is usually given a priori when repeated quality inspection tasks are performed or can be determined by using pose estimation algorithms for rigid objects (cf. Sect. 2.1). These points can be used as starting and end points, i.e. boundary conditions, for three-dimensional ziplock ribbon snakes.

2.2.2.3 Experimental Results on Synthetic Image Data

As a first test, the described algorithm has been applied to synthetically generated image data, for which the ground truth is inherently available. For all examples, a three-dimensional ribbon snake was used. The weight factors of (2.5) were set to $\alpha = 1$, $\beta = 1$, $\gamma = 3$, and $\delta = 0$. Additionally, a hard constraint has been placed on the minimum and maximum ribbon width, which avoids solutions with negative or unrealistically large width. To estimate the reconstruction quality, a synthetically rendered scene was used as a test case, as this allows a direct comparison to the known ground truth. Figures 2.4a and b show the example scene and its three-dimensional reconstruction result. The start and end points of the object and their tangents were specified. In a real-world application these could either be taken from a CAD model, or estimated by pose estimation of the anchoring brackets. The ground truth used to produce the image is known and is compared to the segmented contour. The utilised error measure is the root-mean-square error (RMSE) of the

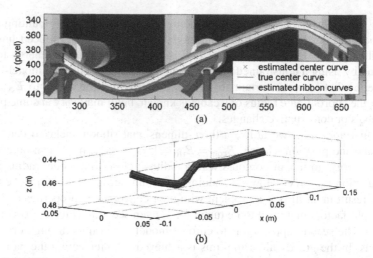

(a)

(b)

Fig. 2.4 (**a**) One of the three artificially rendered input images with the overlaid reprojections of the three-dimensional ribbon snake. A virtual trinocular camera with a resolution of 1024×768 pixels and a base distance of 100 mm has been used to generate the images. (**b**) Reconstructed tube, shown from a different viewpoint. The RMSE between ground truth and reconstruction is 1.5 mm

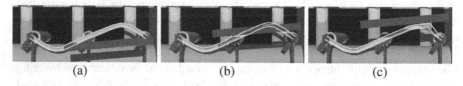

(a)   (b)   (c)

Fig. 2.5 Behaviour of the three-dimensional ziplock ribbon snake algorithm with respect to partial occlusion of the object. A virtual rod is moved across the rendered scene of Fig. 2.4

centre curve of the estimated ribbon snake with respect to the model centre curve. In the example shown in Fig. 2.4, the RMSE amounts to 1.5 mm, which roughly corresponds to 1 pixel disparity error. Subpixel greedy stepwidths and interpolated image energy calculation were used to obtain this result.

The behaviour of the algorithm in the presence of partial occlusions has been tested by moving a virtual rod over the scene, as shown in Fig. 2.5. In Fig. 2.5a, where only a small part of the object is occluded, the RMSE with respect to the ground truth amounts to 1.1 mm, while for stronger occlusions as in Figs. 2.5b and c the RMSE corresponds to 3.1 mm and 3.8 mm, respectively. All described test cases were run on a 1.7 GHz Pentium Mobile Processor. The computation time of the optimisation procedure amounts to between 1 and 23 seconds, depending on the complexity of the scene and the parameters chosen for the optimisation procedure.

The experimental results show that the proposed three-dimensional ziplock ribbon snake algorithm is able to perform a fairly accurate three-dimensional contour segmentation. The stability of the algorithm is mainly due to the usage of model-based constraints and initial contour curves based on model information. However, the proposed method is sensitive to occlusions and self-intersections if they appear excessively. It is limited to lines and tube-shaped objects, which is useful for a variety of applications, e.g. in the field of industrial quality inspection. As real-world applications of the three-dimensional ziplock ribbon snake method, the three-dimensional reconstruction of a cable and of a glue line on a car body part are addressed in Sect. 6.2.

2.2.3 Three-Dimensional Spatio-Temporal Curve Fitting

As an example of three-dimensional pose estimation of articulated objects, this section addresses the problem of markerless pose estimation and tracking of the motion of human body parts in front of a cluttered background. The multiocular contracting curve density (MOCCD) algorithm inspired by Hanek and Beetz (2004) and its spatio-temporal extension, the shape flow algorithm, are introduced by Hahn et al. (2007, 2008b, 2010a) to determine the three-dimensional pose of the hand–forearm limb.

Due to the limited resolution of the trinocular greyscale camera setup it is unfeasible in the system to model each finger of the hand, as is possible e.g. in the work by Stenger et al. (2001). On the other hand, a cylindrical model of the forearm as proposed by Schmidt et al. (2006) is too coarse due to the variability of human appearance, e.g. clothes. Hence, the methods described in this section are based on a three-dimensional hand–forearm model which represents the three-dimensional contour by an Akima spline (Akima, 1970) using control points defined by a parameter vector. The MOCCD algorithm is computationally too expensive to be used in a particle filter framework. Hence, it is integrated into a Kalman filter-based tracking framework which estimates more than one pose hypothesis at a single time step. The presentation in this section is adopted from Hahn et al. (2010a). Further details are provided by Hahn (2011).

2.2.3.1 Modelling the Hand–Forearm Limb

In the application scenario of safe human–robot interaction described in Sects. 7.3 and 7.4, a three-dimensional model of the human hand–forearm limb will be used which consists of a kinematic chain connecting the two rigid elements forearm and hand. The model consists of five truncated cones and one complete cone, as shown in Fig. 2.6. The cones are defined by nine parameters according to

$$\mathbf{T} = [p_{1x}, p_{1y}, p_{1z}, \alpha_1, \beta_1, \alpha_2, \beta_2, r_1, r_4]^T. \tag{2.7}$$

The three-dimensional point $^W\mathbf{p}_1 = [p_{1x}, p_{1y}, p_{1z}]$ defines the beginning of the forearm and is part of the pose parameter vector $\mathbf{T}$. The wrist ($^W\mathbf{p}_2$) and fingertip ($^W\mathbf{p}_3$) positions are computed according to

Fig. 2.6 Hand–forearm model. *Left*: Definition of the cones. *Right*: Dependencies of the radii derived from human anatomy

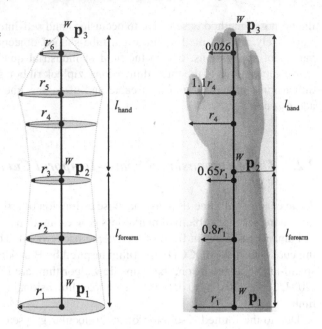

$$^{W}\mathbf{p}_2 = {}^{W}\mathbf{p}_1 + R_Z(\beta_1) \cdot R_Y(\alpha_1) \cdot l_{\text{forearm}} \cdot [1,0,0]^T \tag{2.8}$$

$$^{W}\mathbf{p}_3 = {}^{W}\mathbf{p}_2 + R_Z(\beta_2) \cdot R_Y(\alpha_2) \cdot l_{\text{hand}} \cdot [1,0,0]^T, \tag{2.9}$$

where l_{forearm} and l_{hand} are the predefined lengths of the human hand–forearm limb. The x and y axes are running in the horizontal and vertical directions parallel to the image plane, respectively, while the z axis denotes the depth. The matrix $R_Y(\alpha)$ represents a rotation around the y axis by the angle α, and $R_Z(\beta)$ a corresponding rotation around the z axis.

The lengths l_{hand} and l_{forearm} of the hand and forearm are set to uniform fixed values for all image sequences regarded in the experimental evaluation described in Sect. 7.4. Although human hands and forearms may actually have fairly different lengths, it is shown in Sect. 7.4 that the hand–forearm limb of all test persons is tracked successfully, and we found that differences between the modelled and the actual lengths of 100–200 mm are easily tolerated by the system. Such differences may even occur as short-term variations within a sequence, e.g. when the hand is grabbing, holding, and depositing a tool.

The shapes of the hand and the forearm relative to the maximal radii r_1 and r_4 were derived from human anatomy, as shown in Fig. 2.6, and are defined according to

$$
\begin{aligned}
r_2 &= 0.8 \cdot r_1 \\
r_3 &= 0.65 \cdot r_1 \\
r_5 &= 1.1 \cdot r_4 \\
r_6 &= 0.026 \text{ m} = \text{const.}
\end{aligned}
\tag{2.10}
$$

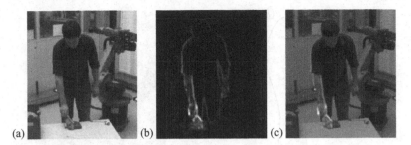

Fig. 2.7 (a) Original 8-bit image I_t. (b) Absolute difference image. (c) Input image I_t^* (scaled to 8 bit) for $\lambda = 1$ according to (2.11)

Hence, in contrast to their lengths, the maximal radii r_1 and r_4 of the hand and the forearm are part of the parameter vector $\mathbf{T}$ and can thus be adapted to the images during the optimisation process.

2.2.3.2   Principles and Extensions of the CCD Algorithm

The CCD algorithm introduced by Hanek (2001) and refined by Hanek and Beetz (2004) adapts a curve model to an image based on the probability distributions of the pixel grey values on the inner and the outer side of the curve. A computationally efficient real-time variant of the CCD algorithm is described by Panin et al. (2006).

A difference to the work of Hanck (2001) is that Hahn et al. (2010a) rely on an extended input image, since in the regarded application scenario the model-based image segmentation is challenging due to noise, a cluttered background, and the coarse object description. In order to obtain an accurate and robust model-based image segmentation, we take advantage of the constant camera position in our application. Our input image $I^*(t)$ is computed by

$$I^*(t) = I(t) + \lambda \big| I(t) - I(t-1) \big|, \qquad (2.11)$$

where $I(t)$ is the image at time step t and $|I(t) - I(t-1)|$ is the absolute difference image of the current and the previous image. The factor λ defines the influence of the absolute difference image. The influence of the absolute difference image increases the pixel values in areas where motion occurs, which allows a more robust segmentation, since the CCD algorithm adapts the curve model by separating the probability distributions of the pixel grey values on the inner and the outer side of the object curve. Another advantage is that if there is no motion, the input image $I^*(t)$ corresponds to the original image $I(t)$ and it is still possible to fit the model. We experimented with different values of λ in the range $[0.5, \ldots, 3]$ and found empirically that the dependence of the segmentation result does not critically depend on the value of λ. For a moving camera, the original image $I(t)$ would have to be used as the input image $I^*(t)$, corresponding to $\lambda = 0$. Figure 2.7 shows the original camera image, the absolute difference image, and the input image obtained for $\lambda = 1$.

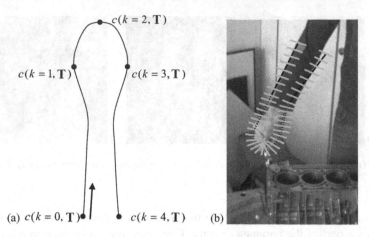

Fig. 2.8 (a) The two-dimensional model curve described by the curve function $c(k, \mathbf{T})$. The parameter k defines a point on the curve, and the vector $\mathbf{T}$ contains the curve parameters. (b) Curve function $c(k, \mathbf{T})$ with the k perpendiculars centred at the curve points

The CCD algorithm fits a parametric curve $c(k, \mathbf{T})$ to the image I^*. The parameter $k \in [0, K]$ of the parametric model curve $c(k, \mathbf{T})$ shown in Fig. 2.8a is incremented with the points defining the curve, and the vector $\mathbf{T}$ denotes the set of estimated curve parameters. The CCD algorithm relies on the image I^* and the initial probability distribution $p(\mathbf{T}) \approx p(\mathbf{T}|\widehat{\mathbf{m}}_\mathbf{T}, \widehat{\Sigma}_\mathbf{T})$ of the parameters $\mathbf{T}$ of the curve model, which is assumed to be Gaussian and is thus given by the mean parameter vector $\widehat{\mathbf{m}}_\mathbf{T}$ and the corresponding covariance matrix $\widehat{\Sigma}_\mathbf{T}$. As initial values, the a priori density parameters $(\widehat{\mathbf{m}}_\mathbf{T}, \widehat{\Sigma}_\mathbf{T})$ are used. The CCD algorithm adapts the model to the image by repeatedly performing steps 1 and 2 described below until the reduction of $\mathbf{m}_\mathbf{T}$ and $\Sigma_\mathbf{T}$ becomes smaller than a predefined value or after a given maximum number of iteration cycles has been performed. This procedure can be summarised by the two steps.

Step 1: Learning Local Probability Distributions   The local probability distributions $S(\mathbf{m}_\mathbf{T}, \Sigma_\mathbf{T})$, which are given by the pixel grey value means and standard deviations, are computed on both sides of the curve.

In this step pixels close to the curve (along the perpendiculars as shown in Fig. 2.8b) are probabilistically assigned to the inner and the outer side of the expected curve. Then the probability distributions $S(\mathbf{m}_\mathbf{T}, \Sigma_\mathbf{T})$ of the pixel grey values on both sides of the curve are computed. For this porpose only pixels on $(K + 1)$ different lines segments are used. Each line segment k is a perpendicular on the curve point $\mathbf{C}_k = c(k, \mathbf{m}_\mathbf{T})$ of the expected curve. In contrast to the original real-time CCD algorithm (Hanek, 2001), the perpendiculars are not chosen to be equally spaced along the curve, because our applied curve model is not a closed curve. Thus there are more perpendiculars on the closed side (hand part) of our curve, to obtain a stronger dependence of the objective function on the shift along the forearm axis (cf. Fig. 2.8b). The length of a perpendicular k depends on the local uncertainty σ_k of the curve given by

$$\sigma_k^2 = \mathbf{n}_k^T \cdot \mathbf{J}_{C_k} \cdot \Sigma_{\mathbf{T}} \cdot \mathbf{J}_{C_k}^T \cdot \mathbf{n}_k \tag{2.12}$$

and changes in each iteration step. The variable $\mathbf{n}_k$ defines the curve normal and $\mathbf{J}_{C_k}$ the Jacobian, i.e. the partial derivative of the curve with respect to the model parameters $\mathbf{T}$. The original real-time CCD algorithm according to Hanek (2001) computes for every perpendicular k a local uncertainty σ_k of the curve. In contrast to Hanek (2001), we apply a fixed local uncertainty for every perpendicular of the curve, thus avoiding a large number of nonlinear function evaluations. The local uncertainties σ_0 and $\sigma_{K/2}$ at the perpendiculars $k = 0$ and $k = K/2$ are computed using (2.12), and the fixed local uncertainty σ results from $\sigma = (\sigma_0 + \sigma_{K/2})/2$. The fixed local uncertainty σ is now used to compute the probabilistic assignment for every point $\mathbf{v}_{k,l}$ on the perpendiculars; l denotes the pixel index on perpendicular k. For every point $\mathbf{v}_{k,l}$ on perpendicular k the probability $a_{l,1}(d_l)$ that the point lies on side 1 (inner side) of the curve (probabilistic assignment) is computed by

$$a_{l,1}(d_l) = \frac{1}{2}\left[\mathrm{erf}\left(\frac{d_l}{\sqrt{2}\sigma} \right) + 1 \right]. \tag{2.13}$$

In (2.13), $\mathrm{erf}(x)$ is the Gaussian error function and $d_l(\mathbf{v}_{k,l}) = \mathbf{n}_k^T (\mathbf{v}_{k,l} - \mathbf{C}_k)$ the signed distance of the pixel coordinate $\mathbf{v}_{k,l}$ from the curve point $\mathbf{C}_k$. The probabilistic assignment $a_{l,2}(d_l)$ of side 2 (outer side) is defined by $a_{l,2}(d_l) = 1 - a_{l,1}(d_l)$.

To compute the two-sided probability distributions of the pixel grey values we follow the suggestions of Hanek (2001) and apply as a weighting function the expression

$$w_{l,s} = w_A(a_{l,s}) \cdot w_B(d_l, \sigma) \cdot w_C(\sigma) \quad \text{with } s \in \{1, 2\}, \tag{2.14}$$

where

$$w_A(a_{l,s}) = \max\left(0, \left[\frac{a_{l,s} - \gamma_1}{1 - \gamma_1} \right]^{(2 \cdot E_A)} \right) \tag{2.15}$$

assesses the probabilistic assignment. The parameter $\gamma_1 \in [0, 1[$ describes the minimum probability $a_{l,s}$ that the pixel is used to compute the probability distributions. We use $\gamma_1 = 0.5$ and $E_A = 3$. The weight $w_B(d_l, \sigma)$ considers the signed distance of the pixel $\mathbf{v}_{k,l}$ to the curve and is given by

$$w_B(d_l, \sigma) = C \cdot \max\left(0, e^{(-d_l^2/(2 \cdot \widehat{\sigma}))} - e^{(-\gamma_4)} \right) \quad \text{with} \tag{2.16}$$

$$\widehat{\sigma} = \gamma_3 \cdot \sigma + \gamma_4. \tag{2.17}$$

Here C is a normalisation constant, where we set $C = 5$. For the other parameters we use $\gamma_2 = 4$, $\gamma_3 = 6$, and $\gamma_4 = 3$. The weighting function $w_C(\sigma)$ evaluates the local uncertainty σ according to

$$w_C(\sigma) = (\sigma + 1)^{-E_C}. \tag{2.18}$$

We recommend the choice $E_C = 4$. Since we consider a fixed local uncertainty σ, the probabilistic assignment and the weights depend only on the signed distance

d_l to the curve, where the sign indicates the side of the curve on which a pixel is located. Hence, the weighting function and the probabilistic assignment need to be computed only once and can be obtained by a distance-dependent look-up operation, thus avoiding a large number of nonlinear function evaluations without loss of accuracy. Based on the weights $w_{l,s}$ we obtain the statistical moments $m_{k,s,o}$ of order $o \in \{0, 1, 2\}$ for every perpendicular k and side $s \in \{1, 2\}$ of the curve, using

$$m_{k,s,0} = \sum_{l=1}^{L_k} w_{l,s} \tag{2.19}$$

$$m_{k,s,1} = \sum_{l=1}^{L_k} w_{l,s} \cdot I_{k,l}^* \tag{2.20}$$

$$m_{k,s,2} = \sum_{l=1}^{L_k} w_{l,s} \cdot I_{k,l}^* \cdot I_{k,l}^{*T} \tag{2.21}$$

with $I_{k,l}^*$ as the pixel value of perpendicular k and pixel index l. The original CCD tracker according to Hanek (2004) uses a spatial and spatio-temporal smoothing of the statistical moments to exploit the spatial and spatio-temporal coherence of pixel values. This improves the robustness of the tracker, since the influence of strong edges and outliers is reduced. In contrast to the original work of Hanek (2004), we apply only a spatial smoothing of the statistical moments, since our input images I^* according to (2.11) are not temporally coherent due to the addition of the absolute difference image. We rely on a blurring with fixed filter coefficients by applying to the statistical moments a Gaussian convolution operator of size 1×5 with a standard deviation of 2 contour points. This leads to the spatially smoothed moments $\tilde{m}_{k,s,o}$ of order $o \in \{0, 1, 2\}$ for every perpendicular k and side $s \in \{1, 2\}$. The local mean vectors $m_{k,s}(t)$ and covariance matrices $\Sigma_{k,s}(t)$ for every perpendicular k at time step t on both sides $s \in \{1, 2\}$ of the curve are computed by

$$m_{k,s}(t) = \frac{\tilde{m}_{k,s,1}(t)}{\tilde{m}_{k,s,0}(t)} \tag{2.22}$$

$$\Sigma_{k,s}(t) = \frac{\tilde{m}_{k,s,2}(t)}{\tilde{m}_{k,s,0}(t)} - m_{k,s}(t) \cdot m_{k,s}^T(t) + \kappa. \tag{2.23}$$

The parameter κ avoids singularities. We set it to $\kappa = 2.5$. The local probability distributions $S(\mathbf{m_T}, \Sigma_\mathbf{T})$ of the pixel grey values which are used in the second step to refine the estimate consist of $(K + 1)$ different local mean vectors $m_{k,s}(t)$ and covariance matrices $\Sigma_{k,s}(t)$. In the following we assume to be at time step t and denote the mean values by $m_{k,s}$ and the covariance matrices by $\Sigma_{k,s}$.

Step 2: Refinement of the Estimate (MAP Estimation)   An update of the parameters $(\mathbf{m_T}, \Sigma_\mathbf{T})$ obtained in step 1, describing the probability distribution of the curve parameters, is performed based on a single Newton-Raphson step which increases the a-posteriori probability according to Eq. (2.24).

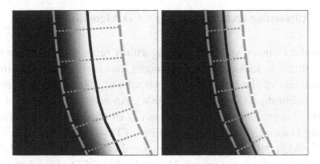

Fig. 2.9 The CCD algorithm determines the parameters of the curve (*black line*) by computing the probability distributions of the pixel grey values in a local neighbourhood of the curve (indicated by the *grey lines*) and by maximising the a posteriori probability of the curve model. Non-optimal (*left*) and optimal (*right*) configuration

The principle of the CCD algorithm is depicted in Fig. 2.9. The CCD algorithm estimates a model pose by computing the maximum of the a posteriori probability according to

$$p(\mathbf{T}|I^*) = p(I^*|\mathbf{T}) \cdot p(\mathbf{T}).\qquad(2.24)$$

Since the probability distributions of $p(\mathbf{T})$ and $p(I^*|\mathbf{T})$ are unknown, they are approximated. The Gaussian a priori density $p(\mathbf{T}) \approx p(\mathbf{T}|\widehat{\mathbf{m}}_\mathbf{T}, \widehat{\Sigma}_\mathbf{T})$ of the model parameters $\mathbf{T}$ is defined by the mean $\widehat{\mathbf{m}}_\mathbf{T}$ and the covariance matrix $\widehat{\Sigma}_\mathbf{T}$. The likelihood function $p(I^*|\mathbf{T})$ is approximated by the Gaussian density function $p(I^*|S(\mathbf{m_T}, \Sigma_\mathbf{T}))$ and describes how well the pixel values along the perpendicular fit estimated probability distributions $S(\mathbf{m_T}, \Sigma_\mathbf{T})$ close to the curve. The observation model, i.e. the likelihood function, is computed by

$$p(I^*|S(\mathbf{m_T}, \Sigma_\mathbf{T})) = \prod_{k,l} \frac{1}{\sqrt{2\pi} \cdot \Sigma_{k,l}} \cdot e^{-\frac{h_k^2}{2\Sigma_{k,l}^2}} \quad \text{with} \qquad (2.25)$$

$$h_k = p(I_{k,l}^*|m_{k,l}, \Sigma_{k,l}) - m_{k,l} \qquad (2.26)$$

where l defines the pixel index on the perpendicular k and $p(I_{k,l}^*|m_{k,l}, \Sigma_{k,l})$ a Gaussian probability density with mean $m_{k,l}$ and covariance $\Sigma_{k,l}$ according to

$$m_{k,l} = a_{l,1} \cdot m_{k,1} + a_{l,2} \cdot m_{k,2} \qquad (2.27)$$
$$\Sigma_{k,l} = a_{l,1} \cdot \Sigma_{k,1} + a_{l,2} \cdot \Sigma_{k,2}. \qquad (2.28)$$

These values depend on the probabilistic assignment $a_{l,s}$ of the pixel with index l and the two-sided probability distributions $S(\mathbf{m_T}, \Sigma_\mathbf{T})$ of the pixel grey values with the mean vector $m_{k,s}$ and covariance matrix $\Sigma_{k,s}$ for perpendicular k.

To increase the numerical stability of the optimisation procedure, the log-likelihood

$$X = -2\ln[p(I^*|S(\mathbf{m_T}, \Sigma_\mathbf{T})) \cdot p(\mathbf{T}|\widehat{\mathbf{m}}_\mathbf{T}, \widehat{\Sigma}_\mathbf{T})], \qquad (2.29)$$

rather than the a posteriori probability according to Eq. (2.24) is computed, and the curve density parameters $(\mathbf{m_T}, \Sigma_\mathbf{T})$ are refined by a single step of a Newton–Raphson optimisation.

2.2.3.3 The Multiocular Extension of the CCD Algorithm

The multiocular extension of the CCD algorithm relies on the projection of the boundary of a three-dimensional contour model into each image. The intrinsic and extrinsic parameters of the camera model (Bouguet, 2007) are obtained by multi-ocular camera calibration (Krüger et al., 2004). An arbitrary number of images N_c can be used for this projection. The input values of the MOCCD algorithm are N_c images and the Gaussian a priori distribution $p(\mathbf{T}) \approx p(\mathbf{T}|\hat{\mathbf{m}}_\mathbf{T}, \widehat{\Sigma}_\mathbf{T})$ of the model parameters $\mathbf{T}$, which define the three-dimensional object model. To achieve a more robust segmentation, the input image $I^*_{c,t}$ of the MOCCD algorithm is computed using (2.11) and the original camera images $I_{c,t}$ with $c \in \{1, \ldots, N_c\}$ at the time steps t and $(t-1)$. Before the first iteration, the MOCCD algorithm is initialised by setting the mean vector and covariance matrix $(\mathbf{m}_\mathbf{T}, \Sigma_\mathbf{T})$ to be optimised to the given a priori density parameters $(\hat{\mathbf{m}}_\mathbf{T}, \widehat{\Sigma}_\mathbf{T})$. The MOCCD algorithm then consists of three steps.

Step 1: Extraction and Projection of the Three-Dimensional Model   The intrinsic and extrinsic camera parameters are used to project the extracted outline of the three-dimensional model to each camera image I^*_c. The MOCCD algorithm extends the CCD algorithm to multiple calibrated cameras by projecting the boundary of a three-dimensional model into each camera image I^*_c. Therefore, the MOCCD algorithm requires the extraction and projection of the outline of the used three-dimensional model.

A three-dimensional hand–forearm model (cf. Sect. 2.2.3.1) is fitted to the images of a trinocular camera. The outline of our three-dimensional model in each camera coordinate system is extracted by computing a vector from the origin of each camera coordinate system to the point in the wrist, e.g. $^{C_1}\mathbf{p}_2$ for camera 1. This vector and the direction vector $\overline{\mathbf{p}_1\mathbf{p}_2}$ of the forearm span a plane. The normal vector of this plane is intersected with the three-dimensional model to yield the three-dimensional outline observed from the camera viewpoint. The extracted three-dimensional contour model for the given camera, which consists of 13 points, is projected into the pixel coordinate system of the camera. The corresponding two-dimensional contour model is computed by an Akima interpolation (Akima, 1970) along the curve with the 13 projected points as control points. Figure 2.10 depicts the extraction and projection of the three-dimensional contour model for camera 1.

Step 2: Learning Local Probability Distributions from all N_c Images   For all N_c camera images I^*_c compute the local probability distributions $S_c(\mathbf{m}_\mathbf{T}, \Sigma_\mathbf{T})$ on both sides of the curve. This step is similar to step 1 of the CCD algorithm; the only difference is that the probability distributions $S_c(\mathbf{m}_\mathbf{T}, \Sigma_\mathbf{T})$ on both sides of the curve are learned for all N_c camera images I^*_c.

Step 3: Refinement of the Estimate (MAP Estimation)   The curve density parameters $(\mathbf{m}_\mathbf{T}, \Sigma_\mathbf{T})$ are refined towards the maximum of (2.30) by performing a

Fig. 2.10 Extraction and projection of the three-dimensional contour model for camera 1

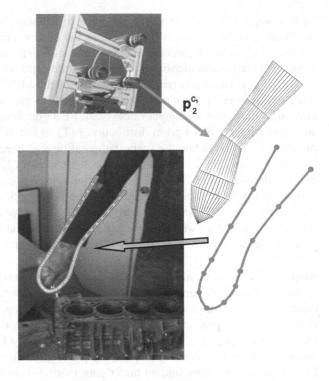

single step of a Newton–Raphson optimisation procedure. The learned probability distributions $S_c(\mathbf{m_T}, \Sigma_{\mathbf{T}})$ are used to maximise the joint probability

$$p\big(\mathbf{T}|i_1^*, \ldots, I_{N_c}^*\big) = \left[\prod_{c=1}^{N_c} p\big(I_c^* | S_c(\mathbf{m_T}, \Sigma_{\mathbf{T}})\big)\right] \cdot p(\mathbf{T}|\widehat{\mathbf{m}}_{\mathbf{T}}, \widehat{\Sigma}_{\mathbf{T}}) \qquad (2.30)$$

with $S_c(\mathbf{m_T}, \Sigma_{\mathbf{T}})$ representing the probability distributions close to the projected curve in image I_c^*. As in the original CCD framework, we optimise the log-likelihood of (2.30) with a Newton–Raphson optimisation step. The MOCCD algorithm can be illustrated as follows: The Gaussian probability densities $p(I^*|S_c(\mathbf{m_T}, \Sigma_{\mathbf{T}}))$ are sensitive with respect to step-like structures along the curve perpendiculars in each image I_c^*, and the three-dimensional model is adapted to the N_c camera images by an implicit triangulation.

2.2.3.4 The Shape Flow Algorithm

The shape flow (SF) algorithm is introduced by Hahn et al. (2008b, 2010a) as a top-down approach for spatio-temporal pose estimation. In contrast to bottom-up motion estimation approaches, like the motion analysis module described in Sect. 2.3.3, the SF algorithm is generally able to estimate the three-dimensional pose parameters $\mathbf{T}$ and the temporal pose derivative $\dot{\mathbf{T}}$ with a spatio-temporal model and the images of

N_t time steps only. With the SF algorithm it is possible to estimate the velocity along the depth axis, which is not possible with the motion analysis module described in Sect. 2.3.3, as the regarded scene flow vectors provide no information about the velocity of the three-dimensional points along the depth axis.

The SF algorithm is a temporal extension of the MOCCD algorithm and fits a three-dimensional spatio-temporal contour model to multiocular images (N_c cameras) at N_t time steps. The input values of the SF algorithm are N_c images at N_t time steps and the Gaussian a priori distribution $p(\mathbf{T}) \approx p(\mathbf{T}|\widehat{\mathbf{m}}_\mathbf{T}, \widehat{\Sigma}_\mathbf{T})$ of the model parameters $\mathbf{T}$, which define the spatio-temporal three-dimensional object model. To achieve a more robust segmentation, the input image $I_{c,t}^*$ of the SF algorithm is computed using (2.11). Here, the SF algorithm is used to estimate the temporal pose derivative $\dot{\mathbf{T}}$ only. Before the first iteration, the SF algorithm is initialised by setting the mean vector and covariance matrix ($\mathbf{m}_\mathbf{T}$, $\Sigma_\mathbf{T}$) to be optimised to a priori density parameters ($\widehat{\mathbf{m}}_\mathbf{T}$, $\widehat{\Sigma}_\mathbf{T}$) which may e.g. be provided by the motion analysis module described in Sect. 2.3.3. The SF algorithm consists of three steps.

Step 1: Projection of the Spatio-Temporal Three-Dimensional Contour Model   Based on the motion model, e.g. with constant velocity, the three-dimensional contour model for all time steps N_t is computed and camera parameters are used to project the extracted outline of the three-dimensional model to each camera image $I_{c,t}^*$. The SF algorithm extends the MOCCD algorithm to the temporal dimension by using a spatio-temporal three-dimensional model, defined by the parameter vector and an underlying motion model, e.g. constant velocity. In this step the observed boundary of the spatio-temporal three-dimensional model is computed for all time steps N_t and projected into each camera image $I_{c,t}^*$. The outline of our three-dimensional model is extracted and projected as described in step 1 of the MOCCD algorithm.

Now we describe the applied motion model and the computation of the spatio-temporal three-dimensional model. Note that the optimised parameter vector in the SF algorithm consists only of the temporal derivative $\dot{\mathbf{T}}(t)$. We assume that the forearm radius r_1 and the hand radius r_4 (cf. Sect. 2.2.3.1) are constant over short periods of time corresponding to a few frames; therefore these radii are not part of the temporal pose derivative $\dot{\mathbf{T}}$. However, the radii r_1 and r_4 are only excluded from the estimation of the temporal pose derivative $\dot{\mathbf{T}}$, not from the estimation of the pose $\mathbf{T}$ itself. Hence, the algorithm is able to adapt itself to short-term changes of the radii within a sequence; only their temporal derivatives are not estimated directly.

The three-dimensional pose $\mathbf{T}(t)$ at time step t is computed at time step t with the MOCCD algorithm or with the fusion module described in Sect. 7.4.3. The temporal pose derivative $\dot{\mathbf{T}}(t)$ at time step t is determined with the SF algorithm and the image triples at the time steps $(t + \Delta t)$ and $(t - \Delta t)$. The spatio-temporal three-dimensional curve model at the time steps $(t \pm \Delta t)$ is computed according to $\mathbf{T}(t) \pm \dot{\mathbf{T}}(t) \cdot \Delta t$, thus assuming constant motion. Figure 2.11 depicts the projected contour model for camera 1 (the one which defines the coordinate system) and the spatio-temporal three-dimensional pose estimation result (a model-based dense

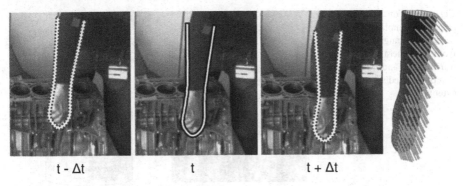

$$t - \Delta t \qquad\qquad t \qquad\qquad t + \Delta t$$

Fig. 2.11 Projected three-dimensional contour model for camera 1 at time steps $(t - \Delta t)$, t, and $(t + \Delta t)$. The *lines* indicate the amount and direction of motion for each point on the model surface

scene flow). At time step t the projected contour of the estimated three-dimensional pose is shown as a solid curve, while the images at the time steps $(t \pm \Delta t)$ depict the projected contour of the pose derivative.

Step 2: Learn Local Probability Distributions from all N_c Images   For all N_c camera images I_c^* and for all N_t time steps, compute the local probability distributions $S_{c,t}(\mathbf{m_T}, \Sigma_\mathbf{T})$ on both sides of the projected three-dimensional contour model, defined by camera c and time step t. This step is similar to step 1 of the CCD algorithm, the only difference is that the probability distributions $S_{c,t}(\mathbf{m_T}, \Sigma_\mathbf{T})$ on both sides of the curve are learned for all N_c cameras images $I_{c,t}^*$ at all N_t time steps.

Step 3: Refine the Estimate (MAP Estimation)   The curve density parameters $(\mathbf{m_T}, \Sigma_\mathbf{T})$ are refined towards the maximum of (2.31) by performing a single step of a Newton–Raphson optimisation procedure. The learned spatio-temporal probability distributions $S_{c,t}(\mathbf{m_T}, \Sigma_\mathbf{T})$ are used to maximise the joint probability

$$p\big(\mathbf{T}|\{I_{c,t}\}\big) = \left[\prod_c \prod_t p\big(I_{c,t}|S_{c,t}(\mathbf{m_T}, \Sigma_\mathbf{T})\big) \right] \cdot p(\mathbf{T}|\widehat{\mathbf{m}}_\mathbf{T}, \widehat{\Sigma}_\mathbf{T}) \qquad (2.31)$$

with $S_{c,t}(\mathbf{m_T}, \Sigma_\mathbf{T})$ representing the probability distributions of the pixel grey values close to the projected curve in image $I_{c,t}$ (camera c, time step t). The underlying assumption is that the images are independent random variables. As in the original CCD framework, a numerically favourable form of (2.31) is obtained by computing the log-likelihood. The SF algorithm can be interpreted as a top-down, model-based spatio-temporal three-dimensional pose estimation approach which determines a three-dimensional pose and its temporal derivative. The advantage is that temporal and spatial constraints are handled directly in the optimisation procedure.

Fig. 2.12 Construction of the reference templates. The forearm rectangle is cropped from all camera images and transformed and interpolated to a predefined size and orientation

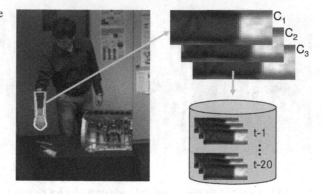

2.2.3.5 Verification and Recovery of the Pose Estimation Results

Pose Verification   To verify and rate a set of calculated pose parameters, three quality measures are used. The first quality criterion is the point distance of the segmented point cloud to the model. Accordingly, a thin hull around the object model is used to determine the points inside the object hull. The weighting value σ_p is the quotient of object points inside the hull and all segmented points.

The second quality criterion is the orientation similarity σ_o, which is computed for a three-dimensional pose by extracting the contour of the three-dimensional model according to Sect. 2.2.3.1 and projecting it into the images acquired by the camera system. For calculating the quality of a contour, the algorithm 'walks along' small perpendiculars in each projected curve point of the contour. For each pixel on the perpendicular the image gradient is calculated. The image gradient orientation, which is between 0° and 180°, is then compared with the orientation of the model contour in the current curve point itself. While the contour gradient describes a reference orientation, the grey image gradient is the compared actual orientation. By simply counting the curve points that do not differ too much and normalising by all projected curve points in all camera images, one obtains an intuitive quality measure in the range $[0 \ldots 1]$.

The third quality criterion is the appearance similarity σ_c for a three-dimensional pose at time step t, which is based on a comparison of the current object appearance with the previous object appearances. With the three-dimensional pose at time step t and the known camera parameters we crop the image of the forearm in all camera images and transform the cropped images to a predefined size and orientation. The final pose estimation result is used to add the current reference template at time step t to a database (cf. Fig. 2.12). This database describes the appearance of the tracked object in the last 20 time steps. The appearance similarity σ_c of a new pose estimation result is computed based on a normalised cross-correlation of the current object appearance at time step t with the previous object appearance at time step $(t - 1)$. Since we have three cameras, there are three correlation results for a pose comparison, where we choose the worst of the three as the final result. The assumptions made for this similarity measure are that

Fig. 2.13 Probability
distribution image for
camera 1, obtained based on
the histogram of the relative
frequency of greyscale pixel
values

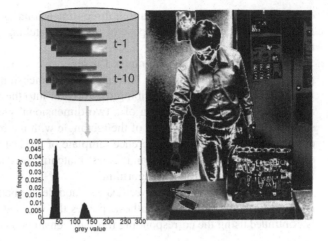

(i) a good three-dimensional pose estimation is available at the first time step and
(ii) that the object appearance does not change considerably over a small period of
time.

To verify an estimated three-dimensional pose, five criteria are used: (i) the temporal variation of the orientation similarity, (ii) the current orientation similarity,
(iii) the temporal variation of the appearance similarity for the three-dimensional
pose $\mathbf{T}(t)$ compared with the pose $\mathbf{T}(t - \Delta t)$, (iv) the appearance similarity for $\mathbf{T}(t)$
compared with $\mathbf{T}(t - \Delta t)$, and (v) the appearance similarity for pose $\mathbf{T}(t)$ compared
with pose $\mathbf{T}(t - 2\Delta t)$.

If the five criteria of a three-dimensional pose pass a set of thresholds, the pose is
defined as valid and the reference template is added to the database. Otherwise, the
tracking can either be stopped with a warning that the object is lost, or a reference
template-based pose recovery stage can be applied.

Pose Recovery on Loss of Object   If the object is deemed to be lost by the verification stage, the pose recovery stage starts at the last valid three-dimensional
pose vector $\mathbf{T}$ and computes two possible pose hypotheses: (i) based on a probability distribution image and (ii) by applying a correlation with the reference templates.

The first pose hypothesis is obtained using the last 10 reference templates of the
forearm to construct a histogram which describes the forearm appearance. The histogram describes the relative frequency of greyscale pixel values (Bradski, 1998)
and is computed only for camera 1. Similar to Bradski (1998), the histogram is used
to compute a probability distribution image for camera 1, as shown in Fig. 2.13.
The last valid three-dimensional pose vector $\mathbf{T}$ is used to project a rectangle circumscribing the forearm into the probability distribution image. A two-dimensional
greedy optimisation in the image plane is applied to find the centre and rotation of
the rectangle with the maximum sum of pixel probabilities. Using the best matching rectangle, we construct a three-dimensional pose under the assumption that the

depth does not change. The resulting three-dimensional pose is computed with the MOCCD algorithm, where the pose of the best matching rectangle is used for initialisation.

The second hypothesis is computed using a two-dimensional correlation-based pose refinement algorithm. The last valid three-dimensional pose vector $\mathbf{T}$ is used to project a rectangle circumscribing the forearm into the image of camera 1. This rectangle is the starting position of a two-dimensional greedy optimisation which searches the centre and rotation of the rectangle with the highest normalised cross-correlation compared to the reference template of the last valid time step. A three-dimensional pose is inferred from the best matching rectangle, which is used as an initialisation for the MOCCD algorithm.

Relying on the criteria of the verification module, the better of the two hypotheses is determined. If the better hypothesis passes the verification module, the tracking is continued using the corresponding three-dimensional pose.

2.3 Point Cloud Segmentation Approaches

For the point-based three-dimensional pose estimation methods outlined in Sect. 2.1, explicit knowledge about correspondences between three-dimensional model points and two-dimensional image points is required. The problem of estimating the pose of an object is then equivalent to that of determining exterior camera orientation (cf. Sect. 1.4). In contrast, appearance-based pose estimation approaches like those described in Sects. 2.1 and 2.2.1.2 do not rely on explicit correspondences but, instead, minimise the difference between the expected appearance of the object according to the estimated pose and the true object appearance.

In many scenarios, a three-dimensional description of the scene is given as a point cloud obtained e.g. by stereo image analysis (cf. Sect. 1.2) or with active sensors such as laser scanning devices. Initially, this point cloud contains no information about objects in the scene. In such cases, an important task is the segmentation of the point cloud into objects, either without using a priori information or based on (weak or strong) model assumptions about the objects found in the scene. A scene segmentation without a priori knowledge can be achieved by clustering methods (Press et al., 2007; Marsland, 2009), while an important approach to model-based segmentation of point clouds is the iterative closest point (ICP) algorithm (Besl and McKay, 1992; Zhang, 1992). Similar methods have been developed in the domain of photogrammetry, e.g. to extract human-made objects such as buildings from topographic maps or terrestrial laser scanner data (Rottensteiner et al., 2005, 2006). We regard in detail a method introduced by Schmidt et al. (2007) for the detection and tracking of objects in a three-dimensional point cloud with motion attributes generated with the spacetime stereo approach described in Sect. 1.5.2.5. This method involves a clustering step relying on the spatial distribution and motion behaviour of the scene points, a subsequent model-fitting stage, and a kernel particle filter for tracking the detected objects.

2.3.1 General Overview

Segmentation of a point cloud corresponds to the subdivision of the cloud into sub-parts that likely represent different objects. Without a priori knowledge about the sizes and shapes of the objects encountered in the scene, i.e. in the absence of model information, an appropriate approach to scene segmentation is clustering, which corresponds to the subdivision of a set of points into parts consisting of mutually similar points (Press et al., 2007; Marsland, 2009). These points may e.g. be three-dimensional points extracted by a scene reconstruction method or three-dimensional points enriched by velocity information such as optical flow or scene flow (cf. Sect. 1.5.2.5), but may also be data points defined in an abstract feature space, where the position in the feature space is associated with certain properties. According to Marsland (2009), the similarity between the points is measured by an appropriately defined metric, where the most common choice is the Euclidean distance between the points. It is important to note that the subdivision of the data set into clusters is performed without information about the class to which each of the individual data points belongs, such that clustering is also termed 'unsupervised learning' (Press et al., 2007).

2.3.1.1 The k-Means Clustering Algorithm

An important hierarchical clustering algorithm is the k-means algorithm introduced by MacQueen (1967). According to Marsland (2009), the number k of clusters has to be given, and k random points are selected as cluster centres. In the first step, each data point is assigned to the cluster centre with the smallest distance. In the second step, the new cluster centres are computed as the averages of the data points according to their assignments in the first step. These two steps are repeated until the assignment of the data points to the established cluster centres (and thus also the cluster centres themselves) remains constant. A new, unknown data point is assigned to the cluster with the smallest distance. Notably, as a consequence of the random initialisation, the k-means algorithm does not necessarily yield the same result for different initialisations.

2.3.1.2 Agglomerative Clustering

According to Press et al. (2007), agglomerative clustering starts with each data point representing a cluster and combines small clusters into larger ones until a dissimilarity criterion between the clusters is met. Press et al. (2007) describe several approaches to determine the distances d_{pk} between a newly formed cluster k and a reference cluster p in comparison to the distances d_{pi} and d_{pj} of the previous cluster pair (i, j) to the same reference cluster as a criterion to combine the cluster pair into a new single cluster. Here, the 'weighted pair group method using arithmetic averages' (WPGMA) implies $d_{pk} = d_{kp} = (d_{pi} + d_{pj})/2$, the 'unweighted pair group method using arithmetic averages' (UPGMA) yields $d_{pk} = d_{kp} = (n_i d_{pi} + n_j d_{pj})/(n_i + n_j)$ with n_i and n_j as the number of data points in the clusters i and j, respectively, the 'single linkage clustering method' relies on the minimum distance $d_{pk} = d_{kp} = \min(d_{pi}, d_{pj})$, and the 'complete linkage clustering method' on the maximum distance $d_{pk} = d_{kp} = \max(d_{pi}, d_{pj})$. For segmentation of a three-dimensional point cloud, the object detection and tracking method by Schmidt et al. (2007) described in Sect. 2.3.4 relies on the complete linkage clustering method.

2.3.1.3 Mean-Shift Clustering

The mean-shift clustering approach is a non-parametric clustering technique which estimates local density maxima of the data points. It is described in detail by Comaniciu and Meer (2002), who mention as precursors to their approach the works by Fukunaga and Hostetler (1975) and Cheng (1995). According to Comaniciu and Meer (2002), the mean-shift algorithm relies on a kernel-based estimation of the density gradient of the distribution of the N data points $\{\mathbf{x}_i\}_{i=1,\dots,N}$. The function $k(x)$ is termed the 'profile' of the kernel function. Several kernel functions are discussed by Cheng (1995). Comaniciu and Meer (2002) state that two important kernel profiles are the Epanechnikov kernel with $k_E(x) = 1 - x$ for $0 \leq x \leq 1$ and $k_E(x) = 0$ otherwise, and the normal kernel $k_N = \exp(-\frac{1}{2}x)$ with $x \geq 0$. The kernel function is assumed to be radially symmetric with $K(\mathbf{x}) = c_{k,d} \, k(\|\mathbf{x}\|^2)$, where d is the feature space dimension and $c_{k,d} > 0$ normalises the kernel function such that its integral over the complete feature space amounts to unity. To estimate the density gradient, Comaniciu and Meer (2002) define $g(x) = -dk(x)/dx$ as the profile of the kernel $G(\mathbf{x}) = c_{g,d} \, g(\|\mathbf{x}\|^2)$. The mean-shift algorithm is then initialised with the position $\mathbf{y}_0$ in the feature space, and the kernel width h needs to be given. The position in the feature space is then updated iteratively for $j > 0$ according to

$$\mathbf{y}_{j+1} = \frac{\sum_{i=1}^{N} \mathbf{x}_i g(\|\frac{\mathbf{y}_j - \mathbf{x}_i}{h}\|^2)}{\sum_{i=1}^{N} g(\|\frac{\mathbf{y}_j - \mathbf{x}_i}{h}\|^2)}. \tag{2.32}$$

Comaniciu and Meer (2002) show that $\mathbf{y}_j$ converges towards a local maximum of the point density as long as the profile $k(x)$ of the kernel $K(\mathbf{x})$ is convex and decreases monotonically with increasing values of x.

2.3.1.4 Graph Cut and Spectral Clustering

A more recent approach to the clustering problem is the normalised graph cuts method introduced by Shi and Malik (1997, 1998, 2000), which is closely related to the method of spectral clustering (Fowlkes et al., 2004). In the context of image segmentation, Shi and Malik (2000) model the image in the form of a weighted undirected graph, where each node is assigned to a pixel while an edge of the graph is defined by a pair of pixels. The similarity between the pixel pair determines the weight of an edge. Removing the edges connecting the segments out of which the image consists leads to a segmentation of the image into disjoint sets. The optimal subdivision is the configuration with the minimal removed edge weights, which is termed the 'cut'. Hence, such techniques are also known as 'graph cut' methods. They have become fairly popular in the domain of image segmentation.

Fowlkes et al. (2004) assume that a number of N image pixels is given by their previously determined properties such as position, grey value, texture, or depth. The basis of spectral clustering is the $N \times N$ symmetric similarity matrix W of the graph. The set of nodes is denoted by V. When a bipartition of V is given by A and B with $A \cup B = V$ and $A \cap B = 0$, the 'cut' is defined by

$$\text{cut}(A, B) = \sum_{i \in A} \sum_{j \in B} W_{ij}. \tag{2.33}$$

The degree d_i of node i corresponds to $d_i = \sum_j W_{ij}$, and the volumes of A and B are given by $\text{vol}(A) = \sum_{i \in A} d_i$ and $\text{vol}(A) = \sum_{i \in B} d_i$. The 'normalised cut' is then defined according to

$$\text{ncut}(A, B) = \frac{2 \, \text{cut}(A, B)}{\text{vol}(A) \| \text{vol}(B)} \tag{2.34}$$

with the harmonic mean $a \| b = 2ab/(a + b)$. At this point it is desired to determine the graph bipartition which minimises the value of $\text{ncut}(A, B)$. A solution of this complex optimisation problem based on an eigenvalue decomposition of the Laplacian matrix $\mathcal{L} = D^{-1/2}(D - W)D^{-1/2}$ with the diagonal matrix D containing the values d_i as diagonal elements is proposed by Shi and Malik (2000). Fowlkes et al. (2004) extend the clustering framework towards more than two groups. The computational effort of the graph cut approach may become considerable, as it increases quadratically with the number of pixels. Hence, Fowlkes et al. (2004) suggest that one utilise the Nyström method to obtain an approximate solution of the eigensystem.

2.3.1.5   The ICP Algorithm

A method to register a point cloud to a geometric object model is the iterative closest point (ICP) algorithm introduced by Besl and McKay (1992). Given an initial estimate of the object pose, the pose parameters are updated by minimising the mean squared distance between the measured data and the model, and a new assignment of measured points to model points is performed. This procedure is applied in an iterative manner. As a result, the algorithm yields the three-dimensional object pose. Besl and McKay (1992) apply this method to point clouds, parametric and non-parametric curves, and to parametric, non-parametric, and triangulated (tessellated) surfaces. In the ICP algorithm proposed by Zhang (1992), the scene points as well as the object model are represented as connected ('chained') points. During each iteration step the pose parameters are updated while at the same time some of the scene points are assigned to the model, based on the distance to the model and the similarity between the directions between neighbouring points for the data and the model curve, such that outliers in the data are not taken into account for matching. The ICP algorithm yields those measured points that can be assigned to the model, i.e. a scene segmentation, along with the pose parameters.

2.3.1.6 Photogrammetric Approaches

In the domain of photogrammetry, an important application which requires the segmentation of three-dimensional point clouds is the three-dimensional reconstruction of buildings, mainly from airborne or terrestrial laser scanner data. Rottensteiner (2006) states that polyhedral models are appropriate for modelling buildings on spatial scales at which topographic mapping is performed, where symmetry constraints or a priori knowledge, e.g. about the orthogonality of walls or the orientation of parts of the building, can be exploited. Rottensteiner (2006) defines one group of common approaches to building extraction as bottom-up methods, where the geometric primitives of the building are constructed from the measured three-dimensional point cloud and are then used to build up a model of the building. This approach is used by Rottensteiner et al. (2005) to determine the roof planes of buildings in three-dimensional point clouds acquired by a laser scanner based on statistical considerations. The second basic class of methods discussed by Rottensteiner (2006) is top-down reconstruction, where given geometric primitives are adapted to parts of the three-dimensional point cloud. A priori knowledge can either be incorporated by 'hard constraints', which are always exactly satisfied by the inferred model, or by 'soft constraints', which allow a residual deviation of the adapted model from the three-dimensional point cloud data.

2.3.2 Mean-Shift Tracking of Human Body Parts

This section describes the mean-shift-based approach of Hahn et al. (2010b) to tracking human body parts, which extracts all moving objects or object parts from the scene based on a simple ellipsoid model. The presentation in this section is adopted from that work. Further details are provided by Hahn (2011).

2.3.2.1 Clustering and Object Detection

Object detection and three-dimensional tracking are based on a scene flow field. We use a combination of dense optical flow and sparse correlation-based stereo. The dense optical flow algorithm described by Wedel et al. (2008a, 2008b) is used to

Fig. 2.14 Reprojected sparse scene flow field

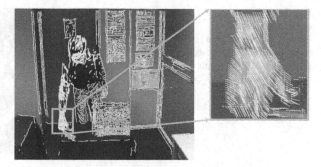

Fig. 2.15 *Left*: Ellipsoid model used for tracking arbitrary objects or object parts in the three-dimensional point cloud.
Right: Reprojection of four tracked objects

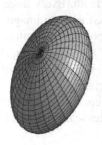

determine the object motion in the image sequence. The optical flow field is combined with the three-dimensional points from the blockmatching stereo algorithm by Franke and Joos (2000) to obtain the scene flow field (cf. Fig. 2.14). The velocity component parallel to the depth axis is not computed.

At each time step, a graph-based clustering stage extracts all moving objects from the scene flow field, essentially separating moving objects from the (stationary or differently moving) background. The computed clusters are approximated as ellipsoids, and the three-dimensional ellipsoid pose $\mathbf{T} = (c_x, c_y, c_z, \beta)^T$ is determined (cf. Fig. 2.15). Only the centre $\mathbf{c} = (c_x, c_y, c_z)^T$ of the ellipsoid and the rotation angle β around the depth axis are part of the pose vector $\mathbf{T}$, since we assume that the approximated objects are parallel to the image plane. The three-dimensional pose update of all tracked objects is based on a two-stage three-dimensional extension of the mean-shift algorithm according to Cheng (1995), Comaniciu et al. (2000). If a tracked object is not moving for more than five time steps it is deleted.

2.3.2.2 Target Model

The target model $\widehat{\mathbf{q}}_{(id)}$ with the object index id is computed based on the first three-dimensional ellipsoid pose $\mathbf{T}^{(id)}$ and is updated at every time step. It consists of a one-dimensional histogram of greyscale values. To compute the histogram $\widehat{\mathbf{q}}_{(id)}$ we place a grid on the surface of the ellipsoid, the resolution of which is equal

Fig. 2.16 Two-stage
mean-shift procedure.
Projected search region (*left*),
three-dimensional probability
grid (*middle*), final result
(*right*)

to the pixel resolution at the current depth. Every three-dimensional point on the
surface grid of the ellipsoid is projected into the images of all three cameras. The
histogram bin of a three-dimensional point $\mathbf{p}$ is obtained with the look-up function
$iBin(\mathbf{p}) = \frac{1}{3}(I_{uv}^{C_1} + I_{uv}^{C_2} + I_{uv}^{C_3})$, where $I_{uv}^{C_c}$ is the greyscale value in the image from
camera c at the projected position (u, v) of the three-dimensional point $\mathbf{p}$. Using
all three-dimensional points on the surface grid of the ellipsoid, a one-dimensional
histogram of the object appearance is computed. A normalisation of the histogram
yields the relative frequency of each greyscale value on the ellipsoid surface, which
is interpreted as a probability.

2.3.2.3 Image-Based Mean-Shift

In the first stage, the mean-shift procedure is applied to a search region, a three-
dimensional plane parallel to the image plane centred at the last object position.
Similar to the method of Bradski (1998) in two dimensions, the target model $\widehat{\mathbf{q}}_{(id)}$
is used as a look-up table to compute the probability value for all three-dimensional
points in the search region. The look-up function $iBin$ is used to obtain a probability
value for each three-dimensional point on the grid. Figure 2.16 (left) depicts the
projected search region in the image of one camera and Fig. 2.16 (middle) shows
the inferred three-dimensional probability grid. The three-dimensional centre point
$\widetilde{\mathbf{c}}$ is estimated with the mean-shift procedure using a geometric ellipse model. The
ellipse orientation β is computed similarly as in Bradski (1998). This mean-shift
stage allows only for an update of the lateral pose of the tracked ellipsoid, since the
probability grid is parallel to the image plane. No information from the scene flow
field is used; thus a pose update of the ellipsoid is computed even if there is no new
three-dimensional information available.

2.3.2.4 Point Cloud-Based Mean-Shift

In this stage all moving three-dimensional points of the scene flow field are used
to update the three-dimensional pose of the tracked ellipsoid. At the first iteration
$j = 1$ of the mean-shift procedure, the ellipsoid centre $\mathbf{c}_{j=1}$ is initialised with the

estimated three-dimensional centre point $\tilde{c}$ of the image-based mean-shift stage. For all subsequent iterations, the ellipsoid model is moved to the new position

$$
\mathbf{c}_{j+1} = \frac{\sum_{n=1}^{N} \mathbf{s}_n \cdot g(\mathbf{s}_n, \mathbf{c}_j) \cdot \widehat{\mathbf{q}}_{(id)}(iBin(\mathbf{s}_n))}{\sum_{n=1}^{N} g(\mathbf{s}_n, \mathbf{c}_j) \cdot \widehat{\mathbf{q}}_{(id)}(iBin(\mathbf{s}_n))},
\tag{2.35}
$$

where $\mathbf{c}_j$ is the previous centre position. In the mean-shift procedure a truncated Gaussian kernel $g(\mathbf{s}_n, \mathbf{c}_j)$ is used according to Cheng (1995), for which the weight decreases with increasing distance from the ellipsoid centre $\mathbf{c}_j$. The mean-shift-based three-dimensional tracking approach incorporates an appearance weighting $\widehat{\mathbf{q}}_{(id)}(iBin(\mathbf{s}_n))$ obtained by looking up the appearance probability of the moving three-dimensional point $\mathbf{s}_n$ in the target model $\widehat{\mathbf{q}}_{(id)}$, such that a three-dimensional point with an appearance similar to the target appearance is assigned a higher weight. Figure 2.16 (right) depicts all moving three-dimensional points and the final result of the two-stage mean-shift procedure for three-dimensional tracking.

2.3.3 Segmentation and Spatio-Temporal Pose Estimation

The problem of three-dimensional scene segmentation along with the detection and pose estimation of articulated objects has been addressed primarily in the context of human motion capture (cf. Sect. 2.2.1.2 for an overview). A technique for model-based three-dimensional human body tracking based on the ICP algorithm is presented by Knoop et al. (2005). Normal optical flow is used by Duric et al. (2002) for positional short-term prediction in an image-based system for the detection and tracking of human body parts. The motion of a camera through a scene is estimated by Gonçalves and Araújo (2002) based on a combined analysis of stereo correspondences and optical flow.

This section describes a vision system for model-based three-dimensional detection and spatio-temporal pose estimation of objects in cluttered scenes proposed by Barrois and Wöhler (2008). The presentation is adopted from that work. Further details are provided by Barrois (2010). As low-level features, this approach requires a cloud of three-dimensional points attributed with information about their motion and the direction of the local intensity gradient. These features are extracted by space-time stereo based on local image intensity modelling according to Sect. 1.5.2.5. After applying a graph-based clustering approach to obtain an initial separation between the background and the object, a three-dimensional model is adapted to the point cloud based on an ICP-like optimisation technique, yielding the translational, rotational, and internal degrees of freedom of the object. An extended constraint line approach is introduced which allows one to estimate the temporal derivatives of the translational and rotational pose parameters directly from the low-level motion information provided by the spacetime stereo data.

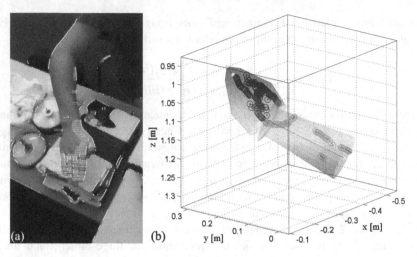

Fig. 2.17 (**a**) Image from a test sequence. Interest pixels for which stereo correspondences are established are shown as *bright dots*. Epipolar velocities are indicated as *white lines*. (**b**) Three-dimensional model adapted to the point cloud

2.3.3.1 Scene Clustering and Model-Based Pose Estimation

An initial segmentation of the attributed three-dimensional point cloud extracted with the spacetime stereo technique is obtained by means of a graph-based unsupervised clustering technique (Bock, 1974) in a four-dimensional space spanned by the spatial coordinates and the epipolar velocity of the three-dimensional points. This clustering stage generates a scene-dependent number of clusters, essentially separating the moving object from the (stationary or differently moving) background. For the first image of a sequence, the approximate position and orientation of the object are estimated based on a principal component analysis of the corresponding cluster points and used as initial values for the model adaptation procedure. For the subsequent images, the initial pose parameters are inferred for the current time step from the previous spatio-temporal pose estimation result, as described later.

We follow the ICP approach according to Zhang (1992) in order to fit a three-dimensional model of the hand–forearm limb (which does not necessarily represent the object at high accuracy) to the three-dimensional points determined to belong to the moving foreground object by the preceding clustering stage. We utilise the hand–forearm model introduced in Sect. 2.2.1.2 (Hahn et al., 2007, 2010a), consisting of a kinematic chain connecting the two rigid elements forearm and hand. The model consists of five truncated cones and one complete cone (cf. Fig. 2.17b). The cone radii corresponding to the hand and the upper end of the forearm are both set to 60 mm, and the lengths of the forearm and the hand are fixed to 220 mm and 180 mm, respectively. The other radii are inferred from human anatomy, as described in Sect. 2.2.1.2. For each of the two rotationally symmetric model parts, the five-dimensional vector **T** of translational and rotational pose parameters is determined. The relative orientation between forearm and hand is described by two an-

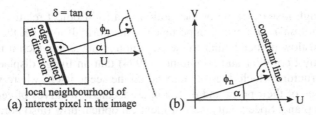

Fig. 2.18 (a) Relation between edge direction δ and normal velocity ϕ_n. (b) Definition of the constraint line in UV space according to Schunck (1989), representing the configurations (U, V) which are consistent with the observed normal velocity ϕ_n

gles, which are included in the model as internal degrees of freedom. In the course of the adaptation process, three-dimensional points not previously determined to belong to the object may be added to it while others may be rejected, resulting in a robust behaviour with respect to errors of the preceding clustering stage. The optimisation procedure is implemented as an M-estimator (Rey, 1983). It is straightforward to utilise the result of this three-dimensional pose estimation procedure as an initialisation for the appearance-based MOCCD technique described in Sect. 2.2.1.2.

2.3.3.2 Estimation of the Temporal Pose Derivatives

Both motion components of a scene point parallel to the image plane can only be recovered from the corresponding local pixel neighbourhood if the intensity pattern around the pixel is corner-like. Edge-like intensity patterns only allow the determination of one velocity component, such as the component parallel to the epipolar lines computed by the spacetime stereo algorithm (cf. Sect. 1.5.2.5). This ambiguity is a consequence of the well-known aperture problem (Horn, 1986). Restricting the stereo and motion analysis to corner-like image features (Franke et al., 2005) may result in fairly sparse depth maps. If edge-like image features are evaluated, as is the case in all image sequences regarded in this study, projecting the determined velocity component onto a line orthogonal to the local edge direction yields the normal velocity ϕ_n, as depicted in Fig. 2.18a. The angle α between the direction of the horizontal epipolar lines and the direction of the normal velocity is given by $\delta = \tan \alpha$ with δ as defined by (1.121) in Sect. 1.5.2.5.

In the following, the translational velocity components of the object parallel to the x, y, and z axes are denoted by U_{obj}, V_{obj}, and W_{obj}, respectively, and expressed in metres per second. A two-dimensional space is spanned by the horizontal and vertical velocity components U and V measured in the scene and expressed in metres per second. This space is termed UV space. Given the observed normal velocity ϕ_n, all consistent configurations (U, V) are represented by the corresponding constraint line in UV space as defined by Schunck (1989) (cf. Fig. 2.18b). Fermüller and Aloimonos (1994) extend the concept of constraint lines towards the analysis of 'image displacement fields', i.e. optical flow and disparity, that arise from the motion of a camera through a static scene or the motion of a rigid object relative to the camera ('rigid motion'). Of special importance is the normal flow, i.e. the component of the optical flow perpendicular to the edge in the image at which it is measured. It is shown by Fermüller and Aloimonos (1994) that an image displacement field displays a structure which does not depend on the scene itself, where vectors with specific values of their norm and direction are located on curves of certain shapes in the image plane. Specifically, sets of identical optical flow (also normal flow) or disparity vectors correspond to conic curves, termed 'iso-motion contours' by Fermüller and Aloimonos (1994). The properties of these curves only depend on the parameters of the three-dimensional rigid motion.

In the spatio-temporal pose estimation scenario regarded in this section, for an object performing a purely translational motion parallel to the image plane all constraint lines belonging to pixels on the object intersect in a single point in UV space. Both components of the translational motion are thus uniquely recovered. For objects with a rotational motion component in the image plane, a case which is not addressed by Schunck (1989), the intersection points between constraint lines are distributed across an extended region in UV space. This situation is illustrated in Fig. 2.19a for an ellipse rotating counterclockwise. The constraint lines belonging to the indicated contour points are shown in Fig. 2.19b. In this example, the U coordinates of the constraint line intersection points are a measure for the mean horizontal velocities of the corresponding pairs of image points. The V coordinates have no such physical meaning. The distribution of intersection points is elongated in vertical direction due to the fact that a vertical edge detector is used for interest pixel extraction and because only image points with associated values of $|\delta| < \delta_{\max}$ with $\delta_{\max}$ typically chosen between 1 and 2 (cf. Sect. 7.3) are selected by the space-time stereo approach. Hence, constraint lines running at small angles to the U axis do not exist.

Figure 2.19c shows a distribution of constraint line intersection points obtained from the scene shown in Fig. 2.17a, typical of a rotationally symmetric and elongated object like the forearm partial model used in this study. The points in UV space are weighted according to the spatial density of the corresponding three-dimensional points along the longitudinal object axis. The mean $(U_{\mathrm{obj}}, V_{\mathrm{obj}})$ of the intersection point distribution, corresponding to the translational motion component of the object, has already been subtracted from the intersection points in Fig. 2.19c. The translational motion component W_{obj} parallel to the z axis is given by the median of the (fairly noisy) values of $\partial z / \partial t$ for all three-dimensional points assigned to the object or object part.

In the example regarded in Fig. 2.19c, scene points near the wrist are moving faster in the image plane than scene points near the elbow. The resulting intersection points are strongly concentrated near the points (U_1, V_1) and (U_2, V_2) depicted in Fig. 2.19c, which represent the motion of the scene points near the elbow and near the wrist. In this scenario, two circular markers attached to the upper and the lower end of the forearm, respectively, would yield two narrow clusters of intersection points in UV space at (U_1, V_1) and (U_2, V_2). Regarding scene points at arbitrary positions on the forearm instead of well-localised markers yields a distribution which is largely symmetric with respect to the line connecting the points

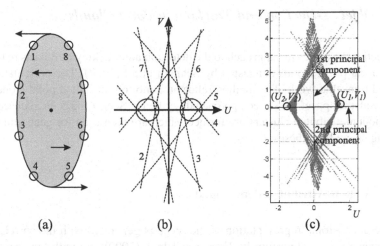

Fig. 2.19 (**a**) Rotating ellipse with *reference points* marked on its boundary. (**b**) Constraint lines resulting from the rotation of the ellipse. (**c**) Typical distribution of constraint *line intersections* in UV space for a real-world image from the first test sequence (cf. Fig. 2.17). The mean of the distribution has been subtracted from all points; the principal components are drawn as *solid black lines*

(U_1, V_1) and (U_2, V_2). The information about the rotational motion of the object is thus contained in the range Δv covered by the projections of the intersection points on the principal component of the distribution which is oriented perpendicular to the longitudinal axis of the object (the second principal component in Fig. 2.19c). The value of Δv then corresponds to the velocity dispersion across the object caused by rotational motion in the image plane. In our system, we robustly estimate Δv based on the 10 % and 90 % quantiles of the distribution of the projection values. The angular velocity ω_p of the object rotation parallel to the image plane is then obtained by $\omega_p = \Delta v / \Delta l$ with Δl as the length interval parallel to the longitudinal object axis covered by the assigned three-dimensional points.

The rotation orthogonal to the image plane is determined based on the values of $\partial z / \partial t$ determined in Sect. 1.5.2.5 for the extracted three-dimensional points. For each model part, the projections $p^{(i)}$ of the assigned three-dimensional points on the longitudinal object axis are computed, and a regression line is fitted to the $(p^{(i)}, \partial z / \partial t^{(i)})$ data points. The slope of the regression line directly yields the velocity dispersion Δw in the z direction and thus the angular velocity ω_o of the object rotation orthogonal to the image plane. Due to the rotational symmetry of the object models regarded in this study, the rotational motion of the object is already fully determined by the two components ω_p and ω_o of the angular velocity.

The technique described in this section allows us to extend the determination of the vector $\mathbf{T}$ of pose parameters by a direct estimation of the temporal pose derivative $\dot{\mathbf{T}}$ without the need for an object tracking stage.

2.3.4 Object Detection and Tracking in Point Clouds

This section describes the approach to the detection and tracking of objects in three-dimensional point clouds suggested by Schmidt et al. (2007). The presentation is adopted from that work. The method relies on a motion-attributed point cloud obtained with the spacetime stereo approach described in Sect. 1.5.2.5. In a subsequent step, motion-attributed clusters are formed which are then used for generating and tracking object hypotheses.

2.3.4.1 Motion-Attributed Point Cloud

A three-dimensional representation of the scene is generated with the correlation-based stereo vision algorithm by Franke and Joos (2000) and with the spacetime stereo algorithm described by Schmidt et al. (2007) (cf. Sect. 1.5.2.5). Both stereo techniques generate three-dimensional points based on edges in the image, especially object boundaries. Due to the local approach they are independent of the object appearance. While correlation-based stereo has the advantage of higher spatial accuracy and is capable of generating more point correspondences, spacetime stereo provides a velocity value for each stereo point. However, it generates a smaller number of points and is spatially less accurate, since not all edges are necessarily well described by the model defined in (1.118). Taking into account these properties of the algorithms, the results are merged into a single motion-attributed three-dimensional point cloud. For each extracted three-dimensional point c_k an average velocity $\bar{v}(c_k)$ is calculated, using all spacetime points s_j, $j \in (1, \ldots, J)$ in an ellipsoid neighbourhood defined by $\delta_S(s_j, c_k) < 1$ around c_k. To take into account the spatial uncertainty in depth direction of the spacetime data, $\delta_S(s_j, c_k)$ defines a Mahalanobis distance whose correlation matrix Σ contains an entry $\Sigma_z \neq 1$ for the depth coordinate which can be derived from the recorded data, leading to

$$\bar{v}(c_k) = \frac{\rho}{J} \sum_{j=1}^{J} v(s_j) \quad \forall s_j : \delta_S(s_j, c_k) < 1. \tag{2.36}$$

The factor ρ denotes the relative scaling of the velocities with respect to the spatial coordinates. It is adapted empirically depending on the speed of the observed objects. This results in a four-dimensional point cloud, where each three-dimensional point is attributed with an additional one-dimensional velocity component parallel to the epipolar lines; see Fig. 2.20d.

A reference image of the observed scene is used to reduce the amount of data to be processed by masking out three-dimensional points that emerge from static parts of the scene, as shown in Figs. 2.20a and b. Furthermore, only points within a given interval above the ground plane are used, as we intend to localise objects and humans and thus always assume a maximum height for objects above the ground.

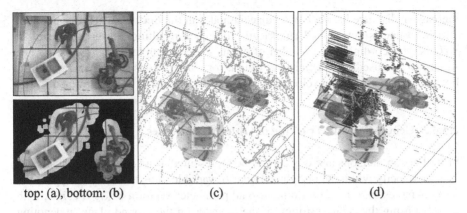

top: (a), bottom: (b)   (c)   (d)

Fig. 2.20 (**a**) Original image (*left camera*). (**b**) Background subtracted image. (**c**) Full point cloud obtained with the correlation-based stereo vision technique. (**d**) Reduced motion-attributed point cloud

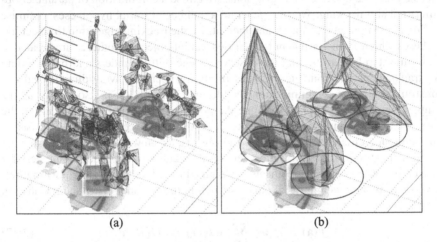

(a)   (b)

Fig. 2.21 (**a**) Over-segmentation and cluster velocities. (**b**) Objects with convex hull

2.3.4.2 Over-Segmentation for Motion-Attributed Clusters

To simplify the scene representation, we apply a hierarchical clustering algorithm, recognising small contiguous regions in the cloud, based on features like spatial proximity or homogeneity of the velocities. This procedure deliberately over-segments the scene, generating motion-attributed clusters. By incorporating velocity information for clustering, we expect an improvement in segmentation at these early stages of the algorithm, without the need for strong models to ensure separation of neighbouring objects. For clustering, we apply the complete linkage algorithm to describe the distance between two clusters. The resulting hierarchical tree is partitioned by selecting a clustering threshold and addressing each subtree as an individual cluster (cf. Fig. 2.21a). The criterion for selecting the threshold is the increase in distance between two adjacent nodes in the tree, for which a maximum allowed value is determined empirically. For each resulting cluster l, the weight $w(l)$ is set according to the number of points P belonging to l as $w(l) = \sqrt{P}$. The square root is used to constrain the weight for clusters consisting of many points. For each cluster the mean velocity of all points belonging to it is determined.

2.3.4.3 Generation and Tracking of Object Hypotheses

From here on, persons and objects can be represented as a collection of clusters of similar velocity within an upright cylinder of variable radius. An object hypothesis $R(a)$ is represented by a four-dimensional parameter vector $\mathbf{a} = (x, y, v, r)^T$, with x and y being the centre position of the cylinder on the ground plane, v denoting the velocity of the object, and r the radius. This weak model is suitable for persons and most encountered objects.

To extract the correct object positions, we utilise a combination of parameter optimisation and tracking. We first generate a number of initial hypotheses, optimise the location in parameter space, and then utilise the tracking algorithm to select hypotheses which form consistent trajectories. Initial object hypotheses are created at each time step by partitioning the observed scene with cylinders and by including the tracking results from the previous frame, respectively. Multidimensional unconstrained nonlinear minimisation (Nelder and Mead, 1965), also known as the simplex algorithm, is applied to refine the position and size of the cylinders in the scene, so that as many neighbouring clusters with similar velocity values as possible can be grouped together to form compact objects, as shown in Fig. 2.21b. An error function $f(\mathbf{a})$ used for optimisation denotes the quality of the grouping process for a given hypothesis. Each hypothesis is weighted based on the relative position, relative velocity, and weight of all clusters l within the cylinder $R(\mathbf{a})$ using Gaussian kernels according to

$$f(\mathbf{a}) = f_r(\mathbf{a}) \sum_{l \in R(\mathbf{a})} w(l) f_d(l, \mathbf{a}) f_v(l, \mathbf{a}) \tag{2.37}$$

with $f_r(\mathbf{a}) = \exp(-\frac{r(\mathbf{a})^2}{2H_{r,\min}^2}) - \exp(-\frac{r(\mathbf{a})^2}{2H_{r,\max}^2})$ keeping the radius in a realistic range, $f_d(l) = \exp(-\frac{[s(l)-s(\mathbf{a})]^2}{2H_d^2})$ reducing the importance of clusters far away from the cylinder centre, and $f_v(l, \mathbf{a}) = \exp(-\frac{[v(l)-v(\mathbf{a})]^2}{2H_v^2})$ masking out clusters having differing velocities. The functions $r(\mathbf{a})$, $s(\mathbf{a})$, and $v(\mathbf{a})$ extract the radius, the two-dimensional position on the ground plane, and the velocity of the hypothesis $\mathbf{a}$, respectively. The kernel widths H are determined empirically. Figure 2.22 shows the error function from (2.37), parameterised for opposing velocities. Local minima are centred on top of the objects of interest.

After optimisation, hypotheses with identical parameterisation are merged and those without any clusters within $R(\mathbf{a})$ are removed. The remaining hypotheses are tracked over time using a particle filter, keeping only object hypotheses forming a

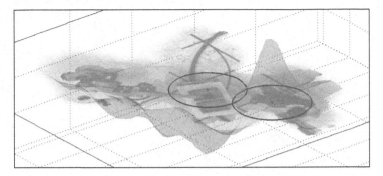

Fig. 2.22 Error function plot for minimisation, showing the error surface for $v = 0.26$ m s^{-1}, $r = 0.53$ m (*lower surface*), and $v = -0.79$ m s^{-1}, $r = 0.53$ m (*upper surface*, values mirrored for clearer display)

Fig. 2.23 Trajectory of the tracked object (*dark grey*) with annotated ground truth (*light grey*) for a tabletop sequence

consistent trajectory. The trajectory of a moving object in a fairly simple tabletop sequence as determined with the proposed algorithm is shown in Fig. 2.23 in comparison with the manually determined ground truth. This example demonstrates that a moving object can be separated from stationary background objects. In Sect. 7.2 we provide a detailed quantitative evaluation of our method in a complex industrial production scenario.

Chapter 3
Intensity-Based and Polarisation-Based Approaches to Three-Dimensional Scene Reconstruction

In contrast to triangulation-based methods, intensity-based approaches to three-dimensional scene reconstruction (also termed 'photometric methods' by d'Angelo and Wöhler, 2008), exploit the pixel grey values in the image to recover the shape of a surface or an object. Shadows in multiple images of a surface acquired under different illumination conditions may contain a significant amount of information about the surface shape (shape from shadow, cf. Sect. 3.1). The pixel grey values can be used to determine the position-dependent surface orientation, which by integration yields a depth map of the surface (shape from shading, cf. Sect. 3.2). Making use of the intensity information contained in multiple images leads to the photometric stereo approach described in Sect. 3.3. Utilising polarisation information of the reflected light instead of its intensity under certain circumstances allows a more accurate determination of surface orientation (shape from polarisation, Sect. 3.4).

3.1 Shape from Shadow

A shadow in the image of a surface contains information about the depth difference on the surface between the starting point of the shadow, e.g. the summit of a mountain, and its end point situated downslope and corresponding to the shadow tip, given that the direction of incident light is known. Determination of a height difference Δz by determination of the shadow length l relies on the relation

$$\Delta z = l \tan \mu, \tag{3.1}$$

where μ is the elevation angle of the light source and l has to be measured along the azimuthal direction of the incident light. Here, the geometric information l is extracted by regarding photometric information, in this case the absence of light in certain parts of the image of the surface. Hence, shadow information can commonly be obtained from an image by a thresholding operation.

C. Wöhler, *3D Computer Vision*, X.media.publishing,
DOI 10.1007/978-1-4471-4150-1_3, © Springer-Verlag London 2013

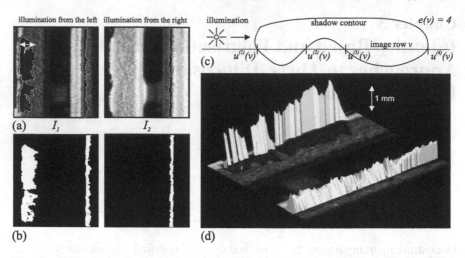

Fig. 3.1 (**a**) Side view of an industrial part (friction plate) displaying two ridges due to technical failure. The ridges are perpendicular to the surface such that they do not appear in the perpendicular (*top*) view, as is the case here. Their shadows on the surface, however, can be clearly distinguished (*dashed contour lines*). (**b**) Binarised ratio images. (**c**) Analysis of the shadow contour. (**d**) Three-dimensional reconstruction of the ridges based on their shadows

3.1.1 Extraction of Shadows from Image Pairs

This section describes a contour-based method for the extraction of shadows from image pairs at subpixel accuracy and the subsequent reconstruction of small-scale surface features. The presentation is adopted from Hafezi and Wöhler (2004). Two images are required which show the same surface region illuminated from oppo-site directions, respectively, and under oblique illumination. Pixels with identical coordinates in these two images must correspond to the same physical points on the surface. Possible ways to achieve this are to move neither the camera nor the object to be reconstructed during image acquisition, or to apply image registration techniques (Gottesfeld Brown, 1992). However, the same approach can be used to extract shadow regions from single images. This section describes how shadow re-gions can be determined from images at subpixel accuracy. Without loss of general-ity, it will always be assumed that the scene is illuminated exactly from the left-hand or the right-hand side.

Figure 3.1a shows two images of the same part of the lateral surface of a friction plate. The scene is illuminated from the left-hand side and from the right-hand side (images I_1 and I_2, respectively). As neither the part nor the camera is moved, no im-age registration step is necessary. In the ratio images I_1/I_2 and I_2/I_1, the shadows cast by the respective light source appear as bright regions, as shown in Fig. 3.1b. This approach has the advantage of being insensitive to albedo variations of the sur-face, because regions of low albedo that might be erroneously taken for shadows appear dark in both images, thus producing no bright region in one of the ratio im-ages. A disadvantage is that surface parts situated in a shadow in both images are discarded—the illumination conditions should therefore be chosen such that this situation does not occur. The bright regions in the ratio images are segmented and analysed using the binary connected component (BCC) analysis algorithm (Mandler and Oberländer, 1990) which yields—among other information—the properties area, centre coordinates, and a pixel contour description for each segmented region. This computation yields n_1 regions in the first and n_2 regions in the second image. The extracted contours are smoothed by B-spline interpolation (Rogers, 2001). Without loss of generality, it is assumed that the scene is illuminated along the image rows. We thus calculate the u (column) coordinates at which the interpolated contour intersects the rows in the v (row) range covered by the corresponding B-spline in order to obtain subpixel accuracy (cf. Sect. 1.5.2.2). Optionally, the B-spline contours can be used as an initialisation to active contour techniques such as the one introduced by Williams and Shah (1992) for further refinement. The contours are represented as sets $\{\mathbf{c}_{1,a}^{(m)}\}$ and $\{\mathbf{c}_{2,b}^{(n)}\}$ of points for the first and the second image, respectively:

$$\mathbf{c}_{1,a}^{(m)} = \left(\hat{u}_{1,a}^{(m)}, \hat{v}_{1,a}^{(m)}\right), \quad a = 1, \ldots, n_1 \tag{3.2}$$

$$\mathbf{c}_{2,b}^{(n)} = \left(\hat{u}_{2,b}^{(n)}, \hat{v}_{2,b}^{(n)}\right), \quad b = 1, \ldots, n_2 \tag{3.3}$$

where a and b are the region indices in the images and m and n the point indices in the respective contours. The values $\hat{u}_{1,a}^{(m)}$ and $\hat{u}_{2,b}^{(n)}$ are real numbers, while the values $\hat{v}_{1,a}^{(m)}$ and $\hat{v}_{2,b}^{(n)}$ denote image rows and therefore are integer numbers.

For each image row v in the range covered by a contour, the number of intersections between the contour and the image row is calculated. These intersection counts are denoted by $e(v)$. Along with these values, the u coordinates of the intersections $u^{(i)}(v)$ with $i = 1, \ldots, e(v)$ are determined. They are known at subpixel accuracy due to the B-spline representation of the contours. For each image row v, the intersections are sorted in ascending order according to their respective $u^{(i)}(v)$ values (Fig. 3.1c). For extraction of ridges of surface features, image rows v with an odd number $e(v)$ of intersections are discarded. For the shadows in image 1 with illumination from the left-hand side, intersections $u^{(i)}(v)$ with even indices i are points at which a shadow ends, while intersections $u^{(i)}(v)$ with odd indices i are ridges that cast a shadow (Fig. 3.1c). The situation is just the inverse in image 2 illuminated from the right-hand side. Hence, the shadow lengths for image row v are

$$l^{(j)}(v) = \left| u^{(j)}(v) - u^{(j-1)}(v) \right| \quad \text{with } j \text{ even.} \tag{3.4}$$

Given the elevation angle μ of the light source with respect to the ground plane, the shadow length $l^{(j)}(v)$ yields information about the difference in depth (in the following denoted by z) at the corresponding pixel positions:

$$(\Delta z)_{\text{shadow}} = \left| z\left(u^{(j)}(v), v\right) - z\left(u^{(j-1)}(v), v\right) \right| = l^{(j)}(v) \tan \mu \quad \text{with } j \text{ even.} \tag{3.5}$$

The sign of the depth difference in (3.5) depends on whether the scene is illuminated from the right-hand or the left-hand side. It is assumed that the incident light is parallel and that the elevation angle μ of the light source with respect to the ground plane is known. For geometrical reasons an 'aperture problem' occurs, since structures that run parallel to the direction of incident light cannot be evaluated.

To extract the bottom of a surface feature, we make use of the fact that a surface region with a slope towards the light source appears brighter than a flat surface region. We thus segment and analyse with the BCC analysis algorithm all regions from image I_1 (I_2) which are brighter than a given threshold θ_1 (θ_2) and which are illuminated in one image while unlighted in the other. For the pixels of these regions, the relations $I_1 > \theta_1$ ($I_2 > \theta_2$) and $I_1/I_2 > \theta_0$ ($I_2/I_1 > \theta_0$) must hold, respectively. The contour lines of these image regions are obtained by BCC analysis and are used as an initialisation to the active contour algorithm described by Williams and Shah (1992), which then adapts them more accurately to the outline of the bottom of the surface feature.

The ridges and bottoms in the two images are merged based on the mutual distance of their centres, measured in pixel coordinates in image I_1 and I_2, respectively, to form complete surface features. As it is not always evident which object in image I_1 belongs to which object in image I_2, the algorithm is implemented such that it may suggest combinations based on their mutual distance that can either be accepted or rejected by the user. Figure 3.1d shows the result of three-dimensional reconstruction by shadow analysis.

3.1.2 Shadow-Based Surface Reconstruction from Dense Sets of Images

Kender and Smith (1987) analyse the shadows cast by a surface on itself to reconstruct its shape, where moving light sources and thus implicitly an infinite number of images acquired under different illumination conditions are assumed. The azimuthal direction of illumination is parallel to the image rows. The method regards the two-dimensional version of the shape from shadow problem; i.e. it reconstructs intersections of the surface with planes perpendicular to the xy plane, which are of the form $z(x)$. Several constraints for the depth values of shadowed and illuminated pixels are formulated. For the surface parts between the starting point x_i and the end point x_e of a shadow, the surface is located below the straight line through the points $z(x_i)$ and $z(x_e)$, while illuminated pixels must be located above that line. Kender and Smith (1987) show that the surface shape can be fully recovered when the shadows are observed for the continuous range of all possible illumination directions. Also for a finite number of observations, many images are necessary to obtain a good reconstruction accuracy. To extend the reconstruction to the full surface $z(x, y)$, Kender and Smith (1987) propose an iterative relaxation method.

Hatzitheodorou (1989) introduces a spline-based representation of the surface in order to reconstruct the three-dimensional surface shape from a set of images displaying shadows acquired under different illumination conditions. It is shown that the illumination angle yields information about the elevation difference between the starting point and the end point of a shadow and about the surface slope in the direction of incident light for the starting point of a shadow. Another constraint taken into account is (similar to Kender and Smith 1987) that the surface between the starting point and the end point of a shadow must be located below the connecting straight line. According to the experimental evaluation, the method of Hatzitheodorou (1989) does not require a continuously moving light source but is able to perform a three-dimensional surface reconstruction based on images in which the surface is illuminated under four to six different illumination angles in the horizontal and the vertical image direction, respectively.

The previously described shadow constraints are formulated as graphs by Yu and Chang (2002). They develop a formal framework to constrain the shape of a surface based on multiple images and show that the surface shape can be reconstructed based on the resulting shadow graph when the set of images acquired under different illumination conditions is infinitely large. To allow a three-dimensional surface reconstruction from a moderate but still considerable number of about 10 images, Yu and Chang (2002) propose a technique to integrate shadow and shading information, for which it is required that the images be illuminated from a large variety of known directions. For a small number of pixels, reasonably good initial depth values should be given, such that the shadow constraints allow one to infer depth bounds for all pixels. Depth values obtained by shape from shading are then made consistent with the bounds derived from shadow information based on a constrained optimisation procedure.

The shape from shadow approach is used in combination with silhouette information by Savarese et al. (2002) to estimate the three-dimensional shape of an object. They apply a technique termed space carving for an initial estimation of the three-dimensional shape of the object relying on a set of silhouette images acquired from different viewpoints. For a refinement of the shape of the object, a second set of images is required where point light sources are used for illumination. Based on the deviations between the self-shadows on the surface which would result from the initially estimated shape and those observed in the images, an adjustment of the object shape is performed to minimise the deviations from the image data. This combined method reveals the object shape much more accurately than shape from silhouettes alone, but it still requires many images to recover fine shape details.

The combination of shadow analysis with other three-dimensional surface reconstruction methods is described in Sect. 5.2.

3.2 Shape from Shading

This section describes methods for three-dimensional reconstruction of object surfaces which are based on the pixel grey values of a single image. Different surface reflectance models are introduced in Sect. 3.2.1. Many intensity-based methods rely on the determination of the surface gradients (cf. Sect. 3.2.2). Early approaches aiming for a reconstruction of height profiles along image rows (photoclinometry) emerged in the domain of remote sensing (Wilhelms, 1964) (cf. Sect. 3.2.2.1). Under certain assumptions about the surface it is also possible to determine a full height

Fig. 3.2 Definition of the surface normal **n**, the illumination direction **s**, the viewing direction **v**, the phase angle α, the polar angle θ_i and azimuth angle ϕ_i of incidence, and the polar angle θ_e and azimuth angle ϕ_e of emission. The vectors **n**, **s**, and **v** are generally not coplanar, such that $\alpha \leq \theta_i + \theta_e$

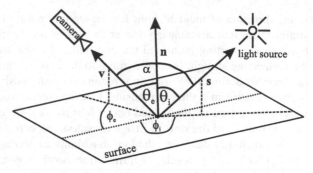

map of the surface visible in the image (cf. Sect. 3.2.2.2). This approach is termed shape from shading (Horn, 1986, 1989; Horn and Brooks, 1989). An overview of the variety of techniques to infer a height map from the determined surface gradients is provided in Sect. 3.2.3.

3.2.1 The Bidirectional Reflectance Distribution Function (BRDF)

Prior to the detailed description of intensity-based three-dimensional surface reconstruction methods we introduce the basic radiometric quantities. The light power incident on the apparent surface, measured in $W\,m^{-2}$, is termed irradiance. The light quantity emitted into a specific direction by a surface is measured in $W\,m^{-2}\,sr^{-1}$ and is termed radiance. The normalisation to unit solid angle is necessary due to the generally direction-dependent emission from the surface (Horn, 1986).

According to Horn (1986), the radiance received by the imaging device is dependent on both the viewing direction and the direction of the incident light. The illumination direction **s** is given by the 'zenith angle' or 'polar angle' θ_i and the 'azimuth angle' ϕ_i of incidence, while the direction **v** into which the reflected light is emitted is denoted by the zenith angle θ_e and the azimuth angle ϕ_e of emission (cf. Fig. 3.2). At this point, the 'bidirectional reflectance distribution function' (BRDF) $f(\theta_i, \phi_i, \theta_e, \phi_e)$ is introduced, which denotes the radiance L_{surf} of a surface viewed from the direction given by (θ_e, ϕ_e) divided by the irradiance E_{illum} due to illumination from the direction given by (θ_i, ϕ_i). Accordingly, the BRDF is defined as

$$f(\theta_i, \phi_i, \theta_e, \phi_e) = \frac{dL_{surf}(\theta_e, \phi_e)}{dE_{illum}(\theta_i, \phi_i)} = \frac{dL_{surf}(\theta_e, \phi_e)}{L_{illum}(\theta_i, \phi_i)\cos\theta_i d\Omega_i} \qquad (3.6)$$

(Nicodemus et al. 1977; Dorsey et al. 2008). In (3.6), $dL_{surf}(\theta_e, \phi_e)$ denotes the differential radiance as perceived by the detector $dE_{illum}(\theta_i, \phi_i) = L_{illum}\cos\theta_i d\Omega_i$ the differential irradiance received from the light source situated in the direction given by (θ_i, ϕ_i) (cf. Fig. 3.3), $L_{illum}(\theta_i, \phi_i)$ the radiance of the light source, and $d\Omega_i$ the differential solid angle under which the regarded surface element appears from the position of the light source (Nicodemus et al. 1977). Horn (1986) states (regarding the Lambertian case) that the factor $\cos\theta_i$ originates from geometrical

Fig. 3.3 Irradiance dE_{illum} due to illumination by a light source with radiance L_{illum} on a surface element covering a solid angle element $d\Omega_i$

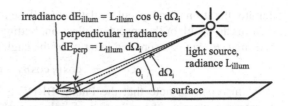

'foreshortening' and furthermore notes that for many surfaces the BRDF does not depend separately on the angles ϕ_i and ϕ_e but only on the difference $(\phi_e - \phi_i)$. This is true for diffusely and specularly reflecting surfaces but e.g. not for surfaces containing oriented microstructures. In the case of dependence of the BRDF on the difference $(\phi_e - \phi_i)$ it is often convenient to express the BRDF in terms of the incidence angle θ_i, the emission angle θ_e, and the 'phase angle' α between the direction $\mathbf{s}$ of incident light and the direction $\mathbf{v}$ into which the reflected light is emitted (Hapke, 1981) (cf. Fig. 3.2 and Sect. 3.2.2.1).

Horn (1986) points out that the amounts of radiation energy exchanged between two surfaces must always be identical in the state of thermal equilibrium. Otherwise, the surface temperatures would change, leading to a deviation from thermal equilibrium which would contradict the second law of thermodynamics. A physically meaningful BRDF must therefore fulfil the Helmholtz reciprocity condition:

$$f(\theta_i, \phi_i, \theta_e, \phi_e) = f(\theta_e, \phi_e, \theta_i, \phi_i). \tag{3.7}$$

In this context, an important special case is the ideal Lambertian surface, which appears equally bright from all directions while reflecting all incident light. For such a surface, the BRDF must be constant, i.e. independent of the angles θ_i, ϕ_i, θ_e, and ϕ_e. To determine the value of that constant, we follow the derivation outlined by Horn (1986). The integral of the radiance of the surface over all directions must be equal to the total irradiance, leading to

$$\int_{-\pi}^{\pi} \int_{0}^{\pi/2} f(\theta_i, \phi_i, \theta_e, \phi_e) E(\theta_i, \phi_i) \cos\theta_i \sin\theta_e \cos\theta_e \, d\theta_e \, d\phi_e = E \cos\theta_i. \tag{3.8}$$

By taking into account that $2\sin\theta_e \cos\theta_e = \sin 2\theta_e$, it follows that $\pi f = 1$ for an ideal Lambertian surface, corresponding to

$$f_{\text{Lambert}}(\theta_i, \phi_i, \theta_e, \phi_e) = \frac{1}{\pi}. \tag{3.9}$$

Hence, the radiance L is obtained from the irradiance E_0 by $L = E_0/\pi$.

A BRDF model which is widely used in the domain of computer graphics to represent smooth surfaces with a diffuse and a specular reflectance component is introduced by Phong (1975). The Phong BRDF is given by the weighted sum of a Lambertian BRDF component and a specular BRDF component according to

$$f_{\text{Phong}}^{\text{spec}}(\theta_i, \theta_r) = \sigma \frac{(\cos\theta_r)^m}{\cos\theta_i} \tag{3.10}$$

with θ_r as the angle between the viewing direction $\mathbf{v}$ and the direction into which an ideal mirror would reflect the incident light (Dorsey et al., 2008). The parameter σ

denotes the strength of specular relative to diffuse reflection, while the parameter m governs the width of the specular reflection. Setting $m \to \infty$ yields an ideal mirror. The angle θ_r can be expressed in terms of the angles θ_i, θ_e, and α by

$$\cos\theta_r = 2\cos\theta_i\cos\theta_e - \cos\alpha. \tag{3.11}$$

It is important to note that the Phong BRDF is not motivated by the physical processes governing the reflection of light at real surface materials. As a consequence, the Helmholtz reciprocity condition (3.7) is not fulfilled by the Phong model.

A physically motivated BRDF model for rough surfaces is introduced by Torrance and Sparrow (1967). It is described in the overview by Meister (2000) that for many rough surfaces the specular reflection component does not reach its peak exactly in the direction corresponding to $\theta_e = \theta_i$, as would be expected from an ideal mirror, but that the maximum occurs for higher values of the emission angle θ_e. Torrance and Sparrow (1967) assume that the surface is composed of a large number of microfacets which reflect the incident light in a mirror-like manner. According to Meister (2000), the corresponding BRDF is given by the weighted sum of a Lambertian component and a specular component f_{TS}^{spec} given by

$$f_{TS}^{spec}(\theta_i, \theta_e, \phi, n, k, w, \delta) = \frac{F(\theta_i, \theta_e, \phi, n, k)G(\theta_i, \theta_e, \phi)\exp(-w^2\delta^2)}{\cos\theta_i\cos\theta_e}. \tag{3.12}$$

In (3.12), the angle ϕ denotes the azimuth difference $(\phi_e - \phi_i)$ and δ the angle of the surface normal of the microfacet with respect to the macroscopic surface normal. The refraction index of the surface is assumed to be complex and amounts to $n + ik$ with k as the attenuation coefficient (cf. also Sect. 3.4.2). The expression $F(\theta_i, \theta_e, \phi, n, k)$ is the Fresnel reflectance (Hapke 1993) and $G(\theta_i, \theta_e, \phi) \in [0, 1]$ the 'geometrical attenuation factor', which takes into account shadows and occlusions. Meister (2000) points out that it is commonly possible to set $G(\theta_i, \theta_e, \phi) = 1$, and he gives the analytical expression

$$G(\theta_i, \theta_e, \phi) = \min\left(1, \frac{2\cos\delta\cos\theta_e}{\cos\theta_i'}, \frac{2\cos\delta\cos\theta_i}{\cos\theta_i'}\right) \tag{3.13}$$

as derived by Nayar et al. (1991) with θ_i' as the local illumination angle of the surface facet. It is furthermore stated that $\cos 2\theta_i' = \cos\theta_i\cos\theta_e - \sin\theta_i\sin\theta_e\cos\phi$. The model by Torrance and Sparrow (1967) that the orientations δ of the normals of the surface facets have a Gaussian distribution proportional to $\exp(-w^2\delta^2)$, where w denotes a width parameter. An analytical expression for δ as a function of θ_i, θ_e, and ϕ is given by Meister (2000).

Simple BRDF models like the Lambertian or the Phong BRDF are generally of limited accuracy when used in the context of three-dimensional surface reconstruction. However, sometimes determination of the parameters of physically motivated BRDFs such as the Torrance-Sparrow model is not possible or requires considerable experimental efforts. Hence, in the application scenario of industrial quality inspection described in detail in Chap. 6 (d'Angelo and Wöhler 2005a, 2005b, 2008;

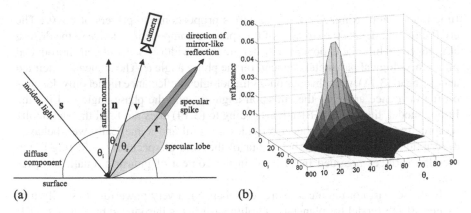

Fig. 3.4 (**a**) Sketch of the three reflectance components according to Nayar et al. (1991) (but without off-specular lobe), modelled by (3.14). The reflectance components are plotted for constant illumination direction **s** and varying viewing direction **v**. (**b**) Measured reflectance of a raw forged iron surface for $\alpha = 75°$

Wöhler and d'Angelo 2009) a phenomenological BRDF model for rough metallic surfaces is used which is an extension of the model by Phong (1975) and has been chosen such that the empirically determined reflectance properties of the material are well represented. Hence, the reflectance of a typical rough metallic surface is assumed to consist of three components according to Nayar et al. (1991): a diffuse (Lambertian) component, the specular lobe, and the specular spike. The diffuse component is generated by multiple scattering processes in the surface material. The specular lobe, which is caused by single reflection at the surface, has a maximum close to the mirror direction and may be rather broad. The specular spike describes reflections in the mirror direction, where the strength decreases strongly already for small deviations from the mirror direction. Figure 3.4a illustrates the three components of the reflectance function. Notably, in the model by Nayar et al. (1991) the maximum of the specular lobe not necessarily coincides with the mirror direction, while such 'off-specular' components are not regarded here. For illustration, Fig. 3.4b shows a reflectance function measured for raw forged iron at a phase angle of $\alpha = 75°$ (as shown in Sect. 3.2.2, for the materials regarded here the reflectance function corresponds to the BRDF multiplied by $\cos\theta_i$). We define an analytical form for the reflectance for which we perform a least-mean-squares fit to the measured reflectance values, depending on the incidence angle θ_i and the angle θ_r between the specular direction **r** and the viewing direction **v** (cf. Fig. 3.4a):

$$f_N^{spec}(\rho, \theta_i, \theta_r, \alpha) = \rho \left[1 + \sum_{n=1}^{N} \sigma_n \cdot \frac{(\cos\theta_r)^{m_n}}{\cos\theta_i} \right]. \qquad (3.14)$$

For $\theta_r > 90°$ only the diffuse component is considered. The reflectance measurement is performed for a small part of the surface, for which the albedo ρ can be assumed to be constant. The shapes of the specular components of the reflectance function are approximated by $N = 2$ terms proportional to powers of $\cos\theta_r$. The coefficients σ_n denote the strength of the specular components relative to the diffuse component, while the exponents m_n denote their widths. Generally, all introduced phenomenological parameters depend on the phase angle α. The angle θ_r is defined according to (3.11), such that our phenomenological reflectance model only depends on the incidence angle θ_i, the emission angle θ_e, and the phase angle α. Like the Phong model, the specular BRDF according to (3.14) does not fulfil the Helmholtz reciprocity condition (3.7), but it provides a useful and numerically well-behaved description of the reflectance behaviour of the kind of specularly reflecting rough metallic surfaces regarded in Chap. 6 in the context of industrial quality inspection.

In the scenario of remote sensing (cf. Chap. 8), a very powerful physically motivated BRDF model for planetary regolith surfaces is introduced by Hapke (1981, 1984, 1986, 1993, 2002). For three-dimensional surface reconstruction, however, it is shown by McEwen (1991) that a very good approximation of the true reflectance behaviour over a wide range of incidence and emission angles and surface orientations is obtained by the phenomenological lunar-Lambert law

$$f_{\mathrm{LL}}(\rho, \theta_i, \theta_r, \alpha) = \rho\left[2L(\alpha)\frac{1}{\cos\theta_i + \cos\theta_e} + \left(1 - L(\alpha)\right)\right] \qquad (3.15)$$

with $L(\alpha)$ as a phase angle-dependent empirical factor determined by McEwen (1991). A more detailed discussion of the Hapke model and the lunar-Lambert BRDF is given in Chap. 8.

3.2.2 Determination of Surface Gradients

3.2.2.1 Photoclinometry

Photoclinometric and shape from shading techniques take into account the geometric configuration of camera, light source, and the object itself, as well as the reflectance properties of the surface to be reconstructed. We always assume parallel incident light and an infinite distance between camera and object as proposed by Horn (1986, 1989), which is a good approximation in the application scenario of industrial quality inspection (cf. Chap. 6) and nearly exactly fulfilled in the remote sensing scenario (cf. Chap. 8). Under these conditions, the intensity I_{uv} of the image pixel located at (u, v) amounts to

$$I_{uv} = R_I(\rho, \mathbf{n}, \mathbf{s}, \mathbf{v}). \qquad (3.16)$$

According to Horn (1986), (3.16) is termed the 'image irradiance equation'. Here, ρ is the surface albedo, $\mathbf{n}$ the surface normal, $\mathbf{v}$ the direction to the camera, $\mathbf{s}$ the direction of incident light, and R_I the reflectance map. The reflectance map indicates the relationship between surface orientation and brightness, based on information about surface reflectance properties and the distribution of the light sources that illuminate the surface. In the example of a Lambertian surface illuminated by a light source of radiance E, the radiance of the surface corresponds to $L = (E/\pi) \cos \theta_i$, where the factor $\cos \theta_i$ is of purely geometrical nature (cf. (3.6)) (Horn, 1986). The factor ρ is a normalisation constant and absorbs several quantities such as the amount of light not reflected by the surface, the absolute irradiance of the light source, and the sensitivity of the camera sensor used to acquire the image of the surface. Hence, the Lambertian reflectance map is given by

$$R_I^{\text{Lambert}}(\rho, \mathbf{n}, \mathbf{s}) = \rho \cos \theta_i, \tag{3.17}$$

where the incidence angle θ_i corresponds to the angle between $\mathbf{n}$ and $\mathbf{s}$ with $\cos \theta_i = \mathbf{n} \cdot \mathbf{s}/(|\mathbf{n}||\mathbf{s}|)$. In many practical applications, the Lambert model does not correspond very well to the true reflectance behaviour of the regarded surface. Hence, we will show in Sects. 6.3 and 8.1 how realistic reflectance maps are obtained in the regarded application scenarios.

The surface is described by the function $z(x, y)$; in practise, however, it turns out to be advantageous to utilise the formulation z_{uv} defined at the discrete pixel positions (u, v). In the following, the surface normal $\mathbf{n}$ is represented in gradient space by the directional derivatives $p = \partial z/\partial x$ and $q = \partial z/\partial y$ of the surface function $z(x, y)$ with $\mathbf{n} = (-p, -q, 1)^T$ (Horn, 1986). In an analogous manner we define $\mathbf{s} = (-p_s, -q_s, 1)^T$ and $\mathbf{v} = (-p_v, -q_v, 1)^T$. In the following we assume an infinite distance between the surface, the light source, and the camera, respectively (Horn 1986, 1989). Accordingly, the reflectance map R_I can be expressed in terms of the surface gradients p_{uv} and q_{uv} at each pixel position and the constant vectors $\mathbf{s}$ and $\mathbf{v}$, leading to the formulation $I_{uv} = R_I(\rho_{uv}, p_{uv}, q_{uv}, \mathbf{s}, \mathbf{v})$.

The angle α between the vectors $\mathbf{s}$ and $\mathbf{v}$ is termed the 'phase angle' (Hapke, 1981). The angle between the vectors $\mathbf{n}$ and $\mathbf{s}$ is given by θ_i and the angle between $\mathbf{n}$ and $\mathbf{v}$ by θ_e, such that these angles can be expressed as

$$\begin{aligned}
\cos \theta_i &= \frac{\mathbf{n} \cdot \mathbf{s}}{|\mathbf{n}| \cdot |\mathbf{s}|} = \frac{1 + p_s p_{uv} + q_s q_{uv}}{\sqrt{1 + p_s^2 + q_s^2}\sqrt{1 + p_{uv}^2 + q_{uv}^2}} \\
\cos \theta_e &= \frac{\mathbf{n} \cdot \mathbf{v}}{|\mathbf{n}| \cdot |\mathbf{v}|} = \frac{1 + p_v p_{uv} + q_v q_{uv}}{\sqrt{1 + p_v^2 + q_v^2}\sqrt{1 + p_{uv}^2 + q_{uv}^2}}
\end{aligned} \tag{3.18}$$

(Horn, 1989). According to (3.16), we attempt to determine two variables p_{uv} and q_{uv} for each pixel from one single measurement, the pixel grey value I_{uv}. Without further assumptions about the surface, this is an ill-posed problem. The photoclinometric approach consists of computing height profiles along image rows under the assumptions that the terrain is gently sloping ($|p|, |q| \ll 1$), the illumination is highly oblique, and the scene is illuminated along the image rows, corresponding to $q_s = 0$. An early description of the principle of photoclinometry is given by Wilhelms (1964). As long as the reflectance is similar to the Lambert law (3.17), it depends much more strongly on p than on q, such that one may set $q = 0$ (Horn, 1989). This approximation is often valid in remote sensing scenarios, e.g. when it is desired to derive a three-dimensional reconstruction of linear ridges or cross sections of craters (Horn, 1989).

Commonly a constant albedo ρ is assumed, and the value of ρ is chosen such that the average surface slope over the region of interest is zero (Wöhler et al., 2006b) or corresponds to a given nonzero value. Alternatively, a non-uniform albedo ρ_{uv} is determined based on a pair of images acquired under different illumination conditions according to Lena et al. (2006) (cf. Sect. 3.3.2). Equation (3.16) is then solved for the surface gradient p_{uv} for each pixel with intensity I_{uv}. For each image row v, a height profile z_{uv} can be readily obtained by integration of the surface gradients p_{uv}.

3.2.2.2 Single-Image Approaches with Regularisation Constraints

The classical shape from shading approach regarded in this section is based on the global optimisation of an energy function according to Horn (1986, 1989) and Horn and Brooks (1989). The presentation in this section is adopted from Wöhler and Hafezi (2005). The described method involves searching for two functions $p(x, y)$ and $q(x, y)$ which imply a surface that generates the observed image intensity $I(x, y)$. The original problem formulation is expressed in the continuous variables x and y, resulting in a variational framework. Here we will, however, immediately deal with finite sums over the image pixels, the positions of which are denoted by the discrete variables u and v, and rewrite the error integrals introduced by Horn (1986) accordingly. Hence, the intensity constraint can be expressed by the minimisation of an intensity error term e_i with

$$e_i = \sum_{u,v} \left[I_{uv} - R_I(p_{uv}, q_{uv}) \right]^2 \qquad (3.19)$$

with $R_I(p_{uv}, q_{uv})$ as the reflectance function of the regarded surface. It is straightforward to extend this error term to two or more light sources (Sect. 3.3). This section, however, concentrates on the single light source scenario. As the correspondingly defined reconstruction problem is ill-posed, we furthermore introduce a regularisation constraint e_s which requires local continuity of the surface. Such a smooth surface implies that the absolute values of the derivatives $\partial p/\partial x$, $\partial p/\partial y$, $\partial q/\partial x$, and $\partial q/\partial y$ are small, which results in an error term e_s with

$$e_s = \sum_{u,v} \left[\left\{ \frac{\partial p}{\partial x} \right\}_{uv}^2 + \left\{ \frac{\partial p}{\partial y} \right\}_{uv}^2 + \left\{ \frac{\partial q}{\partial x} \right\}_{uv}^2 + \left\{ \frac{\partial q}{\partial y} \right\}_{uv}^2 \right]. \qquad (3.20)$$

This leads to a minimisation of the overall error

$$e = e_s + \lambda e_i, \qquad (3.21)$$

where the Lagrange multiplier λ denotes the relative weight of the two error terms e_i and e_s. With the approximations

$$\left\{\frac{\partial p}{\partial x}\right\}_{uv} = \frac{1}{2}(p_{u+1,v} - p_{u-1,v})$$

$$\left\{\frac{\partial p}{\partial y}\right\}_{uv} = \frac{1}{2}(p_{u,v+1} - p_{u,v-1})$$

$$\left\{\frac{\partial q}{\partial x}\right\}_{uv} = \frac{1}{2}(q_{u+1,v} - q_{u-1,v})$$ (3.22)

$$\left\{\frac{\partial q}{\partial y}\right\}_{uv} = \frac{1}{2}(q_{u,v+1} - q_{u,v-1})$$

and the average values

$$\bar{p}_{uv} = (p_{u+1,v} + p_{u-1,v} + p_{u,v+1} + p_{u,v-1})/4$$
$$\bar{q}_{uv} = (q_{u+1,v} + q_{u-1,v} + q_{u,v+1} + q_{u,v-1})/4$$ (3.23)

we obtain an iterative update rule for p_{uv} and q_{uv} by setting the derivatives of e with respect to p_{uv} and q_{uv} to zero, which yields the expressions

$$p_{uv}^{(n+1)} = \bar{p}_{uv}^{(n)} + \lambda\left(I_{uv} - R_I\left(\bar{p}_{uv}^{(n)}, \bar{q}_{uv}^{(n)}\right)\right)\frac{\partial R_I}{\partial p}\bigg|_{\bar{p}_{uv}^{(n)}, \bar{q}_{uv}^{(n)}}$$

$$q_{uv}^{(n+1)} = \bar{q}_{uv}^{(n)} + \lambda\left(I_{uv} - R_I\left(\bar{p}_{uv}^{(n)}, \bar{q}_{uv}^{(n)}\right)\right)\frac{\partial R_I}{\partial q}\bigg|_{\bar{p}_{uv}^{(n)}, \bar{q}_{uv}^{(n)}}$$ (3.24)

(Horn, 1986). The initial values $p_{uv}^{(0)}$ and $q_{uv}^{(0)}$ must be provided based on a priori knowledge about the surface. The surface profile z_{uv} is then derived from the slopes p_{uv} and q_{uv} by means of numerical integration, as outlined in detail in Sect. 3.2.3. Wöhler and Hafezi (2005) suggest that the albedo ρ_{uv} is set to a uniform value, which may be updated using (3.16) and (3.18) in each iteration step based on a certain number of selected pixels (e.g. all pixels of a certain image column)—hence, the iterative update rule (3.24) not only determines the surface gradients p_{uv} and q_{uv} but also the albedo ρ by minimisation of error function (3.21). Section 3.3 describes how a non-uniform albedo ρ_{uv} is taken into account.

The three-dimensional reconstruction algorithm proposed by Horn (1989), which generates an integrable surface gradient vector field, is described as follows. It simultaneously yields the surface gradients p_{uv} and q_{uv} and the depth z_{uv}. Here, the assumption of a smooth surface according to (3.20) is replaced by the departure from integrability error expressed by the error term

$$e_{\text{int}} = \sum_{uv}\left[\left(\left\{\frac{\partial z}{\partial x}\right\}_{uv} - p_{uv}\right)^2 + \left(\left\{\frac{\partial z}{\partial y}\right\}_{uv} - q_{uv}\right)^2\right].$$ (3.25)

Accordingly, the shape from shading problem corresponds to a minimisation of the overall error term

$$f = e_i + \gamma e_{\text{int}}.$$ (3.26)

In the continuous formulation, satisfying the integrability constraint (3.25) corresponds to the variational problem of minimising the functional

$$\iint \left[\left(\frac{\partial z(x, y)}{\partial x} - p(x, y) \right)^2 + \left(\frac{\partial z(x, y)}{\partial y} - q(x, y) \right)^2 \right] dx \, dy \qquad (3.27)$$

with respect to the surface gradients $p(x, y)$ and $q(x, y)$. The Euler equation of this problem is given by

$$\nabla^2 z = \frac{\partial p}{\partial x} + \frac{\partial q}{\partial y}, \qquad (3.28)$$

where $\nabla^2 z$ denotes the Laplace operator applied to z, where (3.28) must hold at each position in the image (Horn, 1986). For discrete pixels, the Laplace operator can be approximated by the expression

$$\{\nabla^2 z\}_{uv} \approx \frac{\kappa}{\varepsilon^2} (\bar{z}_{uv} - z_{uv}), \qquad (3.29)$$

where ε is the lateral extent of the pixels, which is conveniently set to $\varepsilon = 1$ if all pixels are quadratic and of the same lateral extent, and $\kappa = 4$ when the local average $\bar{z}_{uv}$ is computed based on the four nearest neighbours of the pixel (Horn, 1986). According to Horn (1989), setting the derivative of the error term f with respect to p_{uv} and q_{uv} to zero and combining (3.28) and (3.29) then yields the following iteration scheme:

$$p_{uv}^{(n+1)} = \left\{ \frac{\partial z}{\partial x} \right\}_{uv}^{(n)} + \frac{1}{\gamma} (I - R_I) \frac{\partial R_I}{\partial p}$$

$$q_{uv}^{(n+1)} = \left\{ \frac{\partial z}{\partial y} \right\}_{uv}^{(n)} + \frac{1}{\gamma} (I - R_I) \frac{\partial R_I}{\partial q} \qquad (3.30)$$

$$z_{uv}^{(n+1)} = \bar{z}_{uv}^{(n)} - \frac{\varepsilon^2}{\kappa} \left(\left\{ \frac{\partial p}{\partial x} \right\}_{uv}^{(n+1)} + \left\{ \frac{\partial q}{\partial y} \right\}_{uv}^{(n+1)} \right).$$

After each update of the surface gradients p_{uv} and q_{uv}, the corresponding height map z_{uv} is computed by means of a discrete approximation to the solution of the Euler–Lagrange differential equations of the corresponding variational problem (Horn, 1989). For a single light source and oblique illumination, this algorithm gives a good estimate even of the surface gradients perpendicular to the direction of incident light, as it adjusts them to the integrability constraint without affecting the intensity error e_i given by (3.19).

Horn (1989) remarks that even if the iterative update rule (3.24) is initialised with a solution that perfectly fits with the observed pixel grey values, i.e. $e_i = 0$, the algorithm will nevertheless yield a different, smoother surface, since the constraint of small partial derivatives of the surface is a strong restriction and not always physically reasonable. In contrast, the integrability constraint is a much weaker restriction and always physically correct. If the corresponding iterative update rule (3.30) is initialised with a surface for which the associated intensity error e_i is zero, the algorithm will retain this 'perfect' solution. However, the algorithm based on the integrability constraint has the drawback of a small convergence radius, such that it needs to be initialised with a surface profile which is already close to the final solution (Horn, 1989).

In the single-image shape from shading scenario, the surface albedo ρ_{uv} has always been regarded as known. If this is not the case, in many applications the assumption of a uniform albedo ρ is made. Different albedo values yield different solutions of the shape from shading problem, since e.g. increasing ρ will result in a surface inclined away from the light source and vice versa. Hence, it is often necessary to make additional assumptions about the surface, e.g. that the average surface slope is zero or obtains a predefined value. In Sect. 3.3 methods to cope with unknown and non-uniform surface albedos are described.

3.2.3 Reconstruction of Height from Gradients

Local techniques for computation of height from gradients rely on curve integrals and are based on specifying an integration path and a local neighbourhood. According to the technique described by Jiang and Bunke (1997), reconstruction of height is started at a given point (u_0, v_0) of the image, e.g. the centre, for which $z_{u_0,v_0} = 0$ is assumed, and the initial paths are forming a cross along image column u_0 and image row v_0 (cf. also Klette and Schlüns 1996). The image origin is in the upper left corner. For the upper right quadrant, the height value z_{uv} is obtained according to

$$z_{uv} = \frac{1}{2}\left[z_{u-1,v} + \frac{1}{2}(p_{u-1,v} + p_{uv}) + z_{u,v+1} + \frac{1}{2}(q_{u,v+1} + q_{uv}) \right] \quad (3.31)$$

Analogous relations for the remaining three quadrants are readily obtained. In (3.31) deviations of the surface gradient field from integrability are accounted for by averaging over the surface gradients in the horizontal and vertical directions. A drawback of this method is that the resulting height map z_{uv} depends on the initial location (u_0, v_0).

In a more systematic way than in the rather elementary approach by Jiang and Bunke (1997), the three-dimensional reconstruction scheme based on the integrability error outlined in Sect. 3.2.2.2 can be used for adapting a surface to the generally non-integrable surface gradient field obtained by shape from shading. It is desired to obtain a surface z_{uv} with partial derivatives $\{\partial z/\partial x\}_{uv}$ and $\{\partial z/\partial y\}_{uv}$ which come as close as possible to the values p_{uv} and q_{uv} previously obtained by shape from shading, which are assumed to be known and fixed. The depth map z_{uv} is chosen such that the integrability error (3.25) is minimised. Accordingly, it is shown by Horn (1986) that (3.28) and (3.29) directly yield an iterative scheme to determine the height map z_{uv} (cf. also (3.30)):

$$z_{uv}^{(n+1)} = \bar{z}_{uv}^{(n)} - \frac{\varepsilon^2}{\kappa}\left(\left\{ \frac{\partial p}{\partial x} \right\}_{uv} + \left\{ \frac{\partial q}{\partial y} \right\}_{uv} \right). \quad (3.32)$$

The main drawback of this variational approach is the large number of iterations necessary until convergence is achieved. Frankot and Chellappa (1988) and Simchony et al. (1990) propose methods to enforce integrability of the gradient field by performing a least-mean-squares adjustment of an integrable gradient field to the measured, generally non-integrable gradient field. In the approach of Frankot and Chellappa (1988), the basic step consists of computing the Fourier transform of (3.28), which yields

$$Z_{\omega_u \omega_v} = -\frac{i\omega_u P_{\omega_u \omega_v} + i\omega_v Q_{\omega_u \omega_v}}{\omega_u^2 + \omega_v^2}, \tag{3.33}$$

where $i = \sqrt{-1}$, and $P_{\omega_u \omega_v}$, $Q_{\omega_u \omega_v}$, and $Z_{\omega_u \omega_v}$ are the Fourier transforms of p_{uv}, q_{uv}, and z_{uv}. The corresponding depth map z_{uv} is readily obtained by computing the inverse Fourier transform of $Z_{\omega_u \omega_v}$. This concept is extended by Simchony et al. (1990) to solving the Poisson equation $\nabla^2 z = f$ with the Dirichlet boundary condition that z is known on the boundary of the surface.

The Fourier-based approach is extended by Wei and Klette (2004) to a 'strong integrability' error term that additionally takes into account the differences between the second-order derivatives of z_{uv} and the first-order derivatives of p_{uv} and q_{uv} according to

$$e_{\text{int}}^{\text{strong}} = e_{\text{int}} + \delta \sum_{u,v} \left[\left(\left\{ \frac{\partial^2 z}{\partial x^2} \right\}_{uv} - \left\{ \frac{\partial p}{\partial x} \right\}_{uv} \right)^2 + \left(\left\{ \frac{\partial^2 z}{\partial y^2} \right\}_{uv} - \left\{ \frac{\partial q}{\partial y} \right\}_{uv} \right)^2 \right], \tag{3.34}$$

where δ is a weight factor and the 'weak integrability' error term e_{int} is given by (3.25). According to Wei and Klette (2004), minimisation of the error term (3.34) is performed based on a Fourier transform in the continuous image domain, which yields the expression

$$Z_{\omega_u \omega_v} = -\frac{i(\omega_u + \delta\omega_u^3) P_{\omega_u \omega_v} + i(\omega_v + \delta\omega_v^3) Q_{\omega_u \omega_v}}{\omega_u^2 + \omega_v^2 + \delta(\omega_u^4 + \omega_v^4)} \tag{3.35}$$

for the Fourier-transformed depth map $Z_{\omega_u \omega_v}$. Again, the height map z_{uv} is obtained by computing the inverse Fourier transform of $Z_{\omega_u \omega_v}$.

Agrawal et al. (2005) propose an algebraic approach to the reconstruction of height from gradients which exploits the information contained in the 'curl' of the given non-integrable vector field, denoted by $\partial p/\partial y - \partial q/\partial x$. The curl of a vector field denotes the deviation from integrability. The method determines a residual gradient field which is added to the measured gradients p_{uv} and q_{uv} such that an integrable gradient field results. Agrawal et al. (2005) show that the method of Simchony et al. (1990) yields an integrable gradient field, the divergence $\partial p/\partial x + \partial q/\partial y$ of which is identical to that of the measured, non-integrable gradient field. In principle, the residual gradient field can be obtained by solving a set of linear equations, which is, however, ill-posed for shape from shading applications since the curl tends to be nonzero for nearly all pixels. Hence, the number of unknown residual gradient values exceeds the number of pixels by about a factor of

two. In contrast to Simchony et al. (1990), who compute a least-squares solution
of minimum norm, Agrawal et al. (2005) propose that at image locations for which
the curl of the measured surface gradients is below a given threshold, the gradients
remain unchanged. A graph-based optimisation scheme is presented for correcting
a maximum possible number of gradients at image locations with large curl values.

In the applications of three-dimensional surface reconstruction techniques to
real-world problems described in this work (cf. Chaps. 6 and 8) we utilise a computationally efficient implementation of the approach by Simchony et al. (1990) based
on enforcing the 'weak integrability' constraint (3.25). Any physically reasonable
surface z_{uv} must satisfy this constraint. In our application scenarios, computational
efficiency is relevant, since the employed methods require a reconstruction of the
height map z_{uv} from the gradients p_{uv} and q_{uv} at many different intermediate stages
of the optimisation algorithm.

3.2.4 Surface Reconstruction Based on Partial Differential Equations

In the mathematical framework discussed in this section, the observed image intensities are assumed to be represented by a continuous function $I(x, y)$ instead of the
discrete pixel grey values I_{uv}. According to Bruss (1989), for shape from shading
problems involving a reflectance function of the special form $R(p, q) = p^2 + q^2$,
(3.16) becomes

$$p^2 + q^2 = I(x, y) \qquad (3.36)$$

which is referred to as an 'eikonal equation'. Under certain conditions, which are
derived in detail by Bruss (1989), a unique solution for the reconstructed surface
can be obtained from a single image based on (3.36).

According to Bruss (1989), reflectance functions of the form $R(p, q) = f(p^2 + q^2)$ with f as a bijective mapping yield image irradiance equations that can be transformed into a form equivalent to (3.36). An important practically relevant scenario
in which all conditions derived by Bruss (1989) under which a unique solution of
the image irradiance equation is obtained are fulfilled is a Lambertian surface illuminated by a light source, the position of which coincides with that of the camera
(Bruss, 1989; Kimmel and Sethian, 2001). Kimmel and Sethian (2001) point out
that, in this special case, $I(x, y)$ is given by $I(x, y) = 1/\sqrt{1 + p^2 + q^2}$, leading to
the eikonal equation

$$\|\nabla z(x, y)\| = \sqrt{\frac{1}{I(x, y)^2} - 1}. \qquad (3.37)$$

For orthographic projection, i.e. infinite distance between the surface and the camera, and parallel incident light this situation corresponds to the zero phase angle
($\alpha = 0$) case.

Rouy and Tourin (1992) propose a numerical solution for this formulation of the shape from shading problem. More recently, Kimmel and Sethian (2001) have extended the shape from shading approach based on an eikonal equation to the more general scenario of a Lambertian surface observed under oblique illumination. They introduce a numerical approximation of an equation of the form $\|\nabla z(x, y)\| = f(x, y)$ according to

$$\left[\max\left(D_{uv}^{-x}z, -D_{uv}^{+x}z, 0\right)\right]^2 + \left[\max\left(D_{uv}^{-y}z, -D_{uv}^{+y}z, 0\right)\right]^2 = f_{uv}^2, \tag{3.38}$$

where $z_{uv} = z(u\Delta x, v\Delta y)$ is the discretised version of $z(x, y)$ defined on the pixel raster, $D_{uv}^{-x}z = (z_{uv} - z_{u-1,v})/\Delta x$, $D_{uv}^{+x}z = (z_{u+1,v} - z_{uv})/\Delta x$, and the same analogously for the direction parallel to the vertical image axis (y direction). Kimmel and Sethian (2001) state the proof by Rouy and Tourin (1992) that the shape from shading problem can be solved based on this numerical scheme, and they emphasise that while the solution z is built up, small z values have an influence on larger z values but not vice versa. Hence, Kimmel and Sethian (2001) suggest to initialise all z values to infinity except at the local minima, where they are initialised with the correct depth value. If only a single minimum point exists, the surface is initialised with $z_{uv} = \infty$ except for the minimum. If the absolute value of the minimum is unknown (which is commonly the case), it is set to zero. According to Kimmel and Sethian (2001), an update step for z_{uv} then corresponds to

$$z_1 = \min(z_{u-1,v}, z_{u+1,v}), \qquad z_2 = \min(z_{u,v-1}, z_{u,v+1})$$

$$z_{uv} = \begin{cases} \frac{1}{2}\left(z_1 + z_2 + \sqrt{2f_{uv}^2 - (z_1 - z_2)^2}\right) & \text{if } |z_1 - z_2| < f_{uv} \\ \min(z_1, z_2) + f_{uv} & \text{otherwise.} \end{cases} \tag{3.39}$$

Kimmel and Sethian (2001) state that the computational complexity of this scheme is between $\mathcal{O}(N)$ and $\mathcal{O}(N^2)$ depending on the surface, where N is the number of pixels. Furthermore, they utilise the fast marching method by Sethian (1999), which relies on the principle that the solution for z is built up from small values towards large values ('upwinding') and on an efficient scheme for taking into account the updated z values. This approach yields a computational complexity of better than $\mathcal{O}(N \log N)$. The proposed scheme immediately yields the shape from shading solution in the zero phase angle case.

In the more general scenario of a Lambertian surface illuminated by a light source located in a direction which is not identical to that of the camera, the reflectance map is given by the scalar product $I(x, y) = \mathbf{s} \cdot \mathbf{n}$, where the albedo corresponds to unity, and $\|\mathbf{s}\| = \|\mathbf{n}\| = 1$. Kimmel and Sethian (2001) assume that the image is rotated such that the value of s_y is set to zero. However, the described numerical solution scheme for the eikonal equation cannot be used directly to reconstruct the surface. Hence, they transform the observed image into the coordinate system of the light source, leading to the expression

$$\tilde{p}^2 + \tilde{q}^2 = \frac{1}{\tilde{I}(\tilde{x}, y)^2} - 1 \tag{3.40}$$

which formally corresponds to the eikonal equation (3.37). In (3.40), $\tilde{p}$, $\tilde{q}$, $\tilde{x}$, and $\tilde{I}$ are defined in the light source coordinate system. The relation between the original and the transformed image radiance then corresponds to

$$\tilde{I}(\tilde{x}, y) = I(s_z \tilde{x} + s_x \tilde{z}, y). \tag{3.41}$$

Inserting (3.41) into (3.40) allows one to determine the depth values z_{uv} of the surface. As an alternative, Kimmel and Sethian (2001) propose an extended fast marching scheme that directly yields the solution for z_{uv}.

The shape from shading approach based on partial differential equations is extended by Vogel et al. (2008) to a formulation in terms of the Hamilton–Jacobi equation which takes into account a finite distance between the object and the camera, i.e. a full projective camera model, and a non-Lambertian Phong reflectance model. The light source is assumed to be located in the optical centre of the camera, corresponding to a phase angle of $\alpha = 0°$. According to Vogel et al. (2008), the differential equation to be solved for the depth map $z(x, y) = z(\mathbf{x})$ defined in the continuous domain corresponds to

$$\frac{Rb^2}{z} \sqrt{\frac{2}{Q^2} [b^2 \|\nabla z\|^2 + (\nabla z \cdot \mathbf{x})^2] + z^2} = \frac{1}{z^2} \tag{3.42}$$

with R as the reflectance function, b as the camera constant, and $Q = Q(\mathbf{x}) = b/\sqrt{\|\mathbf{x}\|^2 + b^2}$. A discretised solution of the Hamilton–Jacobi equation is obtained using the 'method of artificial time'. The approach is evaluated by Vogel et al. (2008) based on synthetic images with and without noise and on simple real-world images.

The method of Vogel et al. (2008) is applied to more complex real-world images by Vogel et al. (2009b). The object of interest is segmented by subsequently applying the approach of Chan and Vese (2001) for initialisation, which relies on image grey values rather than edges, and the edge-based geodesic active contour method of Caselles et al. (1997) for refinement. A correction for non-uniform surface albedo is performed using a diffusion-based image inpainting method. For several objects with non-Lambertian surfaces (a cup, a computer mouse, and a book with a plastic cover), realistic three-dimensional reconstruction results are obtained. However, no comparison to ground truth data is provided. A computationally highly efficient method for solving the Hamilton–Jacobi equation (3.42) based on a fast marching scheme is developed by Vogel et al. (2009a).

Beyond an integration of the Phong model, Vogel and Cristiani (2011) discuss the approach of Ahmed and Farag (2007), who employ the reflectance model of Oren and Nayar (1995) for shape from shading. The Oren-Nayar model has been developed for rough surfaces composed of small facets which are individually governed by a Lambertian reflectance. Vogel and Cristiani (2011) assume that the light source is located in the optical centre of the camera. They compare the numerical approach used by Ahmed and Farag (2007) with the upwind scheme proposed by Rouy and Tourin (1992), concluding that the upwind scheme converges faster and can be implemented more easily. Furthermore, Vogel and Cristiani (2011) derive upper bounds for the step size of the upwind scheme for the Phong model and the

Oren-Nayar model and state that the upwind scheme can be implemented as a computationally efficient fast marching algorithm for both examined non-Lambertian reflectance models. Experimentally, the results of the proposed numerical methods are compared based on synthetically generated images.

The main advantage of the shape from shading approaches outlined in this section, compared to the variational method described in Sect. 3.2.2, is the fact that they do not require a smoothness or integrability constraint but directly yield a reconstruction of the surface exclusively based on the observed pixel grey values. They are, however, restricted to surfaces with specific, relatively simple reflectance properties and in some cases also to specific illumination conditions, e.g. a light source coincident with the optical centre of the camera, which is a major drawback in complex real-world scenarios (cf. Chaps. 6 and 8).

3.3 Photometric Stereo

The solution of shape from shading based on a single image is ambiguous as long as the surface albedo is unknown and no assumption about the surface can be made. Furthermore, for oblique illumination and reflectance maps similar to the Lambert law (3.17), the surface gradients perpendicular to the direction of incident light are much less well defined than those in the direction of incident light. These drawbacks can be overcome by the analysis of several images, a procedure termed 'photometric stereo' in analogy to standard triangulation-based stereo image analysis techniques.

3.3.1 Photometric Stereo: Principle and Extensions

A straightforward way to extend the shape from shading method outlined in Sect. 3.2.2.2 is to acquire a set of L pixel-synchronous images of the surface under known illumination conditions described by the vectors $\mathbf{s}_l$. The intensity error according to Horn (1986) is extended by Wöhler and Hafezi (2005) as a sum over all L images according to

$$e_i = \sum_{l=1}^{L} \sum_{u,v} \left[I_{uv}^{(l)} - R_I(\mathbf{s}_l, p_{uv}, q_{uv}) \right]^2 \tag{3.43}$$

while the smoothness constraint (3.20) and the integrability constraint (3.25) remain unchanged. The corresponding iterative update schemes for the surface gradients are analogous to (3.24) or (3.30). In this setting we obtain reliable information about the surface gradients in all directions with $L = 2$ light sources, but a known uniform albedo ρ still has to be assumed. In principle, once the value of ρ is determined, it is possible to obtain without further constraints the surface gradients p_{uv} and q_{uv} from the $L = 2$ intensities available for each pixel. In many applications, however, it is advantageous to continue assuming a smooth surface, as this prevents the surface from being strongly influenced by noise or small-scale specular reflections.

The classical approach to photometric stereo for surfaces of non-uniform albedo is the method introduced by Woodham (1980), which relies on three pixel-synchronous images of the surface acquired under different illumination conditions (cf. also Horn 1986, Jiang and Bunke 1997, and Klette et al. 1996), defined by the illumination vectors $\mathbf{s}_l$ with $\|\mathbf{s}_l\| = 1$. The surface is assumed to display a Lambertian reflectance behaviour according to (3.17) and a non-uniform albedo ρ_{uv}. The light sources are situated at infinite distance, and their irradiances are identical. For each pixel (u, v), three intensity values are measured and expressed as the three components of the vector $\mathbf{I}_{uv}$. If the surface normal $\mathbf{n}_{uv}$ is defined as a unit vector, the pixel grey values are given by

$$\mathbf{I}_{uv} = \rho_{uv} S \cdot \mathbf{n}_{uv}, \qquad (3.44)$$

where the rows of the 3×3 matrix S contain the illumination vectors $\mathbf{s}_l$. Taking the norm on both sides of (3.44) immediately yields

$$\rho_{uv} = \left\| S^{-1} \mathbf{I}_{uv} \right\|, \qquad (3.45)$$

and the surface normal amounts to

$$\mathbf{n}_{uv} = \frac{1}{\rho_{uv}} S^{-1} \mathbf{I}_{uv}. \qquad (3.46)$$

This algorithm has the considerable advantage that it copes with surfaces of arbitrary non-uniform surface albedo. However, a drawback is that the inverse matrix S^{-1} exists only if the three illumination vectors $\mathbf{s}_l$ are not coplanar, and that it is restricted to surfaces of purely Lambertian reflectance.

The 'multi-image shape from shading' method proposed by Lohse and Heipke (2003, 2004) and Lohse et al. (2006) relies on the principle of photometric stereo but assumes a uniform surface albedo. This technique is based on the direct reconstruction of the surface in an object-centred coordinate system. It is used to obtain digital elevation models of the lunar polar regions based on images acquired by the Clementine spacecraft (cf. Chap. 8).

A detailed overview of classical and recent photometric stereo methods is given in the survey by Herbort and Wöhler (2011), some of which are described in the following text. Several recent approaches specifically address the problem of reconstructing surfaces with non-Lambertian reflectance functions and moving objects.

A photometric stereo approach is used by Alldrin et al. (2008) to obtain a three-dimensional surface reconstruction along with the locally non-uniform reflectance function. The reflectance function of the surface material is represented by a linear combination of the reflectance functions of several known 'basis materials', where smoothness and monotonicity constraints are imposed on the reflectance function. The experimental evaluation by Alldrin et al. (2008) involves more than 100 images per object acquired under different illumination conditions. Furthermore, it is shown that photorealistic images can be rendered for new viewing directions based on the estimated three-dimensional shapes and reflectance functions.

Goldman et al. (2010) propose a photometric stereo approach which performs a three-dimensional surface reconstruction along with an estimation of the locally

non-uniform reflectance function from a set of images acquired under different illumination conditions. The surface material is assumed to be composed of a small
number of 'fundamental materials', where the material of a specific surface location is additionally constrained to consist of a mixture of only two materials. The
proposed optimisation scheme estimates the surface normals, the reflectance parameters of the fundamental materials, and the pixel-specific material fractions. It
is shown by Goldman et al. (2010) that their approach is especially suitable for
generating synthetically rendered images of the reconstructed objects under illumination and viewing conditions different from those encountered during image
acquisition.

Hernandez et al. (2007) use the method of 'multispectral photometric stereo',
which consists of acquiring three colour channels simultaneously using an RGB
camera, where the surface to be reconstructed is illuminated by a red, a green,
and a blue light source emitting in non-overlapping wavelength ranges. This approach avoids the requirement of classical photometric stereo to acquire the images
subsequently and thus to keep the surface stationary. Under the assumption of a
Lambertian surface with a non-uniform albedo, a photometric stereo scheme similar to the method described at the beginning of this section is applied in order to
obtain the surface gradients. The depth map is then inferred by integration, and a
temporal tracking of the variations of the three-dimensional surface shape is performed, using the surface derived from the first image as a deformable template.
Correspondences between subsequent frames are established based on optical flow
information inferred from the surface gradient images. This method is applied by
Hernandez et al. (2007) to the three-dimensional reconstruction of clothes. The multispectral photometric stereo approach employed using standard RGB cameras does
not yield more than three images, and under these conditions images of complex
surfaces are nearly never shadow-free for all colour channels. Thus Hernandez et
al. (2008) propose a method to obtain unambiguous surface gradients for pixels lying inside shadow areas in one of the images by imposing a combined integrability
and direction-dependent smoothness constraint. The framework of Hernandez et al.
(2007, 2008) is applied by Hernandez and Vogiatzis (2010) to the three-dimensional
reconstruction of faces. Their method is calibrated by estimating the object motion using structure from motion and by applying stereo image analysis to derive a
three-dimensional reconstruction of the face. The reconstruction, which is accurate
on large spatial scales but noisy on small scales, is then used to estimate the light
source directions. A refined three-dimensional reconstruction of the facial surface is
obtained by multispectral photometric stereo with correction for shadows according
to the method of Hernandez et al. (2007, 2008).

3.3.2 Photometric Stereo Approaches Based on Ratio Images

This section regards photometric stereo approaches which are suited for non-
uniform surface albedos, coplanar illumination vectors (which may be of high practical relevance, especially in the field of remote sensing applications, as pointed out

by Wöhler and Hafezi 2005 and Lena et al. 2006), and a much more general class
of reflectance characteristics.

3.3.2.1 Ratio-Based Photoclinometry of Surfaces with Non-uniform Albedo

Similar to the scenario of single-image photoclinometry (cf. Sect. 3.2.2.1), illumination of the scene along the image rows ($q_s = 0$) is assumed. For oblique illumination, the dependence of the reflectance map on p is much more pronounced than the
dependence on q, provided that it has no strongly specular component. Hence, we
again approximate the surface gradient q perpendicular to the direction of incident
light with zero values. The presentation in this section is adopted from Wöhler and
Hafezi (2005) and Lena et al. (2006).

Two images of the surface acquired under different illumination angles are required to separate intensity variations due to topographic relief from those due to
albedo variations. The images have to be pixel-synchronous, which is achieved by
an image registration step (Gottesfeld Brown, 1992). We do not have to restrict our-
selves to Lambertian reflectance; instead we assume a reflectance map of the form

$$R_I(\rho_{uv}, \mathbf{s}, p_{uv}, q_{uv}) = \rho_{uv} \tilde{R}_I(\mathbf{s}, p_{uv}, q_{uv}). \tag{3.47}$$

Photoclinometry is then performed along image rows by extending (3.16) as described by McEwen (1985) and determining p_{uv} such that

$$\frac{I_{uv}^{(1)}}{I_{uv}^{(2)}} = \frac{\tilde{R}_I(\mathbf{s}_1, p_{uv}, q_{uv})}{\tilde{R}_I(\mathbf{s}_2, p_{uv}, q_{uv})}. \tag{3.48}$$

The surface gradients q_{uv} are still kept zero, and the albedo ρ_{uv} cancels out, such
that (3.48) directly yields the surface gradient p_{uv} individually for each pixel. It
is generally not possible to obtain an analytical solution for p_{uv}; thus numerical
techniques like the Newton method have to be used.

When the images are not absolutely calibrated radiometrically, their average pixel
grey values must be adjusted according to the different illumination angles, relying
on the assumption that on the average the surface is flat. As long as $\tilde{R}_I(p, q)$ is not
strongly nonlinear in p and q, it is sufficient to normalise $I_{uv}^{(1)}$ by multiplying its
pixel grey value with the factor

$$\frac{\tilde{R}_I(\mathbf{s}_1, 0, 0)\langle I_{uv}^{(2)}\rangle_{u,v}}{\tilde{R}_I(\mathbf{s}_2, 0, 0)\langle I_{uv}^{(1)}\rangle_{u,v}}.$$

The non-uniform surface albedo ρ_{uv} is then recovered by

$$\rho_{uv} = \frac{1}{L} \sum_{l=1}^{L} \frac{I_{uv}^{(l)}}{\tilde{R}_I(\mathbf{s}_l, p_{uv}, q_{uv})}. \tag{3.49}$$

In the next step, the albedo map ρ_{uv} is inserted into one of the single-image shape
from shading schemes described in Sect. 3.2.2, preferably relying on the image acquired under the more oblique illumination conditions in order to extract the relief

as accurately as possible. The surface gradients p_{uv} determined based on (3.48) are used as initial values for the corresponding iterative update rule (3.24) or (3.30). Accordingly, p_{uv} hardly changes in the course of the iteration process, while q_{uv} obtains values consistent with the smoothness constraint (3.20) or the integrability constraint (3.25).

3.3.2.2 Ratio-Based Variational Photometric Stereo Approach

Another approach to cope with a non-uniform surface albedo ρ_{uv} is to return to the single-image shape from shading schemes in Sect. 3.2.2 and to replace the single-image intensity error term (3.19) by the modified ratio-based error term

$$\tilde{e}_i = \sum_{u,v} \left[\frac{I_{uv}^{(1)} \tilde{R}_I(\mathbf{s}_2, p_{uv}, q_{uv})}{I_{uv}^{(2)} \tilde{R}_I(\mathbf{s}_1, p_{uv}, q_{uv})} - 1 \right]^2 \tag{3.50}$$

as proposed by Wöhler and Hafezi (2005), who infer the ratio-based iterative update rule

$$p_{uv}^{(n+1)} = \bar{p}_{uv}^{(n)} + \lambda \left(\frac{I_{uv}^{(1)} \tilde{R}_I(\mathbf{s}_2, \bar{p}_{uv}^{(n)}, \bar{q}_{uv}^{(n)})}{I_{uv}^{(2)} \tilde{R}_I(\mathbf{s}_1, \bar{p}_{uv}^{(n)}, \bar{q}_{uv}^{(n)})} - 1 \right) \frac{I_{uv}^{(1)}}{I_{uv}^{(2)}} \frac{\partial}{\partial p} \left. \frac{\tilde{R}_I(\mathbf{s}_2, p_{uv}, q_{uv})}{\tilde{R}_I(\mathbf{s}_1, p_{uv}, q_{uv})} \right|_{\bar{p}_{uv}^{(n)}, \bar{q}_{uv}^{(n)}}$$

$$\tag{3.51}$$

$$q_{uv}^{(n+1)} = \bar{q}_{uv}^{(n)} + \lambda \left(\frac{I_{uv}^{(1)} \tilde{R}_I(\mathbf{s}_2, \bar{p}_{uv}^{(n)}, \bar{q}_{uv}^{(n)})}{I_{uv}^{(2)} \tilde{R}_I(\mathbf{s}_1, \bar{p}_{uv}^{(n)}, \bar{q}_{uv}^{(n)})} - 1 \right) \frac{I_{uv}^{(1)}}{I_{uv}^{(2)}} \frac{\partial}{\partial q} \left. \frac{\tilde{R}_I(\mathbf{s}_2, p_{uv}, q_{uv})}{\tilde{R}_I(\mathbf{s}_1, p_{uv}, q_{uv})} \right|_{\bar{p}_{uv}^{(n)}, \bar{q}_{uv}^{(n)}}.$$

The non-uniform albedo ρ_{uv} cancels out and can be recovered by (3.49) after determination of the surface gradients p_{uv} and q_{uv}. The properties of the results obtained with the ratio-based iterative scheme (3.51) are comparable to those obtained by single-image shape from shading analysis, except that one is not restricted to surfaces of uniform albedo. For more than two light sources and images ($L > 2$), the error term (3.50) can be extended to a sum over all $L(L-1)/2$ possible pairs of images, which reveals surface gradients in all directions if the light sources are appropriately distributed.

A drawback of the presented method is the fact that it must be initialised with a surface which is already close to the final solution; otherwise the algorithm diverges or becomes stuck in local minima. Hence, as long as the albedo variations are not strong, it is shown by Wöhler and Hafezi (2005) that it is advantageous to combine the two shape from shading approaches described in this section as follows. First, the surface profile is reconstructed using the multi-image intensity error (3.43), resulting in values for both p_{uv} and q_{uv} and a uniform albedo ρ. As a second step, the iterative update rule (3.51) is initialised with the results of the first step and then started. This procedure changes the surface profile only at the locations of albedo variations. The albedo map ρ_{uv} is then obtained according to (3.49). As a third step, p_{uv} and q_{uv} are recomputed according to (3.43). These three steps are repeated until p_{uv}, q_{uv}, and ρ_{uv} converge towards a self-consistent solution. Experimental results obtained with this approach are described in detail in Sect. 6.3.

3.4 Shape from Polarisation

An important drawback of the single-image shape from shading approach is the fact that an ill-posed problem has to be solved, since it is desired to determine two surface gradients (and sometimes also an albedo value) for each pixel based on a single intensity measurement. This drawback is overcome either by introducing constraints on the reconstructed surface, such as knowledge about the surface at the boundaries, smoothness, or uniform albedo, or by regarding several images of the surface acquired under different illumination conditions.

A further possibility to transform the ill-posed problem into a well-posed one is offered by extending the measurement of intensities to the additional measurement of polarisation properties of the light reflected from the surface. This approach yields up to three measurements per pixel, i.e. intensity, degree of polarisation, and direction of polarisation, which may allow an unambiguous reconstruction of the surface gradient field under the conditions typically encountered in real-world scenarios.

3.4.1 Surface Orientation from Dielectric Polarisation Models

In many shape from shading algorithms a Lambertian reflectance map is explicitly assumed, as is e.g. the case for the photometric stereo method described in Sect. 3.3. The computed surface shape is inaccurate when specular reflections are present in the image. An early approach to incorporate polarisation information into the shape from shading framework consists of the detection and subsequent removal of specular reflections in the image based on the analysis of colour and polarisation data, as proposed by Nayar et al. (1993). They use the degree of polarisation to select pixels characterised by specular reflection and derive a technique to estimate the specular colour. Furthermore, they show that the colour of the diffuse reflection component can be constrained to a one-dimensional colour subspace, based on which neighbouring pixels of similar colour are identified. The result is an image of the surface that displays only the diffuse (Lambertian) component of the reflected light.

The existing methods that aim for a reconstruction of surface shape from polarisation measurements deal with dielectric materials. Wolff (1987) presents a method to estimate the orientation of a surface by polarisation, where the direction of incident light, the viewing direction, and the polarisation behaviour of the surface are assumed to be known. This approach is extended by Wolff (1989) to the estimation of surface orientation based on a stereo pair of polarisation images.

In the approach of Rahmann (1999), a polarisation image is generated by acquiring images of the surface with a camera equipped with a linear polarising filter. The intensity of a pixel depends on the rotation angle ω of the polarising filter according to

$$I(\omega) = I_c + I_v \cos\left[2(\omega - \Phi)\right]. \tag{3.52}$$

In (3.52), I_c denotes the intensity averaged over all orientations of the polarising filter and I_v the intensity amplitude. The polarisation degree D_p is defined as

$$D_p = \frac{I_{\max} - I_{\min}}{I_{\max} + I_{\min}} = \frac{I_v}{I_c}. \tag{3.53}$$

The rotation angle of the polarising filter for which maximum intensity $I_{\max}$ is observed corresponds to the polarisation angle Φ. To determine the polarisation image, at least three pixel-synchronous images of the surface are acquired. For each pixel, (3.52) is fitted to the measured pixel pixel grey values (where Rahmann, 1999 suggests a computationally efficient linear optimisation approach), which yields the parameters I_c, I_v, and Φ.

Atkinson and Hancock (2005a) reconstruct the orientation of dielectric surfaces based on the Fresnel equations. In this scenario, the refraction index n_i of the external medium, e.g. air, can be approximated as $n_i = 1$, while the refraction index of the dielectric material is denoted by n_t. The angle θ_i is the incidence angle as defined in Sect. 3.2.2.1 and θ_t the angle between the surface normal and the direction of the light inside the material. The angles θ_i and θ_t are interrelated by Snellius's refraction law according to

$$n_i \sin \theta_i = n_t \sin \theta_t. \tag{3.54}$$

The Fresnel reflection coefficients are defined as

$$F_\perp = \frac{n_i \cos \theta_i - n_t \cos \theta_t}{n_i \cos \theta_i + n_t \cos \theta_t} \tag{3.55}$$

$$F_\parallel = \frac{n_t \cos \theta_i - n_i \cos \theta_t}{n_t \cos \theta_i + n_i \cos \theta_t}, \tag{3.56}$$

where (3.55) and (3.56) yield the fraction of the amplitude of the electric field of the incident light and that of the light polarised orthogonal and parallel, respectively, with respect to the plane defined by the surface normal $\mathbf{n}$ and the illumination direction $\mathbf{s}$. Since the Fresnel coefficients denote amplitudes, the corresponding intensity ratios are given by $F_\perp^2$ and $F_\parallel^2$.

Based on (3.53) together with $F_\perp^2$ and $F_\parallel^2$ computed according to (3.55), Atkinson and Hancock (2005b) derive a relation between the incidence angle θ_i and the polarisation degree D_p^{spec} for specular reflection, which yields for $n_i = 1$:

$$D_p^{\mathrm{spec}}(\theta_i) = \frac{F_\perp^2 - F_\parallel^2}{F_\perp^2 + F_\parallel^2} = \frac{2 \sin^2 \theta_i \cos \theta_i \sqrt{n_t^2 - \sin^2 \theta_i}}{n_t^2 - \sin^2 \theta_i - n_t^2 \sin^2 \theta_i + 2 \sin^4 \theta_i}. \tag{3.57}$$

Equation (3.57), however, is not valid for diffuse polarisation, which is due to internal scattering of incident light penetrating the surface. Atkinson and Hancock (2005b) state that the light becomes partially polarised after entering into the medium, random internal scattering processes then lead to a depolarisation of the light, and then the light becomes partially polarised again once refraction into the air occurs. Analogous to the case of specular reflection, Snellius's law and the Fresnel equations yield an equation for the degree of polarisation D_p^{diff} of light diffusely scattered by the surface in terms of the emission angle θ_e (again, $n_i = 1$ is assumed):

$$D_p^{\text{diff}} = \frac{(n_t - \frac{1}{n_t})^2 \sin^2 \theta_e}{2 + 2n_t^2 - (n + \frac{1}{n_t})^2 \sin^2 \theta_e + 4 \cos \theta_e \sqrt{n_t^2 - \sin^2 \theta_e}}. \tag{3.58}$$

Rahmann (1999) exploits the fact that, according to the Fresnel equations, light which is specularly reflected by a surface can be decomposed into two components oriented parallel and perpendicular, respectively, relative to the 'reflection plane' spanned by the illumination vector **s** and the viewing direction **v**. For unpolarised incident light, the first component corresponds to the fraction of light which remains unpolarised after reflection from the surface. Rahmann (1999) concludes that the orientation of the polarised component, which is given by the polarisation angle Φ, denotes the direction perpendicular to the reflection plane.

However, this approach can only be applied if it is possible to distinguish specular from diffuse reflection. While this distinction is usually possible for dielectric surfaces, it will be shown in Sect. 3.4.2 that the reflectance behaviour of metallic surfaces is more complex and that they display several specular reflection components which strongly overlap with the diffuse reflection component.

It is favourable to employ polarisation imaging for the reconstruction of specularly reflecting surfaces based on polarisation images, as shown by Rahmann and Canterakis (2001), who utilise for shape recovery the projection of the surface normals directly provided by the polarisation angle. Based on the measured polarisation angle information, iso-depth curves are obtained, the absolute depth of which, however, is unknown. These level curves provide correspondences between the different images, which are in turn used for triangulation, thus yielding absolute depth values. Rahmann and Canterakis (2001) demonstrate that a three-dimensional surface reconstruction is possible based on three polarisation images. By formulating the surface reconstruction problem as a minimisation of an error functional (cf. Sect. 3.2.2.2) describing the mean-squared difference between the observed and the modelled polarisation angle, Rahmann and Canterakis (2001) show that two polarisation images are sufficient for a three-dimensional reconstruction of asymmetrical objects, while the reconstruction of simpler, e.g. spherical, surfaces requires at least three polarisation images.

Atkinson and Hancock (2005a) derive the polarisation degree and the polarisation angle from a set of 36 images acquired under different orientations of the linear polarisation filter mounted in front of the lens. They systematically examine the accuracy of the value of θ_i obtained based on (3.53) and (3.58). The azimuthal component of the surface orientation corresponds (up to an $180°$ ambiguity) to the measured polarisation angle. Furthermore, they utilise the result to estimate the BRDF of the surface material at zero phase angle (parallel illumination vector **s** and viewing direction **v**).

This method to estimate the surface normals based on the Fresnel equations is extended by Atkinson and Hancock (2005b) to a multiple-view framework in which the polarisation information is exploited to establish potential correspondences between different images in the absence of surface texture. Potential correspondences are identified according to similar values of $|\theta_D| = \arctan(\sin \Phi \tan \theta_i)$. A three-dimensional surface reconstruction of the surface sections around the potentially corresponding points is performed, which is then used for matching across the different images. The resulting surface gradient field yields the depth map of the surface according to the algorithm of Frankot and Chellappa (1988). The polarisation-based stereo approach of Atkinson and Hancock (2005b) is applicable to surfaces without texture, for which classical stereo vision approaches would fail.

A polarisation-based method to estimate three-dimensional shape, surface texture and roughness, and the directions of incident light for an object from a single viewpoint is described by Miyazaki et al. (2003). The proposed method performs a three-dimensional reconstruction of the object surface by deriving the surface normals from the measured polarisation properties of the reflected light. The determination of the diffuse reflection component allows one to extract the surface texture. Localising specular highlights yields the directions to the light sources, which also allow an estimation of the surface roughness based on the width of the specular highlights. For this purpose, a simplified version of the reflectance model of Torrance and Sparrow (1967) (cf. Sect. 3.2.1) is used. A transformation of the original colour image into a hue/saturation/intensity space allows the construction of an image from which the specular reflection component is removed when regarding its hue and saturation values. The shape from polarisation approach is extended to transparent objects by Miyazaki et al. (2004), who determine the surface orientation based on the polarisation angle Φ and the specular polarisation degree D_p^{spec} according to (3.57). The twofold ambiguity of the value of θ_i determined from D_p^{spec} is resolved by rotating the object, acquiring two polarisation images, and establishing correspondences between the images, which yields the surface normal unambiguously. This approach is extended by Miyazaki and Ikeuchi (2005), who introduce a technique termed 'polarisation ray tracing'. Their method determines the light path along with the polarisation properties. For this purpose, it takes into account reflection and refraction processes at the surface of the object, which again consists of transparent material, as well as light transmission within the object. A three-dimensional surface reconstruction is performed based on an iterative optimisation approach which adapts the modelled to the measured polarisation properties.

3.4.2 Determination of Polarimetric Properties of Rough Metallic Surfaces for Three-Dimensional Reconstruction Purposes

It is pointed out by Morel et al. (2005) that the specular polarisation degree D_p^{spec} defined according to (3.57) is not valid for metallic surfaces, as metals are characterised by complex refraction indices. Commonly, the notation $\hat{n} = n(1 + ik)$ is used with the imaginary part k as the attenuation index. Morel et al. (2005) approximate the complex refraction index by $|\hat{n}|^2 = n_r^2(1 + k^2) \gg 1$, which is generally true for visible wavelengths, and accordingly obtain the relation

$$D_p^{\text{met}} = \frac{2n \tan \theta_i \sin \theta_i}{\tan^2 \theta_i \sin^2 \theta_i + |\hat{n}|^2} \qquad (3.59)$$

for the polarisation degree in terms of the incidence angle. Equation (3.59) is valid for smooth, specularly reflecting metallic surfaces. Provided that the complex refraction index of the material is known, Morel et al. (2005) compute the surface gradients and determine the depth map of the surface by integration of the gradient field. The surface is illuminated diffusely by a hemispherical dome. The described method is used in the context of quality inspection of very smooth polished metallic surfaces.

According to polarised light scattering measurements performed by Germer et al. (2000), it is questionable, however, if a simple polarisation model like (3.59) can be applied to metallic surfaces. The steel surface samples examined by Germer et al. (2000) were polished with various polishing emulsions, and some were etched in a sulphuric acid solution. In the course of their ellipsometric measurements, they determine the BRDF of the surface, the degree of circular polarisation, the overall degree of polarisation, and the polarisation angle of the light reflected from the surface for a constant incidence and emission angle of $\theta_i = \theta_e = 60°$ over a range of incident polarisation states and azimuthal scattering angles. The surface roughness is determined by means of atomic force microscopy. Germer et al. (2000) compare their polarimetric measurements with theoretical predictions of the scattering behaviour of surfaces exhibiting a roughness on microscopic scales ('microroughness') and a variable subsurface permittivity. For most values of the azimuthal scattering angle, the measurements are neither fully consistent with the microroughness model nor with the subsurface scattering model, which suggests a combination of both mechanisms.

The experimental results of Germer et al. (2000) give an impression of the difficulties encountered when attempting to apply polarisation models to metallic surfaces. This is especially true for rough metallic surfaces. As a consequence, for the raw forged iron surfaces regarded in the industrial quality inspection scenarios described in Sect. 6.3, it was found to be favourable to determine empirically the reflectance and polarisation properties instead of relying on physical models (d'Angelo and Wöhler, 2005a, 2006, 2008).

The measurement procedure employed by d'Angelo and Wöhler (2005a, 2006) for determining the polarisation properties of the surface is similar to the method described by Atkinson and Hancock (2005a). A flat sample part is attached to a goniometer, which allows a rotation of the sample around two orthogonal axes. The corresponding goniometer angles γ_1 and γ_2 can be adjusted at an accuracy of a few arcseconds. As illustrated in Fig. 3.5, adjusting γ_1 is equivalent to rotating the surface normal **n** around an axis perpendicular to the plane spanned by the vectors **s** and **v**, while adjusting γ_2 causes a rotation of **n** around an axis lying in that plane. The phase angle α between **s** and **v** is independent of γ_1 and γ_2, since the centre of rotation lies on the sample surface, and is assumed to be constant

Fig. 3.5 Definition of the
goniometer angles γ_1 and γ_2

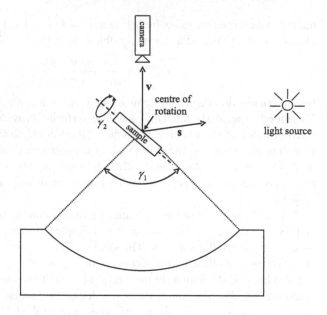

over the image. It is straightforward to determine the surface normal **n**, the incidence angle θ_i, and the emission angle θ_e from the goniometer angles γ_1 and γ_2
and the vectors **s** and **v**. For each configuration of goniometer angles, five images
are acquired through a linear polarisation filter at orientation angles ω of $0°$, $45°$,
$90°$, $135°$, and $180°$. Due to the encountered wide range of reflected intensities, a
high dynamic range image is synthesised from four low dynamic range images acquired with different exposure times. For each filter orientation ω, an average pixel
pixel grey value over an image area containing a flat part of the sample surface is
computed. A sinusoidal function of the form (3.52) is then fitted to the measured
pixel pixel grey values. The filter orientation Φ for which maximum intensity is observed corresponds to the polarisation angle, and the polarisation degree is readily
obtained from the sinusoidal fit according to $D_p = I_v/I_c$ (cf. Sect. 3.4.1). In principle, three measurements would be sufficient to determine the three parameters I_c,
I_v, and Φ, but the fit becomes less noise-sensitive when more measurements are
used.

As is apparent from the previous discussion, no accurate physically motivated
model for the polarisation properties of rough metallic surfaces is available. Hence,
d'Angelo and Wöhler (2005a) fit a phenomenological model, here a polynomial
in terms of the goniometer angles γ_1 and γ_2, to the measured values of the polarisation angle and degree. The polarisation angle is represented by an incomplete
third-degree polynomial of the form

$$R_\Phi(\gamma_1, \gamma_2) = a_\Phi + b_\Phi \gamma_2 + c_\Phi \gamma_1 \gamma_2 + d_\Phi \gamma_1^2 \gamma_2 + e_\Phi \gamma_2^3, \qquad (3.60)$$

which is antisymmetric in γ_2, and $R_\Phi(\gamma_1, 0) = a_\Phi = \text{const}$, corresponding to coplanar vectors **n**, **s**, and **v**. In an analogous manner, the polarisation degree is represented by an incomplete polynomial of the form

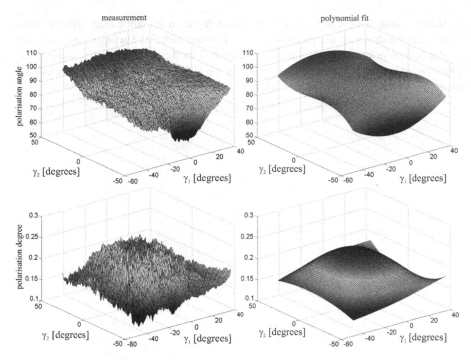

Fig. 3.6 Measured and modelled polarisation properties of a raw forged iron surface at a phase angle of $\alpha = 79°$. *Top*: Polarisation angle. *Bottom*: Polarisation degree

$$R_D(\gamma_1, \gamma_2) = a_D + b_D\gamma_1 + c_D\gamma_1^2 + d_D\gamma_2^2 + e_D\gamma_1^2\gamma_2^2 + f_D\gamma_2^4 + g_D\gamma_1\gamma_2^4$$
$$+ h_D\gamma_1^2\gamma_2^4, \tag{3.61}$$

which is symmetric in γ_2. The symmetry properties are required for geometrical reasons as long as an isotropic interaction between incident light and surface material can be assumed. The polarisation properties of a raw forged iron surface measured at a phase angle of $\alpha = 79°$ are illustrated in Fig. 3.6, along with the polynomial fits according to (3.60) and (3.61). Interestingly, while in the framework based on Fresnel theory outlined in Sect. 3.4.1 the polarisation angle corresponds to the projection of the surface normal into the image plane (up to a 90° phase shift for specular polarisation), a close inspection of the polarisation angle measurements by d'Angelo and Wöhler (2005a) reveals that this simple relation does not hold for rough metallic surfaces.

At this point it is straightforward to determine the surface gradients p and q associated with the goniometer angles γ_1 and γ_2 based on the mechanical setup of the goniometer. Based on the fitted phenomenological laws for the polarisation angle Φ and degree D_p, the functions $R_\Phi(p, q)$ and $R_D(p, q)$ yielding the polarisation properties in terms of the surface gradients p and q are obtained. In analogy to the intensity reflectance map $R_I(p, q)$, $R_\Phi(p, q)$ is termed a polarisation angle reflectance map, and $R_D(p, q)$ a polarisation degree reflectance map. Results concerning three-dimensional reconstruction of rough metallic surfaces based on the evaluation of polarisation features are described in the context of the shape from photopolarimetric reflectance framework in Sect. 5.3 and the application scenario of quality inspection outlined in Sect. 6.3.

Chapter 4
Point Spread Function-Based Approaches to Three-Dimensional Scene Reconstruction

Basically, there are two distinct approaches to utilising focus information for depth estimation. Section 4.1 gives an outline of the concept of the point spread function (PSF) of an optical system. The depth from defocus approach described in Sect. 4.2 consists of acquiring a small number of images at different focus settings, where the differences of the PSF across the set of images are exploited to estimate the depth of scene points. The depth from focus method described in Sect. 4.3 aims for determining depth by acquiring several images at different known focus settings, where the configuration for which the best focused image is observed is used to compute the distance to the scene point based on the known intrinsic camera parameters.

4.1 The Point Spread Function

In contrast to the pinhole camera model assumed in the previous chapters, a real optical system must be described as a two-dimensional linear filter characterised by a (generally spatially non-uniform) point spread function (PSF).

According to the description by Kuhl et al. (2006), for monochromatic light an exact description of the PSF due to diffraction of light at a circular aperture is given by the radially symmetric Airy pattern

$$A(r) \propto \left(\frac{J_1(r)}{r} \right)^2, \tag{4.1}$$

where $J_1(r)$ is a Bessel function of the first kind of first order (Pedrotti, 1993). A cross section of the Airy pattern with its central maximum and concentric rings of decreasing brightness is shown in Fig. 4.1. The central maximum is also called the 'Airy disk'. For practical purposes, however, particularly when a variety of additional lens-specific influencing quantities (e.g. chromatic aberration) is involved, the Gaussian function is a reasonable approximation to the PSF according to

$$G_\sigma(\hat{u}, \hat{v}) = \frac{1}{2\pi\sigma^2} e^{-\frac{(\hat{u}-\hat{u}_c)^2 + (\hat{v}-\hat{v}_c)^2}{2\sigma^2}} \tag{4.2}$$

C. Wöhler, *3D Computer Vision*, X.media.publishing,
DOI 10.1007/978-1-4471-4150-1_4, © Springer-Verlag London 2013

Fig. 4.1 Cross section of the
Airy pattern $A(r)$ according
to (4.1)

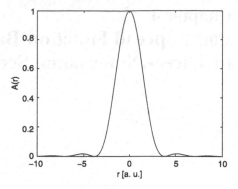

(cf. also Subbarao, 1988; Chaudhuri and Rajagopalan, 1999; McCloskey et al., 2007; and Namboodiri et al., 2008). In (4.2), the centre of the PSF is denoted by $(\hat{u}_c, \hat{v}_c)$. The perceived amount of image blur increases with increasing values of σ. In the following, σ will be referred to as the 'radius' of the PSF.

4.2 Reconstruction of Depth from Defocus

The PSF-based depth from defocus method relies on the fact that the image of a scene point situated at a distance z from the camera becomes more and more blurred, i.e. the PSF radius σ increases, with increasing depth offset $(z - z_0)$ between the scene point at distance z and the plane at distance z_0 on which the camera is focused.

4.2.1 Basic Principles

This introductory section first follows the descriptions by Pentland (1987), Subbarao (1988), and Chaudhuri and Rajagopalan (1999). Accordingly, for an image acquired by a camera with principal distance b, i.e. the distance between the optical centre and the image plane, and focal length f, the depth z_0 of a perfectly focused scene point is given by the lens law

$$\frac{1}{b} + \frac{1}{z_0} = \frac{1}{f} \tag{4.3}$$

(Pedrotti, 1993). Pentland (1987) introduces the concept of the 'blur circle' (also known as the 'circle of confusion') into the depth from defocus framework. Following his derivation, the lens law (4.3) yields for the distance z_0 between the lens and a scene point imaged without blur the   relation $z_0 = f b_0 / (b_0 - f)$, where b_0 is the distance between the optical centre and the image plane without blur and f is the focal length of the lens (cf. Fig. 4.2). For a different distance b between the optical centre and the image plane, an object at distance $z = f b / (b - f)$ appears without

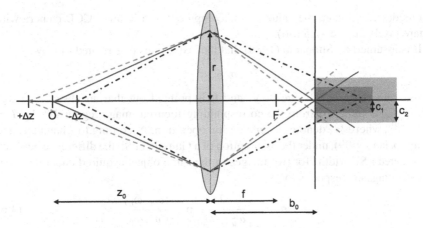

Fig. 4.2 Relation between a depth offset Δz and the resulting circles of confusion with radii c_1 and c_2 according to Pentland (1987)

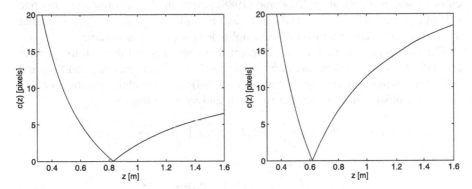

Fig. 4.3 Dependence of the radius c of the circle of confusion on the depth z for a lens of $f = 12$ mm at $\kappa = 1.4$ (*left*) and for a lens of $f = 20$ mm at $\kappa = 2.4$ (*right*). The value of c is given in pixels, where the size of the square pixels corresponds to 4.65 μm. For each configuration, the principal distance b is assumed to be fixed. The image is best focused at a depth of about 0.8 m and 0.6 m, respectively

blur. Figure 4.2 reveals that $r/b = c/(b_0 - b)$ with r as the lens radius and c as the radius of the circle of confusion, i.e. the circle at which the scene point appears in the image plane. According to Pentland (1987), inserting the third into the second relation yields $z = f r b_0 / [r b_0 - f(r + c)]$, corresponding to

$$z = \frac{f b_0}{b_0 - f - 2 c \kappa} \tag{4.4}$$

with $\kappa = f/(2r)$ as the f-stop number of the lens. For illustration, the dependence of the radius c on the depth z for fixed focal length f and principal distance b according to (4.4) is shown for a lens of $f = 12$ mm at $\kappa = 1.4$ and for a lens of $f = 20$ mm at $\kappa = 2.4$ in Fig. 4.3 (to allow a comparison with the experimental results described later, the value of c is computed for a Baumer CCD camera with square pixels of size 4.65 μm).

It is assumed by Subbarao (1988) that the PSF radius σ is related to c by

$$\sigma = \gamma c \tag{4.5}$$

with a camera-specific value of γ, and it is pointed out that an observed image region I_{uv} is obtained from the corresponding focused image region $I^{(0)}$ by $I = G_\sigma * I^{(0)}$, where '*' denotes a convolution operation. According to Chaudhuri and Rajagopalan (1999), under the assumption of a Gaussian PSF the difference between the squared PSF widths for two images of the same object acquired under different focus settings corresponds to

$$\sigma_1^2 - \sigma_2^2 = -\frac{2}{\omega_u^2 + \omega_v^2} \ln \frac{\mathcal{I}_1(\omega_u, \omega_v)}{\mathcal{I}_2(\omega_u, \omega_v)}, \tag{4.6}$$

where $\mathcal{I}_1(\omega_u, \omega_v)$ and $\mathcal{I}_2(\omega_u, \omega_v)$ are the amplitude spectra obtained for the two focus configurations. Note that in frequency space, the convolution becomes an element-wise multiplication. Subbarao (1988) points out that, in principle, only one pair of amplitudes $\mathcal{I}_1(\omega_u, \omega_v)$ and $\mathcal{I}_2(\omega_u, \omega_v)$ is required to compute $(\sigma_1^2 - \sigma_2^2)$, but averaging over a larger domain of the amplitude spectrum is favourable.

For two images blurred due to different focus settings and thus (in the general case) different principal distances b_1 and b_2, different focal lengths f_1 and f_2, and different lens apertures r_1 and r_2, Subbarao (1988) and Chaudhuri and Rajagopalan (1999) establish a linear relation between σ_1 and σ_2 according to

$$\sigma_1 = \alpha \sigma_2 + \beta \quad \text{with } \alpha = \frac{r_1 b_1}{r_2 b_2} \text{ and } \beta = \gamma r_1 b_1 \left(\frac{1}{f_1} - \frac{1}{b_1} - \frac{1}{f_2} + \frac{1}{b_2} \right) \tag{4.7}$$

and derive from (4.7) the relation

$$\sigma_1^2 - \sigma_2^2 = (\alpha^2 - 1)\sigma_2^2 + 2\alpha\beta\sigma_2 + \beta^2. \tag{4.8}$$

The value of σ_2 is then obtained from (4.8) when the value of $(\sigma_1^2 - \sigma_2^2)$ determined according to (4.6) is inserted into (4.8).

Pentland (1987) suggests an approach to determining the amount of defocus in the image which assumes that intensity transitions along object borders are ideal step functions in the real world, which are blurred by the optical system of the camera. For this purpose, Pentland (1987) analyses Laplace-filtered blurred images in order to determine the PSF radius.

As an example, two intensity profiles extracted orthogonal to an object boundary, displaying different amounts of defocus, are shown in Fig. 4.4. According to Krüger and Wöhler (2011), the intensity profile $I(u)$ generated by blurring an ideal edge with a Gaussian PSF can also be represented by a function of the form

$$I(u) = a \, \text{erf}\left(\frac{u - u_0}{\sqrt{2}\sigma} \right) + b \tag{4.9}$$

with u as the pixel coordinate orthogonal to the boundary, a as the amplitude of the edge, b as an offset parameter, u_0 as the position of the steepest brightness

Fig. 4.4 Two intensity profiles, extracted orthogonal to a slightly defocused (*solid curve*) and a strongly defocused (*dashed curve*) object boundary, respectively

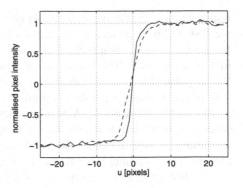

gradient, and σ as the PSF radius in pixel units (cf. Sect. 1.4.8). The error function $\text{erf}(t) = \frac{2}{\sqrt{\pi}} \int_0^t e^{-s^2}\, ds$ is the step response following from the Gaussian PSF. The edge is steep, i.e. well focused, for $\sigma \to 0$, while the amount of defocus increases for increasing σ.

Subbarao and Wei (1992) introduce a computationally efficient method to determine the width of the PSF based on the evaluation of one-dimensional intensity profiles rather than two-dimensional image regions. The one-dimensional profiles are obtained by summing the pixel rows. The fast Fourier transform algorithm used to compute the amplitude spectrum assumes that the image continues periodically at its borders, which may introduce spurious high spatial frequency components when the grey values at the borders are not equal. To circumvent this problem, Subbarao and Wei (1992) perform a pixel-wise multiplication of the grey values of the image with a two-dimensional Gaussian weighting function such that the pixel grey values decrease from the centre of the image towards its borders.

Another computationally efficient scheme to determine the PSF difference between two images, which is based on the inverse S-transform, is introduced by Subbarao and Surya (1994), involving local spatial filtering operations rather than a two-dimensional Fourier transform. Their approach allows PSFs of arbitrary, non-Gaussian shape by introducing a generalisation of the parameter σ as the square root of the second central moment of the arbitrarily shaped PSF.

Watanabe et al. (1996) present a real-time system for estimating depth from defocus which relies on a specially designed telecentric lens which generates two differently focused images using a prism element. A light pattern is projected into the scene being analysed such that depth values can also be obtained for uniform surfaces. The 'pillbox' function, which corresponds to a blur circle of uniform intensity, is used as a PSF instead of a Gaussian function.

Chaudhuri and Rajagopalan (1999) introduce the 'block shift-variant blur model', which takes into account the mutual influences of the PSF widths of neighbouring image regions. Furthermore, a variational approach which enforces a smooth behaviour of the PSF width is introduced. Based on a maximum likelihood approach, a criterion for the optimal relative blurring of the two regarded images is inferred. These frameworks are extended by Chaudhuri and Rajagopalan (1999) to a depth estimation based on several images of the scene acquired at different focus settings. Furthermore, a simulated annealing-based approach for estimating the PSF width based on a focused and a blurred image is developed, and a method for a coupled estimation of the PSF width and the pixel grey values of the focused image is proposed. The mathematical frameworks established by Chaudhuri and Rajagopalan (1999) are especially useful in the presence of a strongly non-uniform PSF or considerable depth discontinuities.

In order to increase the depth accuracy at the borders of objects in the scene, where the depth map is discontinuous, McCloskey et al. (2007) suggest to estimate the amount of image blur based on elliptical regions oriented orthogonal to the direction of the maximum variation of the depth.

Namboodiri et al. (2008) propose a regularisation approach to the estimation of dense depth maps that also applies for scene parts in which no surface structure is present. Based on the framework outlined by Chaudhuri and Rajagopalan (1999), a Markov random field method is developed which allows one to determine the maximum a posteriori solution for the depth map using graph cut-based optimisation.

Section 4.2.2 describes to which extent relatively small depth differences across surfaces can be recovered with the depth from defocus method under realistic circumstances. Section 4.2.3 introduces a framework for the determination of absolute depth values across broad ranges, introducing an appropriate empirical calibration approach.

4.2.2 Determination of Small Depth Differences

For clarity, in this section the radius Σ in frequency space of the Gaussian modulation transfer function (MTF) of the optical system, which results from the Fourier transform of the Gaussian PSF, is utilised as a measure for the image blur. The presentation in this section is adopted from d'Angelo and Wöhler (2005c, 2008). The observed image blur decreases with increasing values of Σ, and it is $\Sigma \propto 1/\sigma$, such that a perfectly sharp image is characterised by $\Sigma \rightarrow \infty$, corresponding to $\sigma = 0$.

The calibration procedure for estimating depth from defocus then involves the determination of the lens-specific characteristic curve $\Sigma(z - z_0)$. For this purpose two pixel-synchronous images of a rough, uniformly textured plane surface consisting of forged iron are acquired, inclined by $45°$ with respect to the optical axis. The image part in which the intensity displays maximum standard deviation (i.e. most pronounced high spatial frequencies) is sharp and thus situated at distance z_0. A given difference in pixel coordinates with respect to that image location directly yields the corresponding depth offset $(z - z_0)$. The first image I_1 is taken with a small aperture, i.e. $f/8$, resulting in virtually absent image blur, while the second image I_2 is taken with a large aperture, i.e. $f/2$, resulting in a perceivable image blur that depends on the depth offset $(z - z_0)$.

The images are partitioned into quadratic windows, for each of which the average depth offset $(z - z_0)$ is known. After Tukey windowing, the MTF radius Σ in frequency space is computed based on the ratio $\mathcal{I}_2(\omega_u, \omega_v)/\mathcal{I}_1(\omega_u, \omega_v)$ of the amplitude spectra of the corresponding windows of the second and the first image,

Fig. 4.5 Enlarged section of the right diagram of Fig. 4.3 ($f = 20$ mm and $\kappa = 2.4$), showing that c is approximately proportional to $|z - z_0|$ for small $|z - z_0|$

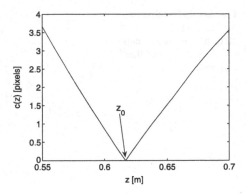

respectively, according to

$$\Sigma^2 = -\left\langle \frac{\omega_u^2 + \omega_v^2}{2 \ln \frac{\mathcal{I}_2(\omega_u, \omega_v)}{\mathcal{I}_1(\omega_u, \omega_v)}} \right\rangle_{\omega_u, \omega_v} \tag{4.10}$$

(cf. also Subbarao, 1988), where $\langle \ldots \rangle_{\omega_u, \omega_v}$ denotes the average over the coordinates ω_u and ω_v in frequency space. Only the range of intermediate spatial frequencies is regarded in order to reduce the influence of noise on the resulting value of Σ. If the amplitude spectrum of the examined image window displays a very low value at (ω_u, ω_v), the corresponding amplitude ratio tends to be inaccurate, which may result in a substantial error of Σ. Hence, we first compute Σ according to (4.10), identify all spatial frequencies (ω_u, ω_v) for which the term in brackets in (4.10) deviates by more than one standard deviation from Σ, and recompute Σ after neglecting these outliers.

For a given value of Σ, the corresponding value of $(z - z_0)$ is ambiguous, since two depth values $z_1 < z_0$ and $z_2 > z_0$ may correspond to the same value of Σ. In our experiments this twofold ambiguity was avoided by placing the complete surface to be reconstructed behind the plane at distance z_0, implying $z > z_0$. One would expect $\Sigma \to \infty$ for $z \to z_0$, since ideally the small-aperture image and the large-aperture image are identical for $z = z_0$. It was found empirically, however, that due to the imperfections of the optical system, even for $z = z_0$ an image window acquired with a larger aperture is slightly more blurred than the corresponding image window acquired with a smaller aperture. This remains true as long as the small aperture is sufficiently large for diffraction effects to be small. As a consequence, Σ obtains a finite maximum value at $z = z_0$ and decreases continuously for increasing z.

The geometric optics-based approach of Pentland (1987) and Subbarao (1988) implies that the radius c of the circle of confusion is proportional to the value of Δb, such that the PSF radius in image space (being proportional to Σ^{-1}) is assumed to be proportional to the radius c of the circle of confusion, implying $\Sigma^{-1} \to 0$ for $z \to z_0$. For the lenses, CCD sensors, and object distances regarded in our experiments (cf. Sect. 6), it follows from the models of Pentland (1987) and Subbarao (1988) that Σ^{-1} is proportional to $|z - z_0|$ for small values of $|z - z_0|$ of some millimetres and for small radii of the circle of confusion of a few pixels (cf. Fig. 4.5). D'Angelo and

Fig. 4.6 Calibration of the depth from defocus algorithm: measurements $(\Sigma^{-1}, (z - z_0))$ and fitted calibration curve

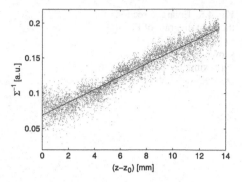

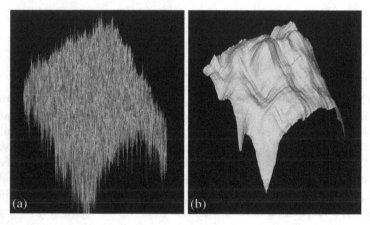

Fig. 4.7 Depth from defocus analysis of a raw forged iron surface. (**a**) Raw measurements. (**b**) Raw measurements smoothed with a median filter of 30×30 pixel size

Wöhler (2008) find that the measured $(\Sigma^{-1}, (z - z_0))$ data points can be represented fairly well by a linear function (cf. Fig. 4.6), displaying a nonzero offset due to the aforementioned imperfections of the optical system. This simple relationship holds due to the regarded small depth range. For larger depth ranges, more appropriate representations of the relationship between PSF radius and depth are introduced in Sect. 4.2.3.

D'Angelo and Wöhler (2008) have acquired images of the raw forged iron surface of a connection rod from a distance of about 450 mm with a lens of $f = 25$ mm focal length at 1032×776 pixel image resolution for $\kappa = 8$ and $\kappa = 2$, respectively (the field of view corresponds to $10°$). The raw depth from defocus measurements are shown in Fig. 4.7a. Smoothing this result by a median filter of 30×30 pixel size yields the surface profile shown in Fig. 4.7b, which provides a reasonable impression of the overall surface shape. However, the profile shows many spurious structures, especially on small scales, such that shape details are not reliably recovered. The standard error of the depth values obtained by depth from defocus corresponds to 1.2 mm (cf. Fig. 4.6), with an average object distance of 450 mm.

Fig. 4.8 Relation between the offset $\Delta b = |b - b_0|$ of the image plane and the radius c of the circle of confusion

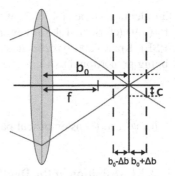

Although this corresponds to an absolute depth error of only 0.3 %, due to the relatively small depth extension of the scene of about 4 mm, the extracted set of three-dimensional points contains reasonably reliable information only about the average surface gradient, not about higher order surface properties. It is shown in Sects. 5.3 and 5.6 that in combination with triangulation-based and intensity-based methods, such depth from defocus measurements may nevertheless contribute useful information to the three-dimensional reconstruction of a surface or an object, as pointed out by d'Angelo and Wöhler (2005c).

4.2.3 Determination of Absolute Depth Across Broad Ranges

According to Kuhl et al. (2006) and Wöhler et al. (2009), in the geometric optics approximation a point in a scene is transformed into a circle of confusion of radius

$$c = \Delta b / (2\kappa) \qquad (4.11)$$

in the image plane, where $\Delta b = |b - b_0|$ and κ is the f-stop number expressing the focal length in terms of the aperture diameter (cf. Fig. 4.8). Empirically, it is found that for small $|\Delta b|$ the resulting amount σ of defocus can be modelled by a zero-mean Gaussian, which is symmetric in $|\Delta b|$:

$$\sigma(\Delta b) = \frac{1}{\phi_1} \exp\left(-\frac{(\Delta b)^2}{\phi_2}\right) + \phi_3. \qquad (4.12)$$

The radius c of the circle of confusion and the PSF radius σ are related to each other in that σ is a monotonically increasing nonlinear function of c. Hence, the symmetric behaviour of $c(\Delta b)$ apparent from Fig. 4.8 implies a symmetric behaviour of $\sigma(\Delta b)$.

Depending on the constructional properties of the lens, analytic forms different from (4.12) but also symmetric in Δb may better represent the observed behaviour of the PSF. For example, Krauß (2006) determines the PSF radius σ based on the adaptation of a function of sigmoidal shape of the form $I(u) = a \, \tanh[\zeta(u - u_0)] + b$, where $\zeta = 1/(2\tilde{\sigma})$ according to (1.90), to an intensity profile extracted orthogonal to an object boundary. Setting $\sigma = \tilde{\sigma}/\sqrt{\pi/8}$ yields an identical slope at $u = u_0$ of the fitted sigmoidal profile and the profile according to (4.9) (cf. Sect. 1.4.8 for representations of an ideal edge blurred by a Gaussian PSF). Krauß (2006) represents the dependence of $1/\sigma$ on Δb for the utilised lens as being proportional to a Lorentz function of the form

$$\frac{\psi_1}{(\Delta b)^2 + \psi_1^2} + \psi_2 \qquad (4.13)$$

with ψ_1 and ψ_2 as empirical parameters.

4.2.3.1 Definition of the Depth–Defocus Function

In order to obtain a relation between the depth of an object and the PSF radius σ according to Kuhl et al. (2006), the image plane is assumed to be fixed while the distance z of the object varies by the amount Δz, such that $\Delta z = 0$ refers to an object in best focus. But since neither z nor Δz is known, the functional relation needs to be modelled with respect to Δb according to

$$\frac{1}{b_0 + \Delta b} + \frac{1}{z} = \frac{1}{f}. \qquad (4.14)$$

A value of $\Delta b \neq 0$ refers to a defocused object point. Solving (4.14) for Δb and inserting Δb in (4.12) yields the 'depth–defocus function'

$$S(z) = \frac{1}{\phi_1} \exp\left(-\frac{1}{\phi_2}\left(\frac{zf}{z-f} - b_0\right)^2\right) + \phi_3. \qquad (4.15)$$

4.2.3.2 Calibration of the Depth–Defocus Function

Stationary Camera   Barrois and Wöhler (2007) propose a depth from defocus calibration approach that requires a stationary camera calibrated geometrically, e.g. with one of the methods described in Sect. 1.4—for all experiments described here, the semi-automatic approach by Krüger et al. (2004) described in Sect. 1.4.7 is employed. Two pixel-synchronous images of the calibration pattern shown in Fig. 4.9 are acquired at a small and a large aperture, respectively, as described in Sect. 4.2.2. The calibration pattern consists of a random noise pattern on the left, which is especially suitable for estimating the PSF radius Σ in frequency space based on Fourier-transformed image windows according to (4.10), and a chequerboard pattern of known size on the right. The pose of the chequerboard pattern is obtained at high accuracy by extracting the corner points and applying bundle adjustment (cf. Sect. 2.1). Hence, the coordinates of each corner point are known in the camera coordinate system. The position of the random dot pattern with respect to the chequerboard pattern and thus the depth z of each pixel on the random dot pattern are also known. A window of size 32×32 pixels is extracted around each pixel on the random dot pattern. Fitting (4.15) with $S(z) = 1/\Sigma(z)$ to the measured (Σ, z) data points yields a depth–defocus function like the one shown in Fig. 4.10.

Fig. 4.9 Pixel-synchronous image pair (*left*: $\kappa = 8$, *right*: $\kappa = 2$) used for calibration of the depth–defocus function with a stationary camera

Fig. 4.10 Depth–defocus function obtained with a stationary camera based on the calibration pattern shown in Fig. 4.9

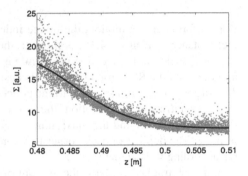

Moving Camera The description of the moving camera setting is adopted from Kuhl et al. (2006). Calibrating the depth-defocus function $\mathcal{S}(z)$ for a given lens corresponds to determining the parameters ϕ_1, ϕ_2, ϕ_3, and f in (4.15). This is achieved by taking a large set of measured (σ, z) data points and performing a least-squares fit to (4.15), where z is the distance from the camera and σ the radius of the Gaussian PSF G_σ used to blur the well-focused image according to

$$I_{ij} = G_\sigma * I_{if_i}. \qquad (4.16)$$

Here, I_{if_i} represents a small region of interest (ROI) around feature i in image f_i in which this feature is best focused, and I_{ij} an ROI of equal size around feature i in image j.

For calibration, an image sequence is acquired while the camera approaches a calibration rig displaying a chequerboard. The sharp black-and-white corners of the chequerboard are robustly and precisely detectable with the method of Krüger et al. (2004), even in defocused images. Small ROIs around each corner allow the estimation of defocus using their grey value variance χ. The better focused the corner, the higher the variance χ.

It was found experimentally that the parameterised defocus model according to (4.15) is also a reasonable description of the dependence of χ on the depth z.

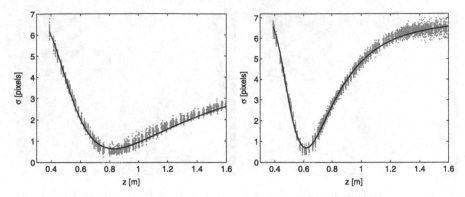

Fig. 4.11 Depth–defocus functions for a lens with $f = 12$ mm and $\kappa = 1.4$ (*left*) and a lens with $f = 20$ mm and $\kappa = 2.4$ (*right*), fitted to the measured data points according to (4.15)

For uniform camera motion, the image index j is strongly correlated with the object distance z. Hence, (4.15) is fitted to the measured (χ, j) data points for each corner i, such that the location of the maximum of S yields the index f_i of the image in which the ROI around corner i is best focused. This ROI corresponds to I_{if_i}. The fitting procedure is applied to introduce robustness with respect to pixel noise. For non-uniform camera motion, the index f_i can be obtained by a parabolic fit to the values of χ around the maximum or by directly selecting the ROI with maximum χ. The depth z of each corner is reconstructed from the pose of the complete rig according to Bouguet (2007).

For each tracked corner i, the amount of defocus is computed for each ROI I_{ij}, i.e. the σ value relative to the previously determined best-focused ROI I_{if_i} according to (4.16). By employing the bisection method, the value of σ is determined for which the root-mean-square deviation between $G_\sigma * I_{if_i}$ and I_{ij} becomes minimal. The depth–defocus function is then obtained by a least-mean-squares fit of (4.15) to all determined (σ, z) data points.

Two examples are shown in Fig. 4.11 for lenses with focal lengths of 12 mm and 20 mm and f-stop numbers of 1.4 and 2.4, respectively. Objects at a distance of about 0.8 m and 0.6 m are in focus, corresponding to the minimum of the curve, respectively. At the minimum of the depth–defocus function one would expect a PSF radius of zero, but the influence of pixel noise may yield small nonzero positive values of σ_{ij} near the minimum, leading to the behaviour observed in Fig. 4.11.

4.2.3.3 Determination of the Depth Map

Stationary Camera   An example result by Barrois and Wöhler (2007) of the depth from defocus method based on a pixel-synchronous pair of images acquired at different f-stop numbers with a stationary camera is shown in Fig. 4.12 for a door hinge. This procedure may be automated using a lens equipped with a motorised

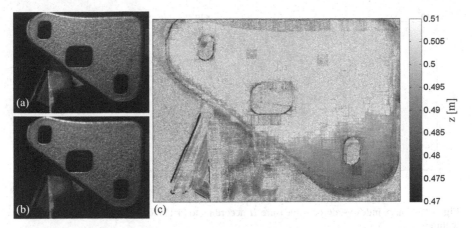

Fig. 4.12 Example of a depth map obtained with the depth from defocus approach based on two images acquired with a stationary camera. (**a**) Sharp input image, acquired at $\kappa = 8$. (**b**) Unsharp input image, acquired at $\kappa = 2$. (**c**) Resulting depth map. For the black pixels no depth value could be computed. The *pixel grey* values are absolutely scaled in metres in the camera coordinate system

iris. The raw cast iron surface of this automotive part displays a sufficient amount of texture to allow a reasonable estimation of the position-dependent PSF radius. The depth from defocus method was calibrated according to the method illustrated in Fig. 4.9. The depth–defocus function shown in Fig. 4.10 was used to determine the depth map in Fig. 4.12c, clearly illustrating that the plane surface is tilted such that its lower part is closer to the camera than its upper part.

Moving Camera The description of the moving camera setting is adopted from Kuhl et al. (2006), who extract salient features from the image sequence. These features are tracked using the technique by Shi and Tomasi (1994) ("KLT tracker", cf. also Lucas and Kanade, 1981), which is based on the Harris corner detector (Harris and Stephens, 1988). A ROI of constant size is extracted around each feature point at each time step. For each tracked feature, the best focused image has to be identified in order to obtain the increase of defocus for the other images. It is found that the grey value variance as a measure of defocus does not perform well on features other than black-and-white corners. Instead, the amplitude spectrum $|\mathcal{I}(\omega_u, \omega_v)|$ of the ROI extracted around the feature position is used by Kuhl et al. (2006). High-frequency components of the amplitude spectrum denote sharp details, whereas low-frequency components refer to large-scale features. Hence, the integral over the high-frequency components can be used as a measure of the sharpness of a certain tracked feature. However, since the highest frequency components are considerably affected by pixel noise and defocus has no perceivable effect on the low-frequency components, a frequency band between ω_0 and ω_1 is taken into account according to

$$H = \iint_{\omega_0}^{\omega_1} \left| \mathcal{I}(\omega_u, \omega_v) \right| d\omega_u \, d\omega_v \qquad (4.17)$$

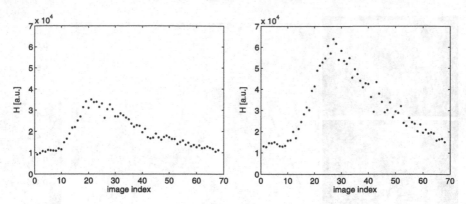

Fig. 4.13 Image index vs. defocus measure H according to (4.17) for two different tracked image features

with $\omega_0 = \frac{1}{4}\omega_{max}$ and $\omega_1 = \frac{3}{4}\omega_{max}$, where ω_{max} is the maximum spatial frequency. The amount of defocus increases with decreasing values of H. The defocus measure H is used to determine the index of the best focused ROI for each tracked feature in the same manner as the grey value variance χ in Sect. 4.2.3.2. Figure 4.13 shows the behaviour of H for two different example features tracked across a sequence. The value of H cannot be used for comparing the amount of defocus among different feature points, since the maximum value of H depends on the image content. The same is true for the grey value variance. Hence, both the integral H of the amplitude spectrum as well as the grey value variance are merely used for determining the index of the image in which a certain feature is best focused. Other defocus measures may be used, as e.g. those regarded by Nayar (1989), but it depends on the individual sequence as to which defocus measure is most useful to determine the sharpest ROI of the sequence.

The PSF radius is then computed relative to the best focused ROI. The depth z is obtained by inverting the depth–defocus function $S(z)$ according to (4.15). The encountered twofold ambiguity is resolved by using information about the direction of camera motion, which is obtained either based on a priori knowledge or by performing a structure from motion analysis, e.g. according to Sect. 1.3, yielding information about the path of the camera. If the estimated value of σ is smaller than the minimum of $S(z)$, the depth is set to the value of z at which the function $S(z)$ obtains its minimum. For an example feature, the computed PSF radii and the inferred depth values are shown in Fig. 4.14, illustrating that the camera moves away from the object at an approximately constant velocity.

An integration of the techniques of depth from defocus based on an image sequence acquired with a moving camera and structure from motion in order to obtain an accurate and absolutely scaled three-dimensional scene reconstruction is described in detail in Sect. 5.1.

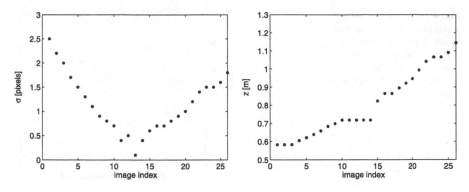

Fig. 4.14 Typical behaviour of the PSF radius σ (*left*) and depth z (*right*) across an image sequence for an example feature

4.2.3.4 Estimation of the Useful Depth Range

At this point it is useful to examine which focal length and lens aperture are required to obtain depth values of a given accuracy with the depth from defocus method. Wöhler et al. (2009) assume that for a lens of focal length f_1, an object is well focused at depth z_0, and a certain amount of defocus is observed at depth hz_0, where the factor h is assumed to be close to 1 with $|h - 1| \ll 1$. The depth offset $\Delta z = (h - 1)z_0$ implies a circle of confusion of radius c_1 with

$$c_1 = \frac{1}{2\kappa}\left(\frac{1}{f_1^{-1} - z_0^{-1}} - \frac{1}{f_1^{-1} - (hz_0)^{-1}}\right). \tag{4.18}$$

Now let the focal length be changed to f_2 and the object depth be set to a larger distance kz_0 with $k > 1$. The radius c_2 of the corresponding circle of confusion is readily obtained by

$$c_2 = \frac{1}{2\kappa}\left(\frac{1}{f_2^{-1} - (kz_0)^{-1}} - \frac{1}{f_2^{-1} - (hkz_0)^{-1}}\right). \tag{4.19}$$

The f-stop number κ and the pixel size remain unchanged. Since the radius of the circle of confusion is a monotonically increasing function of the PSF radius σ, we assume that observing the same amount of defocus in both scenarios implies an identical radius of the corresponding circle of confusion. With the abbreviations

$$
\begin{aligned}
K &= \frac{1}{f_1^{-1} - z_0^{-1}} - \frac{1}{f_1^{-1} - (hz_0)^{-1}} \\
L_1 &= \frac{1 - h^{-1}}{kz_0} \\
L_2 &= \frac{1 + h^{-1}}{kz_0} \\
M &= \frac{1}{hk^2 z_0^2},
\end{aligned}
\tag{4.20}
$$

Fig. 4.15 Focal length f_2 according to (4.21) required to obtain the same relative depth resolution $|h - 1|$ as a lens of $f_1 = 25$ mm at a distance of $z_0 = 0.5$ m (*open circle*)

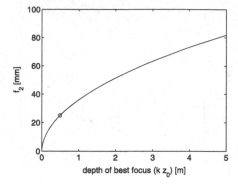

setting $c_1 = c_2$ yields the focal length f_2 according to

$$f_2 = \left(\frac{L_2}{2} \pm \sqrt{\frac{L_1}{K} - M + \frac{L_2^2}{4}} \right)^{-1}. \tag{4.21}$$

Only the solution with the plus sign before the square root yields positive values for f_2. Close inspection of (4.21) reveals that the value of f_2 is approximately proportional to $\sqrt{k}$ independent of the chosen value of h as long as $|h - 1| \ll 1$. Hence, for constant f-stop number κ, constant relative variation $|h - 1|$ of the object depth z, and constant pixel size, the required focal length and thus also the aperture of the lens are largely proportional to $\sqrt{z_0}$. Figure 4.15 depicts the focal length f_2 according to (4.21) required to obtain the same relative depth resolution $|h - 1|$ as a lens of $f_1 = 25$ mm at a distance of $z_0 = 0.5$ m. Hence, the depth from defocus approach is favourably used in the close-range domain as long as standard video cameras and lenses are used, since otherwise the field of view would become too small and the required lens aperture too large.

4.3 Reconstruction of Depth from Focus

In contrast to depth from defocus, depth from focus uses images taken by a single camera at different focus settings to compute depth. The classical depth from focus approach is introduced by Nayar (1989). He points out that the PSF of an optical system not being in focus yields a low-pass filtered version of the original image, where the high spatial frequencies of the original image are suppressed most strongly. Hence, for determining the influence of the PSF, the acquired image of the analysed surface has to display variations of the pixel grey levels on small spatial scales, which is inherently the case for rough surfaces and can be achieved by the projection of light patterns for smooth surfaces. The values of the principal distance b and the focal length f are determined based on a calibration procedure, such that the value of z_0 is directly given by (4.3). If the depth deviates from the value z_0 in (4.3) for which the scene point appears best focused while b and f are kept constant, the image of the scene point becomes blurred. Nayar

(1989) proposes to move the examined object towards the camera in small depth intervals Δz known at high precision. If a point on the surface appears best focused in image n, the corresponding distance to the camera must be z_0, and the index n directly determines the distance between the scene point and the known initial depth.

At this point, Nayar (1989) discusses the quantification of image blur in order to determine the sharpest image, and suggests the 'sum-modified Laplacian' (SML) according to

$$F_{uv} = \sum_{x=u-N}^{u+N} \sum_{y=v-N}^{v+N} \left[\left| \frac{\partial^2 I}{\partial x^2} \right| + \left| \frac{\partial^2 I}{\partial y^2} \right| \right] \tag{4.22}$$

with I as the pixel grey value, where a summand is set to zero when it is smaller than a predefined threshold. The sum is computed over an image window of size $(2N + 1) \times (2N + 1)$ pixels centred around the pixel at position (u, v). The SML focus measure is compared to the grey value variance, the sum of the Laplace-filtered image pixels, and the Tenengrad measure. Nayar (1989) shows that the SML measure for most regarded material samples yields the steepest and most accurately located maximum. The focus measurements are interpolated by fitting a Gaussian function to the maximum SML value and the two neighbouring measurements in order to obtain depth measurements which are more accurate than the interval Δz.

Xiong and Shafer (1993) suggest an efficient search method for determining the maximum of the focus measure based on a Fibonacci search, corresponding to the acquisition of measurements in increasingly smaller depth intervals. It is pointed out by Xiong and Shafer (1993) that this approach is optimal with respect to the required number of measurements as long as the depth-dependent focus measure displays a unimodal behaviour. In the presence of noise, however, the focus measure is not strictly unimodal but may display a large number of local maxima. Hence, Xiong and Shafer (1993) propose to terminate the Fibonacci search for a search interval width below a given threshold and adapt a Gaussian interpolation function to the measurements acquired in this interval.

An advantage of the depth from focus method is that it yields precise depth values. On the other hand, it requires the acquisition of a considerable number of images as well as a highly controlled environment, including accurate knowledge of the intrinsic camera parameters and the relative displacement between the object and the camera. Applications of the depth from focus method include the industrial quality inspection of small parts (Schaper, 2002) and the detection of obstacles in the context of mobile robot guidance (Nourbakhsh et al., 1997).

Chapter 5
Integrated Frameworks for Three-Dimensional Scene Reconstruction

It has been shown in Chaps. 1–4 that the problem of three-dimensional scene reconstruction can be addressed with a variety of approaches. Triangulation-based approaches (cf. Chap. 1) rely on correspondences of points or higher order features between several images of a scene acquired either with a moving camera or with several cameras from different viewpoints. These methods are accurate and do not require a priori knowledge about the scene or the cameras used. On the contrary, as long as the scene points are suitably distributed, they not only yield the scene structure but also the intrinsic and extrinsic camera parameters; i.e. they perform a camera calibration simultaneously with the scene reconstruction. Triangulation-based approaches, however, are restricted to parts of the scene with a sufficient amount of texture to decide which part of a certain image belongs to which part of another image. Occlusions may occur, such that corresponding points or features are hidden in some images, the appearance of the objects may change from image to image due to perspective distortions, and in the presence of objects with non-Lambertian surface properties the observed pixel grey values may vary strongly from image to image, such that establishing correspondences between images becomes inaccurate or impossible.

Intensity-based approaches to three-dimensional scene reconstruction (cf. Chap. 3) exploit the observed reflectance by determining the surface normal for each image pixel. They are especially suited for textureless parts of the scene, but if several images of the scene are available, it is also possible to separate texture from shading effects. The drawbacks are that the reflectance properties of the regarded surfaces must be known, the reconstructed scene structure may be ambiguous, especially with respect to its large-scale properties, and small systematic errors of the estimated surface gradients may cumulate into large depth errors on large scales.

Point spread function (PSF)-based approaches (cf. Chap. 4) directly estimate the depth of scene points based on several images acquired at different focus settings. While the depth from focus method determines depth values based on the configuration of best focus, the problem of depth estimation reduces to an estimation of the PSF difference between images for the depth from defocus method. Depth from defocus can be easily applied and no a priori knowledge about the scene is required,

C. Wöhler, *3D Computer Vision*, X.media.publishing,
DOI 10.1007/978-1-4471-4150-1_5, © Springer-Verlag London 2013

but a sufficient amount of surface texture is required. Due to the fact that estimation of the PSF is sensitive with respect to pixel noise, the resulting depth values tend to be rather inaccurate. Depth from focus is very accurate but also time-consuming due to the large number of images required; thus it should be preferentially applied in measurement applications rather than computer vision scenarios.

These considerations illustrate that each of the approaches described in Chaps. 1–4 has its specific advantages and drawbacks. Some of the techniques are complementary; as an example, triangulation-based methods yield three-dimensional point clouds describing textured parts of the scene while intensity-based methods may be able to reconstruct textureless regions between the points. Hence, just as the human visual system achieves a dense three-dimensional scene reconstruction based on combinations of different cues, it appears to be favourable for computer vision systems to integrate different three-dimensional scene reconstruction methods into a unifying framework. This chapter describes several approaches of this kind and discusses their specific preconditions, advantages, limitations, and preferential application domains.

5.1 Monocular Three-Dimensional Scene Reconstruction at Absolute Scale

This section describes a method for combining triangulation-based and PSF-based methods for monocular three-dimensional reconstruction of static scenes at absolute scale, as introduced by Kuhl et al. (2006) and Wöhler et al. (2009). The presentation in this section is adopted from Wöhler et al. (2009).

The described algorithm relies on a sequence of images of the object acquired by a monocular camera of fixed focal setting from different viewpoints. Object features are tracked over a range of distances from the camera with a small depth of field, leading to a varying degree of defocus for each feature. Information on absolute depth is obtained based on a depth from defocus approach. The parameters of the PSFs estimated by depth from defocus are used as a regularisation term for structure from motion. The reprojection error obtained from bundle adjustment and the absolute depth error obtained from depth from defocus are simultaneously minimised for all tracked object features. The proposed method yields absolutely scaled three-dimensional coordinates of the scene points without any prior knowledge about scene structure and the camera motion. The implementation of the proposed method is described both as an offline and as an online algorithm. Evaluating the algorithm on real-world data, we demonstrate that it yields typical relative scale errors of a few percent. We examine the influence of random effects, i.e. the noise of the pixel grey values, and systematic effects, caused by thermal expansion of the optical system or by inclusion of strongly blurred images, on the accuracy of the three-dimensional reconstruction result.

To our knowledge, prior to the work by Kuhl et al. (2006) no attempt has been made to combine the precise relative scene reconstruction of structure from motion with the absolute depth data of depth from defocus. A work related to the presented approach has been published by Myles and da Vitoria Lobo (1998), where a method to recover affine motion and defocus simultaneously is proposed. However, the spatial extent of the scene is not reconstructed by their method, since it requires planar objects. In contrast, the method described in this section yields a three-dimensional scene reconstruction at absolute scale based on an image sequence acquired with a monocular camera.

5.1.1 Combining Motion, Structure, and Defocus

The structure from motion analysis employed in this section involves the extraction of salient features from the image sequence which are tracked using the KLT technique (Lucas and Kanade, 1981; Shi and Tomasi, 1994). A depth from defocus analysis is performed for these features according to the method introduced by Kuhl et al. (2006), as described in detail in Sect. 4.2.3. We found experimentally that the random scatter of the feature positions extracted by the KLT tracker is largely independent of the image blur for PSF radii smaller than 5 pixels and is always of the order of 0.1 pixel. However, more features are detected and fewer features are lost by the tracker when the tracking procedure is started on a well-focused image. Hence, the tracking procedure is repeated, starting from the sharpest image located near the middle of the sequence which displays the largest value of H according to (4.17) averaged over all previously detected features, proceeding towards either end of the sequence and using the regions of interest (ROIs) extracted from this image as reference patterns. The three-dimensional coordinates $^W\mathbf{x}_k$ of the scene points are then computed by extending the classical bundle adjustment error term (1.25) with an additional error term that takes into account the depth from defocus measurements, leading to the combined error term

$$E_{\text{comb}} = \sum_{i=1}^{L}\sum_{k=1}^{K}\left\|{}^{S_i}_{I_i}T^{-1}\big(\mathcal{Q}\big({}^{C_i}_{W}T, \{c_j\}_i, {}^W\mathbf{x}_k\big)\big) - {}^{S_i}_{I_i}T^{-1}\big({}^{S_i}\mathbf{x}_k\big)\right\|^2$$
$$+ \alpha\big(\mathcal{S}\big([{}^{C_i}_{W}T{}^W\mathbf{x}_k]_z\big) - \sigma_{ik}\big)^2. \tag{5.1}$$

The error term E_{comb} is minimised with respect to the L camera transforms ${}^{C_i}_{W}T$ and the K scene points $^W\mathbf{x}_k$. The value of σ_{ik} corresponds to the estimated PSF radius for feature k in image i, α is a weighting factor, $\mathcal{S}$ the depth–defocus function that yields the expected PSF radius of feature k in image i, and $[{}^{C_i}_{W}T{}^W\mathbf{x}_k]_z$ the z coordinate (depth) of a scene point. The estimated radii σ_{ik} of the Gaussian PSFs define a regularisation term in (5.1), such that absolutely scaled three-dimensional coordinates $^W\mathbf{x}_k$ of the scene points are obtained. The values of $^W\mathbf{x}_k$ are initialised according to the depth values estimated based on the depth from defocus approach. To minimise the error term E_{comb} the Levenberg–Marquardt algorithm (Press et al., 2007) is used, and to reduce the effect of outliers, the M-estimator technique (Rey,

1983) is used. A possible extension of our optimisation technique not regarded in the experiments described in Sect. 5.1.3 is to first weight down errors with a robust estimator, and if after some iteration steps some points are regarded as outliers, to repeat the weighting on the reduced set of observations. Furthermore, it might be favourable to compare the residuals with their individual covariance information, which provides information about how much larger a residual is than it is thought to be determined from the given data. Such techniques are known to improve the convergence behaviour in many applications, but in the experiments regarded in Sect. 4 our simple robust estimator was always sufficient to obtain a solution after a few tens of iterations of the Levenberg–Marquardt scheme.

5.1.2 Online Version of the Algorithm

The integrated three-dimensional reconstruction method described so far is an offline algorithm. The error term (5.1) is minimised once for the complete image sequence after acquisition. This section describes an online version of the proposed combination of structure from motion and depth from defocus as presented by Wöhler et al. (2009), processing the acquired images instantaneously and thus generating a refined reconstruction result as soon as a new image has been acquired. This is a desired property for systems, e.g. in the context of mobile robot navigation, simultaneous localisation and mapping (SLAM), or in situ exploration.

The online version starts by acquiring the current image. Features already present in the previous image are searched by the KLT tracker, and lost features may be replaced with new ones. The amount of defocus is obtained for each feature within the current frame based on the high-frequency integral H of the ROI around the feature position (cf. (4.17)). For each tracked feature, the best focused ROI is determined by fitting a second-degree polynomial to the values of H. Possible candidates that may already have passed their point of best focus are identified based on a threshold rating. The initial depth value is then computed for each tracked feature by estimating the PSF radius σ as outlined in Sect. 4.2.3.2.

The depth values obtained by the depth from defocus method are used to initialise the Levenberg–Marquardt scheme, which determines the camera transforms and three-dimensional feature points that minimise the error function given by (5.1) using an M-estimator as in the offline version. The current optimisation result is used as an initialisation to the subsequent iteration step involving the next acquired image.

5.1.3 Experimental Evaluation Based on Tabletop Scenes

In the tabletop experiments a Baumer industrial CCD camera with an image size of 1032×776 pixels, equipped with a Cosmicar–Pentax video lens of 12 mm focal

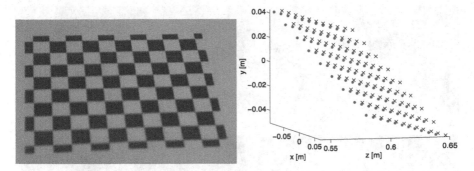

Fig. 5.1 True (*dots*) and reconstructed (*crosses*) three-dimensional pose of the chequerboard, obtained with a weight factor of $\alpha = 0.42$

length, was used. The pixels are skewless and of size $4.65 \times 4.65 \ \mu m^2$. In order to validate our approach, we first reconstructed a planar object with reference points of precisely known mutual distance. A chequerboard, as shown in Fig. 5.1, with 10×8 squares of size $15 \times 15 \ mm^2$, was used. The 99 corners serve as features and were extracted in every image using the method described by Krüger et al. (2004) to ensure subpixel accuracy. The reference pose of the chequerboard was obtained according to Bouguet (2007) based on the given size of the squares (cf. Sect. 2.1). Note that Bouguet (2007) determines the reference pose of the chequerboard by applying a least-mean-squares fit on a single image, whereas the proposed algorithm estimates the three-dimensional structure of a scene by using a least-mean-squares fit applied to the whole image sequence. Comparing the obtained results with the determined reference pose of the object is therefore a comparison between two methods conducting different least-mean-squares fits.

Experiments involving real-world objects were conducted based on image sequences that display a cuboid with markings at known positions, a bottle of known diameter, and a lava stone with a pronounced surface texture. Images from the beginning, the middle, and the end of each sequence are shown in Fig. 5.2 (Wöhler et al., 2009).

5.1.3.1 Evaluation of the Offline Algorithm

To analyse the three-dimensional reconstruction results of the combined structure from motion and depth from defocus approach, we define several error measures. The deviation E_{reconstr} of the reconstructed three-dimensional scene point coordinates $^{W}\mathbf{x}_k$ from the ground truth values $^{W}\mathbf{x}_k^{\mathrm{ref}}$ is given by

$$E_{\mathrm{reconstr}} = \sqrt{\frac{1}{K} \sum_{k=1}^{K} \left\| {}^{W}\mathbf{x}_k - {}^{W}\mathbf{x}_k^{\mathrm{ref}} \right\|^2}, \qquad (5.2)$$

where K denotes the number of scene points. To determine an appropriate weight parameter α in (5.1) we computed E_{reconstr} for different α values in the range between 0 and 1. For $\alpha = 0$ the global minimisation is equivalent to structure from

Fig. 5.2 Images from the *beginning*, the *middle*, and the *end* of (**a**) the cuboid sequence, (**b**) the bottle sequence, and (**c**) the lava stone sequence

motion initialised with the calculated depth from defocus values. One must keep in mind, however, that the absolute scaling factor is then part of the gauge freedom of the bundle adjustment, resulting in a corresponding 'flatness' of the error function. Small α values therefore lead to an unstable convergence. The value of E_{reconstr} levels off to 16 mm for $\alpha \approx 0.3$ and obtains its minimum value of 7 mm for $\alpha = 0.42$. The root-mean-square deviation of the reconstructed size of the squares from the true value of 15 mm then amounts to 0.2 mm or 1.3 %. The most accurate scene reconstruction results are obtained with α between 0.3 and 0.5. The reconstructed three-dimensional scene points $^{W}\mathbf{x}_k$ for $\alpha = 0.42$ are illustrated in Fig. 5.1, the dependence of E_{reconstr} on α in Fig. 5.3 (upper diagram).

In addition to the reconstruction error E_{reconstr}, a further important error measure is the reprojection error

$$E_{\text{reprojection}} = \sqrt{\frac{1}{KL} \sum_{i=1}^{L} \sum_{k=1}^{K} \left\| {}_{I_i}^{S_i} T^{-1} \left(\mathcal{Q} \left({}_{W}^{C_i} T, \{c_j\}_i, {}^{W}\mathbf{x}_k \right) \right) - {}_{I_i}^{S_i} T^{-1} \left({}^{S_i} \mathbf{x}_k \right) \right\|^2 },$$

$$(5.3)$$

Fig. 5.3 Dependence of E_{reconstr} (*upper diagram*), $E_{\text{reprojection}}$ (*lower diagram, dashed curve, left axis*), and E_{defocus} (*lower diagram, solid curve, right axis*) on the weight parameter α

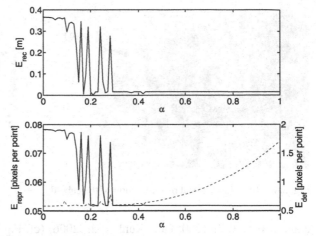

denoting the root-mean-square deviation between the measured two-dimensional feature positions $^{S_i}\mathbf{x}_k$ in the sensor plane after transformation by $^{S_i}_{I_i}T^{-1}$ into the image plane, and the reconstructed three-dimensional scene points $^W\mathbf{x}_k$ reprojected into the images using the reconstructed camera transforms $^{C_i}_WT$. The number of images is denoted by L.

The defocus error denotes the root-mean-square deviation between measured and expected radii σ_{ik} of the Gaussian PSFs according to

$$E_{\text{defocus}} = \sqrt{\frac{1}{KL}\sum_{i=1}^{L}\sum_{k=1}^{K}\left(\mathcal{S}\left(\left[{}^{C_i}_WT{}^W\mathbf{x}_k\right]_z\right) - \sigma_{ik}\right)^2}. \tag{5.4}$$

Figure 5.3 (bottom) shows the relation between the weight parameter α, the reprojection error $E_{\text{reprojection}}$, and the defocus error E_{defocus}. For $\alpha > 0.3$ the defocus error stabilises to 0.58 pixels per feature. Larger α values lead to a stronger influence of the depth from defocus values on the optimisation result, leading to an increasing reprojection error $E_{\text{reprojection}}$ due to the inaccuracy of the estimated σ_{ik} values.

Although the depth values derived by depth from defocus are noisy, they are sufficient to establish a reasonably accurate absolute scale. Hence, this first evaluation shows that the combined approach is able to reconstruct scenes at absolute scale without prior knowledge. As shown in Sect. 4.2.3.4, the described approach is favourably applied in the close-range domain ($z \sim 1$ m) using standard video cameras and lenses (f below $\sim$20 mm, pixel size $\sim$10 µm, image size $\sim$10^6 pixels). For larger distances around 10 m, the focal length required to obtain a comparable relative accuracy of absolute depth is proportional to $\sqrt{z}$, implying a narrow field of view of less than 7° and thus rendering the application of the approach unfeasible from a practical point of view as structure from motion becomes unstable for small intersection angles.

Further experiments regarding several real-world objects are described in the following paragraphs. Here we report results obtained based on the image sequences

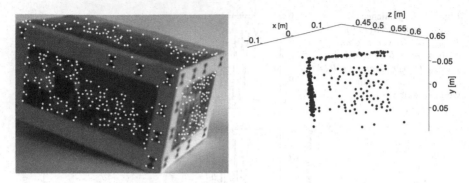

Fig. 5.4 Three-dimensional reconstruction of the cuboid

examined by Kuhl (2005) and Kuhl et al. (2006) (cf. Fig. 5.2), which were refined and extended in later experiments (d'Angelo, 2007; Wöhler et al., 2009). In order to distinguish random fluctuations from systematic deviations, the error measures according to (5.2)–(5.4) were computed for 100 runs for each example. For the utilised camera, the noise of the pixel grey values is proportional to the square root of the grey values themselves. Empirically, we determined for the standard deviation of a pixel with 8-bit grey value $I \in [0 \ldots 255]$ the value $\sigma_I = 0.22\sqrt{I}$. For each of the 100 runs, we added a corresponding amount of Gaussian noise to the images of the sequence. The noise leads to a standard deviation of the feature positions $^{S_i}\mathbf{x}_k$ obtained by the KLT tracker of 0.1 pixel.

Cuboid Sequence To demonstrate the performance of our approach on a non-planar test object of known geometry, it was applied to the cuboid-shaped object shown in Fig. 5.2a. This object displays a sufficient amount of texture to generate 'good features to track' (Shi and Tomasi, 1994). In addition, black markers on white background with known mutual distances are placed near the edges of the cuboid. The three-dimensional coordinates of the scene points are obtained by minimising the error term E_{comb} according to (5.1) with $\alpha = 0.5$ as the weight parameter. This value of α is used in all subsequent experiments. Tracking outliers are removed by determining the features with reprojection errors of more than $3E_{\mathrm{reprojection}}$ and neglecting them in a subsequent second bundle adjustment step.

The three-dimensional reconstruction result for the cuboid sequence is shown in Fig. 5.4. The reprojection error amounts to $E_{\mathrm{reprojection}} = 0.642$ pixel and the defocus error to $E_{\mathrm{defocus}} = 0.64$ pixel. In order to verify the absolute scale, we compared the reconstructed pairwise distances between the black markers on the object (as seen e.g. in the top right corner of the front side) to the corresponding true distances. For this comparison we utilised a set of six pairs of markers with an average true distance of 32.0 mm. The corresponding reconstructed average distance amounts to 34.1 mm (cf. Table 5.1).

Bottle Sequence As a further real-world object, a bottle displaying a cylindrically shaped lower half of 80.0 mm diameter has been regarded (cf. Fig. 5.2b). No

Table 5.1 Summary of the evaluation results for the offline version of the combined structure from motion and depth from defocus algorithm. The indicated error intervals correspond to the standard deviations

Sequence	Length (images)	$E_{\text{reprojection}}$ (pixels)	E_{defocus} (pixels)	Reference length (mm)	
				Ground truth	Reconstruction
Cuboid	46	0.642	0.636	32.0	34.1 ± 1.6
Bottle	26	0.747	0.387	80.0	82.8 ± 1.4
Lava stone	15	0.357	0.174	60.0	58.3 ± 0.8

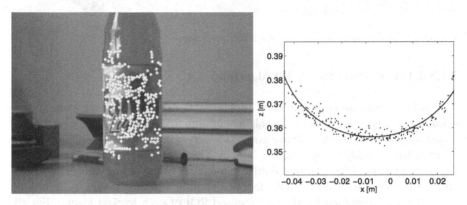

Fig. 5.5 Three-dimensional reconstruction of the lower, cylindrical part of the bottle

background features are selected, since none of these features obtains its maximum sharpness in the acquired sequence. The three-dimensional reconstruction result is shown in Fig. 5.5. The resulting reprojection error corresponds to $E_{\text{reprojection}} = 0.75$ pixel and the defocus error to $E_{\text{defocus}} = 0.39$ pixel. For analysing the absolute scale, the reconstructed three-dimensional point cloud was projected on the ground plane, and a circle was adapted to the projected points. The resulting bottle diameter corresponds to 82.8 mm, which is consistent with the true diameter of 80.0 mm (cf. Fig. 5.5 and Table 5.1).

Lava Stone Sequence As a further real-world object, the lava stone shown in Fig. 5.2c is examined. The three-dimensional reconstruction result is shown in Fig. 5.6. A Delaunay triangulation of the three-dimensional point cloud was used to generate the shaded view of the object. The cusp visible in the left part of the reconstructed surface is the result of three outlier points generated by inaccurately determined feature positions. The resulting reprojection error corresponds to $E_{\text{reprojection}} = 0.357$ pixel and the defocus error to $E_{\text{defocus}} = 0.174$ pixel. As a reference for the absolute scale, a pair of well-defined points with a true distance of 60.0 mm was chosen. The estimated distance corresponds to 58.3 mm, which is in reasonable correspondence with the true value (cf. Table 5.1).

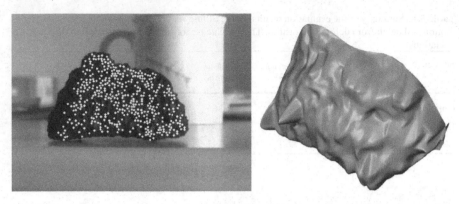

Fig. 5.6   Three-dimensional reconstruction of the lava stone

5.1.3.2 Evaluation of the Online Algorithm

The online algorithm is evaluated by Wöhler et al. (2009), where the same image sequences are used as for the offline algorithm. Initially, the three-dimensional point cloud reconstructed by the online algorithm is very noisy, as only a small number of features have already reached their best focus. The three-dimensional reconstruction result then becomes increasingly similar to the result of the offline algorithm, where small differences remain due to the fact that slightly different indices f_i according to (4.16) are determined for the best focused ROI of each tracked feature. For all image sequences, the same reference distances as for the evaluation of the offline algorithm were used (distances between reference points for the cuboid sequence and for the lava stone sequence, bottle diameter for the bottle sequence). The error bars in Figs. 5.7, 5.9, and 5.10 denote the standard deviations over 100 online runs, respectively, where Gaussian noise was added to the images before each online run.

For the cuboid sequence (cf. Fig. 5.8), the first three-dimensional reconstruction result is obtained when 21 images are processed. In Fig. 5.7, the estimated distance between pairs of reference points is shown as soon as they have passed their respective point of best focus. The correspondingly estimated distances are used to determine the average relative scale error shown in Fig. 5.7. An intuitive finding indicated by Fig. 5.8 is that the three-dimensional reconstruction result becomes more and more accurate with increasing number of processed images and tracked features having passed their point of best focus.

Similar evaluations were performed for the bottle sequence and for the lava stone sequence (cf. Fig. 5.9). The estimated absolute scale of the bottle deviates by less than 3.0 % from the true scale once 12 images have been processed, then decreases further and increases slightly again, while the standard deviation decreases constantly. When all images of the sequence are processed, the error of the estimated absolute scale corresponds to 1.9 standard deviations.

For the lava stone sequence, the absolute scale is reconstructed at a relative accuracy of 1.2 %, corresponding to one standard deviation, after 12 processed images. However, when the image sequence is processed completely, the deviation between

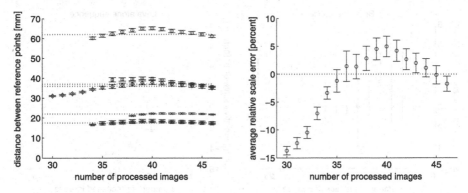

Fig. 5.7 *Left*: Distances between pairs of reference points on the cuboid surface estimated based on the online algorithm in comparison with the ground truth values (*dotted horizontal lines*). The *error bars* indicate standard deviations across 100 online runs. *Right*: Average relative deviations between the estimated and the true pairwise distances for those reference points which have already passed their location of best focus

Fig. 5.8 Three-dimensional reconstruction of the cuboid, obtained with the online algorithm after 5 (*crosses*), 9 (*stars*), and 25 (*dots*) processed images

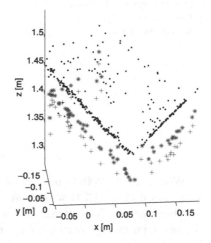

the estimated and the true absolute scale is larger than 5 %, corresponding to about 4 standard deviations, which indicates the influence of systematic effects on the three-dimensional reconstruction result (cf. Sect. 5.1.3.3).

5.1.3.3 Random Errors vs. Systematic Deviations

For the offline algorithm, the relative differences between the ground truth and the reconstructed absolute scale always amount to less than 3 %, corresponding to 1–2 standard deviations (cf. Table 5.1). Presumably, both random errors and small systematic effects contribute to the observed deviations.

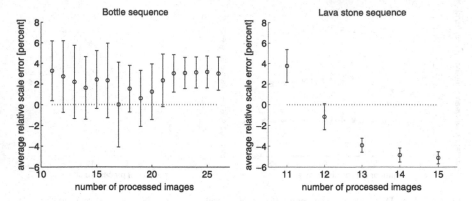

Fig. 5.9 Dependence of the relative deviation between the estimated and the true absolute scale on the number of processed images. *Left*: Bottle sequence. *Right*: Lava stone sequence

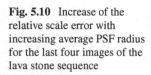

Fig. 5.10 Increase of the relative scale error with increasing average PSF radius for the last four images of the lava stone sequence

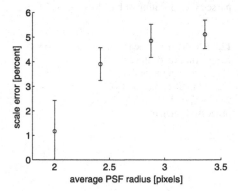

Wöhler et al. (2009) point out that random errors are mainly due to the grey value noise of the CCD sensor, which affects the estimated PSF radius and also produces random fluctuations of the positions of the extracted feature points of about 0.1 pixel. Further systematic effects are to be expected when the typically strongly blurred last images of the sequences are included in the analysis. The accuracy of the KLT tracker was found to remain stable for PSF radii of up to 5 pixels. However, the Depth-Defocus-Function $S(z)$ according to (4.15) shows a strong gradient and thus allows an accurate estimate of the PSF radius σ only for small and intermediate values of σ. This effect becomes apparent from Fig. 4.11, where the 'usable' σ range is between 2 and 3 pixels.

The estimation of z is based on the inverse nonlinear depth–defocus function (4.15). This may result in further systematic effects, since the scatter of the $z(\sigma)$ measurements cannot be described by a symmetric distribution of zero mean such as a Gaussian distribution, even when the scatter of the $\sigma(z)$ measurements can be described by a Gaussian distribution. The nonlinearity of $S(z)$ implies that the average deviation between the measurements of the depth z and the values predicted by $S(z)$ is nonzero, which becomes especially relevant for large PSF radii where the

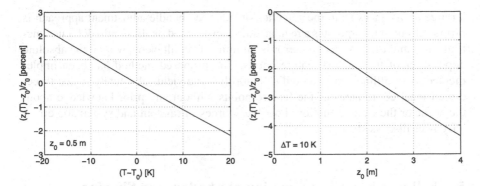

Fig. 5.11 Temperature-induced relative systematic error of the depth from defocus measurements, corresponding to $(z_f(T) - z_0)/z_0$. The focal length is set to $f = 20$ mm

curvature of $\mathcal{S}(z)$ is high (cf. Fig. 4.11). This effect can be observed when the on-line algorithm is applied to the lava stone sequence, for which Fig. 5.10 shows the correlation between the error of the estimated absolute scale and the average PSF radius σ. Measurement errors occurring when the last three images are included, which are strongly blurred with $\sigma > 2$ pixels, appear to have a substantial effect on the accuracy of the estimated absolute scale. These considerations suggest that features with large associated PSF radii σ should be excluded from the analysis, where the favourable σ range depends on the depth–defocus function $\mathcal{S}(z)$.

According to Wöhler et al. (2009), systematic errors may also be introduced by the thermal expansion of the body of the lens, which leads to a temperature-dependent principal distance $b(T)$ and thus a temperature-dependent depth $z_f(T)$, which yields a sharp image. The resulting 'shift' of the depth–defocus function (4.15) along the z axis leads to a relative systematic depth error of $[z_f(T) - z_0]/z_0$. As long as $|T - T_0| \ll T_0$ and $z_0 \gg f$, this systematic error is proportional to z_0 and $(T - T_0)$ (cf. Fig. 5.11). For a lens with $f = 20$ mm, a temperature difference of $T - T_0 = 10$ K leads to systematic deviations of the estimated absolute scale of a few percent when the lens body is assumed to consist of aluminium with a typical relative thermal expansion coefficient of 2.3×10^{-5} K^{-1}.

Other sources of systematic deviations are variations of the appearance of the extracted ROIs across the image sequence, especially when the surface exhibits specular reflectance properties.

5.1.4 Discussion

This section has described a method for combining triangulation-based and PSF-based methods for monocular three-dimensional reconstruction of static scenes at absolute scale. The proposed algorithm is based on a sequence of images of the object acquired by a monocular camera from different viewpoints under constant focus settings. A varying degree of defocus is obtained by tracking feature points over a range of distances from the camera. An extended bundle adjustment approach is proposed which incorporates a regularisation term based on the depth–defocus function, such that the reprojection error is minimised simultaneously with the absolute depth error of the tracked feature points. The proposed method has been implemented as an offline and as an online algorithm and yields absolutely scaled three-dimensional coordinates of the feature points without any prior knowledge about the scene or the camera motion. Possible sources of random and systematic errors have been discussed.

5.2 Self-consistent Combination of Shadow and Shading Features

Information inferred from the analysis of shadows in an image (cf. Sect. 3.1) may be favourably used for refining the three-dimensional shape of a surface obtained by other methods.

Schlüns (1997) uses shadow information in the context of photometric stereo (cf. Sect. 3.3) with multiple light sources in order to derive a unique solution for the surface normal of those pixels for which only two rather than three intensity values are available due to the presence of a shadow (classical photometric stereo requires at least three intensity measurements per pixel to obtain a unique solution for the surface normal, cf. Sect. 3.3). This approach incorporates shadow information qualitatively rather than quantitatively in order to remove the ambiguity of a surface reconstruction result obtained by photometric stereo resulting from the missing intensity information.

Hogan and Smith (2010) propose a method to refine digital elevation models of mountainous areas of the Earth constructed by synthetic aperture radar using information about the surface obtained from shadow analysis. Shadows are extracted from multispectral satellite images based on the assumption that they appear dark in all spectral bands. The refinement relies on geometric considerations inferred from the shadow areas, taking into account the direction of the surface normal with respect to the light source, the depth difference indicated by the shadow, the upper bound imposed on the depth between the starting point and the end point of a shadow, and the gradient and second derivative of the surface at the starting point of a shadow. For adjusting the elevation data to the shadow information, the reliability of the radar measurements is taken into account.

This section describes a framework for three-dimensional surface reconstruction by self-consistent fusion of shading and shadow features introduced by Wöhler and Hafezi (2005). The presentation in this section is adopted from that work. Based on the analysis of at least two pixel-synchronous images of the scene acquired under different illumination conditions, this framework combines a shape from shading approach (cf. Sect. 3.2) for estimating surface gradients and depth variations on small scales with a shadow analysis method (cf. Sect. 3.1) that allows the determination of the large-scale properties of the surface. As a first step, the result of the

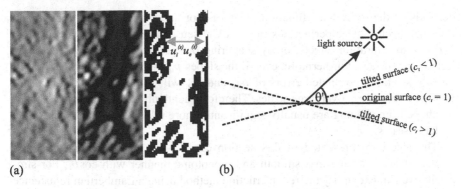

Fig. 5.12 (**a**) Definition of a shadow line. *Left*: Image used for shape from shading analysis. *Middle*: Image used for shadow analysis. *Right*: Binarised ratio image (shadow shown in *white*), the arrow indicating shadow line s ranging from $u_i^{(s)}$ to $u_e^{(s)}$. (**b**) Illustration of the adjustment factor c_t defined in (5.7)

shadow analysis is used to select a consistent solution of the shape from shading reconstruction algorithm. As a second step, an additional error term derived from the fine structure of the shadow is incorporated into the reconstruction algorithm. This approach is extended to the analysis of two or more shadows under different illumination conditions, leading to an appropriate initialisation of the shape from shading algorithm.

5.2.1 Selection of a Shape from Shading Solution Based on Shadow Analysis

This section introduces a self-consistent fusion scheme that combines the shape from shading approach based on a single light source (cf. Sect. 3.2) with the result of shadow analysis. Two images of the scene are registered at subpixel accuracy such that a pixel at position (u, v) corresponds to the same surface point in both images (Gottesfeld Brown, 1992). One of the images, called the shading image, is essentially shadow-free, while the other one shows one or several shadow areas and is therefore termed the shadow image. The shadow pixels are segmented either by binarisation of the shadow image itself with a suitable threshold or by binarisation of the ratio image. The latter approach is insensitive to albedo variations on the surface and is therefore used throughout this section and in the applications regarded in Chaps. 6 and 8.

According to Fig. 5.12a, the shadow is regarded as being composed of a number of S shadow lines. Shadow line s begins at pixel position $(u_i^{(s)}, v^{(s)})$ and ends at position $(u_e^{(s)}, v^{(s)})$ with $u_i^{(s)} \leq u_e^{(s)}$. The information about depth differences derived from the shadow is quite accurate, but it is available only for a small fraction of pixels. The depth information derived from shape from shading is dense, but it strongly depends on the reflectance function, which is not necessarily exactly known, and may be affected by imperfections of the CCD sensor used for image acquisition, e.g. due to saturation effects, or by scattering or specular reflection of incoming light at the surface. Furthermore, even if the slopes p_{uv} and q_{uv} are reasonably well known, small but correlated errors of p_{uv} and q_{uv} will cumulate and finally result in large errors of z_{uv} over large scales. Therefore, depth differences estimated based on shape from shading are usually significantly more reliable on small scales than on large scales.

The algorithm presented in this section copes with any reflectance function $R(p, q)$ that is varying in a smooth and monotonic manner with $\cos \theta_i$. For simplicity we will exemplify the reconstruction method using a Lambertian reflectance function, keeping in mind that the proposed framework is suitable for arbitrary reflectance functions with physically reasonable properties (cf. Chap. 8), in order to illustrate how to incorporate a shadow-related error term into the shape from shading formalism. For the application scenario of three-dimensional reconstruction of small sections of the lunar surface as described in Chap. 8, the Lambertian reflectance values may be inaccurate by a few percent, but this error is usually smaller than the errors caused by nonlinearities and other imperfections of the CCD sensor. Anyway, the shadow-related error term permits significant deviations of the reconstruction result from the solution obtained from reflectance only.

For reflectance functions accurately modelling the photometric surface properties of planetary bodies, one should refer to the detailed descriptions by Hapke (1981, 1984, 1986, 2002) or by McEwen (1991) (cf. Sect. 8.1.2). For the metallic surfaces of the industrial parts examined in Sect. 6.3, we performed measurements which indicate that, for moderate surface gradients, viewing directions roughly perpendicular to the surface, and oblique illumination, the assumption of a Lambertian reflectance function is a good approximation. For shallow slopes ($p, q \ll 1$) and oblique illumination, many realistic reflectance functions can be approximated over a wide range in terms of a linear expansion in p and q at a good accuracy. Sophisticated shape from shading algorithms have been developed for this important class of reflectance functions by Horn (1989), which should all be applicable within the presented framework for surfaces with shallow slopes, perpendicular view, and oblique illumination.

With a Lambertian reflectance function, the result of the iterative shape from shading scheme according to (3.24) depends on the initial values $p_{uv}^{(0)}$ and $q_{uv}^{(0)}$ of the surface gradients and on the value chosen for the surface albedo ρ. A different initialisation usually yields a different result of the algorithm, because although the regularisation (e.g. smoothness or integrability) constraint strongly reduces the range of possible solutions, it still allows for an infinite number of them. Without loss of generality, it is assumed that the scene is illuminated exactly from the right-hand or the left-hand side.

To obtain a solution for z_{uv} which both minimises the error term (3.21) and is at the same time consistent with the average depth difference derived from shadow analysis, we propose an iterative procedure.

1. As the regarded applications deal with relatively smooth and flat surfaces, the initial values $p_{uv}^{(0)}$ and $q_{uv}^{(0)}$ in (3.24) are set to zero. The iteration index m is set to $m = 0$. The surface gradients are then computed according to (3.24). Subsequently, the initial surface profile $z_{uv}^{(m)}$ is reconstructed by numerical integration of the obtained values of p_{uv} and q_{uv} according to Jiang and Bunke (1997) as described in Sect. 3.2.3.

2. The average depth difference $(\Delta z)_{\text{shadow}}^{\text{ave}}$ based on shadow analysis is given by

$$(\Delta z)_{\text{shadow}}^{\text{ave}} = \frac{1}{S} \sum_{s=1}^{S} (|u_e^{(s)} - u_i^{(s)}| + 1) \tan \mu_{\text{shadow}}. \qquad (5.5)$$

In (5.5) the effective shadow length is given by $(|u_e^{(s)} - u_i^{(s)}| + 1)$, such that the shadow length is 1 if $u_i^{(s)} = u_e^{(s)}$; i.e. a single pixel along the direction of incident light lies in the shadow. The corresponding depth difference $(\Delta z)_{\text{sfs}}^{\text{ave}}$ given by the shape from shading analysis is obtained by

$$(\Delta z)_{\text{sfs}}^{\text{ave}} = \frac{1}{S} \sum_{s=1}^{S} [z_m (u_e^{(s)}, v^{(s)}) - z_m (u_i^{(s)}, v^{(s)})]. \qquad (5.6)$$

At the pixels marking the ridge that casts the shadow, denoted by $(u_i^{(s)}, v^{(s)})$ or $(u_e^{(s)}, v^{(s)})$ depending on the direction of illumination, the surface gradient p in the horizontal image direction corresponds to $\tan \mu_{\text{shadow}}$. These values are kept constant throughout the following steps.

3. Assuming that the scene is illuminated exactly in the horizontal image direction, the shape from shading analysis cannot yield reliable information about the surface gradient q_{uv} in the vertical image direction. Especially for small illumination angles μ, changing q_{uv} for a certain surface element does not significantly change the angle θ_i between the corresponding surface normal $\mathbf{n}$ and the direction of illumination $\mathbf{s}$, which results in a small value of $\partial R/\partial q$ in (3.24) for Lambertian reflection. Once the initial values of q_{uv} are small, they remain small during the iteration process according to (3.24). The angle θ_i is mainly governed by the surface gradient p_{uv} in the horizontal image direction. Hence, for all surface elements the angle $\theta_i' = \pi/2 - \theta_i$ between the respective surface element (not its surface normal) and the illumination direction $\mathbf{s}$ is multiplied by a constant factor c_t such that $(\Delta z)_{\text{shadow}}^{\text{ave}} = (\Delta z)_{\text{sfs}}^{\text{ave}}$. For small values of q_{uv}, the horizontal surface gradient p_{uv} is replaced by the new value $\tilde{p}_{uv}$ according to

$$\tilde{p}_{uv} = -\cot\left(\mu + \frac{\pi}{2} - c_t \theta_i'\right) \quad \text{and} \quad \theta_i' = \mu \pm \frac{\pi}{2} + \arctan \frac{1}{p_{uv}}. \qquad (5.7)$$

In (5.7) the plus sign is used for $p_{uv} < 0$ and the minus sign for $p_{uv} > 0$. The surface is tilted away from the light source if $c_t < 1$ and towards the light source if $c_t > 1$, as illustrated in Fig. 5.12b. The value of c_t necessary to adjust the value of $(\Delta z)_{\text{sfs}}^{\text{ave}}$ to that of $(\Delta z)_{\text{shadow}}^{\text{ave}}$ is determined by means of the bisection method. This procedure has the strong advantage that for small illumination angles μ, small surface gradients p_{uv}, and thus small angles θ_i' between the surface and the illumination direction $\mathbf{s}$, changing p_{uv} to $\tilde{p}_{uv}$ according to (5.7) hardly changes the resulting relative pixel grey values. The corresponding Lambertian reflectance is given by $\tilde{\rho}\sin(c_t\theta_i') \approx \rho\sin\theta_i'$ with $\tilde{\rho} = \rho/c_t$, resulting in a new value $\tilde{\rho}$ for the surface albedo but almost unchanged relative intensities throughout the image. The new gradient $\tilde{p}_{uv}$ along with the new albedo $\tilde{\rho}$ is still a near-optimum configuration if $\theta_i \ll \pi/2$, which also remains true if $R(p, q)$ contains higher order terms in $\cos\theta_i$. Hence, the iterative update rule (3.24) is expected to converge quickly.

4. The iterative update rule (3.24) is initialised with $p_{uv}^{(0)} = \tilde{p}_{uv}$, and the iteration procedure is started. After execution, the iteration index m is incremented ($m \leftarrow m+1$), and the surface profile $z_{uv}^{(m)}$ is computed by numerical integration of p_{uv} and q_{uv}.

5. Steps 2, 3, and 4 are repeated until the average change of the surface profile falls below a user-defined threshold Θ_z, i.e. until $\langle(z_{uv}^{(m)} - z_{uv}^{(m-1)})^2\rangle_{u,v}^{1/2} < \Theta_z$. In all described experiments a value of $\Theta_z = 0.01$ pixel is used.

As long as the lateral pixel resolution in metric units is undefined, the depth profile z_{uv} is computed in pixel units. However, multiplying these values by the lateral pixel resolution on the reconstructed surface (e.g. measured in metres per pixel) readily yields the depth profile in metric units.

5.2.2 Accounting for the Detailed Shadow Structure in the Shape from Shading Formalism

This section describes how the detailed shadow structure rather than the average depth difference derived from shadow analysis is incorporated into the shape from shading formalism. The depth difference $(\Delta z)_{\text{shadow}}^{(s)}$ along shadow line s amounts to

$$(\Delta z)_{\text{shadow}}^{(s)} = \left(\left|u_e^{(s)} - u_i^{(s)}\right| + 1\right)\tan\mu_{\text{shadow}}. \qquad (5.8)$$

In the reconstructed profile, this depth difference is desired to match the depth difference

$$(\Delta z)_{\text{sfs}}^{(s)} = z\left(u_e^{(s)}, v^{(s)}\right) - z\left(u_i^{(s)}, v^{(s)}\right) \qquad (5.9)$$

obtained by the shape from shading algorithm. Therefore, it is useful to add a shadow-related error term to (3.21), leading to

$$e = e_s + \lambda e_i + \eta e_z \quad \text{with } e_z = \sum_{s=1}^{S}\left[\frac{(\Delta z)_{\text{sfs}}^{(s)} - (\Delta z)_{\text{shadow}}^{(s)}}{|u_e^{(s)} - u_i^{(s)}| + 1}\right]^2. \qquad (5.10)$$

The scene is supposed to be illuminated from either the right-hand or the left-hand side. The depth difference $(\Delta z)_{\text{sfs}}^{(s)}$ can be derived from the surface gradients by means of a discrete approximation of the total differential $dz = \frac{\partial z}{\partial x}dx + \frac{\partial z}{\partial y}dy$.

Hence, as depth differences are evaluated along image rows only, the second term becomes zero, and we obtain

$$(\Delta z)_{\text{sfs}}^{(s)} = \sum_{u=u_i^{(s)}}^{u_e^{(s)}} p\big(u, v^{(s)}\big). \qquad (5.11)$$

The derivative of e_z for pixel (u, v) with respect to the surface gradients p and q is then

$$\frac{\partial e_z}{\partial p}\bigg|_{u,v} = \begin{cases} 2\frac{(\Delta z)_{\text{sfs}}^{(s)} - (\Delta z)_{\text{shadow}}^{(s)}}{(|u_e^{(s)} - u_i^{(s)}| + 1)^2} & \text{if } u_i^{(s)} \leq u \leq u_e^{(s)} \text{ and } v = v^{(s)} \\ 0 & \text{otherwise} \end{cases} \qquad (5.12)$$

$$\frac{\partial e_z}{\partial q}\bigg|_{u,v} = 0.$$

This leads to an extended update rule for the surface gradient p (cf. (3.24)):

$$p_{uv}^{(n+1)} = \bar{p}_{uv}^{(n)} + \lambda\big(I - R(\bar{p}_{uv}^{(n)}, \bar{q}_{uv}^{(n)})\big)\frac{\partial R}{\partial p}\bigg|_{\bar{p}_{uv}^{(n)}, \bar{q}_{uv}^{(n)}} - \eta\frac{\partial e_z}{\partial p}\bigg|_{u,v}. \qquad (5.13)$$

The update rule for q in (3.24) remains unchanged. The iteration is initialised with the result of the algorithm described in Sect. 5.2.1. After each iteration step the depth profile z_{uv} needs to be reconstructed by numerical integration based on the current values of $p_{uv}^{(n)}$ and $q_{uv}^{(n)}$ (cf. Sect. 3.2.3) in order to determine the values of $(\Delta z)_{\text{sfs}}^{(s)}$ for the next iteration step.

A further condition is that if pixel (u, v) is outside the shadow, the angle between surface normal $\mathbf{n}$ and vector $\mathbf{s}$ of incident light must be less than $\pi/2$, and the values p_{uv} of the pixels outside the shadow have to be limited accordingly during the iteration process. This means that p_{uv} and q_{uv} must fulfil the condition $\mathbf{n} \cdot \mathbf{s}_{\text{shadow}} > 0$, which for incident light from the left- or right-hand side (zero component of $\mathbf{s}_{\text{shadow}}$ in the vertical image direction) becomes $p_{uv} < \tan\mu_{\text{shadow}}$ if $\mu_{\text{shadow}} \in [0, \ldots, \pi/2[$ and $p_{uv} > \tan\mu_{\text{shadow}}$ if $\mu_{\text{shadow}} \in]\pi/2, \ldots, \pi]$.

It is important to note that the shadow-related error term can be incorporated into any error function applied to a variational optimisation scheme, an overview of which is given in Sect. 3.2. In particular, the iterative update rule (3.30) based on the integrability error term (3.25) is readily extended to take into account depth differences indicated by shadow analysis in a manner analogous to (5.13). Three-dimensional reconstruction results of lunar tectonic faults and a wrinkle ridge obtained with this approach are presented in Sect. 8.3.

5.2.3 Initialisation of the Shape from Shading Algorithm Based on Shadow Analysis

In this section, the integration of shading and shadow features described in Sect. 5.2.1 is modified in that two or more shadows are used to initialise the shape

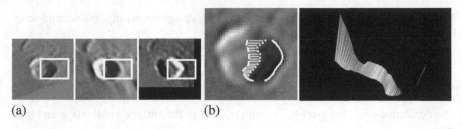

(a)   (b)

Fig. 5.13 Initialisation of the shape from shading algorithm by shadow analysis according to Sect. 5.2.3. (**a**) The *images to the left* in the middle are evaluated with respect to shadow, the *image to the right* with respect to shading. The reconstructed surface part is marked by a *white rectangle*. (**b**) Surface patch between the two shadow lines (*hatched*) along with the initial surface profile derived from shadow analysis

from shading algorithm and compute a reliable value for the surface albedo ρ. The basic idea is developed based on the example of lunar surface reconstruction with a single light source used for the shape from shading analysis, but the proposed method can also be used with shape from shading algorithms that rely on multiple light sources. The shape from shading analysis is performed by making use of error function (5.10) described in Sect. 5.2.2, which takes into account the fine structure of the shadow along with the shading information. The approach described in this section is applicable to arbitrary reflectance functions $R(p, q)$, but for simplicity we again assume Lambertian reflectance.

Figure 5.13 shows a lunar crater (Theaetetus) at sunrise (illumination from the right) at solar elevation angles $\mu_{\text{shadow}}^{(1)} = 17.9°$ and $\mu_{\text{shadow}}^{(2)} = 12.2°$ and at sunset (illumination from the left) at a solar elevation angle of $\mu = 165.0°$. The third image is used as the shading image; the eastern (right) half of the crater is reconstructed as indicated by the rectangular boxes in Fig. 5.13a. To achieve this, we again follow an iterative approach.

1. Initially, it is assumed that the depths of the ridges casting the shadows are constant and identical. The iteration index m is set to $m = 0$. Based on the depth differences with respect to the ridges, the three-dimensional profile $\tilde{z}_m(u, v)$ of the small surface patch between the two shadow lines can be derived from the shadow lengths measured according to Sect. 5.2.1 (cf. Fig. 5.13b).

2. The surface profile $\tilde{z}_m(u, v)$ directly yields the slopes $p_{uv}^{(0)}$ and $q_{uv}^{(0)}$ in the horizontal and vertical image directions, respectively, for all pixels belonging to the surface patch between the shadow lines. The known values of $p_{uv}^{(0)}$ and $q_{uv}^{(0)}$ are used to compute the albedo ρ, and they serve as initial values inside the surface patch between the two shadow lines for the shape from shading algorithm. These values are kept constant throughout the following steps of the algorithm. Outside the region between the shadow lines, the initial values of $p_{uv}^{(0)}$ and $q_{uv}^{(0)}$ are set to zero.

3. Using the shape from shading algorithm with the initialisation applied in the previous step, the complete surface profile $z_{uv}^{(m)}$ is reconstructed based on the

shading image. In general, the resulting depths of the ridges casting the shadows are not identical any more—they are extracted from the reconstructed surface profile $z_{uv}^{(m)}$. This yields a new profile $\tilde{z}_{m+1}(u, v)$ for the surface patch between the shadow lines.

4. The iteration index m is incremented: $m \leftarrow m + 1$.
5. Steps 2, 3, and 4 are repeated until the criterion $\langle (z_{uv}^{(m)} - z_{uv}^{(m-1)})^2 \rangle_{u,v}^{1/2} < \Theta_z$ is fulfilled. Again, the threshold value $\Theta_z = 0.01$ pixel is used.

This iterative algorithm mutually adjusts in a self-consistent manner the depth profiles of the floor and the ridges that cast the shadows. It allows one to determine not only the surface gradients p_{uv} in the direction of the incident light, which can be achieved by shape from shading alone, but to estimate the surface gradients q_{uv} in the perpendicular direction as well. It is especially suited for surface reconstruction under coplanar light sources. Furthermore, the algorithm does not require any special form of the shape from shading algorithm or the reflectance function used; thus it can be extended in a straightforward manner to more than two shadows and to shape from shading algorithms based on multiple light sources.

5.2.4 Experimental Evaluation Based on Synthetic Data

To demonstrate the accuracy of the surface reconstruction techniques presented in the previous section, they are applied to synthetic data for which the ground truth is known. A Lambertian reflectance function is assumed. In all examples of Fig. 5.14 we made use of the smooth surface constraint (3.20). In Figs. 5.14a–c, the true surface profile is shown to the left along with the synthetically generated images used for reconstruction, the reconstructed profile in the middle, and the deviation $(z - z_{\text{true}})$ between reconstructed and true depth to the right, respectively. The directions of illumination for the shading images are indicated by arrows. Figure 5.14a illustrates the result of the method described in Sect. 5.2.2 based on one shading and one shadow image. Consequently, the surface gradients in the vertical image direction are slightly under-estimated. In Fig. 5.14b, two shading images and one shadow image are employed, and a uniform surface albedo is used. This yields a very accurate reconstruction result. The same illumination setting is assumed in Fig. 5.14c, but the albedo is strongly non-uniform. Here, the algorithm described in Sect. 3.3.2 based on the ratio of the images is employed, yielding a less accurate but still reasonable reconstruction result. The computed albedo map is shown next to the reconstructed surface profile. Figure 5.14d illustrates the performance of the algorithm proposed in Sect. 5.2.3 on a synthetically generated object (left). In contrast to traditional shape from shading, the surface gradients perpendicular to the direction of incident light are revealed (middle). The single-image error term (3.19) was then replaced by the ratio-based error term (3.50) for a reconstruction of the same synthetic object but now with a non-uniform albedo (right). Consequently, two shading images are used in combination with the shadow information. As a result, a similar surface profile is obtained along with the surface albedo. Refer to Table 5.2 for a detailed comparison between ground truth and reconstruction results in terms of the root-mean-square error (RMSE).

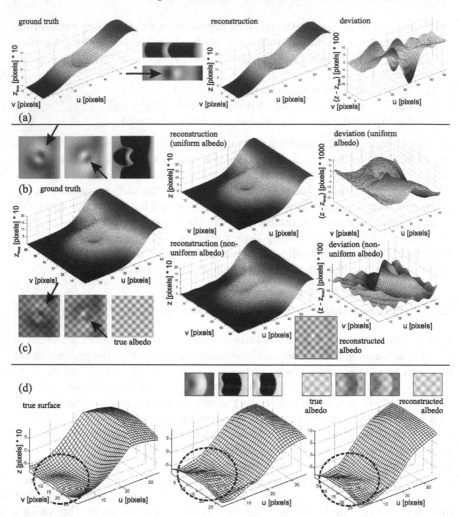

Fig. 5.14 Reconstruction results for synthetic data. (**a**) Surface reconstruction by a combined analysis of one shading and one shadow image according to Sect. 5.2.1, with uniform surface albedo. (**b**) Surface reconstruction by photometric stereo (two shading images) according to Sect. 3.3.1 and one shadow image, with uniform surface albedo. (**c**) Same as (**b**), but with non-uniform surface albedo. (**d**) Surface reconstruction by shadow-based initialisation of the surface profile according to Sect. 5.2.3, with uniform (*middle*) and non-uniform (*right*) surface albedo. The label of the z axis of the *left plot* is valid for all three plots. For detailed comments, cf. Sect. 5.2.4 and Table 5.2

5.2.5 Discussion

In this section we have described a self-consistent scheme for the integration of shading and shadow features based on at least two pixel-synchronous images of the same surface part under different illumination conditions. For a small number

Table 5.2 Comparison of reconstruction results to ground truth data for the synthetic data examples given in Fig. 5.14

Example	μ_1	μ_2	$\mu_{shadow}^{(1)}$	$\mu_{shadow}^{(2)}$	z RMSE (pixels)	ρ RMSE (percent)
(a)		4°		2.5°	0.043	2.0
(b)	6°	8°		2.5°	0.008	0.2
(c)	6°	8°		2.5°	0.052	5.3
(d)		5°	4°	5°	0.135	1.3
					0.174	1.1

of surface points, the shadow analysis yields accurate depth differences. Dense but less accurate depth information is obtained with the shape from shading approach; however, it permits an infinite number of solutions even with the regularisation constraint of a smooth or integrable surface. As a first step, a solution which is consistent with the average depth difference determined by shadow analysis is selected using the presented iterative scheme. As a second step, the error function to be minimised is extended by an error term that takes into account the detailed structure of the shadow.

The second described approach for combining shading and shadow features is especially suitable for surface reconstruction under coplanar light sources. It is based on the initialisation of the surface profile by analysis of at least two shadows observed at different illumination angles. In this setting, shadow analysis allows for deriving the surface gradients in both the horizontal and the vertical image direction along with the surface albedo for a small surface patch between the shadow lines. The surface profile is iteratively reconstructed based on the first proposed algorithm, relying on one shading and one shadow image, which is initialised with the previously obtained result of the analysis of two or more shadows.

Based on synthetic data, we have shown that a high accuracy can be achieved with the proposed reconstruction techniques. This first evaluation is extended to the three-dimensional reconstruction of metallic surfaces in Chap. 6 and lunar surface regions in Chap. 8.

5.3 Shape from Photopolarimetric Reflectance and Depth

This section introduces an image-based three-dimensional surface reconstruction method based on simultaneous evaluation of intensity and polarisation features (shape from photopolarimetric reflectance) and its combination with absolute depth data (shape from photopolarimetric reflectance and depth). The description is adopted from d'Angelo and Wöhler (2005a, 2005b, 2005c, 2006, 2008).

A number of approaches for combining stereo and shape from shading have been proposed in the literature. Cryer et al. (1995) combine depth data on large spatial scales obtained by stereo analysis with depth data on small spatial scales determined by shape from shading. Their approach, however, requires dense depth data and integrates the independently obtained results of two separate algorithms.

Samaras et al. (2000) introduce a surface reconstruction algorithm that performs stereo analysis of a scene and quantifies the reliability of the stereo data using a 'minimum description length metric', such that shape from shading is applied to unstructured surface parts selectively. A surface model described by facets is adjusted to minimise a combined error term relying on the depth inferred by stereo analysis, shape from shading using Lambertian reflectance with an additional constant term, and the smoothness of the surface.

A related approach by Fassold et al. (2004) integrates stereo depth measurements into a variational shape from shading algorithm and estimates surface shape, illumination conditions, and the parameters of an empirically modified Lambertian reflectance function. In their approach, the influence of a depth point is restricted to a small local neighbourhood of the corresponding image pixel.

Horovitz and Kiryati (2004) propose a method that incorporates sparse depth point data into the gradient field integration stage of the shape from shading algorithm. It involves a heuristically chosen parameterised weight function governing the local influence of a depth point on the reconstructed surface. A second approach is proposed by Horovitz and Kiryati (2004), suggesting a subtraction of the large-scale deviation between the depth data independently obtained by stereo and shape from shading, respectively, from the shape from shading solution. For sparse stereo data, the large-scale deviation is obtained by fitting a sufficiently smooth parameterised surface model to the depth difference values. Both approaches combine the independently obtained results of two separate algorithms.

The method of Nehab et al. (2005) combines directly measured surface normals obtained e.g. by photometric stereo with dense depth data directly measured with a range scanning device. The surface obtained by integration of the measured surface normals is assumed to be inaccurate on large spatial scales, while the surface normals inferred from the measured depth data tend to be inaccurate on small spatial scales. In the first step, Nehab et al. (2005) combine the high-pass filtered component of the measured surface normals with the low-pass filtered component of the surface normals inferred from the depth data, which results in corrected surface normals. In the second step, the final surface is constructed by simultaneously minimising its deviation from the measured depth data and the deviation from orthogonality between its gradients and the corrected surface normals determined in the first step. This approach is formulated as a computationally efficient linear optimisation scheme.

A method to simultaneously estimate the depth on small spatial scales along with the albedo map of the surface based on a single image is introduced by Barron and Malik (2011). The proposed approach relies on a training procedure during which the statistical properties of the albedo map and those of the depth map are inferred from a set of examples. A Lambertian reflectance function is assumed. Large-scale depth information obtained by other methods, such as stereo image analysis or active range scanning, can be integrated into the optimisation procedure and thus combined with the inferred small-scale depth information.

The technique proposed in this section is based on the analysis of single or multiple intensity and polarisation images. To compute the surface gradients, we present a global optimisation method based on a variational framework and a local optimisation method based on solving a set of nonlinear equations individually for each image pixel. These approaches are suitable for strongly non-Lambertian surfaces and those of diffuse reflectance behaviour and can also be adapted to surfaces of non-uniform albedo. We describe how independently measured absolute depth data are integrated into the shape from photopolarimetric reflectance framework in order to increase the accuracy of the three-dimensional reconstruction result. In this context we concentrate on dense but noisy depth data obtained by depth from defocus and on sparse but accurate depth data obtained by stereo or structure from motion analysis. We show that depth from defocus information should preferentially be used for initialising the optimisation schemes for the surface gradients. For integration of sparse depth information, we suggest an optimisation scheme that simultaneously adapts the surface gradients to the measured intensity and polarisation data and to the surface slopes implied by depth differences between pairs of depth points. Furthermore, Sect. 5.5 describes a related method for combining image intensity information with active range scanning data.

5.3.1 Shape from Photopolarimetric Reflectance

In our scenario we assume that the surface $z(x, y)$ to be reconstructed is illuminated by a point light source and viewed by a camera, both situated at infinite distance in the directions **s** and **v**, respectively (cf. Fig. 3.2). The xy plane is parallel to the image plane. Parallel unpolarised incident light and an orthographic projection model are assumed. For each pixel location (u, v) of the image we intend to derive a depth value z_{uv}. The surface normal **n**, the illumination vector **s**, the vector **v** to the camera, the incidence and emission angles θ_i and θ_e, the phase angle α, and the surface albedo ρ_{uv} are defined according to Sect. 3.2.

In the framework of shape from photopolarimetric reflectance (SfPR) according to d'Angelo and Wöhler (2005a,b), the light reflected from a surface point located at the world coordinates (x, y, z) with corresponding image coordinates (u, v) is described by the observed pixel grey value I_{uv}, the polarisation angle Φ_{uv} (i.e. the direction in which the light is linearly polarised), and the polarisation degree D_{uv}. This representation is analogous to the one chosen in the context of shape from shading (cf. Sect. 3.2) and photometric stereo (cf. Sect. 3.3). The measurement of polarisation properties is thus limited to linear polarisation; circular or elliptic polarisation is not taken into account. It is assumed that models are available that express these photopolarimetric properties in terms of the surface orientation **n**, illumination direction **s**, and viewing direction **v**. These models may either be physically motivated or empirical (cf. Sects. 3.2.1 and 3.4.2) and are denoted here by R_I (intensity reflectance), R_Φ (polarisation angle reflectance), and R_D (polarisation degree reflectance). The aim of surface reconstruction in the presented framework is to determine for each pixel (u, v) the surface gradients p_{uv} and q_{uv}, given the illumination direction $\mathbf{s}$ and the viewing direction $\mathbf{v}$, such that the modelled photopolarimetric properties of a pixel correspond to the measured values:

$$I_{uv} = R_I(p_{uv}, q_{uv}, \mathbf{s}, \mathbf{v}) \tag{5.14}$$

$$\Phi_{uv} = R_\Phi(p_{uv}, q_{uv}, \mathbf{s}, \mathbf{v}) \tag{5.15}$$

$$D_{uv} = R_D(p_{uv}, q_{uv}, \mathbf{s}, \mathbf{v}). \tag{5.16}$$

The reflectance functions (5.14)–(5.16) may depend on further, e.g. material-specific, parameters which possibly in turn depend on the pixel coordinates (u, v), such as the surface albedo ρ_{uv} which influences the intensity reflectance R_I.

As long as a single light source is used, it is possible without loss of generality to define the surface normal in a coordinate system with positive x and zero y components of the illumination vector $\mathbf{s}$, corresponding to $p_s < 0$ and $q_s = 0$ with a surface normal $\mathbf{n} = (-p, -q, 1)^T$. Furthermore, for simplicity we always choose the z axis such that the viewing direction corresponds to $\mathbf{v} = (0, 0, 1)^T$. The surface normal $\tilde{\mathbf{n}} = (-\tilde{p}, -\tilde{q}, 1)^T$ in the world coordinate system, in which the azimuth angle of the light source is denoted by ψ, is related to $\mathbf{n}$ by a rotation around the z axis, leading to

$$\tilde{p} = p \cos\psi - q \sin\psi \quad \text{and} \quad \tilde{q} = p \sin\psi + q \cos\psi. \tag{5.17}$$

It is generally favourable to define the reflectance functions R_I, R_Φ, and R_D in the coordinate system in which $q_s = 0$. If several light sources with different azimuth angles are used, one must then remember to take into account the transformation between the two coordinate systems according to (5.17).

In the following paragraphs we describe a global and a local approach to solve the problem of shape from photopolarimetric reflectance (SfPR), i.e. to adapt the surface gradients p_{uv} and q_{uv} to the observed photopolarimetric properties I_{uv}, Φ_{uv}, and D_{uv} by solving the (generally nonlinear) system of equations (5.14)–(5.16). The three-dimensional surface profile z_{uv} is then obtained by integration of the surface gradients according to the method proposed by Simchony et al. (1990) as described in Sect. 3.2.3.

5.3.1.1 Global Optimisation Scheme

The first solving technique introduced by d'Angelo and Wöhler (2005a) is based on the optimisation of a global error function simultaneously involving all image pixels, an approach described in detail by Horn (1986, 1989), Horn and Brooks (1989), and Jiang and Bunke (1997) (cf. Sect. 3.2). One part of this error function is the intensity error term (3.19). As the pixel grey value information alone is not necessarily sufficient to provide an unambiguous solution for the surface gradients p_{uv} and q_{uv}, a regularisation constraint e_s is introduced which requires smoothness of the surface, e.g. small absolute values of the directional derivatives of the surface gradients. We therefore make use of the additional smoothness error term (3.20) (Horn, 1986, 1989; Horn and Brooks, 1989; Jiang and Bunke, 1997). In the scenarios regarded in this work, the assumption of a smooth surface is realistic. For wrinkled surfaces, where using (3.20) leads to an unsatisfactory result, it can be replaced by the departure from integrability error term (3.25) as discussed in detail in Sect. 3.2.3.

In our scenario, the incident light is unpolarised. For smooth metallic surfaces the light remains unpolarised after reflection at the surface. Rough metallic surfaces, however, partially polarise the reflected light, as shown e.g. by Wolff (1991). When observed through a linear polarisation filter, the reflected light has a transmitted radiance that oscillates sinusoidally as a function of the orientation of the polarisation filter between a maximum I_{max} and a minimum I_{min}. The polarisation angle $\Phi \in [0°, 180°]$ denotes the orientation under which the maximum transmitted radiance I_{max} is observed. The polarisation degree is defined by $D = (I_{max} - I_{min})/(I_{max} + I_{min}) \in [0, 1]$ (cf. Sect. 3.4.2 for details). Like the reflectance of the surface, both polarisation angle and degree depend on the surface normal $\mathbf{n}$, the illumination direction $\mathbf{s}$, and the viewing direction $\mathbf{v}$. No sufficiently accurate physical model exists so far which is able to describe the polarisation behaviour of light scattered from a rough metallic surface. We therefore determine the functions $R_\Phi(\mathbf{n}, \mathbf{s}, \mathbf{v})$ and $R_D(\mathbf{n}, \mathbf{s}, \mathbf{v})$, describing the polarisation angle and degree of the material, respectively, for the phase angle α between the vectors $\mathbf{s}$ and $\mathbf{v}$ over a wide range of illumination and viewing configurations. To obtain analytically tractable relations rather than discrete measurements, phenomenological models are fitted to the obtained measurements (cf. Sect. 3.4.2).

To integrate the polarisation angle and degree data into the three-dimensional surface reconstruction framework, we define two error terms e_Φ and e_D which denote the deviations between the measured values and those computed using the corresponding phenomenological model, respectively:

$$e_\Phi = \sum_{l=1}^{L} \sum_{u,v} \left[\Phi_{uv}^{(l)} - R_\Phi \left(\theta_i^{(l)}(u,v), \theta_e(u,v), \alpha^{(l)} \right) \right]^2 \tag{5.18}$$

$$e_D = \sum_{l=1}^{L} \sum_{u,v} \left[D_{uv}^{(l)} - R_D \left(\theta_i^{(l)}(u,v), \theta_e(u,v), \alpha^{(l)} \right) \right]^2. \tag{5.19}$$

Based on the feature-specific error terms e_I, e_Φ, and e_D, a combined error term e is defined which takes into account both reflectance and polarisation properties:

$$e = e_s + \lambda e_I + \mu e_\Phi + \nu e_D. \tag{5.20}$$

Minimising error term (5.20) yields the surface gradients p_{uv} and q_{uv} that optimally correspond to the observed reflectance and polarisation properties, where the Lagrange parameters λ, μ, and ν denote the relative weights of the individual reflectance-specific and polarisation-specific error terms. With the discrete approximations $\{\frac{\partial p}{\partial x}\}_{uv} = [p_{u+1,v} - p_{u-1,v}]/2$ and $\{\frac{\partial p}{\partial y}\}_{uv} = [p_{u,v+1} - p_{u,v-1}]/2$ for the second derivatives of the surface z_{uv} and $\bar{p}_{uv}$ as the local average over the four nearest neighbours of pixel (u, v) we obtain an iterative update rule for the surface gradients by setting the derivatives of the error term e with respect to p and q to zero, resulting in

$$p_{uv}^{(n+1)} = \bar{p}_{uv}^{(n)} + \lambda \sum_{l=1}^{L} \left(I - R_I \left(\bar{p}_{uv}^{(n)}, \bar{q}_{uv}^{(n)} \right) \right) \frac{\partial R_I}{\partial p} + \mu \sum_{l=1}^{L} \left(\Phi - R_\Phi \left(\bar{p}_{uv}^{(n)}, \bar{q}_{uv}^{(n)} \right) \right) \frac{\partial R_\Phi}{\partial p}$$

$$+ \nu \sum_{l=1}^{L} \left(D - R_D \left(\bar{p}_{uv}^{(n)}, \bar{q}_{uv}^{(n)} \right) \right) \frac{\partial R_D}{\partial p}, \tag{5.21}$$

where n denotes the iteration index. A corresponding expression for q is obtained in an analogous manner (cf. also Sect. 3.2.2). The initial values $p_{uv}^{(0)}$ and $q_{uv}^{(0)}$ must be provided based on a priori knowledge about the surface or on independently obtained depth data (cf. Sect. 5.3.3). The partial derivatives in (5.21) are evaluated at $(\bar{p}_{uv}^{(n)}, \bar{q}_{uv}^{(n)})$, respectively, making use of the phenomenological model fitted to the measured reflectance and polarisation data. The surface profile z_{uv} is then derived from the resulting gradients p_{uv} and q_{uv} by means of numerical integration of the gradient field according to the method suggested by Simchony et al. (1990).

Note that for the computation of the derivatives of R_I, R_Φ, and R_D with respect to the surface gradients p and q, as required to apply the iterative update rule (5.21), (5.17) must be taken into account if the azimuth angles of the light sources are different from zero.

5.3.1.2 Local Optimisation Scheme

Provided that the model parameters of the reflectance and polarisation functions $R_I(p_{uv}, q_{uv})$, $R_\Phi(p_{uv}, q_{uv})$, and $R_D(p_{uv}, q_{uv})$ are known and measurements of intensity and polarisation properties are available for each image pixel, d'Angelo and Wöhler (2005b, 2008) show that the surface gradients p_{uv} and q_{uv} can be obtained by solving the nonlinear system of equations (5.14)–(5.16) individually for each pixel. For this purpose they make use of the Levenberg–Marquardt algorithm (Press et al., 2007). In the overdetermined case, the root of (5.14)–(5.16) is computed in the least-squares sense. The contributions from the different terms are then weighted according to the corresponding measurement errors. In the application scenario regarded in Sect. 6.3, these standard errors have been empirically determined to $\sigma_I \approx 10^{-3} I_{\text{spec}}$ with I_{spec} as the intensity of the specular reflections, $\sigma_\Phi \approx 0.1°$, and $\sigma_D \approx 0.02$. The surface profile z_{uv} is again derived from the resulting gradients p_{uv} and q_{uv} by means of numerical integration of the gradient field (Simchony et al., 1990).

It is straightforward to extend this approach to photopolarimetric stereo, because each light source provides an additional set of equations. Equation (5.14) can only be solved, however, when the surface albedo ρ_{uv} is known for each surface point. A constant albedo can be assumed in many applications. If this assumption is not valid, albedo variations strongly affect the accuracy of surface reconstruction. In Sect. 3.3.2 it is shown that as long as the surface albedo can be assumed to be of the form (3.47), it is then possible to utilise two images $I_{uv}^{(1)}$ and $I_{uv}^{(2)}$ acquired under different illumination conditions. Equation (5.14) can then be replaced by the ratio-based relation (3.48) such that the albedo cancels out (McEwen, 1985; Wöhler and Hafezi, 2005; Lena et al., 2006).

An advantage of the described local approach is that the three-dimensional reconstruction result is not affected by additional constraints such as smoothness of the
surface but directly yields the surface gradient vector for each image pixel. A drawback, however, is the fact that due to the inherent nonlinearity of the problem, existence and uniqueness of a solution for p_{uv} and q_{uv} are not guaranteed for both the
albedo-dependent and the albedo-independent case. However, in the experiments
presented in Sect. 5.3.4 and Chap. 6 we show that in practically relevant scenarios
a reasonable solution for the surface gradient field and the resulting depth z_{uv} is
obtained, even in the presence of noise.

5.3.2 Estimation of the Surface Albedo

For the specular surfaces regarded for the experimental evaluations based on synthetic data (cf. Sect. 5.3.4) and on real-world objects in the context of industrial
quality inspection (cf. Chap. 6), the three-component reflectance function according
to (3.14) is used by d'Angelo and Wöhler (2005a, 2005b, 2005c, 2008), corresponding to the reflectance function

$$R_I(\theta_i, \theta_e, \alpha) = \rho \left[\cos\theta_i + \sum_{n=1}^{N} \sigma_n \cdot (2\cos\theta_i \cos\theta_e - \cos\alpha)^{m_n} \right] \qquad (5.22)$$

with $N = 2$. The term in round brackets corresponds to $\cos\theta_r$ with θ_r as the angle between the direction $\mathbf{v}$ from the surface to the camera and the direction of
mirror-like reflection (cf. (3.11)). For $\theta_r > 90°$ only the diffuse component is considered. This reflectance function consists of a Lambertian component, a specular
lobe, and a specular spike (Nayar et al., 1991). For a typical rough metallic surface,
the measured reflectance function is shown in Fig. 3.4, where the material-specific
parameters according to (5.22) are given by $\sigma_1 = 3.85$, $m_1 = 2.61$, $\sigma_2 = 9.61$, and
$m_2 = 15.8$. The specular lobe is described by σ_1 and m_1, and the specular spike by
σ_2 and m_2, respectively.

One possible way to determine a uniform surface albedo ρ is its estimation based
on the specular reflections in the images used for three-dimensional reconstruction,
which appear as regions of maximum intensity $I_{spec}^{(l)}$ as long as the reflectance behaviour is strongly specular, i.e. at least one of the parameters σ_n is much larger
than 1. Note that the pixel grey values of these regions must not be oversaturated.
For these surface points we have $\theta_r = 0$ and $\theta_i^{(l)} = \alpha^{(l)}/2$. Relying on the previously
determined parameters σ_n, (5.22) yields

$$\rho = \frac{1}{L} \sum_{l=1}^{L} I_{spec}^{(l)} \cdot \left[\cos\left(\frac{\alpha^{(l)}}{2}\right) + \sum_{n=1}^{N} \sigma_n(\alpha^{(l)}) \right]^{-1}. \qquad (5.23)$$

In principle, a single image is already sufficient to determine the value of ρ as long
as it contains specular reflections. Note that in (5.23) the dependence of the parameters of the reflectance function on the phase angle α is explicitly included.

An albedo estimation according to (5.23) is not possible when the maximum intensity in the image does not correspond to specular reflection with $\theta_r = 0$. In the global optimisation scheme the surface albedo ρ can then be estimated in each iteration step n simultaneously along with the surface gradients. This is achieved by solving (5.22) for ρ_{uv} individually for each pixel (u, v) based on the values of $p_{uv}^{(n)}$ and $q_{uv}^{(n)}$ according to

$$\rho_{uv}^{(n)} = \frac{I_{uv}}{\tilde{R}(p_{uv}^{(n)}, q_{uv}^{(n)})} \tag{5.24}$$

with $\tilde{R}(p, q)$ defined according to (3.47). The uniform albedo ρ is then obtained by computing an appropriate average of the computed values of $\rho_{uv}^{(n)}$. For the strongly specular surfaces regarded in our experiments, we found that the median of $\rho_{uv}^{(n)}$ provides a more robust estimate of ρ than the mean, since a small number of pixels with inaccurately estimated surface gradients (which occur especially at the beginning of the iteration procedure) leads to a significant shift of the mean value while leaving the median value largely unaffected. If no a priori information about the surface gradients is available, the initial guess of ρ, which in turn depends on the initial guesses $p_{uv}^{(0)}$ and $q_{uv}^{(0)}$ of the surface gradients, has a strong influence on the solution found by the global optimisation scheme. Such a priori information can be obtained based on independently measured depth data, as described in the next section.

5.3.3 Integration of Depth Information

Since the obtained solution of shape from shading and, to a lesser extent, SfPR may be ambiguous as long as single images are regarded, integrating additional information into the surface reconstruction process should improve the reconstruction result. For example, a sparse three-dimensional point cloud of the object surface can be reconstructed by stereo vision, laser triangulation, or shadow analysis. Previous approaches either merge the results of stereo and shape from shading (Cryer et al., 1995) or embed the shape from shading algorithm into stereo (Samaras et al., 2000) or structure from motion (Lim et al., 2005) algorithms.

The description in this section is adopted from d'Angelo and Wöhler (2006, 2008), who show how independently acquired additional depth information can be integrated into the SfPR framework outlined in Sect. 5.3.1. It was found that the fusion between SfPR and depth-measuring algorithms is especially useful if the depth data are dense but display a considerable amount of noise, or if they are accurate but only available for a sparse set of surface points. Hence, the description concentrates on dense but noisy depth information, examining as an example the monocular depth from defocus technique, and on reasonably accurate but sparse depth information, e.g. obtained by stereo image analysis or structure from motion.

5.3.3.1 Fusion of SfPR with Depth from Defocus

To obtain a dense depth map of the surface, we employ the two-image depth from defocus method described in Sect. 4.2.2. Once the characteristic curve $\sigma(z - z_0)$ which relates the PSF radius σ to the depth offset $(z - z_0)$ is known (cf. Fig. 4.6), it is possible to extract a dense depth map from a pixel-synchronous pair of images of a surface of unknown shape, provided that the images are acquired at the same focus setting and with the same apertures as the calibration images. The resulting depth map z_{uv}^{DfD}, however, tends to be very noisy as illustrated in Fig. 4.7 (variables representing results obtained by depth from defocus are marked by the index 'DfD'). It is therefore favourable to fit a plane $\tilde{z}_{uv}^{\mathrm{DfD}}$ to the computed depth points, since higher order information about the surface is usually not contained in the noisy depth from defocus data. This procedure reveals information about the large-scale properties of the surface (d'Angelo and Wöhler, 2005c). Approximate surface gradients can then be obtained by computing the partial derivatives $p_{uv}^{\mathrm{DfD}} = \partial \tilde{z}_{uv}^{\mathrm{DfD}}/\partial x$ and $q_{uv}^{\mathrm{DfD}} = \partial \tilde{z}_{uv}^{\mathrm{DfD}}/\partial y$.

In many cases there exists no unique solution for the surface gradients p_{uv} and q_{uv} within the SfPR framework, especially for highly specular reflectance functions. This applies both to the global (Sect. 5.3.1.1) and to the local (Sect. 5.3.1.2) optimisation schemes. Therefore, the obtained solution tends to depend strongly on the initial values $p_{uv}^{(0)}$ and $q_{uv}^{(0)}$. As we assume that no a priori information about the surface is available, we initialise the optimisation scheme with $p_{uv}^{(0)} = p_{uv}^{\mathrm{DfD}}$ and $q_{uv}^{(0)} = q_{uv}^{\mathrm{DfD}}$, thus making use of the large-scale surface gradients obtained by the depth from defocus analysis. The ambiguity of the solution of the global optimisation scheme is even more pronounced when no a priori knowledge about both the surface gradients and the albedo is available. In such cases, which are often encountered in practically relevant scenarios, an initial albedo value is computed according to (5.24) based on the initial surface gradients p_{uv}^{DfD} and q_{uv}^{DfD}. We found experimentally that it is advantageous to keep this albedo value constant during the iteration process as long as no additional constraints can be imposed on the surface, since treating the albedo as a further free parameter in the iteration process increases the manifold of local minima of the error function.

The depth from defocus data are derived from two images acquired with a large and a small aperture, respectively. In practise, it is desirable but often unfeasible to use the well-focused image acquired with small aperture for three-dimensional reconstruction—the image brightness then tends to become too low to obtain reasonably accurate polarisation data. The surface reconstruction algorithm thus may have to take into account the position-dependent PSF. We incorporate the depth from defocus information into the global optimisation scheme, since it is not possible to introduce PSF information (which applies to a local neighbourhood of a pixel) into an approach based on the separate evaluation of each individual pixel. The error terms (3.19), (5.18), and (5.19) of the SfPR scheme described in Sect. 5.3.1 are modified according to

$$e_I^{PSF} = \sum_{u,v}\left[I_{uv} - G_{uv} * R_I(\rho_{uv}, p_{uv}, q_{uv}, \alpha)\right]^2 \qquad (5.25)$$

$$e_\Phi^{PSF} = \sum_{u,v}\left[\Phi_{uv} - G_{uv} * R_\Phi(p_{uv}, q_{uv}, \alpha)\right]^2 \qquad (5.26)$$

$$e_D^{PSF} = \sum_{u,v}\left[D_{uv} - G_{uv} * R_D(p_{uv}, q_{uv}, \alpha)\right]^2 \qquad (5.27)$$

describing the mean square deviation between the observed intensity and polarisation values and the modelled reflectances convolved with the PSF G_{uv} extracted from the image as described in Sect. 4.2.2. This approach is related to the shape from shading scheme for blurred images introduced by Joshi and Chaudhuri (2004). In that work, however, the PSF radius is estimated simultaneously with the surface gradients, while we independently determine the PSF radius for every position in the image during the depth from defocus analysis. The iterative update rule (5.21) then becomes

$$p^{(n+1)} = \bar{p}^{(n)} + \lambda(I - G * R_I)G * \frac{\partial R_I}{\partial p} + \mu(\Phi - G * R_\Phi)G * \frac{\partial R_\Phi}{\partial p}$$

$$+ \nu(D - G * R_D)G * \frac{\partial R_D}{\partial p}, \qquad (5.28)$$

where the dependence of the surface gradients and the PSF on u and v has been omitted for clarity. An analogous expression is readily obtained for q.

5.3.3.2 Integration of Accurate but Sparse Depth Information

One possible method to obtain depth information about the surface is stereo image analysis. In the experiments by d'Angelo and Wöhler (2008), the correlation-based blockmatching method described in Sect. 1.5.2 is used. Apart from blockmatching techniques, one might think of employing a dense stereo algorithm which computes a depth value for each image pixel independent of the presence of texture (Horn, 1986; Scharstein and Szeliski, 2001; Hirschmüller, 2006). However, parts of the surface may show no surface texture at all, or corresponding parts of the stereo image pair do not display a similar structure. The latter behaviour occurs e.g. as a consequence of specular reflectance properties leading to a different appearance of the respective surface part in the stereo images. In such cases of missing or contradictory texture information, dense stereo algorithms usually interpolate the surface across the ambiguous image parts, leading to an inaccurate three-dimensional reconstruction result for the corresponding region. Hence, we prefer to compute depth points only in places where point correspondences can be established unambiguously and accurately and to compute dense depth data in a subsequent step based on an integration of the available photometric or photopolarimetric information.

Another technique well suited to determine a three-dimensional point cloud of the surface to be combined with the SfPR analysis is structure from motion (cf.

Sect. 1.3). The unknown scaling factor may be determined based on a priori knowledge about the scene such as the average pixel scale.

In the framework by Horovitz and Kiryati (2004), the locality of the influence of the depth points on the gradient field is only partially removed. Hence, the approach by d'Angelo and Wöhler (2006, 2008) incorporating sparse depth information into the global optimisation scheme presented in Sect. 5.3.1.1 consists of defining a depth error term based on the surface gradient field and depth differences between sparse three-dimensional points. The depth difference between two three-dimensional points at image positions (u_i, v_i) and (u_j, v_j) is given by

$$(\Delta z)_{ij} = z_{u_j v_j} - z_{u_i v_i}.$$ (5.29)

The corresponding depth difference of the reconstructed surface gradient field is calculated by integration along a path C_{ij} between the coordinates (u_i, v_i) and (u_j, v_j):

$$(\Delta z)_{ij}^{\text{surf}} = \int_{C_{ij}} (p\, dx + q\, dy).$$ (5.30)

In our implementation the path C_{ij} is approximated by a list of K discrete pixel positions (u_k, v_k) with $k = 1, \ldots, K$. While in principle any path C_{ij} between the points (u_i, v_i) and (u_j, v_j) is possible, the shortest integration path, a straight line between (u_i, v_i) and (u_j, v_j), is used here. Longer paths tend to produce larger depth difference errors because the gradient field is not guaranteed to be integrable.

Using these depth differences, it is possible to extend the global optimisation scheme introduced in Sect. 5.3.1 by adding the error term e_z which minimises the squared distance between all N depth points according to

$$e_z = \sum_{i=1}^{N} \sum_{j=i+1}^{N} \frac{((\Delta z)_{ij} - (\Delta z)_{ij}^{\text{surf}})^2}{\|(u_j, v_j) - (u_i, v_i)\|_2},$$ (5.31)

where $\|\ldots\|_2$ denotes the Euclidean distance in the image plane in pixel units. The iterative update rule (5.21) then becomes

$$p_{uv}^{(n+1)} = \bar{p}_{uv}^{(n)} + \lambda \frac{\partial e_I}{\partial p} + \mu \frac{\partial e_\Phi}{\partial p} + \nu \frac{\partial e_D}{\partial p}$$

$$+ 2\chi \sum_{i=1}^{N} \sum_{j=i+1}^{N} \left[\frac{(\Delta z)_{ij} - (\Delta z)_{ij}^{\text{surf}}}{\|(u_j, v_j) - (u_i, v_i)\|_2} \right] \frac{\partial (\Delta z)_{ij}^{\text{surf}}}{\partial p} \bigg|_{u,v}.$$ (5.32)

An analogous expression is obtained for q. The derivatives of $(\Delta z)_{ij}^{\text{surf}}$ with respect to p and q may only be nonzero if the pixel (u_k, v_k) belongs to the path C_{ij} and are zero otherwise. They are computed based on the discrete gradient field. The derivative depends on the direction $(d_u^{(k)}, d_v^{(k)})$ of the integration path at pixel location (u_k, v_k) with $d_u^{(k)} = u_{k+1} - u_k$ and $d_v^{(k)} = v_{k+1} - v_k$ according to

$$\left. \frac{\partial (\Delta z)_{ij}^{\text{surf}}}{\partial p} \right|_{u_k, v_k} = d_u^{(k)} p_{u_k v_k}$$

$$\left. \frac{\partial (\Delta z)_{ij}^{\text{surf}}}{\partial q} \right|_{u_k, v_k} = d_v^{(k)} q_{u_k v_k}. \tag{5.33}$$

The update of the surface gradient at position (u, v) is then normalised with the number of paths to which the corresponding pixel belongs. Error term (5.31) leads to the evaluation of $N(N - 1)/2$ lines at each update step and becomes prohibitively expensive for a large number of depth measurements. Therefore, only a limited number of randomly chosen lines is used during each update step. Due to the discrete pixel grid, the width of each line can be assumed to correspond to one pixel. It is desirable for a large fraction of the image pixels to be covered by the lines. For randomly distributed points and square images of size $w \times w$ pixels, we found that about 70 % of all image pixels are covered by the lines when the number of lines corresponds to $\sim 10w$.

This method is termed 'shape from photopolarimetric reflectance and depth' (SfPRD). It is related to the approach by Wöhler and Hafezi (2005) described in Sect. 5.2 combining shape from shading and shadow analysis using a similar depth difference error term, which is, however, restricted to depth differences along the light source direction. The method proposed by Fassold et al. (2004) directly imposes depth constraints selectively on the sparse set of surface locations with known depth. As a consequence, in their framework the influence of the depth point on the reconstructed surface is restricted to its immediate local neighbourhood. Horovitz and Kiryati (2004) reduce this effect based on a surface which interpolates the sparse depth points. In their framework, the influence of the three-dimensional points on the reconstructed surface is better behaved but still decreases considerably with increasing distance. In contrast, our method effectively transforms sparse depth data into dense depth difference data as long as a sufficiently large number of paths C_{ij} is taken into account. The influence of the depth error term is thus extended across a large number of pixels by establishing large-scale surface gradients based on depth differences between three-dimensional points.

5.3.4 Experimental Evaluation Based on Synthetic Data

To examine the accuracy of the three-dimensional surface reconstruction methods described in Sects. 5.3.1 and 5.3.3 in comparison to ground truth data and to reveal possible systematic errors, the algorithms are tested on synthetically generated surfaces.

The evaluation by d'Angelo and Wöhler (2005c) regards the integration of depth from defocus into the SfPR framework based on the synthetically generated surface shown in Fig. 5.15a. For simplicity, to generate the locally non-uniform blur, for the PSF radius σ the relation $\sigma \propto |z - z_0|$ according to Sect. 4.2.1 is assumed (Pentland, 1987; Subbarao, 1988). To obtain a visible surface texture in the photopolarimetric

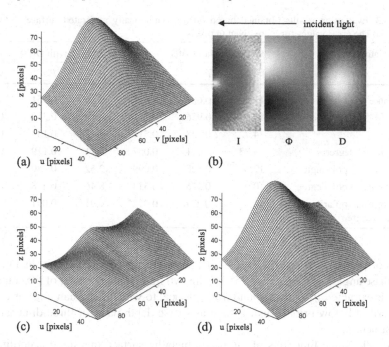

Fig. 5.15 Three-dimensional reconstruction of a synthetically generated surface. (**a**) Ground truth. (**b**) Intensity I, polarisation angle Φ, and polarisation degree D images. The three-dimensional reconstruction result was obtained based on photopolarimetric analysis (**c**) without and (**d**) with depth from defocus information

images, random fluctuations of z_{uv} of the order of 0.1 pixel are introduced. A perpendicular view on the surface along the z axis with $\mathbf{v} = (0, 0, 1)^T$ is assumed. The surface is illuminated from the right-hand side at a phase angle of $\alpha = 75°$. The surface albedo ρ was computed from (5.23) based on the specular reflections. We set $p_{uv}^{(0)} = p_{uv}^{\text{DfD}}$ and $q_{uv}^{(0)} = q_{uv}^{\text{DfD}}$ in (5.21) when using depth from defocus information; otherwise, the PSF G is set to unity and the surface gradients are initialised with zero values due to the lack of prior information. Figures 5.15c–d illustrate that the main benefit of depth from defocus analysis comes from the improved initialisation, which prevents the SfPR algorithm from converging towards a local, suboptimal minimum of the error function. The best results are obtained by utilising a combination of polarisation angle and degree, of reflectance and polarisation angle, or a combination of all three features (cf. Table 5.3).

To examine the behaviour of the local and global optimisation schemes and their combination with sparse depth data, dependent on how many images based on certain reflectance and polarisation features are used, d'Angelo and Wöhler (2008) apply the developed algorithms to the synthetically generated surface shown in Fig. 5.16a. We again assume a perpendicular view on the surface along the z axis, corresponding to $\mathbf{v} = (0, 0, 1)^T$. The scene is illuminated sequentially by $L = 2$ light sources under an angle of 15° with respect to the horizontal plane at azimuth

Table 5.3 Evaluation results obtained based on the synthetically generated surface shown in Fig. 5.15a. The error values for z are given in pixels

Utilised information	RMSE (without DfD)			RMSE (with DfD)		
	z	p	q	z	p	q
Reflectance	11.6	0.620	0.514	9.62	0.551	0.514
Pol. angle	17.0	0.956	0.141	6.62	0.342	0.069
Pol. degree	4.72	0.138	0.514	4.73	0.135	0.514
Pol. angle and degree	1.83	0.121	0.057	1.71	0.119	0.056
Reflectance and pol. angle	12.0	0.528	0.099	2.52	0.280	0.055
Reflectance and pol. degree	10.9	0.575	0.514	8.46	0.418	0.517
Reflectance and polarisation (angle and degree)	10.2	0.277	0.072	0.91	0.091	0.050

angles of $\psi^{(1)} = -30°$ and $\psi^{(2)} = +30°$, respectively. This setting results in identical phase angles $\alpha^{(1)} = \alpha^{(2)} = 75°$ for the two light sources. A set of 500 random points is extracted from the ground truth surface, to which Gaussian noise is added as described below prior to using them as sparse depth data for three-dimensional reconstruction.

The reflectance functions of the rough metallic surface measured according to Sects. 3.2.1 and 3.4.2 were used to render the synthetic images shown in Fig. 5.16c. Gaussian noise is applied with a standard deviation of 5×10^{-4} for the intensity I, where the maximum grey value is about 6×10^{-2}, $1°$ for the polarisation angle Φ, and 0.4 pixel for the depth values (z between 0 and 6 pixels). The weights for the error terms according to (5.32) are set to $\lambda = 450$, $\mu = 40$, $\nu = 100$, and $\chi = 1$. The surface gradients are initialised with zero values.

Figure 5.16 shows the reconstruction results on noisy synthetic images, where the plots (d)–(f), (j), and (k) were obtained by applying SfPR alone, while the plots (g)–(i) depict the results obtained based on integration of sparse depth data into the SfPR framework. The respective reconstruction errors are given in Table 5.4. It is apparent that the shape from shading reconstruction using a single light source fails to reconstruct the surface (Fig. 5.16d), while the surface shape can be reconstructed approximately using a single intensity and polarisation angle image (Fig. 5.16f). To reach similar reconstruction accuracy without polarisation information, illumination from two different directions is required (Fig. 5.16e). Table 5.4 illustrates that using intensity and polarisation degree in the three-dimensional reconstruction process leads to poor accuracy both for the global and the local approach, while using intensity and polarisation angle yields a high accuracy which does not further increase when the polarisation degree is additionally used. The reason for this behaviour is the fact that intensity and polarisation degree contain somewhat redundant information, since both display a maximum in or near the specular direction ($\theta_r = 0°$) and decrease in a qualitatively similar lobe-shaped manner for increasing values of θ_r. The dependence on surface orientation, however, is much stronger for the intensity than for the polarisation degree, while the measurement error tends

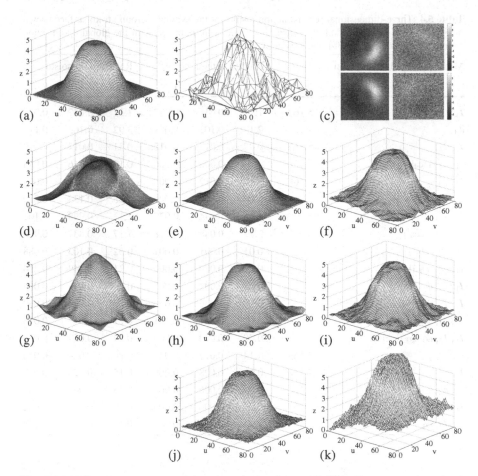

Fig. 5.16 Three-dimensional reconstruction results for a synthetically generated surface. (**a**) Ground truth. (**b**) Noisy depth data. (**c**) Noisy intensity and polarisation angle images, based on measured reflectance functions of a raw forged iron surface. The reconstruction result for noisy images of a surface with uniform albedo, obtained by SfPR with global optimisation without integration of sparse depth data, is shown in (**d**) using a single intensity image, in (**e**) using both intensity images, and in (**f**) using one intensity and one polarisation angle image. (**g**) Reconstructed surface obtained based on noisy sparse depth data alone. (**h**) Reconstruction result using sparse depth data and intensity. (**i**) Reconstruction result using sparse depth data, intensity, and polarisation angle. For comparison, the reconstruction result obtained based on SfPR with local optimisation and without sparse depth data is shown in (**j**) using both intensity images and in (**k**) using one intensity and one polarisation angle image

to be significantly lower for the intensity. The local optimisation approach according to Sect. 5.3.1.2 provides a very accurate reconstruction for the noise-free case, but performs worse than the global approach on noisy data (cf. Figs. 5.16j–k). This property can be observed clearly by comparing the corresponding reconstruction errors of p and q given in Table 5.4. With intensity and polarisation angle images,

Table 5.4 Three-dimensional reconstruction results for the synthetic ground truth surface shown in Fig. 5.16a. If not identified otherwise, the results were obtained with the global optimisation approach. The error values for z are given in pixels

Method, utilised information	Figure	RMSE (without noise)			RMSE (with noise)		
		z	p	q	z	p	q
I_1	5.16d	1.11	0.046	0.077	1.11	0.047	0.077
ϕ_1	–	2.13	0.102	0.059	3.92	0.163	0.117
I_1, I_2	5.16e	0.22	0.012	0.018	0.21	0.014	0.019
I_1, I_2 (local)	5.16j	0.00	0.000	0.000	0.19	0.046	0.088
I_1, ϕ_1	5.16f	0.17	0.012	0.007	0.19	0.040	0.065
I_1, ϕ_1 (local)	5.16k	0.00	0.000	0.000	0.28	0.134	0.210
I_1, D_1	–	1.11	0.044	0.077	1.13	0.098	0.102
I_1, D_1 (local)	–	2.12	0.088	0.178	7.17	0.837	0.928
I_1, ϕ_1, D_1	–	0.01	0.001	0.001	0.52	0.103	0.088
I_1, ϕ_1, D_1 (local)	–	0.00	0.000	0.000	0.31	0.149	0.214
I_1, I_2, ϕ_1	–	0.11	0.009	0.005	0.20	0.034	0.066
I_1, I_2, ϕ_1 (local)	–	0.00	0.000	0.000	0.35	0.074	0.099
I_1, I_2, ϕ_1, ϕ_2	–	0.01	0.001	0.001	0.21	0.056	0.078
I_1, I_2, ϕ_1, ϕ_2 (local)	–	0.00	0.000	0.000	0.24	0.057	0.079
z	5.16g	0.14	0.012	0.013	0.20	0.034	0.036
I_1, z	5.16h	0.11	0.008	0.009	0.15	0.023	0.028
I_1, ϕ_1, z	5.16i	0.09	0.006	0.005	0.13	0.042	0.065
I_1, I_2, ϕ_1, z	–	0.09	0.006	0.005	0.15	0.036	0.062
$I_1, I_2, \phi_1, \phi_2, z$	–	0.07	0.004	0.003	0.11	0.052	0.078

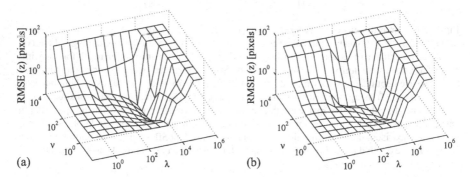

Fig. 5.17 Dependence of the reconstruction error of the SfPR approach on the weight parameters λ and μ according to (5.21) and (5.32) for the synthetic example shown in Fig. 5.16a without noise (*left*) and with noise (*right*)

the reconstruction result becomes very accurate. Similarly accurate reconstruction results, however, are already obtained based on a single intensity and polarisation image.

Figure 5.16g shows the reconstruction result using only the sparse depth values, effectively smoothing and interpolating the sparse depth values shown in Fig. 5.16b. The overall shape is correct, but smaller details like the flattened top of the object are missing in the reconstructed three-dimensional profile. Adding intensity and polarisation terms improves the results and captures the finer details which are not visible in the sparse depth data (cf. Figs. 5.16h–i).

The values for the weight parameters of the error terms according to (5.21) and (5.32) are related to the magnitudes of the intensity and polarisation features and their measurement uncertainties. The influence of the weight parameters on the reconstruction accuracy has been evaluated using the previously described synthetic data. As a typical example, Fig. 5.17 shows the root-mean-square depth error of the reconstructed surface profile obtained from one intensity and one polarisation angle image for different weight parameters λ and μ. For noise-free image data, the reconstruction error decreases with increasing λ and μ until the algorithm starts to diverge at fairly well-defined critical values. For noisy input images (cf. Fig. 5.16c) the reconstruction error displays a weaker dependence on λ and μ and a less pronounced minimum. This is a favourable property, since small changes in the weight parameters do not lead to large differences in the reconstruction accuracy as long as the values chosen for λ and μ are well below their critical values for which the algorithm begins to diverge.

5.3.5 Discussion

In this section we have presented an image-based three-dimensional surface reconstruction method relying on simultaneous evaluation of intensity and polarisation features and its combination with depth data.

The shape from photopolarimetric reflectance (SfPR) technique is based on the analysis of single or multiple intensity and polarisation images. The surface gradients are determined based on a global optimisation method involving a variational framework and based on a local optimisation method which consists of solving a set of nonlinear equations individually for each image pixel. These approaches are suitable for strongly non-Lambertian surfaces and surfaces of diffuse reflectance behaviour.

The shape from photopolarimetric reflectance and depth (SfPRD) method integrates independently measured absolute depth data into the SfPR framework in order to increase the accuracy of the three-dimensional reconstruction result. In this context we concentrated on dense but noisy depth data obtained by depth from defocus and on sparse but more accurate depth data obtained e.g. by stereo analysis or structure from motion. However, our framework is open for independently measured three-dimensional data obtained from other sources such as laser triangulation.

We have shown that depth from defocus information can be used for determining the large-scale properties of the surface and for appropriately initialising the surface gradients. At the same time it provides an estimate of the surface albedo. For integration of sparse depth information, we have suggested an optimisation scheme that simultaneously adapts the surface gradients to the measured intensity and polarisation data and to the surface slopes implied by depth differences between pairs of depth points. This approach transforms sparse depth data into dense depth difference data, leading to a non-local influence of the depth points on the reconstructed surface profile.

The experimental evaluation based on synthetic data illustrates that including polarisation information into the three-dimensional reconstruction scheme significantly increases the accuracy of the reconstructed surface. The main benefit arises from taking into account polarisation angle data, while intensity and polarisation degree tend to contain redundant information. We found that taking into account dense but noisy depth from defocus data may be helpful in estimating the surface albedo and in avoiding local minima of the error function. The integration of sparse but accurate depth data significantly increases the three-dimensional reconstruction accuracy, especially on large scales.

5.4 Stereo Image Analysis of Non-Lambertian Surfaces

This section describes a framework for the stereo analysis of non-Lambertian surfaces. The presentation is adopted from Wöhler and d'Angelo (2009). A general drawback of all methods for stereo image analysis mentioned in Sect. 1.5 is the fact that they implicitly assume Lambertian reflectance properties of the object surfaces. Two images of the surface are acquired from different viewpoints, and two image parts are assumed to correspond to the same physical surface point if their appearances are similar. This is only the case for Lambertian surfaces, where the surface brightness is independent of the viewpoint. However, even in the Lambertian case geometric distortions between the two images occur, which may be taken into account by estimating an affine transformation between the views (Shi and Tomasi, 1994). A method for three-dimensional reconstruction of objects from image sequences that accounts for the changing camera viewpoint by a combination of structure from motion and photometric stereo is presented by Lim et al. (2005). The reflectance behaviour of the surface, however, is still explicitly assumed to be Lambertian.

Since specular reflections are viewpoint dependent, they may cause large intensity differences at corresponding image points. As a consequence of this behaviour, stereo analysis is often unable to establish correspondences at all, or the inferred disparity values tend to be inaccurate, or the established correspondences do not belong to the same physical surface point. Only a few methods that specifically address the three-dimensional reconstruction of specular surfaces have been proposed in the literature. Lowitzsch et al. (2005) introduce a technique based on deflectometry, i.e. projection of light patterns on the surface and analysis of the deformations of their reflections, which is restricted to mirror-like surfaces. Bhat and Nayar (1998) infer a relationship between the relative angle between the optical axes of a pair of stereo cameras, the roughness of the surface, and the probability of the correctness of an established stereo correspondence. This approach attempts to minimise the influence of specular reflections on the images by choosing an appropriate configuration of the stereo camera pair but does not quantitatively consider the effect of specular reflections for establishing stereo correspondences.

A method for separating the specular from the Lambertian reflectance component based on the 'dichromatic reflection model' is described by Klette et al. (1999). The surface material is assumed to be dielectric and to consist of a coloured medium and an interface. Body reflection, i.e. reflection of incident light at the optically neutral medium, is diffuse, while reflection at the interface is specular. The resulting surface radiance is characterised by two components, the 'interface reflection colour' and the 'body reflection colour'. Klette et al. (1999) show that the RGB colour values of the light reflected from the surface lie in the 'dichromatic plane'. Clustering in this plane allows one to construct an image which only displays the diffuse reflectance component, which can then be used for three-dimensional surface reconstruction based on shape from shading or photometric stereo.

Lohse et al. (2006) propose the 'multi-image shape from shading' method, which can in principle be used with an arbitrary but precisely known reflectance function. A three-dimensional reconstruction of the surface is performed directly in the world coordinate system along with an estimation of the reflectance parameters based on an optimisation procedure, where a uniform surface albedo is assumed. This method is favourably used under an oblique viewing geometry since under such conditions small depth differences more strongly translate into offsets in the image coordinates and thus have a more pronounced influence on the utilised error function. However, the experimental evaluation by Lohse et al. (2006) does not involve specular surfaces.

Stereo image analysis which is independent of the reflectance function can be achieved by taking into account the Helmholtz reciprocity condition (cf. (3.7)), which states that the value of the bidirectional reflectance distribution function (BRDF) does not change upon exchange of the camera and the light source (Magda et al., 2001; Zickler et al., 2002, 2003a, 2003b). This approach, however, requires a considerable instrumental effort. The Helmholtz stereopsis method introduced by Zickler et al. (2002) consists of combining each camera with a point light source in order to acquire 'reciprocal image pairs', such that the image taken by the first camera is illuminated by the second light source and vice versa. As a consequence, identical radiances are received by the first and the second camera, respectively, where Zickler et al. (2002) point out that one pair of images is generally not sufficient to obtain a three-dimensional scene reconstruction.

Other methods for BRDF independent stereo image analysis are based on variations of the illumination intensity; i.e. the light sources are kept at fixed locations while the emitted intensity distribution is changed. This is the case e.g. for the projection of light patterns, termed 'coded structured light' by Batlle et al. (1998), and also the spacetime stereo framework introduced by Davis et al. (2005) (cf.

Sect. 1.5.2.5). Wolff and Angelopoulou (1994) propose a method to obtain dense stereo correspondences based on photometric ratios. Two stereo image pairs of the scene are acquired, where the camera positions remain fixed but the illumination conditions change. The surfaces are assumed to be smooth and to consist of dielectric material, such that a special reflectance model can be used which is more complex than the Lambertian reflectance but does not represent specular reflections. Wolff and Angelopoulou (1994) show that the pair of ratio images obtained by dividing two stereo image pairs acquired under different illumination conditions by each other is invariant with respect to the exposure time and gain of the camera, the viewpoint, and the albedo of the surface as long as no specular reflections occur. Stereo correspondences between the computed pair of ratio images are established by a pixel-wise comparison of the ratio values.

Jin et al. (2003) show that for several images acquired from different viewpoints, the rank of the matrix containing the radiance values measured in all images for a local neighbourhood of a certain pixel is not larger than two. As a reflectance function, the fairly complex model of Ward (1992) is used, which is composed of a diffuse and a specular component. Jin et al. (2003) utilise this constraint for the three-dimensional reconstruction of non-Lambertian surfaces based on a level set approach.

For images acquired from different viewpoints, where the scene is illuminated by several light sources at fixed positions with variable irradiance values, Wang et al. (2007) rely on the 'light transport constancy' to establish stereo correspondences. They show that the matrix containing the scene radiance values observed by the cameras under the different illumination conditions has a rank which is lower than the number of light sources. They introduce a criterion for establishing stereo correspondences which is based on the singular values of that matrix and show that it is equivalent to evaluating ratio images similar to the method of Wolff and Angelopoulou (1994). The method by Wang et al. (2007) is not restricted to Lambertian surfaces but can be applied to surfaces with arbitrary reflectance functions. In their experiments, variations of the illumination conditions are generated by two projectors.

In the following, the method of Wöhler and d'Angelo (2009) for the three-dimensional reconstruction of surfaces with non-Lambertian reflectance properties based on stereo image analysis is described. Using the SfPRD technique described in Sect. 5.3 as a basis, triangulation-based cues are combined with photopolarimetric information into an iterative framework that allows one to establish stereo correspondences in accordance with the specular reflectance behaviour and at the same time to determine the surface gradient field based on the known photometric and polarimetric reflectance properties. Illumination by a single point light source is sufficient; no variable illumination is required. Disparities are refined based on a comparison between observed and modelled pixel brightnesses. The approach yields a dense three-dimensional reconstruction of the surface which is consistent with the observed data.

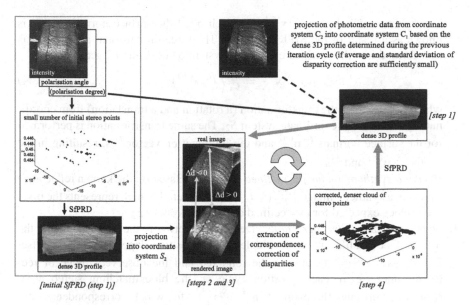

Fig. 5.18 Schematic description of the specular stereo algorithm

5.4.1 Iterative Scheme for Disparity Estimation

We utilise a correlation-based blockmatching stereo algorithm (cf. Sect. 1.5.2) to obtain depth information about the surface. The images are rectified to standard stereo geometry, resulting in epipolar lines corresponding to the image rows (cf. Sect. 1.5). Directly applying the stereo algorithm to an image pair of a rough metallic surface usually results in a fairly sparse disparity map due to limited texture, repeating patterns, or a different appearance of corresponding surface parts in the stereo images as a consequence of the strongly specular reflectance behaviour.

The coordinate systems of the two cameras are denoted by the indices C_1 (left camera) and C_2 (right camera), the corresponding rectified coordinate systems by R_1 (left rectified camera) and R_2 (right rectified camera). The transformations between these coordinate systems and therefore also the viewing directions $^{C_1}\mathbf{v}_1$ and $^{C_1}\mathbf{v}_2$ of the cameras are known from the extrinsic camera calibration; e.g. let us look at coordinate system C_1. We assume that the surface is illuminated with a point light source situated at infinite distance in a direction given by the vector $^{C_1}\mathbf{s}$. The intensity and polarisation angle reflectance functions R_I and R_Φ are assumed to be known from a reference measurement. The proposed stereo image analysis method for non-Lambertian surfaces is termed specular stereo. It consists of the following steps (cf. also Fig. 5.18).

1. *Compute a three-dimensional surface profile based on SfPRD*: A three-dimensional surface profile is computed with the SfPRD method based on the intensity and polarisation data of camera 1 and the depth points $^{C_1}\mathbf{r}_j^{(m)}$ obtained by stereo analysis, where m denotes the iteration cycle index. Each pixel is regarded as

a three-dimensional point $^{C_1}\mathbf{x}_i^{(m)}$. For each pixel the surface normal $^{C_1}\mathbf{n}_i^{(m)}$ is known as a result of the SfPRD method. The three-dimensional point cloud is transformed into the rectified coordinate system S_2 of camera 2 according to

$$^{S_2}\mathbf{x}_i^{(m)} = {}^{S_2}_{C_1}\mathcal{T}\big({}^{C_1}\mathbf{x}_i^{(m)}\big), \qquad (5.34)$$

where $^{S_2}_{C_1}\mathcal{T}$ denotes the transformation (a rotation and a translation) from coordinate system C_1 into coordinate system S_2. The same transformation is performed for the surface normals $^{C_1}\mathbf{n}_i^{(m)}$ and the illumination vector $^{C_1}\mathbf{s}$, resulting in the vectors $^{S_2}\mathbf{n}_i^{(m)}$ and $^{S_2}\mathbf{s}$.

2. *Render a synthetic image for rectified camera 2*: Based on the known reflectance function, a synthetic image $R_I^{(m)}({}^{S_2}u, {}^{S_2}v)$ is rendered, which represents the pixel grey values expected for the rectified coordinate system S_2.

3. *Determine disparity corrections*: Deviations between the estimated and the true surface profile are now revealed by a position-dependent lateral offset $\Delta d_j^{(m)}({}^{S_2}u_j^{(m)}, {}^{S_2}v_j^{(m)})$ between the rendered and the observed image of rectified camera 2. In each iteration cycle m, the blockmatching stereo algorithm re-determines the pixels $({}^{S_2}u_j^{(m)}, {}^{S_2}v_j^{(m)})$ for which correspondences between the rendered and the observed image in the rectified coordinate system S_2 can be established. Due to the chosen standard geometry, a depth error of a pixel in the image of camera 1 translates into an offset along the corresponding epipolar line, i.e. image row, in the rectified image of camera 2. The value of $\Delta d_j^{(m)}({}^{S_2}u_j^{(m)}, {}^{S_2}v_j^{(m)})$ corresponds to the disparity error of the pixel at $({}^{S_2}u_j^{(m)}, {}^{S_2}v_j^{(m)})$ in the rectified image of camera 2. We determine the offset based on the same correlation-based blockmatching approach as utilised for the initial stereo image analysis.

4. *Compute corrected three-dimensional points*: The positions $({}^{S_2}u_j^{(m)}, {}^{S_2}v_j^{(m)})$ and disparities $d_j^{(m)}$ of all pixels for which the blockmatching technique is able to determine a value $\Delta d_j^{(m)}$ are updated according to

$$
\begin{aligned}
{}^{S_2}u_j^{(m),\text{corr}} &= {}^{S_2}u_j^{(m)} - \Delta d_j^{(m)} \\
{}^{S_2}v_j^{(m),\text{corr}} &= {}^{S_2}v_j^{(m)} \\
d_j^{(m),\text{corr}} &= d_j^{(m)} + \Delta d_j^{(m)}.
\end{aligned}
\qquad (5.35)
$$

The corrected three-dimensional point cloud $^{S_2}\mathbf{r}_j^{(m+1)}$ is obtained from the corrected pixel positions $({}^{S_2}u_j^{(m),\text{corr}}, {}^{S_2}v_j^{(m),\text{corr}})$ and disparities $d_j^{(m),\text{corr}}$ determined according to (5.35), relying on the basic equations of stereo analysis in standard epipolar geometry (Horn, 1986). Transformed into the coordinate system of camera 1, the corrected three-dimensional points are denoted by $^{C_1}\mathbf{r}_j^{(m+1)}$. Finally, the iteration cycle index m is incremented: $m \leftarrow m + 1$.

5. Iterate steps 1–4 until the average and the standard deviation of the disparity corrections $\Delta d_j^{(m)}$ are of the order of 1 pixel. Note that the disparities $d_j^{(m)}$ are

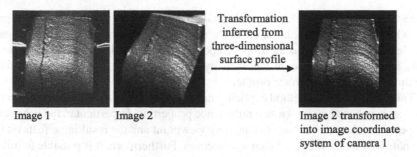

Image 1   Image 2   Image 2 transformed
                                                     into image coordinate
                                                     system of camera 1

Fig. 5.19 Transformation of image 2 into the image coordinate system of camera 1 after the average and the standard deviation of the disparity correction Δd_j have decreased to less than about one pixel

measured between the observed rectified images with coordinate systems S_1 and S_2, while the disparity corrections $\Delta d_j^{(m)}$ are measured between the rendered and the observed image in the rectified coordinate system S_2.

Once this degree of self-consistency is reached, it is favourable to additionally take into account the photopolarimetric information of camera 2. In our experiments (cf. Sect. 6.3.4), we do not acquire a second polarisation image—it would be necessary to perform the difficult task of absolutely calibrating the rotation angles of two polarising filters with respect to each other—but merely use the intensity information of camera 2. In (5.20), the intensity error e_I then consists of two parts according to $e_I = e_I^{(1)} + e_I^{(2)}$. For this purpose, the image of camera 2 is transformed during step 1 of the iteration scheme from coordinate system C_2 to C_1 (cf. Fig. 5.19). In iteration cycle m, the appropriate transformation is obtained based on the three-dimensional surface profile defined by the points $^{C_2}\mathbf{x}_i^{(m-1)}$ obtained during the previous iteration cycle. The resulting transformed image of camera 2 and the image of camera 1 are pixel-synchronous at reasonable accuracy due to the already achieved smallness of the disparity corrections.

Including the accordingly transformed intensity information of camera 2 into the optimisation scheme corresponds to a photometric stereo approach which exploits the effect of different viewpoints on the measured brightness of the surface, while the direction of illumination remains constant. This technique does not provide additional photometric constraints for Lambertian surfaces, as their brightness is independent of the viewing direction, which is the main reason why traditional photometric stereo (Horn, 1986) relies on multiple illumination directions rather than multiple viewpoints.

The described iterative scheme for specular stereo analysis is visualised in Fig. 5.18 for the connection rod example regarded in detail in Sect. 6.3.4. The initial SfPRD step according to the left part of Fig. 5.18 (marked as step 1) yields a dense three-dimensional surface profile which results in a rendered image in the rectified camera coordinate system S_2 (step 2) that does not correspond very well with the rectified image observed by camera 2. Determining correspondences between the rendered and the observed image (step 3) and generating an accordingly corrected three-dimensional point cloud (step 4) yields a dense three-dimensional surface profile which displays a similar small-scale structure as the initial three-dimensional profile but a lower large-scale slope. Repeating steps 1–4 during subsequent iterations and taking into account the intensity information of camera 2 further refines the three-dimensional surface profile.

The specular stereo method explicitly models the appearance of the surface in the two cameras based on the known reflectance properties. In particular, the behaviour of specular reflections subject to changing viewpoint and the resulting effects on the estimation of disparities are taken into account. Furthermore, it is possible to utilise the method for large baseline stereo, where the stereo baseline is comparable to the object distance, as the differences in perspective introduced by the strongly different viewpoints are explicitly considered as well. All available triangulation-based and photopolarimetric information is utilised for the purpose of three-dimensional surface reconstruction.

The iterative optimisation scheme described in this section assumes convergence. However, the solution is not guaranteed to converge, since the triangulation-based and photopolarimetric information may in principle be contradictory, e.g. due to camera calibration errors or inaccurate knowledge of the illumination direction. However, we observed that in all experiments regarded in Sect. 6.3.4 convergence is achieved after 4–8 iteration cycles. Self-consistent measures for assessing the three-dimensional reconstruction accuracy and convergence behaviour are discussed in Sect. 6.3.4.3.

5.4.2 Qualitative Behaviour of the Specular Stereo Algorithm

Figure 5.20 shows the observed vs. the rendered images of the specular surface of the connection rod. While initially in camera 1 the rendered image is very similar to the observed image since the initial SfPRD step aims for obtaining a small value of e_I according to (3.19), the differences between the observed image in camera 2 and the correspondingly rendered image are evident. During the initial SfPRD step, the intensity information of image 2 is not taken into account. The differences in surface shape occur because the large-scale surface slope in the vertical image direction is inaccurately estimated by the initial SfPRD step—for only less than 0.5 % of the image pixels can an initial disparity value be determined. Differences in surface brightness (the right third of the surface profile appears bright in the observed image but fairly dark in the rendered image) are due to the same large-scale inaccuracies of the initial three-dimensional shape estimate, which result in inaccurate surface gradients and thus estimated surface brightness.

After 8 cycles of the iterative scheme proposed in Sect. 5.4.1, the geometric appearance of the surface and the distribution of surface brightness in both rendered images closely resemble the corresponding observed images. Now a disparity value can be determined for 18 % of the image pixels. This example qualitatively illustrates the convergence behaviour of the proposed algorithm. Section 6.3.4 provides

observed images   rendered images (initial)   rendered images (8 iterations)

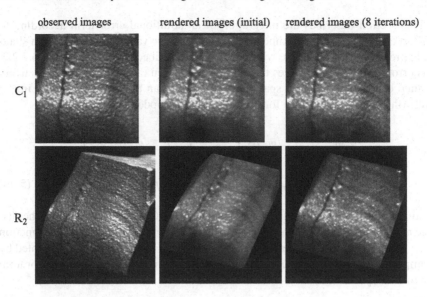

Fig. 5.20 Observed (*left*) vs. rendered (*middle*, *right*) images for the connection rod example in camera coordinate system C_1 and in rectified coordinate system R_2, respectively, shown before the first iteration cycle and after 8 iteration cycles

a more detailed experimental evaluation in the application scenario of industrial quality inspection.

5.5   Combination of Shape from Shading and Active Range Scanning Data

In application domains such as industrial metrology or remote sensing, an alternative to passive stereo image analysis is active range scanning. In industrial metrology, a state-of-the-art approach is the projection of structured light, where the three-dimensional shape of the surface is inferred from the deformations of the projected light pattern observed in the camera image (Batlle et al., 1998). An important remote sensing technique is light detection and ranging (LIDAR), which relies on depth measurement based on the time of flight of emitted light pulses (Schowengerdt, 2006).

Actively scanned three-dimensional data commonly have a high absolute depth accuracy but an effective lateral resolution which is lower than that of images acquired from the same viewpoint. For example, range scanning data obtained by the projection of structured light tend to display a considerable amount of noise on small spatial scales, which results in a decreased effective lateral resolution. LIDAR measurements usually have a high depth accuracy, but the lateral density of the measured points may be low except when the surface is scanned several times.

This section describes the integration of an additional error term according to Herbort et al. (2011) and Grumpe et al. (2011) into the variational shape from shading approach of Horn (1989), which has been described in detail in Sect. 3.2.2.2. This error term e_{DEM} measures the deviation between the gradients of the actively scanned depth data z_{uv}^{DEM} on spatial scales larger than the extension of the image pixels (the index DEM stands for 'digital elevation model') and is defined as

$$e_{\text{DEM}} = \sum_{uv} \left(\left[f_{\sigma_{\text{DEM}}} \left(\left\{ \frac{\partial z^{\text{DEM}}}{\partial x} \right\}_{uv} \right) - f_{\sigma_{\text{DEM}}}(p_{uv}) \right]^2 \right.$$
$$\left. + \left[f_{\sigma_{\text{DEM}}} \left(\left\{ \frac{\partial z^{\text{DEM}}}{\partial y} \right\}_{uv} \right) - f_{\sigma_{\text{DEM}}}(q_{uv}) \right]^2 \right), \tag{5.36}$$

where, in contrast to the continuous formulation by Grumpe et al. (2011), the discrete notation in terms of the pixel coordinates u and v is used. In (5.36), the function $f_{\sigma_{\text{DEM}}}$ denotes a low-pass filter which is in principle arbitrary but is implemented by Grumpe et al. (2011) as a Gaussian filter of half width σ_{DEM}. The overall error term g then corresponds to

$$g = e_i + \gamma e_{\text{int}} + \delta e_{\text{DEM}}, \tag{5.37}$$

with γ and δ as weight factors, where e_i and e_{int} are defined by (3.19) and (3.25), respectively. According to Grumpe et al. (2011), setting the derivatives of g with respect to the surface gradients p and q to zero results in an iterative update rule according to

$$p_{uv}^{(n+1)} = z_x^{(n)} + \frac{1}{\gamma} \left[I_{uv} - R_{uv}\left(z_x^{(n)}, z_y^{(n)}\right) \right] \frac{\partial R_{uv}}{\partial p} \bigg|_{z_x^{(n)}}$$
$$+ \frac{\delta}{\gamma} \sum_{ij} \left[f_{\sigma_{\text{DEM}}} \left(\left\{ \frac{\partial z^{\text{DEM}}}{\partial x} \right\}_{ij} \right) - f_{\sigma_{\text{DEM}}}\left(z_x^{(n)}\right) \right]$$
$$\times \left\{ \frac{\partial f_{\sigma_{\text{DEM}}}(p_{uv})}{\partial p} \right\}_{ij}\bigg|_{z_x^{(n)}}$$
$$z_{uv}^{(n+1)} = \bar{z}_{uv}^{(n)} - \frac{\epsilon^2}{\kappa} \left[\left\{ \frac{\partial p^{(n+1)}}{\partial x} \right\}_{uv} + \left\{ \frac{\partial q^{(n+1)}}{\partial y} \right\}_{uv} \right] \tag{5.38}$$

with $\bar{z}_{uv}^{(n)}$ as the average over the κ nearest neighbours of the regarded pixel and ϵ as the lateral extent of the pixels. Equation (5.38) is an extension of the iterative update rule introduced by Horn (1989) for determining an integrable surface. An expression for $q_{uv}^{(n+1)}$ analogous to the first part of (5.38) is obtained in a straightforward manner. Non-uniform lateral pixel extensions or unequal lateral extensions of the pixels in the horizontal and vertical image directions (as is the case for certain map projections) must be taken into account by replacing ϵ by appropriately chosen pixel-specific values.

The sum over u and v in the first part of (5.38) corresponds to the partial derivative $\partial e_{\text{DEM}}/\partial p$. At this point it is favourable to introduce the $K \times L$ filter matrix $F_{\sigma_{\text{DEM}}}$, leading to the expression

$$\left.\frac{\partial e_{\text{DEM}}}{\partial p}\right|_{u_0,v_0} = -\sum_{uv}\left[\sum_{k=-K/2}^{K/2}\sum_{l=-L/2}^{L/2}F_{\sigma_{\text{DEM}}}(k,l)\left(\left\{\frac{\partial z^{\text{DEM}}}{\partial x}\right\}_{u+k,v+l} - p_{u+k,v+l}\right)\right]$$
$$\times\left[\sum_{k=-K/2}^{K/2}\sum_{l=-L/2}^{L/2}F_{\sigma_{\text{DEM}}}(k,l)\left.\frac{\partial p_{u+k,v+l}}{\partial p_{uv}}\right|_{u_0,v_0}\right]\epsilon^2 \tag{5.39}$$

for the pixel at (u_0, v_0). Equation (5.39) corresponds to a correlation operation. The terms of the sum over u and v in (5.39) are zero except for $u_0 = u+k$ and $v_0 = v+l$. Omitting the zero terms in (5.39) yields

$$\left.\frac{\partial e_{\text{DEM}}}{\partial p}\right|_{u_0,v_0} = -\sum_{i=-K/2}^{K/2}\sum_{j=-L/2}^{L/2}F_{\sigma_{\text{DEM}}}(-u_0,-v_0)\left[\sum_{k=-K/2}^{K/2}\sum_{l=-L/2}^{L/2}F_{\sigma_{\text{DEM}}}(k,l)\right.$$
$$\times\left.\left(\left\{\frac{\partial z^{\text{DEM}}}{\partial x}\right\}_{u_0+k+i,v_0+l+j} - p_{u_0+k+i,v_0+l+j}\right)\right]\epsilon^2. \tag{5.40}$$

In an analogous manner, it follows that

$$\left.\frac{\partial e_{\text{DEM}}}{\partial q}\right|_{u_0,v_0} = -\sum_{i=-K/2}^{K/2}\sum_{j=-L/2}^{L/2}F_{\sigma_{\text{DEM}}}(-u_0,-v_0)\left[\sum_{k=-K/2}^{K/2}\sum_{l=-L/2}^{L/2}F_{\sigma_{\text{DEM}}}(k,l)\right.$$
$$\times\left.\left(\left\{\frac{\partial z^{\text{DEM}}}{\partial y}\right\}_{u_0+k+i,v_0+l+j} - q_{u_0+k+i,v_0+l+j}\right)\right]\epsilon^2. \tag{5.41}$$

Hence, the terms $\partial e_{\text{DEM}}/\partial p$ and $\partial e_{\text{DEM}}/\partial q$ can be determined based on a subsequent correlation and convolution operation as long as the function $f_{\sigma_{\text{DEM}}}$ is a linear filter, allowing a computationally efficient implementation of the iterative update rule (5.38).

The described algorithm is not only able to perform a three-dimensional surface reconstruction but also to estimate the non-uniform albedo map ρ_{uv}, even if only a single image is available. For this purpose, Grumpe et al. (2011) propose an embedding of (5.38) into an iterative scheme as follows.

1. Initialise the iteration index $m = 0$ and set the surface $z_{uv}(0)$ to the initial surface, e.g. $z_{uv}(0) = z_{uv}^{\text{DEM}}$ or $z_{uv}(0) = z_{uv}^{\text{PHCL}}$ (see below).
2. Determine the incidence angle $\theta_i^{(m)}$ and the emission angle $\theta_e^{(m)}$ for each pixel based on $z_{uv}(m)$ and the corresponding surface gradients.
3. Compute the non-uniform surface albedo $\rho_{uv}^{(m)}$ by determining a pixel-wise solution of $R_{uv}(\rho_{uv}^{(m)}, \theta_i^{(m)}, \theta_e^{(m)}, \alpha) = I_{uv}$ with respect to $\rho_{uv}^{(m)}$.
4. Set the albedo of the next iteration to $\rho_{uv}^{(m+1)} = g_{\sigma_\rho^{(m)}} * \rho_{uv}^{(m)}$, where $g_{\sigma_\rho^{(m)}}$ is a Gaussian low-pass filter of half width $\sigma_\rho^{(m)}$ and '$*$' denotes a convolution.
5. Apply the iterative update rule according to (5.38) in order to determine the surface $z_{uv}(m+1)$.
6. Set $\sigma_\rho^{(m+1)}$ to a value smaller than $\sigma_\rho^{(m)}$.

7. Increase the iteration index: $m \leftarrow m + 1$.
8. Repeat steps 2–7 until topography-related artifacts begin to appear in the albedo map $\rho_{uv}^{(m)}$.

At this point it is important to take into account the smoothing effect of the update rule for z_{uv} in (5.38), which is due to the use of the local average $\bar{z}_{uv}$ in the discrete approximation of the Laplace operator by Horn (1989) occurring as a result of the inclusion of the integrability error e_{int}. If the algorithm is initialised by a smooth surface, small surface details tend to be less pronounced in the final solution than their real counterparts. Hence, Grumpe and Wöhler (2011) propose an extended photoclinometry approach which performs a pixel-wise independent minimisation of the error term

$$\tilde{g} = e_i + \delta e_{\text{DEM}} \tag{5.42}$$

with respect to the surface gradients p_{uv}^{PHCL} and q_{uv}^{PHCL} based on an optimisation by gradient descent. The surface is initialised with z_{uv}^{DEM}, while the albedo map is obtained based on the surface gradients derived from to z_{uv}^{DEM} according to steps 2–4 described above. The corresponding surface z_{uv}^{PHCL} is then obtained using the iterative scheme of Horn (1986) according to (3.32). Generally, the appearance of small-scale details is more realistically pronounced in z_{uv}^{PHCL} than in the solution obtained by (5.38) initialised with a smooth surface. Hence, the surface z_{uv}^{PHCL} obtained by the extended photoclinometry scheme is favourably used as an initialisation to the variational approach described above.

The extended shape from shading method described in this section, which relies on the integration of dense depth data with an effective lateral resolution which is significantly lower than that of the available images, will be applied to the three-dimensional reconstruction of metallic surfaces in an industrial metrology scenario in Sect. 6.3.5 and to the construction of DEMs of the lunar surface in Sects. 8.2 and 8.4.

5.6 Three-Dimensional Pose Estimation Based on Combinations of Monocular Cues

This section describes the integrated approach to the problem of three-dimensional pose estimation (cf. Sect. 2.1) proposed by Barrois and Wöhler (2007). The presentation in this section is adopted from that work. Most appearance-based approaches to three-dimensional pose estimation explicitly rely on point features or edges. However, in the presence of a cluttered background or low contrast between object and background, edge information tends to be an unreliable cue for pose estimation. This method applies the principles of combining several sources of complementary information for three-dimensional surface reconstruction, which have been derived in the previous sections of this chapter, to the problem of three-dimensional pose estimation. It relies on the comparison of the input image to synthetic images generated by an OpenGL-based renderer using model information about the object provided by CAD data. The comparison provides an error measure which is minimised by an iterative optimisation algorithm. Although all six degrees of freedom are esti- mated, the described approach requires only a monocular camera, circumventing disadvantages of multiocular camera systems such as the need for extrinsic cam- era calibration. The framework is open for the inclusion of independently acquired depth data. A first evaluation is performed based on a simple but realistic example object.

Classical monocular pose estimation approaches have in common that they are not able to estimate the distance to the object at reasonable accuracy, since the only available information is the scale of a known object in the resulting image. Scale information yields no accurate results, since for small distance variations the object scale does not change significantly. In comparison, for a convergent stereo setup with a baseline similar to the object distance, for geometrical reasons a depth ac- curacy of the same order as the lateral translational accuracy is obtainable. For this reason, a variety of three-dimensional pose estimation methods relying on multiple images of the scene have been proposed (cf. Sect. 2 for an overview). However, from a practical point of view, using a monocular camera system is often favourable (cf. Sect. 6.1), although a high pose estimation accuracy may be required, e.g. to detect subtle deviations between the true and desired object poses. In this section we therefore regard a monocular configuration.

5.6.1 Photometric and Polarimetric Information

The first source of information we exploit is the intensity reflected from the object surface. For this purpose, we make use of the two-component specular reflectance function inspired by Nayar et al. (1991) and defined by (5.22). The unknown surface albedo ρ is estimated by the optimisation algorithm described below. Although we regard objects of uniform surface albedo in our experiments, our framework would in principle allow us to render and investigate objects with a textured surface by using texture mapping in combination with an estimation of the factor ρ. The other parameters of the reflectance function are determined empirically as described in Sect. 3.2.1, regarding a sample of the corresponding surface material attached to a goniometer.

The determined parameters of the reflectance function and a CAD model of the object are used to generate a synthetic image of the observed scene. For this pur- pose, an OpenGL-based renderer has been implemented. The surface orientation is required for each point of the object surface to compute a reflectance value accord- ing to (5.22), but OpenGL does not directly provide this information. Hence, the technique developed by Decaudin (1996) is used to calculate the surface normal for every pixel based on three rendered colour images obtained by a red, a green, and a blue virtual light source appropriately distributed in space. Afterwards, the reflectance function (5.22) is used to compute the predicted intensity for each pixel.

We obtain a photorealistic image $R_I(p_{uv}, q_{uv})$ which can be compared with the input image I_{uv}, resulting in the intensity error term

$$e_I = \sum_{u,v} \left[I_{uv} - R_I(p_{uv}, q_{uv}) \right]^2. \qquad (5.43)$$

The summation is carried out for the rendered pixels representing the object surface. A disadvantage of the technique proposed by Decaudin (1996) is the fact that no shadow information is generated for the scene. Hence, shadows are computed in a further ray tracing step after the photorealistic rendering process.

Furthermore, we introduce an analogous error term e_Φ taking into account the polarisation angle Φ_{uv} of the light reflected from the object surface. We utilise the polarisation reflectance function $R_\Phi(p_{uv}, q_{uv})$ according to (3.60) as defined in Sect. 3.4.2 with empirically determined parameters. The renderer then predicts the polarisation angle for each pixel, resulting in the error term

$$e_\Phi = \sum_{u,v} \left[\Phi_{uv} - R_\Phi(p_{uv}, q_{uv}) \right]^2. \qquad (5.44)$$

In principle, a further error term denoting the polarisation degree might be introduced at this point. However, in all our experiments we found that the polarisation degree is an unreliable feature with respect to three-dimensional pose estimation of objects with realistic surfaces, as it depends more strongly on small-scale variations of the microscale roughness of the surface than on the surface orientation itself.

5.6.2 Edge Information

To obtain information about edges in the image, we compute a binarised edge image from the observed intensity image using the Canny edge detector (Canny, 1986). In a second step, a distance transform image C_{uv} is obtained by computing the chamfer distance for each pixel (Gavrila and Philomin, 1999). As our approach compares synthetically generated images with the observed image, we use a modified chamfer matching technique. The edges in the rendered image are extracted with a Sobel edge detector, resulting in a Sobel magnitude image E_{uv}, which is not binarised. To obtain an error term which gives information about the quality of the match, a pixel-wise multiplication of C_{uv} by E_{uv} is performed. The advantage of omitting the binarisation is the continuous behaviour of the resulting error function with respect to the pose parameters, which is a favourable property regarding the optimisation stage. If the edge image extracted from the rendered image were binarised, the error function would become discontinuous, making the optimisation task more difficult. Accordingly, the edge error term e_E is defined as

$$e_E = - \sum_{u,v} C_{uv} E_{uv}, \qquad (5.45)$$

where the summation is carried out over all image pixels (u, v). The minus sign in (5.45) arises from the fact that our optimisation scheme aims to determine the minimum of the error function.

5.6.3 Defocus Information

We utilise the depth from defocus technique described in Sect. 4.2.3.2 to estimate depth values from the amount of defocus. This approach requires two pixel-synchronous images; one is acquired with a small aperture ($\kappa = 8$), while the second one is acquired with a large aperture ($\kappa = 2$). This procedure may be automated using a lens equipped with a motorised iris. For the first image we assume that no perceivable amount of defocus is present. The images are partitioned into windows of size 32×32 pixels. The PSF radius Σ in frequency space is computed by fitting a Gaussian to the ratio of the amplitude spectra of the corresponding windows of the first and the second image, respectively. Only the range of intermediate spatial frequencies is regarded in order to reduce the influence of noise on the resulting value of Σ. The depth–defocus function according to (4.15) is calibrated using the combined chequerboard and random dot pattern shown in Fig. 4.9.

5.6.4 Total Error Optimisation

To start the optimisation process, an initial object pose has to be provided. With this pose a first set of images (intensity, polarisation angle, edges, and depth map) is rendered. Each measured cue provides an error term, denoted by e_I, e_Φ, e_E, and e_D, respectively. We use these error terms to compute an overall error e_T which is minimised in order to obtain the object pose. As the individual error terms are of different orders of magnitude, we introduce the weight factors β_I, β_Φ, β_E, and β_D to appropriately take into account the individual terms in the total error e_T according to

$$e_T = \beta_I e_I + \beta_\Phi e_\Phi + \beta_E e_E + \beta_D e_D. \tag{5.46}$$

The individual error terms are not independent of each other, such that they have to be minimised simultaneously via minimisation of the total error e_T. This may become a fairly intricate nonlinear optimisation problem. The value of each weight factor is chosen inversely proportional to the typical relative measurement error, respectively. However, we found that the influence on the observed intensity, polarisation, edge, and depth cues is different for small variations of each pose parameter (cf. Table 5.5). For example, a slight lateral translation has a strong influence on the edges in the image but may leave the observed intensity and polarisation angle largely unchanged. On the other hand, under certain viewing conditions, rotations around small angles are hardly visible in the edge image and yet have a significant effect on the observed intensity or polarisation behaviour.

Table 5.5 Influence of small changes of the pose parameters on the observed edge, photopolarimetric, and depth cues

	Intensity, polarisation	Edges	Depth
Rotation angles	Strong	Weak	Weak
Lateral translation (x, y)	Weak	Strong	Weak
Translation in z	Weak	Weak	Strong

For minimisation of the overall error e_T we use an iterative gradient descent approach. We have chosen this algorithm because of its stable convergence behaviour, but other optimisation methods are possible. It is impossible to calculate analytically the derivatives of the total error term with respect to the pose parameters, as the error term is computed based on rendered images; thus the gradient is evaluated numerically. If a certain cue does not provide useful information (which may e.g. be the case for polarisation data when the surface material only weakly polarises the reflected light, or for edges in the presence of a cluttered background), this cue can be neglected in the optimisation procedure by setting the corresponding weight factor in (5.46) to zero. It is shown experimentally in this section and in Sect. 6.1 that pose estimation remains possible when relying on merely two or three different cues.

Our framework requires a priori information about the object pose for initialisation of the nonlinear optimisation routine, and thus it is especially useful for pose refinement. In comparison, the template matching-based approach of von Bank et al. (2003) yields five pose parameters without a priori knowledge about them, while the sixth parameter, the distance to the object, is assumed to be exactly known. In the addressed application domain of industrial quality inspection, a priori information about the pose is available from the CAD data of the part itself and the workpiece to which it is attached. Here it is not necessary to detect the part in an arbitrary pose, but rather to measure small differences between the reference pose parameters and those desired according to the CAD data. Hence, when applied in the context of industrial quality inspection, our method should be initialised with the pose given by the CAD data, and depending on the tolerances stored in the CAD data, a production fault is indicated when the deviation of one or several pose parameters exceeds the tolerance value. The experimental evaluation presented in the next section shows that our framework is able to detect small differences between the true and desired object poses.

5.6.5 Experimental Evaluation Based on a Simple Real-World Object

For a first evaluation of the performance of the presented approach we estimated the pose of a simple cuboid-shaped real-world object (a rubber) and compared the results to the independently derived ground truth. The images were taken with a

Fig. 5.21 Input intensity images for pose 1 (*left*) and pose 2 (*right*) of the rubber (cf. Table 5.6)

Baumer industrial CCD camera of 1032×776 pixel image size, equipped with a $f = 25$ mm lens. The approximate distance to the object was 0.5 m. The coordinate system was chosen such that the x and y axes correspond to the horizontal and vertical image axis, respectively, while the z axis is parallel to the optical axis. The scene was illuminated with a LED point light source located at a known position. The algorithm was initialised with four different poses, differing by several degrees in the rotation angles and a few millimetres in translation. As a result of the pose estimation we adopted the minimisation run yielding the lowest residual error according to (5.46).

The reflectance function R_I was determined with a goniometer by estimating the parameters according to (5.22). At the same time we found that the polarisation degree of the light reflected from the surface is so small that it cannot be reliably determined. Hence, the input data for pose estimation are limited to intensity, edges, and depth.

For our evaluation, we attached the rubber with its lateral surface to the goniometer table and oriented it in two different poses relative to the camera. The angular difference between the two poses is only a few degrees (cf. Fig. 5.21). For the determination of the ground truth, we replaced the rubber for each pose by a chequerboard of known geometry. The chequerboard was attached to the goniometer table, and its pose was estimated using the rig finder algorithm described by Krüger et al. (2004), which is based on a bundle adjustment approach for camera calibration purposes. Due to the simple cuboid shape of the rubber, the chequerboard pattern could be aligned at high accuracy into the same direction as the lateral surfaces of the rubber, such that the chequerboard pose could be assumed to be identical with the pose of the rubber.

The results of this experiment are shown in Table 5.6. The deviations between the measured and the true pose parameters are only a few tenths of a degree for the rotation angles and a few tenths of a millimetre for the lateral translations. The translation in z is determined at an accuracy of about 4 mm (which is about an order of magnitude lower than the lateral accuracy) or 1 %. This is a reasonable result, given that only monocular image data are available.

Table 5.6 Estimated pose and ground truth (GT) for the rubber example

Parameter	Pose 1	GT 1	Pose 2	GT 2
Roll (°)	13.3	13.5	16.7	16.3
Pitch (°)	−18.2	−18.9	−18.6	−19.7
Yaw (°)	59.4	58.6	59.2	58.5
t_x (mm)	−3.6	−3.2	−2.8	−2.5
t_y (mm)	2.3	2.3	1.3	1.7
t_z (mm)	451.5	454.3	457.5	453.9

5.6.6 Discussion

The three-dimensional pose estimation approach described in this section is based on photometric, polarimetric, edge, and defocus cues. A correspondingly defined error function is minimised by comparing the observed data to their rendered counterparts, where an accurate rendering of intensity and polarisation images is performed based on the material-specific reflectance functions determined with a goniometer. If a certain cue cannot be reliably measured or does not yield useful information, it can be neglected in the optimisation procedure.

A pose estimation accuracy comparable to the one obtained in the simple rubber example is achieved for more difficult objects in the context of industrial quality inspection, as described in Sect. 6.1. It turns out that this accuracy is comparable to or higher than that of the monocular template matching approach of von Bank et al. (2003) (cf. Sect. 2.1), which exclusively relies on edge information and estimates only five degrees of freedom. The depth from defocus method has proven to be a useful instrument for the estimation of object depth in close range at an accuracy of about 1 %.

Part II
Application Scenarios

Chapter 6
Applications to Industrial Quality Inspection

Industrial quality inspection is an important application domain for three-dimensional computer vision methods. Traditional vision-based industrial quality inspection systems primarily rely on two-dimensional detection and pose estimation algorithms, e.g. relying on the detection of point and line features, the extraction of blob features from binarised images, or two-dimensional grey value correlation techniques (Demant, 1999). More advanced vision-based quality inspection systems employ three-dimensional methods in order to detect production faults more reliably and robustly. In this section we regard applications in the automobile industry of the methods for three-dimensional pose estimation of rigid and articulated objects described in Chap. 2.

A typical area of interest is checking for completeness of a set of small parts attached to a large workpiece, such as plugs, cables, screws, and covers mounted on a car engine. A different task is the inspection of the position and orientation of parts, e.g. checking if they are correctly mounted but also checking for proper grasping and transport with an industrial robot.

Section 6.1 regards the three-dimensional pose estimation of rigid parts in the context of quality inspection of car engine components. The approach of object detection by pose estimation without a priori knowledge about the object pose is analysed in Sect. 6.1.1, while the technique of pose refinement based on an appropriate initial pose is regarded in Sect. 6.1.2. Here we adopt the presentation of von Bank et al. (2003) and Barrois and Wöhler (2007), respectively (cf. Sects. 2.1 and 5.6). The three-dimensional pose estimation of tubes and cables in the scenario of car engine production is analysed in Sect. 6.2 according to d'Angelo et al. (2004) (cf. Sect. 2.2.1.2). For each scenario we compare our evaluation results to results reported in the literature for systems performing similar inspection tasks. Section 6.3 describes applications of the integrated approaches introduced in Sects. 5.1–5.4 (Wöhler and Hafezi, 2005; d'Angelo and Wöhler, 2005a, 2005b, 2005c, 2006, 2008; Wöhler and d'Angelo, 2009; Herbort et al., 2011) to the three-dimensional reconstruction of rough metallic surfaces.

C. Wöhler, *3D Computer Vision*, X.media.publishing,
DOI 10.1007/978-1-4471-4150-1_6, © Springer-Verlag London 2013

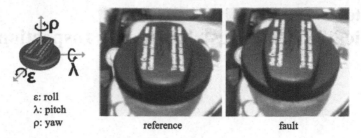

ε: roll
λ: pitch
ρ: yaw   reference   fault

Fig. 6.1 *Left*: Definition of the roll, pitch, and yaw angles ε, λ, and ρ. *Centre* and *right*: Reference pose of the oil cap and typical fault

6.1 Inspection of Rigid Parts

The first typical quality inspection scenario involving the three-dimensional pose estimation of rigid parts is detection by pose estimation (cf. Sect. 6.1.1), corresponding to a simultaneous detection of the presence and estimation of the pose of an object of known three-dimensional geometry. In the second scenario, pose refinement (cf. Sect. 6.1.2), a reasonably accurate initial pose of the object is required which is then refined further.

Many applications of pose estimation methods for quality inspection purposes impose severe constraints on the hardware to be used with respect to robustness and easy maintenance. Hence, it is often difficult or even impossible to utilise stereo camera systems, since they have to be recalibrated regularly, especially when the sensor unit is mounted on an industrial robot. In this section we therefore describe applications of the monocular pose estimation methods by von Bank et al. (2003) and by Barrois and Wöhler (2007) (cf. Sects. 2.1 and 5.6) in the automobile production environment.

6.1.1 Object Detection by Pose Estimation

The inspection task addressed in this section is to detect the presence and to estimate the three-dimensional pose of the oil cap shown in Fig. 6.1 based on the method of von Bank et al. (2003). To generate real-world images with well-defined ground truth poses, we made use of a calibrated robot system. The accuracy of calibration with respect to the world coordinate system is about 0.1° with respect to camera orientation and 0.1 mm with respect to camera position. As the engine itself is not part of the robot system, the relation between world coordinate system and engine coordinate system has to be established separately, which reduces the accuracies stated above by about an order of magnitude.

First, the difference between the measured and the true pose of the correctly assembled oil cap is determined depending on the camera viewpoint and the illumination conditions. The scene is illuminated by a cylindric lamp around the

Table 6.1 Properties of the three oil cap template hierarchies (ranges of pose angles ρ, ε, λ, and grid sizes in degrees). Hierarchy 1 consists of 4550 templates, hierarchies 2 and 3 of 1331 templates, respectively

Hierarchy	ρ range	$\Delta\rho$	ε range	$\Delta\varepsilon$	λ range	$\Delta\lambda$
1	$0°\ldots180°$	$2°$	$18°\ldots72°$	$6°$	$-12°\ldots+12°$	$6°$
2	$0°\ldots20°$	$2°$	$30°\ldots50°$	$2°$	$-10°\ldots+10°$	$2°$
3	Same as 2, but without writing modelled					

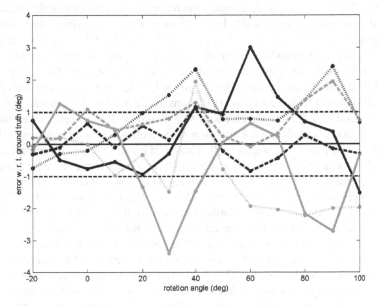

Fig. 6.2 Deviations of ε (*solid lines*), ρ (*dashed lines*), and λ (*dotted lines*) from their ground truth values. Illumination is with cylindric lamp only (*black lines*) and with both cylindric and halogen lamps (*grey lines*). The true roll angle is constantly set to $\varepsilon = 70°$

camera lens (confocal illumination) and a halogen spot. The background of the scene may be fairly cluttered. The distance to the object amounts to 200 mm and is assumed to be known, such that only five degrees of freedom are to be estimated. The resolution of the utilised images corresponds to about 0.4 mm per pixel.

For this examination we use template hierarchy 1 (cf. Table 6.1). The angle ε denotes the roll angle, λ the pitch angle, and ρ the yaw angle. For camera viewpoints with $-10° \leq \rho \leq 10°$ and $50° \leq \varepsilon \leq 60°$, the measured pose lies within the calibration accuracy interval of $1°$ for all three angles. Figure 6.2 shows that for $\varepsilon = 70°$, this is even true for $-20° \leq \rho \leq 20°$. This implies that from a correspondingly chosen viewpoint, the algorithm is highly sensitive with respect to deviations from the reference pose. Hence, it is possible to determine the pose of the oil cap to an accuracy of about $1°$. Significantly changing the illumination conditions by switching off the halogen lamp does not affect the pose estimation results. The computation time of the system amounts to about 200 ms on a Pentium IV 2.4 GHz processor.

As the described system aims at distinguishing incorrect from correct poses, i.e. performing a corresponding classification of the inspected object, the rate of correctly recognised faults (the rate of incorrectly assembled oil caps which are recognised as such by the inspection system) is determined vs. the rate of correctly assembled objects erroneously classified as incorrectly assembled (false positive rate). This representation of the system behaviour is termed the receiver operating characteristics (ROC) curve. We determined the recognition behaviour of the system for three different camera viewpoints. Here we concentrate on a typical fault situation showing angle differences $\Delta\rho = 0°$, $\Delta\varepsilon = 2.5°$, $\Delta\lambda = -3.5°$ with respect to the reference pose. In the production environment, the engine and thus the attached oil cap are positioned with a tolerance of about 1 cm with respect to the camera. This positional variation was simulated by acquiring 125 different images of each examined fault situation from 125 camera positions inside a cube of 1 cm size which are equally spaced by 2.5 mm in each coordinate direction. This offset is taken into account appropriately in the pose estimation based on the measured position of the oil cap in the image. As a first step, a fault is assigned based on each of the three angles separately if the corresponding angle deviates from the reference value by more than a given threshold. By varying this threshold, an ROC curve is generated for each angle separately, as shown in Figs. 6.3a–c. We then generate a combined ROC curve by assuming that the oil cap is assembled incorrectly if the deviation of at least one of the pose angles is larger than the corresponding threshold. These thresholds are then adjusted such that the area under the ROC curve becomes maximum. This combination generally yields an ROC curve showing very few misclassifications on the acquired test set, as illustrated in Fig. 6.3d. Both with template hierarchy 1, which covers a wide range of pose angles with a large grid size, and with hierarchy 2, covering a region on the viewing sphere close to the reference view with a small grid size (cf. Table 6.1), very high recognition rates close to 100 % are achieved. With hierarchy 3, which is identical to hierarchy 2 except that the writing on top of the oil cap has been omitted, the performance decreases, but not significantly: At a false positive rate of zero, a rate of correctly recognised faults of 98.4 % is still achieved.

In the second scenario, dealing with the inspection of an ignition plug, we regard three fault configurations in addition to the reference configuration: The clip is not fixed, the plug is loose, and the plug is missing (Fig. 6.4). The connector and the plug are modelled as two separate objects such that the offset of the plug in the vertical direction can be used to distinguish fault configurations from the reference configuration. The matching results in Fig. 6.4 show that the vertical position of the plug relative to the connector can be determined at an accuracy of about 0.5 mm, which is sufficient to faithfully distinguish correctly from incorrectly assembled ignition plugs.

Comparison with Other Pose Estimation Methods   At this point, a comparison of the achieved pose estimation accuracy with other systems is illustrative.

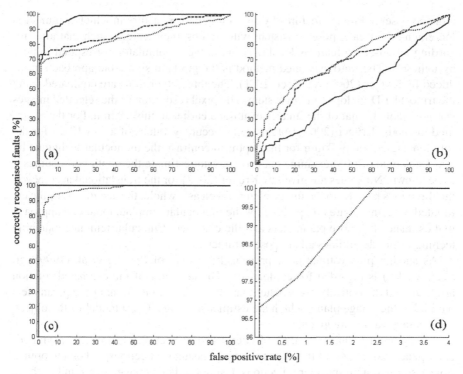

Fig. 6.3 ROC curves of the inspection system, based on the measured values of (**a**) the roll angle ε, (**b**) the yaw angle ρ, (**c**) the pitch angle λ, (**d**) all three pose angles. *Solid*, *dashed*, and *dotted lines* denote three different camera viewpoints. Note that the axis scaling in (**d**) is different from that in (**a**)–(**c**)

Fig. 6.4 Ignition plug inspection: Reference configuration (*left*) and three fault configurations with the corresponding matching results, using two templates. Image scale is 0.2 mm per pixel

Krüger (2007) uses the oil cap described above as a test object to evaluate the performance of three multiocular three-dimensional pose estimation methods developed in his work. The first regarded approach is the multiocular template matching technique introduced by Krüger (2007). As a comparison, Krüger (2007) develops and evaluates a multiocular extension of the feature pose map algorithm introduced by Westling and Davis (1996) (Westling and Davis 1996 associate pose parameters and observed image features by an accumulator structure in which a counter is incremented for each pose consistent with an observed feature, such that after regarding all observed features local maxima in the accumulator correspond to pose hypotheses). The third evaluated method is the gradient sign table approach introduced by Krüger (2007) (cf. Sect. 2.1.1). The three algorithms are compared using the trinocular Digiclops camera system. The pixel resolution of the regarded images is comparable to that of the images examined earlier in this section. For the examined methods, Krüger (2007) obtains mean accuracy values of about 1°–2° for the rotation angles and 3–7 mm for the depth. In contrast, the monocular technique by von Bank et al. (2003) examined above does not estimate the depth but assumes it to be known. No values are given by Krüger (2007) for the translational accuracy in the directions parallel to the image plane. Taken as a whole, the accuracies of the estimated pose angles are comparable for the monocular template matching approach that estimates five pose parameters and the extended, trinocular template matching technique that determines all six pose parameters.

As another pose estimation approach, the system of Bachler et al. (1999) (cf. Sect. 2.1.1.2) is regarded for comparison. The accuracy of the estimated rotation angle around the optical axis is better than 3°. For the translational pose parameters parallel to the image plane, which are estimated using a CAD model of the object, no accuracy values are given.

The system of Chang et al. (2009) described in Sect. 2.1.1.2 relies on synthetically generated images of the object showing specular reflections and on the optical flow associated with specular reflections. Using synthetic images as ground truth, an average translational accuracy parallel to the image plane of better than 0.5 mm is obtained, while no depth value is determined. The rotational accuracy typically corresponds to 2.5°–5°. The presented qualitative evaluation on real images suggests that these accuracy values are also realistic for real images.

The system of Collet et al. (2011) described in Sect. 2.1.1.2 is based on a single or several calibrated images of the scene. A resolution of about 1 mm per pixel can be inferred from the given image size of 640 × 480 pixels and the apparent size of the objects in the images shown. In a monocular setting, the translational pose estimation error is below 15 mm and decreases to below 5 mm when three images are used. The rotational accuracy corresponds to about 6° for the monocular setting and to about 3.5°–6° for three images, depending on how the pose estimation results inferred from the individual images are combined.

6.1.2 Pose Refinement

This section examines the application of the appearance-based approach described in Sect. 5.6 to three-dimensional pose estimation of automotive parts. The description in this section is adopted from Barrois and Wöhler (2007), whose method combines monocular photopolarimetric, edge, and defocus information. As a first example, the oil cap is regarded again (cf. Fig. 6.5). The experimental setup is the

Fig. 6.5 Example of a high dynamic range intensity image (*left*, grey values are displayed logarithmically) and a polarisation angle image (*right*, grey value map is scaled in degrees)

Fig. 6.6 Intensity images of the oil cap for pose 1 (*left*) and pose 2 (*right*). Grey values are displayed in logarithmic scale

same as in Sect. 5.6 (Baumer industrial CCD camera, 1032×776 pixel image size, $f = 25$ mm, object distance around 0.5 m). To increase the signal-to-noise ratio of the intensity and polarisation data, the images were downscaled to 258×194 pixels, corresponding to a lateral resolution of about 0.4 mm per pixel. A depth from defocus analysis was performed based on the full-resolution images acquired at apertures of f/8 and f/2, respectively.

The system performs pose refinement with four initial poses differing by several degrees in the rotation angles and a few millimetres in translation. The minimisation run yielding the lowest residual error is adopted as the pose estimation result. Due to its complex shape, this object cannot be attached to the goniometer table in a reproduceable manner; thus we determined the ground truth pose in this experiment based on a stereoscopic bundle adjustment tool which exploits manually established point correspondences between a calibrated stereo image pair and the CAD model of the object. As in the first experiment, the goniometer was used to determine the intensity and polarisation angle reflectance functions R_I and R_Φ. The light reflected by the plastic surface of the oil cap is partially polarised by 10–20 %, such that the polarisation angle can be used in addition to intensity, edges, and depth. The intensity images of the two regarded poses are shown in Fig. 6.6, illustrating that at some places, especially near the right image border, the edges are not well defined, such that the pose estimation algorithm must largely rely on intensity and polarisation information. The comparison to the ground truth is shown in Table 6.2, demonstrating

Table 6.2 Estimated pose and ground truth (GT) for the oil cap example

Parameter	Pose 1	GT 1	Pose 2	GT 2
Roll (°)	233.2	234.5	230.7	232.1
Pitch (°)	1.3	2.3	0.9	2.4
Yaw (°)	57.3	55.2	56.8	56.0
t_x (mm)	14.7	14.7	15.0	14.8
t_y (mm)	2.1	2.8	2.0	2.5
t_z (mm)	512.9	509.2	512.7	509.2

Fig. 6.7 Intensity images of the door hinge for pose 1 (*left*) and pose 2 (*right*). Grey levels are displayed in logarithmic scale

that the object pose can be determined with an accuracy of 1°–2° for the rotation angles, some tenths of a millimetre for the lateral translations, and several millimetres or about 1 % for the object distance. Small deviations of the rotation angles can be compensated by correspondingly adjusting the albedo factor ρ, leading to a lower accuracy of the rotation angles, compared to the rubber example. Due to the somewhat ill-defined edges the pose estimation fails when only edge information is used, as no convergence of the minimisation routine is achieved.

For the oil cap example, it is possible to directly compare the results of the method of Barrois and Wöhler (2007) to those of the monocular edge-based template matching method proposed by von Bank et al. (2003), since in that work the same object and the same CAD model are regarded. The deviation of the rotation angles estimated by von Bank et al. (2003) from the corresponding ground truth is typically around 1°–2° but may also become larger than 3°. In contrast to the method of Barrois and Wöhler (2007), it is assumed by von Bank et al. (2003) that the distance to the object is known, i.e. only five rather than six degrees of freedom are estimated by von Bank et al. (2003). On the other hand, that method does not require a priori information about the object pose.

In a further experiment another automotive part is regarded, a door hinge consisting of cast metal with a rough and strongly specular surface (cf. Fig. 6.7). The light from the point light source is specularly reflected into the camera. The Canny edge detector yields a very large number of edges (cf. Fig. 6.8), thus providing no reliable information about the object pose. As a consequence, our approach fails when we

Fig. 6.8
Distance-transformed edge
image of the door hinge

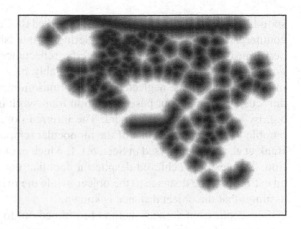

Table 6.3 Estimated pose
differences and ground truth
for the door hinge example

Parameter difference	Result	GT
$\Delta\varepsilon$ (°) (roll)	4.15	4.23
$\Delta\lambda$ (°) (pitch)	2.06	1.69
$\Delta\rho$ (°) (yaw)	0.22	0.58
Δt_x (mm)	0.71	0.06
Δt_y (mm)	1.88	2.33
Δt_z (mm)	3.82	0.16

attempt to perform a pose estimation of the hinge based on the extracted edge information. The surface of the hinge does not perceivably polarise the reflected light. Hence, we only use intensity and defocus data as input information for our algorithm. The obtained results illustrate that our algorithm also works in the absence of some of the input cues and that it is suitable for pose estimation of objects with a strongly specular surface.

In this experiment, the chequerboard method could not be used for determining the ground truth, since the hinge could not be attached to the goniometer in a reproduceable manner; it was not possible to place it in a known position relative to the chequerboard and the goniometer. Similarly, the bundle adjustment tool based on manually established point correspondences could not be used since, unlike the oil cap, the hinge does not display well-defined corner points. Hence, the estimated poses are compared with the difference imposed by the two chosen goniometer settings, which are given at high accuracy. The estimated pose differences and the corresponding ground truth values are shown in Table 6.3. Although not all geometric, photometric, and depth cues are available, the obtained results are comparable to or better than those obtained in the previous experiments (some tenths of a degree for the rotation angles, some tenths of a millimetre for the lateral translation, and some millimetres for the object distance).

The examined monocular pose estimation framework is based on photometric, polarimetric, edge, and defocus cues. The pose is obtained by minimising a correspondingly defined error function. The observed data are compared to their rendered counterparts, where an accurate rendering of intensity and polarisation images is performed based on the material-specific reflectance functions determined with a goniometer. If a certain cue cannot be reliably measured or does not yield useful information, it can be neglected in the optimisation procedure. Beyond depth from defocus, in principle our pose estimation framework is open for depth data obtained e.g. by active range measurement. The inferred pose refinement accuracy is comparable to or higher than that of the monocular template matching approach by von Bank et al. (2003) analysed in Sect. 6.1.1, which exclusively relies on edge information. This result is achieved despite the fact that our method additionally provides an estimate of the distance to the object, while the method of von Bank et al. (2003) assumes that the object distance is known.

The depth from defocus method has turned out to be a useful instrument for the estimation of object depth in close range, at an accuracy of about 1 %. We have demonstrated the usefulness of our method under conditions typically encountered in industrial quality inspection scenarios such as the assembly of complex parts. Here, the desired pose of the whole workpiece or part of it is given by the CAD data, and the inspection system has to detect small differences between the actual and the desired pose.

Comparison with Other Pose Refinement Methods   It is again interesting to compare the accuracy of our method with that achieved by other pose refinement approaches. For their proposed monocular pose refinement method (cf. Sect. 2.1.1), Kölzow and Ellenrieder (2003) determine the absolute accuracy of the pose parameters based on synthetic images of the oil cap also regarded by von Bank et al. (2003), where the background is uniform (the given image dimensions and the known object size allow one to estimate an approximate pixel scale of 0.7 mm per pixel). Accordingly, the mean rotational accuracy of the method by Kölzow and Ellenrieder (2003) is better than 1°, the mean translational accuracy is better than 1 mm parallel to the image plane, and the mean depth accuracy corresponds to 2.6 mm. The standard deviation, indicating the uncertainty of a single measurement, is better than 2° for the rotation, better than 1 mm for the translation parallel to the image plane, and about 4 mm for the depth. Regarding real images of the oil cap with a complex background, the standard deviations of the estimated pose parameters across subsequent images of a sequence are comparable to the standard deviations obtained for the synthetic images.

The monocular system of Nomura et al. (1996) (cf. Sect. 2.1.1) uses synthetic edge and intensity images generated based on an object model. At an image resolution of about 2 mm per pixel, the rotational accuracy is better than 0.5°, the translational accuracy parallel to the image plane corresponds to 0.04 mm, and the accuracy of the estimated depth amounts to 5.19 mm.

The system of Yoon et al. (2003) (cf. Sect. 2.1.1) performs a pose estimation of industrial parts in real time in stereo images. The objects are located at distances of 600–800 mm, and a resolution of approximately 0.9 mm per pixel can be inferred from the presented example images. Yoon et al. (2003) report an accuracy of better than 1.5° and 2.5 mm for the three rotation angles and the three translational pose parameters, respectively.

The system of Stößel (2007) (cf. Sect. 2.2) has been developed for estimation of the pose parameters of articulated objects in monocular images. When applied to the real-world oil cap data by von Bank et al. (2003), the full extended kernel particle filter approach shows the highest performance of the system configurations examined by Stößel (2007), yielding a mean error between 0.1° and 0.3° for the three rotation angles. Due to the stochastic nature of the employed optimisation algorithm, however, the result of an optimisation run is non-deterministic. Hence, the uncertainty of an individual rotation angle measurement amounts to 0.9–1.5°. Stößel (2007) does not report accuracy values for the translational degrees of freedom.

This comparison illustrates that the pose refinement approach of Barrois and Wöhler (2007) based on multiple monocular cues is able to estimate the rotational pose parameters at an accuracy which is of the same order of magnitude as the mean error of the method proposed by Stößel (2007), even under viewing directions where geometric cues alone do not allow one to recover the object pose reliably. It should be noted, however, that the uncertainty of an individual measurement by Stößel (2007) is nearly an order of magnitude higher than the mean error. Presumably, the high accuracy of the estimated rotational pose parameters achieved by our method is due to the integration of photopolarimetric information. The translational accuracy of our method in directions parallel to the image plane, which is largely determined by the available edge information, is comparable to or slightly higher than that observed for other pose refinement systems, which all rely to a considerable extent on edge information. The accuracy of the values obtained for the object depth with the monocular depth from defocus technique comes close to that of the system of Yoon et al. (2003), which is based on the evaluation of stereo image pairs.

6.2 Inspection of Non-rigid Parts

In this section the three-dimensional active contour algorithm of d'Angelo et al. (2004) described in Sect. 2.2.2 is applied to the reconstruction of a cable, using images acquired with a Digiclops trinocular camera system at a distance to the object of about 1 m, as shown in Fig. 6.9. A three-dimensional ziplock ribbon snake has been used in these examples. The approximate ribbon radius was used as model information, and constraints for the upper and lower bound of the ribbon width were applied. The segmented contour part is displayed from a slightly different viewing angle to show the spatial segmentation. The accuracy of reconstruction compared to ground truth obtained with a calliper gauge is about 1 mm, corresponding to 1.5 pixels, in this example.

A different inspection scenario is the three-dimensional reconstruction of a glue line on the non-planar free-form surface of a car body part, as shown in Fig. 6.10.

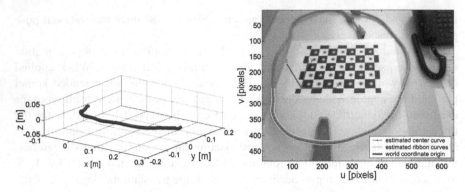

Fig. 6.9 Cable Scene. It is evident that the reconstructed cable is located above the table plane ($z \doteq 0$). The world coordinate system has been defined by estimating the pose of the chequerboard

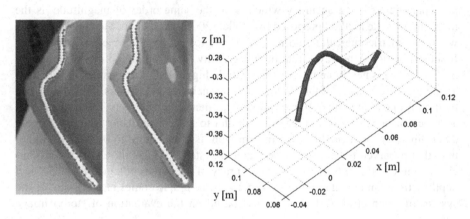

Fig. 6.10 Three-dimensional reconstruction of a glue line on the non-planar surface of a car body part (*left*), resulting three-dimensional ziplock ribbon snake (*right*)

Although the object is not flexible, a pose estimation method for rigid objects cannot be applied due to the lack of an accurate geometry model. Hence, the multiocular ziplock ribbon snake algorithm is an adequate approach to reconstruct the three-dimensional shape of the glue line. Again, the images were acquired with the Digiclops system, and the object was situated at a distance of about 0.7 m to the camera. The accuracy of the reconstruction result compared to ground truth obtained with a calliper gauge amounts to 1 mm, corresponding to 1.5 pixels.

A scenario that goes beyond mere quality inspection is illustrated in Fig. 6.11 in a laboratory environment. A bar code is desired to be read by a monocular camera (camera 2 in Fig. 6.11a) but is partially occluded by a cable. The trajectory of the cable is reconstructed with the multiocular ziplock snake method (cf. Fig. 6.11b–c) using the Digiclops trinocular camera system (camera 1 in Fig. 6.11a). As soon as the three-dimensional pose estimation has been performed as indicated in Fig. 6.11c, the industrial robot grasps the cable and holds it aside, as shown in

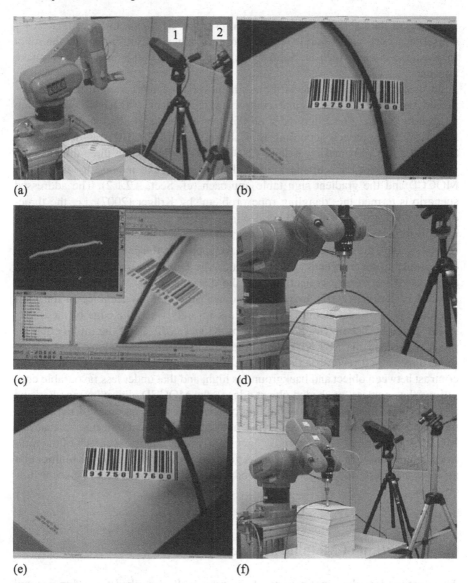

Fig. 6.11 Industrial robot grasping a cable. (**a**) The pose of the cable is estimated based on trinocular image data acquired with a Digiclops system (*1*). The image of the bar code is taken by a monocular camera (*2*). (**b**) The bar code cannot be read due to the cable partially occluding it. (**c**) The three-dimensional pose of the cable is estimated. (**d**) The robot grasps the cable and holds it aside. (**e**) Now the bar code can be read. (**f**) The robot places the cable back into its original position

Fig. 6.11d. For this purpose, the robot needs to be calibrated with respect to the coordinate system of the trinocular camera. In the image of the monocular camera, the bar code is now unoccluded and can be read (cf. Fig. 6.11e). Finally, the robot places the cable back to its original position, as shown in Fig. 6.11f. A lo-calisation accuracy of 1 mm is required for mechanical reasons to enable the robot to grasp the cable, which is faithfully achieved by the multiocular ziplock snake approach.

In the application scenario of three-dimensional reconstruction of tubes, a sim-plified variant of the multiocular contracting curve density (MOCCD) algorithm is used by Krüger and Ellenrieder (2005). An extensive evaluation based on the full MOCCD approach according to Hahn et al. (2007, 2010a) as described in Sect. 2.2.1.2 is provided by Krüger (2007), who compares the three-dimensional reconstruction accuracy of the multiocular ziplock snake method to that of the MOCCD and the gradient sign table approach (cf. Sect. 2.2.1.2). The addressed scenario is termed the 'dangling rope problem' by Krüger (2007), i.e. the three-dimensional position of the non-rigid object and its tangential direction is known a priori for only one of its ends (in the application scenarios regarded in this sec-tion to evaluate the multiocular ziplock snake approach, this information has always been available for both ends of the objects). The Digiclops trinocular camera sys-tem is used for image acquisition, and the distance to the object corresponds to about 1 m. Krüger (2007) arrives at the conclusion that the accuracy of the mul-tiocular ziplock snake method degrades less strongly when the edge of the object in the image is incomplete. It is shown by Krüger (2007) that the multiocular zi-plock snake and the MOCCD yield comparable average deviations between the three-dimensional reconstruction and the ground truth of 1–3 mm as long as the contrast between object and background is high, and that under less favourable con-ditions (low contrast or shaded object edges), the MOCCD algorithm may become more accurate than the multiocular ziplock snake by up to an order of magnitude, while the multiocular ziplock snake permits smaller apparent object sizes than the MOCCD algorithm. Furthermore, Krüger (2007) finds that the accuracy of the mul-tiocular gradient sign tables approach is generally similar to that of the multiocular ziplock snake and the MOCCD but tends to be more robust with respect to low contrast.

6.3 Inspection of Metallic Surfaces

This section describes applications of the previously described three-dimensional surface reconstruction methods to the inspection of metallic surfaces mainly of au-tomotive parts. Where possible, the results are compared to independently derived ground truth values obtained by a laser profilometer or by tactile measurement.

Traditionally, photometric three-dimensional surface reconstruction techniques such as shape from shading have been regarded as being unsuitable for industrial applications (Mühlmann, 2002). State-of-the-art commercial three-dimensional sur-face reconstruction systems for industrial quality inspection purposes are based on active scanning techniques such as projection of coded structured light. It is shown in this section, however, that especially for metallic surfaces, taking into

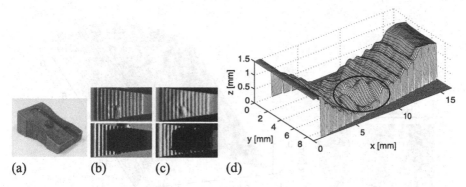

Fig. 6.12 Three-dimensional reconstruction of the lateral surface of a sharpener, based on the integration of shadow and shading features according to Sect. 5.2. (**a**) The sharpener. (**b**) Images used for three-dimensional reconstruction. (**c**) Images rendered based on the reconstruction result. (**d**) Three-dimensional surface reconstruction. A surface defect of 0.5 mm depth is marked by an ellipse

account photometric image information during the reconstruction process under well-controlled conditions yields three-dimensional reconstruction results that are at least comparable to those obtained with active scanning devices while requiring significantly less complex and expensive instrumental configurations.

6.3.1 Inspection Based on Integration of Shadow and Shading Features

Wöhler and Hafezi (2005) regard the three-dimensional reconstruction of the lateral surface of a sharpener consisting of aluminium. Due to the perpendicular view and strongly oblique illumination, the specular components in the reflectance function (3.14) are negligible as $\cos \theta_r \ll 1$, such that Lambertian reflectance is a reasonable approximation to the true reflectance behaviour. The result of the combined shadow and shading approach according to Sect. 5.2, relying on one shadow and one shading image, is shown in Fig. 6.12. The surface displays a regularly striped structure and a small surface defect, which are well visible in the reconstruction result. The depth of the surface defect marked by an oval in Fig. 6.12d of approximately 0.5 mm corresponds within 0.1 mm to the value derived by tactile measurement. This example illustrates that even in the absence of accurate knowledge about the surface reflectance the combined shadow and shading approach yields a quantitatively fairly accurate three-dimensional reconstruction result.

6.3.2 Inspection of Surfaces with Non-uniform Albedo

An application in which the three-dimensional reconstruction approach must cope with a non-uniform surface albedo is the inspection of uncoated steel sheet surfaces.

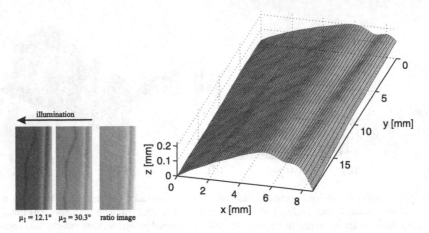

Fig. 6.13 Three-dimensional reconstruction of a metallic surface of non-uniform albedo (*dark line* traversing the *left half of the image from top to bottom*). A constriction is visible at the *right image* border. The input images (*left*) are acquired at illumination angles of 12.1° and 30.3°, respectively. The surface reconstruction (*right*) is obtained by applying the ratio-based iterative update rule (3.51)

This scenario is addressed by Wöhler and Hafezi (2005), and the presentation in this section is adopted from that work. The surface shown in Fig. 6.13 displays a dark line in the left half of the image, which is an acceptable surface property that may be due to small particles deposited on the surface during the production process, and a constriction in the right half of the image, which is a defective thinning of the sheet metal that may lead to mechanical instabilities.

The three-dimensional reconstruction of the surface is performed relying on the ratio-based intensity error term (3.50) and the ratio-based iterative update rule according to (3.51). The specular component of the surface reflectance was found to be weak, such that it could be neglected for the viewing and illumination geometry applied to acquire the images shown in Fig. 6.13. Under a perpendicular view on the surface, two images were acquired at phase angles of 77.9° and 59.7°. This configuration corresponds to elevation angles of the light source of 12.1° and 30.3° above the average surface plane, respectively. In the ratio image, the dark line disappears while the constriction stands out clearly. The reconstructed surface profile shows that the constriction with a depth of less than 0.1 mm is recovered, while no artefacts occur at the location of the dark line. Hence, the ratio-based approach achieves successful separation of pixel brightness variations due to non-uniform albedo from those caused by changing surface gradients.

As another example, Fig. 6.14 shows the reconstructed surface of a steel sheet with a shallow deformation along with the corresponding albedo map ρ_{uv}. The surface profile was obtained by extending the fusion scheme for shading and shadow features outlined in Sect. 5.2 to several light sources as pointed out in Sect. 3.3. The reconstruction procedure consisted of applying the ratio-based iterative update rule equation (3.51) including the shadow-related error term (5.10), and subsequently

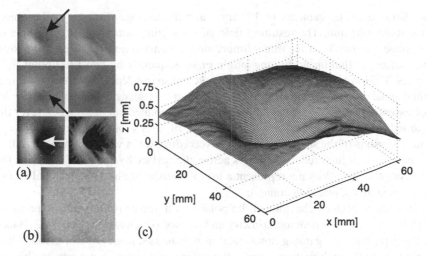

Fig. 6.14 Three-dimensional surface reconstruction of a steel sheet with a deformation. (**a**) Two shading images and one shadow image with their simulated counterparts. Illumination direction is as indicated by the *arrows*. (**b**) Albedo map computed according to (3.49). (**c**) Reconstructed surface profile, shown with respect to the fitted reference plane. The depth of the deformation corresponds to 0.36 mm

the iterative update rule equation (5.13) with the error term (3.43) for multiple light sources. As the average inclination of the reconstructed part of the surface with respect to the ground plane amounts to several degrees, a reference plane was fitted to the reconstructed profile. In Fig. 6.14c, this reference plane has been subtracted from the reconstruction result. In the albedo map, variations appear that correspond to dark and bright spots and lines. Again, intensity changes in the image which are caused by shading effects have been separated from those due to variations of the surface albedo.

6.3.3 Inspection Based on SfPR and SfPRD

The surface reconstruction algorithms described in Sect. 5.3 were applied by d'Angelo and Wöhler (2005b, 2006, 2008) to the raw forged iron surface of a connection rod. This section describes their three-dimensional reconstruction results and compares them to a ground truth cross section of the same surface, measured with a scanning laser focus profilometer. The second inspected part is a slightly damaged section of the raw surface of a flange also consisting of forged iron. Its surface shows several small deformations. The depths of these deformations inferred from the three-dimensional reconstruction results are compared to ground truth values obtained by tactile measurement. The presentation in this section is adopted from d'Angelo and Wöhler (2008).

A convergent stereo setup is utilised, consisting of two CCD cameras of 1032 × 776 pixel image resolution, equipped with lenses of 25 mm focal length. The baseline distance of the cameras is 320 mm, and the average distance to the object amounts to 480 mm. The resulting field of view corresponds to 10°. The size of the image sections used for three-dimensional reconstruction is 240×240 pixels. The surface is illuminated by one single or subsequently by two LED point light sources. The intensity I, polarisation angle Φ, and sparse depth Z are used for three-dimensional reconstruction. In addition to the fact that intensity and polarisation degree essentially provide redundant information, as pointed out in Sect. 5.3.4, for the regarded rough metallic surfaces the behaviour of D is strongly affected by small-scale variations of the surface roughness. Accordingly, the value of the polarisation degree D for specular reflection varies across the surface by up to 20 %. Hence, the polarisation degree does not represent a useful feature for three-dimensional reconstruction in this application context.

This unfavourable behaviour of the polarisation degree is known from previous work in the domain of photopolarimetry and has been discussed in Sect. 3.4.2. Based on the experiments regarding raw forged iron materials, however, it was found that in contrast to the polarisation degree, the polarisation angle is not perceivably influenced by slight variations of the surface roughness. As a consequence, the polarisation degree is a feature which may be useful for determination of the surface orientation only for smooth dielectric surfaces, which can be accurately described in terms of the Fresnel equations as shown by Atkinson and Hancock (2005b).

6.3.3.1 Results Obtained with the SfPR Technique

For three-dimensional surface reconstruction of the raw forged iron surface of the connection rod with the local SfPR approach according to d'Angelo and Wöhler (2005b) described in Sect. 5.3.1.2, two intensity images and one polarisation angle image were employed. Figure 6.15a shows a flawless part and a part that displays a surface deformation. The ratio-based and thus albedo-independent intensity error term according to (3.48) was used. The deviation between the flawless and the deformed surface becomes evident in Figs. 6.15b–c. The comparison between the ground truth and the corresponding cross section extracted from the reconstructed profile yields a root-mean-square error (RMSE) of 220 μm.

Two experiments concerning the application of the global SfPR approach to the connection rod surface were performed by d'Angelo and Wöhler (2008). In the first experiment, we initialised the surface gradients by zero values and determined the uniform surface albedo ρ_0 according to (5.23), relying on specular reflections. The reflectance and the polarisation angle image as well as the stereo reconstruction result are shown in Fig. 6.16. The dashed line indicates the cross section for which ground truth data are available. Cross sections extracted from the corresponding reconstructed surface profiles and their comparison to ground truth are shown in Fig. 6.17. The RMSE values are 56 μm for the SfPR approach and 281 μm for the shape from shading approach which neglects polarisation information. While the SfPR approach yields a very accurate reconstruction of the surface, the shape from shading approach estimates a largely uniform value of the surface gradient

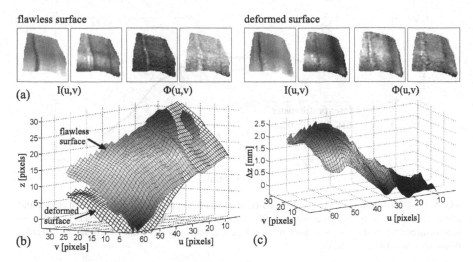

Fig. 6.15 Application of the local SfPR algorithm to the raw forged iron surface of the connection rod (d'Angelo and Wöhler, 2005b). (**a**) Images of a flawless and of a deformed surface. (**b**) Comparison of the three-dimensional surface profiles obtained with the local optimisation scheme. (**c**) Difference between the two profiles

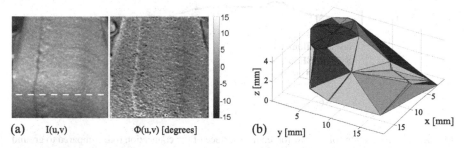

Fig. 6.16 (**a**) Reflectance and polarisation angle images of the raw forged iron surface of the connection rod. (**b**) Triangulated stereo reconstruction result

perpendicular to the direction of incident light due to the minor influence of this gradient on the error function.

In the second experiment, we initialised the global optimisation scheme with the surface gradients p_{uv}^{DfD} and q_{uv}^{DfD} inferred from the depth from defocus result as described in Sect. 5.3.3.1. To calibrate the depth from defocus algorithm, a linear function was fitted to the $(\Sigma, (z - z_0))$ data points (cf. Sect. 4.2.2). The calibration curve is shown in Fig. 4.6, and for illustration purposes, the raw and median-filtered depth from defocus measurements are shown in Fig. 4.7 (cf. Sect. 4.2.2). The profile shows many spurious structures, especially on small scales, such that shape details are not reliably recovered. Three-dimensional reconstruction was performed based on a combination of intensity and polarisation angle (Fig. 6.16a). The albedo ρ_0 was estimated based on all image pixels according to (5.24) with the surface gradi-

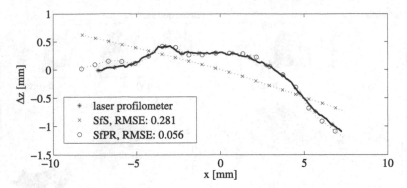

Fig. 6.17 Cross sections of the raw forged iron surface of the connection rod, compared to ground truth (RMSE in mm), obtained with the SfPR and the shape from shading approach (SfS), no stereo information, initialisation with zero surface gradients, albedo estimated based on specular reflections according to (5.23)

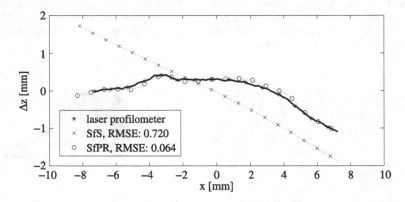

Fig. 6.18 Cross sections of the raw forged iron surface of the connection rod, compared to ground truth (RMSE in mm). SfPR and shape from shading approach (SfS), no stereo information, initialisation with surface gradients obtained by depth from defocus, albedo estimated based on all image pixels according to (5.24)

ents set to p_{uv}^{DfD} and q_{uv}^{DfD} and was kept constant during the iteration process. Cross sections extracted from the corresponding reconstructed surface profiles and their comparison to ground truth are shown in Fig. 6.18. The RMSE values are 64 μm for the SfPR approach and 720 μm for the shape from shading approach. The shape from shading approach again does not correctly estimate the surface gradients perpendicular to the direction of incident light, which results in a large RMSE value. Including polarisation information yields largely the same result as obtained with the albedo estimated from specular reflections, but without requiring the presence of specular reflections in the image.

For the flange, as shown in Fig. 6.19a, the global SfPR approach was initialised with zero surface gradients, and the uniform surface albedo ρ_0 was determined ac-

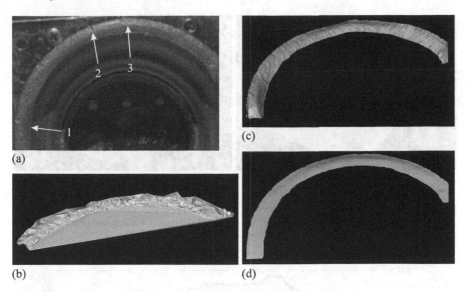

Fig. 6.19 (**a**) High dynamic range image of the flange, displayed at logarithmic scale. Three-dimensional reconstruction is performed for the ring-shaped surface part. The depths of the indicated dents were measured on the reconstructed surface profile and compared to ground truth data. (**b**) Triangulated stereo reconstruction result. (**c**) SfPR, no stereo information. (**d**) Shape from shading, no stereo information. Albedo estimated based on specular reflections according to (5.23)

cording to (5.23), relying on specular reflections. The three-dimensional reconstruction is performed for the ring-shaped part only, as the neighbouring parts are situated in the shadow and only visible due to secondary reflections (Fig. 6.19a is a high dynamic range image displayed at logarithmic scale). What is more, the surface normals of the neighbouring parts are nearly orthogonal to the viewing direction. Our goniometer setup for measuring the intensity and polarisation reflectance functions does not cope with such an extreme viewing geometry, such that in this range the reflectance function values are unknown. Furthermore, photometric surface reconstruction techniques are most favourably applied when the view on the surface is largely perpendicular (McEwen, 1991). Although the small-scale deformations of the surface are clearly apparent in the SfPR result (cf. Fig. 6.19c) and to a lesser extent also in the shape from shading result (cf. Fig. 6.19d), large-scale deviations from the essentially flat true surface shape are apparent.

6.3.3.2   Results Obtained with the SfPRD Technique

The convergent stereo setup employed by d'Angelo and Wöhler (2006, 2008) was calibrated with the automatic camera calibration system described by Krüger et al. (2004). After acquisition of the images, they were rectified to standard epipolar geometry. Effectively, this results in typical disparity values of around 4000 pixels at the object distance in the rectified stereo image pairs. Experiments with synthetic

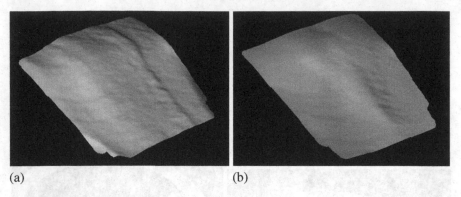

(a)   (b)

Fig. 6.20 Reconstructed surface profile of the connection rod. (**a**) SfPRD and (**b**) shape from shading approach using stereo information, albedo estimated during the iteration process based on all image pixels according to (5.24)

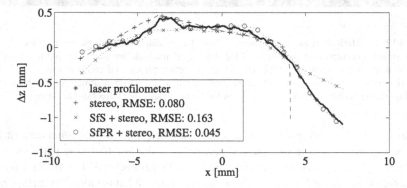

Fig. 6.21 Cross sections of the raw forged iron surface, compared to ground truth (RMSE in mm). SfPRD and shape from shading approach using stereo information, albedo estimated during the iteration process based on all image pixels according to (5.24)

data have shown that the standard deviation of the disparity amounts to 0.3 pixel, resulting in a standard deviation of 30 μm of the resulting depth points. One of the stereo cameras is equipped with a rotating linear polarisation filter and is used to acquire the images required for SfPR according to Sect. 5.3.1. Due to the highly specular reflectance of the metallic surfaces, usually only a sparse set of depth points can be reliably extracted using the blockmatching stereo algorithm.

For the raw forged iron surface of the connection rod, Fig. 6.16a shows the intensity and polarisation angle image and Fig. 6.16b the triangulated stereo reconstruction result (d'Angelo and Wöhler, 2006). The surface albedo was estimated based on (5.24) during each step of the iteration process. We found that the RMSE between the corresponding cross section extracted from our reconstructed three-dimensional profile and the ground truth amounts to 45 μm (Figs. 6.20a and 6.21). If the shape from shading approach is used such that polarisation information is not taken into account, the RMSE is 163 μm (cf. Fig. 6.20b). The RMSE of the combined shape

Table 6.4 Three-dimensional reconstruction results for the raw forged iron surface of the connection rod, obtained based on comparison of the cross section shown in Fig. 6.16a. Albedo determination marked as 'initial' denotes that the albedo was estimated prior to the iteration process either based on specular reflections or based on depth from defocus data and was not changed afterwards, while 'adapted' denotes an estimation of the albedo during the iteration process

Utilised information	Albedo determination	Figure	z RMSE (µm)
SfS	Equation (5.23), initial	6.17	281
SfPR	Equation (5.23), initial	6.17	56
SfS, DfD	Equation (5.24), initial	6.18	1153
SfPR, DfD	Equation (5.24), initial	6.18	55
Stereo	–	6.21	80
SfS, stereo	Equation (5.24), adapted	6.21	50 (163)
SfPR, stereo	Equation (5.24), adapted	6.21	45

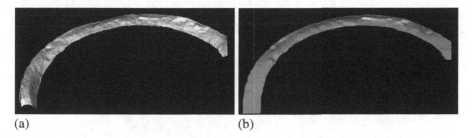

(a)   (b)

Fig. 6.22 Reconstructed surface profile of the flange. (**a**) SfPRD and (**b**) shape from shading approach using stereo information, albedo estimated during the iteration process based on all image pixels according to (5.24)

from shading and stereo approach is larger than that of the stereo reconstruction alone, corresponding to 80 µm, since no stereo data are available for the rightmost 3.2 mm of the cross section. Neglecting this margin yields a much smaller RMSE of 50 µm. For the examined strongly specular surface, Figs. 6.20a and 6.20b illustrate that, in contrast to the shape from shading approach, the SfPR method reveals a large amount of small scale surface detail. The results of the comparison to ground truth data are summarised in Table 6.4.

Figure 6.22 shows the three-dimensional reconstruction of the flange surface calculated using one intensity and one polarisation angle image along with stereo depth information. The triangulated set of stereo depth points is shown in Fig. 6.19b. As in the previous example, the surface albedo was estimated during the iteration process according to (5.24). In contrast to the first experiment, it was not possible in the second experiment to determine accurate ground truth values for a cross section through the surface because the laser profilometer is not suitable for acquiring measurements of such a large and curved surface section. Instead, we regarded the depths of the three dents indicated in Fig. 6.19a, for which ground truth values were obtained by tactile measurement and compared to the reconstructed depth differ-

Fig. 6.23 Stereo image pairs of the star pattern (*left*) and the ring-shaped flange (*right*). These examples illustrate that, due to the specular reflectance behaviour of the surface, corresponding surface parts do not necessarily have a similar appearance in the images

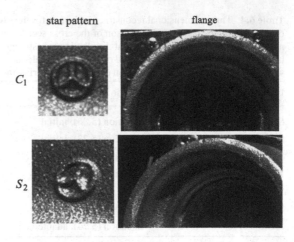

star pattern   flange

C_1

S_2

ences. Due to the small size of the surface defects, the accuracy of the tactile depth measurement only amounts to 0.05 mm. The true depth of the dent 1 is 1.2 mm, the reconstructed depth 1.3 mm. Dents 2 and 3 each have a true depth of 0.25 mm, while the corresponding depth on the reconstructed surface profile amounts to 0.30 mm and 0.26 mm, respectively. On large scales, our three-dimensional reconstruction correctly displays a flat surface. These comparisons indicate a good correspondence between the true surface and our reconstruction results.

6.3.4 Inspection Based on Specular Stereo

In this section the specular stereo method of Wöhler and d'Angelo (2009) described in Sect. 5.4 is applied to the three-dimensional reconstruction of rough metallic surfaces displaying a weak diffuse reflection component along with considerable specular lobes and spikes. The same experimental setup as in Sect. 6.3.3.2 is used. The surface of the connection rod, a cast iron surface displaying a star pattern, and the ring-shaped surface part of the flange are examined. The first and third examples have also been regarded in Sect. 6.3.3.2. The presentation in this section is adopted from Wöhler and d'Angelo (2009).

6.3.4.1 Qualitative Discussion of the Three-Dimensional Reconstruction Results

Figure 5.20 displays a stereo image pair of the connection rod, while in Fig. 6.23 the stereo image pairs of the star pattern and the ring-shaped flange examples are shown. The appearance of the surface of the star pattern differs so strongly between

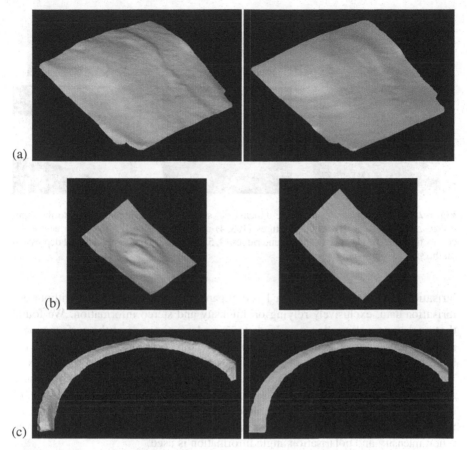

Fig. 6.24 Three-dimensional reconstruction results for (**a**) the connection rod, (**b**) the star pattern, and (**c**) the ring-shaped flange. The *images in the left column* display the results obtained based on intensity and polarisation angle as photometric information, while for the *images in the right column* the polarisation information was neglected

the two images that initially only one single stereo point can be determined.[1] In the flange example, the brightness distribution across the surface is also fairly different for the stereo images, but the appearance of the surface is sufficiently similar to obtain initial three-dimensional points for about 10 % of the image pixels situated on the ring section.

Figure 6.24 shows the final three-dimensional reconstruction results for the three regarded examples. In each case, the three-dimensional profile obtained using po-

---

[1]In all experiments, the same blockmatching threshold was used. Slightly decreasing this threshold for the star pattern example would have resulted in more than one initial three-dimensional point. However, this somewhat extreme configuration was used intentionally in order to illustrate that this information is sufficient to obtain convergence of the specular stereo scheme.

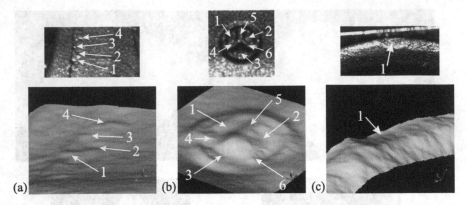

Fig. 6.25 Close-up views of the three-dimensional surface profiles in comparison to the input images. (**a**) Small positive relief structures $(1, 3, 4)$ and a depression (2) on the surface of the connection rod. (**b**) Low parts $(1, 2, 3)$ and ridges $(4, 5, 6)$ of the star pattern. (**c**) Small depression on the surface of the ring-shaped flange

larisation angle data from camera 1 is compared to the result obtained without po-larisation data, exclusively relying on intensity and stereo information. We found that neglecting polarisation data leads to an under-estimation of the surface slopes in the direction perpendicular to the illumination direction, such that details like the bending in the leftmost part of the flange surface in Fig. 6.24c tend to disappear. This effect is due to the illumination by a single light source (Horn, 1989). These results illustrate that the pixel grey value $I(u, v)$ and the polarisation angle $\Phi(u, v)$ contain complementary information about the surface gradients $p(u, v)$ and $q(u, v)$, which is the main reason why a better three-dimensional reconstruction is achieved when intensity and polarisation angle information is used.

Figure 6.25 shows close-up views of the three-dimensional surface profiles in comparison to the input images, clearly indicating that mesoscopic and macroscopic structures which appear as dark and bright spots in the input images can be recon-structed. Figure 6.25a displays several small positive relief structures $(1, 3, 4)$ and a depression (2) on the surface of the connection rod. In Fig. 6.25b the low parts of the star pattern are indicated by 1, 2, and 3 and the ridges by 4, 5, and 6. Fig-ure 6.25c illustrates how the specular stereo method recovers a shallow depression on the surface of the ring-shaped flange (cf. also Sect. 6.3.4.2).

6.3.4.2 Comparison to Ground Truth Data

For the connection rod example a highly accurate reference profile was measured with a laser profilometer for a cross section of the surface, as indicated in Fig. 6.26. The root-mean-square deviation between the result of the specular stereo method and the ground truth amounts to 55 µm, which is somewhat smaller than the average lateral extension of the image pixels of 86 µm.

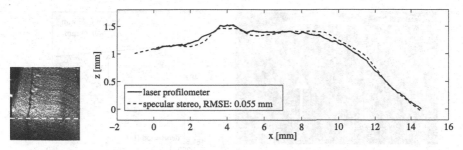

Fig. 6.26 Comparison of a cross section through the three-dimensional surface profile obtained by specular stereo, relying on intensity and polarisation angle data, and the ground truth determined with a laser profilometer (connection rod example)

Fig. 6.27 Comparison of height differences on the surface obtained by specular stereo and the corresponding ground truth values determined based on tactile measurement (star pattern example)

For the star pattern example it was not possible to obtain ground truth values with the laser profilometer, as the depth differences across the profile are too large and the surface slopes are too steep. Hence, we determined height differences at two representative locations on the surface by tactile measurement (cf. Fig. 6.27). At both locations, the correspondence between the specular stereo reconstruction and the ground truth is better than 0.1 mm. For the ring-shaped flange example, a similar technique was used to examine the surface reconstruction accuracy.

For the shallow depression marked in the lower right point cloud in Fig. 6.28, a depth of 0.23 mm was obtained by specular stereo, which is in good agreement with the ground truth value of 0.25 mm obtained by tactile measurement. The same depth value was inferred from the dense surface profile shown in Fig. 6.24 obtained based on the stereo point cloud and the available photometric and polarimetric data.

6.3.4.3 Self-consistency Measures for Three-Dimensional Reconstruction Accuracy

The specular stereo algorithm of Wöhler and d'Angelo (2009) yields several self-consistency measures which provide an impression of how accurately the surface

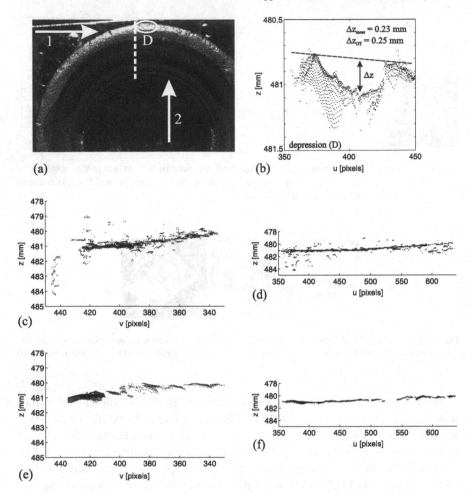

Fig. 6.28 Three-dimensional point clouds generated by the initial blockmatching stereo and by the specular stereo algorithm (flange example). For clarity, in all diagrams only the part of the point cloud right of the *dashed line* marked in (**a**) is shown. (**a**) Viewing directions into the point cloud. A shallow depression in the surface is marked by '*D*'. (**b**) Enlarged part of the three-dimensional point cloud generated by specular stereo as seen from direction 2, showing a side view of the shallow depression. (**c**) View from direction 1 and (**d**) from direction 2 into the initial three-dimensional point cloud. (**e**) View from direction 1 and (**f**) from direction 2 into the three-dimensional point cloud generated by the specular stereo algorithm

is reconstructed. These quantities describe how consistent the geometric and the photopolarimetric data are with each other, given the result of the specular stereo algorithm.

An intuitive measure for reconstruction accuracy is the appearance of the three-dimensional point cloud obtained by stereo analysis. In Fig. 6.28 two views into the three-dimensional point cloud of the ring-shaped flange are shown for the initial blockmatching stage and for the final result of the specular stereo method. The initial blockmatching stage yields a large number of three-dimensional points (cf. centre row in Fig. 6.28) which appear to form a plane surface. The depth values are fairly noisy, and some outliers are apparent which deviate from the plane by several millimetres. This behaviour presumably results from points on the surface appearing more or less strongly dissimilar in the stereo images. The point cloud obtained by specular stereo (bottom row) is significantly less noisy, and the bent cross section of the ring-shaped surface is clearly apparent. The shallow depression in the surface is also visible (it has already been shown above that its reconstructed depth is in good correspondence with tactile measurement).

For the connection rod and the star pattern, the initially very small fraction of image pixels for which a stereo correspondence can be established increases by several orders of magnitude in the course of the iteration process (cf. left row of Fig. 6.29, top). For the ring-shaped flange, the number of (initially very noisy) three-dimensional points decreases by about a factor of 2, but the accuracy of the measured depth values significantly increases. At the end of the iteration process, the average disparity correction is smaller than 0.7 pixel for all three examples (cf. Fig. 6.29, left row, middle). A nonzero average value of Δd corresponds to a uniform offset of the surface profile in the z direction. Another important self-consistency measure is the standard deviation $\sigma_{\Delta d}$ of the disparity correction, which directly quantifies how closely the rendered images derived from the reconstructed surface match the observed stereo images (cf. Fig. 6.29, left row, bottom). Initially, $\sigma_{\Delta d}$ is larger than 8 pixels for the connection rod, while it amounts to about 3 pixels for the star pattern and the flange. These fairly large values indicate large-scale discrepancies between the initial three-dimensional reconstruction and the stereo images. The specular stereo algorithm yields values for $\sigma_{\Delta d}$ of about 1 pixel for the connection rod and the flange and 0.4 pixel for the star pattern (for our stereo configuration, a disparity difference of 1 pixel corresponds to a depth difference of 0.135 mm in the regarded range of depth values). If the polarisation information is neglected, the self-consistency measures still show a similar behaviour (cf. right column in Fig. 6.29).

As a whole, the average values and the standard deviations of the disparity correction inferred for the three examples provide self-consistency measures for the accuracy of the three-dimensional reconstruction result of the specular stereo algorithm that indicate residual errors which are comparable to the deviations between the three-dimensional reconstruction result and independently measured ground truth data.

6.3.4.4 Consequences of Poorly Known Reflectance Parameters

The specular stereo algorithm of Wöhler and d'Angelo (2009) requires knowledge about the parameters of the photometric and polarimetric reflectance functions. This section discusses the behaviour of the specular stereo algorithm for poorly known reflectance parameters, regarding the connection rod example. For the reflectance function according to (3.14) we determined the parameters $\sigma_1 = 3.85$ and $m_1 = 2.61$

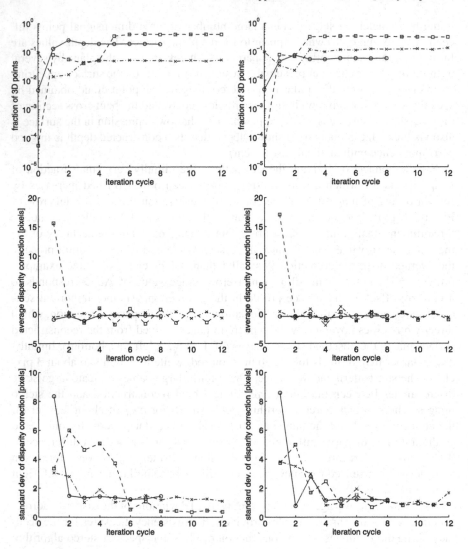

Fig. 6.29 Fraction of three-dimensional points relative to the number of pixels (*top row*), average disparity correction (*centre row*), and standard deviation of the disparity correction (*bottom row*) during the iteration process for the connection rod example (*solid curve, circles*), the star pattern example (*dashed curve, squares*), and the flange example (*dashed-dotted curve, crosses*). *Left column*: Results obtained based on intensity and polarisation angle information. *Right column*: Results obtained based on intensity information alone

for the specular lobe and $\sigma_2 = 9.61$ and $m_2 = 15.8$ for the specular spike based on a reference measurement. In the first experiment we omitted the specular spike by setting $\sigma_2 = 0$, which results in the three-dimensional profile shown in Fig. 6.30a. If we additionally decrease the intensity and increase the width of the specular lobe by setting σ_1 and m_1 to 0.5 times their true values, respectively, we obtain the three-

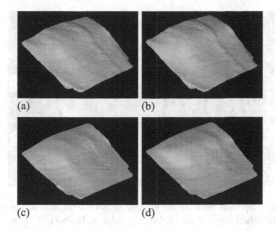

Fig. 6.30 Three-dimensional reconstruction result for poorly known reflectance parameters (connection rod example, cf. also Fig. 6.24). (**a**) Reflectance function with $\sigma_2 = 0$ (i.e. specular spike omitted) and correct parameters for the specular lobe. Polarisation angle data are used. (**b**) Reflectance function with $\sigma_2 = 0$ and σ_1 and m_1 decreased by a factor of 0.5, respectively. Polarisation angle data are used. (**c**), (**d**) Same reflectance parameters as in (**a**) and (**b**), but without taking into account polarisation angle data

dimensional profile shown in Fig. 6.30b. If furthermore the polarisation information is neglected, the three-dimensional profiles shown in Figs. 6.30c–d are obtained.

Compared to the reconstruction results shown in Fig. 6.24 obtained with the correct reflectance parameters, the three-dimensional profiles shown in Fig. 6.30 are tilted towards the light source. Hence, the SfPRD algorithm attempts to generate the large pixel brightness values observed in the images for specular reflections by decreasing the incidence angle between the normals of the corresponding surface parts and the direction of incident light. However, we observe a graceful degradation of the three-dimensional reconstruction result, even when the assumed reflectance parameters strongly deviate from their true values.

6.3.5 Inspection Based on Integration of Photometric Image Information and Active Range Scanning Data

Sections 6.3.3 and 6.3.4 describe a methodical framework for three-dimensional surface reconstruction which requires that the illumination conditions as well as the material-specific reflectance properties are known. Alternatively, a three-dimensional surface reconstruction can be obtained by the triangulation-based evaluation of fringe or coded patterns projected on the surface, as described in detail e.g. in the surveys by Batlle et al. (1998) and Beraldin (2004). However, it is well known that the three-dimensional surface reconstruction results provided by such active range scanning systems are usually fairly noisy and tend to display gaps for which no depth data are available when strongly specular surfaces are regarded. This

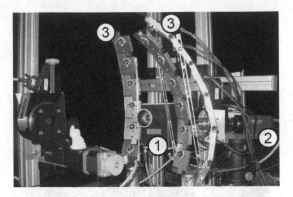

Fig. 6.31 Hardware setup employed for the three-dimensional reconstruction of an embossing on the surface of the dumbbell-shaped object. Image credit: S. Herbort. A light pattern is projected on the surface by the projector (*1*), and the fringe patterns are observed by the camera (*2*), which also acquires images of the surface illuminated from a variety of directions using the LED light sources (*3*)

behaviour is due to the strong intensity variations across the images of the projected pattern. Saturation occurs where the projected light is reflected specularly into the camera, while the pattern is invisible when the diffuse reflectance component is faint and most of the projected light is reflected past the camera. Hence, it is beneficial in such application scenarios to combine depth data obtained by active range scanning devices with image data according to the extended photometric stereo method proposed by Herbort et al. (2011) described in Sect. 5.5.

The part regarded in this section is a dumbbell-shaped object consisting of dark, rough cast iron. A three-dimensional reconstruction of an embossing on its surface is performed based on the method of Herbort et al. (2011) using the reflectance function (3.14). The hardware setup is illustrated in Fig. 6.31. As the same camera is used for the evaluation of the projected light patterns and the acquisition of the images for photometric stereo analysis, the actively scanned depth data and the images are pixel-synchronous. The reconstructed surface part is indicated in Fig. 6.32a. A set of twelve pixel-synchronous images were acquired under different illumination conditions, four of which are shown in Fig. 6.32b. The lateral resolution of the images corresponds to 42 μm per pixel. The very noisy depth data determined based on projection of structured light are shown in Fig. 6.32c.

A resolution pyramid with n_{pyr} pyramid levels is applied, which starts at a resolution of $1/2^{n_{pyr}}$ of the original image resolution. The three-dimensional reconstruction result on one level is used as an initialisation for the next level of double resolution until the full image resolution is reached. As described in detail by Herbort and Wöhler (2012), the reflectance parameters of the surface according to (3.14) are estimated on each resolution level based on the corresponding three-dimensional surface reconstruction result, where for the lowest resolution level the active range scanning data downsampled by a factor of $1/2^{n_{pyr}}$ are used. The estimated reflectance parameters are used to obtain the three-dimensional surface reconstruction on the next level, resulting in a self-consistent optimisation scheme.

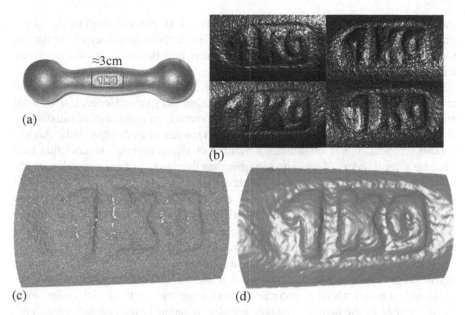

Fig. 6.32 Three-dimensional reconstruction results of an embossing on a dark, rough cast iron surface. Image credit: S. Herbort. (**a**) Dumbbell-shaped object. The reconstructed surface part is marked. (**b**) Four images from the set of twelve images acquired under different illumination conditions. (**c**) Shaded view of the depth data determined based on projection of structured light. The *white areas* denote gaps in the data. (**d**) Shaded view of the three-dimensional reconstruction result obtained with the combined method described in Sect. 5.5

The three-dimensional reconstruction result obtained with the combined method has a high lateral resolution and reveals both the shape of the surface on large spatial scales and most small-scale surface details visible in the acquired images (cf. Fig. 6.32d). The height of the embossing has been determined to 0.67 ± 0.02 mm by tactile measurement with a caliper gauge. The combined three-dimensional reconstruction method yields a consistent height value of 0.69 mm.

6.3.6 Discussion

It has been shown in Sect. 6.3.1 that the image-based approach suggested by Wöhler and Hafezi (2005) can be used for three-dimensional surface reconstruction in the context of industrial quality inspection. The shadow information provides depth information on large spatial scales, while fine surface details are revealed by the shading information.

The combined framework for three-dimensional surface reconstruction based on photopolarimetric information and independently measured depth data proposed by d'Angelo and Wöhler (2008) can be favourably used in the application scenario of industrial quality inspection (cf. Sect. 6.3.3). The accuracy of depth differences on the surface measured with the SfPRD method is about twice as high as the lateral pixel resolution of the utilised images. To obtain depth from defocus information, the acquisition of two images at different apertures may be automated using a motor iris lens.

Large-scale deviations of the estimated three-dimensional surface shape from the true shape may occur if the available depth data are too sparse. Hence, if traditional stereo analysis techniques do not yield three-dimensional point data of satisfactory accuracy or density, the specular stereo method suggested by Wöhler and d'Angelo (2009) (cf. Sect. 6.3.4) establishes a number of stereo correspondences that may become several orders of magnitude higher than the number of correspondences obtained by classical blockmatching. The three-dimensional point cloud obtained with the specular stereo method is less noisy, contains a negligible number of outliers, and shows significantly more surface detail than the point cloud obtained by classical blockmatching. For poorly known reflectance parameters, a graceful degradation of the accuracy of the three-dimensional reconstruction result is observed.

The approach proposed by Herbort et al. (2011) (cf. Sect. 6.3.5), which combines active range scanning data with photometric stereo, yields a three-dimensional reconstruction result which is accurate on both large and small spatial scales. Most details visible in the acquired images are also apparent in the reconstructed depth map, while the strong noise in the active range scanning data is removed and the gaps are filled. The accuracy of the three-dimensional surface reconstruction result is about twice as high as the lateral pixel resolution of the images.

Chapter 7
Applications to Safe Human–Robot Interaction

This chapter addresses the scenario of safe human–robot interaction in the industrial production environment. For example, in car manufacturing, industrial production processes are characterised by either fully automatic production sequences carried out solely by industrial robots or fully manual assembly steps where only humans work together on the same task. Close collaboration between humans and industrial robots is very limited and usually not possible due to safety concerns. Industrial production processes may increase their efficiency by establishing a close collaboration of humans and machines exploiting their unique capabilities, which requires sophisticated techniques for human–robot interaction. In this context, the recognition of interactions between humans and industrial robots requires vision methods for three-dimensional pose estimation and tracking of the motion of human body parts based on three-dimensional scene analysis.

Section 7.1 gives an overview of vision-based safe human–robot interaction and illustrates the importance of gesture recognition in the general context of human–robot interaction. In Sect. 7.2 the performance of the three-dimensional approach of Schmidt et al. (2007) in the detection and tracking of objects in point clouds (cf. Sect. 2.3) in a typical industrial production environment is evaluated. In Sects. 7.3–7.5, the methods of Barrois and Wöhler (2008) and Hahn et al. (2010a, 2010b) for the three-dimensional detection, pose estimation, and tracking of human body parts (cf. Sect. 2.2.1.2) as well as the approach suggested by Hahn et al. (2009, 2010b) for recognising the performed actions are evaluated in similar scenarios.

7.1 Vision-Based Human–Robot Interaction

Vision-based systems for detecting the presence of humans in the workspace of an industrial robot and safeguarding the cooperation between a human and an industrial robot are described in Sect. 7.1.1. These systems take into account the approximate shape of the human but do not determine the motion behaviour of human body parts. Section 7.1.2 provides an overview of methods for the recognition of ges-

C. Wöhler, *3D Computer Vision*, X.media.publishing,
DOI 10.1007/978-1-4471-4150-1_7, © Springer-Verlag London 2013

tures performed by humans in the application context of human–robot interaction, concentrating on pointing gestures and the interaction with objects.

7.1.1 Vision-Based Safe Human–Robot Interaction

In the safety system described by Vischer (1992) in the context of a robotic system for object manipulation, the expected position of an industrial robot is verified, and persons in the neighbourhood of the robot are localised in a camera image. A background image is subtracted from the current image of the workspace, where a method which behaves robustly with respect to changing illumination is applied.

A robotic system for grasping objects is described by Schweitzer (1993), which partially builds upon the work by Vischer (1992). Schweitzer (1993) points out that this system is equipped with two safety systems developed by Baerveldt (1992), where one safety system consists of accelerometers which detect exceedingly fast robot movements, while the other system is based on a camera, comparing the expected robot position to the position inferred from the image and estimating the position of a human in the neighbourhood of the robot. According to Schweitzer (1993), the robot may be stopped if necessary, or an alternate path can be defined in order to avoid endangerment of the human.

Ebert and Henrich (2003) describe the SIMERO system for safe human–robot interaction, which provides an integrated image-based framework for safeguarding the collaboration between a human and an industrial robot. A background subtraction is performed for the acquired images of the workspace based on a reference image, resulting in a silhouette of the human. A robot modelling stage yields a silhouette of the robot relying on its joint angles. The extracted silhouettes of the human and the robot are used to predict collisions without extracting the three-dimensional structure of the scene. Subsequently, the path of the robot is planned.

Gecks and Henrich (2005) regard the problem of 'pick-and-place operations' during which objects are manipulated, leading to changes in the background or reference image used for object detection. Hence, an algorithm for adapting the reference image to changed object positions is introduced. Based on the object detection results, a robot path is determined that does not lead to collisions. The system relies on several cameras, but does not perform an actual three-dimensional reconstruction of the workspace.

The safety system of Kuhn et al. (2006) concentrates on movements of a robot guided by a person, where several camera images are combined with data of a force/torque sensor attached to the robot. Object detection is performed based on background subtraction of each image, and the three-dimensional positions of the objects are estimated. A collision-free robot path is determined, where the maximum permissible robot speed depends on the relative positions of the robot and the objects.

Henrich et al. (2008) propose a safety system which relies on several calibrated cameras used to obtain a three-dimensional reconstruction of the workspace.

Change detection methods are used to detect objects in the images. The background is modelled based on a clustering approach. The velocity of the robot is adapted according to its distance to a person in the workspace, and the path of the robot can be updated continuously, where guided robot movements are also taken into account. In addition to cameras, time-of-flight-based active range scanning sensors are examined.

A similar approach for the three-dimensional detection of obstacles in the workspace around an industrial robot is proposed by Henrich and Gecks (2008). A difference image technique is the basis for a distinction between pixels belonging to the static scene without unknown objects and pixels indicating the approximate shape of unknown objects, where the classification is performed by a Bayes classifier. The result is used by Henrich and Gecks (2008) to construct an image of the current robot configuration and an image denoting the obstacle. Taking into account future configurations of the robot, the system then performs a test to determine if the robot may interfere with the obstacle. Regions possibly occluded by the robot are marked as potentially belonging to an obstacle, which allows a refined collision detection and a refined update of the reference image. The described system is also able to determine a robot path which avoids collisions with obstacles in the scene but nevertheless permits close encounters.

The image-based approach to the detection of obstacles in the neighbourhood of an industrial robot is extended by Fischer and Henrich (2009) to a system consisting of several colour cameras and range sensors observing the workspace, where the data are processed in a distributed manner in on-board units associated with the individual sensors. This system describes an object by its convex hull but does not reconstruct parts of the human body.

For a safety system capable of monitoring an extended workspace around an industrial robot or a machine and precisely predicting possible collisions with a human, a three-dimensional reconstruction of the scene is highly beneficial. As a consequence, the camera-based SafetyEYE system has been created in cooperation between the Mercedes-Benz production facilities in Sindelfingen, Daimler Group Research and Advanced Engineering in Ulm, and the company Pilz GmbH & Co. KG, a manufacturer of safe automation systems (cf. Winkler 2006, who provides a detailed introduction to the SafetyEYE system, the cooperation in which it has been developed and commercialised, application-oriented engineering aspects concerning the integration of the system into automobile production facilities, and future extensions). The stereo vision and camera calibration algorithms for the SafetyEYE system have been developed in a research project led by Dr. Lars Krüger and the author. The SafetyEYE system consists of a calibrated trinocular camera sensor, which monitors the protection area around the machine (cf. Fig. 7.1), and two industrial PCs. Two different algorithms for stereo image analysis determine a three-dimensional point cloud describing the structure of the scene being monitored. As soon as a certain number of three-dimensional points is detected inside the protection area, the system initiates the protective measures necessary to prevent an accident, either by slowing down or by stopping the machine. The system is installed by defining the three-dimensional virtual protection areas with a configuration software. Setting up a traditional safety system consisting of several components such

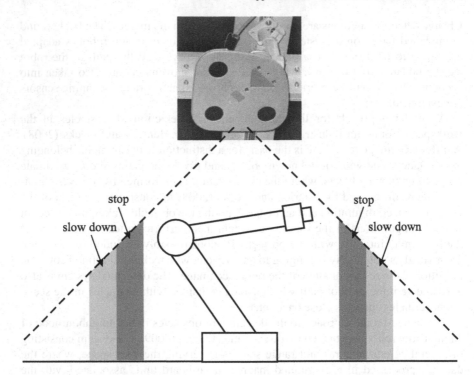

Fig. 7.1 The SafetyEYE system. The trinocular camera sensor (*top*) observes the scene. Once a person or an object enters the virtual protection areas, the robot slows down (*light grey areas*) or stops (*dark grey areas*)

as metal fences, light barriers, and laser scanners often takes as long as one day, while the three-dimensional protection areas of the SafetyEYE system are usually configured within a few hours. A typical industrial scene is shown in Fig. 7.2. The system is designed to comply with safety requirements according to the regulations EN 954-1 and SIL 2 EN 62061.

In its first version, the SafetyEYE system aims at preventing hazardous interferences between humans and robots. Hence, although it is more flexible than typical modern safety systems usually consisting of different components, its behaviour is still similar to traditional systems in that its main task is to strictly separate the human from the machine, slowing down and eventually stopping the machine if a human enters the protection area. The capabilities of future systems might be extended beyond the generation of a three-dimensional point cloud to a distinction between persons and objects. This would be a step towards collaborative working environments in which persons and machines are able to work simultaneously on the same workpiece.

For such complex scenarios, it is necessary to perform a segmentation of the three-dimensional point cloud and a detection of objects in it, as is achieved by the method introduced by Schmidt et al. (2007) outlined in Sect. 2.3 (cf. the evaluation

Fig. 7.2 Trajectories of tracked objects (*dark grey*) with annotated ground truth (*light grey*) for a typical industrial scene

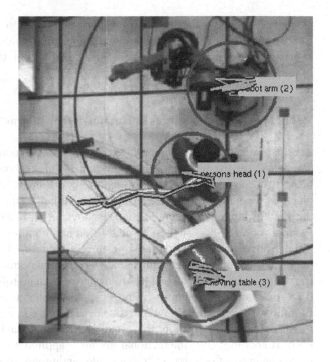

in Sect. 7.2 regarding the industrial production environment). Furthermore, to precisely predict possible collisions between the human and the robot while they are working close to each other, it is necessary to detect parts of the human body, especially the arms and hands of a person working next to the robot, and to determine their three-dimensional trajectories in order to predict collisions with the robot. Section 7.1.2 gives an overview of existing methods in the field of vision-based gesture recognition. These approaches are certainly useful for the purpose of human–robot interaction, but since many of them are based on two-dimensional image analysis and require an essentially uniform background, they are largely insufficient for safety systems. In contrast, the three-dimensional approaches introduced by Hahn et al. (2007, 2010a) and by Barrois and Wöhler (2008) outlined in Sects. 2.2.1.2 and 2.3 yield reasonably accurate results for the pose of the hand–forearm limb independent of the individual person, even in the presence of a fairly cluttered background (cf. Sects. 7.3 and 7.4).

7.1.2 Pose Estimation of Articulated Objects in the Context of Human–Robot Interaction

Gesture recognition is strongly related to the pose estimation of articulated objects. An overview of important methods in this field is given in Sect. 2.2.1.2. Three-dimensional pose estimation results obtained for the human body or parts of it are commonly used as a starting point for gesture recognition, which may in turn be an important element of human–robot interaction. Hence, this section provides a short overview of gesture recognition methods, including pointing gestures and interactions with objects.

7.1.2.1 The Role of Gestures in Human–Robot Interaction

A broad overview of the importance of gestures as a 'communication channel' or 'modality' for the interaction between humans and robots is given by Hofemann (2007). Accordingly, classical seminal works are those by Turk (2005), who emphasises the general high relevance of non-verbal modalities such as gestures in the field of human–robot interaction, Pavlovic et al. (1997), and Nehaniv (2005). Pavlovic et al. (1997) suggest a subdivision into communicative gestures and manipulative gestures. They define a gesture as the temporal behaviour of the time-dependent vector of model parameters over a certain period of time. Nehaniv (2005) introduces five classes of gestures relevant for human–robot interaction, including (i) ' "irrelevant"/manipulative gestures', such as unintentional arm movements while running; (ii) 'side effects of expressive behaviour', e.g. hand, arm, and face movements during a conversation; (iii) 'symbolic gestures' having a clear interpretation, such as nodding; (iv) 'interactional gestures' applied e.g. for beginning or terminating an interaction; and (v) 'referential/pointing gestures', also known as deictic gestures, such as pointing to an object in order to provide a reference while communicating.

It is shown in the following sections that the recognition of the movements and postures of humans, especially their hands and arms, in the context of manipulative gestures is also highly relevant in the context of systems that safeguard human–robot interaction in the industrial production environment. Hence, the algorithms required for such systems are closely related to those used for gesture recognition.

7.1.2.2 Recognition of Gestures

Black and Jepson (1998) model the movements of human body parts as 'temporal trajectories', i.e. the behaviour of a set of pose parameters. These trajectories are characteristic for specific gestures. For the adaptation of trajectory models to observed data, Black and Jepson (1998) use an extension of the CONDENSATION algorithm (Blake and Isard, 1998). The trajectories are represented by the time-dependent velocity in the horizontal and vertical directions. The trajectory-based approach of Black and Jepson (1998) has inspired many later works. As an example, joint angle trajectories inferred from the monocular, kernel particle filter-based body pose estimation system of Schmidt et al. (2006) are utilised by Hofemann (2007) for gesture recognition.

In contrast, in the classical work by Campbell et al. (1996), measurements of the motion of features belonging to the head and the hand are used to recognise Tai Chi gestures using hidden Markov models (HMMs), where the head and the hands are tracked with a stereo blob tracking algorithm. Similarly, Nickel et al. (2004) and Nickel and Stiefelhagen (2004) assign pointing gestures to different classes relying on an HMM approach. HMMs are also used by Li et al. (2006) to classify hand trajectories of manipulative gestures, where the object context is taken into account. A particle filter provides a framework to assign the observations to the HMM.

More recently, an HMM-based approach to the recognition of gestures represented as three-dimensional trajectories has been introduced by Richarz and Fink (2001). The person and the hands performing a gesture are detected in colour images based on the head–shoulder contour using histograms of oriented gradients as features and a multilayer perceptron as a classification stage. The mean-shift method is used for tracking the upper human body. For each image, a two-dimensional trajectory of the moving hand is extracted. As the images are not acquired synchronously, a temporal interpolation scheme is applied to infer a three-dimensional trajectory from the individual two-dimensional trajectories acquired from different viewpoints. Richarz and Fink (2001) observe that many gestures are performed in an 'action plane', into which they project the three-dimensional trajectories. For classification, Richarz and Fink (2001) extract various features from the projected trajectories, such as (among others) the trajectory normalised with respect to the height of the person, represented in Cartesian as well as in polar coordinates, the time-dependent velocity of the moving hand, and the curvature of the trajectory. Based on the inferred feature representations, an HMM is used to distinguish between nine classes of gestures. Furthermore, long trajectories which comprise sequences of different gestures are divided into segments corresponding to movements not representing a gesture and to individual gestures, respectively.

A broad overview of early and recent research works addressing the visual recognition of actions performed by the full human body, which is methodically closely related to the field of gesture recognition, is provided in the recent survey by Poppe (2010) (which, however, does not cover the recognition of gestures performed by parts of the human body).

7.1.2.3 Including Context Information: Pointing Gestures and Interactions with Objects

Gesture recognition algorithms are an important part of cognitive systems, which communicate or interact with their environment and users rather than merely acquiring information about their surroundings (Bauckhage et al., 2005; Wachsmuth et al., 2005). In this context, the accurate determination of the pointing gesture as well as interactions between humans and objects are essential issues.

To estimate the pointing direction, Nickel et al. (2004) propose to combine the direction of the line connecting the head and the hand and the direction in which the head is oriented to accurately and robustly infer the object at which the interacting user is pointing. The two-dimensional positions of the head and the hand in the image are extracted based on skin colour analysis. An HMM is used to assign pointing gestures to different classes.

In the mobile robotic system of Groß et al. (2006), a particle filter for tracking several objects simultaneously is used in combination with the Adaboost face detector (Viola and Jones, 2001). Cylinder models are adapted to depth data acquired with a laser scanner, while images are acquired with a fisheye camera and a standard camera. The distribution of positions of persons in the vicinity of the robot is modelled by a mixture of Gaussians, leading to a Bayesian framework which allows one to integrate all available sensor information in order to accept or reject object hypotheses. When a person is detected, the system attempts to recognise a deictic gesture and to infer the pointing direction from the available monocular image data. Using the position of the head as a reference, an image region containing the head and another region containing the arm are determined. The distance and the direction of the position to which the person is pointing are determined subsequently using multilayer perceptron classification and regression. The achieved accuracy of the distance typically corresponds to about 50–200 mm and the angular accuracy to approximately $10°$.

Fritsch et al. (2004) rely on the extraction of skin-coloured regions to determine spatial trajectories and recognise activities based on a particle filter approach. They include the integration of knowledge about the object with which an interaction is performed, which they term 'context information'. A gesture is assumed to occur in a 'situational context', given by the conditions to be fulfilled for it to be performed and by its impact on the environment, as well as in a 'spatial context', i.e. the spatial relations between the hand trajectories and the objects in the scene, e.g. denoting which object is being gripped. A 'context area' in the image is given by the part of the scene in which objects are expected to be manipulated. Fritsch et al. (2004) integrate the situational context by restricting the particles to those consistent with the requirements of the action, while the spatial context is considered by suppressing particles that disagree with the observed object information. Bauckhage et al. (2005) describe an integration of these concepts into a cognitive vision system for the recognition of actions, also addressing the issue of evaluation.

7.1.2.4 Discussion in the Context of Industrial Safety Systems

Based on the previously described methods, it is possible to recognise the meaning of observed gestures, and it has been shown that it is possible to incorporate contextual information such as relations between the hand and objects in the scene.

Many of the systems described above rely on a detection of the hand based on skin colour. An important drawback of these approaches is the fact that colour-based segmentation tends to be unstable in the presence of variable illumination, especially changing spectral characteristics of the incident light. Although adaptively modelling the colour distribution in the image may partially solve this problem, skin colour cues are not suitable for detecting humans in the industrial production environment, since in many domains of industrial production dedicated work clothes such as gloves are obligatory. An industrial safety system thus must be able to recognise the human body or parts of it based on shape cues alone. Furthermore, the recognition performance should not decrease in the presence of a cluttered background displaying arbitrary colours. It is thus favourable to abandon the assumption of a specific colour distribution separating relevant from background objects.

Many systems for estimating the three-dimensional pose of the human body or parts of it require a user-dependent configuration and calibration stage. An industrial safety system, however, must be able to detect and localise arbitrary humans without relying on any kind of a priori knowledge about them, as a large number of persons may have access to the workspace to be safeguarded by the system. As a consequence, we will see in the following sections that it is favourable to utilise person-independent models of the human body and its parts rather than attempting to adapt a highly accurate person-specific model to the observations.

In the systems described above, multiple hypothesis tracking is a fairly common technique, but most existing systems merely evaluate two-dimensional cues. In many cases this is sufficient for interpreting gestures for enabling an interaction between a human and a robotic system. However, for an industrial system for safeguarding large workspaces it is required to acquire accurate three-dimensional data of the scene of considerably high spatial resolution and assign them to specific parts of the human body in order to be able to reliably avoid collisions or other hazardous interferences between the human and the machine.

In the following sections of this chapter, the issue of user-independent three-dimensional detection and tracking of persons and human body parts not involving skin colour cues is addressed in the context of safe human–robot interaction in the industrial production environment.

7.2 Object Detection and Tracking in Three-Dimensional Point Clouds

This section describes the evaluation of the method for three-dimensional detection and tracking of persons in three-dimensional point clouds introduced by Schmidt et al. (2007) as described in Sect. 2.3 in an industrial production scenario, involving a workspace with a human worker, a robot, and a moving platform. The presentation in this section is adopted from Schmidt et al. (2007). Stereo image sequences recorded with a Digiclops CCD camera system with an image size of 640×480 pixels, a pixel size of 7.4 μm, and a focal length of 4 mm were used. The stereo baseline corresponds to 100 mm. The average distance to the scene amounts to 5.65 m.

A three-dimensional point cloud of the scene is generated by combining the correlation-based stereo technique of Franke and Joos (2000) and the spacetime stereo approach outlined in Sect. 1.5.2.5 as described in Sect. 2.3. We empirically found for the correlation matrix element Σ_z in (2.36) the value $\Sigma_z = 0.292$, regarding a set of three-dimensional points obtained with the spacetime stereo algorithm and belonging to a plane scene part, while $\Sigma_x = \Sigma_y = 1$ are equally scaled. The velocity scaling factor is set to $\rho = 380$ s, where the velocity is expressed in metres per second and the spatial coordinates in metres. The kernel widths for (2.37) are

Table 7.1 Tracking results compared to ground truth. RMSE values are in millimetres

Sequence	# images	Object	With velocity		Without velocity	
			RMSE	Tracked fraction (%)	RMSE	Tracked fraction (%)
Industrial 1	69	Person	265	100.0	383	84.8
		Table	603	100.0	218	69.7
		Robot	878	95.5	1118	98.5
Industrial 2	79	Person	427	100.0	318	94.8
		Table	435	100.0	275	100.0
		Robot	121	98.7	177	96.1
Industrial 3	24	Person	196	100.0	147	100.0
		Table	249	100.0	225	90.9
		Robot	171	100.0	293	100.0
Industrial 4	39	Person	247	75.7	352	89.2
		Table	270	100.0	245	97.3
		Robot	91	100.0	200	97.3
Industrial 5	24	Person	208	90.9	254	81.8
		Table	219	100.0	329	100.0
		Robot	86	77.3	331	100.0

chosen as $H_{r,\max} = 1.88$ m, $H_{r,\min} = 0.135$ m, $H_d = 0.113$ m, and $H_v = 0.188$ m for the industrial scenes. While the object sizes as well as the overall size of the scenes are far different, the kernel widths merely need to be scaled by an empirical uniform factor, such that the relative parameter values remain constant. The value of ρ depends on the typical velocities encountered in the scene. Hence, we set for the tabletop scene $H_{r,\max} = 4.14$ m, $H_{r,\min} = 0.297$ m, $H_d = 0.249$ m, $H_v = 0.414$ m, and $\rho = 3200$ s. For each sequence, ground truth was generated manually by marking the centre of the objects of interest in each frame, i.e. the head of the person, and transforming them into three-dimensional coordinates using the known geometry of the scene and the objects, e.g. the height of the person and the position of the ground plane. The trajectories of the tracked objects are compared to the ground truth based on the corresponding value of the root-mean-square error (RMSE) in world coordinates. Figure 7.2 shows a typical tracking result achieved by our system. The results in Table 7.1 illustrate that objects can be tracked in a stable manner at reasonable accuracy. Using epipolar velocity as an additional feature yields a more accurate localisation result for 10 of 16 detected objects, and detection is usually possible in a larger fraction of the frames. For four other objects the RMSE but also the detection rate are lower when the velocity information is neglected. The system is designed to segment the point cloud into clusters of differing velocity. As a consequence, the proposed system works best for objects with homogeneous velocity. For exam-

Fig. 7.3 Determination of
the ground truth

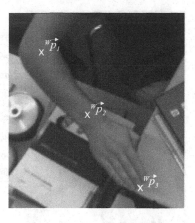

ple, we observed that for a walking person moving the arms backwards the object hypothesis does not include the arms due to their velocity.

The experimental evaluation shows that the proposed method is a promising technique for applications in the field of human–robot interaction in industrial production scenarios. It does not rely on colour cues, and the objects in the scene are detected and tracked based on a weak model (a cylinder) which does not require any a priori knowledge about the objects.

7.3 Detection and Spatio-Temporal Pose Estimation of Human Body Parts

In this section, which is adopted from Barrois and Wöhler (2008), their method for model-based object detection and spatio-temporal three-dimensional pose estimation (cf. Sect. 2.2.1.2) is evaluated by analysing three realistic image sequences displaying a hand–forearm limb moving at non-uniform speed in front of a complex cluttered background (cf. Figs. 2.17 and 7.4). The distance of the hand–forearm limb to the camera amounts to 0.85–1.75 m, the image resolution to 2–3 mm per pixel. For acquisition of stereo image pairs a Digiclops CCD camera system is used. The time step between subsequent image pairs amounts to $\Delta t = 50$ ms. Spacetime stereo information according to Sect. 1.5.2.5 is determined based on triples of subsequent stereo image pairs, where we have set $\delta_{max} = 2$. Ground truth information has been determined based on three markers attached to points located on the upper forearm ($^W\mathbf{p}_1$), the wrist ($^W\mathbf{p}_2$), and the front of the hand ($^W\mathbf{p}_3$) as depicted in Fig. 7.3. The three-dimensional coordinates of the markers were determined by bundle adjustment.

For each of the two parts of the hand–forearm model, the corresponding 5 translational and rotational pose parameters (denoted by the vector $\mathbf{T}$) are determined independently. For the evaluation, our method is employed as a 'tracking by detection' system; i.e. the pose $\mathbf{T}(t)$ and the pose derivative $\dot{\mathbf{T}}(t)$ are used to compute a

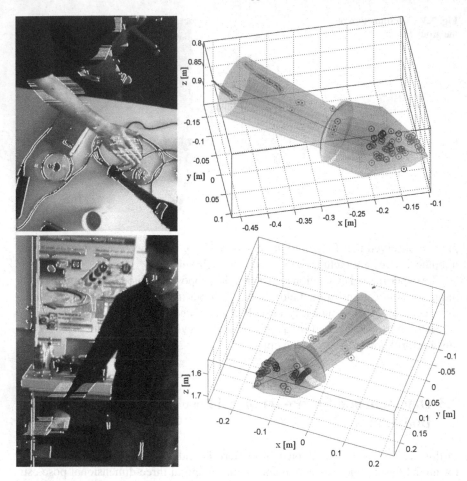

Fig. 7.4 Spacetime stereo and model adaptation results for example images from the second (*top*) and the third (*bottom*) test sequence. Three-dimensional points are indicated by *bright dots*, epipolar velocities by *white lines*

pose $\mathbf{T}_{\text{init}}(t + n\Delta t) = \mathbf{T}(t) + \dot{\mathbf{T}}(t) \cdot (n\Delta t)$ for the next time step $(t + n\Delta t)$ at which a model adaptation is performed. The pose $\mathbf{T}_{\text{init}}(t + n\Delta t)$ is used as an initialisation for the model adaption procedure. The temporal derivatives of the pose parameters are determined independently for each model part, where the translational motion is constrained such that the two model parts are connected with each other at the point $^{W}\mathbf{p}_{2}$. Ground truth values were obtained by manually marking the reference points on the hand–forearm limb according to Fig. 7.3.

For each sequence, the evaluation is performed for different values of n. The highest regarded value is $n = 16$, corresponding to an effective rate of only 1.25 frames per second. As a measure for the accuracy of the estimated pose, the mean Euclidean distances in the scene between the estimated and the ground truth positions are shown for $^{W}\mathbf{p}_{1}$ (circles), $^{W}\mathbf{p}_{2}$ (squares), and $^{W}\mathbf{p}_{3}$ (diamonds) column-

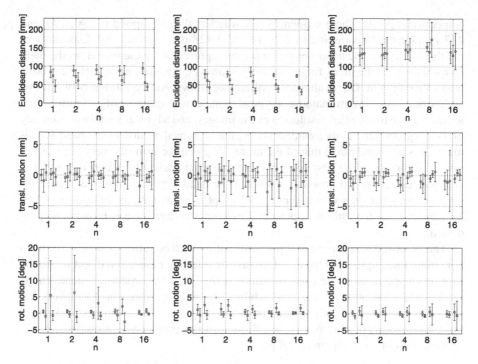

Fig. 7.5 Evaluation results, displayed column-wise for the three test sequences. 'Motion' refers to the pose variation between subsequent images

wise for the three test sequences in the first row of Fig. 7.5. The second row shows the mean errors and standard deviations of the translational motion components U_{obj} (circles), V_{obj} (squares), and W_{obj} (diamonds) per time step. For each value of n, the left triple of points denotes the forearm and the right triple the hand. The third row displays the mean errors and standard deviations of the rotational motion components ω_p (circles) and ω_o (squares). For each value of n, the left pair of points denotes the forearm and the right pair the hand.

The Euclidean distances between the estimated and true reference points typically amount to 40–80 mm and become as large as 150 mm in the third sequence, which displays a pointing gesture (cf. Fig. 7.4). Being independent of n, the values are comparable to those reported by Hahn et al. (2007, 2010a). The deviations measured for our system are comparable to the translational accuracy of about 70 mm achieved by the stereo-based upper body tracking system proposed by Ziegler et al. (2006). Furthermore, the average joint angle error of 25.7° determined in that work for the lower arm is equivalent to a translational error of about 100 mm, using our assumed forearm length of 220 mm, which is slightly higher than, but comparable to, the deviations obtained for our system.

The discrepancies observed for our system are to some extent caused by a shift of the model along the longitudinal object axis but also by the fact that the lengths of the partial models of the forearm and the hand are fixed to 220 and 180 mm, respectively. For the three sequences, the true lengths correspond to 190, 190, and 217 mm for the forearm and to 203, 193, and 128 mm for the hand. Especially in the third sequence the hand posture is poorly represented by the model, as the hand forms a fist with the index finger pointing. However, this does not affect the robustness of the system. Our evaluation furthermore shows that the motion between two subsequent images is estimated at a typical translational accuracy of 1–3 mm, which is comparable to the pixel resolution of the images, and a typical rotational accuracy of 1–3 degrees. Due to its roundish shape, the rotational motion of the hand is estimated less accurately than that of the more elongated forearm (the very large errors observed for ω_p in the first sequence are due to sporadically occurring outliers). A robust detection and pose estimation of the hand–forearm limb is achieved for time intervals between subsequent model adaptations as long as 800 ms ($n = 16$). The accuracy of the estimated pose and its temporal derivative is largely independent of n.

The proposed spatio-temporal pose estimation method relies on a new extended constraint line approach introduced to directly infer the translational and rotational motion components of the objects based on the low-level spacetime stereo information. Our evaluation of this approach in a 'tracking by detection' framework has demonstrated that a robust and accurate estimation of the three-dimensional object pose and its temporal derivative is achieved in the presence of a cluttered background without requiring an initial pose.

7.4 Three-Dimensional Tracking of Human Body Parts

In this section, the three-dimensional pose estimation and tracking system described in Sect. 2.2.3 are evaluated quantitatively and compared with the individual components based on a trinocular small-baseline data set. The mean-shift tracking method outlined in Sect. 2.3.2 is evaluated on the same image sequences. A description of the data set, an evaluation of different system configurations, and a discussion of the obtained experimental results are provided. The presentation is adopted from Hahn et al. (2010a) (cf. Sects. 7.4.1–7.4.6) and from Hahn et al. (2010b) (cf. Sect. 7.4.7). Further details are provided by Barrois (2010) and Hahn (2011).

7.4.1 Image Acquisition

To obtain reliable depth information of the investigated scene, a trinocular camera system (cf. Fig. 7.6) similar to the SafetyEYE protection system is used. From the perspective of the desired application of the camera system as a safety system in an industrial environment, it is required that no in situ calibration is performed but that the camera system is calibrated once immediately after it has been built. This

Fig. 7.6 Arrangement of the
trinocular camera system

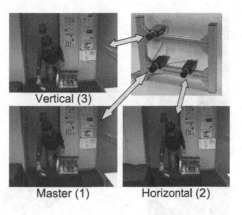

Vertical (3)

Master (1)   Horizontal (2)

requirement is due to the fact that a calibration in the industrial environment, e.g.
by a robot showing a calibration target to the cameras, would require a stop of the
production line, which is unacceptable in practise. Furthermore, an appropriately
constructed trinocular small-baseline system of three cameras mounted inside a single housing remains mechanically stable for a considerable period of time, i.e. several years. In contrast, multi-view systems built up of several disconnected cameras
regularly need an in situ recalibration due to mechanical or thermal stress, which is
unacceptable in an industrial environment. Furthermore, if the camera system needs
to be exchanged, installing a single-housing calibrated camera system of moderate
size is much easier and less expensive than setting up and calibrating a system of
many distributed cameras—for the latter, a stop of the production line would again
be necessary.

In the proposed system, the multiocular contracting curve density (MOCCD)-
based techniques (cf. Sect. 2.2.3) directly use the three synchronously acquired images, whereas the scene flow algorithm uses the images as two stereo pairs. The
two stereo pairs are perpendicularly arranged in order to circumvent the aperture
problem, such that we have a horizontal and a vertical stereo pair.

Since it is desired to obtain metric measurements from the images, the intrinsic
and extrinsic parameters of the camera system need to be known. Therefore the
cameras are calibrated (Krüger et al., 2004), and the image sequences are rectified
using the method of Fusiello et al. (2000) prior to applying the stereo algorithm. The
three-dimensional points determined by the scene flow algorithm of the horizontal
and the vertical stereo pair are both transformed back into the coordinate system
of the master camera (cf. Fig. 7.6). This yields three-dimensional points from all
three cameras in the same coordinate system as the one used by the MOCCD-based
techniques.

7.4.2 Data Set Used for Evaluation

The evaluation is based on nine test sequences which display five different test persons performing complex movements similar to motion patterns typically occurring

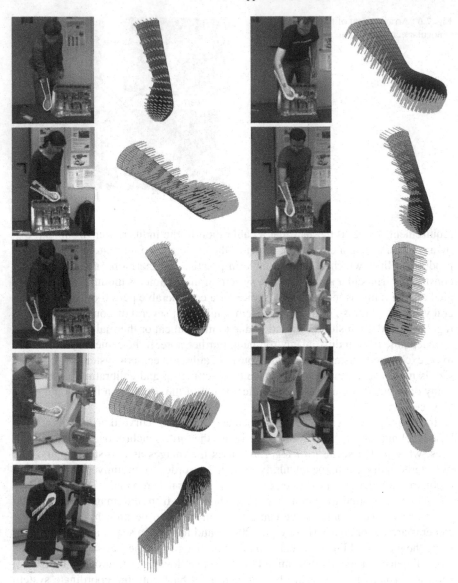

Fig. 7.7 Typical spatio-temporal three-dimensional pose estimation results for system configuration 5

in an industrial production environment. Sequences 1–5 display various persons working in an office environment, while sequences 6–9 show persons working in a typical industrial production environment. A sample image of each sequence along with the corresponding spatio-temporal pose estimation result is shown in Fig. 7.7. In order to illustrate that our system can also be used with object models other than the hand–forearm model described in Sect. 2.2.3.1, three-dimensional pose estima-

Fig. 7.8 Typical
three-dimensional pose
estimation results for the head
and shoulders part of a person
using system configuration 1

tion results for the head and shoulders part of a person obtained using a correspondingly adapted articulated object model are shown in Fig. 7.8.

In all sequences, the background is fairly cluttered, and the contrast between the
persons and the background tends to be low. The persons are wearing various kinds
of clothes with long and short sleeves, with and without work gloves. For each
system configuration, the parameter setting is the same for all sequences, respectively.

The image sequences were acquired with the trinocular colour camera system
shown in Fig. 7.6, where the horizontal and vertical baseline amounts to 150 mm.
The time interval between subsequent image triples amounts to $\Delta t = 71$ ms. Each
sequence consists of at least 300 image triples. The average distance of the test persons to the camera system varies from 2.7 m to 3.3 m. The ground truth data consist
of the coordinates of three reference points in the world coordinate system, which
correspond to the points ${}^W\mathbf{p}_1$, ${}^W\mathbf{p}_2$, and ${}^W\mathbf{p}_3$ of the three-dimensional model of
the hand–forearm limb. To extract the ground truth, three markers were attached
to the tracked limb. The positions of the markers in the images were measured
with the chequerboard corner localisation routine by Krüger and Wöhler (2011)
(cf. Sect. 1.4.8), and their three-dimensional coordinates were determined based on
bundle adjustment.[1]

7.4.3 Fusion of the ICP and MOCCD Poses

The structure of the fusion stage, which combines the ICP and the MOCCD results, is shown in Fig. 7.9. First, the initial pose parameters are used for both pose
estimation algorithms to start their respective optimisation. To verify and rate the
calculated pose parameters we use the quality measures described in Sect. 2.2.3.5.
These three criteria are calculated for the pose results of both algorithms separately.
Afterwards, the weighting values are summed to a weighting factor w_{ICP} for the ICP
result and another weighting factor w_{MOCCD} for the MOCCD result according to

$$w_{\text{ICP}} = \sigma_{p|\mathbf{T}_{\text{ICP}}} + \sigma_{o|\mathbf{T}_{\text{ICP}}} + \sigma_{c|\mathbf{T}_{\text{ICP}}} \tag{7.1}$$

$$w_{\text{MOCCD}} = \sigma_{p|\mathbf{T}_{\text{MOCCD}}} + \sigma_{o|\mathbf{T}_{\text{MOCCD}}} + \sigma_{c|\mathbf{T}_{\text{MOCCD}}}. \tag{7.2}$$

---

[1] The image sequences and ground truth data are accessible at http://aiweb.techfak.uni-bielefeld.de/
content/hand-forearm-limb-data-set.

Fig. 7.9 Overview of the fusion stage

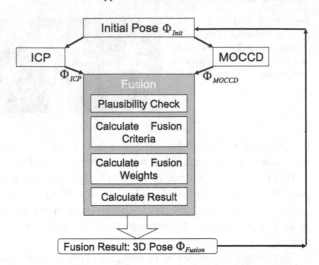

Fig. 7.10 Convergence behaviour of the ICP–MOCCD fusion stage. The *first column* illustrates the ICP results for each iteration and the *second column* the MOCCD results. In the *last column* the fusion result is shown for each iteration

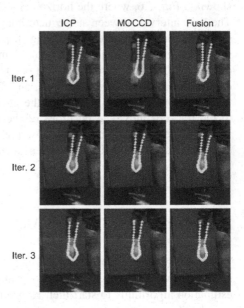

The two pose updates $\Delta\mathbf{T}_{\text{ICP}}$ and $\Delta\mathbf{T}_{\text{MOCCD}}$ of the pose estimation algorithms are then used together with the calculated weighting factor to compute the fusion pose parameter vector $\mathbf{T}_{\text{fusion}}$ according to

$$\mathbf{T}_{\text{fusion}} = \mathbf{T}_{\text{init}} + \frac{w_{\text{ICP}}}{w_{\text{ICP}} + w_{\text{MOCCD}}} \Delta\mathbf{T}_{\text{ICP}} + \frac{w_{\text{MOCCD}}}{w_{\text{ICP}} + w_{\text{MOCCD}}} \Delta\mathbf{T}_{\text{MOCCD}}. \quad (7.3)$$

This procedure is performed several times using the fusion result as a new initialisation for the next pose estimation stages, until the pose parameters converge (cf. Fig. 7.10).

7.4.4 System Configurations Regarded for Evaluation

Several system configurations are evaluated by Hahn et al. (2010a), including different combinations of three-dimensional pose estimation and tracking modules.

Configuration 1: Tracking Based on the MOCCD   The first system configuration is based on the MOCCD algorithm. To start tracking, a coarse initialisation of the model parameters at the first time step is required. We apply three instances of the MOCCD algorithm in a multi-hypothesis Kalman filter framework. Each MOCCD instance is associated with a Kalman filter, where each Kalman filter implements a different kinematic model assuming a different object motion. The idea behind this kinematic modelling is to provide a sufficient amount of flexibility for changing hand–forearm motion. It is required for correctly tracking reversing motion, e.g. that which occurs during tightening of a screw. A winner-takes-all component selects the best-fitting model at each time step using the following criteria: (i) the confirmation measurement, (ii) the quality of the prediction, and (iii) the difference of the probability distributions of the pixel grey values along the model curve. The confirmation measurement is introduced by Hanek (2004) and is an indicator of the convergence of the optimisation. The second criterion describes the similarity of the prediction and the pose measurement. With the third criterion it is ensured that the MOCCD algorithm separates probability distributions along the projected curve. A hypothesis that is better than any other in at least two criteria is deemed the winner. It is important to note that the Kalman filter is only used for initialisation purposes, while the evaluation refers to the actual MOCCD measurements.

Configuration 2: Tracking Based on the Shape Flow Method   The second configuration is based on the shape flow (SF) method. Similar to configuration 1, tracking starts with a user-defined parameter vector $\mathbf{T}(t = 1)$. A hierarchical approach is used to determine the three-dimensional pose $\mathbf{T}$ and its temporal derivative $\dot{\mathbf{T}}$. The three-dimensional pose $\mathbf{T}(t)$ at time step t is computed using the MOCCD algorithm. The temporal pose derivative $\dot{\mathbf{T}}(t)$ at time step t is determined with the SF algorithm as described in Sect. 2.2.3.4 using the images at the time steps $(t + \Delta t)$ and $(t - \Delta t)$. To achieve a temporally stable and robust tracking, we rely on two pose hypotheses, where a winner-takes-all component selects the best-fitting spatio-temporal model at each time step using the same criteria as for configuration 1. The prediction of the parameter vector for the first hypothesis is computed with a constant velocity model, and for the second hypothesis we apply a constant position model. These predictions are used at time step $(t + \Delta t)$ as initialisations for the MOCCD and SF instances. The idea behind this two-hypothesis approach is to provide a sufficient amount of flexibility for changing hand–forearm motion without requiring a large number of MOCCD and SF evaluations.

Configuration 3: ICP-Based Tracking   This configuration applies an ICP-based 'tracking by detection' approach for which no pose initialisation at the first time step is required. The three-dimensional model according to Sect. 2.2.3.1 is adapted to the motion-attributed three-dimensional point cloud based on the ICP-like optimisation technique described in Sect. 2.3.3. Prediction of the three-dimensional pose to the next time step is performed using the ICP-based motion analysis technique described in Sect. 2.3.3.2.

In contrast to the evaluation of this method in Sect. 7.3, which relies on the space-time stereo approach of Schmidt et al. (2007) (cf. Sect. 1.5.2.5), in this section a combination of dense optical flow information determined based on the method of Wedel et al. (2008a) and sparse stereo information obtained with the correlation-based approach of Franke and Joos (2000) is used. The flow vectors are two dimensional, such that, in contrast to a full scene flow computation as performed e.g. by Huguet and Devernay (2007) or Wedel et al. (2011), the velocity component parallel to the depth axis is missing. We favour the direct combination of optical flow and stereo due to its high computational efficiency. In principle, motion parallel to the depth axis can be estimated using the stereo information of two consecutive frames and the corresponding optical flow fields based on the disparity difference between the two points connected by an optical flow vector. This information, however, turned out to be rather unreliable due to the disparity noise, which is of the order of 0.2 pixel. Hence, motion along the depth axis will be recovered on the object level using the SF technique (cf. configuration 5).

Configuration 4: Fusion of ICP and MOCCD   This configuration corresponds to the fusion approach described in Sect. 7.4.3, where the three-dimensional pose is predicted based on the ICP approach but without using the SF algorithm.

Configuration 5: Fusion of ICP, MOCCD, and SF   This configuration corresponds to the fusion approach described in Sect. 7.4.3, where the SF algorithm is used for predicting the three-dimensional pose.

7.4.5 Evaluation Results

The three-dimensional pose estimation accuracy of the described configurations is quantified by the average Euclidean distances between the measured three-dimensional positions of the reference points and the corresponding ground truth data, along with the standard deviations obtained for each sequence. The average Euclidean distances can largely be attributed to inaccurate modelling of the hand–forearm limb as identical model parameters are used for all test persons, while the standard deviations mainly result from the inaccuracy of the pose estimation itself. The estimated temporal derivatives of the pose parameters are evaluated by determining the mean error and standard deviation of the error for the three velocity components of each reference point, using the discrete temporal derivatives of the ground truth positions as ground truth data for the velocity components.

According to Fig. 7.11, the positional error of configuration 1 (MOCCD algorithm) with respect to the average Euclidean distance between measured and ground

Fig. 7.11 Three-dimensional
pose estimation results for
configuration 1 using
greyscale images. The *labels
above the error bars* denote
the fraction of images on
which the object is tracked

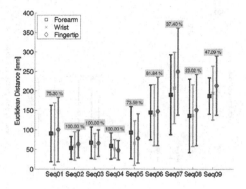

truth positions of the reference points amounts to 50–100 mm for sequences 1–5
and to 120–250 mm for sequences 6–9. The standard deviations correspond to 50–
100 mm. For several sequences the tracking process is interrupted and the object is
lost rather early, as illustrated by the percentages indicated on the labels above the
error bars.

The average positional error of configuration 2 (SF algorithm) on greyscale images (cf. Fig. 7.12) is somewhat lower than that of configuration 1 for all sequences,
and the fraction of images in which the object is tracked is always higher or comparable. The component-wise average velocity errors of configuration 2 show no
systematic offsets. The standard deviations of the velocity errors are slightly lower
for sequences 1–5 than for sequences 6–9, corresponding to about 10 and 15 mm per
time step, respectively. When colour images are used instead of greyscale images,
the average positional error decreases to below 50 mm for sequences 1–5, where the
object is tracked across all images, but remains largely unchanged for sequences 6–
9 (cf. Fig. 7.13). The standard deviations of the component-wise velocity errors are
also similar to those obtained for greyscale images.

For configuration 3 (ICP algorithm with constraint line-based motion analysis)
the average positional errors obtain values between 50 and 200 mm with standard
deviations between 50 and 100 mm (cf. Fig. 7.14). In comparison with configura-

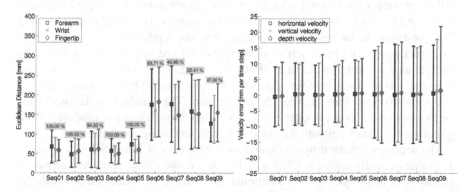

Fig. 7.12 Spatio-temporal three-dimensional pose estimation results for configuration 2 using
greyscale images

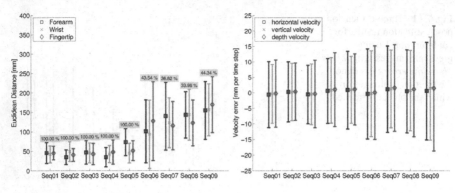

Fig. 7.13 Spatio-temporal three-dimensional pose estimation results for configuration 2 using colour images

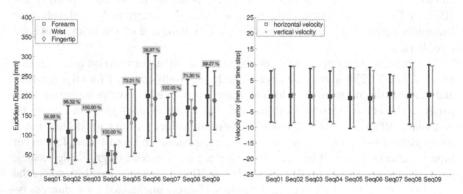

Fig. 7.14 Spatio-temporal three-dimensional pose estimation results for configuration 3 using greyscale images

tion 2, the fraction of images in which the object is tracked is lower for sequences 1, 2, 5, and 6 but higher for the more 'difficult' sequences 7–9. The standard deviations of the component-wise lateral velocity errors are lower than for configuration 2 and correspond to 7–10 mm per time step for all sequences. However, configuration 3 does not determine the velocity component along the depth axis.

A tracking of the object across all images of all test sequences is achieved by configuration 4 (fusion of ICP and MOCCD, cf. Fig. 7.15). The average positional error amounts to 40–70 mm for sequences 1–5 and 80–100 mm for sequences 6–9 with standard deviations between 20 and 50 mm. The standard deviations of the component-wise lateral velocity errors correspond to 6–10 mm per time step. Configuration 4 does not estimate the velocity component along the depth axis.

The accuracy achieved by configuration 5 (fusion of ICP and SF) is very similar to that of configuration 4 (cf. Fig. 7.16). Again, the object is tracked across all images of all test sequences. As additional information, configuration 5 reveals the velocity component along the depth axis, which is determined at an accuracy of 8–15 mm per time step.

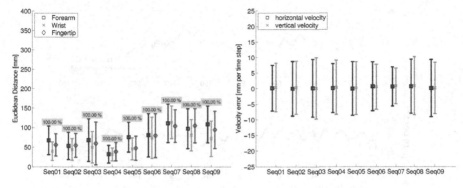

Fig. 7.15 Spatio-temporal three-dimensional pose estimation results for configuration 4 using greyscale images

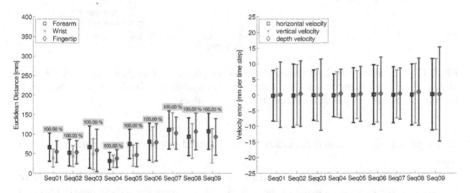

Fig. 7.16 Spatio-temporal three-dimensional pose estimation results for configuration 5 using greyscale images

In the context of the envisioned application scenario of safe human–robot interaction, the achieved accuracies of pose and motion estimation are clearly high enough for the prevention of hazardous situations in the industrial production scenario.

In our Matlab implementation, the computation time of the most complex system, configuration 5, amounts to 20 s per image triple. A speed of 3–5 image triples per second for a C++ implementation of the full system on standard PC hardware can be expected when no hardware-specific optimisation efforts are made.

Instantaneous motion information can also be obtained by directly computing the temporal derivatives of the poses obtained with the MOCCD and the ICP algorithms, respectively, without applying a specific motion analysis stage. However, in comparison with system configuration 5, the standard deviations of the errors of the velocity components obtained based on the directly computed temporal pose derivatives are higher by a factor of about two for the MOCCD and three for the ICP algorithm. Our proposed motion analysis techniques thus lead

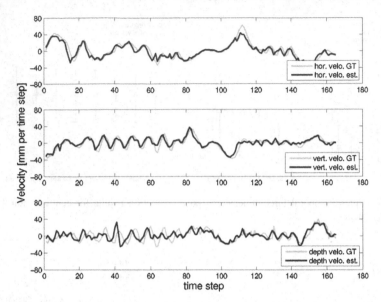

Fig. 7.17 Estimation of the instantaneous velocity components $\dot{x}$ (*top*), $\dot{y}$ (*middle*), and $\dot{z}$ (*bottom*) of the reference point in the wrist, obtained using configuration 5. *Dark grey lines* indicate the measurements, *light grey lines* the ground truth ('GT') values

to a significantly increased accuracy of the inferred instantaneous motion information.

Given the small baselines of the trinocular camera system, it is a remarkable result that the measurement error of the velocity along the depth axis is nearly identical to that of the lateral velocity components. Figure 7.17 depicts the estimated velocity components of the reference point at the wrist (dark grey curves) and the corresponding ground truth values (label 'GT', light grey curves) for a part of sequence 4, illustrating the accuracy of the motion information obtained by configuration 5. The absence of a 'phase shift' between the estimated motion and the ground truth in Fig. 7.17 confirms that the motion estimation stages described in Sect. 2.3.3.2 are able to provide information about the instantaneous motion properties of the object.

7.4.6 Comparison with Other Methods

At this point it is instructive to compare the obtained evaluation results with the metric accuracies achieved by other body tracking systems. However, this comparison is difficult due to the rather special application scenario of the work and also because no large amount of quantitative evaluation data can be found in the literature. Often the fraction of images for which tracking results are obtained is determined, but the metric accuracies are only rarely given.

It is shown by Hahn et al. (2007) that the MOCCD algorithm yields significantly more accurate and robust tracking results than the three-dimensional extension of the contour tracking approach of Blake and Isard (1998) and the three-dimensional active contour technique of d'Angelo et al. (2004), especially because the latter two tracking systems tend to lose the object after a few tens of frames.

A direct comparison is possible with the monocular approach of Schmidt et al. (2006). Their system is evaluated by Schmidt (2009) on an image sequence which is similar to our sequence 1; it was acquired with the same camera system as the one used in this section and shows the same test person and the same background at the same distance. The only difference is that Schmidt (2009) uses the original colour images. The system is initialised manually and obtains an average positional error of 210 mm on the monocular colour image sequence, which is about three times larger than the errors of our configurations 4 and 5. Not surprisingly, the positional error of the monocular system is most pronounced in the direction parallel to the depth axis, where it amounts to 160 mm on average. Furthermore, the system is unable to detect slight movements of the hand, e.g. those that occur when tightening a screw.

Further quantitative comparisons are only possible with systems using long-baseline multiple-camera setups. Rosenhahn et al. (2005) compare their tracking results obtained with a four-camera setup with ground truth data recorded by a marker-based system relying on eight cameras. In their scenario, the test persons wear tight-fitting clothes and the body model is adapted to each individual test person. The obtained accuracies are much higher than those achieved in this section. The average error of the elbow joint angle amounts to only 1.3°, which is mainly due to the detailed modelling of the test person, the fairly simple background, and the long-baseline multiple camera setup which strongly alleviates the problem of occlusions. Similar accuracies are obtained in the presence of more complex backgrounds by Rosenhahn et al. (2008a, 2008b), who also rely on individually calibrated body models.

Mündermann et al. (2008) examine camera configurations with 4, 8, 16, 32, and 64 cameras. The average positional error of their system corresponds to 10–30 mm, where the accuracy increases with an increasing number of cameras. Their positional accuracies are again higher than those achieved in this section, which is mainly due to our restriction to the small-baseline camera system required by our application scenario.

A three-camera setup with baselines of several metres is used by Hofmann and Gavrila (2009), who evaluate their system on 12 test persons and obtain an average positional accuracy of 100–130 mm in a fairly complex real-world environment. Their results are comparable to those obtained in this section, although the baseline of their camera setup is wider by a factor of 10–30. On the other hand, the distance of the test persons to the camera corresponds to approximately 10–15 m, which is higher by about a factor of three than in our scenario.

On the HumanEva data set (Sigal and Black, 2006), an average positional error of 30–40 mm with a standard deviation of about 5 mm is obtained by Gall et al. (2009). In particular, the small standard deviation illustrates the high robustness of their approach. However, similar to Rosenhahn et al. (2005, 2008a, 2008b), their system

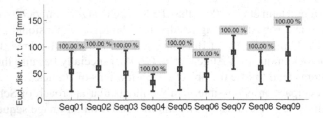

Fig. 7.18 Positional error of the mean-shift tracking stage (Euclidean distance with respect to ground truth data (GT)) for the nine test sequences. The '100 %' labels indicate that the method is able to track the hand performing the working actions completely across all test sequences

requires detailed person-specific modelling, more cameras, much wider baselines, and less complex backgrounds than the small-baseline approaches proposed in this section.

7.4.7 Evaluation of the Three-Dimensional Mean-Shift Tracking Stage

This section describes the evaluation of the mean-shift tracking method described in Sect. 2.3.2 on the same data set as the one described in Sect. 7.4.2, where only the greyscale versions of the images are used. The presentation is adopted from Hahn et al. (2010b).

In the test sequences, an average number of 6.3 objects are tracked simultaneously by the mean-shift method. These objects always comprise the right hand of the person (which performs the working actions). The ellipsoid associated with the right hand is indicated manually once for the first image of the sequence. When tracking fails and the hand gets lost, the corresponding ellipsoid is re-initialised based on the ellipsoid located closest to the last known hand position. The average Euclidean distances between the estimated hand position and the ground truth data (here: the coordinates of the wrist point) along with the corresponding standard deviations are depicted for each test sequence in Fig. 7.18. Due to the re-initialisation step, our system is able to track the hand performing the working actions completely across all test sequences, as indicated by the labels on top of the error bars in Fig. 7.18. The average Euclidean distance corresponds to 45–90 mm, the standard deviation to 16–50 mm. The metric accuracy of the hand position estimated by the three-dimensional mean-shift approach is thus comparable to the accuracy of the wrist point estimated by the SF method on the same data set. In the latter work, however, the full three-dimensional pose of the articulated hand–forearm limb, including internal degrees of freedom, is determined along with its temporal derivative.

Figure 7.19 illustrates the results of the mean-shift tracking approach for four test sequences. In part, large values of the Euclidean distance between the estimated hand position and the ground truth data may result from the fact that the centre of

Fig. 7.19 Example results of
the mean-shift tracking
algorithm for four test
sequences. *Left column*:
Reprojected ellipsoid
associated with the person's
right hand. *Right column*:
Moving three-dimensional
points in the scene along with
the tracking result

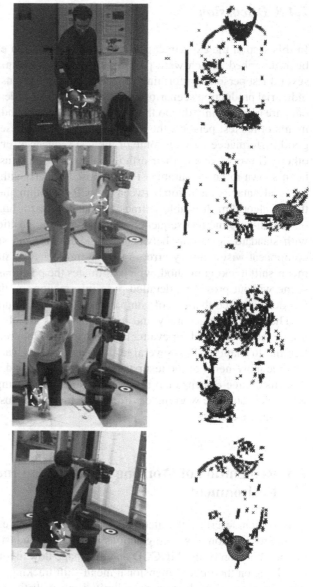

the ellipsoid associated with the hand does not necessarily correspond to the wrist
but rather to the middle of the hand (cf. second example in Fig. 7.19).

The average runtime of the Matlab implementation of the three-dimensional
mean-shift tracking algorithm corresponds to 260 ms per tracked ellipsoid on a
2.4 GHz Core 2 Duo processor. For a C++ implementation, frame rates around
10 frames per second can be expected for the same hardware.

7.4.8 Discussion

In this section the experimental investigations by Hahn et al. (2010a, 2010b) have been described, which were performed on real-world image sequences displaying several test persons performing different working actions typically occurring in an industrial production scenario. For evaluation, independently obtained ground truth data are used. Mainly due to the cluttered background and fast discontinuous movements of the test persons, the individual algorithms presented in this study show a good performance only on some of the test sequences, encountering difficulties on others. However, due to their orthogonal properties, a fusion of the algorithms has been shown to be favourable. The proposed system with the highest performance takes advantage of a fusion between the ICP algorithm, the MOCCD algorithm, and the SF algorithm. It is able to track the hand–forearm limb across all images of all our small-baseline test sequences with an average positional error of 40–100 mm with standard deviations between 20 and 50 mm and standard deviations of the component-wise velocity errors of 6–10 mm per time step. The evaluation of the mean-shift tracking method, which estimates the positions of moving objects in the scene without providing detailed pose information, on the same image sequences has demonstrated that it is of comparable positional accuracy.

The reasonable accuracy and high robustness are obtained even though (i) the image sequences used for evaluation all display a cluttered background, (ii) the system has to adapt itself to several test persons wearing various kinds of clothes, and (iii) the movements of the test persons may be rapid and discontinuous. Hence, the described three-dimensional pose estimation and tracking framework is a step towards collaborative working environments involving close interaction between humans and machines.

7.5 Recognition of Working Actions in an Industrial Environment

This section describes the methods developed by Hahn et al. (2008a, 2009, 2010b) for the recognition of working actions in a realistic industrial environment based on the combination of the MOCCD and the shape flow algorithm (Hahn et al., 2010a) or relying on the three-dimensional mean-shift tracking stage (Hahn et al., 2010b). An experimental evaluation on a limited but realistic data set is also performed. Further details are provided in Hahn (2011).

In the system described in Hahn et al. (2008a), trajectories are generated with the MOCCD-based approach of Hahn et al. (2007, 2010a) (cf. Sects. 2.2.1.2 and 7.4). After a normalisation procedure with respect to the length of the trajectory and its position and orientation in space, classification is performed with a nearest-neighbour approach. Furthermore, the classification result is used for a prediction of the hand position based on the corresponding reference trajectory, which is demonstrated to be significantly more accurate than a Kalman filter-based prediction.

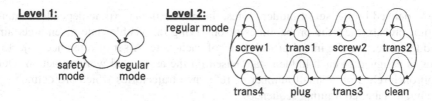

Fig. 7.20 Two-level architecture of the action recognition stage

Hahn et al. (2009, 2010b) propose a recognition stage for working actions, the description of which is adopted here from Hahn et al. (2010b). The method is based on the classification and matching of three-dimensional trajectories given by the sequence of three-dimensional positions of the hand. When the mean-shift method is used, the trajectories of all moving objects in the scene are analysed. The cyclic sequence of working actions in an engine assembly scenario is known to the system but may be interrupted by 'unknown' motion patterns. To allow an online action recognition, a sliding window approach is applied. Due to the fact that the system is designed for safe human–robot interaction, a recognition stage with two levels is implemented (Fig. 7.20). At the first level, a decision is made as to whether the human worker performs a known working action (regular mode) or an unknown motion (safety mode) based on a set of trajectory classifiers. In the safety mode (level 1), the system may prepare to slow down or halt the industrial robot. The regular mode (level 2) defines the cyclic working process performed by the human worker. It is implemented as an HMM in which the hidden state is continuously estimated by a particle filter.

The state of level 1 according to Fig. 7.20 is determined by a set of classifiers based on features extracted from the trajectory data in the sliding window of a size of eight time steps for all tracked objects. Movements between two working actions (transfer motion) are recognised by a transfer classifier. Since it is known at which position the worker has to tighten a screw or to fit a plug, a second classifier (working action classifier) is used for recognising working actions by incorporating spatial context for the actions 'screw 1', 'screw 2', 'clean', and 'plug'. The reference locations are obtained based on the known three-dimensional pose of the engine. A third classifier (distance classifier) is applied to the result of the working action classifier and decides whether the recognised working action is a known one, since such motion patterns can only occur close to the three-dimensional object associated with that action. The combination of the three classifiers results in an output discriminant vector for the six classes.

According to the description by Hahn et al. (2010b), the decision as to whether the system is in safety mode or in regular mode is made based on the result of the distance classifier and the matching accuracy of the particle weights in level 2, where the observed trajectories are analysed with respect to the occurrence of known working actions. Similar to the work of Li et al. (2006), a particle filter-based matching of a non-stationary HMM is applied in order to recognise the sequence of working actions. The HMM of level 2 (cf. Fig. 7.20) is derived from the known cyclic working task, defined by the set of hidden states, the non-stationary (time-dependent) transition probabilities, the probabilities of observing the visible state given a certain hidden state, and the initial probabilities of each state. A set of reference trajectories is assigned to each hidden state based on the associated working action. Our approach relies on a small number of reference trajectories which are defined by manually labelled training sequences.

Besides an estimate of the class to which the observed trajectory belongs, the trajectory classifier also yields the phase of the working action, i.e. the fraction by which it has been completed. While a working action is performed, the estimated phase governs the non-stationary transition probabilities, which are assumed to increase with increasing phase.

The evaluation of the action recognition stage relies on 20 trinocular real-world test sequences acquired from different viewpoints. The sequences contain working actions performed by eight different test persons in front of a complex cluttered working environment. The distance of the test persons to the camera system amounts to 2.2–3.3 m. For training, only two sequences in which the working actions are performed by two different well-trained individuals (teachers) were used. The teacher-based approach is motivated by the application scenario, in which workers are generally trained by only a few experts. Ground truth labels were assigned manually to all images of the training and test sequences.

It is demonstrated by Hahn et al. (2009, 2010b) that the system achieves an average action recognition rate of more than 90 % on the test sequences independent of whether the combination of MOCCD and shape flow algorithm or the mean-shift tracking approach is used. The average word error rate, which is defined as the sum of insertions, deletions, and substitutions, divided by the total number of test patterns, amounts to less than 10 %. Beyond the recognition of working actions, the system is able to recognise disturbances, which occur e.g. when the worker interrupts the sequence of working actions by blowing his nose. The system then enters the safety mode and returns to the regular mode as soon as the working actions continue. On the average, the system recognises the working actions with a temporal offset of several tenths of a second when compared to the manually defined beginning of an action (which is not necessarily provided at high accuracy), where the standard deviations are always larger than or comparable to the mean values.

Chapter 8
Applications to Lunar Remote Sensing

The application of three-dimensional computer vision methods to the domain of lunar remote sensing addressed in this chapter concentrates on the derivation of digital elevation models (DEMs) of small parts of the lunar surface at high lateral resolution and high vertical accuracy. Section 8.1 provides a general overview of existing methods used for constructing DEMs of planetary bodies and the corresponding data sets. The three-dimensional reconstruction of lunar craters at high resolution, i.e. beyond a determination of their depth and rim height, is regarded in Sect. 8.2, while Sect. 8.3 discusses the three-dimensional reconstruction of lunar wrinkle ridges and tectonic faults. Section 8.4 describes the generation of DEMs of lunar domes, subtle volcanic features on the Moon.

8.1 Three-Dimensional Surface Reconstruction Methods for Planetary Remote Sensing

A general overview of activities in the field of topographic mapping of planetary bodies in the inner and the outer solar system is provided in Sect. 8.1.1.1. The utilised methods can be divided into active approaches, shadow length measurements, classical photogrammetric techniques, and photoclinometric approaches. Section 8.1.2 describes how the reflectance behaviour of planetary regolith surfaces encountered for bodies without an atmosphere in the inner solar system, i.e. Mercury, the Moon, and the asteroids, is modelled in the context of three-dimensional reconstruction of such surfaces based on intensity-based methods. These models are a basis for the work about topographic mapping of the lunar surface described in Sects. 8.2–8.4.

8.1.1 Topographic Mapping of the Terrestrial Planets

8.1.1.1 Active Methods

Three-dimensional reconstruction of planetary surfaces can be performed by either active or passive methods. Active methods mainly involve radar or laser altimetry.

C. Wöhler, *3D Computer Vision*, X.media.publishing,
DOI 10.1007/978-1-4471-4150-1_8, © Springer-Verlag London 2013

According to Wu and Doyle (1990), ground-based radar observations of Mercury, Venus, and Mars were performed for the first time in the early 1970s, providing surface cross sections with vertical accuracies of 100–150 m. From orbit, the three-dimensional surface profile of Venus has been explored by radar measurements of the Pioneer 10 Venus Orbiter (Pettengill et al., 1980; Wu and Doyle, 1990). Later radar-based topographic measurements of Mercury are described by Harmon and Campbell (1988).

The laser altimeters on the Apollo 15–17 spacecrafts provided lunar topographic data for surface points at a high accuracy of 2 m (Wu and Doyle, 1990). The lunar surface has been globally mapped at a lateral resolution of 0.25° in longitude and latitude, i.e. better than 7.5 km, by laser altimetry from the Clementine spacecraft (Bussey and Spudis, 2004). According to Araki et al. (2009), a global topographic map of the Moon with a standard deviation of the elevation values of 4.1 m has been constructed using the Laser Altimeter (LALT) instrument on board the Kaguya (SE-LENE) spacecraft. The Lunar Reconnaissance Orbiter (LRO) carries the Lunar Orbiter Laser Altimeter (LOLA), which provides elevation data with a standard deviation of 90 mm (Riris et al., 2010). The LOLA elevation measurements have been re-sampled into global topographic maps ('gridded data record') of 4, 16, 64, 128, and 256 pixels per degree nominal lateral resolution (Neumann, 2009). With increasing number of elevation measurements, topographic maps of 512 and 1024 pixel per degree nominal lateral resolution have also been made available.[1] However, in many lunar regions the true lateral resolution of these topographic maps is much lower than the nominal one, as they tend to contain a significant number of interpolation artefacts.

The surface of Mars has been mapped almost entirely at a nominal lateral resolution of 463 m at the equator and an elevation accuracy of about 10 m by the Mars Orbiter Laser Altimeter (MOLA) carried by the Mars Global Surveyor Orbiter spacecraft (Gwinner et al., 2010).

8.1.1.2 Shadow Length Measurements

The classical passive approach to determine height differences on planetary surfaces is the measurement of shadow lengths. This method dates back to Herschel's visual telescopic observations in the year 1787 (Wu and Doyle, 1990). Modern shadow length measurements have been systematically performed using spacecraft imagery of the Moon (Wood, 1973; Wood and Andersson, 1978), Mercury (Pike, 1988), and Mars (Cintala et al., 1976) to determine the depths and rim heights of craters and the heights of their central peaks.

---

[1] The LOLA topographic maps are accessible on the NASA Planetary Data System at http://pds-geosciences.wustl.edu/missions/lro/lola.htm.

8.1.1.3 Stereo and Multi-image Photogrammetry

Elevation maps of about a quarter of the lunar surface are provided by the Lunar Topographic Orthophotomap (LTO) series generated based on orbital imagery acquired by the Apollo 15–17 command modules with modified aerial cameras, where the spacecraft motion allowed the acquisition of images under multiple viewing directions.[2] These topographic maps were computed based on stereophotogrammetry, where the standard deviation of the elevation values corresponds to 30 m (Wu and Doyle, 1990). A three-dimensional reconstruction of lunar surface regions not covered by the LTO series is performed by Cook et al. (1999) based on correlation-based stereoscopic analysis of images acquired by the Lunar Orbiter and Clementine spacecraft from the orbit around the Moon. The lateral resolution of the obtained surface profiles corresponds to about 1 km.

Scholten et al. (2011) present the Global Lunar 100 Meter Raster DTM (GLD100), a global topographic map of the Moon derived by stereoscopic analysis of images taken by the Wide Angle Camera (WAC) on board the LRO spacecraft.[3] The nominal lateral resolution corresponds to 100 m, while the elevation accuracy amounts to 23 m.

Wu and Doyle (1990) describe the topographic maps of the surface of Mars constructed by Wu et al. (1982) based on photogrammetric analysis of Viking Orbiter imagery with their vertical accuracies of 30–60 m, and point out that local elevation maps obtained by stereoscopic evaluation of Viking lander imagery reach accuracies between 0.1 and 0.7 m.

More recent efforts to generate a global topographic map of Mars are based on images of the High Resolution Stereo Camera (HRSC), a line scan camera installed on the Mars Express spacecraft. An in-depth discussion of the HRSC experiment is given by Jaumann et al. (2007). A software system to generate a global topographic map of scale 1 : 200000 is presented by Gehrke et al. (2006), where larger scales of 1 : 100000 and 1 : 50000 can also be obtained if images of sufficiently high resolution are available. The mapping system is demonstrated based on the region Iani Chaos, for which images of a lateral resolution of 12 metres per pixel are available.

The dense stereo algorithm based on semi-global matching introduced by Hirschmüller (2006), which was originally developed for the three-dimensional reconstruction of surfaces with pronounced depth discontinuities from satellite images, such as urban areas with buildings (cf. Sect. 1.5), is applied to HRSC images by Hirschmüller et al. (2007). A comparison between the inferred topographic maps and MOLA data yields an average difference of 9 m and a root-mean-square deviation of 51 m at a lateral image resolution of 15 m. A lower image quality leads to deviations which are about five times as high.

---

[2]The Lunar Topographic Orthophotomap (LTO) series is accessible at http://www.lpi.usra.edu/resources/mapcatalog/LTO.

[3]The GLD100 is accessible at http://wms.lroc.asu.edu/lroc/global_product/100_mpp_DEM (NASA/GSFC/Arizona State University).

A more recent HRSC-based global topographic map of Mars is described by Gwinner et al. (2010); it has an average lateral resolution ('grid spacing') of 93.1 m and exhibits an average absolute difference with respect to the MOLA topographic map of 29.2 m and a corresponding root-mean-square deviation of 49.9 m.

8.1.1.4 Photoclinometry and Shape from Shading

While the lateral resolution of a topographic map generated by stereophotogrammetric techniques is generally significantly lower than the pixel resolution of the images from which it has been produced, the technique of photoclinometry described in Sect. 3.2.2.1 can be used to generate cross-sectional profiles of planetary surfaces at a resolution comparable to that of the available images. It has been pointed out in Sect. 3.2.2.1 that photoclinometric methods yield a fairly accurate representation of depth differences on small scales but tend to produce systematic depth errors on scales much larger than the pixel resolution. Early work by Wilhelms (1964) describes the photoclinometric determination of the statistical distribution of small-scale slopes on the lunar surface, using telescopic photographic lunar images. Photoclinometry is used by Mouginis-Mark and Wilson (1979) to measure crater depths on Mercury, relying on Mariner 10 images. Howard et al. (1982) apply a photoclinometry technique to Viking orbiter images of the northern polar region of Mars, revealing elevation variations of a few hundred metres on horizontal scales of about 10 km.

More recent work by Fenton and Herkenhoff (2000) describes the determination of topographic data for the 'layered deposits' situated in the northern polar region of Mars. They use three-dimensional points determined by stereophotogrammetry as an absolute reference for three-dimensional profiles obtained by photoclinometry, where a constant surface albedo is assumed and an approximate correction of the influence of the atmosphere is performed. The results are compared with MOLA data. The photoclinometric measurements reveal thicknesses of individual layers of the order of some tens of metres. Beyer and McEwen (2002) use a photoclinometry technique to examine the suitability of selected regions on the Martian surface as landing sites for rover missions by determining surface gradients on spatial scales of several metres. Herkenhoff et al. (2002) estimate the roughness of the 'residual ice cap' in the northern polar region of Mars, i.e. the ice persisting during the Martian summer, in order to examine its suitability as a landing site. They determine the statistical distribution of surface slope angles inferred by photoclinometry. Lohse et al. (2006) apply their 'multi-image shape from shading method' (cf. Sect. 5.4) to construct topographic maps of the lunar surface based on Clementine images. A similar approach is used by Gaskell et al. (2007) for a three-dimensional reconstruction of the asteroid Eros, relying on Near-Earth Asteroid Rendezvous (NEAR) spacecraft image. Grieger et al. (2008) propose a photometric stereo approach for constructing a DEM of the region around the lunar south pole based on several partially overlapping images acquired by the SMART-1 AMIE camera under different illumination conditions.

8.1.2 Reflectance Behaviour of Planetary Regolith Surfaces

When the inner planets of the solar system formed, all of them underwent internal differentiation processes which led to the formation of a core mainly consisting of iron and nickel, a mantle consisting of dense silicate rock, and a silicic crust. In the absence of an atmosphere, the rocky surfaces were shattered by meteorite impacts over billions of years. At the same time, they were eroded in a less spectacular but also fairly efficient manner by the particles of the solar wind, e.g. highly energetic protons, which cause slow chemical changes in the material directly exposed to them. As a consequence, the uppermost layer of an atmosphereless planetary body, which mainly consists of silicate minerals, is made up by a material termed 're-golith' which is highly porous and is composed of fine grains. This has been shown directly by the drilling experiments performed during some of the Apollo missions to the Moon (McKay et al., 1991).

A reflectance function for planetary regolith surfaces is introduced by Hapke (1981) according to

$$R_{H81}(\theta_i, \theta_e, \alpha) = \frac{w \cos \theta_i}{4\pi (\cos \theta_i + \cos \theta_e)} ([1 + B(\alpha)] p(\alpha) - 1 + H(\cos \theta_i) H(\cos \theta_e)).$$

$$(8.1)$$

The parameter w corresponds to the 'single-scattering albedo', i.e. the reflectivity of a single surface grain. The function $p(\alpha)$ specifies the phase angle-dependent scattering behaviour of a single particle. The function $B(\alpha)$ describes the 'opposition effect', a strong increase in the intensity of the light reflected from the surface for phase angles smaller than about a few degrees. According to Hapke (1986, 2002), the opposition effect has two major sources. The shadow-hiding opposition effect is due to the fact that regolith surfaces are porous, and under moderate and large phase angles the holes between the grains are filled by shadows. These shadows disappear for small phase angles, leading to an increased intensity of the light reflected from the surface (Hapke, 1986). The coherent backscatter opposition effect is due to coherent reflection of light at the surface particles under low phase angles (Hapke, 2002). The function $B(\alpha)$ can be expressed as

$$B(\alpha) = \frac{B_0}{1 + \tan(\alpha/2)/h},$$

$$(8.2)$$

where B_0 governs the strength and h the width of the peak (Hapke, 1986). If the opposition effect were exclusively due to shadow hiding, one would expect a value of B_0 between 0 and 1. However, values of B_0 larger than 1 are commonly allowed to additionally take into account the coherent backscatter opposition effect (Warell, 2004), as it is difficult to separate the two contributions.

For the particle angular scattering function $p(\alpha)$, McEwen (1991) uses the phase function introduced by Henyey and Greenstein (1941) involving a single asymme-

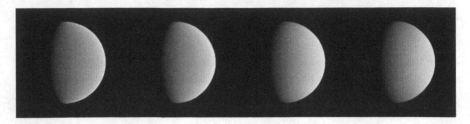

Fig. 8.1 Intensity across a planetary disk of uniform albedo for a phase angle of $\alpha = 70°$ for macroscopic roughness parameters $\bar{\theta}$ of (*from the left*) $0°$, $10°$, $20°$, and $30°$, computed based on the reflectance function introduced by Hapke (1984). The other parameters of the Hapke model have been chosen according to solution 1 obtained for the Moon by Warell (2004)

try parameter. However, it is commonly more favourable, as discussed by Warell (2004), to adopt the double Henyey–Greenstein formulation

$$p_{2HG}(\alpha) = \frac{1+c}{2} \frac{1-b^2}{(1-2b\cos\alpha+b^2)^{3/2}} + \frac{1-c}{2} \frac{1-b^2}{(1+2b\cos\alpha+b^2)^{3/2}} \quad (8.3)$$

introduced by McGuire and Hapke (1995), modelling a backward and a forward scattered lobe. In (8.3), the width of the two lobes is denoted by the value of b, which may lie in between 0 and 1. The parameter c denotes the relative strengths of the two lobes (McGuire and Hapke, 1995).

The function $H(x)$ in (8.1) takes into account multiple scattering processes. It is tabulated by Chandrasekhar (1950), and a first-order approximation is given by Hapke (1981) according to

$$H(x) \approx \frac{1+2x}{1+2x\sqrt{1-w}}. \quad (8.4)$$

An improved, second-order approximation of $H(x)$ is introduced by Hapke (2002), which is relevant essentially for high-albedo surfaces. Only very small differences, however, are observed compared to the formulation in (8.4) for low-albedo surfaces like that of the Moon.

An extension of (8.1) is introduced by Hapke (1984) to take into account the roughness of the surface on spatial scales between the submillimetre range and the resolution limit of the imaging device. It is shown by Helfenstein (1988), based on the analysis of close-range stereo images of the lunar surface acquired during the Apollo missions, that the strongest influence on the reflectance behaviour comes from surface roughness on the submillimetre and millimetre scales. The full form of the reflectance function including the macroscopic roughness $\bar{\theta}$ is given by Hapke (1984). For illustration, modelled planetary disks are shown in Fig. 8.1 for values of $\bar{\theta}$ between $0°$ and $30°$. The other parameters of the reflectance functions are set to $w = 0.168$, $b = 0.21$, $c = 0.7$, $h = 0.11$, and $B_0 = 3.1$ according to Warell (2004) (cf. Table 1 in that study, Moon solution 1 therein). For the angular scattering function, the formulation according to (8.3) has been used. Figure 8.1 illustrates that the Hapke model yields an unrealistically bright rim around the limb of the planetary disk for $\bar{\theta} = 0°$, i.e. when the macroscopic surface roughness is not taken into

Fig. 8.2 Image of the lunar disk, acquired under a phase angle of $\alpha = 59.6°$. No bright rim at the limb of the disk is apparent

account—cf. Fig. 8.2 for a real image of the lunar disk, in which no bright rim is visible at the limb. The bright rim disappears more and more for increasing values of $\bar{\theta}$, and for the phase angle configuration shown in Fig. 8.1, the observed intensity increasingly resembles that of a Lambertian surface. Most planetary surfaces display macroscopic roughness values between 10° and 30° (Hapke, 1984; Helfenstein, 1988; Veverka et al., 1988; Warell, 2004).

It is not straightforward, however, to apply the reflectance function introduced by Hapke (1981, 1984, 1986) to three-dimensional surface reconstruction using intensity-based methods. According to McEwen (1991), a reflectance function that fairly well describes the reflectance behaviour of dark regolith surfaces is of the form

$$R_{\mathrm{L}}(\theta_i, \theta_e, \alpha) = f(\alpha) \frac{\cos \theta_i}{\cos \theta_i + \cos \theta_e}, \tag{8.5}$$

with the phase angle-dependent factor $f(\alpha)$. For constant $f(\alpha)$, (8.5) corresponds to the Lommel–Seeliger reflectance law (Lohse and Heipke, 2004). For large phase angles approaching 180°, the reflectance of the lunar surface becomes increasingly Lambertian. McEwen (1991) proposes the lunar-Lambert function, which is a combination of the Lommel–Seeliger and the Lambertian reflectance function according to

$$R_{\mathrm{LL}}(\theta_i, \theta_e, \alpha) = \rho \left(2L(\alpha) \frac{\cos \theta_i}{\cos \theta_i + \cos \theta_e} + \left(1 - L(\alpha)\right) \cos \theta_i \right) \tag{8.6}$$

with ρ as an albedo parameter that also absorbs quantities specific to the image acquisition process and $L(\alpha)$ as an empirical phase angle-dependent parameter (cf. Sect. 3.2.1 for the corresponding bidirectional reflectance distribution function (BRDF)). The formulation in (8.6) has the advantage that it can be used directly for ratio-based photoclinometry and shape from shading methods as described in Sect. 3.3.2.1, as the surface albedo ρ then cancels out for each image pixel.

To obtain a function $L(\alpha)$ that provides a realistic description of the reflectance behaviour of the lunar surface, McEwen (1991) computes intensity profiles for the 'photometric equator' (the great circle on the planetary sphere which contains the point on the sphere in which the Sun is located in the zenith, i.e. the 'subsolar point', and the point exactly below the observer) and the 'mirror meridian' (the great circle orthogonal to the photometric equator on which $\theta_i = \theta_e$). The intensity values are then extracted in photometric longitude (the angle measured along the photometric equator) and photometric latitude (the angle measured along the mirror meridian). According to McEwen (1991), the opposition effect parameters B_0 and h have a significant influence on the observed reflectance only for phase angles below about 5°, where it is not favourable to apply photoclinometric techniques also with respect to illumination and viewing geometry. As it tends to be difficult to adapt the lunar-Lambert function to the Hapke function near the limb of the planetary disk, values of $\theta_e > 70° + \alpha/9$ are not taken into account for the parameter estimation. This is no restriction, because photoclinometric methods are preferentially applied for small values of θ_e, corresponding to a viewing direction approximately perpendicular to the surface.

The behaviour of $L(\alpha)$ is illustrated by McEwen (1991) as a sequence of reference diagrams for different values of the single-scattering albedo w, different parameter values of the function $p(\alpha)$, and macroscopic roughness values between 0° and 50°. For low-albedo surfaces with $w \approx 0.1$ and macroscopic roughness values $\bar{\theta}$ larger than about 10°, the shape of the angular scattering function has only a minor influence on $L(\alpha)$. For small phase angles, $L(\alpha)$ is always close to 1, while it approaches zero for phase angles larger than about 140°. For intermediate phase angles, the behaviour of $L(\alpha)$ strongly depends on the value of $\bar{\theta}$, where in the practically relevant range for values of $\bar{\theta}$ between 0° and 30°, $L(\alpha)$ monotonously decreases with increasing $\bar{\theta}$. As a consequence, the reflectance behaviour becomes increasingly Lambertian for increasing phase angles and $\bar{\theta}$ values (cf. Fig. 8.1). For the lunar surface, the behaviour of $L(\alpha)$ can also be expressed as a third-order polynomial in α (McEwen, 1996). The lunar-Lambert reflectance function with $L(\alpha)$ as established by McEwen (1991) is used in Sects. 8.2 and 8.4 for the three-dimensional reconstruction of lunar craters and lunar volcanic features.

8.2 Three-Dimensional Reconstruction of Lunar Impact Craters

8.2.1 Shadow-Based Measurement of Crater Depth

The depth of a crater can be estimated based on the length of the shadow cast by the crater rim, when the shadow ends near the crater centre (Pike, 1988). A method generally applicable to images acquired under oblique viewing conditions is described by Pike (1988) (cf. Appendix A by Clow and Pike therein), who utilises it for measuring the depths of simple bowl-shaped craters and the heights of their rims above the surrounding surface in Mariner 10 images of the planet Mercury and obtains a depth–diameter relation for Mercurian craters.

A sketch of depth–diameter relations for impact craters on Mercury, the Moon, Mars, and the Earth established by Pike (1980) is shown in Fig. 8.3. It has been observed by Pike (1980, 1988) and also in previous classical works, e.g. by Wood

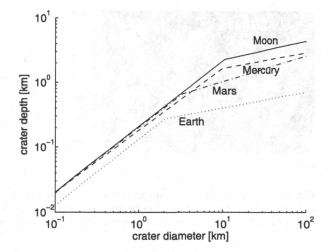

Fig. 8.3 Depth–diameter relations for Mercury, the Moon, the Earth, and Mars (adapted from Pike, 1980).

(1973) and Wood and Andersson (1978), that the slope in the double-logarithmic diagram displays a sudden change at a planet-specific critical diameter value, which marks what is called the simple-to-complex transition. In the recent work by Salamunićcar et al. (2012), such data are extracted automatically based on an analysis in terms of orbital imagery and topographic data obtained by laser altimetry, relying on pattern recognition methods. Craters with diameters exceeding the critical value are not bowl-shaped any more but, depending on their diameter, display complex structures such as flat floors, central peaks, or inner walls with terraces (Pike, 1980). A discussion of the geological factors influencing the dependence of the crater depth on the diameter is provided e.g. by Cintala et al. (1976) and Pike (1980).

8.2.2 Three-Dimensional Reconstruction of Lunar Impact Craters at High Resolution

This section describes results obtained by Hafezi and Wöhler (2004), Wöhler and Hafezi (2005), d'Angelo and Wöhler (2008), and Herbort et al. (2011) for the three-dimensional reconstruction of lunar impact craters at high resolution based on the methods discussed in Chaps. 3 and 5. The presentation in this section is adopted from those works.

The telescopic images utilised by Hafezi and Wöhler (2004) and Wöhler and Hafezi (2005) were acquired with ground-based telescopes of 125 mm and 200 mm aperture equipped with a CCD camera (Philips ToUCam). Each image was generated by stacking several hundreds of video frames. For this purpose we made use of the Registax and Giotto software packages, employing a cross-correlation technique similar to the one described by Baumgardner et al. (2000). In that work, however, digitised analog video tapes were processed, while we directly acquired digital video frames. The scale of our images is between 500 and 800 m per pixel on the lunar

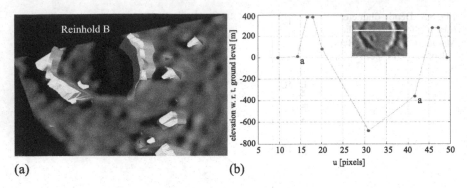

(a)   (b)

Fig. 8.4 (a) Shadow-based three-dimensional reconstruction of the crater Reinhold B according to Sect. 3.1.1. (b) Cross section through the crater floor, obtained based on shadow length measurements in three images acquired at different illumination conditions

surface. Due to atmospheric seeing, however, the effective resolution (denoted by the diameter of the point spread function rather than the spatial resolution per pixel) of our best images approximately corresponds to 1 km on the lunar surface. All other telescopic lunar images regarded in this section were acquired with the same technique.

As an example of a complex crater shape not immediately revealed by the image data, Hafezi and Wöhler (2004) examine the lunar crater Reinhold B (cf. Fig. 8.4a). Due to the fact that the time intervals between the images used for extraction of shadow information typically amount to several weeks, the relative position of camera and object cannot be kept constant during acquisition of all necessary images of the scene; thus an image registration procedure (Gottesfeld Brown, 1992) becomes inevitable to obtain pixel-synchronous images.

Although the floor of the crater Reinhold B looks flat, shadow analysis based on two images according to Sect. 3.1.1 reveals that the elevation difference between the ridge of the eastern (right) crater rim and the centre of the crater floor amounts to 1000 m and is thus 700 m larger than the elevation difference between the ridge of the western (left) rim, while the ridges of both rims are 300–400 m above the level of the environment. This means that the western part of the crater floor is on about the same level as the environment, while its central part is 700 m deeper. Hence, the western half of the crater floor is inclined by an angle of approximately 4°, given the crater diameter of 19 km. Figure 8.4b shows a cross section of Reinhold B which additionally contains the results of shadow analysis obtained with a third image obtained at again different illumination conditions (marked by 'a'). Here, an identical ground level east and west of the crater has been assumed (Hafezi and Wöhler, 2004). For comparison, Fig. 8.5 shows the LOLA DEM of Reinhold B, which also reveals the slight asymmetry of the crater floor in the east–west direction.

Wöhler and Hafezi (2005) construct high-resolution local DEMs of lunar impact craters with the integrated method based on shadow and shading described in Sect. 5.2. It is not possible, however, to obtain the required images from existing image archives of lunar spacecraft missions, as these generally do not contain

Fig. 8.5 Perspective view of
the LOLA DEM of the crater
Reinhold B from
southwestern direction. The
vertical axis is six times
exaggerated

several images of a surface region under sufficiently different illumination conditions. Hence, telescopic lunar CCD images were used again. Selenographic positions were obtained from Rükl (1999). The three-dimensional reconstruction approach described in Sect. 5.2 assumes that the grey value I of a pixel is proportional
to the incident flux F. However, for many cameras it is possible to adjust the gamma
value γ manually from within the camera control software, causing the grey value
I to be proportional to F^γ. Hence, a calibration of the gamma scale in the camera
control software was performed by evaluating flat-field frames of different intensities acquired through different neutral density filters with known transmission coefficients, then fitting a characteristic curve of the form $I = aF^\gamma$ to the measured
flat-field intensities.

In the scenario of three-dimensional reconstruction of small regions of the lunar surface under roughly perpendicular view and oblique illumination, $\cos\theta_e$ in
the lunar-Lambert reflectance function (8.6) hardly deviates from its average value
$\langle\cos\theta_e\rangle \approx 1$. Since $\cos\theta_i \ll 1$, changes in θ_i do not significantly influence the value
of the denominator $(\cos\theta_e + \cos\theta_i)$; thus it can be approximated by the constant
value $(\langle\cos\theta_e\rangle + \langle\cos\theta_i\rangle)$ as long as the surface gradients are small. This results
in an effective albedo $\rho_{\text{eff}} = \rho[\frac{2L(\alpha)}{\langle\cos\theta_e\rangle+\langle\cos\theta_i\rangle} + 1 - L(\alpha)]$. This approximation is
acceptable for the lunar impact craters regarded here, because the regions examined
in this section are not close to the limb of the lunar disk, and the observed surface
slopes are usually smaller than about $10°$. Furthermore, the average depth deviation between the surface profile computed with a lunar-Lambert reflectance function from the Lambertian solution is always well within the error range of shadow
analysis in the example scenes. In the examples of Fig. 8.6a, the root-mean-square
deviation is smaller than 40 m for $L(\alpha)$ in the range $-0.1, \ldots, 1$. If, however, the
surface is imaged under a more oblique viewing angle, as is the case for some of
the lunar domes regarded in Sect. 8.4, it is important to fully take into account the
lunar-Lambert reflectance function.

For each examined crater, the obtained surface profile is checked by Wöhler and
Hafezi (2005) for consistency with the image data by means of a ray tracing software. The appearance of the surface profile under solar elevation angles μ (shading
image) and μ_{shadow} (shadow image) is simulated assuming a Lambertian surface.
For all examples, both simulated images are satisfactorily similar to the corresponding real images. A good cross-check is provided by the rendered shadow image due
to the fact that the shape of the simulated shadow is highly sensitive with respect to
small deviations of the surface profile from the correct shape. Additionally, we have
shown (see the beginning of Sect. 5.2) that the quality of reconstruction is hardly
affected by inaccurate knowledge of the reflectance function.

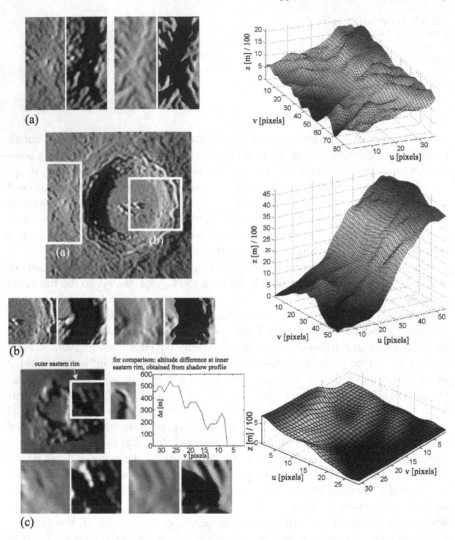

Fig. 8.6 Three-dimensional reconstruction of lunar craters by combined shading and shadow analysis according to Sect. 5.2. The original shading and shadow images are shown *on the left*, respectively, along with the obtained three-dimensional surface profile and the corresponding rendered images, given the same illumination conditions as used for shading and shadow analysis. (**a**) Outer western rim of lunar crater Copernicus. (**b**) Inner eastern rim of lunar crater Copernicus. (**c**) Outer eastern rim of lunar crater Wolf

Figure 8.6a shows the three-dimensional surface reconstruction of the outer western rim of the lunar crater Copernicus, obtained by employing the technique outlined in Sects. 5.2.1 and 5.2.2 that consists of selecting a shape from shading solution consistent with shadow analysis in a first step and taking into account the detailed shadow structure in a second step. The shading image alone does not reveal the large-scale eastward slope of the profile, which can only be derived from the shadow image. Effectively, the shadow allows one to adjust the albedo ρ such that the shape from shading algorithm yields a surface profile consistent with both the small-scale depth variations evident in the shading image and the large-scale slope derived from the shadow image. Figure 8.6b shows the inner eastern rim of the lunar crater Copernicus. The surface profile reveals terraces and small craters in the crater wall. The performance of the reconstruction algorithm is slightly decreased by small shadows in the shading image cast by the central peaks. The correspondence of the simulated shadow contour with its real counterpart is reasonable. In Fig. 8.6c, the outer eastern rim of the lunar crater Wolf is shown along with the depth differences at the corresponding inner rim obtained by shadow analysis alone. A comparison reveals that the crater floor is lying on the same level as the surrounding mare surface. The simulated shadow shows all features displayed by the real shadow image.

Figure 8.7 shows the reconstructed surface profile of the floor of the lunar crater Theaetetus, which has a diameter of 25 km. It was generated by the technique described in Sect. 5.2.3 that relies on an initialisation of the shape from shading algorithm by surface gradients obtained by the analysis of several shadows observed under different illumination conditions. Both the simulated shading image and the contours of the simulated shadows correspond well with their real counterparts. Even the ridge crossing the crater floor, which is visible in the upper left corner of the region of interest in Fig. 8.7a and in the Lunar Orbiter photograph shown in Fig. 8.7c for comparison, is apparent in the reconstructed surface profile (arrow). Hence, the reconstruction technique reliably indicates even small-scale structures on the surface that cover only a few pixels. Furthermore, it turns out that the crater floor is inclined from the north to the south, and a low central elevation (rising to about 250 m above the floor level) becomes apparent in the reconstructed surface profile. Such features are important for a geological interpretation of the crater, as they essentially mark the difference between simple bowl-shaped craters and more complex craters such as Theaetetus (Spudis, 1993). This central elevation does not appear in the images in Fig. 8.7a used for reconstruction but is clearly visible in the telescopic image of Theaetetus acquired at a solar elevation angle of $\mu = 28.7°$ shown in Fig. 8.7e (lower arrow). The corresponding simulated image (lower part of Fig. 8.7e) is very similar to the real image, although that image has not been used for reconstruction. This kind of comparison is suggested by Horn (1989) as an independent test of reconstruction quality. For comparison, traditional shape from shading as outlined in Sect. 3.2.2.2 yields an essentially flat crater floor and no ridge (Fig. 8.7f). This shows that the traditional approach is obviously not able to extract reliable information about surface gradients perpendicular to the azimuthal direction of illumination under the given illumination conditions.

As an independent comparison, Fig. 8.8a shows a three-dimensional reconstruction of the eastern half of Theaetetus extracted from the topographic maps provided by Cook (2007). These topographic data have a lateral resolution of 1 km and were computed with the stereophotogrammetric approach described by Cook et al. (1999), relying on Clementine orbital imagery. The DEM in Fig. 8.8a is fairly noisy and contains some spike artefacts on the crater rim. Furthermore, for some points

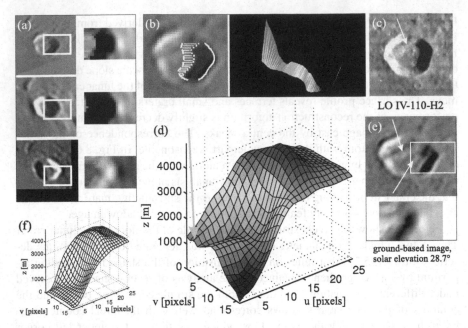

Fig. 8.7 Three-dimensional reconstruction of the eastern half of lunar crater Theaetetus based on the initialisation of the shape from shading algorithm by shadow analysis according to Sect. 5.2.3. (**a**) The *two upper images* are evaluated with respect to shadow, the third one with respect to shading. The reconstructed surface part is marked by a *white rectangle*, respectively, the corresponding simulated images are shown *to the right*. (**b**) Surface patch between the two shadow lines (*hatched*) along with the initial surface profile derived from shadow analysis. (**c**) Section from Lunar Orbiter photograph IV-110-H2, shown for comparison. Image credit: NASA/USGS. (**d**) Reconstructed surface profile. Although the marked ridge is hardly visible in the three ground-based images used for surface reconstruction, it clearly appears in the reconstructed surface profile due to its effect on the shadows. (**e**) Further ground-based image of Theaetetus shown for comparison, not used for reconstruction, along with the simulated image derived from the reconstruction result. The ridge crossing the crater and the low central elevation are marked by *arrows*. (**f**) Three-dimensional reconstruction result obtained with traditional shape from shading, selecting the solution consistent with the first shadow image. None of the previously mentioned details on the crater floor is visible

on the crater floor no data are available. No small-scale structures appear on the crater floor. The LOLA DEM in Fig. 8.8b shows a hint of the central elevation of the crater but no details on the inner crater rim due to the presence of broad interpolation artefacts. In the DEM shown in Fig. 8.7d obtained with the combined method of Wöhler and Hafezi (2005) based on shadow and shading features, the size of the central elevation is somewhat overestimated when compared to the LOLA DEM and the GLD100 (cf. Fig. 8.8c). Both the LOLA DEM and the GLD100 clearly show the ridge in the northern part of the crater floor (cf. arrow in Fig. 8.7d). The overall crater depth according to Fig. 8.7d is in good correspondence with the depths indicated by the stereophotogrammetric DEM by Cook (2007), the LOLA DEM, and the GLD100 shown in Fig. 8.8.

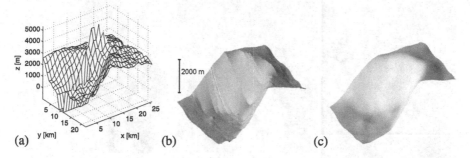

Fig. 8.8 (**a**) Perspective view of the DEM of the eastern half of Theaetetus, extracted from the topographic data by Cook (2007). (**b**) Perspective view of the LOLA DEM and (**c**) the GLD100 of the eastern half of Theaetetus from southwestern direction. The vertical axis is three times exaggerated

As an example of the combination of shape from shading with sparse depth data, d'Angelo and Wöhler (2008) analyse a sequence of five images of the lunar crater Kepler acquired by the SMART-1 spacecraft on January 13, 2006, from heights above the lunar surface between 1613 and 1702 km (European Space Agency, 2006) using the method described in Sect. 5.3.3. The crater diameter amounts to 32 km. During image acquisition the spacecraft flew over the crater and at the same time rotated around its axis, such that the crater remained in the field of view over a considerable period of time (European Space Agency, 2006). The first and last images of the sequence are shown in Fig. 8.9a. The image size is 512×512 pixels. Figure 8.9b shows the reconstructed part of the surface, which is smaller than the complete field of view, as the surface albedo becomes non-uniform at larger distances from the crater. The image is rotated such that north is to the top and west to the left. Relying on a structure from motion analysis based on bundle adjustment (cf. Sect. 1.3), a three-dimensional point cloud is extracted from the image sequence, as shown in Fig. 8.9c after Delaunay triangulation. Since no lens calibration data are available, it is assumed that the lens can be described by the pinhole model with the principal point in the image centre. The image scale amounts to 146 m per pixel (European Space Agency, 2006), such that the scaling constant can be readily determined for the structure from motion result.

Since no polarisation information is available, d'Angelo and Wöhler (2008) combine the shape from shading method with the result of structure from motion (cf. Sect. 5.3.3), making use of the lunar-Lambert reflectance function according to (8.6). The viewing direction was determined according to the normal vector of a plane fitted to the three-dimensional point cloud extracted by structure from motion analysis. For this non-specular surface, the uniform albedo ρ was estimated based on all image pixels in the course of the iteration process according to (5.24) as explained in Sect. 5.3.2. Saturated (white) pixels were excluded from the shape from shading analysis.

The three-dimensional reconstruction result shown in Fig. 8.10a distinctly reveals the uneven crater floor of Kepler as well as the material that has slumped down the

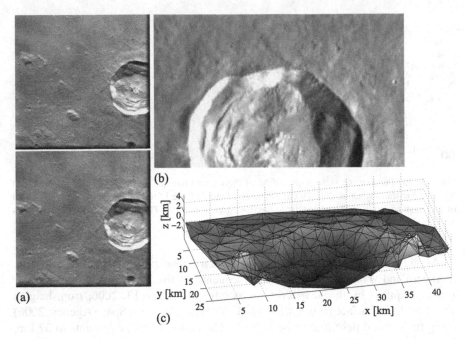

Fig. 8.9 Lunar crater Kepler. (**a**) First and last images of a five-image sequence acquired by the SMART-1 spacecraft, published by European Space Agency (2006). Image credit: ESA/J.-L. Josset. (**b**) Region selected for three-dimensional reconstruction, oriented such that north is *to the top* and west *to the left*. (**c**) Three-dimensional reconstruction obtained by structure from motion (triangulated three-dimensional point cloud)

inner crater wall at several places, especially at the northern rim. The reconstructed surface obtained with the combined structure from motion and shape from shading approach reveals much finer detail than the structure from motion data alone. The typical depth difference between crater floor and rim amounts to about 2850 m. A crater depth of 2750 m is reported in the lunar atlas by Rükl (1999). D'Angelo and Wöhler (2008) do not provide a more detailed evaluation due to the lack of high-resolution topographic data. However, the recently released LOLA DEM, from which the northern part of Kepler has been extracted and displayed as a perspective view as shown in Fig. 8.10b, also yields an average crater depth of 2750 m and displays many of the small-scale details visible in Fig. 8.10a. The same is true for the GLD100 of the northern part of Kepler shown in Fig. 8.10c.

According to d'Angelo and Wöhler (2008), this example demonstrates the usefulness of the combination of intensity data and sparse depth data obtained from a camera moving in an uncontrolled manner, regarding a surface with well-defined reflectance properties under accurately known illumination conditions. The self-consistent solution for the three-dimensional surface profile obtained according to Sect. 5.3.3 yields a crater rim of largely uniform height, indicating that the estimated surface gradients in the horizontal and in the vertical image direction are essentially correct. In contrast, surface reconstruction by shape from shading alone based on

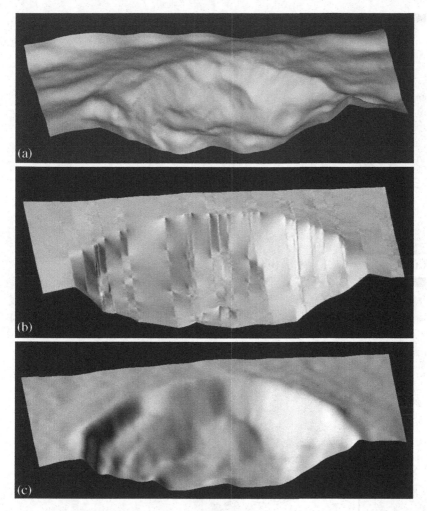

Fig. 8.10 Lunar crater Kepler. (**a**) Dense three-dimensional reconstruction using the combination of structure from motion with shape from shading (cf. Fig. 8.9). (**b**) Perspective view of the LOLA DEM and (**c**) of the GLD100 of the same region. The vertical axis is two times exaggerated

images acquired under identical illumination conditions is not able to simultaneously estimate both surface gradients for each pixel as long as no boundary values are known for the surface to be reconstructed. What is more, the sparse depth points do not introduce spurious artefacts into the reconstructed surface profile despite the considerable noise in the three-dimensional point cloud (cf. Fig. 8.9c) extracted by structure from motion.

Figure 8.11 shows a DEM of the eastern part of the crater Alphonsus obtained using the approach by Herbort et al. (2011) and Grumpe and Wöhler (2011), which is based on a combination of the LOLA DEM on large spatial scales and shape from shading on small spatial scales (cf. Sect. 5.5). The DEM has been constructed rely-

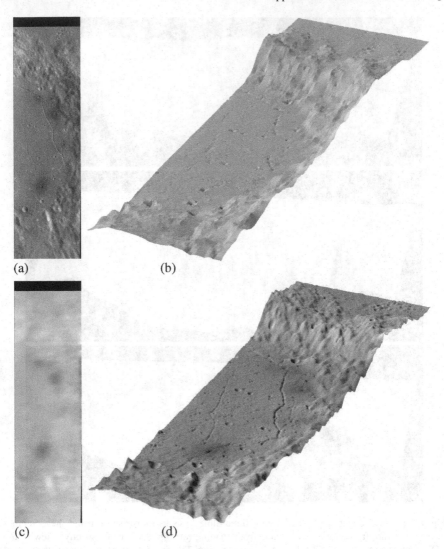

Fig. 8.11 (**a**) M^3 image at 1978 nm of the eastern part of the crater Alphonsus. Image credit: NASA/JPL-Caltech. (**b**) Perspective view of the LOLA DEM of the region. (**c**) Single-scattering albedo map at 1978 nm (grey value range 0–0.6). (**d**) Perspective view of the refined DEM, displayed with the albedo-dependent modelled reflectance used as an overlay. The vertical axis is three times exaggerated

ing on a single Chandrayaan-1 M^3 image, but this method nevertheless allows one to determine a map of the non-uniform surface albedo along with the DEM. The reflectance model by Hapke (1981, 1984, 1986) has been used, such that the albedo values in Fig. 8.11c correspond to the physical single-scattering albedo, while the other parameters of the Hapke model were assumed to be constant and were chosen according to Warell (2004). The low-albedo patches are dark lunar pyroclastic de-

Fig. 8.12 Enlarged perspective views of a section of the floor of Alphonsus, obtained based on (**a**) the LOLA DEM, (**b**) the GLD100, and (**c**) the method described in Sect. 5.5 using Chandrayaan-1 M^3 imagery in combination with LOLA data. The size of the region corresponds to about 42×42 km^2. For generating the perspective views, a constant surface albedo has been assumed. The vertical axis is three times exaggerated

posits consisting of volcanic ash, which are mentioned e.g. by Gaddis et al. (2000, 2003), while high-albedo regions correspond to parts of the crater rim consisting of bright highland material. The amount of small-scale detail in the refined DEM is much higher than in the LOLA DEM of the same region. Figure 8.12 compares enlarged DEMs of a section of the floor of Alphonsus, covering an area of about 42×42 km^2, obtained based on LOLA data, the GLD100, and the method described in Sect. 5.5 using Chandrayaan-1 M^3 imagery in combination with LOLA data. The amount of detail is much higher in Fig. 8.12c than in Figs. 8.12a and b.

8.2.3 Discussion

The DEMs of lunar craters presented in this section obtained based on photometric three-dimensional reconstruction methods all have a lateral resolution that comes close to the respective pixel resolution. The method of Herbort et al. (2011) (cf. Sect. 5.5) allows one to estimate the non-uniform surface albedo even when only a single image is available. When hyperspectral images are available, as is the case for M^3 data, the obtained albedo values of all channels can be used to compute surface reflectances normalised to a standard illumination and viewing geometry (however, the parameters of the Hapke model apart from the single-scattering albedo then must be assumed constant). Wöhler and Grumpe (2012) show that, even after such a normalisation procedure, an influence of the topography on the pixel-wise spectra is still apparent. This leads to slight topography-dependent distortions of the spectra which result in a strong dependence of diagnostic spectral features, such as the wavelength or depth of characteristic absorptions, on the surface gradients. DEMs of high lateral resolution will thus be useful for a correction of such topographic effects on hyperspectral data.

Another domain in which highly resolved DEMs are beneficial is the automatic detection of lunar craters; this is of high geological relevance, as the determination of crater densities is a common method for estimating ages of planetary surfaces (Hiesinger et al., 2003). Salamunićcar et al. (2012) propose a classification-based crater detection algorithm which relies on the combined analysis of images and

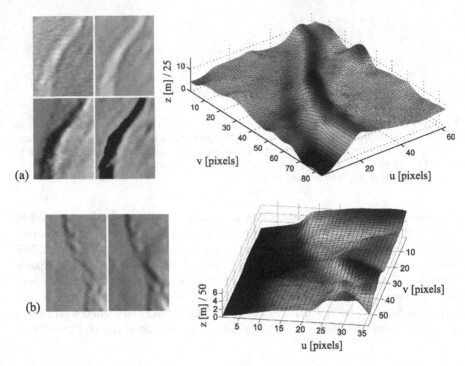

Fig. 8.13 Telescopic CCD images, rendered counterparts, and three-dimensional reconstruction result for (**a**) a mare ridge or fault southwest of the crater Aristarchus and (**b**) the end of a lunar lava flow at the border between Mare Imbrium and Mare Serenitatis

topographic data. Salamunićcar et al. (2011) demonstrate that using a DEM constructed with the method described in Sect. 5.5 instead of the LOLA DEM yields a significantly higher detection rate especially for small craters of about 1–2 km diameter or less, thus allowing the determination of reliable statistics especially for small crater sizes.

8.3 Three-Dimensional Reconstruction of Lunar Wrinkle Ridges and Faults

The mare regions of the Moon display many low wrinkle ridges ('dorsa') and a small number of tectonic faults ('rupes'). Wrinkle ridges were formed due to the contraction of cooling mare lava. Tectonic faults are linear structures at which the surface elevation changes suddenly. Their occurrence is due to the basin-forming impacts on the Moon (Wilhelms, 1987). This section describes three-dimensional reconstruction results according to Wöhler and Hafezi (2005) and Wöhler et al. (2006a) for some typical wrinkle ridges and tectonic faults. The presentation in this section is adopted from those works.

The results shown in Figs. 8.13, 8.14 and 8.15 were obtained by Wöhler and Hafezi (2005). Figure 8.13a shows a structure situated southwest of the crater

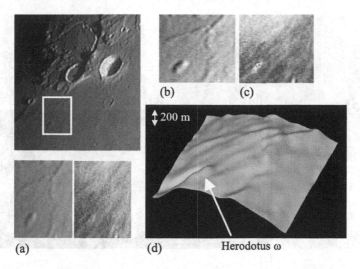

Fig. 8.14 Reconstruction of the region around lunar dome Herodotus ω based on two images acquired at different illumination conditions ($\mu_1 = 5.0°$, $\mu_2 = 15.5°$) and ratio-based intensity error term (3.50). (**a**) Scene at lower (*left image*) and higher (*right image*) solar elevation. Contrast has been enhanced. (**b**) Ratio image $I_{uv}^{(1)}/I_{uv}^{(2)}$. Due to the distance of the surface region from the centre of the Moon's apparent disk, the image has been correspondingly scaled. (**c**) Albedo map obtained according to (3.49). (**d**) Reconstructed surface profile, shown as shaded relief to accentuate subtle surface structures. Along with the actual surface features, the bending of the surface due to the spherical shape of the Moon is visible in the horizontal image direction

Aristarchus which appears to be a wrinkle ridge. Three-dimensional surface reconstruction was performed based on the approach described in Sect. 5.2 combining shadow and shading information. The initial adaptation of the surface profile according to Sect. 5.2.1 was skipped, and the surface was reconstructed by directly applying the algorithm described in Sect. 5.2.2 that takes into account the detailed shadow structure, making use of integrability constraint (3.25). The surface profile reveals a step-like structure of this mare ridge, elevated by 250 m and 180 m above the terrain to its west and east, respectively. The elevation difference indicates that this structure is probably a fault rather than a typical wrinkle ridge.

It is possible to employ the reconstruction technique described in Sect. 5.2 even when no shadow image is available, by setting the value of $(\Delta z)_{\text{shadow}}^{\text{ave}}$ (cf. (5.5) in Sect. 5.2.1) according to a priori knowledge about the large-scale behaviour of the surface profile. Such large-scale depth information may also be obtained from space-based radar or laser altimetry measurements. The surface profile of a step-like structure between Mare Serenitatis and Mare Imbrium shown in Fig. 8.13b has been derived by setting $(\Delta z)_{\text{shadow}}^{\text{ave}} = 0.2$ pixel ≈ 160 m, corresponding to the average height of the step. This fault-like formation is not of tectonic origin but is the end of a lunar lava flow.

Figure 8.14 displays the three-dimensional reconstruction result for a section of the lunar surface southwest of the crater Aristarchus with its bright ray system. This surface part displays a strongly non-uniform albedo. In this example, surface recon-

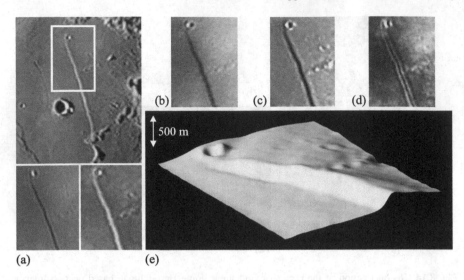

Fig. 8.15 DEM of the northern part of the tectonic fault Rupes Recta based on two images acquired at different illumination conditions ($\mu_1 = 13.7°$, $\mu_2 = 175.6°$) by first applying the ratio-based intensity error term (3.50) with smoothness and shadow constraints (3.20) and (5.10), then using the resulting surface profile and albedo map as an initialisation to the shape from shading scheme that involves integrability constraint (3.25). (**a**) Scene illuminated from the east (*left image*) and from the west (*right image*). (**b**) Shadow image. (**c**) Ratio image. (**d**) Albedo map obtained according to (3.49). (**e**) Reconstructed surface profile, shown as *shaded relief* to accentuate subtle surface structures. Along with the actual surface features, the bending of the surface due to the Moon's spherical shape is visible in the horizontal image direction

struction is performed based on two images taken at different solar elevation angles $\mu_1 = 5.0°$ and $\mu_2 = 15.5°$ but virtually identical solar azimuth angles, using error term (3.50). The average pixel pixel grey value $\langle I_{uv}^{(1)} \rangle$ of the first image is scaled such that $\langle I_{uv}^{(1)} \rangle / \langle I_{uv}^{(2)} \rangle = \sin \mu_1 / \sin \mu_2$, which means that on the average, the surface section is assumed to be flat. A large-scale surface slope of angle δ in the direction of incident light might be imposed by setting $\langle I_{uv}^{(1)} \rangle / \langle I_{uv}^{(2)} \rangle = \sin(\mu_1 + \delta) / \sin(\mu_2 - \delta)$—with an absolutely calibrated CCD sensor one might think of deriving such a large-scale slope directly from the surface reconstruction procedure. The reconstructed surface profile contains several low ridges with altitudes of roughly 50 m along with the lunar dome Herodotus ω. The albedo map obtained according to (3.49) displays a gradient in surface brightness from the lower right to the upper left corner along with several ray structures running radial to the crater Aristarchus.

Figure 8.15 shows the northern part of the lunar tectonic fault Rupes Recta. The images shown in Fig. 8.15a were acquired at solar elevation angles $\mu_1 = 13.7°$ and $\mu_2 = 175.6°$, which means that the scene is illuminated from opposite directions. The scene was reconstructed by first applying the ratio-based intensity error (3.50) with smoothness and shadow constraints (3.20) and (5.10), then using the resulting surface profile and albedo map obtained by (3.49) as an initialisation to the shape from shading scheme that involves integrability constraint (3.25). A third image

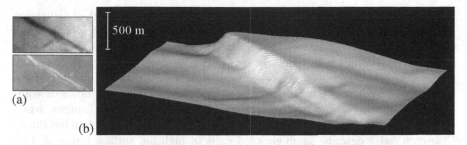

Fig. 8.16 (**a**) Pixel-synchronous pair of images of the central part of Rupes Cauchy, acquired at local sunrise (*top*) and at local sunset (*bottom*). Image credit: P. Lazzarotti. (**b**) Perspective view of the DEM obtained based on combined shadow and shading analysis according to Sect. 5.2. The vertical axis is 10 times exaggerated. The curvature of the lunar surface has been subtracted

(cf. Fig. 8.15b) provides the required shadow information. The height of the reconstructed part of Rupes Recta ranges from 200 m to about 400 m, which is well consistent with the shadow length in Fig. 8.15b. The albedo map ρ_{uv} shows bright spots in the lower part and especially in the upper right part of the image. The linear structures in the albedo map along Rupes Recta are artefacts; presumably, ρ_{uv} is not very accurate at places where the surface strongly bends and the residual intensity error $\tilde{e}_i$ according to (3.50) is comparably large due to the regularisation constraints.

A three-dimensional reconstruction of the central part of the lunar tectonic fault Rupes Cauchy obtained by Wöhler et al. (2006a) based on a combined shadow and shading analysis according to Sect. 5.2 is shown in Fig. 8.16. The upper image in Fig. 8.16a acquired at local sunrise was used for extracting shadow information. The resulting DEM reveals that the elevation of the fault is not constant, obtaining values of more than 350 m in its highest parts. In the southern part of the DEM small structures appear on the slope of the fault, reaching a height of about 100 m relative to the surface level to the west.

8.4 Three-Dimensional Reconstruction of Lunar Domes

8.4.1 General Overview of Lunar Domes

This section provides a short description of the characteristics of lunar volcanic domes. According to Head and Gifford (1980), lunar mare domes are low elevations of mostly circular shape located in the mare plains. They have smooth surfaces and low flank slopes of typically less than a few degrees. Presumably, most of them were formed by the effusion of basaltic lava (Wilhelms, 1987). The highest frequencies of lunar domes are observed in several parts of Oceanus Procellarum, especially in the Marius region and between the craters Hortensius, Milichius, and Tobias Mayer, and in Mare Tranquillitatis. Other mare regions on the lunar nearside display individual domes (Head and Gifford, 1980).

Head and Gifford (1980) provide a qualitative morphological classification scheme for lunar domes. Their classes 1–3 refer to largely symmetric volcanic features resembling terrestrial shield volcanoes, displaying comparably steep flanks (class 1), flat profiles with relatively steep margins (class 2), and very low flank slopes (class 3). Domes of class 4 appear close to mare ridges and may have been formed by intrusive magmatic processes, bending the surface upwards without the eruption of lava on the surface, or may also be structural features, while class 5 domes are assumed to represent highland terrain over which lava has flown. Classes 6 and 7 describe small elevated parts of highland surface surrounded by mare basalt and complex edifices of irregular outline, respectively.

Lunar highland domes are larger and steeper than mare domes. They were formed of highly viscous, presumably silicic lavas (Wilson and Head, 2003). Typical examples are the Gruithuisen and Mairan domes in northern Oceanus Procellarum (Wilson and Head, 2003; Kusuma et al., 2012) and Mons Hansteen in southwestern Oceanus Procellarum (Hawke et al., 2003).

8.4.2 Observations of Lunar Domes

This section describes spacecraft and telescopic observations of lunar domes, adopting the presentation by Wöhler et al. (2006b) but also taking into account more recent spacecraft data acquired by LRO and Chandrayaan-1.

8.4.2.1 Spacecraft Observations of Lunar Mare Domes

Most lunar mare domes can only be observed under oblique illumination due to the low slopes of their flanks. Consequently, the Lunar Orbiter images[4] mostly acquired at solar elevation angles between 20° and 30° display steeper effusive mare domes, like e.g. some (but not all) of the domes near Milichius (cf. Fig. 8.17a), the Hortensius dome field (cf. Fig. 8.17b), the Marius Hills, the domes in Mare Undarum (cf. Fig. 8.18a), and the Mons Rümker complex (cf. Fig. 8.18b). The lower domes in Mare Tranquillitatis, however, are invisible in the Lunar Orbiter images; only some of their summit pits are apparent (cf. Fig. 8.17c). What is more, these images are not suitable for photogrammetric analysis aiming for generating topographic data due to the lack of geometric and photometric calibration; the relation between incident flux and pixel grey value is nonlinear and unknown, because the images were acquired on photographic film scanned on board the spacecraft.

An orbital Apollo 15 photograph[5] of the large dome complex Mons Rümker situated in northern Oceanus Procellarum is shown in Fig. 8.19. It was acquired on

---

[4]Digitised Lunar Orbiter images scanned at high resolution are accessible at http://astrogeology.usgs.gov/Projects/LunarOrbiterDigitization.

[5]Digitised Apollo images are accessible at http://www.apolloarchive.com.

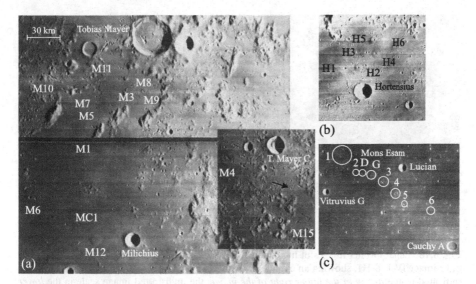

Fig. 8.17 Lunar Orbiter images of lunar mare domes. Image credit: NASA/USGS. (**a**) Lunar Orbiter images IV-133-H2 and IV-126-H2, showing the mare dome field between Milichius and Tobias Mayer. (**b**) Lunar Orbiter image IV-133-H1, showing the domes near Hortensius. (**c**) Lunar Orbiter image IV-073-H2, showing the domes Diana (D) and Grace (G) and the domes of the Northern Tranquillitatis Alignment (NTA). *Circles* indicate dome diameters. The images are reproduced at uniform scale, north is *to the top* and west *to the left*

film with a hand-held Hasselblad camera from the Apollo 15 command module and is therefore also unsuitable for a photometric evaluation. However, this image qualitatively reveals the large-scale shape of Mons Rümker, indicating that the western part of the plateau is more elevated than its eastern part (cf. Sect. 8.4.3.1).

While the Apollo images used for preparing the Lunar Topographic Orthophotomaps are virtually distortion-free, they cannot be used for photoclinometric analysis, again due to an unknown nonlinear relation between incident flux and film density, and many of them were acquired at high solar elevation angles. The morphometric properties of a limited number of lunar volcanic edifices have been derived from the Lunar Topographic Orthophotomaps by Pike and Clow (1981).

The fact that nearly all Clementine images were acquired at local lunar noon implies high illumination angles for the equatorial regions of the Moon, where the mare domes are situated. Consequently, for the important lunar dome fields these images are neither suitable for stereophotogrammetry nor photoclinometry or shape from shading.

More recent spacecraft images of lunar mare and highland domes are shown in Fig. 8.20. The images in Figs. 8.20a, b, and d were extracted from data acquired by the Chandrayaan-1 Moon Mineralogy Mapper (M^3). The M^3 images are made up (in global mode) by 85 channels with centre wavelengths between 461 and 2976 nm at a

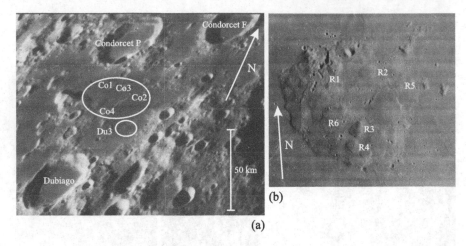

Fig. 8.18 Lunar Orbiter images of lunar mare domes. Image credit: NASA/USGS. (**a**) Lunar Orbiter image IV-178-H1, showing an oblique view on Mare Undarum with its dome field. North is indicated by the *arrow in the upper right of the image*, the undistorted image scale in the *lower right*. (**b**) Lunar Orbiter image IV-163-H2, showing the lunar dome complex Mons Rümker. The labels R1–R6 indicate individual volcanic edifices

Fig. 8.19 Section from Apollo 15 orbital image AS15-97-13252, showing an oblique view of the lunar dome complex Mons Rümker from southern direction. Image credit: NASA

pixel resolution of 140 m.[6] The original images were mapped to a simple cylindrical projection. A detailed description of the M^3 instrument is given by Pieters et al. (2009). Figures 8.20c, e, and f are excerpts from the Lunar Reconnaissance Orbiter Camera (LROC) WAC global mosaic.[7] A detailed description of the LROC WAC

---

[6]The Chandrayaan-1 M^3 hyperspectral image data archive is accessible at http://m3.jpl.nasa.gov/m3data.html.

[7]The LROC WAC image archive is accessible at http://wms.lroc.asu.edu/lroc. The LROC WAC global mosaic is available at http://wms.lroc.asu.edu/lroc/wac_mosaic.

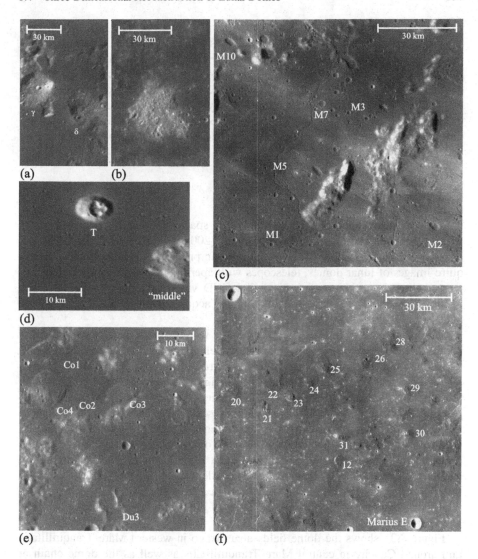

Fig. 8.20 Chandrayaan-1 M^3 and LROC WAC images of lunar mare and highland domes. M^3 image credit: NASA/JPL-Caltech. LROC WAC image credit: NASA/GSFC/Arizona State University. (**a**) M^3 image at 1978 nm wavelength of the Gruithuisen highland domes. (**b**) M^3 image at 1978 nm wavelength of the highland dome Mons Hansteen. (**c**) Mare domes between the craters Milichius and T. Mayer. Section from the global LROC WAC mosaic. (**d**) M^3 image at 1978 nm wavelength of the highland domes Mairan T and Mairan 'middle'. (**e**) Lunar domes in Mare Undarum. Section from the global LROC WAC mosaic. (**f**) Northern part of the Marius Hills region. Section from the global LROC WAC mosaic

instrument is provided by Robinson et al. (2010). The identification numbers of the domes in the Marius Hills region shown in Fig. 8.20f are according to the study of that region by Lena et al. (2009).

The illumination angles of the LROC WAC global mosaic and most M^3 images are too steep to clearly reveal low mare domes (cf. Fig. 8.20). However, the highland domes are well visible in these images. Hence, Herbort et al. (2011) rely on M^3 data for shape from shading based DEM construction (cf. Sect. 5.5) as the M^3 data set provides radiance images, allowing one to apply the Hapke model (Hapke, 1981, 1984, 1986) to the resulting absolute physical reflectance values, along with the pixel-wise illumination, viewing, and phase angles. DEMs of lunar highland domes recently obtained with the method of Herbort et al. (2011) are presented in Sect. 8.4.3.1.

8.4.2.2 Telescopic CCD Imagery

Due to the lack of photometrically calibrated spacecraft imagery acquired under strongly oblique illumination, Wöhler et al. (2006b) utilise telescopic CCD images for the determination of the morphometric properties of lunar domes. To acquire images of lunar domes, telescopes with apertures between 200 and 400 mm were utilised in combination with digital CCD video cameras of different types (Atik, ToUCam, Lumenera), relying on the acquisition technique described in Sect. 8.2.2.

The images shown in Figs. 8.21b and 8.22c were taken in the Johnson I band, a bandpass filter transmitting near-infrared wavelengths between 700 and 1100 nm, while the other telescopic images were acquired in integral visible light through a UV+IR block filter which transmits wavelengths between 400 and 700 nm. The telescopic CCD images in Figs. 8.21–8.25 are not geometrically rectified, which implies a non-uniform direction-dependent pixel scale. The scale bars in these figures therefore indicate the average pixel scale for each image. Labels without brackets denote that a three-dimensional reconstruction of the corresponding dome has been performed based on the respective image data, while labels in brackets are merely shown for comparison. For our set of lunar domes, the image sections used for three-dimensional reconstruction were extracted from the telescopic CCD images rectified to perpendicular view. A correction of the gamma value of the camera has been performed as described in Sect. 8.2.2.

Figure 8.21 shows the dome fields near Arago in western Mare Tranquillitatis and around Cauchy in central Mare Tranquillitatis as well as the dome chain at the northern border of Mare Tranquillitatis termed 'Northern Tranquillitatis Alignment' (NTA) by Wöhler et al. (2007b). The dome fields situated in Mare Insularum near the craters Hortensius, Milichius, and Tobias Mayer are shown in Fig. 8.22, while Fig. 8.23 displays the dome field in Mare Undarum (Lena et al., 2008) and the large volcanic complex Mons Rümker in northern Oceanus Procellarum (Wöhler et al., 2007a). For comparison, several isolated domes situated outside the large dome fields are shown in Fig. 8.24, while Fig. 8.25 shows a dome at the southern rim of the crater Petavius which is associated with a pyroclastic deposit composed of dark material distributed across the surface by a violent volcanic eruption. This pyroclastic deposit is also mentioned by Gaddis et al. (2000).

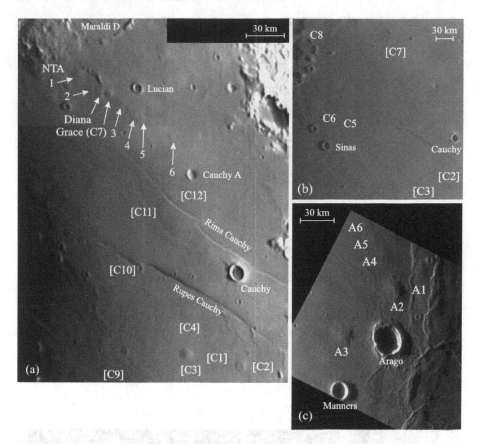

Fig. 8.21 (a) Telescopic CCD image of the northern part of Mare Tranquillitatis, showing the dome field around the crater Cauchy and the NTA domes. (b) Telescopic CCD image of the north–western part of Mare Tranquillitatis, showing further domes in the Cauchy region. (c) Telescopic CCD image of the region around Arago. Image credit: P. Lazzarotti. North is *to the top* and west *to the left*

8.4.3   Image-Based Determination of Morphometric Data

This section describes the construction of DEMs of lunar domes, relying on telescopic CCD images and also recent spacecraft images. An estimation of the error interval of the morphometric parameters (e.g. the dome height) inferred from the DEMs is performed, and the obtained dome heights are compared to other, independently obtained height measurements. The description is mainly adopted from Wöhler et al. (2006b) and also discusses results of further studies.

8.4.3.1 Construction of DEMs

A robust method for estimating elevation differences on the lunar surface is the analysis of shadow lengths as described in Sect. 3.1. In the CCD images, the diameter D

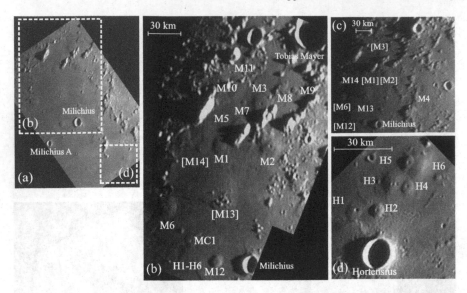

Fig. 8.22 Telescopic CCD images of the Hortensius and Milichius/Tobias Mayer dome fields.
(**a**) Low-resolution image for orientation. (**b**) Dome field between Milichius and Tobias Mayer.
Image credit: J. Phillips. (**c**) Region north of Milichius. (**d**) Dome field north of Hortensius. Image
credit: M. Wirths. North is *to the top* and west *to the left*

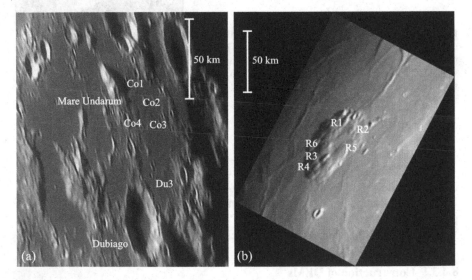

Fig. 8.23 (**a**) Telescopic CCD image of the dome field in Mare Undarum. Image credit: P. Lazzarotti. (**b**) Dome complex Mons Rümker in northern Oceanus Procellarum. Image credit:
K.C. Pau. North is *to the top* and west *to the left*

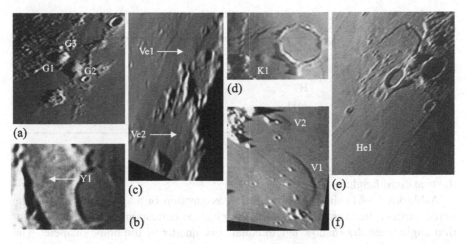

Fig. 8.24 Isolated mare domes in various regions of the Moon, examined for comparison. (a) Highland domes Gruithuisen γ (G1), δ (G2), and NW (G3). (b) Mare dome Yerkes 1 near crater Yerkes in Mare Crisium. (c) Mare domes Vendelinus 1 and 2 near the western rim of Vendelinus. Image credit: J. Phillips. (d) Mare dome Kies π (K1). (e) Mare dome Herodotus ω (He1). (f) Valentine dome V1 and its northern neighbour V2. Image credit: K.C. Pau

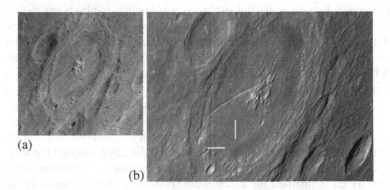

Fig. 8.25 (a) Image of the crater Petavius under moderately high solar illumination, showing two dark pyroclastic deposits located at its southern and its northern rim, respectively. (b) Image of Petavius, showing the dome associated with the southern pyroclastic deposit (marked by *white lines*). Image credit: P. Lazzarotti. In both images, north is *to the top* and west *to the left*

of the dome and the length l of its shadow were measured in pixels. The corresponding image scale in kilometres per pixel was obtained by measuring the diameters of craters of known size in the field of view. The possible effect of sloping terrain has to be carefully considered, as the measured shadow length is longer for downward slopes and shorter for upward slopes, compared to horizontal terrain. A further problem arising especially for low domes is that even under strongly oblique illumination the shadow does not begin at the dome summit but at some point on its flank,

Table 8.1 Flank slope and	Dome	Slope (°)	Height (m)
height values for several mare domes, determined using the			
shadow-based method of	C11	0.6	60
Ashbrook (1961)	A2 (Arago α)	1.5	310
	H7	1.5	100
	M11	3.0	150
	M12 (Milichius π)	2.7	230

such that the determined height difference value merely represents a lower limit to the true dome height.

Ashbrook (1961) shows that under the assumption of a spherical shape of the dome surface, the average value of the flank slope corresponds to the solar elevation angle when the shadow length equals one quarter of the dome diameter. The observer determines the moment in time, corresponding to a solar elevation angle $\tilde{\mu}$, for which $l = D/4$ is given, leading to a dome height $h = (D/2) \tan \tilde{\mu}$. The Ashbrook method has primarily been devised for visual observations. The assumption of spherical dome shape, however, represents a significant restriction to its applicability. Here it was used to determine the heights of domes C11, A2, H7, M11, and M12 (cf. Table 8.1).

Photometric three-dimensional surface reconstruction methods are more generally applicable to the determination of the morphometric properties of lunar domes. In a first step, the photoclinometric approach (cf. Sect. 3.2.2.1) is taken, which consists of computing depth profiles along image rows. For all regarded domes, the terrain is gently sloping, i.e. $|p|, |q| \ll 1$, the illumination is highly oblique, and the scene is illuminated nearly exactly from the east or the west, corresponding to $q_s = 0$. The lunar-Lambert reflectance (8.6) thus depends much more strongly on the surface gradient p in the east–west direction than on the gradient q in the north–south direction, such that we may initially set $q = 0$. Note that this approximation is exact for cross sections in the east–west direction through the summit of a feature, while it is otherwise a reasonable approximation. A constant albedo ρ is assumed, which is justified for all examined domes, as they are virtually indistinguishable from their surroundings in Clementine 750 nm images. The value of ρ is chosen such that the average surface slope over the region of interest is zero. Under these assumptions, (3.16) is solved for the surface gradient p_{uv} for each pixel with intensity I_{uv}.

The result of photoclinometry is used as an initialisation to the shape from shading scheme according to Horn (1989) described in Sect. 3.2.2.2. The ground-based CCD images are affected by a slight blur due to atmospheric seeing. Hence, the observed image I_{uv} is assumed to be a convolution of the true image with a Gaussian point spread function (PSF) G_σ (cf. Chap. 4). The PSF radius σ is determined from the intensity profile of shadows cast by steep mountains, e.g. crater rims, where an abrupt transition from illuminated surface to darkness is expected. Convolving a synthetically generated abrupt change in intensity with a Gaussian PSF and comparing the result with the intensity profile observed in the image allows for an estimation of the PSF radius σ. A similar method is used by Baumgardner et al. (2000) to estimate the PSF for ground-based Mercury images, using the limb of the planetary disk as a reference. Then the PSF-dependent intensity error term proposed by Joshi and Chaudhuri (2004) is used:

$$e_i = \sum_{u,v} \left[I_{uv} - G_\sigma * R(\rho, p_{uv}, q_{uv}) \right]^2 \qquad (8.7)$$

(Joshi and Chaudhuri, 2004). The uniform surface albedo ρ and approximate values for the surface gradients p_{uv} in the east–west direction are estimated using the method described in Sect. 3.2.2.1, obtained there under the assumption of zero values of the surface gradients q_{uv} in the north–south direction. The surface profile z_{uv} is computed such that the integrability error term (3.25) is minimised.

To obtain a DEM of the dome in the southern part of the crater Petavius shown in Fig. 8.25, Lena et al. (2006) employ the ratio-based photoclinometry approach described in Sect. 3.3.2, relying on the image shown in Fig. 8.25b and a further image acquired under lower solar illumination. The albedo map ρ_{uv} determined according to (3.49) was then inserted into the single-image shape from shading scheme described in Sect. 3.2.2, making use of the integrability constraint (3.25). The surface gradients p_{uv} determined by ratio-based photoclinometry based on (3.48) were used as initial values for the iterative update rule (3.30).

The image scale in kilometres per pixel is determined for the telescopic images relying on craters of known diameters. The dome diameter D is measured in pixels, where for non-circular domes the geometric mean of the major and the minor axis is used. The height h of a dome is obtained by measuring the depth difference in the reconstructed three-dimensional profile between the dome summit and the surrounding surface, taking into account the curvature of the lunar surface. The average flank slope ζ is then obtained by

$$\zeta = \arctan \frac{2h}{D}. \qquad (8.8)$$

The dome volume V is computed by integrating the DEM over an area corresponding to a circular region of diameter D around the dome centre. If only a part of the dome can be reconstructed, as is the case for a few domes in the Milichius field due to shadows cast on the dome surfaces by nearby hills, rotational symmetry is assumed, such that the volume can be estimated based on the rotational body formed by a cross section through the dome centre.

DEMs obtained by Wöhler et al. (2006b) for the regarded lunar domes are shown in Fig. 8.26, illustrating the rich variety of three-dimensional shapes occurring in the examined four lunar dome fields. For example, dome C1 near Cauchy is remarkably low but clearly effusive due to its summit pit. The nearby domes C2 and C3, traditionally known as Cauchy ω and τ, are steeper but quite different in shape, since C2 clearly displays a flattened top with a summit pit while C3 is of more conical shape. The large edifices A2 and A3, traditionally designated Arago α and β, are somewhat irregularly shaped, while dome A1 next to A2, situated near a mare ridge, is of regular conical shape. The domes near Hortensius have large and deep summit

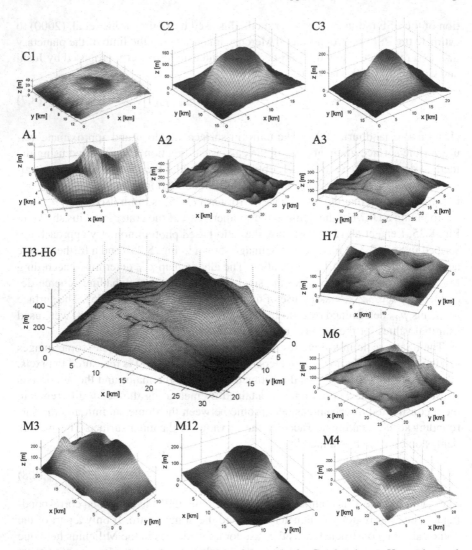

Fig. 8.26 Perspective views of typical DEMs of domes in the Cauchy, Arago, Hortensius, and Milichius/Tobias Mayer dome fields. The dome identification according to Wöhler et al. (2006b) is indicated in the *upper left of each plot*, respectively. For C1, C2, and C3, the vertical axis is exaggerated by a factor of 50, for the other domes by a factor of 30

pits. This is true even for the comparably low dome H7 displaying a summit pit with a depth corresponding to about at least half the height of the dome. The domes near Milichius show remarkably manifold three-dimensional shapes. Examples are M3 with its pancake-like shape, M4 and M6 with their rougher and more strongly textured surfaces, and M12 showing a very regular, flattened shape which is quite similar to that of C2, with a central summit pit.

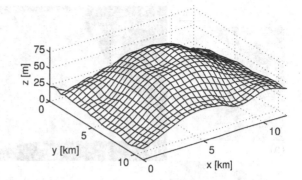

Fig. 8.27 Perspective view of the DEM of the very low dome NTA3, viewed from southwestern direction. The vertical axis is 50 times exaggerated

The aligned domes making up the NTA examined by Wöhler et al. (2007b) are very low, except for Diana and Grace. As an example, a DEM of the dome NTA3 is shown in Fig. 8.27, illustrating its low profile. A summit pit is clearly visible on top of NTA3.

Lena et al. (2008) examine the domes Condorcet 1–4 and Dubiago 3, which are situated in Mare Undarum near the eastern limb of the apparent lunar disk. A DEM of a part of this dome field is shown in Fig. 8.28, revealing that the flank slope of Condorcet 4 is quite steep, while Condorcet 2 and 3 are lower and have a more pancake-like cross-sectional profile. Under the oblique viewing and illumination angles and low phase angles encountered for these domes, the reflectance behaviour of the lunar surface largely obeys the Lommel–Seeliger law—for the lunar macroscopic surface roughness estimated by Warell (2004), a value of $L(\alpha) = 0.9$ in the lunar-Lambert reflectance function (8.6) is indicated by McEwen (1991). Hence, the dependence of the surface reflectance on the incidence angle and in turn on the surface slope is much less pronounced than for Lambertian reflectance. As a consequence, the heights of the domes in Mare Undarum obtained assuming Lambertian reflectance are too low by about a factor of two, compared to the values derived with the lunar-Lambert reflectance law.

The DEM of the large dome complex Mons Rümker shown in Fig. 8.29b is constructed by Wöhler et al. (2007a) by employing the described combined photoclinometry and shape from shading technique as a multi-resolution approach to

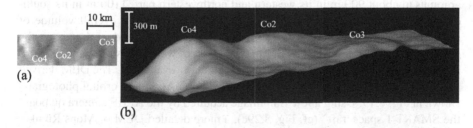

Fig. 8.28 (a) Telescopic CCD image of the domes Condorcet 2–4, situated in Mare Undarum. The image is rectified to perpendicular view, north is *to the top* and west *to the left*. Image credit: P. Lazzarotti. (b) Perspective view of the DEM of Condorcet 2–4, viewed from southwestern direction. The vertical axis is 10 times exaggerated, the curvature of the lunar surface has been subtracted

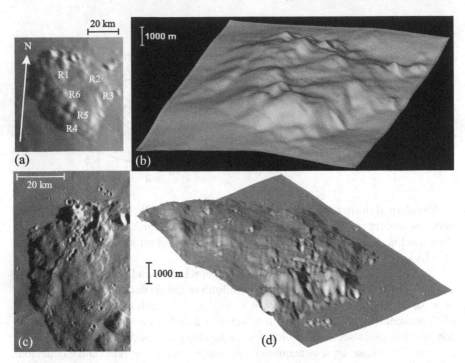

Fig. 8.29 (**a**) Telescopic CCD image of the dome complex Mons Rümker, situated in northwest-ern Oceanus Procellarum. The individual edifices R1–R6 are indicated. The image is rectified to perpendicular view, north is indicated by the *white arrow*. Image credit: K.C. Pau. (**b**) Perspective view of the DEM of Mons Rümker obtained based on the image shown in (**a**) (from southeastern direction). The vertical axis is 10 times exaggerated, the curvature of the lunar surface has been subtracted. (**c**) Section from SMART-1 AMIE image LR3-R01914-00017-00100. The image reso-lution corresponds to 218 m per pixel. Image credit: ESA/J.-L. Josset/B. Grieger. (**d**) Perspective view of the DEM of Mons Rümker obtained based on the image shown in (**c**) (from northeastern direction). The vertical axis is 10 times exaggerated, the curvature of the lunar surface has been subtracted

stabilise the convergence behaviour and facilitate at the same time the reconstruc-tion of small-scale surface features. The DEM shows that the height of the plateau amounts to about 900 m in its western and northwestern part, 1100 m in its south-ern part, and 650 m in its eastern and northeastern part. The overall volume of erupted lava corresponds to about 1800 km^3. About 30 individual domes on the Rümker plateau are described by Smith (1974), six of which are sufficiently well re-solved in the telescopic CCD image for morphometric evaluation. The DEM derived for Mons Rümker is qualitatively consistent with the Apollo 15 orbital photograph shown in Fig. 8.19. Using a low-Sun image acquired by the AMIE camera on board the SMART-1 spacecraft[8] (cf. Fig. 8.29c), a more detailed DEM of Mons Rümker

---

[8]The SMART-1 AMIE images are accessible at the ESA Planetary Science Archive at http://www.rssd.esa.int/index.php?project=PSA.

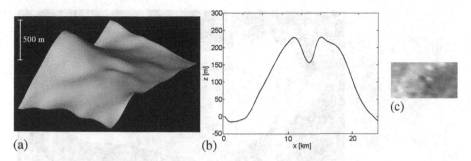

Fig. 8.30 (a) Perspective view of the DEM of the dome at the southern rim of Petavius, viewed from northwestern direction. The vertical axis is ten times exaggerated. (b) Cross section in east––west direction through the summit pit of the dome. (c) Albedo map obtained by (3.49)

could be constructed based on photoclinometry and shape from shading analysis, which is shown in Fig. 8.29d.

Lena et al. (2006) construct a DEM of the dome at the southern rim of Petavius, situated in a region of non-uniform albedo characterised by a dark pyroclastic deposit. It is shown in Fig. 8.30a. The cross section through the summit pit (cf. Fig. 8.30b) reveals that the dome summit is elevated by 240 m above the surrounding surface. To the south of the pit, the terrain rises further up to a height of 530 m. The albedo map of the region covered by the DEM is shown in Fig. 8.30c, clearly indicating the dark pyroclastic material. The average flank slope of the higher summit south of the dome amounts to 3.1°, and parts of the flank are even steeper than 4°. Hence, it is probably too high and too steep to be of volcanic origin. The interpretation by Lena et al. (2006) is that the dome is placed adjacent to a hummocky, impact-related deposit, which is supported by the close proximity of this region to the rugged inner crater rim of Petavius.

A DEM of the Valentine dome is shown in Fig. 8.31. This large dome is of possibly intrusive origin. Its shape is asymmetric; its eastern edge is fairly pronounced and steep, while the western edge merges smoothly with the surrounding mare surface. The dome surface displays several protrusions and is traversed by a curved rile.

The approach introduced by Grumpe et al. (2011) described in Sect. 5.5, which relies on the integration of shape from shading with active range scanning data (here: the LOLA DEM), has been used for the construction of DEMs and albedo maps of the highland domes Gruithuisen γ and δ, Mons Hansteen, and Mairan T and 'middle'. The analysis is based on M^3 imagery (cf. Figs. 8.20a, b, and d) and on the LOLA DEM with $1/512°$ nominal lateral resolution, corresponding to about 60 m at the lunar equator. However, as indicated by the excerpts from the LOLA DEM shown in Figs. 8.8b and 8.10b, the true lateral resolution of the LOLA DEM is generally much lower than the indicated nominal lateral resolution. The obtained DEMs are shown in Fig. 8.32 as perspective views with the albedo-dependent modelled reflectance used as an overlay, where the reflectance model by Hapke (1981, 1984, 1986) has been used for shape from shading analysis. The albedo maps reveal the extraordinary brightness of the dome surfaces.

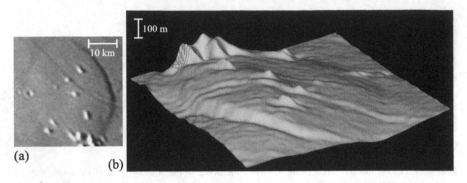

Fig. 8.31 (a) Telescopic CCD image of the Valentine dome, situated at the western border of Mare Serenitatis and possibly of intrusive origin. The image is rectified to perpendicular view, north is *to the top* and west *to the left*. Image credit: K.C. Pau. (b) Perspective view of the DEM of the Valentine dome, viewed from northeastern direction. The vertical axis is 30 times exaggerated, the curvature of the lunar surface has been subtracted

8.4.3.2 Error Estimation

According to the analysis by Wöhler et al. (2006b), three main sources of error can be identified in the context of image-based three-dimensional reconstruction of lunar domes based on photoclinometry and shape from shading (this analysis does not refer to the method by Grumpe et al. (2011), which also relies on laser altimetry data). The parameter $L(\alpha)$ of the reflectance function is not exactly known and may show variations over the surface for different terrain types. A standard error of $L(\alpha)$ of 0.15 is assumed, an error range that also includes larger values of the macroscopic surface roughness $\bar{\theta}$ of up to 20° (McEwen, 1991, Fig. 16 therein). The radius σ of the Gaussian PSF for the telescopic CCD images could be estimated at an accuracy of about 0.5 pixel. The uncertainties in $L(\alpha)$ and σ affect the measured height values of the lunar domes by no more than a few metres and can therefore be regarded as irrelevant. The influence of the PSF can be expected to become more important for strongly wrinkled surfaces.

A more important issue is the slight nonlinearity of the CCD sensor, which is compensated by the gamma calibration procedure described in Sect. 8.2.2. The uncertainty of the determined gamma values approximately amounts to 0.05 for the Atik and the ToUCam CCD cameras. The Lumenera CCD camera has a linear ($\gamma = 1.0$) characteristic curve. The uncertainty in γ results in a relative standard error of the dome height h of 10 %, which is independent of the height value itself. The dome diameter D can be measured at an accuracy of 5 %, since the outer rim is not well defined for most domes. Based on experiments, it is shown that these uncertainties in h and D lead to a typical standard error of the edifice volume V, computed by integration of the three-dimensional profile, of about 20 %.

Experiments regarding synthetic image data have shown that the proposed combined photoclinometry and shape from shading approach does not produce systematic errors as long as the gamma value of the camera, the reflectance function, and the PSF radius are known.

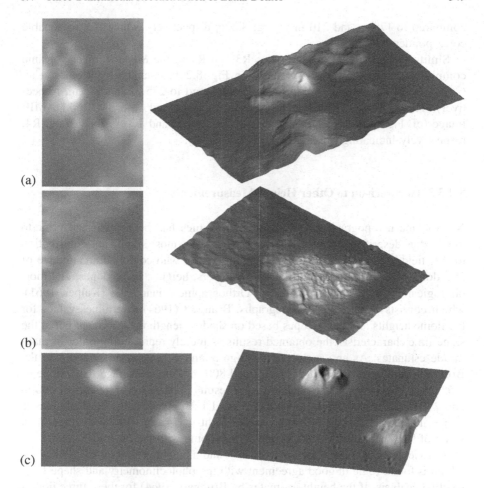

Fig. 8.32 Single-scattering albedo maps and perspecitive views of DEMs of lunar highland domes, constructed based on Figs. 8.20a, b, and d. (**a**) Gruithuisen γ and δ. The albedo map refers to 1210 nm wavelength, the grey value range is 0–0.4. (**b**) Mons Hansteen. The albedo map refers to 1978 nm wavelength, the grey value range is 0–0.55. (**c**) Mairan T and Mairan 'middle'. Image credit: A. Grumpe. The albedo map refers to 1978 nm wavelength, the grey value range is 0–0.55. The DEMs are shown as perspective views with the albedo-dependent modelled reflectance used as an overlay. The vertical axis is three times exaggerated

The dome height values independently obtained based on shadow length measurement according to Ashbrook (1961) may be used for comparison, yielding a good consistency with the corresponding values obtained by photoclinometry and shape from shading (cf. Table 8.1).

When no ground truth is available, the consistency of height measurements across several images is a further good indicator of their reliability. Height values of the domes M3 and M12 were determined based on the images in Figs. 8.22b and 8.22c, which were acquired with different telescopes and CCD cameras from different locations. The obtained dome heights are 190 m and 230 m in Fig. 8.22b, compared to 170 m and 210 m in Fig. 8.22c, respectively, which is a reasonable correspondence.

Similarly, the heights of the domes R3 and R4 in the Mons Rümker volcanic complex according to the DEM shown in Fig. 8.29b, obtained by Wöhler et al. (2007a) using a telescopic CCD image, correspond to 275 m and 185 m, respectively. The DEM shown in Fig. 8.29d, constructed based on a SMART-1 AMIE image (cf. Fig. 8.29c), yields height values of 240 m and 170 m for R3 and R4, respectively, indicating a high degree of consistency.

8.4.3.3 Comparison to Other Height Measurements

Not too much topographic data about lunar domes had been published prior to the studies described in the previous sections. The most significant contribution to this field has been provided by Brungart (1964), who compiled a catalogue of 261 domes reporting their coordinates, diameters, heights, flank slopes, and morphological characteristics, utilising the Orthographic Lunar Atlas (Kuiper, 1961), which consists of telescopic photographs. Brungart (1964) determines values for the dome heights and flank slopes based on shadow length measurement but at the same time characterises the obtained results as merely representing order of magnitude estimates. As an example, for Arago α and β (entries no. 3 and 4 in the Brungart catalogue) a height of 700 m and 800 m with an average flank slope of 5.5° and 6.0° is reported, respectively. Our results indicate lower heights of 330 m and 270 m along with flank slopes of 1.5° and 1.3°, respectively. For Milichius π (entry no. 190), Brungart (1964) states a height of 742 m with an average flank slope of 9°. An estimate of the height of this dome with the method of Ashbrook (1961) yields an average slope angle of 2.7° and a height of 230 m (cf. Table 8.1), which is found to be in good agreement with the photoclinometry and shape from shading analysis. If the height estimates by Brungart (1964) for these three domes were correct, the domes would have to display shadows of length 13.5 km, 9.9 km, and 15.7 km in Figs. 8.21c and 8.21a, respectively, which is clearly not the case. Similarly, the height estimates for the domes H1–H6 near Hortensius are systematically higher than those obtained based on photoclinometry and shape from shading by a factor of two and more, and for the flank slopes values of up to 20° are stated. The height and flank slope values given by Brungart (1964) for these domes would imply large shadows of a length of up to 25 km for the domes in Fig. 8.22b, which do not exist. From these results it can be concluded that the height estimates of Brungart (1964) are systematically too high by a significant amount. This finding clearly shows how difficult it is to accurately measure shadow lengths in high-contrasted photographic reproductions, since shading effects are easily confused with black shadows, leading to a systematic overestimation of height and flank slope.

Accurate height measurements of lunar volcanic edifices are presented by Pike and Clow (1981). Their data set primarily contains lunar cones, but they have also

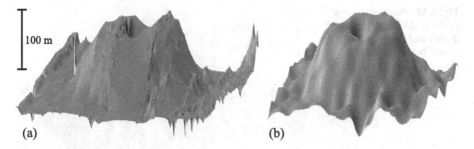

(a)   (b)

Fig. 8.33 Perspective view of (**a**) the LOLA DEM and (**b**) the GLD100 of the mare dome Cauchy ω (C2) from southeastern direction. The vertical axis is 50 times exaggerated

Fig. 8.34 High-resolution Lunar Topophotomap LT 61A2S1 (50), showing the dome pair Diana and Grace. The contour interval corresponds to 20 m, the diameter of the dome Grace is 8 km. Image credit: NASA/LPI

determined the height of the mare dome Cauchy ω (C2) situated in Mare Tranquillitatis, stating a value of 116 m. The LOLA DEM and the GLD100 of Cauchy ω are shown in Fig. 8.33. They both yield a height value of 120 m. The dome height of 125 m obtained by means of photoclinometry and shape from shading analysis is in good agreement. For comparison, the corresponding height value by Brungart (1964) of 306 m (entry no. 36) is again too large.

Fig. 8.35 Perspective view of the GLD100 of Diana (*left dome*) and Grace (*right dome*) from southeastern direction. The vertical axis is 30 times exaggerated

Table 8.2 Comparison of shape from shading-based dome heights obtained by Wöhler et al. (2006b, 2007b) (index 'sfs') and height values inferred from the GLD100 constructed by Scholten et al. (2011)

Dome	$h_{sfs}(m)$	h_{GLD100} (m)	Dome	h_{sfs} (m)	h_{GLD100} (m)
A2 (Arago α)	330	350	C4	50	51
A3 (Arago β)	270	275	K1 (Kies π)	160	180
C1	25	23	M12 (Milichius π)	230	225
C2 (Cauchy ω)	125	120	Diana	70	80
C3 (Cauchy τ)	190	209	Grace	140	144

The domes Diana and Grace appear in the high-resolution Lunar Topophotomap LT 61A2S1 (50) (cf. Fig. 8.34).[9] For Diana, this topographic map yields an elevation difference with respect to the surrounding mare plain of 80 m on the western and 50 m on the eastern flank. The corresponding values for Grace are 100 m on the western and 140 m on the eastern flank. The GLD100 yields height values of 80 m and 144 m for Diana and Grace, respectively (cf. Fig. 8.35). Based on the telescopic CCD image shown in Fig. 8.21a, the photoclinometry and shape from shading analysis yields height values of 70 m and 140 m for Diana and Grace, respectively, which is in good accordance with the results derived from orbital imagery.

For several domes, Table 8.2 provides a comparison between the heights determined by Wöhler et al. (2006b, 2007b) based on shape from shading analysis using telescopic CCD images and those inferred from the GLD100. Given the 10 % error interval derived in Sect. 8.4.3.2 for the shape from shading-based measurements and the elevation accuracy of the GLD100 of 23 m stated by Scholten et al. (2011), the height values are generally consistent.

---

[9]The Lunar Topophotomap series is accessible at http://www.lpi.usra.edu/resources/mapcatalog/topophoto/.

8.4.4 Discussion

Topographic mapping of planetary bodies is no end in itself but—especially for the Moon—a precondition for a deeper understanding of the geophysical processes that occurred in their early geologic history and formed their surfaces.

A novel classification scheme for 'monogenetic' lunar mare domes, which were formed during a single eruption event, is introduced by Wöhler et al. (2006b, 2007b). It refines the classes 1–3 by Head and Gifford (1980) based on the morphometric properties, i.e. the diameter, height, average flank slope, and volume of the volcanic edifice measured by shape from shading analysis, as well as on the spectral properties of the dome surface inferred from multispectral images of the Clementine spacecraft. This classification scheme suggests a division into four classes, three of which are further subdivided into two subclasses, respectively (cf. Fig. 8.36 for an overview). The morphologically more complex mare domes in the Marius Hills region and near the crater Arago are assigned to two separate classes, while they comprise one class in the scheme by Head and Gifford (1980). The morphometric properties inferred for the examined set of mare domes are used to estimate the viscosity of the dome-forming magma, its effusion rate, and the duration of the effusion process, using a model originally developed by Wilson and Head (2003) for lunar highland domes. It is mentioned qualitatively by Weitz and Head (1999) that the flank slopes of lunar domes increase with increasing lava viscosity and decreasing lava effusion rate. These relations are confirmed quantitatively by the modelling analyses of Wilson and Head (2003) and Wöhler et al. (2006b). Similar analyses are performed by Lena et al. (2009) for the volcanic edifices in the Marius Hills region.

According to Wilson and Head (1996, 2002), the magma was under pressure and formed narrow, elongated crustal fractures, called dikes, during its ascent to the surface. Based on a dike model introduced by Rubin (1993) and applied to lunar highland domes by Wilson and Head (2003), the dimensions of the dikes that formed lunar mare domes are estimated by Wöhler et al. (2007b) along with the velocity at which the magma ascended through them. By comparing the time scales of magma ascent through a dike with the time scales on which heat was conducted from the magma into the surrounding rock, evidence is found that the importance of 'magma evolution' processes during ascent such as cooling and crystallisation increases with increasing lava viscosity.

The study by Wöhler and Lena (2009) regards elongated lunar mare domes with very low flank slopes of typically only some tenths of a degree. These domes were not formed by lava effusion but possibly by an uplift of small parts of the lunar crust by pressurised magma which had intruded between rock layers below the surface. Such magmatic intrusions are termed 'laccoliths'. These 'candidate intrusive domes' (cf. the Valentine dome shown in Fig. 8.24f as an example) are examined in terms of the classical laccolith model introduced by Kerr and Pollard (1998) in order to estimate the intrusion depth and the magma pressure based on the morphometric properties inferred from shape from shading anal-

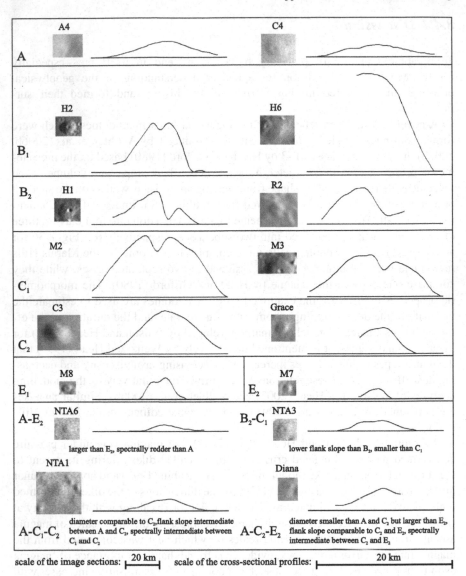

scale of the image sections: |—20 km—| scale of the cross-sectional profiles: |————20 km————|

Fig. 8.36 Images and cross sections of typical representatives of the monogenetic mare dome classes and the continuum between them according to Wöhler et al. (2007b). The image sections were extracted from the telescopic images shown in Figs. 8.21–8.25. The horizontal extension of all cross sections is 20 km, their vertical axes are 30 times exaggerated

ysis. Relying on these morphometric data, Michaut (2010) performs a numerical analysis of the growth of lunar laccoliths in comparison to terrestrial laccoliths.

It is important to note that these fairly detailed geophysical conclusions about lunar domes and the mechanisms behind their formation could only be drawn based on morphometric properties obtained by image-based three-dimensional surface reconstruction methods.

Chapter 9
Conclusion

This work has described the state of the art in three-dimensional computer vision as well as achievements which have resulted from a variety of newly introduced methods. In this final chapter we discuss the main contributions of this work and possible future research directions.

The first part of this work has discussed three very general classes of three-dimensional computer vision methods. As a first class of methods for three-dimensional scene reconstruction, triangulation-based approaches have been regarded. We have seen that three-dimensional scene reconstruction based on point correspondences between a set of images is a problem for which theoretically well-founded mathematical frameworks are available in the contexts of classical bundle adjustment and projective geometry. Similarly, intrinsic and extrinsic camera calibration and self-calibration are solved problems for which many different solutions exist. As a general rule, camera calibration based on linear methods in the framework of projective geometry should be refined by a bundle adjustment stage. The relative accuracies of linear projective geometry methods and bundle adjustment approaches for three-dimensional scene reconstruction and camera calibration strongly depend on the utilised camera system and on the application at hand, such that general rules are hard to obtain.

A major drawback even for recent camera calibration systems is the fact that the calibration rig has to be identified more or less manually in the images. At this point important progress has been achieved in this work by introducing a graph-based method for the automatic detection of the calibration rig and its orientation. It has been shown that for wide-angle lenses with strong distortions or non-pinhole optical systems such as fisheye lenses or catadioptric omnidirectional cameras, it is preferable to use chequerboard patterns instead of photogrammetric retro-reflective markers as calibration rigs. For such optical systems, nontrivial corrections need to be applied to the measured centres of circular markers while chequerboard corner locations are point features and thus bias-free. A method for the localisation of chequerboard corners at high accuracy based on a physical model of the point spread function of the lens has been introduced; this method yields an accuracy comparable to that of a circular marker detector under favourable illumination conditions while showing a significantly more robust behaviour in the presence of low contrast or non-uniform illumination. At the same time, the proposed approach is clearly superior to previous chequerboard corner localisation techniques.

In the context of stereo vision, various blockmatching, feature-based, dense, and spacetime methods have been described. A contour-based approach to the determination of accurate disparity values has been proposed for camera-based safeguarding of workspaces in the industrial production scenario. Spacetime stereo approaches which determine motion information along with the three-dimensional scene structure have recently emerged but are not yet often applied in computer vision systems. In this context, a novel spacetime stereo method based on local intensity modelling has been introduced. Along with the three-dimensional position of a scene point, the model adaptation yields information about the motion along the epipolar line and along the depth axis. Furthermore, a generally applicable framework for suppressing false stereo correspondences due to repetitive structures in the scene has been proposed.

An introduction to methods for three-dimensional pose estimation of rigid, non-rigid, and articulated objects has been provided. A template-based monocular approach for pose estimation of rigid objects has been proposed which relies on CAD data of the object and does not require a priori information about the pose. To determine the three-dimensional structure of non-rigid objects in the scene, which display an infinite number of degrees of freedom, a multiple-view ziplock ribbon snake technique has been developed. For segmenting moving objects from a three-dimensional point cloud and tracking them over time, an approach based on the mean-shift clustering method has been described. For the pose estimation of articulated objects such as human body parts, consisting of several rigid parts related to each other by internal degrees of freedom, the multiocular contracting curve density (MOCCD) algorithm has been proposed as a robust appearance-based approach. Provided that an initial guess of the pose parameters is available, it allows one to refine the pose of an object and track it over time at high accuracy in the presence of a strongly cluttered scene background and low contrast between the object and the background. To address the problem of three-dimensional pose estimation of articulated objects in the absence of prior knowledge, a further proposed approach performs a model-based segmentation of a motion-attributed point cloud along with an estimation of the object pose and its temporal derivative. This method relies on the disparity values and the low-level motion information extracted by spacetime stereo. Another proposed point cloud segmentation approach relies on the extraction of motion-attributed clusters from spacetime stereo data, which are then used for generating and tracking object hypotheses based on a kernel particle filter framework. In this context, a general insight is that using motion-attributed three-dimensional point cloud data is favourable, if not essential, for performing robust segmentation and tracking of objects in three-dimensional point clouds.

The second class of three-dimensional scene reconstruction methods regarded in this work are intensity-based methods, where we have concentrated on approaches related to shadow analysis, photoclinometry, shape from shading, photometric stereo, and shape from polarisation. It has been shown that photoclinometric approaches that aim for a reconstruction of cross-sectional surface profiles, which were originally developed in the domain of planetary remote sensing in the middle of the twentieth century, are closely related to the shape from shading methods developed about three decades ago in the domain of computer vision. If information about the reflectance properties of the surface is available, intensity-based approaches may provide fairly accurate information about the surface gradients, which in turn yield the three-dimensional surface shape. However, a drawback of most shape from shading methods is that they only converge towards a solution if additional constraints such as smoothness or integrability of the surface are applied. Furthermore, the determined solution is generally not unique. Shape from shading methods which yield a unique solution based on a partial differential equation approach are restricted to Lambertian surfaces and require a priori knowledge about the position of local minima of the surface, which is not necessarily straightforward to obtain.

Some of these drawbacks are alleviated when several pixel-synchronous images acquired under different illumination conditions are available for an evaluation in terms of photometric stereo. The classical approach relies on three pixel-synchronous images of the scene acquired under different illumination conditions and yields a unique configuration of albedo and surface gradients for each pixel, which can be computed by a pixel-wise matrix inversion procedure as long as the surface is Lambertian. The described ratio-based photoclinometric and photometric stereo methods relying on two pixel-synchronous images are suitable for a more general class of reflectance functions. In contrast to the classical photometric stereo approach, they can be used in the presence of the coplanar illumination vectors often encountered in remote sensing scenarios.

Furthermore, an extension of the shape from shading framework to the determination of surface orientation from polarisation information has been described. Accurate and physically well-defined polarisation models based on the Fresnel theory are available for smooth dielectric surfaces. An approximate description can still be obtained according to the refraction law for smooth, specularly reflecting metallic surfaces. Rough metallic surfaces, however, have a more complex polarisation behaviour for which no accurate physical models are available so far. Hence, we have proposed an empirical framework to determine the dependence between the polarisation properties of rough metallic surfaces and the observing and illumination geometry.

The third examined class of three-dimensional reconstruction methods is that of the point spread function (PSF)-based approaches. They exploit the dependence of the PSF on the distance between the camera and the object. Depth from defocus approaches measure the width of the PSF and infer the object depth based on a previously determined relation between these two values. While classical PSF-based methods assume that this dependence can be well described in terms of geometric optics, this work has shown that an empirical approach based on a suitable calibration of the lens (which may be performed simultaneously with geometric camera calibration) is preferable. The depth–defocus function introduced in this context has been shown to represent the observed relation between object depth and width of the PSF much better than the relation inferred from geometric optics. A general property of the depth from defocus approach is that it yields dense but fairly inaccurate and noisy depth maps. It has been demonstrated analytically that depth from defocus should be preferentially utilised in close-range scenarios. A further class of PSF-based methods, depth from focus techniques, search for the point of best focus by moving the camera or the object and are thus accurate but slow.

The described classes of three-dimensional reconstruction methods all have their specific advantages and drawbacks. Some of the techniques have complementary properties—triangulation-based methods determine three-dimensional point clouds describing textured parts of the scene, while intensity-based methods may be able to reconstruct textureless regions. Hence, it is favourable for computer vision systems to integrate different three-dimensional scene reconstruction methods into a unifying framework. The first described integrated approach combines structure from motion and depth from defocus and yields a three-dimensional point cloud of the scene along with the absolute scaling factor without the need for a priori knowledge about the scene or the camera motion. Several quantities that influence the accuracy of this approach, such as pixel noise, the nonlinearity of the depth–defocus function, and temperature effects, are discussed. Another integrated approach combines shadow and shading features for three-dimensional surface reconstruction, alleviating the ambiguity of the shape from shading solution. The shape from photopolarimetric reflectance and depth method integrates photopolarimetric information with depth information that can in principle be obtained from arbitrary sources. In this context, depth from defocus information can be favourably used to determine the large-scale properties of the surface, to appropriately initialise the surface gradients, and to estimate the surface albedo. Sparse depth information is incorporated by transforming it into dense depth difference information, such that the three-dimensional reconstruction accuracy is significantly increased, especially on large scales. The shape from photopolarimetric reflectance and depth method has been extended to an iterative scheme for stereo image analysis of non-Lambertian surfaces. This approach overcomes the general drawback of classical stereo approaches, which implicitly assume a Lambertian surface reflectance when establishing point correspondences between images. Disparity estimation is performed based on a comparison between the observation and the surface model, leading to a refined disparity map with a strongly reduced number of outliers. Furthermore, the combination of active range scanning data with photometric image information has been demonstrated to perform a three-dimensional surface reconstruction at high lateral and depth resolution. Another integrated approach has been introduced to address the problem of monocular three-dimensional pose refinement of rigid objects based on photopolarimetric, edge, and depth from defocus information. It has been demonstrated that the combination of various monocular cues allows one to determine all six pose parameters of a rigid object at high accuracy.

The second part of this work has addressed several scenarios in which three-dimensional computer vision methods are favourably applied. The first regarded application scenario is quality inspection of industrial parts. For the three-dimensional pose estimation of rigid parts, the proposed combined methods have turned out to yield rotational pose parameters of an accuracy of a few tenths of a degree. It has been shown that these accuracies are significantly higher than those obtained with previously existing methods that mostly rely on edge information. This favourable behaviour can be attributed to the inclusion of photopolarimetric information. The accuracy of the determined lateral object position is largely given by the pixel resolution of the image. The depth accuracy obtained from defocus information comes close to the accuracies reported in the literature for systems performing pose estimation in stereo image pairs.

The three-dimensional pose estimation of non-rigid parts (cables and tubes) has been demonstrated based on the multiocular ziplock ribbon snake method. It has been employed in a robot-based system in which the result of pose estimation is utilised for gripping a non-rigid object. The localisation accuracy of this approach has been shown to be comparable to the pixel resolution of the image.

The integrated frameworks involving the combination of shadow and shading features, shape from photopolarimetric reflectance and depth, and specular stereo have been applied to the three-dimensional reconstruction of rough metallic surfaces. The accuracy of depth differences on the surface is typically better than the lateral pixel resolution of the utilised images. For poorly known reflectance parameters, a graceful degradation of the reconstruction accuracy is observed. For the combination of intensity-based methods with depth data acquired by active range scanning devices, similar accuracies have been obtained.

A different application scenario is safe human–robot interaction in the industrial production environment. Existing camera-based safety systems which are either still under investigation or already commercially available have been discussed. Furthermore, an overview of vision-based gesture recognition methods for human–robot interaction has been provided. This discussion has led to the conclusion that most of the existing approaches are not well suitable for safety systems. Their performance tends to decrease in the presence of a cluttered background, many of them depend on skin colour cues, which are unsuitable for detecting humans in the industrial production environment, and a high accuracy of the localisation and pose estimation of the hand is often only obtained if a user-specific model is available. Hence, we have evaluated the proposed methods for segmentation of three-dimensional point clouds and model-based object localisation and pose estimation in the context of human–robot interaction. Merely relying on coarse object models, the motion of a human through an industrial workspace as well as the motion of the hand–forearm limb through a scene with a cluttered background can be reliably tracked. It is not necessary to adapt these systems to the individual human being regarded. Similarly, encouraging results have been obtained for the MOCCD and the shape flow algorithm, which are used for tracking the hand–forearm limb through highly complex cluttered scenes. Based on the obtained three-dimensional reconstruction results, it has been demonstrated that a robust automatic recognition of a sequence of working actions is possible in a realistic industrial environment.

The third application scenario refers to the generation of topographic maps in the domain of lunar remote sensing. Methods based on radar and laser altimetry, shadow length measurements, stereo and multi-image photogrammetry, and photoclinometry are well established with respect to the extraction of regional or global topographic data of various solar system bodies. Global lunar digital elevation models (DEMs) obtained based on laser altimetry and stereophotogrammetry have become available recently. To construct local DEMs of the lunar surface of high lateral resolution, we have applied the proposed intensity-based methods to the three-dimensional reconstruction of lunar craters, low wrinkle ridges and faults, and domes, mainly based on telescopic lunar images acquired with CCD cameras but also utilising recent images by the SMART-1 and Chandrayaan-1 spacecraft. In this context we have given an introduction to the reflectance behaviour of planetary regolith surfaces. The presented digital elevation maps of lunar craters are of higher resolution than the available topographic maps, while the extracted basic features (e.g. crater depth) are consistent with the existing data. A direct comparison has shown that for the examined lunar domes, the height values obtained with the proposed intensity-based methods based on telescopic CCD imagery are comparable to those inferred from recent topographic spacecraft data.

In light of the described progress in the field of three-dimensional computer vision methods and their extensive evaluation in several strongly different real-world application scenarios, future research directions emerge.

For example, the proposed frameworks for three-dimensional reconstruction of metallic surfaces should be extended to a determination of the (generally spatially non-uniform) reflectance properties in parallel with the three-dimensional surface reconstruction. Furthermore, it will be necessary to take into account interreflections for increasing the three-dimensional reconstruction accuracy.

In the domain of safe human–robot interaction, the presented methods for action recognition based on the extracted three-dimensional reconstruction results should be developed further to increase the contextual and situational knowledge of the safety system.

The encouraging results obtained with the proposed integrated frameworks for three-dimensional surface reconstruction furthermore suggest that photometric image information should be utilised in combination with classical triangulation-based photogrammetric evaluation techniques for the purpose of regional or global topographic mapping of planetary bodies in the context of future mapping activities. Possible examples are the construction of detailed topographic maps of the planet Mercury based on image data from the MESSENGER spacecraft or of asteroids using images acquired by the Dawn spacecraft. For the Moon, it will be possible to significantly increase the resolution of existing topographic maps by incorporating photometric image information.

References

Abdel-Aziz, Y. I., Karara, H. M., 1971. Direct linear transformation from comparator coordinates into object space coordinates in close-range photogrammetry. Proc. of Symp. on Close-Range Photogrammetry, American Society of Photogrammetry, Falls Church, pp. 1–18.

Agrawal, A., Chellappa, R., Raskar, R., 2005. An algebraic approach to surface reconstruction from gradient fields. Proc. Int. Conf. on Computer Vision, Beijing, China, vol. 1, pp. 174–181.

Ahmed, A., Farag, A., 2007. Shape from shading under various imaging conditions. Proc. IEEE Int. Conf. on Computer Vision and Pattern Recognition, pp. 1–8.

Akima, H., 1970. A new method of interpolation and smooth curve fitting based on local procedures. J. Assoc. Comput. Mach. 17(4), pp. 589–602.

Alldrin, N., Zickler, T., Kriegman, D., 2008. Photometric stereo with non-parametric and spatially varying reflectance. Proc. IEEE Int. Conf. on Computer Vision and Pattern Recognition, Anchorage, USA.

Amberg, B., Blake, A., Fitzgibbon, A., Romdhani, S., Vetter, T., 2007. Reconstructing high quality face-surfaces using model based stereo. Proc. Int. Conf. on Computer Vision, pp. 1–8.

Ando, S., Kusachi, Y., Suzuki, A., Arakawa, K., 2005. Appearance based pose estimation of 3D object using support vector regression. Proc. IEEE Int. Conf. on Image Processing, I, pp. 341–344.

Araki, H., Tazawa, S., Noda, H., Ishihara, Y., Goossens, S., Kawano, N., Sasaki, S., Kamiya, I., Otake, H., Oberst, J., Shum, C. K., 2009. The lunar global topography by the laser altimeter (LALT) onboard Kaguya (SELENE): results from the one year observation. Lunar Planet. Sci. XXXX, abstract #1432.

Aschwanden, P. F., 1993. Experimenteller Vergleich von Korrelationskriterien in der Bildanalyse. Hartung-Gorre-Verlag, Konstanz.

Ashbrook, J., 1961. Dimensions of the Lunar Dome Kies 1. J. Assoc. Lunar Planet. Obs. 15(1–2), pp. 1–3.

Atkinson, G. A., Hancock, E. R., 2005a. Analysis of directional reflectance and surface orientation using Fresnel theory. Proc. Iberoamerican Congress on Pattern Recognition, Beijing, pp. 103–111.

Atkinson, G. A., Hancock, E. R., 2005b. Multi-view surface reconstruction using polarization. Proc. Int. Conf. on Computer Vision, Beijing, pp. 309–316.

Bachler, G., Berger, M., Röhrer, R., Scherer, S., Pinz, A., 1999. A vision driven automatic assembly unit. Proc. International Conference on Computer Analysis of Images and Patterns, Ljubljana, Slovenia, pp. 375–382.

Baerveldt, A.-J., 1992. A safety system for close interaction between man and robot. Proc. IFAC Int. Conf. on Safety, Security and Reliability of Computers, Zurich, Switzerland.

Baker, H. H., Binford, T. O., 1981. Depth from edge and intensity based stereo. Proc. Int. Joint Conf. on Artificial Intelligence, Vancouver, Canada, pp. 631–636.

Barrois, B., 2010. Analyse der Position, Orientierung und Bewegung von rigiden und artikulierten Objekten aus Stereobildsequenzen. Doctoral Dissertation, Technical Faculty, Bielefeld University, Germany.

Barrois, B., Wöhler, C., 2007. 3D pose estimation based on multiple monocular cues. ISPRS Workshop Towards Benchmarking Automated Calibration, Orientation and Surface Reconstruction from Images (BenCOS), held in conjunction with CVPR 2007, Minneapolis, USA.

Barrois, B., Konrad, M., Wöhler, C., Groß, H.-M., 2010. Resolving stereo matching errors due to repetitive structures using model information. Pattern Recognit. Lett. 31, pp. 1683–1692.

Barrois, B., Wöhler, C., 2008. Spatio-temporal 3D pose estimation of objects in stereo images. In: Gasteratos, A., Vincze, M., Tsotsos, J. (eds.), Proc. Int. Conf. on Computer Vision Systems, Santorini, Greece. Lecture Notes in Computer Science 5008, pp. 507–516, Springer, Berlin.

Barron, J. T., Malik, J., 2011. High-frequency shape and albedo from shading using natural image statistics. Proc. IEEE Int. Conf. on Computer Vision and Pattern Recognition, pp. 2521–2528.

Barrow, H., 1977. Parametric correspondence and chamfer matching: two new techniques for image matching. Proc. Int. Joint Conf. on Artificial Intelligence, pp. 659–663.

Batlle, J., Mouaddib, E., Salvi, J., 1998. Recent progress in coded structured light as a technique to solve the correspondence problem: a survey. Pattern Recognit. 31(7), pp. 963–982.

Bauckhage, C., Hanheide, M., Wrede, S., Käster, T., Pfeiffer, M., Sagerer, G., 2005. Vision systems with the human in the loop. EURASIP J. Appl. Signal Process. 2005(14), pp. 2375–2390.

Baumgardner, J., Mendillo, M., Wilson, J. K., 2000. A digital high definition imaging system for spectral studies of extended planetary atmospheres, 1. Initial result in white light showing features on the hemisphere of Mercury unimaged by Mariner 10. Astron. J. 119, pp. 2458–2464.

Beraldin, J.-A., 2004. Integration of laser scanning and close-range photogrammetry—the last decade and beyond. Proc. 20th Int. Soc. for Photogrammetry and Remote Sensing Congress, Commission VII, pp. 972–983.

Besl, P. J., McKay, N. D., 1992. A method for registration of 3-D shapes. IEEE Trans. Pattern Anal. Mach. Intell. 14(2), pp. 239–256.

Beyer, R. A., McEwen, A. S., 2002. Photoclinometric measurements of meter-scale slopes for the potential landing sites of the 2003 Mars Exploration Rovers. Proc. Lunar Planet. Sci. XXXIII, abstract #1443.

Bhat, D. N., Nayar, S. K., 1998. Stereo and specular reflection Int. J. Comput. Vis. 26(2), pp. 91–106.

Biber, P., Andreasson, H., Duckett, T., Schilling, A., 2004. 3D modeling of indoor environments by a mobile robot with a laser scanner and panoramic camera. Proc. IEEE/RSJ Int. Conf. Intell. Robots Syst., 4, pp. 3430–3435.

Birchfield, S., 1998. An Introduction to Projective Geometry (for Computer Vision). http://www.ces.clemson.edu/stb/projective/ (accessed October 16, 2007).

Black, M. J., Jepson, A. D., 1998. A probabilistic framework for matching temporal trajectories: CONDENSATION-based recognition of gestures and expressions. Proc. Europ. Conf. on Computer Vision, LNCS 1406, pp. 909–924, Springer, Berlin.

Blake, A., Isard, M., 1998. Active Contours. Springer, London.

Bock, H. H., 1974. Automatische Klassifikation. Vandenhoeck & Ruprecht, Göttingen.

Bouguet, J.-Y., 1999. Visual Methods for Three-Dimensional Modeling. PhD thesis, California Institute of Technology, Pasadena.

Bouguet, J.-Y., 2007. Camera Calibration Toolbox for Matlab. http://www.vision.caltech.edu/bouguetj/calib_doc/ (accessed September 04, 2007).

Bradski, G. R., 1998. Real time face and object tracking as a component of a perceptual user interface. Proc. Workshop on Appl. of Computer Vision, pp. 214–219.

Bronstein, I. N., Semendjajew, K. A., 1989. Taschenbuch der Mathematik. Verlag Harri Deutsch, Frankfurt a. M.

Brown, D. C., 1966. Decentering distortion of lenses. Photom. Eng. 32(3), pp. 444–462.

Brown, D. C., 1971. Close-range camera calibration. Photom. Eng. 37(8), pp. 855–866.

Brox, T., Rosenhahn, B., Cremers, D., 2008. Contours, optic flow, and prior knowledge: cues for capturing 3D human motion from videos. In: Rosenhahn, B., Klette, R., Metaxas, D. (eds.), Human Motion: Understanding, Modelling, Capture and Animation. Springer, Dordrecht.

Brungart, D. L., 1964. The Origin of Lunar Domes. M.Sc. thesis, Airforce Institute of Technology, Wright Patterson Air Force Base, Ohio, USA.

Bruss, A., 1989. The eikonal equation: some results applicable to computer vision. In: Horn, B. K. P., Brooks, M. (eds.). Shape from Shading. MIT Press, Cambridge.

Bussey, C., Spudis, P., 2004. The Clementine Atlas of the Moon. Cambridge University Press, Cambridge.

Campbell, L. W., Becker, D. A., Azarbayejani, A., Bobick, A., Pentland, A., 1996. Invariant features for 3-D gesture recognition. Proc. Int. Workshop on Face and Gesture Recognition, Killington, USA, pp. 157–162.

Cañero, C., Radeva, P., Toledo, R., Villanueva, J. J., Mauri, J., 2000. 3D curve reconstruction by biplane snakes. Proc. Int. Conf. on Pattern Recognition, Barcelona, Spain, vol. 4, pp. 4563–4567.

Canny, J., 1986. A computational approach to edge detection. IEEE Trans. Pattern Anal. Mach. Intell. 8, pp. 679–698.

Caselles, V., Kimmel, R., Sapiro, G., 1995. Geodesic active contours. Proc. Int. Conf. on Computer Vision, Boston, USA, pp. 694–699.

Caselles, V., Kimmel, R., Sapiro, G., 1997. Geodesic active contours. Int. J. Comput. Vis. 22, pp. 61–79.

Chan, T., Vese, L., 2001. Active contours without edges. IEEE Trans. Image Process. 10(2), pp. 266–277.

Chandrasekhar, S., 1950. Radiative Transfer. Oxford University, London.

Chang, J. Y., Raskar, R., Agrawal, A., 2009. 3D pose estimation and segmentation using specular cues. Proc. IEEE Conf. on Computer Vision and Pattern Recognition, pp. 1706–1713.

Chaudhuri, S., Rajagopalan, A. N., 1999. Depth from Defocus: A Real Aperture Imaging Approach. Springer, New York.

Chen, D., Zhang, G., 2005. A new sub-pixel detector for x-corners in camera calibration targets. Proc. 13th International Conference in Central Europe on Computer Graphics, Visualization and Computer Vision.

Cheng, Y., 1995. Mean shift, mode seeking, and clustering. IEEE Trans. Pattern Anal. Mach. Intell. 17, pp. 790–799.

Cintala, M. J., Head, J. W., Mutch, T. A., 1976. Craters on the Moon, Mars, and Mercury: a comparison of depth/diameter characteristics. Proc. Lunar Planet. Sci. VII, pp. 149–151.

Cipolla, R., Drummond, T., Robertson, D., 1999. Camera calibration from vanishing points in images of architectural scenes. Proc. 10th British Machine Vision Conference, Nottingham, UK, pp. 382–391.

Clarke, T. A., Fryer, J. F., 1998. The development of camera calibration methods and models. Photogramm. Rec. 16(91), pp. 51–66.

Cohen, L. D., 1991. On active contour models and balloons. CVGIP, Image Underst. 53(2), pp. 211–218.

Cohen, L. D., Cohen, I., 1993. Finite element methods for active contour models and balloons for 2d and 3d images. IEEE Trans. Pattern Anal. Mach. Intell. 15(11), pp. 1131–1147.

Collet, A., Martinez, M., Srinivasa, S., 2011. The MOPED framework: object recognition and pose estimation for manipulation. Int. J. Robot. Res. 30(10), pp. 1284–1306.

Comaniciu, D., Meer, P., 2002. Mean shift: a robust approach toward feature space analysis. IEEE Trans. Pattern Anal. Mach. Intell. 24(5), pp. 603–619.

Comaniciu, D., Ramesh, V., Meer, P., 2000. Real-time tracking of non-rigid objects using mean shift. Proc. IEEE Conf. on Computer Vision and Pattern Recognition, 2, pp. 142–149.

Cook, A. C., 2007. Lunar Digital Elevation Models. http://users.aber.ac.uk/atc/dems.html (accessed November 05, 2007).

Cook, A. C., Spudis, P. D., Robinson, M. S., Watters, T. R., Bussey, D. B. J., 1999. The topography of the lunar poles from digital stereo analysis. Proc. Lunar Planet. Sci. XXX, abstract #1154.

Cox, I., Hingorani, S., Rao, S., 1996. A maximum likelihood stereo algorithm. Comput. Vis. Image Underst. 63(3), pp. 542–567.

Craig, J. J., 1989. Introduction to Robotics, Mechanics and Control. Addison-Wesley, Reading.

Cryer, J.E., Tsai, P.-S., Shah, M., 1995. Integration of shape from shading and stereo. Pattern Recognit., 28(7), pp. 1033–1043.

d'Angelo, P., 2007. 3D Scene Reconstruction by Integration of Photometric and Geometric Methods. Doctoral Dissertation, Technical Faculty, Bielefeld University, Germany.

d'Angelo, P., Wöhler, C., Krüger, L., 2004. Model based multi-view active contours for quality inspection. Proc. Int. Conf. on Computer Vision and Graphics, Warszaw, Poland.

d'Angelo, P., Wöhler, C., 2005a. 3D reconstruction of metallic surfaces by photopolarimetric analysis. In: Kalviainen, H., Parkkinen, J., Kaarna, A. (eds.), Proc. 14th Scand. Conf. on Image Analysis, Joensuu, Finland. Lecture Notes in Computer Science 3540, pp. 689–698, Springer, Berlin.

d'Angelo, P., Wöhler, C., 2005b. 3D surface reconstruction based on combined analysis of reflectance and polarisation properties: a local approach. ISPRS Workshop Towards Benchmarking Automated Calibration, Orientation and Surface Reconstruction from Images (BenCOS), Beijing, China.

d'Angelo, P., Wöhler, C., 2005c. 3D surface reconstruction by combination of photopolarimetry and depth from defocus. In: Kropatsch, W., Sablatnig, R., Hanbury, A. (eds.). Pattern Recognition, Proc. 27th DAGM Symposium, Vienna, Austria. Lecture Notes in Computer Science 3663, pp. 176–183, Springer, Berlin.

d'Angelo, P., Wöhler, C., 2006. Image-based 3D surface reconstruction by combination of sparse depth data with shape from shading and polarisation. ISPRS Conf. on Photogrammetric Computer Vision, Bonn, Germany.

d'Angelo, P., Wöhler, C., 2008. Image-based 3D surface reconstruction by combination of photometric, geometric, and real-aperture methods. ISPRS J. Photogramm. Remote Sens. 63(3), pp. 297–321.

Davis, T., 2001. Projective Geometry. http://www.geometer.org/mathcircles/projective.pdf (accessed February 09, 2012).

Davis, J., Nehab, D., Ramamoorthi, R., Rusinkiewicz, S., 2005. Spacetime stereo: a unifying framework for depth from triangulation. IEEE Trans. Pattern Anal. Mach. Intell. 27(2), pp. 296–302.

Decaudin, P., 1996. Cartoon Looking Rendering of 3D Scenes. INRIA Research Report 2919.

Demant, C., 1999. Industrial Image Processing. Springer, Berlin.

Deutscher, J., Blake, A., Reid, I., 2001. Articulated body motion capture by annealed particle filtering. Proc. IEEE Conf. on Computer Vision and Pattern Recognition, Kauai, Hawaii, USA, vol. 2, pp. 2126–2133.

Di Stefano, L., Marchionni, M., Mattoccia, S., 2004. A PC-based real-time stereo vision system. Int. J. Mach. Graph. Vision 13(3), 197–220.

Dorsey, J., Rushmeier, H., Sillion, F., 2008. Digital Modeling of Material Appearance. Morgan Kaufmann, Burlington.

Duric, Z., Li, F., Sun, Y., Wechsler, H., 2002. Using normal flow for detection and tracking of limbs in color images. Proc. Int. Conf. on Pattern Recognition, Quebec City, Canada, vol. 4, pp. 268–271.

Durucan, E., 2001. Low Computational Cost Illumination Invariant Change Detection for Video Surveillance by Linear Independence. Thèse no. 2454, Ecole Polytechnique Fédérale de Lausanne.

Ebert, D., Henrich, D., 2003. SIMERO: Sichere Mensch-Roboter-Koexistenz. Proc. Workshop für OTS-Systeme in der Robotik – Mensch und Roboter ohne trennende Schutzsysteme, Stuttgart, Germany, pp. 119–134.

Ellenrieder, M. M., 2004. Shape reconstruction of flexible objects from monocular images for industrial applications. Proc. SPIE Electronic Imaging, Computational Imaging II, San Jose, USA, SPIE 5299, pp. 295–303.

Ellenrieder, M. M., 2005. Optimal Viewpoint Selection for Industrial Machine Vision and Inspection of Flexible Objects. Doctoral Dissertation, Technical Faculty, Bielefeld University, Germany. VDI Fortschritt-Berichte, Reihe 10, no. 763, VDI-Verlag, Düsseldorf.

Erol, A., Bebis, G., Nicolescu, M., Boyle, R. D., Twombly, X., 2007. Vision-based hand pose estimation: a review. Comput. Vis. Image Underst. 108(1–2), pp. 52–73.

European Space Agency, 2006. Kepler Crater as Seen by SMART-1 (June 30, 2006). http://www.esa.int/SPECIALS/SMART-1/SEMBGLVT0PE_2.html (accessed August 22, 2006).

Fassold, H., Danzl, R., Schindler, K., Bischof, H. 2004. Reconstruction of archaeological finds using shape from stereo and shape from shading. Proc. 9th Computer Vision Winter Workshop, Piran, Slovenia, pp. 21–30.

Faugeras, O., 1993. Three-Dimensional Computer Vision (Artificial Intelligence). MIT Press, Cambridge.

Faugeras, O., Hotz, B., Mathieu, H., Viéville, T., Zhang, Z., Fua, P., Théron, E., Moll, L., Berry, G., Vuillemin, J., Bertin, P., Proy, C., 1993. Real Time Correlation-Based Stereo: Algorithm, Implementations and Applications. INRIA Technical report no. 2013. http://perception.inrialpes.fr/Publications/1993/FHMVZFTMBVBP93/RR-2013.pdf (accessed February 10, 2012).

Fenton, L. K., Herkenhoff, K. E., 2000. Topography and stratigraphy of the northern martian polar layered deposits using photoclinometry, stereogrammetry, and MOLA altimetry. Icarus 147(2), pp. 433–443.

Fermüller, C., Aloimonos, Y., 1994. On the geometry of visual correspondence. Int. J. Comput. Vis. 21(3), pp. 223–247.

Fielding, G., Kam, M., 1997. Applying the Hungarian method to stereo matching. Proc. IEEE Conf. on Decision and Control, pp. 549–558.

Fischer, M., Henrich, D., 2009. Surveillance of robots using multiple colour or depth cameras with distributed processing. Proc. ACM/IEEE Int. Conf. on Distributed Smart Cameras.

Fischler, M. A., Bolles, R. C., 1981. Random sample consensus: a paradigm for model fitting with applications to image analysis and automated cartography. Commun. ACM 24(6), pp. 381–395.

Fowlkes, C., Belongie, S., Chung, F., Malik, J., 2004. Spectral grouping using the Nyström method. IEEE Trans. Pattern Anal. Mach. Intell. 26(2), pp. 214–225.

Franke, U., Gavrila, D., Görzig, S., Lindner, F., Paetzold, F., Wöhler, C., 1999. Autonomous driving approaches downtown. IEEE Intell. Syst. 13(6), pp. 40–48.

Franke, U., Joos, A., 2000. Real-time stereo vision for urban traffic scene understanding. Proc. IEEE Conf. on Intelligent Vehicles, Detroit, pp. 273–278.

Franke, U., Kutzbach, I., 1996. Fast stereo based object detection for stop&go traffic. IEEE Int. Conf. on Intelligent Vehicles, Tokyo, pp. 339–344.

Franke, U., Rabe, C., Badino, H., Gehrig, S. K., 2005. 6D-vision: fusion of stereo and motion for robust environment perception. In: Kropatsch, W., Sablatnig, R., Hanbury, A. (eds.). Pattern Recognition, Proc. 27th DAGM Symposium, Vienna, Austria. Lecture Notes in Computer Science 3663, pp. 216–223, Springer, Berlin.

Frankot, R. T., Chellappa, R., 1988. A method for enforcing integrability in shape from shading algorithms. IEEE Trans. Pattern Anal. Mach. Intell. 10(4), pp. 439–451.

Fritsch, J., Hofemann, N., Sagerer, G., 2004. Combining sensory and symbolic data for manipulative gesture recognition. Proc. Int. Conf. on Pattern Recognition, Cambridge, UK, vol. 3, pp. 930–933.

Fua, P., 1993. A parallel stereo algorithm that produces dense depth maps and preserves image features. Mach. Vis. Appl. 6, 35–49.

Fua, P., Brechbühler, C., 1996. Imposing hard constraints on soft snakes. Proc. Europ. Conf. on Computer Vision, Cambridge, UK, vol. 2, pp. 495–506.

Fua, P., Leclerc, Y. G., 1990. Model driven edge detection. Mach. Vis. Appl. 3(1), pp. 45–56.

Fukunaga, K., Hostetler, L. D., 1975. The estimation of the gradient of a density function, with applications in pattern recognition. IEEE Trans. Inf. Theory 21, pp. 32–40.

Fusiello, A., Trucco, E., Verri, A., 2000. A compact algorithm for rectification of stereo pairs. Mach. Vis. Appl. 12, pp. 16–22.

Gaddis, L. R., Tyburczy, J. A., Hawke, B. R., 2000. Mafic characteristics of lunar pyroclastic deposits. Lunar Planet. Sci. XXXI, abstract #1700.

Gaddis, L. R., Staid, M. I., Tyburczy, J. A., Hawke, B. R., Petro, N. E., 2003. Compositional analyses of lunar pyroclastic deposits. Icarus 161, pp. 262–280.

Gall, J., Rosenhahn, B., Brox, T., Seidel, H.-P., 2009. Optimization and filtering for human motion capture—a multi-layer framework. Int. J. Comput. Vis. 87(1–2), pp. 75–92.

Gambini, J., Mejail, M., Jacobo-Berlles, J., Delrieux, C., 2004. SAR image segmentation through B-spline deformable contours and fractal dimension. Proc. 20th ISPRS Congress, XXXV(3), pp. 1159–1163.

Gaskell, R. W., Barnoiun-Jha, O. S., Scheeres, D. J., 2007. Modeling Eros with stereophotoclinometry. Proc. Lunar Planet. Sci. XXXVIII, abstract #1333.

Gavrila, D. M., Davis, L. S., 1996. 3D model-based tracking of humans in action: a multi-view approach. Proc. IEEE Conf. on Computer Vision and Pattern Recognition, pp. 73–80.

Gavrila, D. M., Philomin, V., 1999. Real-time object detection for "smart" vehicles. Proc. Int. Conf. on Computer Vision, Kerkyra, Greece, pp. 87–93.

Gecks, T., Henrich, D., 2005. Human–robot cooperation: safe pick-and-place operations. Proc. IEEE Int. Workshop on Robot and Human Interactive Communication, Nashville, USA.

Gehrke, S., Lehmann, H., Wahlisch, M., Albertz, J., 2006. New large-scale topographic maps of planet mars. Proc. Europ. Planetary Science Congress, Berlin, Germany, p. 228.

Germer, T. A., Rinder, T., Rothe, H., 2000. Polarized light scattering measurements of polished and etched steel surfaces. Scattering and Surface Roughness III, SPIE 4100, pp. 148–155

Gövert, T., 2006. Konzeption und Implementierung eines Systems zur raumzeitlichen konturbasierten 3D-Stereoanalyse im Produktionsszenario. Diplom Thesis, Technical Faculty, Bielefeld University, Germany.

Goldman, B., Curless, B., Hertzmann, A., Seitz, S., 2010. Shape and spatially varying BRDFs from photometric stereo. IEEE Trans. Pattern Anal. Mach. Intell. 32(6), pp. 1060–1071.

Gonçalves, N., Araújo, H., 2002. Estimation of 3D motion from stereo images—differential and discrete formulations. Proc. Int. Conf. on Pattern Recognition, Quebec City, Canada, vol. 1, pp. 335–338.

Gottesfeld Brown, L., 1992. A survey of image registration techniques. ACM Comput. Surv. 24(4), pp. 325–376.

Grammatikopoulos, L., Karras, G., Petsa, E., 2004. Camera calibration combining images with two vanishing points. Int. Archives of the Photogrammetry, Remote Sensing and Spatial Information Sciences XXXV-5, pp. 99–104.

Grammatikopoulos, L., Karras, G., Petsa, E., Kalisperakis, I., 2006. A unified approach for automatic camera calibration from vanishing points. Int. Archives of the Photogrammetry, Remote Sensing and Spatial Information Sciences XXXVI-5.

Grebner, K., 1994. Wissensbasierte Entwicklungsumgebung für Bildanalysesysteme aus dem industriellen Bereich. Doctoral Dissertation, Technical Faculty, Bielefeld University, Germany.

Grest, D., Koch, R., 2008. Motion capture for interaction environments. In: Rosenhahn, B., Klette, R., Metaxas, D. (eds.), Human Motion: Understanding, Modelling, Capture and Animation, Springer, Dordrecht.

Grieger, B., Beauvivre, S., Despan, D., Erard, S., Josset, J.-L., Koschny, D., 2008. Investigating a peak of (almost) eternal light close to the lunar south pole with SMART-1/AMIE images. Proc. European Planetary Science Congress, EPSC2008-A-00205, Münster, Germany.

Groß, H.-M., Richarz, J., Mueller, S., Scheidig, A., Martin, C., 2006. Probabilistic multi-modal people tracker and monocular pointing pose estimator for visual instruction of mobile robot assistants. Proc. IEEE World Congress on Computational Intelligence and Int. Conf. on Neural Networks, pp. 8325–8333.

Grumpe, A., Herbort, S., Wöhler, C., 2011. 3D reconstruction of non-Lambertian surfaces with non-uniform reflectance parameters by fusion of photometrically estimated surface normal data with active range scanner data. Proc. Oldenburger 3D-Tage, Oldenburg, Germany, pp. 54–61.

Grumpe, A., Wöhler, C., 2011. DEM construction and calibration of hyperspectral image data using pairs of radiance images. Proc. Int. Symp. on Image and Signal Processing and Analysis, Special Session on Image Processing and Analysis in Lunar and Planetary Science, Dubrovnik, Croatia, 2011.

Gwinner, K., Scholten, F., Preusker, F., Elgner, S., Roatsch, T., Spiegel, M., Schmidt, R., Oberst, J., Jaumann, R., Heipke, C., 2010. Topography of Mars from global mapping by HRSC high-resolution digital terrain models and orthoimages: characteristics and performance. Earth Planet. Sci. Lett. 294, pp. 506–519.

Hafezi, K., Wöhler, C., 2004. A general framework for three-dimensional surface reconstruction by self-consistent fusion of shading and shadow features and its application to industrial quality inspection tasks. Photonics Europe, Strasbourg, SPIE 5457, pp. 138–149.

Hahn, M., 2011. Raum-zeitliche Objekt- und Aktionserkennung: Ein statistischer Ansatz für reale Umgebungen. Doctoral Dissertation, Technical Faculty, Bielefeld University, Germany.

Hahn, M., Barrois, B., Krüger, L., Wöhler, C., Sagerer, G., Kummert, F., 2010a. 3D pose estimation and motion analysis of the articulated human hand-forearm limb in an industrial production environment. 3D Research 03, 03.

Hahn, M., Krüger, L., Wöhler, C., Groß, H.-M., 2007. Tracking of human body parts using the multiocular contracting curve density algorithm. Proc. Int. Conf. on 3-D Digital Imaging and Modeling, Montréal, Canada.

Hahn, M., Krüger, L., Wöhler, C., 2008a. 3D action recognition and long-term prediction of human motion. In: Gasteratos, A., Vincze, M., Tsotsos, J. (eds.), Proc. Int. Conf. on Computer Vision Systems, Santorini, Greece. Lecture Notes in Computer Science 5008, pp. 23–32, Springer, Berlin.

Hahn, M., Krüger, L., Wöhler, C., 2008b. Spatio-temporal 3D pose estimation of human body parts using the shape flow algorithm. Proc. Int. Conf. on Pattern Recognition, Tampa, USA.

Hahn, M., Krüger, L., Wöhler, C., Kummert, F., 2009. 3D action recognition in an industrial environment. In: Ritter, H., Sagerer, G., Dillmann, R., Buss, M. (eds.), Proc. 3rd Int. Workshop on Human-Centered Robot Systems, Bielefeld, Germany. Cognitive Systems Monographs 6, pp. 141–150, Springer, Berlin.

Hahn, M., Quronfuleh, F., Wöhler, C., Kummert, F., 2010b. 3D mean-shift tracking and recognition of working actions. In: Salah, A. A., Gevers, T., Sebe, N., Vinciarelli, A. (eds.), Proc. Int. Workshop on Human Behaviour Understanding, held in conjunction with ICPR 2010, Istanbul, Turkey. Lecture Notes on Computer Science 6219, pp. 101–112, Springer, Berlin.

Hanek, R., 2001. The contracting curve density algorithm and its application to model-based image segmentation. Proc. IEEE Conf. on Computer Vision and Pattern Recognition, pp. 797–804.

Hanek, R., 2004. Fitting Parametric Curve Models to Images Using Local Self-adapting Separation Criteria. Doctoral Dissertation, Technical University of Munich.

Hanek, R., Beetz, M., 2004. Fitting Parametric Curve Models to Images Using Local Self-adapting Separation Criteria. Int. J. Comput. Vis. 59, pp. 233–258.

Hapke, B. W., 1981. Bidirectional reflectance spectroscopy 1: Theory. J. Geophys. Res. 86, pp. 3039–3054.

Hapke, B. W., 1984. Bidirectional reflectance spectroscopy 3: correction for macroscopic roughness. Icarus 59, pp. 41–59.

Hapke, B. W., 1986. Bidirectional reflectance spectroscopy 4: the extinction coefficient and the opposition effect. Icarus 67, pp. 264–280.

Hapke, B. W., 1993. Theory of Reflectance and Emittance Spectroscopy. Cambridge University Press, Cambridge.

Hapke, B. W., 2002. Bidirectional reflectance spectroscopy 5: the coherent backscatter opposition effect and anisotropic scattering. Icarus 157, pp. 523–534.

Haralick, R., Joo, H., Lee, C., Zhuang, X., Vaidya, V., Kim, M., 1989. Pose estimation from corresponding point data. IEEE Trans. Syst. Man Cybern. 19(6), pp. 1426–1446.

Harmon, J. K., Campbell, D. B., 1988. Radar observations of Mercury. In: Vilas, F., Chapman, C. R., Shapley Matthews, M. (eds.), Mercury, The University of Arizona Press, Tucson.

Harris, C., Stephens, M., 1988. A combined corner and edge detector. Proc. 4th Alvey Vision Conf., pp. 189–192.

Hartley, R., 1997. Kruppa's equations derived from the fundamental matrix. IEEE Trans. Pattern Anal. Mach. Intell. 21, pp. 133–135.

Hartley, R., Zisserman, A., 2003. Multiple View Geometry in Computer Vision (2nd Edition). Cambridge University Press, Cambridge.

Hatzitheodorou, M., 1989. The derivation of 3-d surface shape from shadows. Proc. Image Understanding Workshop, Palo Alto, pp. 1012–1020.

Hawke, B. R., Lawrence, D. J., Blewett, D. T., Lucey, P. G., Smith, G. A., Spudis, P. D., Taylor, G. J., 2003. Hansteen alpha: a volcanic construct in the lunar highlands. J. Geophys. Res. 108(E7), CiteID 5069, doi:10.1029/2002JE002013.

Head, J. W., Gifford, A., 1980. Lunar mare domes: classification and modes of origin. Moon Planets 22, pp. 235–257.

Heap, T., Hogg, D., 1996. Toward 3D hand tracking using a deformable model. Proc. IEEE Int. Conf. on Automatic Face and Gesture Recognition, pp. 140–145.

Heikkilä, J., Silvén, O., 1997. A four-step camera calibration procedure with implicit image correction. Proc. IEEE Conf. on Computer Vision and Pattern Recognition, pp. 1106–1112.

Heisele, B., 1998. Objektdetektion in Straßenverkehrsszenen durch Auswertung von Farbbildfolgen. Doctoral Dissertation, Faculty of Electrical Engineering, Stuttgart University. Fortschritt-Berichte VDI, Reihe 10, no. 567.

Helfenstein, P., 1988. The geological interpretation of photometric surface roughness. Icarus 73, pp. 462–481.

Henrich, D., Fischer, M., Gecks, T., Kuhn, S., 2008. Sichere Mensch/Roboter-Koexistenz und Kooperation. Proc. Robotik 2008, München, Germany.

Henrich, D., Gecks, T., 2008. Multi-camera collision detection between known and unknown objects. Proc. ACM/IEEE International Conference on Distributed Smart Cameras.

Henyey, L. G., Greenstein, J. L., 1941. Diffuse radiation in the Galaxy. Astrophys. J. 93, pp. 70–83.

Herbort, S., Grumpe, A. & Wöhler, C., 2011. Reconstruction of non-Lambertian surfaces by fusion of shape from shading and active range scanning. Proc. IEEE Int. Conf. Image Process.

Herbort, S., Wöhler, C., 2011. An introduction to image-based 3d surface reconstruction and a survey of photometric stereo methods. 3D Research 02, 03004.

Herbort, S., Wöhler, C., 2012. Self-consistent 3D surface reconstruction and reflectance model estimation of metallic surfaces. Proc. Int. Conf. on Computer Vision Theory and Applications, Rome, Italy.

Herkenhoff, K. E., Soderblom, L. A., Kirk, R. L., 2002. MOC photoclinometry of the north polar residual cap on Mars. Proc. Lunar Planet. Sci. XXXIII, abstract #1714.

Hernandez, C., Vogiatzis, G., Brostow, G. J., Stenger, B., Cipolla, R., 2007. Non-rigid photometric stereo with colored lights. Proc. Int. Conf. on Computer Vision.

Hernandez, C., Vogiatzis, G., Cipolla, R., 2008. Shadows in three-source photometric stereo. Proc. Europ. Conf. on Computer Vision, pp. 290–303.

Hernandez, C., Vogiatzis, G., 2010. Self-calibrating a real-time monocular 3D facial capture system. Proc. Int. Symp. on 3D Data Processing, Visualization and Transmission.

Hiesinger, H., Head, J. W., Wolf, U., Jaumann, R., Neukum, G., 2003. Ages and stratigraphy of mare basalts in Oceanus Procellarum, Mare Nubium, Mare Cognitum, and Mare Insularum. J. Geophys. Res. 108(E7), pp. 5065–5091.

Hinz, M., Toennies, K. D., Grohmann, M., Pohle, R., 2001. Active double-contour for segmentation of vessels in digital subtraction angiography. Proc. SPIE, 4322, pp. 1554–1562.

Hirschmüller, H., 2001. Improvements in real-time correlation-based stereo vision. Proc. IEEE Workshop on Stereo and Multi-Baseline Vision, Kauai, pp. 141–148.

Hirschmüller, H., Innocent, P. R., Garibaldi, J., 2002. Real-time correlation-based stereo vision with reduced border errors. Int. J. Comput. Vis. 47(1/2/3), pp. 229–246.

Hirschmüller, H., 2005. Accurate and efficient stereo processing by semi-global matching and mutual information. Proc. IEEE Conf. on Computer Vision and Pattern Recognition, pp. 807–814.

Hirschmüller, H., 2006. Stereo vision in structured environments by consistent semi-global matching. Proc. IEEE Conf. on Computer Vision and Pattern Recognition, 2, pp. 2386–2393.

Hirschmüller, H., Mayer, H., Neukum, G., and the HRSC CoI team, 2007. Stereo processing of HRSC Mars express images by semi-global matching. Symposium of ISPRS Commission IV/7, Goa, India.

Hirschmüller, H., 2008. Stereo processing by semiglobal matching and mutual information. IEEE Trans. Pattern Anal. Mach. Intell. 30(2), pp. 328–341.

Hofemann, N., 2007. Videobasierte Handlungserkennung für die natürliche Mensch-Maschine-Interaktion. Doctoral Dissertation, Technical Faculty, Bielefeld University, Germany.

Hofmann, M., Gavrila, D. M., 2009. Multi-view 3D human pose estimation combining single-frame recovery, temporal integration and model adaptation. Proc. IEEE Conf. on Computer Vision and Pattern Recognition, pp. 2214–2221.

Hogan, J., Smith, W. A. P., 2010. Refinement of digital elevation models from shadowing cues. Proc. IEEE Int. Conf. on Computer Vision and Pattern Recognition, pp. 1181–1188.

Horn, B. K. P., 1986. Robot Vision. MIT Press, Cambridge.

Horn, B. K. P., 1989. Height and Gradient from Shading. MIT Technical Report, AI memo, no. 1105A.

Horn, B. K. P., 2000. Tsai's Camera Calibration Method Revisited. MIT Technical Report. http://people.csail.mit.edu/bkph/articles/Tsai_Revisited.pdf (accessed September 04, 2007).

Horn, B. K. P., Brooks, M., 1989. The variational approach to shape from shading. In: Horn, B. K. P., Brooks, M. (eds.), Shape from Shading. MIT Press, Cambridge.

Horovitz, I., Kiryati, N., 2004. Depth from gradient fields and control points: bias correction in photometric stereo. Image Vis. Comput. 22, pp. 681–694.

Howard, A. D., Blasius, K. R., Cutts, J. A., 1982. Photoclinometric determination of the topography of the martian north polar cap. Icarus 50, pp. 245–258.

Huguet, F., Devernay, F., 2007. A variational method for scene flow estimation from stereo sequences. Proc. Int. Conf. on Computer Vision, pp. 1–7.

Isard, M., Blake, A., 1998. CONDENSATION—conditional density propagation for visual tracking. Int. J. Comput. Vis. 29, pp. 5–28.

Jähne, B., 2005. Digitale Bildverarbeitung. Springer, Berlin.

Jaumann, R., et al., 2007. The high-resolution stereo camera (HRSC) experiment on Mars Express: instrument aspects and experiment conduct from interplanetary cruise through the nominal mission. Planet. Space Sci. 55(7–8), pp. 928–952.

Jiang, X., Bunke, H., 1997. Dreidimensionales Computersehen. Springer, Berlin.

Jin, H., Soatto, S., Yezzi, A., 2003. Multi-view stereo beyond lambert. Proc. IEEE Conf. on Computer Vision and Pattern Recognition, pp. 171–178.

Joshi, M. V., Chaudhuri, S., 2004. Photometric stereo under blurred observations. Proc. Int. Conf. on Pattern Recognition, Cambridge, UK, vol. 3, pp. 169–172.

Kung, I.-K., Lacroix, S., 2001. A robust interest points matching algorithm. Proc. Int. Conf. on Computer Vision, Vancouver, Canada, pp. 538–543.

Kass, M., Witkin, A., Terzopoulos, D., 1988. Snakes: active contour models. Int. J. Comput. Vis. 1(4), pp. 321–331.

Kender, J. R., Smith, E. M., 1987. Shape from darkness: deriving surface information from dynamic shadows. Proc. Int. Conf. on Computer Vision, London, UK, pp. 539–546.

Kerr, A. D., Pollard, D. D., 1998. Toward more realistic formulations for the analysis of laccoliths. J. Struct. Geol. 20(12), pp. 1783–1793.

Kimmel, R., Sethian, J. A., 2001. Optimal algorithm for shape from shading and path planning. J. Math. Imaging Vis. 14(3), pp. 237–244.

Klette, R., Koschan, A., Schlüns, K., 1996. Computer Vision: Räumliche Information aus digitalen Bildern. Vieweg Verlag, Braunschweig.

Klette, R., Kozera, R., Schlüns, K., 1999. Shape from shading and photometric stereo methods. In: Jähne, B., Haussecker, H., Geissler, P. (eds.), Signal Processing and Pattern Recognition, Handbook of Computer Vision and Applications 2, pp. 532–590, Academic Press, San Diego.

Klette, R., Schlüns, K., 1996. Height data from gradient fields. Machine Vision Applications, Architectures, and Systems Integration V, Boston, Proc. Photonics East, SPIE 2908, pp. 204–215.

Knoop, S., Vacek, S., Dillmann, R., 2005. Modeling joint constraints for an articulated 3D human body model with artificial correspondences. ICP. Proc. Int. Conf. on Humanoid Robots, Tsukuba, Japan.

Kölzow, T., Ellenrieder, M., 2003. A general approach for multi-feature, multi-sensor classification and localization of 3D objects in 2D image sequences. Proc. SPIE-IS&T Electronic Imaging, SPIE 5014, pp. 99–110.

Krauß, M., 2006. Integration von Depth-from-Defocus und Shape-from-Polarisation in einen Pose-Estimation-Algorithmus. Diplom Thesis, Faculty of Computer Science and Automation, Technical University of Ilmenau.

Krüger, L., 2007. Model Based Object Classification and Localisation in Multiocular Images. Doctoral Dissertation, Technical Faculty, Bielefeld University, Germany.

Krüger, L., Ellenrieder, M. M., 2005. Pose estimation using the multiocular contracting curve density algorithm. Proc. 10th Int. Fall Workshop on Vision, Modeling, and Visualization, Erlangen, Germany.

Krüger, L., Wöhler, C., Würz-Wessel, A., Stein, F., 2004. In-factory calibration of multiocular camera systems. Proc. SPIE Photonics Europe (Optical Metrology in Production Engineering), Strasbourg, pp. 126–137.

Krüger, L., Wöhler, C., 2011. Accurate chequerboard corner localisation for camera calibration. Pattern Recognit. Lett. 32, pp. 1428–1435.

Kruppa, E., 1913. Zur Ermittlung eines Objektes aus zwei Perspektiven mit innerer Orientierung. Sitzungsberichte der Mathematisch Naturwissenschaftlichen Kaiserlichen Akademie der Wissenschaften 122, pp. 1939–1948.

Kuhl, A., 2005. Spatial Scene Reconstruction by Combined Depth-from-Defocus and Shape-from-Motion. Diplom Thesis, Faculty of Computer Science and Automation, Technical University of Ilmenau.

Kuhl, A., Wöhler, C., Krüger, L., Groß, H.-M., 2006. Monocular 3D scene reconstruction at absolute scales by combination of geometric and real-aperture methods. In: Franke, K., Müller, K.-R., Nickolay, B., Schäfer, R. (eds.), Pattern Recognition, Proc. 28th DAGM Symposium, Heidelberg, Germany. Lecture Notes in Computer Science 4174, pp. 607–616, Springer, Berlin.

Kuhn, H. W., 1955. The Hungarian method for the assignment problem. Nav. Res. Logist. Q. 2, pp. 83–97.

Kuhn, S., Gecks, T., Henrich, D., 2006. Velocity control for safe robot guidance based on fused vision and force/torque data. Proc. IEEE Conf. on Multisensor Fusion and Integration for Intelligent Systems, Heidelberg, Germany.

Kuiper, G. P., 1961. Orthographic Atlas of the Moon. University of Arizona Press, Tucson.

Kusuma, K. N., Sebastian, N., Murty, S. V. S., 2012. Geochemical and mineralogical analysis of Gruithuisen region on Moon using M3 and Diviner images. Planet. Space Sci. 67(1), pp. 46–56.

Kwon, Y.-H., 1998. DLT Method. http://www.kwon3d.com/theory/dlt/dlt.html (accessed October 16, 2007).

Lagger, P., Salzmann M., Lepetit, V., Fua, P., 2008. 3D pose refinement from reflections. Proc. IEEE Conf. on Computer Vision and Pattern Recognition, Anchorage, USA.

Lamdan, Y., Wolfson, H., 1988. Geometric hashing: a general and efficient model-based recognition scheme. Proc. IEEE Conf. on Computer Vision and Pattern Recognition, pp. 238–249.

Lange, C., Hermann, T., Ritter, H., 2004. Holistic body tracking for gestural interfaces. Gesture-Based Communication in Human-Computer Interaction, selected and revised papers of the 5th Int. Gesture Workshop, Genova, Italy. Lecture Notes in Computer Science 2915, pp. 132–139, Springer, Berlin.

Lee, J., Kunii, T., 1993. Constraint-based hand animation. Models and Techniques in Computer Animation, Springer, Tokyo, pp. 110–127.

Lena, R., Wöhler, C., Bregante, M. T., Fattinnanzi, C., 2006. A combined morphometric and spectrophotometric study of the complex lunar volcanic region in the south of Petavius. J. R. Astron. Soc. Can. 100(1), pp. 14–25.

Lena, R., Wöhler, C., Bregante, M. T., Lazzarotti, P., Lammel, S., 2008. Lunar domes in Mare Undarum: spectral and morphometric properties, eruption conditions, and mode of emplacement. Planet. Space Sci. 56, pp. 553–569.

Lena, R., Wöhler, C., Phillips, J., 2009. Marius Hills: morphometry, rheology, and mode of emplacement. Proc. European Planetary Science Congress, EPSC2009-262, Potsdam, Germany.

Li, M., Lavest, J.-M., 1995. Some Aspects of Zoom-Lens Camera Calibration. Technical Report ISRN KTH/NA/P-95/03-SE, Royal Institute of Technology (KTH), Stockholm, Sweden.

Li, Z., Fritsch, J., Wachsmuth, S., Sagerer, G., 2006. An object-oriented approach using a top-down and bottom-up process for manipulative action recognition. In: Franke, K., Müller, K.-R., Nickolay, B., Schäfer, R. (eds.), Pattern Recognition, Proc. 28th DAGM Symposium, Heidelberg, Germany. Lecture Notes in Computer Science 4174, pp. 212–221, Springer, Berlin.

Lim, J., Jeffrey, H., Yang, M., Kriegman, D., 2005. Passive photometric stereo from motion. Proc. IEEE Int. Conf. Computer Vision, II, pp. 1635–1642.

Lohse, V., Heipke, C., 2003. Derivation of digital terrain models by means of multi-image shape-from-shading: results using Clementine images. ISPRS Workshop High Resolution Mapping from Space, Hannover, Germany.

Lohse, V., Heipke, C., 2004. Multi-image shape-from-shading. Derivation of planetary digital terrain models using Clementine images. Int. Arch. Photogramm. Remote Sens. XXXV(B4), pp. 828–833.

Lohse, V., Heipke, C., Kirk, R. L., 2006. Derivation of planetary topography using multi-image shape-from-shading. Planet. Space Sci. 54, pp. 661–674.

Lourakis, M., Argyros, A., 2004. The Design and Implementation of a Generic Sparse Bundle Adjustment Software Package Based on the Levenberg-Marquardt Algorithm. Technical Report 340, Institute of Computer Science—FORTH, Heraklion, Crete, Greece.

Lowe, D. G., 1987. Three-dimensional object recognition from single two-dimensional images. Artif. Intell. 31(3), pp. 355–395.

Lowe, D. G., 1991. Fitting parameterized three-dimensional models to images. IEEE Trans. Pattern Anal. Mach. Intell. 13(5), pp. 441–450.

Lowitzsch, S., Kaminski, J., Knauer, M. C., Häusler, G., 2005. Vision and modeling of specular surfaces. Proc. 10th Int. Fall Workshop on Vision, Modeling, and Visualization, Erlangen, Germany.

Lu, Y., Zhang, J. Z., Wu, Q. M. J., Li, Z. N., 2004. A survey of motion-parallax-based 3-D reconstruction algorithms. IEEE Trans. Syst. Man Cybern., Part C, Appl. Rev. 34(4), pp. 532–548.

Lucas, B. D., Kanade, T., 1981. An iterative image registration technique with an application to stereo vision. Proc. Int. Joint Conf. on Artificial Intelligence, Vancouver, pp. 674–679.

Lucchese, L., Mitra, S., 2002. Using saddle points for subpixel feature detection in camera calibration targets. Proc. Asia-Pacific Conference on Circuits and Systems, pp. 191–195.

Luhmann, T., 2006. Nahbereichsphotogrammetrie. Grundlagen, Methoden und Anwendungen. 2nd Edition, Wichmann, Heidelberg.

MacQueen, J. B., 1967. Some methods for classification and analysis of multivariate observations. Proc. 5th Berkeley Symposium on Mathematical Statistics and Probability, pp. 281–297, University of California Press, Berkeley.

Magda, S., Zickler, T., Kriegman, D., Belhumeur, P., 2001. Beyond Lambert: reconstructing surfaces with arbitrary BRDFs. Proc. Int. Conf. on Computer Vision, pp. 291–302.

Mallon, J., Whelan, P. F., 2006. Which pattern? Biasing aspects of planar calibration patterns and detection methods. Pattern Recognit. Lett. 28(8), pp. 921–930.

Mandler, E., Oberländer, M., 1990. One pass encoding of connected components in multi-valued images. Proc. IEEE Int. Conf. on Pattern Recognition, Atlantic City, pp. 64–69.

Marr, D., Poggio, T., 1979. A computational theory of human stereo vision. Proc. R. Soc. Lond. B, Biol. Sci., 204(1156), pp. 301–328.

Marsland, S., 2009. Machine Learning: An Algorithmic Perspective. Chapman & Hall/CRC Machine Learning & Pattern Recognition Series.

Mason, S., 1994. Expert System Based Design of Photogrammetric Networks. Doctoral Dissertation, ETH Zürich.

McCloskey, S., Langer, M., Siddiqi, K., 2007. Evolving measurement regions for depth from defocus. Proc. Asian Conf. on Computer Vision. Lecture Notes on Computer Science 4844, pp. 858–868, Springer, Berlin.

McEwen, A. S., 1985. Albedo and topography of Ius Chasma, Mars. Proc. Lunar Planet. Sci. XVI, pp. 528–529.

McEwen, A. S., 1991. Photometric functions for photoclinometry and other applications. Icarus 92, pp. 298–311.

McEwen, A. S., 1996. A precise lunar photometric function. Proc. Lunar Planet. Sci. XXVII, pp. 841–842.

McKay, D. S., Heiken, G., Basu, A., Blanford, G., Simon, S., Reedy, R., French, B. M., Papike, J., 1991. The Lunar regolith. In: Heiken, G., Vaniman, D., French, B. M. (eds.), Lunar Sourcebook, Cambridge University Press, Cambridge.

McGuire, A. F., Hapke, B. W., 1995. An experimental study of light scattering by large, irregular particles. Icarus 113, pp. 134–155.

Medioni, G., Nevatia, R., 1985. Segment-based stereo matching. Comput. Vis. Graph. Image Process. 31, pp. 2–18.

Meister, G., 2000. Bidirectional Reflectance of Urban Surfaces. Doctoral Dissertation, Hamburg University.

Michaut, C., 2010. Dynamics of laccolith intrusions, with applications to Earth and Moon. Lunar Planet. Sci. XXXXI, abstract #1084.

Miyazaki, D., Tan, R. T., Hara, K., Ikeuchi, K., 2003. Polarization-based inverse rendering from a single view. Proc. IEEE Int. Conf. on Computer Vision, Nice, vol. 2, pp. 982–987.

Miyazaki, D., Kagesawa, M., Ikeuchi, K., 2004. Transparent surface modeling from a pair of polarization images. IEEE Trans. Pattern Anal. Mach. Intell. 26(1), pp. 73–82.

Miyazaki, D., Ikeuchi, K., 2005. Inverse polarization raytracing: estimating surface shape of transparent objects. Proc. IEEE Int. Conf. on Computer Vision and Pattern Recognition, San Diego, vol. 2, pp. 910–917.

Moeslund, T. B., Hilton, A., Krüger, V., 2006. A survey of advances in vision-based human motion capture and analysis. Comput. Vis. Image Underst. 104(2), pp. 90–126.

Mongkolnam, P., Dechsakulthorn, T., Nukoolkit, C., 2006. Image shape representation using curve fitting. Proc. WSEAS Int. Conf. on Signal, Speech and Image Processing, Lisbon, Portugal.

Mouginis-Mark, P. J., Wilson, L., 1979. Photoclinometric measurements of Mercurian landforms. Proc. Lunar Planet. Sci. X, pp. 873–875.

Morel, O., Meriaudeau, F., Stolz, C., Gorria, P., 2005. Polarization imaging applied to 3D reconstruction of specular metallic surfaces. Machine Vision Applications in Industrial Inspection XIII. SPIE 5679, pp. 178–186.

Mühlmann, K., 2002. Design und Implementierung eines Systems zur schnellen Rekonstruktion dreidimensionaler Modelle aus Stereobildern. Doctoral Dissertation, Faculty of Science, Mannheim University.

Mündermann, L., Corazza, S., Andriacchi, T. P., 2008. Markerless motion capture for biomechanical applications. In: Rosenhahn, B., Klette, R., Metaxas, D. (eds.), Human Motion: Understanding, Modelling, Capture and Animation, Springer, Dordrecht.

Murray, D., Little, J. J., 2004. Segmenting correlation stereo range images using surface elements. Proc. 2nd Int. Symp. on 3D Data Processing, Visualization, and Transmission, pp. 656–663.

Myles, Z., da Vitoria Lobo, N., 1998. Recovering affine motion and defocus blur simultaneously. IEEE Trans. Pattern Anal. Mach. Intell. 20(6), pp. 652–658.

Namboodiri, V. P., Chaudhuri, S., Hadap, S., 2008. Regularized depth from defocus. Proc. IEEE Int. Conf. on Image Processing, pp. 1520–1523.

Nayar, S., 1989. Shape from Focus. Carnegie Mellon University, Technical Report CMU-RI-TR-89-27.

Nayar, S. K., Ikeuchi, K., Kanade, T., 1991. Surface reflection: physical and geometrical perspectives. IEEE Trans. Pattern Anal. Mach. Intell. 13(7), pp. 611–634.

Nayar, S. K., Fang, X.-S., Boult, T., 1993. Removal of specularities using color and polarization. Proc. IEEE Int. Conf. on Computer Vision and Pattern Recognition, New York, pp. 583–590.

Nayar, S. K., Bolle, R. M., 1996. Reflectance based object recognition. Int. J. Comput. Vis. 17(3), pp. 219–240.

Nelder, J. A., Mead, R., 1965. A simplex method for function minimization. Comput. J. 7, pp. 308–313.

Nehab, D., Rusinkiewicz, S., Davis, J., Ramamoorthi, R., 2005. Efficiently combining positions and normals for precise 3D geometry. ACM Trans. Graph. 24, pp. 536–543.

Nehaniv, C. L., 2005: Classifying types of gesture and inferring intent. Proc. Symp. on Robot Companions: Hard Problems and Open Challenges in Robot–Human Interaction, pp. 74–81. The Society for the Study of Artificial Intelligence and the Simulation of Behaviour.

Neuenschwander, W., Fua, P., Iverson, L., Szekely, G., Kubler, O., 1997. Ziplock snakes. Int. J. Comput. Vis. 25(3), pp. 191–201.

Neumann, G. A., 2009. Lunar Orbiter Laser Altimeter Raw Data Set, LRO-L-LOLA-4-GDR-V1.0, NASA Planetary Data System. http://pds-geosciences.wustl.edu/missions/lro/lola.htm (accessed November 01, 2011)

Nevatia, R., Babu, K. R., 1980. Linear feature extraction and description. Comput. Graph. Image Process. 13, pp. 257–269.

Nickel, K., Seemann, E., Stiefelhagen, R., 2004. 3D-tracking of head and hands for pointing gesture recognition in a human–robot interaction scenario. Proc. IEEE Int. Conf. on Automatic Face and Gesture Recognition, Seoul, Korea, pp. 565–570.

Nickel, K., Stiefelhagen, R., 2004. Real-time person tracking and pointing gesture recognition for human–robot interaction. Proc. Europ. Conf. on Computer Vision, Workshop on HCI, Prague, Czech Republic. Lecture Notes in Computer Science 3058, pp. 28–38, Springer, Berlin.

Nicodemus, F. E., Richmond, J. C., Hsia, J. J., Ginsberg, I. W., Limperis, T., 1977. Geometrical considerations and nomenclature for reflectance. US Department of Commerce, National Bureau of Standards, Washington, DC, USA.

Niemann, H., Hornegger, J., 2001. A novel probabilistic model for object recognition and pose estimation. Int. J. Pattern Recognit. Artif. Intell. 15(2), pp. 241–253.

Nomura, Y., Zhang, D., Sakaida, Y., Fujii, S., 1996. 3-d object pose estimation based on iterative image matching: shading and edge data fusion. Proc. IEEE Int. Conf. on Computer Vision and Pattern Recognition, pp. 866–871.

Nourbakhsh, I. R., Andre, D., Tomasi, C., Genesereth, M. R., 1997. Mobile robot obstacle avoidance via depth from focus. Robot. Auton. Syst. 22, pp. 151–158.

Olague, G., Hernández, B., 2005. A new accurate and flexible model based multi-corner detector for measurement and recognition. Pattern Recognit. Lett. 26(1), pp. 27–41.

Oren, M., Nayar, S., 1995. Generalization of the Lambertian model and implications for machine vision. Int. J. Comput. Vis. 14(3), pp. 227–251.

Panin, G., Ladikos, A., Knoll, A., 2006. An efficient and robust real-time contour tracking system. Proc. IEEE Int. Conf. on Computer Vision Systems, New York, USA, pp. 44–51.

Pavlovic, V., Sharma, R., Huang, T. S., 1997. Visual interpretation of hand gestures for human–computer interaction: a review. IEEE Trans. Pattern Anal. Mach. Intell. 19(7), pp. 677–695.

Pedrotti, F. L., 1993. Introduction to Optics. 2nd Edition, Prentice Hall, New York.

Pentland, A., 1987. A new sense for depth of field. IEEE Trans. Pattern Anal. Mach. Intell. 9, pp. 523–531.

Pettengill, G. H., Eliason, E., Ford, P. G., Loriat, G. B., 1980. Pioneer Venus radar results: altimetry and surface properties. J. Geophys. Res. 85, pp. 8261–8270.

Pieters, C. M., et al., 2009. The Moon mineralogy mapper (M3) on Chandrayaan-1. Curr. Sci. 96(4), 500–505.

Pike, R. J., Clow, G., 1981. Revised Classification of Terrestrial Volcanoes and Catalogue of Topographic Dimensions, with new Results of Edifice Volume. US Geological Survey Open-File Report 81-1038.

Phong, B. T., 1975. Illumination for computer generated pictures. Commun. ACM 18(6), pp. 311–317.

Phong, T. Q., Horaud, R., Yassine, A., Tao, P. D., 1996. Object pose from 2-D to 3-D point and line correspondences. Int. J. Comput. Vis. 15(3), pp. 225–243.

Pike, R. J., 1980. Control of crater morphology by gravity and target type: Mars, Earth, Moon. Proc. Lunar Planet. Sci. XI, pp. 2159–2189.

Pike, R. J., 1988. Geomorphology of impact craters on Mercury. In: Vilas, F., Chapman, C. R., Shapley Matthews, M. (eds.), Mercury, The University of Arizona Press, Tucson.

Plänkers, R., Fua, P., 2003. Articulated soft objects for multiview shape and motion capture. IEEE Trans. Pattern Anal. Mach. Intell. 25(9), pp. 1182–1187.

Pons, J.-P., Keriven, R., Faugeras, O., 2005. Modelling dynamic scenes by registering multi-view image sequences. Proc. IEEE Conf. on Computer Vision and Pattern Recognition, 2, pp. 822–827.

Pons-Moll, G., Baak, A., Gall, J., Leal-Taixé, L., Müller, M., Seidel, H.-P., Rosenhahn, B., 2011. Outdoor human motion capture using inverse kinematics and von Mises-Fisher sampling. Proc. IEEE Int. Conf. on Computer Vision, Barcelona, Spain.

Poppe, R., 2010. A survey on vision-based human action recognition. Image Vis. Comput. 28, pp. 976–990.

Press, W. H., Teukolsky, S. A., Vetterling, W. T., Flannery, B. P., 2007. Numerical Recipes. The Art of Scientific Computing. 3rd Edition, Cambridge University Press, Cambridge.

Rahmann, S., 1999. Inferring 3D scene structure from a single polarization image. Polarization and Color Techniques in Industrial Inspection, SPIE 3826, pp. 22–33.

Rahmann, S., Canterakis, N., 2001. Reconstruction of specular surfaces using polarization imaging. Proc. Int. Conf. on Computer Vision and Pattern Recognition, Kauai, vol. I, pp. 149–155.

Rey, W. J. J., 1983. Introduction to Robust and Quasi-robust Statistical Methods. Springer, Berlin.

Richarz, J., Fink, G. A., 2001. Visual recognition of 3D emblematic gestures in an HMM framework. J. Ambient Intell. Smart Environ. 3(3), pp. 193–211. Thematic Issue on Computer Vision for Ambient Intelligence.

Riris, H., Cavanaugh, J., Sun, X., Liiva, P., Rodriguez, M., Neumann, G., 2010. The Lunar Orbiter Laser Altimeter (LOLA) on NASA's Lunar Reconnaissance Orbiter (LRO) Mission. Proc. Int. Conf. on Space Optics, Rhodes, Greece.

Robinson, M. S., et al., 2010. Lunar Reconnaissance Orbiter Camera (LROC) instrument overview. Space Sci. Rev. 150, 81–124.

Rogers, D. F., 2001. An Introduction to NURBS. Academic Press, San Diego.

Rosenhahn, B., Perwass, C., Sommer, G., 2003. Pose estimation of free-form surface models. In: Michaelis, B., Krell, G. (eds.), Pattern Recognition, Proc. 25th DAGM Symposium, Magdeburg, Germany. Lecture Notes in Computer Science 2781, pp. 574–581, Springer, Berlin.

Rosenhahn, B., Kersting, U., Smith, A., Gurney, J., Brox, T., Klette, R., 2005. A system for markerless human motion estimation. In: Kropatsch, W., Sablatnig, R., Hanbury, A. (eds.), Pattern Recognition, Proc. 27th DAGM Symposium, Vienna, Austria. Lecture Notes in Computer Science 3663, pp. 230–237, Springer, Berlin.

Rosenhahn, B., Brox, T., Cremers, D., Seidel, H.-P., 2006. A comparison of shape matching methods for contour based pose estimation. Combinatorial Image Analysis, Lecture Notes in Computer Science 4040, pp. 263–276, Springer, Berlin.

Rosenhahn, B., Kersting, U. G., Powell, K., Brox, T., Seidel, H.-P., 2008a. Tracking Clothed People. In: Rosenhahn, B., Klette, R., Metaxas, D. (eds.), Human Motion: Understanding, Modelling, Capture and Animation, Springer, Dordrecht.

Rosenhahn, B., Schmaltz, C., Brox, T., Weickert, J., Cremers, D., Seidel, H.-P., 2008b. Markerless motion capture of man–machine interaction. Proc. IEEE Conf. on Computer Vision and Pattern Recognition.

Rottensteiner, F., Trinder, J., Clode, S., Kubik, K., 2005. Automated delineation of roof planes in LIDAR data. Int. Archives of the Photogrammetry, Remote Sensing and Spatial Information Sciences, XXXVI-3/W19, pp. 221–226.

Rottensteiner, F., 2006. Consistent estimation of building parameters considering geometric regularities by soft constraints. Int. Archives of the Photogrammetry, Remote Sensing and Spatial Information Sciences XXXVI-3, pp. 13–18.

Roy, S., Cox, L., 1998. A maximum-flow formulation of the N-camera stereo correspondence problem. Proc. Int. Conf. on Computer Vision, Bombay, pp. 492–499.

Rubin, A. S., 1993. Tensile fracture of rock at high confining pressure: implications for dike propagation. J. Geophys. Res. 98, pp. 15919–15935.

Rükl, A., 1999. Mondatlas. Verlag Werner Dausien, Hanau.

Rouy, E., Tourin, A., 1992. A viscosity solutions approach to shape-from-shading. SIAM J. Numer. Anal. 29(3), pp. 867–884.

Sagerer, G., 1985. Darstellung und Nutzung von Expertenwissen für ein Bildanalysesystem. Springer, Berlin.

Salamunićcar, G., Lončarić, Grumpe, A., Wöhler, C., 2011. Hybrid method for detection of Lunar craters based on topography reconstruction from optical images. Proc. IEEE Int. Symp. on Image and Signal Processing and Analysis, Dubrovnik, Croatia, pp. 597–602.

Salamunićcar, G., Lončarić, Mazarico, E., 2012. LU60645GT and MA132843GT catalogues of Lunar and Martian impact craters developed using a crater shape-based interpolation crater detection algorithm for topography data. Planet. Space Sci. 60(1), pp. 236–247.

Salvi, J., Armangu, X., Batlle, J., 2002. A comparative review of camera calibrating methods with accuracy evaluation. Pattern Recognit. Lett. 35(7), pp. 1617–1635.

Salzmann, M., Urtasun, R., 2010. Combining discriminative and generative methods for 3D deformable surface and articulated pose reconstruction. Proc. IEEE Conf. on Computer Vision and Pattern Recognition, San Francisco, USA, pp. 647–654.

Samaras, D., Metaxas, D., Fua, P., Leclerc, Y.G., 2000. Variable Albedo surface reconstruction from stereo and shape from shading. Proc. IEEE Conf. on Computer Vision and Pattern Recognition, I, pp. 480–487.

Savarese, S., Rushmeier, H., Bernardini, F., Perona, P., 2002. Implementation of a shadow carving system for shape capture. Proc. Int. Symp. on 3D Data Processing, Visualization and Transmission, Padua, Italy, pp. 107–114.

Schaper, D., 2002. Automated quality control for micro-technology components using a depth from focus approach. Proc. 5th IEEE Southwest Symp. on Image Analysis and Interpretation, pp. 50–54.

Scharstein, D., Szeliski, R., 2001. A taxonomy and evaluation of dense two-frame stereo correspondence algorithms. Int. J. Comput. Vis. 47(1/2/3), pp. 7–42.

Schlüns, K., 1997. Shading based 3D shape recovery in the presence of shadows. Proc. First Joint Australia & New Zealand Biennial Conference on Digital Image & Vision Computing: Techniques and Applications, Auckland, New Zealand, pp. 195–200.

Schmidt, J., 2009. Monokulare Modellbasierte Posturschätzung des Menschlichen Oberkörpers. Proc. Oldenburger 3D-Tage, Oldenburg, Germany, pp. 270–280.

Schmidt, J., Fritsch, J., Kwolek, B., 2006. Kernel particle filter for real-time 3d body tracking in monocular color images. Proc. IEEE Int. Conf. on Automatic Face and Gesture Recognition, pp. 567–572.

Schmidt, J., Wöhler, C., Krüger, L., Gövert, T., Hermes, C., 2007. 3D scene segmentation and object tracking in multiocular image sequences. Proc. Int. Conf. on Computer Vision Systems, Bielefeld, Germany.

Scholten, F., Oberst, J., Matz, K.-D., Roatsch, T., Wählisch, M., Robinson, M. S., and the LROC Team, 2011. GLD100—the global lunar 100 meter raster DTM from LROC WAC stereo models. Lunar Planet. Sci. XXXXII, abstract #2046.

Schowengerdt, R. A., 2006. Remote Sensing: Models and Methods for Image Processing. Academic Press, San Diego.

Schreer, O., 2005. Stereoanalyse und Bildsynthese. Springer, Berlin.

Schunck, B. G., 1989. Image flow segmentation and estimation by constraint line clustering. IEEE Trans. Pattern Anal. Mach. Intell. 11(10), pp. 1010–1027.

Schweitzer, G., 1993. High-performance applications: robot motions in complex environments. Control Eng. Pract. 1(3), pp. 499–504.

Sepehri, A., Yacoob, Y., Davis, L. S., 2004. Estimating 3d hand position and orientation using stereo. Proc. 4th Indian Conf. on Computer Vision, Graphics and Image Processing, pp. 58–63.

Sethian, J., 1999. Level Set Methods and Fast Marching Methods: Evolving Interfaces in Computational Geometry, Fluid Mechanics, Computer Vision, and Materials Science. Cambridge University Press, Cambridge.

Shi, J., Malik, J., 1997. Normalized cuts and image segmentation. IEEE Conf. on Computer Vision and Pattern Recognition, San Juan, Puerto Rico, pp. 731–737.

Shi, J., Malik, J., 1998. Motion segmentation and tracking using normalized cuts. Proc. Int. Conf. on Computer Vision, Bombay, India, pp. 1154–1160.

Shi, J., Malik, J., 2000. Normalized cuts and image segmentation. IEEE Trans. Pattern Anal. Mach. Intell. 22(8), pp. 888–905.

Shi, J., Tomasi, C., 1994. Good features to track. IEEE Conf. on Computer Vision and Pattern Recognition, Seattle, USA, pp. 593–600.

Sigal, L., Black, M. J., 2006. Human Eva: Synchronized Video and Motion Capture Dataset for Evaluation of Articulated Human Motion. Technical Report CS-06-08, Brown University.

Simchony, T., Chellappa, R., Shao, M., 1990. Direct analytical methods for solving poisson equations in computer vision problems. IEEE Trans. Pattern Anal. Mach. Intell. 12(5), pp. 435–446.

Sminchisescu, C., 2008. 3D human motion analysis in monocular video: techniques and challenges. In: Rosenhahn, B., Klette, R., Metaxas, D. (eds.), Human Motion: Understanding, Modelling, Capture and Animation, Springer, Dordrecht.

Smith, E. I., 1974. Rümker hills: a lunar volcanic dome complex. The Moon 10(2), pp. 175–181.

Smith, S. M., Brady, J. M., 1997. SUSAN—a new approach to low level image processing. Int. J. Comput. Vis. 23(1), pp. 45–78.

Spudis, P. D., 1993. The Geology of Multi-ring Impact Basins. Cambridge University Press, Cambridge.

Stein, F., 2004. Efficient computation of optical flow using the census transform. In: Rasmussen, C. E., Bülthoff, H. H., Giese, M. A., Schölkopf, B. (eds.), Pattern Recognition, Proc. 26th DAGM Symposium, Tübingen, Germany. Lecture Notes in Computer Science 3175, pp. 79–86, Springer, Berlin.

Stenger, B., Mendonça, P. R. S., Cipolla, R., 2001. Model-based hand tracking using an unscented kalman filter. Proc. British Machine Vision Conference, Manchester, UK, vol. I, pp. 63–72.

Stößel, D., 2007. Automated Visual Inspection of Assemblies from Monocular Images. Doctoral Dissertation, Technical Faculty, Bielefeld University, Germany.

Subbarao, M., 1988. Parallel depth recovery by changing camera parameters. Proc. Int. Conf. on Computer Vision, pp. 149–155.

Subbarao, M., Surya, G., 1994. Depth from defocus: a spatial domain approach. Int. J. Comput. Vis. 13(3), pp. 271–294.

Subbarao, M., Wei, T.-C., 1992. Depth from defocus and rapid autofocusing: a practical approach. Proc. IEEE Conf. on Computer Vision and Pattern Recognition, pp. 773–776.

Tonko, M., Nagel, H. H., 2000. Model-based stereo-tracking of non-polyhedral objects for automatic disassembly experiments. Int. J. Comput. Vis. 37(1), pp. 99–118.

Torrance, K., Sparrow, E., 1967. Theory for off-specular reflection from rough surfaces. J. Opt. Soc. Am. 57(9), pp. 1105–1114.

Triggs, W., McLauchlan, P. F., Hartley, R. I., Fitzgibbon, A. W., 2000. Bundle adjustment—a modern synthesis. Proc. Int. Workshop on Vision Algorithms, pp. 298–372, Springer, London.

Tsai, R. Y., 1987. A versatile camera calibration technique for high-accuracy 3D machine vision metrology using off-the-shelf TV cameras and lenses. IEEE J. Robot. Autom. 3(4), pp. 323–344.

Turk, M., 2005. Multimodal human computer interaction. In: Kisacanin, B., Pavlovic, V., Huang, T. S. (eds.), Real-Time Vision for Human–Computer Interaction, Springer, Berlin, pp. 269–283.

Van der Mark, W., Gavrila, D. M., 2006. Real-time dense stereo for intelligent vehicles. IEEE Trans. Intell. Transp. Syst. 7(1), pp. 38–50.

Vedula, S., Baker, S., Rander, P., Collins, R., Kanade, T., 2005. Three-dimensional scene flow. IEEE Trans. Pattern Anal. Mach. Intell. 27(3), pp. 475–480.

Veverka, J., Helfenstein, P., Hapke, B. W., Goguen, J. D., 1988. Photometry and polarimetry of Mercury. In: Vilas, F., Chapman, C. R., Shapley Matthews, M. (eds.), Mercury, The University of Arizona Press, Tucson.

Vincent, E., Laganière, R., 2001. Matching feature points in stereo pairs: a comparative study of some matching strategies. Comput. Vis. Image Underst. 66(3), pp. 271–285.

Viola, P. A., Jones, M. J., 2001. Rapid object detection using a boosted cascade of simple features. Proc. IEEE Conf. on Computer Vision and Pattern Recognition, pp. 511–518.

Vischer, D., 1992. Cooperating robot with visual and tactile skills. Proc. IEEE Int. Conf. on Robotics md Automation, pp. 2018–2025.

Vogel, O., Breuß, M., Weickert, J., 2008. Perspective shape from shading with non-Lambertian reflectance. In: Rigoll, G. (ed.), Pattern Recognition, Proc. 30th DAGM Symposium, Munich, Germany. Lecture Notes in Computer Science 5096, pp. 517–526, Springer, Berlin.

Vogel, O., Breuß, M., Leichtweis, T., Weickert, J., 2009a. Fast shape from shading for Phong-type surfaces. In: Tai, X.-C., Morken, K., Lysaker, M., Lie, K.-A. (eds.), Scale Space and Variational Methods in Computer Vision. Lecture Notes in Computer Science 5567, pp. 733–744, Springer, Berlin.

Vogel, O., Valgaerts, L., Breuß, M., Weickert, J., 2009b. Making shape from shading work for real-world images. In: Denzler, J., Notni, G., Süße, H. (eds.), Pattern Recognition, Proc. 31st DAGM Symposium, Jena, Germany. Lecture Notes in Computer Science 5748, pp. 191–200, Springer, Berlin.

Vogel, O., Cristiani, E., 2011. Numerical schemes for advanced reflectance models for shape from shading. Proc. IEEE Int. Conf. on Image Processing, pp. 5–8.

von Bank, C., Gavrila, D. M., Wöhler, C., 2003. A visual quality inspection system based on a hierarchical 3D pose estimation algorithm. In: Michaelis, B., Krell, G. (eds.), Pattern Recognition, Proc. 25th DAGM Symposium, Magdeburg, Germany. Lecture Notes in Computer Science 2781, pp. 179–186, Springer, Berlin.

Wachsmuth, S., Wrede, S., Hanheide, M., Bauckhage, C., 2005. An active memory model for cognitive computer vision systems. KI Journal 19(2), pp. 25–31. Special Issue on Cognitive Systems.

Wang, L., Yang, R., Davis, J. E., 2007. BRDF invariant stereo using light transport constancy. IEEE Trans. Pattern Anal. Mach. Intell. 29(9), pp. 1616–1626.

Ward, G. J., 1992. Measuring and modeling anisotropic reflection. Proc. Ann. Conf. on Computer Graphics and Interactive Techniques (SIGGRAPH '92), pp. 265–272.

Warell, J., 2004. Properties of the Hermean regolith: IV. Photometric parameters of Mercury and the Moon contrasted with Hapke modelling. Icarus 167(2), pp. 271–286.

Watanabe, M., Nayar, S. K., Noguchi, M., 1996. Real-time computation of depth from defocus. Proc. SPIE Three-Dimensional and Unconventional Imaging for Industrial Inspection and Metrology, SPIE 2599, pp. 14–25.

Wedel, A., Rabe, C., Vaudrey, T., Brox, T., Franke, U., Cremers, D., 2008a. Efficient dense scene flow from sparse or dense stereo data. Proc. Europ. Conf. on Computer Vision, pp. 739–751.

Wedel, A., Vaudrey, T., Meissner, A., Rabe, C., Brox, T., Franke, U., Cremers, D., 2008b. An evaluation approach for scene flow with decoupled motion and position. In: Revised Papers Int. Dagstuhl Seminar on Statistical and Geometrical Approaches to Visual Motion Analysis, pp. 46–69, Springer, Berlin.

Wedel, A., Brox, T., Vaudrey, T., Rabe, C., Franke, U., Cremers, D., 2011. Stereoscopic scene flow computation for 3D motion understanding. Int. J. Comput. Vis. 95, pp. 29–51.

Wei, T., Klette, R., 2004. Fourier transform based methods for height from gradients. Proc. Control, Automation, Robotics and Vision Conference, Kunming, China, vol. 1, pp. 85–91.

Weitz, C. M., Head, J. W., 1999. Spectral properties of the Marius Hills volcanic complex and implications for the formation of lunar domes and cones. J. Geophys. Res. 104(E8), pp. 18933–18956.

Westling, M., Davis, L., 1996. Object recognition by fast hypothesis generation and reasoning about object interactions. Proc. Int. Conf. on Pattern Recognition, IV, pp. 148–153.

Wilhelms, D. E., 1964. A photometric technique for measurement of lunar slopes. Astrogeologic Studies, Annual Progress Report, Part D: Studies for Space Flight Program, USGS Preliminary Report, pp. 1–12.

Wilhelms, D. E., 1987. The Geologic History of the Moon. USGS Prof. Paper 1348, USGS, Flagstaff, USA.

Williams, D. J., Shah, M., 1992. A fast algorithm for active contours and curvature estimation. CVGIP, Image Underst. 55, pp. 14–26.

Wilson, L., Head, J. W., 1996. Lunar linear rilles as surface manifestations of dikes: theoretical considerations. Proc. Lunar Planet. Sci. XXVII, abstract #1445.

Wilson, L., Head, J. W., 2002. Tharsis-radial graben systems as the surface manifestations of plume-related dike intrusion complexes: models and implications. J. Geophys. Res. 107(E8), p. 5057.

Wilson, L., Head, J. W., 2003. Lunar Gruithuisen and Mairan domes: rheology and mode of emplacement. J. Geophys. Res. 108(E2), pp. 5012–5018.

Winkler, K. (ed.), 2006. Three Eyes Are Better than Two. SafetyEYE uses technical image processing to protect people at their workplaces. DaimlerChrysler Hightech Report 12/2006, DaimlerChrysler AG Communications, Stuttgart, Germany.

Wöhler, C., d'Angelo, P., 2009. Stereo image analysis of non-Lambertian surfaces. Int. J. Comput. Vis. 81(2), pp. 172–190.

Wöhler, C., d'Angelo, P., Krüger, L., Kuhl, A., Groß, H.-M., 2009. Monocular 3D scene reconstruction at absolute scale. ISPRS J. Photogramm. Remote Sens. 64, pp. 529–540.

Wöhler, C., Grumpe, A., 2012. Integrated DEM construction and calibration of hyperspectral imagery: a remote sensing perspective. In: Breuss, M., Bruckstein, A., Maragos, P. (eds.), Innovations for Shape Analysis: Models and Algorithms. Revised contributions to Dagstuhl Seminar. Mathematics and Visualization, Springer, to appear.

Wöhler, C., Hafezi, K., 2005. A general framework for three-dimensional surface reconstruction by self-consistent fusion of shading and shadow features. Pattern Recognit. 38(7), pp. 965–983.

Wöhler, C., Krüger, L., 2003. A contour based stereo vision algorithm for video surveillance applications. SPIE Visual Communication and Image Processing Lugano 5150(3), pp. 102–109.

Wöhler, C., Lena, R., 2009. Lunar intrusive domes: morphometric analysis and laccolith modelling. Icarus 204(2), pp. 381–398.

Wöhler, C., Lena, R., Bregante, M. T., Lazzarotti, P., Phillips, J., 2006a. Vertical studies about Rupes Cauchy. Selenology 25(1), pp. 7–12.

Wöhler, C., Lena, R., Lazzarotti, P., Phillips, J., Wirths, M., Pujic, Z., 2006b. A combined spectrophotometric and morphometric study of the lunar mare dome fields near Cauchy, Arago, Hortensius, and Milichius. Icarus 183, pp. 237–264.

Wöhler, C., Lena, R., Pau, K. C., 2007a. The lunar dome complex Mons Rümker: morphometry, rheology, and mode of emplacement. Proc. Lunar Planet. Sci. XXXVIII, abstract #1091.

Wöhler, C., Lena, R., Phillips, J., 2007b. Formation of lunar mare domes along crustal fractures: rheologic conditions, dimensions of feeder dikes, and the role of magma evolution. Icarus 189(2), pp. 279–307.

Wolff, L. B., 1987. Shape from polarization images. Comput. Vis. Workshop 87, pp. 79–85.

Wolff, L. B., 1989. Surface orientation from two camera stereo with polarizers. Optics, Illumination, Image Sensing for Machine Vision IV, SPIE 1194, pp. 287–297.

Wolff, L. B., 1991. Constraining object features using a polarization reflectance model. IEEE Trans. Pattern Anal. Mach. Intell. 13(7), pp. 635–657.

Wolff, L. B., Angelopoulou, E., 1994. Three-dimensional stereo by photometric ratios. J. Opt. Soc. Am. 11(11), pp. 3069–3078.

Wood, C. A., 1973. Moon: central peak heights and crater origins. Icarus 20, pp. 503–506.

Wood, C. A., Andersson, L., 1978. New morphometric data for fresh lunar craters. Proc. Lunar Planet. Sci. IX, pp. 3369–3389.

Woodham, R. J., 1980. Photometric method for determining surface orientation from multiple images. Opt. Eng. 19(1), pp. 139–144.

Wu, S. S. C., Elassal, A. A., Jordan, R., Schafer, F. J., 1982. Photogrammetric application of Viking orbital photography. Planet. Space Sci. 30(1), pp. 45–55.

Wu, S. S. C., Doyle, F. J., 1990. Topographic mapping. In: Greeley, R., Batson, R. M. (eds.), Planetary Mapping, Cambridge University Press, Cambridge.

Xiong, Y., Shafer, S., 1993. Depth from focusing and defocusing. DARPA Image Understanding Workshop, Palo Alto, California, USA, pp. 967–976.

Xu, C., Prince, J. L., 1998. Snakes, shapes, and gradient vector flow. IEEE Trans. Image Process. 7(3), pp. 359–369.

Ye, Q. Z., Ong, S. H., Han, X., 2001. A stereo vision system for the inspection of IC bonding wires. Int. J. Imaging Syst. Technol. 11(4), pp. 254–262.

Yoon, Y., DeSouza, G. N., Kak, A. C., 2003. Real-time tracking and pose estimation for industrial objects using geometric features. Proc. Int. Conf. on Robotics and Automation, pp. 3473–3478.

Yu, Y., Chang, J. T., 2002. Shadow graphs and surface reconstruction. Europ. Conf. on Computer Vision, Copenhagen, pp. 31–45.

Zabih, R., Woodfill, J., 1994. Non-parametric transforms for computing visual correspondence. Proc. Europ. Conf. on Computer Vision, pp. 151–158.

Zhang, Z., 1992. Iterative Point Matching for Registration of Free-form Curves. Technical Report No. 1658, Institut National de Recherche en Informatique et en Automatique (INRIA), Sophia Antipolis, France.

Zhang, Z., 1998. A Flexible New Technique for Camera Calibration. Microsoft Research Technical Report MSR-TR-98-71.

Zhang, Z., 1999a. Flexible camera calibration by viewing a plane from unknown orientations. Proc. Int. Conf. on Computer Vision, pp. 666–673.

Zhang, Z., 1999b. Iterative point matching for registration of free-form curves and surfaces. Int. J. Comput. Vis. 13(2), pp. 119–152.

Zhang, L., Curless, B., Seitz, S., 2003. Spacetime stereo: shape recovery for dynamic scenes. Proc. Computer Vision and Pattern Recognition, 2, pp. 367–374.

Zhang, J. Q., Gimel'farb, G. L., 1999. On Detecting Points-of-Interest for Relative Orientation of Stereo Images. Technical Report CITR-TR-51, Computer Science Department of The University of Auckland. http://citr.auckland.ac.nz/techreports/1999/CITR-TR-51.pdf (accessed February 06, 2012)

Zickler, T., Belhumeur, P. N., Kriegman, D. J., 2002. Helmholtz stereopsis: exploiting reciprocity for surface reconstruction. Proc. Europ. Conf. on Computer Vision, pp. 869–884.

Zickler, T., Belhumeur, P. N., Kriegman, D. J., 2003a. Toward a stratification of Helmholtz stereopsis. Proc. IEEE Conf. on Computer Vision and Pattern Recognition, pp. 548–554.

Zickler, T., Ho, J., Kriegman, D. J., Ponce, J., Belhumeur, P. N., 2003b. Binocular Helmholtz stereopsis. Proc. Int. Conf. on Computer Vision, pp. 1411–1417.

Ziegler, J., Nickel, K., Stiefelhagen, R., 2006. Tracking of the articulated upper body on multi-view stereo image sequences. Proc. IEEE Conf. on Computer Vision and Pattern Recognition, 1, pp. 774–781.